国际犯罪学大师系列

GUOJI FANZUIXUE DASHI XILIE

国际犯罪学大师论

犯罪控制科学

1

Master Criminologists on the
Science of Crime Control (Volume 1)

主编◉刘建宏

副主编◉金诚

人民出版社

编者简介

刘建宏　博士
Jianhong Liu

　　刘建宏教授 1988 年取得南开大学硕士学位后赴美留学，于
1993 年春获美国纽约州立大学博士学位，之后在美国任教多年，
2002 年获终身正教授。2007 年起任澳门大学教授。现任亚洲
犯罪学学会会长，西南政法大学讲席教授，博士生导师，博士
后导师。主要研究领域为刑事司法、犯罪学、毒品犯罪、社会
科学方法论与社会统计学等。刘建宏教授应邀担任《定量犯罪
学》(SSCI) 编委，《犯罪、法律与社会变迁》(SSCI) 编委，《国
际罪犯矫治与比较犯罪学》(SSCI) 专刊特邀编辑及副编辑，《澳
大利亚与新西兰犯罪学杂志》(SSCI) 专刊特邀编辑。2005 年
起任《亚洲犯罪学》总顾问编辑，2009 年起任《亚洲犯罪学》
主编。

　　刘建宏教授曾获国际犯罪学会青年学者奖。曾与美国犯罪
学学会副会长史蒂文·F. 梅斯纳教授等共获美国国家科学研究
基金奖在中国进行犯罪学研究。2006 年获美国国务院福布莱
特学者奖。自 2009 年起当选为世界著名学术组织"康拜尔合
作组织犯罪和司法领导委员会"委员。2011 年 6 月、2012 年 6
月两次应邀在"斯德哥尔摩犯罪学奖"学术大会上做主题发言。

　　刘建宏教授长期活跃在国际前沿学术领域，并在努力消除
西方社会对中国的偏颇认识、积极促进中外学者合作交流方面
做出了有益的贡献。

金　诚　教授

Cheng Jin

编者简介

金诚，浙江警察学院教授、治安系副主任，澳门大学博士候选人。现任亚洲犯罪学学会理事、中国预防青少年犯罪研究会理事、浙江省青少年犯罪研究会秘书长、《预防青少年犯罪研究》杂志编委。2004 年，澳大利亚新南威尔士州警察学院访问学者；2006 至 2007 年，美国山姆·休斯敦州立大学刑事司法学院访问教授。先后被授予全国公安模范教育训练工作者、浙江省高校中青年学科带头人、浙江省高校优秀留学回国人员等称号；主持国家社科基金项目、教育部人文社科研究规划基金项目、浙江省社科规划课题等项目。曾在国内外学术刊物上发表论文 40 余篇，多篇论文被《人大复印资料》、《高等学校文科学报文摘》（CUPA）全文转载。曾组织" 中美青少年团伙犯罪问题研究 "研讨会、公安部引智项目"犯罪控制与警务战略 "国际高峰论坛等国际学术会议。

大卫·P.法林顿 博士

David P. Farrington, Ph.D

作者简介

　　现为英国剑桥大学犯罪学研究所心理犯罪学教授，同时担任英国学院、医学科学研究院、英国心理协会、美国犯罪学学会、心理科学协会和侵害行为国际研究协会研究员。英国犯罪学会和心理学学会法医心理终身荣誉会员；康拜尔合作组织犯罪和司法领导委员会委员。担任《犯罪行为与精神健康》杂志联合主编以及其他 17 本学术期刊的编委。曾任欧洲心理学和法学协会、英国犯罪学学会、实验犯罪学学会主席、美国犯罪学学会主席（北美以外的第一人被选为这一职位）。曾荣获美国犯罪学会塞林·格卢克奖，以表彰他对犯罪学的国际贡献。他的主要研究兴趣是发展犯罪学，同时担任在剑桥大学研究违法发展项目总监，该项目对 400 多名 8 至 48 岁的伦敦男性开展纵向调查。发表论文以及有关犯罪学和心理学的书籍章节 556 篇，出版专著和政府刊物 89 部。

Dr. David P. Farrington is Professor of Psychological Criminology at the Institute of Criminology, Cambridge University. He is a Fellow of the British Academy, of the Academy of Medical Sciences, of the British Psychological Society, of the American Society of Criminology, of the Association for Psychological Science, and of the International Society for Research on Aggression. He is also an Honorary Life Member of the British Society of Criminology and of the British Psychological Society Division of Forensic Psychology. He is a member of the Campbell Collaboration Crime and Justice Group Steering Committee, joint editor of the Journal Criminal Behavior and Mental Health, and a member of the editorial boards of 17 other journals. He has been President of the European Association of Psychology and Law, President of the British Society of Criminology, President of the Academy of Experimental Criminology, President of the American Society of Criminology(the first person from outside North America to be elected to this office). He has received the Sellin—Glueck Award of the American Society of Criminology for international contributions to criminology, the Sutherland Award of the American Society of Criminology for outstanding contributions to criminology. His major research interest is in developmental criminol- ogy, and he is Director of the Cambridge Study in Delinquent Development, which is a prospective longitudinal survey of over 400 London males from age 8 to age 48. In addition to 556 published journal articles and book chapters on criminological and psychological topics, he has published 89 books, monographs and government publications.

菲德律·洛赛尔 博士

Friedrich Lösel, Ph.D

作者简介

　　现为英国剑桥大学犯罪学研究所所长、德国埃朗根·纽伦堡大学心理学教授、剑桥大学沃尔夫森学院院士。研究领域涉及未成年人犯罪、监狱学、罪犯治疗、球迷闹事、学校欺负、人格紊乱罪犯、虐待儿童和家庭教育与评价方法等。发表论文300余篇，出版著作18部。曾任欧洲心理学和法学协会主席、德语国家犯罪学会主席、康拜尔合作组织犯罪和司法领导委员会委员，美国乔治梅森大学循证犯罪政策中心委员，德国犯罪学协会副主席。同时担任各种国际期刊的编委。曾荣获包括欧洲心理学和法学协会终身成就奖、美国犯罪学学会塞林·格卢克奖、格拉斯哥·卡里多尼亚大学科学名誉博士、犯罪学斯德哥尔摩奖和德国心理学奖。还当选为实验犯罪学研究院院士。

Dr. Friedrich Lösel is Director of the Institute of Criminology at the University of Cambridge, and Professor of Psychology at the University of Erlangen–Nuremberg, Germany. He is also a Fellow of Wolfson College, Cambridge. He has carried out research on juvenile delinquency, prisons, offender treatment, football hooliganism, school bullying, personality disordered offenders, child abuse, and family education and evaluation methodology. He has published approximately 300 journal articles and book chapters and is the author or editor of 18 books. Professor Friedrich Lösel has been President of the European Association of Psychology and Law, President of the Criminological Society of the German–speaking Countries, the member of the Steering Committee of the Campbell Crime and Justice Group, Member of the Advisory Board of the Centre of Evidence–Based Crime Policy at George Mason University (U.S.), and vice–president of the German Criminological Society. He also serves on the editorial boards of various international journals. In recognition of his scientific work, he has received various honours including the Award for Lifetime Achievement of the European Association of Psychology and Law, the Sellin–Glueck Award of the American Society of Criminology, an honorary Doctor of Science from Glasgow Caledonian University, the Stockholm Prize in Criminology, and the German Psychology Prize. He was also elected as a Fellow of the Academy of Experimental Criminology.

编 者 的 话

在国际学术领域中,犯罪控制科学的研究由来已久。近几十年来,其成果尤为突飞猛进,已达到了很高的科学水平,其科学成果在发达国家政府有关犯罪控制政策的制订中普遍受到高度重视。"他山之石,可以攻玉"。有选择地、系统地介绍和引进一些国外有影响的,尤其是公认的大师级学者的研究成果,对于我们推动当前我国犯罪控制政策制定的科学化,提升我国社会管理的科学水平,具有十分重要的意义。这就是编写本套丛书的主要目的。

为此目的,浙江警察学院、亚洲犯罪学会、浙江省青少年犯罪研究会于2011年5月在杭州成功举办了"犯罪控制与警务战略"国际高峰论坛。本次论坛邀请数位国际犯罪学界大师级犯罪学家作了精彩的主题演讲,这些犯罪学家包括:原美国犯罪学会会长、原英国犯罪学会会长、剑桥大学心理学教授大卫·P. 法林顿(David P. Farrington);2007年犯罪学最高奖项斯德哥尔摩犯罪学奖获得者、英国剑桥大学犯罪学研究所所长、教授菲德律·洛赛尔(Friedrich Lösel);2010年犯罪学最高奖项斯德哥尔摩犯罪学奖获得者、美国乔治梅森大学教授、以色列希伯莱大学教授大卫·威斯勃德(David Weisburd);亚洲犯罪学会会长、澳门大学教授刘建宏。国内50余位专家、学者参加了论坛。

本次论坛反响热烈，影响深远，得到了国内新闻媒体的广泛关注。新华通讯社、人民公安报等媒体对论坛进行了宣传报道，报道先后被凤凰网、中国日报网、北国网等10余家网站转载。本套丛书的第一部（共二册）以本次高峰论坛上几位犯罪学大师的讲稿为基础，进而收录了他们其他若干相关的学术论文。刘建宏教授在高峰论坛的发言作为本书的序言。浙江警察学院院长、教授级高级工程师傅国良担任本书的学术顾问。

本书的翻译工作由浙江警察学院金诚教授、丁靖艳讲师、展万程副教授负责完成。浙江警察学院国家级"国际警务合作人才培养模式创新实验区"项目赴美留学区队学生沈宜嘉、翁一帆、吴胜淼、沈如意、张宙跹、赵超颜、叶威明、袁立华、陈韵汝、张雪、陈朦朦、刘可忻、倪彤等同学协助完成了论文的初稿翻译工作。全书由金诚教授负责校译审核全稿。

本书的翻译和出版，得到了人民出版社、浙江警察学院的大力支持。在此，我们表示衷心的感谢！

2012 年 3 月

目　　录

中国犯罪控制政策的科学化（代序）

刘 建 宏

一、绪 论

犯罪控制对任何国家而言，都是一个非常重要的政策问题。各国在与犯罪做斗争的历史过程中，都会形成一些自己的办法。在比较发达的国家中，解决犯罪问题和解决其他社会问题通常都形成了一套政策体系，我把这个体系大致概括为四个层次。

（一）犯罪控制政策体系的四个层次

第一个层次是观点层次。主导的观点或者大部分人认同的观点可能成为对犯罪问题的基本理解，影响其他各层次的犯罪控制政策的建设和执行。

第二个层次是与犯罪控制有关的法律法规。包括刑事法律法规和在特定历史时期为处理某一特定犯罪问题通过的特殊法案或者单行法规。

第三个层次是犯罪控制机构的行政设置及其建立的各种政策。这些行政设置可以是在中央设立的，也可以是在地方设置的。一些发达国家往往会就某一特定问题通过单行法案，并拨付相应的预算，设立相应的行政机构来执行这些法案。

本文根据刘建宏教授于 2011 年 5 月在杭州举办的"犯罪控制与警务战略"高峰论坛上的讲话整理而成。

第四个层次是政策项目层次。政策通常是通过具体项目来体现的,项目的概念可以很宽泛,可以是很大的项目,也可以是很具体的小项目,在西方往往用 program 这个概念来表示。这些体系有些是建立在比较充分的科学研究基础之上的,而更多的是在政治及其他方面考虑的基础上建立的。

这个体系中第一层次中的观点和理论方针可以是来自科学理论研究的结果,其他几个政策层次可以是来自于以科学评估为核心的研究活动基础上,科学研究可以成为犯罪控制理论政策和实践的科学基础。

(二)我国犯罪控制政策框架

过去几十年来,在我国,特别是自改革开放三十年来,犯罪问题与犯罪率,特别是青少年犯罪,出现了较为明显的增加,日益成为政府和广大公众关注的重要问题。中国的犯罪控制和犯罪学取得了长足发展,犯罪控制领域的理论和实践都取得了重要的成就。我国政府也已建立了自己的犯罪控制体系。

1. 在观点层次上,国家确定了社会治安综合治理的方针。可以说,我国犯罪控制政策框架主要是以社会治安综合治理这个基本方针为中心的政策体系,这个政策框架首先包含着中央政府对犯罪控制的基本指导思想。

中共中央 1979 年 8 月在批转中央宣传部、教育部、文化部、公安部、国家劳动总局、全国总工会、共青团中央、全国妇联等 8 个单位《关于提请全党重视解决青少年违法犯罪问题的报告》时明确指出,解决青少年的违法犯罪问题,必须实行党委领导,全党动员,依靠学校、工厂、机关、部门、街道、农村社队等城乡基层组织和全社会的力量。绝不能就事论事,孤立对待,而应当同加快经济发展,加强思想政治工作,健全民主与法制,搞好党风、民风,狠抓青少年教育等工作结合进行。这是最早见于中央文件中的有关对社会治安问题实行综合治理的指导思想。

社会治安综合治理,是指在党和政府的领导下,依靠国家政权、社会团体和广大人民群众的力量,各部门协调一致,齐抓共管,运用政治的、经济的、行政的、法律的、文化的、教育的等多种手段,整治社会治安,打击犯罪和预防犯罪,保障社会稳定,防止被害,为我国社会主义现代化建设和改革开放创造良好的社会环境(康树华,2001)。

2. 法律、法规层面,1991 年 3 月 2 日,第七届全国人大常委会第十八次会议通过了《全国人大常委会关于加强社会治安综合治理的决定》。

3. 犯罪控制组织机构,例如中央、各地专门设立综治委等机构,并进一步颁布了各种具体政策,领导、组织各种具体项目的实施,形成了一个具有相当规模的犯罪控制体系。

4. 在政策项目层次上,从中央至地方多年来提出了很多政策项目,如打击犯罪、预防犯罪、矫治罪犯、刑事司法过程、社区参与、化解矛盾冲突、情景犯罪预防。具体实施的政策项目,大到多部门治理,小到具体犯罪干预项目。

我国学者也对犯罪治理政策做了大量研究。如研究对政府理论观点的形成等,这些对政策的制定也都有着重要的影响。我国学者也对主要的政策项目做了一些有价值的评估研究。

(三)我国犯罪控制政策的问题与挑战

目前,我国在经济社会发展各个方面取得了重大成就,同时我们也面临许多的犯罪控制问题与挑战,在社会基本稳定的大前提下,大量不安定的风险因素和社会矛盾普遍存在。

1. 刑事案件仍在上升

随着经济社会发展、改革开放深入、市场化深化,有关犯罪控制的社会管理任务十分艰巨,除了传统类型的犯罪和治安案件仍在持续上升,一些特别严重的犯罪问题也对我们提出重大挑战,例如不断发展的有组织犯罪问题、毒品犯罪问题、拐卖妇女儿童犯罪问题等,发展趋势都相当严峻。从警务战略的角度看,如何以有限的警务资源有效地应对这些挑战,不断总结经验,提出创新,发展出有效果又有效益的各种政策项目,维护好社会治安,保证国家经济建设、人民生活安定,我们面临十分艰巨的任务。

单位:件

图1 1999—2009 年我国公安机关立案的刑事案件

中国综合治理犯罪框架下公安机关是犯罪控制的领导力量和中坚力量。公安部门设计并执行的政策项目就是严打。

2.1983 年以来的严打等政策项目

"严打"是依法从重从快严厉打击刑事犯罪分子活动的简略表述,是为解决一定时期中突出的社会治安问题而依法进行的打击严重刑事犯罪的活动。①

1983 年 9 月,全国人大常委会通过了两个决定,即《全国人民代表大会常务委员会关于严惩严重危害社会治安的犯罪分子的决定》和《全国人民代表大会常务委员会关于迅速审判严重危害社会治安的犯罪分子的程序的决定》,这两个决定为"严打"活动提供了合法的依据。第一个决定体现出"从严",而第二个决定表现的是"从快"。

从 1983 年 8 月上旬开始到 1984 年 7 月,各地公安机关迅速开展严厉打击刑事犯罪活动的第一战。迟志强就是这次战役中最著名的一个案例。

严打虽严,却反弹很快。这里有一组数字。在 1983 年到 1987 年第一次"严打"期间,刑事犯罪确实得到了抑制,"严打"期间,从各类报道中不仅可以看到各种公共场所治安良好,连女工上下夜班、女学生下晚自习也不再需要家人接送了。但是,在"严打"后,刑事案件的立案数一下子由 1987 年的 57 万件上升到 1988 年的 83 万多件——三年的"严打"并没有达到预期的长效目标。②

严打政策项目、严打刑事犯罪使犯罪在一定程度上得以抑制,但也收到很多批评,很多学者,包括政府和学界普遍认为严打并不能达到社会控制的长效目的。总之,犯罪控制是一个重要题目,我们社会若要长治久安就要做好犯罪控制。

(四)社会管理科学化的提出

面对严峻挑战探讨应对思路是十分重要的,我们的长期目标是长治久安,短期目标是对突发出现的严重问题提出及时有效的应对措施以及干预项目。胡锦涛总书记提出的未来犯罪控制思路有什么新的思考方向?一个重要思考方向就是要在科学基础上建立和完善犯罪控制政策的体系、政策和有效的干预项目。2011 年初胡锦涛总书记提出了社会管理机制创新,为犯罪控制政策研究指出了未来的方向。

2011 年 2 月 19 日上午,中国省部级主要领导干部社会管理及其创新专题研讨班开班式在中央党校举行。中共中央总书记、国家主席、中央军委主席胡锦涛发表重要讲话,提出了关于加强和改善社会管理格局、维护群众权益机制、公共安全体系、基

---

① 百度百科名片,"严打",http://baike.baidu.com/view/9917.htm,2011 年 5 月 14 日访问。
② 1983 年严打的法制缺陷,http://www.wyzxsx.com/Article/Class14/201008/170374.html,2011 年 5 月 14 日访问。

层社会管理和服务、思想道德建设等社会管理机制创新的八点建议。

中共中央政治局常委、中央政法委书记周永康也发表文章指出我国要从实际出发，总结我国社会管理经验，借鉴国外有益成果，不断提高社会管理科学化水平。

国家领导人关于社会管理科学化的要求，指明了我国未来犯罪控制理论实践的发展方向是科学化。

胡锦涛总书记提出了下一步的科学管理目标，指明了未来发展方向。什么是科学管理？我们现在犯罪控制政策和管理是否已经是科学的管理呢？我个人理解是要看如何定义科学的概念。科学概念的定义可以很宽泛、冗长，也可以很简单，但核心精神就是要依靠事实和证据说话，依靠严格分析、科学收集的资料来发现解决问题的办法。

宽泛的科学概念可以包括一切依靠事实和证据来做结论的活动和成果。我们所讲的实践是检验真理的标准，在精神上就属于这种科学概念。但是在西方科学界，科学的概念是指一个更加具体的、狭义的概念，即指经验科学的概念，"科学"二字，通常是经验科学的简称。经验科学指的是以可观察、可感知的事实为基础建立的认识，科学事实是指以科学的方法系统地收集严格、可靠的经验事实。以科学为基础的管理政策就是指以经验科学研究为基础建立起来的政策。西方的管理理论就是以经验科学研究为基础建立起来的理论，已经达到了非常发达的程度。跟随自然科学的蓬勃发展，社会科学也已在 20 世纪发展成为高度发达的经验科学。我个人认为，未来实现胡锦涛主席提出的科学管理目标的一个主要途径就是建立或完善以经验科学研究为基础的一套犯罪控制体系，它包括科学研究基础上形成的观点、理论和政策以及实施这些政策的具体项目。这套体系依靠可靠性日益提高的数据，严格程度日益提高的分析技术，对政策项目的科学评估，做出正确的政策决定，即达到对犯罪控制的科学管理。

二、犯罪控制政策科学化的重要性

实践证明，自然科学和社会科学领域取得了巨大的成就，管理科学与经济科学也取得了突飞猛进的发展，这些成绩的取得，离不开科学作用的发挥。自然科学发展证明，科学发展是一种巨大的力量，科学发展过程是人类认识发展的必然过程。对自然科学的重要性鲜少有人质疑，但对社会科学的重要性，尤其是经验研究的重要性在早期的发展过程中各国都常常有质疑的声音。最典型的一个质疑就是很多科学研究的结论往往与通过某些个人经验得到的结论相差不远,体现不出科学研究的特殊价值。为增强对科学研究重要性的认识,我们简单地就这个质疑做些初步的回答,并从科学发展不同阶段特点的角度来说明这个问题。

(一)科学发现与主观洞察力

1. 科学发现的客观性

从长远看,科学发现结论在有些方面与有经验者判断无异,在有的方面差别巨大,科学发现是中性客观的。

2. 科学发现的累积性

从长远看,科学方法不断进步,精确度不断提高,但靠常识却不能提高,经验很难传承,人生经历的经验积累走不了多远。自然科学领域,计算机、航空器等的研制说明,科学发展是必然的趋势,当然社会科学领域不可能对用科学方法从事的研究视而不见。金融、经济、管理方法单靠个人经验、洞察力无法具有说服力。

3. 科学方法的深层揭示功能

人类的洞察力,个人的洞察力相当有限,统计方法有发现的功能。在复杂数据中,常常蕴藏着我们不能从表面窥视的深刻内容,通过统计的方法把人们完全看不到的深层内容通过科学方法加以揭示呈现。

4. 科学方法的精确性

个人的洞察力精确度不够,统计分析经验在使用过程中不断提升。

5. 科学发现的价值中立性

科学精神要追求尽可能的客观,不带任何个人偏好的发现,人的判断总是避免不了受价值判断的影响,要有科学精神。不管个人的洞察力强弱,总是掺杂主观想象的成分。这个毕竟不是事实,分析的事实哪怕简单也是客观的,主观与客观是一致的;性质也是不同的,层次高的人观点,如果不是科学的,也可能是主观的;普通的人员经过分析的结果也是科学的,不排除有人用客观形式装扮主观意图。在科学评估研究设计中,科学共同体要做到双盲评估(double blinded),所谓双盲评估是受测人不知道,测试人也不知道是哪组,结果说了算。

(二)西方犯罪学发展的三个阶段

对18世纪晚期以来的犯罪学研究如何划分阶段或时期,犯罪学家们有不同的看法。对西方犯罪学史历史发展阶段的划分,最有代表性的观点可能是德国出生的英国犯罪学家赫尔曼·曼海姆(Hermann Mannheim)(1889—1974)提出来的。曼海姆认

为,过去200多年间犯罪学研究的历史发展,可以大致划分为三个阶段:①

1. 前科学阶段

前科学阶段(the pre-scientific stage),既没有系统阐述假设,也没有检验假设。人们并没有试图公正地解决他们所遇到的问题,没有研究他们所发现的事实,这并不意味着那时的一些探讨是无价值的。相反,尽管18世纪和19世纪上半期的大部分刑罚学文献属于前科学阶段的范围,但是,我们现在的刑罚制度中的人道主义进步,在很大程度上应归功于前科学阶段的努力。

2. 准科学阶段

准科学阶段(the semi-scientific stage)从19世纪中期开始。在这个阶段,提出了大量明确的或含糊的假设,但是,许多假设过于宽泛和模棱两可,以至于经不起精确的检验。而且,在这一阶段,也没有可以使用的公认的科学检验手段。

3. 科学阶段

科学阶段(the scientific stage),来源于某个一般性理论的假设,必须通过正确使用一种或几种普遍承认的方法检验,其结果应当得到无偏见的解释和验证。如果有必要的话,应当根据研究结果修改最初的假设,形成新的假设。

在科学阶段,并不排斥使用直觉方法,但是,"我们的直觉必须接受检验"。如果说迄今为止概括出来的所有要求在科学阶段都已经实现了,那是不可能的,只能是一种理想。

笔者认为,前科学、准科学与科学的区别如下:

(1)是否以证据/经验证据为基础不同。科学化以证据/经验证据为基础。

(2)使用的经验证据质量不同。科学使用的经验证据质量和严格程度远远高于前科学或准科学。

(3)证据系统性有别。科学证据的系统性强于前科学、准科学。

(4)存在着科学基础上差别。科学研究以实证的、观察的经验为基础。

按照前述的科学概念,一个学科从理论层面上升到有关政策层面通常要经历科学发展的三个阶段,按照曼海姆的科学阶段划分,我国目前的水平严格来讲还没有进阶科学阶段。

(三)科学化与科学证据的概念

强调证据和追求严格的经验科学。我们强调过经验科学的核心概念是证据,经

---

① Hermann Mannheim, *Comparative Criminology*: *A Text Book*, Volume one, London: Routledge & Kegan Paul, 1965, pp. 84–86.

验科学就是通过对科学的证据进行严格的分析以达到可信的结论。

理论领域与政策领域具有循证性(Evidence-based)。经验科学的活动可以分为两大领域,第一大领域是理论领域,第二大领域是政策领域。在理论领域里通行的做法是依靠严格的经验验证来建立理论,这其中包括以严格的科学方法系统地收集证据、收集资料,通过使用各种经验验证方法包括使用统计模型和计算来检验理论在观察层面上的预见是否成立。政策领域中核心的科学活动就是对现实存在中的政策和政策项目进行评估,并以评估提供的证据为基础调整、改善或放弃已有的政策,从而实现科学的管理。

在这些科学活动过程中,管理者和科学家所追求的目标就是日益提高的证据的可靠程度和日益提高的证据分析严格程度,从而实现结论的可靠程度。正是在这些科学活动中,社会科学家发挥了极大的创造力,在过去一个世纪中,发展出了一套十分专业化的技术体系,建立了真正意义上的社会科学,包括犯罪学理论和社会控制政策的实践研究。

分析技术的发展主要依赖于统计学的迅速发展,各种功能强大的统计技术、统计模型日新月异,同时借助于计算机运算功能的快速发展,使过去无法实现抑或需要相当时间完成的运算任务现在已经可以转瞬完成,从而为数据分析实践中的疑难提供了多种解决渠道。

三、什么是科学化
——犯罪控制的科学分析技术

如前所述,科学是基于经验证据及对其的严格分析而产生的,经验证据有不同程度,用非科学方式和科学方式搜集到的证据的可靠性不同,从而形成了证据质量的区别。科学分析的技术也决定了科学结论的严格有效程度。社会科学发展的过程就是一个社会科学家收集经验证据的技术和分析经验数据的技术越来越严谨的发展过程。

(一)高新数据收集技术的发展

证据效力的核心是数据收集,收集数据是根据研究目的所需回答的科学问题来进行研究设计的。数据搜集技术的核心内容是严格遵循逻辑思维及不断发展的方法论研究成果,来实现数据质量的不断提高。

数据收集实践中,基于数据收集的实际发展出许多克服难题的新方法。常见的数据搜集技术方法,相信已为很多人了解和掌握,实验研究方法、问卷调查方法、田野调查方法等等,科学完整的数据可靠度高,精确性强,当然,这些都离不开方法论的前沿成果。

例如,我前些年在西南政法大学某讲座中曾提出统计技术量表设计方案,问题中的4个选项依次是从最赞成到最不赞成。当时,有学者提出:"为什么不将问卷题目设计成包含同意或者不同意的选项呢?"这点也恰恰反映了统计量表技术的重要发现,方法论学家对问卷设计进行区别研究发现不设计中间选项(是非选项)的问卷,即对很多问题都不是这种赞成或者不赞成的可以从二者中不加思索地选出其一,而是通过不包含中间选择问题的问卷可以得出的研究结果远比含有该种中间选择问题问卷的信息丰富。因为唯有这样,才有助于迫使调查对象进行认真思考,从众多的选项中选择能表达自己真实态度的内容,进而做出有信息效果的回答。当问卷中包含是非选择,很多人出于便利考虑,会对其进行选择,这样选择的结果使信息量大幅减少。当然,方法论专家仍在不断探索、积累数据收集的技术,使科学研究的基础更加牢靠。

(二)高新数据分析技术的发展

日新月异的数据分析技术每一步的进步发展都在不断纠正旧的分析方法和可能存在的偏差,从而使分析结论更可靠、更精确。通过科学的统计方法得出的分析才具有更强的证明力。

作为一名在美国从事犯罪学研究的学者,适时地更新自己的专业理论知识是极为重要的,否则就有可能在很短的时间内落后于当下科学研究的发展进度。数据分析技术的发展主要依赖于统计学的迅速发展,各种功能强大的统计技术、统计模型日新月异,同时借助于计算机运算功能的快速发展,使过去无法实现抑或需要相当时间完成的运算任务现在已经可以转瞬完成,从而为数据分析实践中的疑难提供了多种解决渠道。

未曾深入地了解统计技术的学者可能会产生质疑,搞如此复杂的统计技术真的有用吗?回答当然是肯定的,因为科学数据分析技术每一步的发展都在不断纠正旧有的分析方法和可能存在的偏差,从而使分析结论更可靠、更精确。因此,所有技术上的发展都是为了一个目标,使我们获得的数据和分析结论更加精确可靠。例如,在统计技术中由于因变量的性质可能不同,各种精细的不同层次的设计模型被发展出来,比如当因变量为累犯、再犯时,即以前曾经犯过罪现又犯罪,将过去和现在犯罪的次数作为因变量,这种因变量就成为一个累犯、再犯对某种问题的态度在统计中的反映。同种显示形态传递的性质信息非常不同,次数反映的数量结果是1、2、3、4、5……态度可能是从最不赞成到赞成再到非常赞成,用0、1、2、3、4表示,在统计意义上,其性质完全不同。亦如从同意到不同意符合泊松分布(Poisson distribution),分布可以近似为一个正态分布,所以答案都是1—4等。但是要通过不同统计分析方法、模型才能得出更加可靠、准确的结论。分布不同,模型不同,通常人或许依据自己经验认为是正态分布的数据,但科学统计分析方法得出的结论实际上并非如此,这些通过科学的统计方法得出的分析才具有更强的证明力。

(三)评估研究(Evaluation Research)

1. 评估研究在管理科学化中的中心地位

(1)任何的政策、项目必须经过评估。通过评估,评价政策项目的效度,才知晓理论是否正确、政策是否有效并且经济上是否合算。

(2)评估阶段是研究设计的组成部分,犯罪控制项目只有通过评价,才能得知项目是否达到预先设定的目的。

(3)评估内容包括证据是否真实、证据质量如何、证据证明力大小、样本是否具有代表性、内部效力如何等。

方案实施以后,任何人可以使用设计方案中搜集的资料、数据验证方案是否有实效,例如安装CCTV前、后都要测量,未安装的邻近区域也应监测。

2. 评估的科学标准

我们什么时候才能对报道的犯罪预防项目的评估结论建立信心呢?不管他们提出是否产生有效、无效,或者更糟糕的负面效果,这些结果可信吗?这是基于证据方法来研究犯罪预防的重要问题。

可以肯定的是并非所有的犯罪预防项目的评估效度都是相同的,评估质量的方法存在巨大差别,根据Cook and Campbell(1979)和Shadish等人(2002)的研究,评估研究的质量有四项标准:

(1)统计结论效度(Statistical conclusion validity);

(2)内部效度(Internal validity);

(3)建构/构造效度(Construct validity);

(4)外部效度(External validity)。

下面逐项对评估方面的4个质量标准进行阐释:

(1)统计结论效度。统计结论效度关注的是假定因素(干预因素)和假定效果

（统计结果）之间是否具有关联。对该类效度的主要威胁，来自于统计功效（正确地否定错误的虚假假设的可能性）的低下以至于无法发现效果（例如较低的样本规模），以及统计方法的不当使用。

（2）内部效度。内部效度，是指在多大程度上，研究明确地指明了原因（例如父母教育）对结果的影响（例如越轨行为）。在这里，某种控制条件是十分必要的。该条件用以判断如果原因没有被施加于实验单位（如人口或地区），该单位将会发生怎样的变化。这又被称为"反事实推理"。

影响内部效度的因素是：

①人为选择：实验条件与控制条件之间的先在差异的影响。

②历史：与干预同时发生的某些事件造成的影响。

③自然成熟：对先在趋势的延续性的反映，例如正常的人生成长。

④测量工具：结果测量方法的改变所产生的影响。

⑤测量：前测对后测的改变。

⑥统计回归效应：在那些将干预应用于超常的高分值单位（如高犯罪率地区）的地方，自然波动也会在后测中引起分值的回落，而这种自然波动造成的效应会被错误地解释为干预的影响。另外，将干预应用于低犯罪率或低分值人群中，则会引起相反的效果（分值提升）。

⑦差异耗损：实验条件与控制条件之间的单位（如人群）差异损失所造成的影响。

⑧按时间发生的顺序：介入因素是否在结果发生之前出现这是不清楚的。

（3）建构/构造效度

建构/构造效度，指对干预与结果的理论建构进行操作化定义和测量的程度。例如，如果有一个项目旨在调查有关犯罪的人与人之间训练技巧的结果，训练项目确实针对和改变人际技巧，应作为罪犯被逮捕吗？这种效度形式的主要威胁在于干预在多大程度上成功改变了本应发生的变化，以及度量结果的效度和信度。

（4）外部效度

外部效度，指在多大程度上，对结果的干预所造成的效应能够在不同条件下推广或者重复实现：不同的介入因素操作定义和各种不同结果、不同民族、不同环境等等。在一项研究评估中很难调查这些全部内容。外部效度可以更有说服力地建立在一些研究评估的系统检查和元分析中（见下述）。沙迪什（Shadish）（2002, p. 87）等认为，这种效度形式的主要威胁是原因（民族类型、背景、介入因素）和结果（影响大小）相互作用的结果。例如，一个介入因素的设计目的是减少犯罪，可能对于某些人或者在某些地区起作用,对其他人或者在其他地区可能情况就会不同。问题的关键是是否由于研究执行的人对于研究结果有某种利害关系造成了影响大小的不同。

如果一个犯罪预防项目的评估过程是遵循高度内部效度、结构效度和统计结论效度,则通常被认为是高质量的。也就是说,如果项目评估设计中对这三种效度形式的主要威胁进行控制,一个人可以对介入因素可被观察的效果有充足的信心。实验(随机实验和非随机实验)和准实验研究设计是可以使设计评估类型最大限度地达到这样的目的。

(四)行动研究(Action Research)

近20年来,在犯罪控制政策研究方面的新动向是把数据收集、分析与犯罪控制项目的政策制定完全地统一起来,尤其在犯罪预防项目设计与实施方面表现得尤为突出。此前,从事数据收集与统计分析的专家与从事犯罪控制的实际部门缺乏有效的联系,导致这些科研部门和实际部门互不知晓除本部门以外的真实情况。

随着犯罪控制政策制定、贯彻、执行、评估等科学化阶段的进展,原先的做法逐渐被新方式取代,从事数据搜集,统计分析的学术专家与刑事司法等控制犯罪的实际部门密切结合,形成犯罪控制合力,这样,项目从开始设计之初直至项目实施整个过程均贯穿科学研究的基础,并不断吸收实际部门的深刻实践经验,共同开发设计。总体设计中,包括在实施过程中每阶段数据收集、数据分析、项目实施与项目评估等。由于在每阶段对评估所需要的数据收集都包含必要的实施安排,因此,使项目的严格科学评估成为可能。

如前所述,评估阶段是犯罪控制政策科学化的核心所在,学术研究人员全程参加到刑事司法项目实施评估中,这对保证整个项目的科学化程度产生作用。项目在实施过程中及实施过程以后,科学评估结果又会被及时反馈到下一轮项目的评估设计修订及实施中去,这种科学与实践一体化的过程,在西方称为行动研究。指专家与刑事司法等控制犯罪的实际部门密切结合,项目从开始设计之初直至项目实施整个过程均贯穿科学研究。总体设计中,包括在实施过程中每阶段数据收集、数据分析、项目实施与项目评估等。

行动研究可以用下图表示。

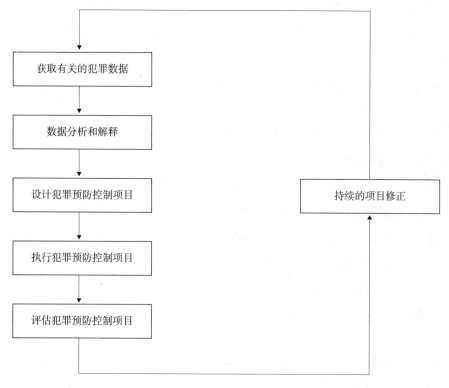

图2 犯罪控制政策行动研究程序图示

四、怎样实现中国犯罪控制政策的科学化
——国际经验及市场化路线

如前所述,犯罪控制的制度体系包括按理论观点建立起来的制度体系。我国已根据国情在历史发展的背景下建立了自己的制度体系。为实现犯罪控制科学管理的目标,我们需要根据新的情况不断完善这一制度体系。

(一)美国犯罪控制政策的科研管理体制

用怎样的体制、组织来保证科学技术的最新发展成果应用到犯罪控制政策的制定中,并被刑事司法实践吸收,促进犯罪控制技术不断向前发展,美国这方面的做法普遍得到承认。美国科研管理体制有三个主要特点:

1. 依靠科学的管理理念在政府中深入人心

科学对社会各项管理工作的基础作用,在美国社会从上到下已经普遍为大家接受。这与美国传统实用主义哲学有密切关系,通常认为有用和实在的理论与实践才能为我所用。科学研究部门的科学家经常成为美国政府中主要领导的人选。

美国犯罪控制主要研究机构是司法部下设司法项目办公室(OJP Office of Justice Programs),司法项目办公室管理所有有关科学研究与实际政策的司法项目。国际司法研究中心设在 OJP 中,由 OJP 管理。

司法部主管各种司法科研项目,下设若干不同分部。其中与刑事司法和犯罪控制的科学研究组织管理有关的两个主管科学研究的机构是国家(刑事)司法(科学)研究院(NIJ national institute of justice)和国家司法统计局(BJS bureau of justice statistics)。美国的 BJS 和 NIJ 是主管科研的机构,这两个机构负责政策、项目的投标、竞标、管理事宜。BJS 主管全国司法统计资料,BJS 可以组织从事大型调查,是直接从事调查研究的机构。NIJ 下面设很多部门,分设自然科学部和社会科学部,NIJ 主管 BJS 之外的科研工作,不直接从事研究,主要负责管理、组织经费的使用,通过美国政策将科研经费划拨给使用机构。

主管 BJS 工作的是詹姆士·林奇(James Linch),主管 NIJ 的领导是约翰·劳布(John Laub),约翰·劳布(John Laub)是 2011 年斯德哥尔摩犯罪学奖的获得者,上述两个研究院的主管负责人/主任都是著名的美国犯罪学家,是经美国国会确认,美国总统奥巴马任命的。

BJS 的研究项目有国家犯罪被害人调查(NCVS, National Crime Victim Security),这个项目从 1972 年开始,一直持续到现在,目前仍在进行。

2011 年,约翰·劳布(John Laub)上任后发表演讲,提出 NIJ 的十项工作目标,直接与提高研究管理水平有关的有五项,包括科学研究知识向犯罪控制领域的应用与转化。[①]

美国实用主义哲学深入人心,主要思想表现在,重视科学机构的组织、科研经费的使用、科研负责人的任命。在美国纯粹的表达并不受重视,重要的是看证据、证据效力,是美国对科学的崇尚,对真理的不懈追求精神的体现。这不仅体现在美国司法部门,其他部门包括国防部、农业部、商业部、健康与社会服务部等,始终充盈着对科学的热情追求与信任。

从美国政府任命的犯罪学家、从事科学研究的人员,从办公机构的组织设计上,均反映出重视科学、哲学、实用主义并重证据、证据效力,可靠严格的证据思想突出。

2. 科学研究机构多元、独立、分散

在美国从事科学研究的机构众多,而不是由一家或者两家机构垄断。从事一般

---

① 见会刊 *The Criminologist* 3—4(2011 年第 2 期)。

科学研究的机构是多元、独立的,有政府直接领导的机构,有私营企业、高等院校以及社会上非营(盈)利的研究机构。

犯罪控制政策的研究主要是依靠高等院校和社会上非营利机构完成的,非营利的组织、机构是专门从事社会科学研究的大型机构,许多重大的项目都是由非营利机构承担,如 RAND(兰德公司)、NORC(National Opinion Research Center)、波士顿的 ABT, West at(西部统计), Urban Institute(城市研究院), RTI(Research Triangle Institute)等大型、非营利性社会科学研究机构。

3. 市场化的学术竞争机制

美国重视科研创新经费的支出,1993 年,美国用于科研的经费为 1600 余亿美元,根据年 5% 的增长率,现在美国每年用于科研的经费在 2000 亿美元上下。用在犯罪控制研究方面亦占相当比重,以 2007 年 NIJ 预算为例,2007 年日常研究经费是 5400 万美元,其中用于自然科学(如 DNA 研究)的经费为 3500 万美元,用于社会科学的经费是 1200 万美元。但日常经费只是全部经费的一小部分,另有根据单行法案额外拨款的经费。单行法案中包含拨款项目,有执行内容法律要拨款,国会从财政部拨款,单行法规、政策通过具有法律性质的法案,美国对某一事项通过一个法律,美国家安全法,拨款根据提出的法案,通过的法案都不是空的,美国非常实际,通过法律同时拨付经费。具体执行由司法部负责。

在 2007 年用于法案(legislative project)等项目额外拨款研究经费额度为 20 亿美元,远远超过美国日常的研究经费支出。这些追加的法定项目费用用于美国国会通过的法律,如 DNA 数据库建设,防弹预算,城市安全预算等等。犯罪分布,地图定位,地图数据库,全国犯人 DNA 数据库,防弹技术,警察保护项目,警察技术中心拨款。NIJ 管理、组织、监督事项的进行情况和经费的使用情况,NIJ 执行法律。

每年,政府以发布项目招标公告方式向具有科研能力的部门了解社会各方面需要掌握的信息及其运行情况。实践中主要是政府、企业、高校、非营利机构这四类组织,通过投标、中标,研究报告等反映调查研究结果。

科学研究的管理部门(如 NIJ)以研究资金或研究合同形式,将科研资金分配给优胜者,并对研究过程和资金使用全程监管。

这种市场化的学术竞争机制可以鼓励先进技术的产生、鼓励使用先进技术、鼓励创新,能够保证最有能力的科学家和组织使用最先进的技术,领衔从事犯罪控制的科学研究工作项目。

首先,由专家依据一定的标准对竞争各方写出研究计划进行综合评定,筛选出中标方。然后,科学研究资金的管理部门(如 NIJ)将用于科学研究的资金通过向中标者拨付,或者通过与中标者签订科学研究合同形式,将一定数额的科研资金分配给在竞争投标中被选出的获胜方。

分配科研资金的依据是竞争投标中的获胜方,项目设计是否先进,是否包含评估,都是竞标成功的重要因素。因此,通过招投标方式决定由哪一方从事研究项目,可以鼓励先进技术、人员使用新技术、新思想进行创新,因唯有此,才可能在竞争中获赢夺标。这不但鼓励科学研究机构创新赢得目标,不断推动工作创新;另一方面,也能够保证最优最先进的技术,最有能力的科学家和组织领衔从事科学研究工作项目。

研究机构都是独立、分散的。机构根据规定提出研究方式,资金使用通过投标取得,竞标过程中 NIJ 组织专家评定,当然,也可以自选认为重要的题目,研究资金有相当的部分用在评估上。

NIJ 一定要看到项目体现出评估写在竞标方案中,保证科学创新不息,控罪控制政策越来越好。

美国科学研究管理的体制保证了科学的发展,从其组织和体制保证的阐述中,我们可以看到其可取之处,这些虽不必然完全适用中国,但"他山之石可以攻玉",我们可以借鉴适合我国体制的部分,依此提升我国的犯罪控制的理论和实践水平。

(二)中国犯罪学发展道路的建议

作为从事犯罪学研究的学者,我认为犯罪学家目前在我国还没有应有的地位。在世界上的许多国家,犯罪学并不被社会广泛了解。与临近学科例如法律相比较,犯罪学家的社会地位并不高。

1. 中国犯罪控制研究科学化路线之探索

犯罪学是一门学问,只有不断发展才能保证它的成功。犯罪学存在于现实世界,它往往带来意想不到的影响和成功。以下我从犯罪学存在的大环境中初步分析影响成功之路的主要概念要素,从一些实际的方面探讨我们通往成功的道路,提出一些值得考虑并切实可行的步骤,使我国犯罪学走向成功。

(1)犯罪学的资源。犯罪学领域中的关键概念之一是资源。因为我国资源不足,所以在世界各国影响力有限。资源就是力量,资源左右影响力的分配,反之亦然。另外,我们需要财务资源来保障科学研究顺利进行,我们需要政治资源影响政府的决策,我们需要社会资源创造并提高犯罪学的影响和认可度。

(2)犯罪学的市场。犯罪学发展另一个关键概念是市场。资源和影响力在市场中进行分配。市场占有率决定一个组织的影响力,犯罪学也不例外。市场能够左右专业群体的社会阶层划分并且决定他们的影响力。市场的这个作用是客观的,犯罪

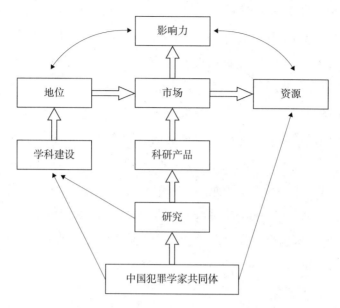

图3　中国犯罪控制研究科学化路线图示

学家更无法控制。为了提高犯罪学的影响力,我们要尊重市场的需求。

　　犯罪学的市场中政府是最关键的市场。制定政策,包括法律法规,警察、法庭和矫治机构的政策项目,干预项目等。非官方组织是另一个主要市场。私营企业有犯罪预防和安全需要,社区、学校、家庭以及个人也有犯罪预防和安全需要。

　　犯罪学共同体的主要使命是提供专业水平的知识产品,而这种产品的使用价值取决于它是否能够满足公共或非公共领域的犯罪控制与社会安全需求。这种需求与犯罪共同体的供给共同组成了我国犯罪学的市场。

　　以市场作为犯罪学发展的支点,意味着用竞争引擎启动犯罪学的学术航路。市场占有率决定组织影响力,左右专业阶层的划分,但是,市场的本意是要尊重和满足各种特定的需求,而这种需求的存在,是我国犯罪学进一步拓展和深化发展领域的基础。

　　我国是否存在发展犯罪学的需求? 答案是肯定的。城市化不仅仅带来了高度发达的物质文明,也带来日益繁重的犯罪问题。2004年的严打运动,2009年的重庆打黑,说明在现代城市当中,如何应对和控制犯罪,是现代社会生活的重要方面,这恰恰是专业化犯罪学知识需求的主要来源。

　　那么,谁需要犯罪学知识呢? 政府是最为传统的消费者。政府在制定法规政策,改进警务机构,推动司法改革等方面,是非常需要高水平的、专业化的犯罪学知识作为参考的,这将大大有益于社会科学化管理水平的提升。除此之外,非公共领域当中,对犯罪学的需求也是不可忽视的。随着城市建设的扩张,城市新兴社区正在不断形成。为了社区安定,需要构建新型的社区治安保障体系。这种体系建设需要大量的犯罪控制知识作为支撑。比如,犯罪的情景预防措施当中,迪斯尼乐园在娱乐项目、建筑布局和工作人员设置与职责安排时,安全与犯罪控制也是重要的考量要素。水池、喷泉和花园既是艺术品,也是在紧急状态下作为地标使用。

(3)犯罪学的科研产品。犯罪学领域还有一个关键概念是科研产品。为了生存并取得成功,我国犯罪学必须拿出高质量的研究成果来满足市场的需求。政府方面犯罪学的研究成果包括,法律法规、政策、项目策划、咨询服务。非官方组织方面犯罪学的研究成果有犯罪防治、安全措施、社会项目等。

总体而言,犯罪学在我国仍然没有得到充分的发展,影响力有待进一步提高。发展我国犯罪学,使之达到世界先进水平,提升犯罪学在我国学术界的影响力,我国犯罪学者担负着不容推卸的历史重任。

2. 中国犯罪控制政策

我国在警务项目方面证明已经取得了成功,是不是我们已经以科学为基础了呢?中国也讲犯罪控制效果的客观性、真实性,也注重实践。但是中国的犯罪控制政策有没有科学化? 够不够科学化? 由谁来决定是否科学化? 用什么方法评估科学化程度? 科学的犯罪控制政策讲证据。

大多数中国的犯罪学理论没有以经验为基础。如刘晓梅、储槐植复述了中国很多的犯罪学理论,没有经验证据,没有对理论证据进行验证。学者刘晓梅指出,中国从理论、经验和实践上都没有科学化。

通过评估,才知晓理论、政策是否科学。中国的理论政策没有评估,基本是领导人(层)的意志决定一切。比如中国的犯罪率在一定时期内发生变化,呈现下降趋势,能不能想当然地认为国家施行的犯罪控制政策在起作用,也许是人的素质普遍提高等其他因素对犯罪率产生了影响。没有进行评估,无法轻率地得出任何结论。

前面已讲到科学方法包括两个方面的重要内容,即理论层面和实践层面。

中国科学研究证据不是高质量证据,样本不具有。中国人是否相信科学化? 中国人是否愿意科学化?

关于中国犯罪控制政策的具体运行,有政府做的,也有委托高校做的,其中局限性如下:

(1)中国犯罪控制政策的缺陷

中国犯罪控制政策不是为了打击犯罪目的,有些政策新瓶装旧酒,虎头蛇尾,没有复制,评估结果不一定权威,评估方法不够科学,例如犯罪率下降,可能是多种因素共同作用的结果,而非单一因素造成。

（2）中国与美国的科研管理体制存在巨大差距

美国政府重视科研,科学在政府管理中深入人心,崇尚科学成为精神。我国重自然科学轻社会科学,殊不知犯罪政策从头至尾都是科学。

美国核心研究机构如 NIJ、BJS 的主要管理者是犯罪学家,犯罪学在美国的地位不容忽略。中国犯罪学和中国犯罪学家目前不能引起足够的重视;美国主要从事刑事司法研究的机构多元、独立、分散。美国政府、企业、高校、非营利机构从事刑事司法研究。NIJ 管理科研,只从事少量的科研,大部分项目被非配到广泛非营利企业中,没有垄断。我国从事相关研究的机构存在垄断的现象,集中于高等院校与政府。犯罪控制运用科学的管理体制,采用招标投标的方式。

五、结　语

在社会管理向科学化方向发展的今天,犯罪学的建设和刑事政策的制定与实施应当遵循科学的轨道。犯罪与刑事司法科学的国内外既往发展,在理论、方法与实践上提供着重要的借鉴。在市场化竞争机制的指引下,融会了实业家精神的中国犯罪学,必将迎来蓬勃发展的春天!

违法与反社会行为的预防

大卫·P. 法林顿（David P. Farrington）

剑桥大学

这篇论文的目的是简要总结一些最有效的预防违法犯罪和反社会行为的项目，这些项目的有效性已经为高质量评估研究所证实。我关注的是经过大样本随机试验评估的项目，因为任何违法行为干预策略的成效能够在这些实验中得到有效的检验（Farrington and Welsh, 2006）。减少犯罪的主要方法可以分为发展性预防、社区预防、情境预防和刑事司法预防（Tonry and Farrington, 1995）。

刑事司法预防是指传统的具有威慑力、消除犯罪能力和改造罪犯的策略，是由执法和刑事司法机构执行实施的。社区预防指在社区内干预能够影响违法行为发生的社会环境与组织机构（如家庭，同伴，社会标准，俱乐部，组织）（Hope, 1995）。这些预防以诸如凝聚力和无序等社区危险性因素和社会环境为关注目标。情境预防指以减少犯罪机会和增加违法行为得逞的难度与风险为目标的预防（Clarke, 1995）。发展预防指遏制个人的潜在犯罪倾向的增长，尤其关注那些在研究人类发展中发现的目标危害性因素和保护性因素（Tremblay and Craig, 1995）。在这篇论文中我所关注的是发展性或聚焦风险的预防。

一、聚焦风险的预防

发展的或聚焦风险的预防，其基本内容很简单：发现滋生犯罪行为的主要风险因素,采取预防措施来遏制它们。经常性地努力致力于发现制约违法犯罪行为的保护性因素并采取预防手段来强化这些保护性因素。纵向调查研究用于不断更新风险因素和保护因素的知识和信息,实验研究和准实验研究用于预防和干预手段、措施的有效性。

聚焦风险的预防由戴维·霍金斯(David Hawkins)和理查德·卡塔拉诺(Richard Catalano)(1992)等先驱们从医药学与公共卫生领域引入犯罪学。这种方法已经成功地在治疗诸如癌症和心脏病等疾病上运用多年。例如,已查明的引发心脏病的风险因素包括抽烟、过量饮食和缺少锻炼。这些危害因素可以通过鼓励人们戒烟、养成健康的饮食习惯、加强锻炼得到消除。

聚焦风险的预防实现了理论解释和实际预防的联系,基础研究和应用研究的联系,学者、政策制定者和执行者之间的联系。《把儿童从犯罪中拯救出来:早期风险因素和有效干预》(Farrington and Welsh,2007)一书对此方法做了详尽的描述。重要的是,聚焦风险的预防易于为人们理解和传播,而且很快为决策者、执行者和大众所接受。风险因素及其预防都是基于经验研究而不是基于理论。这种方法避免了对哪些危险因素产生因果效应这一棘手的理论问题做出回答。

二、什么是风险因素?

从定义上看,风险因素预示着今后违法行为发生的高可能性(Kazdin *et al.*,1997)。例如,贫穷人家出身的儿童随着年龄的增长日后违法犯罪行为发生的可能性也会增加。剑桥大学在研究违法犯罪行为的发展情况时,对伦敦 400 名男性进行了从 8 岁到 48 岁的纵向调查研究。结果表明,在 8 岁时父母监护缺失的人中,到 50 岁的时候,其中有61%的人有过犯罪经历,而其余 8 岁时父母监护良好的人当中这一比例仅为36%,两者存在显著差异(Farrington *et al.*,2006)。既然风险因素的确定基于其对今后违法行为发生的预测能力,那么,运用纵向研究对构建它们是非常必要的。

违法行为风险因素中最重要的已众所周知(Farrington,2007)。它们包括个体因素,如易冲动,智力低下;家庭因素,如父母监护差,过分严厉和摇摆不定的家教;同伴因素,比如和有违法行为的朋友为伍;学校因素,如就读于一所违法犯罪行为频发的学校;社会经济因素,如低收入和居住条件差;邻里和社区因素,居住于一个高犯罪频率社区。我重点关注那些可以通过预防来改变的风险因素。另外,也有对能够阻止犯罪行为发生的保护性因素的研究,但很少为人们所了解。

违法犯罪、暴力、吸毒、逃学与失业等不同的违法犯罪行为,导致其产生的风险因素往往相同。这是一个好消息,因为对任意违法行为奏效的干预措施很可能也适用于其余的。

三、基于家庭的预防

如果父母的监护差和不能够长期保持的规则是导致了违法行为发生的原因,那么基于家庭的预防措施就能有效地减少违法行为的发生。杰拉尔德·帕特森(Gerald Patterson)(1982)在俄勒冈州主持的关于父母抚育行为的培训是最有影响的方法之一。他对父母和子女的相互作用的细密观察表明,反社会儿童的父母在抚养方法上存在缺陷。这些父母没有告诉子女们期望他们应有的行为是怎样的,没有使这种期望持续下去或没有以这种期望来督促提醒子女们认识到这种期望是必要的,并且没有用迅速、适当的奖励或惩罚来保证家教的实施。反社会子女的父母往往使用过多的惩罚(如责骂、大喊大叫、威胁),但没有视子女的表现而制定家教或没有把家教长期坚持下去。

帕特森(Patterson)的方法包含了前行为、行为和结果。他试图教给父母们有效的教养子女方法,即关注孩子在干什么,长期监督孩子的行为,清楚明白地告诉孩子们家教规则,视孩子的表现长期给以奖励和惩罚,消除父母和孩子间的分歧来避免冲突与危机的升级。

短期小样本研究表明,他的治疗对减少儿童偷窃和反社会行为是有效的(Dishion *et al.*,1992;Patterson *et al.*,1992)。然而,这个试验对3—10岁的儿童最为有效,而对年龄较大的青少年效果就不明显了。另外,难以获得有过最困难经历的家庭的合作,尤其是靠社会福利生活的单身母亲们。她们的压力太大,很难做到长期使用适当的方法教养子女。

现在我来回顾一遍已经被评定为最重要的基于家庭的干预策略:包括家庭访问方案(尤其是戴维·奥尔兹(David Olds)的工作),父母培训方案(尤其是卡洛琳·韦伯斯特-斯特拉顿(Carolyn Webster-Stratton),史蒂芬·司各特(Stephen Scott)和马修·桑德斯(Matthew Sanders)运用的方案),针对年龄较大孩子的家庭或社区方案(尤其是詹姆斯·亚历山大(James Alexander)和帕特丽夏·张伯伦(Patricia Chamberlain)运用的方案),多系统治疗方案或 MST(司各特·亨格勒(Scott

Henggeler)和艾莉森·坎宁安(Alison Cunningham)运用的方案)。

四、家庭访问方案

在最著名的深度家庭访问方案(现在叫做保育员—家庭合作关系)中,戴维·奥尔兹(David Olds)和他的同事们(1986)在埃尔迈拉(纽约州)把400位母亲随机地分配到三组,一组在怀孕期间接受保育员的拜访,另一组在怀孕期和孩子出生后的两年内都接受拜访,还有一个实验对照组,组里的母亲们不接受拜访。每一次拜访持续1个小时15分钟,母亲们平均每隔两星期被拜访一次。拜访者们给母亲们以婴儿产前及产后抚养上的建议、有关婴儿成长的知识、正确的营养和在怀孕期间戒烟戒酒的重要性。因此,这是一项通用的父母教育方案。

结果表明,产后拜访使子女在最初的两年内的身体虐待和疏忽的记录有所降低,尤其是那些贫困的未婚先孕的少年母亲,接受拜访组中的此类母亲有4%对子女有虐待和疏忽等犯罪行为,而控制组拜访中的这一比例则为19%。最后的结果最为重要,因为儿童时期受到虐待或疏忽的儿童长大后往往成为暴力罪犯(Widom,1989)。在随后的15年里,研究的重点放在了社会底层的未婚母亲身上。在她们中间,与那些只接受产前拜访或没有接受任何拜访的母亲相比,那些同时接受产前和产后拜访的母亲有较少的违法行为,更少的逮捕率(Olds *et al.*,1997)。另外,那些接受产前产后拜访或者只接受产后拜访的母亲抚养的孩子的违法犯罪记录比那些没有接受任何拜访的母亲抚养的孩子违法犯罪记录少一半多(Olds *et al.*,1998)。随后19年的调查表明这种方案对减少犯罪,尤其是女性犯罪非常有效(Eckenrode *et al.*,2010)。根据格林伍德(Greenwood)等人(2001)和奥斯(Aos)等人(2004)的数据,在这个方案上每投资一美元,就会节省三到四美元。

五、父母管理训练方案

最为著名的父母培训方案之一("艰难的岁月")是卡洛林·韦伯斯特-斯特拉顿(Carolyn Webster-Stratton)(1998)在西雅图实施的。她随机地把426名4岁的孩子(绝大多数孩子的母亲都单身且靠社会福利生活)分成两个组,一个实验组,接受家长培训,另一个是控制组,不接受培训。实验组的母亲们每隔一个星期进行一个聚会,这种聚会持续了八九个星期。她们观看介绍教养方法的录像后进行集中讨论。这些主题包括怎样与子女游戏,帮助子女学习,鼓励他们展现出他们最棒的那一面,有效地建立限制,纠正不端正行为,教给他们解决问题的方法,怎样给予和获得帮助。家庭观察表明实验组的孩子比控制组的孩子表现要好。

卡洛林·韦伯斯特-斯特拉顿(Carolyn Webster-Stratton)和玛丽·哈蒙德(Mary Hammond)也通过 100 名西雅图儿童(平均年龄为 5 岁),验证了父母培训与儿童技能培训方案的有效性。这些孩子因为行为表现存在问题曾经接受过医生治疗。这些孩子及其父母们被随机地分到四个组接受一下培训:(a)父母接受培训,(b)儿童接受技能培训,(c)同时接受父母培训和儿童技能培训,(d)控制组,即不接受任何培训。技能培训的目的是用视频示范来培养子女的亲社会行为和人际交往能力,而父母培训则是在持续的 22—24 周内,父母与治疗专家们每周一次面谈。父母报告和家庭观察表明,无论是在实验刚刚结束还是实验后一年,三个实验组的孩子们与实验对照组的孩子们相比,有较少的问题行为发生。尽管那些同时接受父母培训和子女技能培训的儿童在接下来的一年内行为表现有最明显的进步,但是这三个实验组的结果不存在明显的差异。可以得出一个普遍性结论,即同时进行父母和子女两方面的干预比进行单一方面的干预要有效。

斯蒂芬·司各特(Stephen Scott)和他的同事们(2001)在伦敦和奇切斯特评估了韦伯斯特—斯特拉顿的父母培训方案。来自下层社会家庭贫困的近 140 名 3—8 岁的曾被社会认为有反社会行为的儿童被随机地分到接受父母培训组和控制组。这个父母培训方案以观看录像为主要手段,包括对子女的奖励与惩罚,制定家庭规则,纠正子女不良行为。随后对父母做访谈和观察表明,与控制组的儿童相比,试验组的儿童有反社会行为次数显著地降低了。另外,经过这种干预之后,试验组的父母给予子女更多的鼓励,使他们朝被期望的目标努力,运用有效的命令使子女顺从。

马修·桑德斯(Matthew Sanders)和他的同事们(2000)在澳大利亚的布里斯旺市开展了积极父母管理方案(Positive Parenting Programme,简称 3P 方案)项目,这个方案既可以通过媒体的宣传影响而作为主要预防策略被应用于整个社区,也可以作为辅助预防策略应用于高危险或需要医学治疗的样本。桑德斯(Matthew Sanders)评价了这个策略的有效性,他把那些高危险的三岁儿童随机分为接受 W 的实验组和实验对照组两组。这项方案教给父母 17 种儿童监护策略,这些策略包括与孩子沟通,给予身心关爱和关注,树立好的榜样,制定家教规则,给以明确的指示,对错误行为采取适当的惩罚措施。("隔离处分",或让孩子返回他或她的房间)。这个评估表明 3P 策略在减少儿童反社会行为上很成功。托马斯(Thomas)和奇默(Zimmer-Gembeck)

（2007）的元分析也证实了这一点。

六、其他父母养育干预

另一个被称为功能性家庭治疗的父母养育干预,由詹姆斯·亚历山大（James Alexander）在美国的犹他州实施的（Alexander and Parsons,1973）。这个策略旨在调节家庭相互作用的方式,通过树立榜样,督促和强化,鼓励家庭成员之间在要求和解决问题的时候有明确的交流沟通,家庭冲突尽量最小化。所有的家庭成员都接受培训,如何进行有效沟通,明确规定权利和责任,运用一定的技术使彼此之间互相促进。通过随机地把86个有违法行为的儿童分配到实验组和实验对照组,对这个策略进行了评估。结果表明,与其他途径（以委托人为中心的或心理动力疗法）相比这种方法使轻微犯罪行为的再犯率减少了一半。一个以同样方法进行,对有严重犯罪行为的青少年进行的研究表明,这种方案同样有效。

帕特丽夏·张伯伦（Patricia Chamberlain）和约翰·里德（John Reid）（1998）在美国俄勒冈州评估了医治促进抚养方案（TFC,Treat Foster Care）,这是一种可以作为拘留监管青少年犯罪者的替代手段。拘留未成年罪犯被认为不尽如人意,尤其是罪犯同伴互相会产生不良影响。方案实施时,社区中家长们会被召集起来接受培训,为青少年罪犯提供一个环境。参加方案的青年在家里、社区和学校都受到严密的监管,他们与青少年罪犯同伴的接触机会被降低到最小。负责教养的父母们提供一个结构化、条理化的生活环境:有明确的规则、限制,针对违犯行为有长期的纪律,实行一对一的监督。青少年们被鼓励锻炼他们的学术能力,培养理想的工作习惯。

在这个评估中,79名男性青少年惯犯被随机地分配到实验组中,或固定的团体性家庭中与其他青少年罪犯生活在一起。随后一年的研究表明TPC男孩们的犯罪记录和自我报告的违法行为都有所减少。因此,这个方案看起来对减少违法行为是有效的。

七、多系统治疗方案

多系统治疗方案（MST）是一种重要的多元家庭保护项目,它是由司各特·亨格勒（Scott Henggeler）和他的同事们（1998）在南卡罗莱纳发展起来的。这个项目是根据青少年的特殊需要而确定的。因此,治疗的特点是因人而异的。这一方法在青年人的家庭,学校和社区中实施。通常,这种方法包括家庭干预、同伴干预和学校干预。家庭干预提升家长监督和约束青少年的能力,同伴干预鼓励青少年选择亲近社会的朋友,学校干预提升胜任力和学业成绩。

在司各特和他的同事们(1993)的评估中,84 个有严重不良倾向的少年(平均 15 岁)被随机地分配接受多系统方法或普通方法(主要包括让青少年离开家庭)的治疗。在随后的紧跟采访中发现接受多系统方法的青年有更少的人被逮捕,或更少的自我报告犯罪的行为。另外一个在密苏里州的评估中,查尔斯·布德林(Charles Borduin)和他的同事们(1995)把 176 个少年犯(平均年龄为 14 岁)随机分配接受多系统方法治疗和个人治疗,后者以个人、家庭和学校因素为关注点。四年之后,接受多系统方法的少年犯中只有 29% 的被再次逮捕,接受个人治疗方法的少年犯中却有 74% 的被再次逮捕。

遗憾的是,艾伦·理查德(Alan Leschied)和埃里森·坎宁安(Alison Cunningham)在加拿大进行的对 MST 更大规模的评估却得出了令人失望的结果(2002)。400 多个少年犯或有犯罪倾向的青年人被随机分配接受多系统方法或是其他普通方法(典型的是缓刑管制)。六个月后,28% 的接受多系统方法治疗的青少年再次获罪,31% 的接受其他方法的再次获罪,两者不存在显著差异。所以,我们并不清楚多系统方法在单独使用时究竟有多有效。两个对于 MST 的元分析得出了相反的结论:尼古拉·柯蒂斯(Nicola Curtis)和她的同伴(2004)发现 MST 是有效的,而茱莉亚·里特尔(Julia Littell)却发现它并没有效。

八、基于家庭的干预是有效的吗?

对基于家庭干预方案有效性的评估产生了令人鼓舞和令人失望两种结果。为了根据大量的评估结果对方案的有效性进行评价,布兰登·威尔士(Brandon Welsh)和我校阅了 40 个对家庭干预方案的评估,每一评估样本量实验组和控制组相加至少有 50 人(Farrington and Welsh,2003)。所有这些评估的输出都是对违法或反社会儿童行为的测量。在对 19 项输出为违法行为的研究中,有 10 项研究支持了家庭干预的影响是显著的结论,而其他 9 项研究没有得到显著的结果。幸运的是,没有研究证明家庭干预有巨大的负面影响。

在全部 19 项研究中,平均效果值(d,标准化均数差)为 0.32。这显然大于零。

当我们把它转换成再犯罪百分比时,一个标准化平均差 0.32 相当于再犯罪率的百分比从 50% 下降至 34%。因此,我们认为,把所有 19 个研究结果综合起来,它们证明以家庭为基础的干预有大量理想的效果。其他元分析(Piquero *et al.*,2008;Manning *et al.*,2010)也表明,早期发展性预防方案是有效的。

九、以学校为基础的预防策略

我现在来介绍一些以学校为基础的预防策略,这些方案中大多数都有一部分是以家庭为基础的。我会首先介绍佩里的学前教育项目,这也许是最有影响力的早期预防项目,因为它的结果表明项目的实施上每花费一美元就节省七美元。然后,我会介绍把儿童技能培训和家长培训结合起来的著名项目,这个项目曾在由理查德·特朗布莱(Richard Tremblay)在蒙特利尔实施,由戴维·霍金斯(David Hawkins)在西雅图实施。我也会介绍由丹·奥尔维斯(Dan Olweus)在挪威和彼得·史密斯(Peter Smith)在英国实施的反欺侮项目。

十、学前教育项目

最著名的智力开发项目是佩里规划,它是由劳伦斯·施魏因豪特(Lawrence Schweinhart)与戴维·魏卡特(David Weikart)(1980)在密歇根的伊普西兰蒂实施的。实质上这是一个针对处于弱势群体的非裔美国儿童展开的学前启蒙教育。一共 123 名孩子(基本上是随机抽取的)分派到实验组与实验对照组。实验组的青少年参加一个日常的学前项目,辅以两年内的每周家访(年龄在 3—4 岁),这个项目"计划—实施—回顾"的主要目的是提供智力激励、增加思考与推理能力,以及提高今后的学习成绩。

这个实验有着良好的长期效果。约翰·贝吕埃-克雷孟特(John Berrueta-Clement)与他的同事(1984)表明:实验组的十九岁学生更容易就业、更有可能完成高中学业、更有希望能够接受大学或专业教育,却很少有违法被逮捕的可能。直到 27 岁,实验组的被逮捕人数累计起来平均只有对照组的一半(Schweinhart *et al.*,1993)。另外,他们明显有高收入和最有可能是业主,实验组的大多女性都已婚,并且她们很少是未婚生育。

在他们年满 40 岁的最新跟踪调查发现,参与者仍然在随后的生活中表现出极大的不同(Schweinhart et al., 2005)。那些接受项目的人员因暴力犯罪(32% vs. 48%)、财产犯罪(36% vs. 56%)、毒品使用(14% vs. 34%)而被终身逮捕显著少于对照组。他们也很少会被判刑五次或更多(36% vs. 55%)。在生命周期中的其他重要方面的改善同样有记录。例如,与对照组相比,实验组中有更多的人受过高等教育(77% vs. 60% 从高中毕业)、工作较好(76% vs. 62%)、有较高年收入,这些差异是显著的。

多项经济分析显示这个项目的经济收益远远高于其投入。裴里(Perry)项目的自我估算(Barnett, 1993)包括犯罪与非犯罪收益、对受害者的无形成本,甚至包含 27 岁以上人员的规划性养老金收益。于是,项目产生了收益与成本比率为 7 : 1 的结果。绝大部分收益(65%)源于犯罪在受害者身上的投入节约。最近的一项针对 40 岁人员的调查发现投入与产出为 1 : 17。

十一、学校方案

蒙特利尔的纵向实验研究结合了儿童技能培训与父母培训。理查德·特伦布莱(Richard Tremblay)与他的同事们(1995)找出 300 名六岁具有破坏性的(攻击性或亢奋的)儿童,把他们随机分派到实验组与对照组。在他们 7 岁至 9 岁时,实验组学生接受旨在提高社会技能与自制力方面的培训。专家指导、同伴榜样、角色扮演和强化偶然事件等手段被运用到小组讨论中,围绕"怎样提供帮助"、"生气时该做什么"、"怎样回应戏弄"这些话题展开小组讨论。同时,他们的父母将接受杰拉尔德·帕特森(Gerald Patterson)(1982)的父母管理培训技巧的培训(1992)。

这项预防项目是成功的。直到 12 岁,与对照组相比较,实验组男孩很少有偷盗行为、很少酗酒、很少参与打架斗殴(根据自我报告)。同时,实验组男生有着良好的学习成绩。从 10—15 岁的每一个年龄段与对照组相比,实验组男生的自我报告犯罪记录较少。有趣的是,随着后续调查的进行,发现在反社会行为上,实验组与对照组之间的差别有所增加。到 24 岁时,实验组男生很少有犯罪记录(布瓦若利等,2007)。

最重要的一个基于学校的预防实验由戴维·霍金斯(David Hawkins)与他的同事在西雅图展开(1991)。他们实施了一项把家长培训、教师培训和儿童技能培训结合起来的方案。八个学校 21 个班级的大约 500 名一年级学生(6 岁)被随机地安排在实验班与对照班。实验班的学生将在家中或学校接受专门的培训来加强他们与父母、与学校的亲密关系。另外,他们接受了人际认知方面的问题解决训练。他们的父母将在"发现他们好的那一面"这个项目中注意并强化孩子的符合社会期望的行为。教师们在课堂管理方面得到培训,例如:清晰地指导或提出期望,对期望的行为参与给予奖励,教育学生亲社会性(社会所期望的)的问题解决方法。

这个项目有着长效收益。截止到六年级(12 岁),实验组的男生很少有主动性违法犯罪行为,而女生很少有主动性吸毒的(O'Donnell et al. ,1995)。在后来的随访中戴维·霍金斯(David Hawkins)与他的同事(1999)发现,在他们 18 岁时,全程干预组的青少年(从一年级开始接受干预一直到六年级)与后期干预组(仅限 5 到 6 年级)或控制组相比,他们更少使用暴力、酗酒,更少性伴侣。到 27 岁,干预组(实验组)有良好的学习成绩和健康的心理,少有犯罪与吸毒等行为(Hawkins et al. ,2008)。

十二、反欺负方案

校园欺负行为理所当然的是引起违法犯罪的危险因素(法林顿,1993)。一些基于学校的预防项目在减少学校欺凌方面成效显著。最著名的一项由丹·奥尔韦乌斯(Dan Olweus)(1994)在挪威实施的。这个项目的基本原理是:创造一种充满成人关怀、对儿童感兴趣并使儿童积极参与的环境,实行包括关怀、严格指导与密切监督等手段在内的权威式子女教养方法,因为这种教养方式与学校欺负相关(Baldry and Farrington,1998);对不被允许的欺负行为进行严格限制;对违规行为实行一贯的非肢体处罚;加强对儿童行为的监督,尤其是在操场;减少欺负行为发生的机会或对欺负行为给予鼓励。

奥尔韦乌斯项目的目的在于提高老师、家长和孩子们对校园欺负行为的关注和认识,使他们放弃关于欺负的种种误解与无知。一本 30 页的小册子被发放到挪威的所有学校,里面包含了对欺负的阐释,向老师和家长推荐了减少欺负行为可采取的措施以及实施步骤。另外,一份长达 25 分钟关于欺负的录像也发放到各个学校。之后,学校向家长们分发了有四页内容的文件夹,里面包含关于欺负行为的资料以及怎样减少欺负的建议。另外,还要求学生们匿名完成关于暴力的自我报告的问卷。

在专门的学校研讨会上,每个学校都通过调查问卷收到了关于青少年欺负普遍性和被欺负受害者的反馈信息。另外,鼓励老师们制定详细的制止欺负行为的规则(如自觉避免实施欺负行为,当欺凌行为发生时及时通知他人,欺凌行为是不可忍受的,试着帮助欺负行为受害者,试着关心那些被同学们冷落的孩子),以观看录像和角色扮演的方式在班级里展开对欺负行为的讨论。另外,鼓励老师加强对孩子们的监督管理,尤其是在体育课上。

在 42 所卑尔根(挪威港口城市)学校进行的对这项反欺负项目的效果进行了评估。丹·奥尔韦乌斯(Dan Olweus)通过孩子们的自我报告问卷对试验前后欺负行为盛行情况作了比较。因为所有的学校都实施了这一方案,因此没有实验对照学校。然而,奥尔韦乌斯(Olweus)将在这个项目实施之前某一年龄的孩子(例如 13 岁)和实验之后作了比较。总体上,这个项目非常成功,因为欺负行为减少了一半。

彼得·史密斯(Peter Smith)和索尼娅·夏普(Sonia Sharp)(1994)在 23 个谢菲尔德市(英国城市)的学校中实施了相似的方案。这个核心方案包括确立全校范围内的反欺负政策,增强对欺负行为的意识,师生应当正确定位自己的角色,明确自己的职责,从而每个人都明白欺负是什么以及怎样应对。另外,对专门为个别的学校提供的可供选择的干预措施:课程工作(比如读书,观看录像),直接指导学生(例如,对那些受到欺负的学生进行自信心训练),操场训练(例如,训练午餐管理者)。这个项目对于减少小学校园内的欺负行为(减少了 15%)非常成功,但是在中学里几乎没有什么影响(只减少了 5%)。法林顿(Farrington)和托菲(Ttofi)(2009)重新评估了 44个反欺负项目,得出结论:欺负行为和受害情况平均减少了 20%。

十三、社区管理策略

为了使有效性最大化,所需要的是一个基于社区的多元层次干预策略,包括上面列出的几个成功的干预措施。在本章中回顾的许多策略都是这一类型。然而,社区护理(CTC)有很多吸引人的地方(Farrington,1996)。或许比起任何其他策略,它更多地以证据为基础,具有系统性:干预策略的选取对某一特定社区来说什么是重要的危险性和保护性因素以及关于策略是否有效的经验证据(Sherman et al.,2002)。它已经在英格兰,苏格兰和威尔士,以及荷兰和澳大利亚至少 35 个地区实施(社区关怀,1997 年)。在由霍金斯(Hawkins)等人进行的大规模的评估中(2009 年)发现,美国 24 个社区因使用 CTC 而减少了犯罪和毒品滥用。

CTC 计划是由戴维·霍金斯(David Hawkins)和理查德·卡塔拉诺(Richard Catalano)开发的基于聚焦风险的预防策略(1992 年),它是美国少年司法与犯罪预防办公室(OJJDP 's)应对严重暴力和长期性青少年犯罪的综合策略的核心内容

（Wilson and Howell，1993）。CTC 是依据组织危险性和保护性因素的理论（社会发展模型）建立的。该干预手段适用于每个特定社区的需要。"社区"可以是一个城市，一个县，一个小镇，甚至邻里或一所房产。该计划旨在通过实施特殊的预防策略来减少青少年犯罪和毒品使用。这一预防策略已证明在减少危害因素或加强保护因素方面有效。它是参考大型社区性的公众健康计划而设计的，这种计划旨在通过解决主要危害性因素来减少疾病如冠心病的发生。CTC 方案强调强化保护性因素和构建优势，部分原因在于对社区来说这比化解危险因素更具吸引力。但是，诚然，一般促进健康改善比疾病预防更有效（Kaplan，2000 年）。

CTC 方案以社会动员为开端。主要社区领导人（例如选出的代表、教育官员、警察长官、商界领袖）被召集在一起，目的是让他们赞同预防计划的目标，同意实施干预策略。主要领导人随后成立一个社区的委员会并对它负责。它由邻里居民和各机构（如学校、警察、市政、缓刑司法、医疗卫生、家庭、青年团体、商界、教堂、媒体）的代表组成。社区委员会代表社区负责社区预防。

随后，社区委员会对社区进行风险性因素与保护性因素评价，找出这个社区需要解决的关键风险性因素和需要强化的保护性因素。对风险性因素的评估可能会涉及警察、学校、社会或人口普查记录，或对当地邻里或学校进行的调查。确定关键的风险性与保护性因素后，社区委员会评估现有资源，规划干预策略。在专家的技术援助和指导下，他们从一系列方案策略中选择那些已经在精心设计的评估研究中被证明是有效的方案。

由霍金斯和卡特拉诺列举的策略清单（1992）包括产前及产后家庭拜访计划，学前智力增进计划，父母培训，学校组织与课程建设，师资培训，媒体运动。其他策略包括孩子技能培训、学校的反欺负计划、情境预防和警务战略。预防策略的选择是基于行之有效的应对每一特定风险性因素的实验证据，但是它也取决于什么被确定为该社区最大的问题。虽然这种方法并不是无懈可击的，但它基于经验性证据汇集了在多个领域最有效的预防计划，所以它非常有望能够减少犯罪和创建更安全的社区。

十四、结　论

高质量的评价性研究显示许多项目都能有效地减少青少年违法犯罪和反社会行为，并且在很多情况下，这些项目的经济收益超过它们的项目支出。最好的方案包括一般性家长教育、家长管理培训、学前智力提升方案、孩子技能训练、师资训练、反欺负方案和 MST。

对于减少犯罪方案有效性的高质量实验和准实验评估在所有国家都是需要的。大多数关于预防策略有效性的知识,如认知行为的技能培训、父母培训和学前智力提升方案,是基于美国的研究取得的,但尚不清楚美国研究的结果在多大程度上可推广应用到其他国家。

在所有国家建立一个大规模的基于证据的,包含严格的评价要求的综合性国家策略来减少犯罪和相关的社会问题的时机已经成熟。这就应该实施这些计划来抑制风险性因素,强化保护性因素,它也同样基于"社区关怀"。初级预防已经有力地改善了人的健康,那么它就可以同样在所有国家有效减少违法犯罪和反社会行为。

[参考文献见英文原作]

（丁靖艳　张宙跫　译）

Prevention of Delinquency
and Antisocial Behaviour

David P. Farrington

University of Cambridge

The main aim of this paper is to summarize briefly some of the most effective programmes for preventing delinquency and antisocial behaviour whose effectiveness has been demonstrated in high quality evaluation research. My focus is especially on programmes evaluated in randomized experiments with reasonably large samples, since the effect of any intervention on delinquency can be demonstrated most convincingly in such experiments (Farrington and Welsh, 2006). The major methods of reducing crime can be classified as developmental, community, situational and criminal justice prevention (Tonry and Farrington, 1995).

Criminal justice prevention refers to traditional deterrent, incapacitative and rehabilitative strategies operated by law enforcement and criminal justice system agencies. Community prevention refers to interventions designed to change the social conditions and institutions (e. g. families, peers, social norms, clubs, organizations) that influence offending in residential communities (Hope, 1995). These interventions target community risk factors and social conditions such as cohesiveness or disorganisation. Situational prevention refers to interventions designed to prevent the occurrence of crimes by reducing opportunities and increasing the risk and difficulty of offending (Clarke, 1995).

Developmental prevention refers to interventions designed to prevent the development of criminal potential in individuals, especially those targeting risk and protective factors discovered in studies of human development (Tremblay and Craig, 1995). My focus in this paper is on developmental or risk-focussed prevention.

RISK-FOCUSSED PREVENTION

The basic idea of developmental or risk-focussed prevention is very simple: Identify the key risk factors for offending and implement prevention techniques designed to counteract them. There is often a related attempt to identify key protective factors against offending and to implement prevention techniques designed to enhance them. Longitudinal surveys are used to advance knowledge about risk and protective factors, and experimental and quasi-experimental methods are used to evaluate the impact of prevention and intervention programmes.

Risk-focussed prevention was imported into criminology from medicine and public health by pioneers such as David Hawkins and Richard Catalano (1992). This approach has been used successfully for many years to tackle illnesses such as cancer and heart disease. For example, the identified risk factors for heart disease include smoking, a fatty diet, and lack of exercise. These can be tackled by encouraging people to stop smoking, to have a more healthy low-fat diet, and to take more exercise.

Risk-focussed prevention links explanation and prevention, links fundamental and applied research, and links scholars, policy makers, and practitioners. The book *Saving Children From a Life of Crime: Early Risk Factors and Effective Interventions* (Farrington and Welsh, 2007) contains a detailed exposition of this approach. Importantly, risk-focussed prevention is easy to understand and to communicate, and it is readily accepted by policy makers, practitioners, and the general public. Both risk factors and interventions are based on empirical research rather than on theories. This approach avoids difficult theoretical questions about which risk factors have causal effects.

WHAT IS A RISK FACTOR?

By definition, a risk factor predicts a high probability of later offending (Kazdin et al., 1997). For example, children who experience poor parental supervision have an increased risk of committing criminal acts later on. In the Cambridge Study in Delinquent

Development, which is a prospective longitudinal survey of 400 London males from age 8 to age 48, 61% of those experiencing poor parental supervision at age 8 were convicted up to age 50, compared with 36% of the remainder, a significant difference (Farrington et al., 2006). Since risk factors are defined by their ability to predict later offending, it follows that longitudinal studies are needed to establish them.

The most important risk factors for delinquency are well known (Farrington, 2007). They include individual factors such as high impulsiveness and low intelligence; family factors such as poor parental supervision and harsh or erratic parental discipline; peer factors such as hanging around with delinquent friends; school factors such as attending a high delinquency-rate school; socio-economic factors such as low income and poor housing; and neighbourhood or community factors such as living in a high-crime neighbourhood. My focus is on risk factors that can be changed by interventions. There is also a focus on protective factors that predict a low probability of offending, but less is known about them.

Risk factors tend to be similar for many different outcomes, including delinquency, violence, drug use, school failure and unemployment. This is good news, because a programme that is successful in reducing one of these outcomes is likely to be successful in reducing the others as well.

FAMILY-BASED PREVENTION

If poor parental supervision and inconsistent discipline are causes of delinquency, it is plausible that family-based prevention should succeed in reducing offending. The behavioural parent management training developed by Gerald Patterson (1982) in Oregon is one of the most influential approaches. His careful observations of parent-child interaction showed that parents of antisocial children were deficient in their methods of child-rearing. These parents failed to tell their children how they were expected to behave, failed to use it consistently or monitor their behaviour to ensure that it was desirable, and failed to enforce rules promptly and unambiguously with appropriate rewards and penalties. The parents of antisocial children used more punishment (such as scolding, shouting or threatening), but failed to use it consistently or make it contingent on the child's behaviour.

Patterson's method involved linking antecents, behaviours and consequences. He attempted to train parents in effective child rearing methods, namely noticing what a child is doing, monitoring the child's behaviour over long periods, clearly stating house rules, making rewards and punishments consistent and contingent on the child's behaviour, and negotiating disagreements so that conflicts and crises did not escalate.

His treatment was shown to be effective in reducing child stealing and antisocial behaviour over short periods in small-scale studies (Dishion *et al.* , 1992; Patterson *et al.* , 1992). However, the treatment worked best with children aged 3—10 and less well with adolescents. Also, there were problems of achieving cooperation from the families experiencing the worst problems. In particular, single mothers on welfare were experiencing so many different stresses that they found it difficult to use consistent and contingent child-rearing methods.

I will now review the most important types of family-based programmes that have been evaluated. These are home visiting programmes (and especially the work of David Olds) , parent training programmes (especially those used by Carolyn Webster-Stratton, Stephen Scott and Matthew Sanders) , home or community programmes with older children (especially those implemented by James Alexander and Patricia Chamberlain) and Multi-Systemic Therapy or MST (used by Scott Henggeler and Alison Cunningham).

HOME VISITING PROGRAMMES

In the most famous intensive home visiting programme (now called the " Nurse Family Partnership") , David Olds and his colleagues (1986) in Elmira (New York State) randomly allocated 400 mothers either to receive home visits from nurses during pregnancy, or to receive visits both during pregnancy and during the first two years of life, or to a control group who received no visits. Each visit lasted about one and a quarter hours, and the mothers were visited on average every two weeks. The home visitors gave advice about prenatal and postnatal care of the child, about infant development, and about the importance of proper nutrition and avoiding smoking and drinking during pregnancy. Hence, this was a general parent education programme.

The results of this experiment showed that the postnatal home visits caused a decrease in recorded child physical abuse and neglect during the first two years of life, especially by poor unmarried teenage mothers; 4% of visited versus 19% of non-visited mothers of this type were guilty of child abuse or neglect. This last result is important because children who are physically abused or neglected tend to become violent offenders later in life (Widom, 1989). In a 15-year follow-up, the main focus was on lower class unmarried mothers. Among these mothers, those who received prenatal and postnatal home visits had fewer arrests than those who received prenatal visits or no visits (Olds et al. , 1997). Also, children of these mothers who received prenatal and/or postnatal home visits had less than half as many arrests as children of mothers who received no visits (Olds et al. , 1998). Also, a 19-year follow-up showed that it was effective in reducing arrests, especially of females (Eckenrode et al. , 2010). For every $1 spent on the programme, $3—$4 were saved, according to Greenwood et al. (2001) and Aos et al. (2004).

PARENT MANAGEMENT TRAINING

One of the most famous parent training programmes ("The Incredible Years") was developed by Carolyn Webster-Stratton (1998) in Seattle. She evaluated its success by randomly allocating 426 children aged 4 (most with single mothers on welfare) either to an experimental group which received parent training or to a control group which did not. The experimental mothers met in groups every week for 8 or 9 weeks, watched videotapes demonstrating parenting skills, and then took part in focussed group discussions. The topics included how to play with your child, helping your child learn, using praise and encouragement to bring out the best in your child, effective setting of limits, handling misbehaviour, how to teach your child to solve problems, and how to give and get support. Observations in the home showed that the experimental children behaved better than the control children.

Carolyn Webster-Stratton and Mary Hammond (1997) also evaluated the effectiveness of parent training and child skills training with about 100 Seattle children (average age 5) referred to a clinic because of conduct problems. The children and their parents were randomly allocated to receive either (a) parent training, (b) child skills training, (c) both parent and child training, or (d) to a control group. The skills training aimed to foster prosocial behaviour and interpersonal skills using video modelling, while the parent training involved weekly meetings between parents and therapists for 22—24 weeks. Parent reports and home observations showed that children in all three experimental conditions had fewer behaviour problems than control children, both in an immediate and in a one-year follow-up. There was little difference between the three experimental conditions, although the combined parent and child training condition produced the most significant improvements in child behaviour at the one-year follow-up. There is a general finding, that combined parent and child interventions are more effective than either one alone.

Stephen Scott and his colleagues (2001) evaluated the Webster-Stratton parent training programme in London and Chichester. About 140 mainly poor, disadvantaged children aged 3—8 who were referred for antisocial behaviour were randomly assigned to receive parent training or to be in a control group. The parent training programme, based on videotapes, covered praise and rewards, setting limits, and handling misbehaviour. Follow-up parent interviews and observations showed that the antisocial behaviour of the experimental children decreased significantly compared to that of the controls. Furthermore, after the intervention, experimental parents gave their children more praise to encourage desirable behaviour, and used more effective commands to obtain compliance.

Matthew Sanders and his colleagues (2000) in Brisbane, Australia, developed the Triple-P Positive Parenting programme. This programme can either be delivered to the whole community in primary prevention using the mass media or can be used in secondary prevention with high-risk or clinic samples. Sanders evaluated the success of Triple-P with high-risk children aged 3 by randomly allocating them either to receive Triple-P or to be in control group. The Triple-P programme involves teaching parents 17 child management strategies including talking with children, giving physical affection, praising , giving attention, setting a good example, setting rules, giving clear instructions, and using appropriate penalties for misbehaviour ("time-out", or sending the child to his or her room). The evaluation showed that the Triple-P programme was successful in reducing children's antisocial behaviour. A meta-analysis by Thomas and Zimmer-Gembeck (2007) confirms the effectiveness of Triple-P in improving child behaviour.

OTHER PARENTING INTERVENTIONS

Another parenting intervention, termed functional family therapy, was developed by James Alexander in Utah (Alexander and Parsons, 1973). This aimed to modify patterns of family interaction by modelling, prompting and reinforcement, to encourage clear communication between family members of requests and solutions, and to minimize conflict. Essentially, all family members were trained to negotiate effectively, to set clear rules about privileges and responsibilities, and to use techniques of reciprocal reinforcement with each other. The programme was evaluated by randomly allocating 86 delinquents to experimental or control conditions. The results showed that this technique halved the recidivism rate of minor delinquents in comparison with other approaches (client-centred or psychodynamic therapy). Its effectiveness with more serious offenders was confirmed in a replication study using matched groups (Barton *et al.*, 1985).

Patricia Chamberlain and John Reid (1998) in Oregon evaluated treatment foster care (TFC), which was used as an alternative to custody for delinquents. Custodial sentences for delinquents were thought to have undesirable effects especially because of the bad influence of delinquent peers. In treatment foster care, families in the community were recruited and trained to provide a placement for delinquent youths. The TFC youths were cLösely supervised at home, in the community, and in the school, and their contacts with delinquent peers were minimized. The foster parents provided a structured daily living environment, with clear rules and limits, consistent discipline for rule violations and one-to-one monitoring. The youths were encouraged to develop academic skills and desirable work habits.

In the evaluation, 79 chronic male delinquents were randomly assigned to treatment foster care or to regular group homes where they lived with other delinquents. A one-year follow-up showed that the TFC boys had fewer criminal referrals and lower self-reported delinquency. Hence, this programme seemed to be an effective treatment for delinquency.

MULTI-SYSTEMIC THERAPY

Multi-Systemic Therapy (MST) is an important multiple-component family preservation programme that was developed by Scott Henggeler and his colleagues (1998) in South Carolina. The particular type of treatment is chosen according to the particular needs of the youth. Therefore, the nature of the treatment is different for each person. MST is delivered in the youth's home, school and community settings. The treatment typically includes family intervention to promote the parent's ability to monitor and discipline the adolescent, peer intervention to encourage the choice of prosocial friends, and school intervention to enhance competence and school achievement.

In the evaluation by Scott Henggeler and his colleagues (1993), 84 serious delinquents (with an average age of 15) were randomly assigned either to receive MST or the usual treatment (which mostly involved placing the juvenile outside home). The results showed that the MST group had fewer arrests and fewer self-reported crimes in a one-year follow-up. In another evaluation in Missouri, Charles Borduin and his colleagues (1995) randomly assigned 176 juvenile offenders (with an average age of 14) either to MST or to individual therapy focussing on personal, family and academic issues. Four years later, only 29% of the MST offenders had been rearrested, compared with 74% of the individual therapy group.

Unfortunately, disappointing results were obtained in a large-scale independent evaluation of MST in Canada by Alan Leschied and Alison Cunningham (2002). Over 400 youths who were either offenders or at risk of offending were randomly assigned to receive either MST or the usual services (typically probation supervision). Six months after treatment, 28% of the MST group had been reconvicted, compared with 31% of the control group, a non-significant difference. Therefore, it is unclear how effective MST is when it is implemented independently. Two meta-analyses of the effectiveness of MST reached contradictory conclusions. Nicola Curtis and her colleagues (2004) found that it was effective, but Julia Littell (2005) found that it was not.

IS FAMILY-BASED INTERVENTION EFFECTIVE?

Evaluations of the effectiveness of family-based intervention programmes have produced both encouraging and discouraging results. In order to assess effectiveness according to a large number of evaluations, Brandon Welsh and I reviewed 40 evaluations of family-based programmes each involving at least 50 persons in experimental and control groups combined (Farrington and Welsh, 2003). All of these had outcome measures of delinquency or antisocial child behaviour. Of the 19 studies with outcome measures of delinquency, 10 found significantly beneficial effects of the intervention and 9 found no significant effect. Happily, no study found a significantly harmful effect of family-based treatment.

Over all 19 studies, the average effect size (d, the standardized mean difference) was .32. This was significantly greater than zero. When we converted it into the percentage reconvicted, a d value of .32 corresponds to a decrease in the percentage reconvicted from 50% to 34%. Therefore, we concluded that, taking all 19 studies together, they showed that family-based intervention had substantial desirable effects. Other meta-analyses (e.g. Piquero *et al.*, 2008; Manning *et al.*, 2010) also show that early developmental prevention programmes are effective.

SCHOOL-BASED PREVENTION

I now turn to school-based prevention programmes, most of which also had a family-based component. I will first of all review the Perry pre-school programme, which is perhaps the most influential early prevention programme, because it concluded that $7 were saved for ever $1 expended. Then I will review the famous programmes combining child skills training and parent training, implemented in Montreal by Richard Tremblay and in Seattle by David Hawkins. I will also review anti-bullying programmes by Dan Olweus in Norway and Peter Smith in England.

PRE-SCHOOL PROGRAMMES

The most famous pre-school intellectual enrichment programme is the Perry project carried out in Ypsilanti (Michigan) by Lawrence Schweinhart and David Weikart (1980). This was essentially a "Head Start" programme targeted on disadvantaged African American children. A small sample of 123 children were allocated (approximately at random) to experimental and control groups. The experimental children attended a daily pre-school programme, backed up by weekly home visits, usually lasting two years (covering ages 3—4). The aim of the "plan-do-review" programme was to provide intellectual stimulation, to increase thinking and reasoning abilities, and to increase later school achievement.

This programme had long-term benefits. John Berrueta-Clement and his colleagues (1984) showed that, at age 19, the experimental group was more likely to be employed, more likely to have graduated from high school, more likely to have received college or vocational training, and less likely to have been arrested. By age 27, the experimental group had accumulated only half as many arrests on average as the controls (Schweinhart et al., 1993). Also, they had significantly higher earnings and were more likely to be home-owners. More of the experimental women were married, and fewer of their children were born to unmarried mothers.

The most recent follow-up of this programme at age 40 found that it continued to make an important difference in the lives of the participants (Schweinhart et al., 2005). Compared to the control group, those who received the programme had significantly fewer life-time arrests for violent crimes (32% vs. 48%), property crimes (36% vs. 56%), and drug crimes (14% vs. 34%), and they were significantly less likely to be arrested five or more times (36% vs. 55%). Improvements were also recorded in many other important life course outcomes. For example, significantly higher levels of schooling (77% vs. 60% graduating from high school), better records of employment (76% vs. 62%), and higher annual incomes were reported by the programme group compared to the controls.

Several economic analyses show that the financial benefits of this programme outweighed its costs. The Perry project's own calculation (Barnett, 1993) included crime and non-crime benefits, intangible costs to victims, and even included projected benefits beyond age 27. This generated the famous benefit-to-cost ratio of 7 to 1. Most of the benefits (65%) were derived from savings to crime victims. The most recent cost-benefit analysis at age 40 found that the programme produced $17 in benefits per $1 of cost.

SCHOOL PROGRAMMES

The Montreal longitudinal-experimental study combined child skills training and parent training. Richard Tremblay and his colleagues (1995) identified disruptive (aggressive or hyperactive) boys at age 6, and randomly allocated over 300 of these to experimental or control conditions. Between ages 7 and 9, the experimental group received training designed to foster social skills and self-control. Coaching, peer modelling, role playing and reinforcement contingencies were used in small group sessions on such topics as "how to help", "what to do when you are angry" and "how to react to teasing". Also, their parents were trained using the parent management training techniques developed by Gerald Patterson (1982).

This prevention programme was successful. By age 12, the experimental boys committed less burglary and theft, were less likely to get drunk, and were less likely to be involved in fights than the controls (according to self-reports). Also, the experimental boys had higher school achievement. At every age from 10 to 15, the experimental boys had lower self-reported delinquency scores than the control boys. Interestingly, the differences in antisocial behaviour between experimental and control boys increased as the follow-up progressed. Up to age 24, fewer experimental boys had a criminal record (Boisjoli *et al.* , 2007).

One of the most important school-based prevention experiments was carried out in Seattle by David Hawkins and his colleagues (1991). They implemented a multiple component programme combining parent training, teacher training and child skills training. About 500 first grade children (aged 6) in 21 classes in 8 schools were randomly assigned to be in experimental or control classes. The children in the experimental classes received special treatment at home and school which was designed to increase their attachment to their parents and their bonding to the school. Also, they were trained in interpersonal cognitive problem-solving. Their parents were trained to notice and reinforce socially desirable behaviour in a programme called "Catch them being good". Their teachers were trained in classroom management, for example to provide clear instructions and expectations to children, to reward children for participation in desired behaviour, and to teach children prosocial (socially desirable) methods of solving problems.

This programme had long-term benefits. By the sixth grade (age 12), experimental boys were less likely to have initiated delinquency, while experimental girls were less likely to have initiated drug use (O'Donnell et al., 1995). In a later follow-up, David Hawkins and his colleagues (1999) found that, at age 18, the full intervention group (those who received the intervention from grades 1—6) admitted less violence, less alcohol abuse and fewer sexual partners than the late intervention group (grades 5—6 only) or the control group. Up to age 27, the intervention group was better on educational attainment and mental health, but not on crime or substance use (Hawkins et al., 2008).

ANTI-BULLYING PROGRAMMES

School bullying, of course, is a risk factor for offending (Farrington, 1993). Several school-based programmes have been effective in reducing bullying. The most famous of these was implemented by Dan Olweus (1994) in Norway. The general principles of the programme were: to create an environment characterized by adult warmth, interest in children, and involvement with children; to use authoritative child-rearing, including warmth, firm guidance, and close supervision, since authoritarian child-rearing is related to child bullying (Baldry and Farrington, 1998); to set firm limits on what is unacceptable bullying; to consistently apply non-physical sanctions for rule violations; to improve monitoring and surveillance of child behaviour, especially in the playground; and to decrease opportunities and rewards for bullying.

The Olweus programme aimed to increase awareness and knowledge of teachers, parents and children about bullying and to dispel myths about it. A 30-page booklet was distributed to all schools in Norway describing what was known about bullying and recommending what steps schools and teachers could take to reduce it. Also, a 25-minute video about bullying was made available to schools. Simultaneously, the schools distributed to all parents a four-page folder containing information and advice about bullying. In addition, anonymous self-report questionnaires about bullying were completed by all children.

Each school received feedback information from the questionnaire, about the prevalence of bullies and victims, in a specially arranged school conference day. Also, teachers were encouraged to develop explicit rules about bullying (e. g. do not bully, tell someone when bullying happens, bullying will not be tolerated, try to help victims, try to include children who are being left out) and to discuss bullying in class, using the video and role-playing exercises. Also, teachers were encouraged to improve monitoring and supervision of children, especially in the playground.

The effects of this anti-bullying programme were evaluated in 42 Bergen schools. Dan Olweus measured the prevalence of bullying before and after the programme using self-report questionnaires completed by the children. Since all schools received the programme, there were no control schools. However, Olweus compared children of a certain age (e. g. 13) before the programme with children of the same age after the programme. Overall, the programme was very successful, because bullying decreased by half.

A similar programme was implemented in 23 Sheffield schools by Peter Smith and Sonia Sharp (1994). The core programme involved establishing a "whole-school" anti-bullying policy, raising awareness of bullying and clearly defining roles and responsibilities of teachers and students, so that everyone knew what bullying was and what they should do about it. In addition, there were optional interventions tailored to particular schools: curriculum work (e. g. reading books, watching videos), direct work with students (e. g. assertiveness training for those who were bullied) and playground work (e. g. training lunch-time supervisors). This programme was successful in reducing bullying (by 15%) in primary schools, but had relatively small effects (a 5% reduction) in secondary schools. Farrington and Ttofi (2009) reviewed 44 anti-bullying programmes and concluded that, on average, bullying and victimization were reduced by about 20%.

COMMUNITIES THAT CARE

In the interests of maximizing effectiveness, what is needed is a multiple-component community-based programme including several of the successful interventions listed above.

Many of the programmes reviewed in this chapter are of this type. However, *Communities That Care* (CTC) has many attractions (Farrington, 1996). Perhaps more than any other programme, it is evidence-based and systematic: the choice of interventions depends on empirical evidence about what are the important risk and protective factors in a particular community and on empirical evidence about "What works" (Sherman *et al.*, 2002). It has been implemented in at least 35 sites in England, Scotland and Wales, and also in the Netherlands and Australia (Communities that Care, 1997). In a large scale evaluation, Hawkins *et al.* (2009) found that, in 24 American communities, CTC was followed by reductions in delinquency and substance use.

CTC was developed as a risk-focussed prevention strategy by David Hawkins and Richard Catalano (1992), and it is a core component of the U. S. Office of Juvenile Justice and Delinquency Prevention's (OJJDP's) Comprehensive Strategy for Serious, Violent and Chronic Juvenile Offenders (Wilson and Howell, 1993). CTC is based on a theory (the social development model) that organizes risk and protective factors. The intervention techniques are tailored to the needs of each particular community. The "community" could be a city, a county, a small town, or even a neighbourhood or a housing estate. This programme aims to reduce delinquency and drug use by implementing particular prevention strategies that have demonstrated effectiveness in reducing risk factors or enhancing protective factors. It is modelled on large-scale community-wide public health programmes designed to reduce illnesses such as coronary heart disease by tackling key risk factors. There is great emphasis in CTC on enhancing protective factors and building on strengths, partly because this is more attractive to communities than tackling risk factors. However, it is generally true that health promotion is more effective than disease prevention (Kaplan, 2000).

CTC programmes begin with community mobilization. Key community leaders (e. g. elected representatives, education officials, police chiefs, business leaders) are brought together, with the aim of getting them to agree on the goals of the prevention programme and to implement CTC. The key leaders then set up a Community Board that is accountable to them, consisting of neighbourhood residents and representatives from various agencies (e. g. school, police, social services, probation, health, parents, youth groups, business, church, media). The Community Board takes charge of prevention on behalf of the community.

The Community Board then carries out a risk and protective factor assessment, identifying key risk factors in that particular community that need to be tackled and key protective factors that need enhancing. This risk assessment might involve the use of police, school, social or census records or local neighbourhood or school surveys. After identifying key risk and protective factors, the Community Board assesses existing resources and develops a plan of intervention strategies. With specialist technical assistance and guidance, they choose programmes from a menu of strategies that have been shown to be effective in well-designed evaluation research.

The menu of strategies listed by Hawkins and Catalano (1992) includes prenatal and postnatal home visiting programmes, pre-school intellectual enrichment programmes, parent training, school organization and curriculum development, teacher training and media campaigns. Other strategies include child skills training, anti-bullying programmes in schools, situational prevention, and policing strategies. The choice of prevention strategies is based on empirical evidence about effective methods of tackling each particular risk factor, but it also depends on what are identified as the biggest problems in the community. While this approach is not without its challenges, an evidence-based approach that brings together the most effective prevention programmes across multiple domains offers the greatest promise for reducing crime and building safer communities.

CONCLUSIONS

High quality evaluation research shows that many programmes are effective in reducing delinquency and antisocial behaviour, and that in many cases the financial benefits of these programmes outweigh their financial costs. The best programmes include general parent education, parent management training, pre-school intellectual enrichment programmes, child skills training, teacher training, anti-bullying programmes, and MST.

High quality experimental and quasi-experimental evaluations of the effectiveness of crime reduction programmes are needed in all countries. Most knowledge about the effectiveness of prevention programmes, such as cognitive-behavioural skills training, parent training and pre-school intellectual enrichment programmes, is based on American research, but it is not clear how far American results can be replicated in other countries.

The time is ripe to mount a large-scale evidence-based integrated national strategy for the reduction of crime and associated social problems, including rigorous evaluation requirements, in all countries. This should implement programmes to tackle risk factors and strengthen protective factors, and it could be based on "Communities That Care". Primary prevention has been effective in improving health, and it could be equally effective in reducing delinquency and antisocial behaviour in all countries.

References

Alexander, J. F. and Parsons, B. V. (1973) Short-term behavioral intervention with delinquent families: Impact on family process and recidivism. *Journal of Abnormal Psychology*, 81, 219－225.

Aos, S., Lieb, R., Mayfield, J., Miller, M. and Pennucci, A. (2004) *Benefits and Costs of Prevention and Early Intervention Programs for Youth*. Olympia, Washington: Washington State Institute for Public Policy.

Baldry, A. C. and Farrington, D. P. (1998) Parenting influences on bullying and victimization. *Legal and Criminological Psychology*, 3, 237－254.

Barnett, W. S. (1993) Cost-benefit analysis. In L. J. Schweinhart, H. V. Barnes and D. P. Weikart, *Significant Benefits: The High/Scope Perry Preschool Study Through Age 27* (pp. 142－173). Ypsilanti, Michigan: High/Scope Press.

Barton, C., Alexander, J. F., Waldron, H., Turner, C. W. and Warburton, J. (1985) Generalizing treatment effects of functional family therapy: Three replications. *American Journal of Family Therapy*, 13, 16－26.

Berrueta-Clement, J. R., Schweinhart, L. J., Barnett, W. S., Epstein, A. S. and Weikart, D. P. (1984) *Changed Lives: The Effects of the Perry Preschool Program on Youths Through Age 19*. Ypsilanti, Michigan: High/Scope Press.

Boisjoli, R., Vitaro, F., Lacourse, E., Barker, E. D., and Tremblay, R. E. (2007) Impact and clinical significance of a preventive intervention for disruptive boys. *British Journal of Psychiatry*, 191, 415－419.

Borduin, C. M., Mann, B. J., Cone, L. T., Henggeler, S. W., Fucci, B. R., Blaske, D. M. and Williams, R. A. (1995) Multisystemic treatment of serious juvenile offenders: Long-term prevention of criminality and violence. *Journal of Consulting and Clinical Psychology*, 63, 569－587.

Chamberlain, P. and Reid, J. B. (1998) Comparison of two community alternatives to incarceration for chronic juvenile offenders. *Journal of Consulting and Clinical Psychology*, 66, 624 – 633.

Clarke, R. V. (1995) Situational crime prevention. In M. Tonry and D. P. Farrington (Eds.) *Building a Safer Society: Strategic Approaches to Crime Prevention* (pp. 91 – 150). Chicago: University of Chicago Press.

Communities that Care (1997) *Communities that Care (UK): A New Kind of Prevention Programme.* London: Communities that Care.

Curtis, N. M., Ronan, K. R. and Borduin, C. M. (2004) Multisystemic treatment: A meta-analysis of outcome studies. *Journal of Family Psychology*, 18, 411 – 419.

Dishion, T. J., Patterson, G. R. and Kavanagh, K. A. (1992) An experimental test of the coercion model: Linking theory, measurement and intervention. In J. McCord and R. E. Tremblay (Eds.) *Preventing Antisocial Behavior: Interventions from Birth through Adolescence* (pp. 253 – 282). New York: Guilford.

Eckenrode, J., Campa, M., Luckey, D. W., Henderson, C. R., Cole, R., Kitzman, H., Anson, E., Sidora-Arcoleo, K., Powers, J. and Olds, D. (2010) Long-term effects of prenatal and infancy nurse home visitation on the life course of youths: 19-year follow-up a randomized trial. *Archives of Pediatrics and Adolescent Medicine*, 164, 9 – 15.

Farrington, D. P. (1993) Understanding and preventing bullying. In M. Tonry and N. Morris (Eds.) *Crime and Justice*, vol. 17 (pp. 381 – 458). Chicago: University of Chicago Press.

Farrington, D. P. (1996) *Understanding and Preventing Youth Crime.* York: Joseph Rowntree Foundation.

Farrington, D. P. (2007) Childhood risk factors and risk-focussed prevention. In M. Maguire, R. Morgan and R. Reiner (Eds.) *The Oxford Handbook of Criminology* (4th ed., pp. 602 – 640). Oxford: Oxford University Press.

Farrington, D. P., Coid, J. W., Harnett, L., Jolliffe, D., Soteriou, N., Turner, R. and West, D. J. (2006) *Criminal Careers and Life Success: New Findings from the Cambridge Study in Delinquent Development.* London: Home Office (Research Findings No. 281).

Farrington, D. P. and Ttofi, M. M. (2009) *School-Based Programmes to Reduce Bullying and Victimization.* Campbell Systematic Reviews 2009;6.

Farrington, D. P. and Welsh, B. C. (2003) Family-based prevention of offending: A meta-analysis. *Australian and New Zealand Journal of Criminology*, 36, 127 – 151.

Farrington, D. P. and Welsh, B. C. (2006) A half-century of randomized experiments on crime and justice. In M. Tonry (Ed.) *Crime and Justice*, vol. 34 (pp. 55 – 132). Chicago: University of Chicago Press.

Farrington, D. P. and Welsh. B. C. (2007) *Saving Children from a Life of Crime: Early Risk Factors and Effective Interventions.* Oxford: Oxford University Press.

Greenwood, P. W., Karoly, L. A., Everingham, S. S., Houbé, J., Kilburn, M. R., Rydell, C. P., Sanders, M. and Chiesa, J. (2001) Estimating the costs and benefits of early childhood interventions: Nurse home visits and the Perry Preschool. In B. C. Welsh, D. P. Farrington, and L. W. Sherman (Eds.) *Costs and Benefits of Preventing Crime* (pp. 123 – 148). Boulder, Colorado: Westview Press.

Hawkins, J. D. and Catalano, R. F. (1992) *Communities that Care.* San Francisco: Jossey-Bass.

Hawkins, J. D., Catalano, R. F., Kosterman, R., Abbott, R. and Hill, K. G. (1999) Preventing adolescent health risk behaviors by strengthening protection during childhood. *Archives of Pediatrics and Adolescent Medicine*, 153, 226 – 234.

Hawkins, J. D., Kosterman, R., Catalano, R. F., Hill, K. G. and Abbott, R. D. (2008) Effects of social development intervention in childhood 15 years later. *Archives of Pediatrics and Adolescent Medicine*, 162, 1133 – 1141.

Hawkins, J. D., Oesterle, S., Brown, E. C., Arthur, M. W., Abbott, R. D., Fagan, A. A. and Catalano, R. F. (2009) Results of a Type 2 translational research trial to prevent adolescent drug use and delinquency. *Archives of Pediatrics and Adolescent Medicine*, 163, 789 – 798.

Hawkins, J. D., Von Cleve, E. and Catalano, R. F. (1991) Reducing early childhood aggression: Results of a primary prevention program. *Journal of the American Academy of Child and Adolescent Psychiatry*, 30, 208 – 217.

Henggeler, S. W., Melton, G. B., Smith, L. A., Schoenwald, S. K. and Hanley, J. H. (1993). Family preservation using multisystematic treatment: Long-term follow-up to a clinical trial with serious juvenile offenders. *Journal of Child and Family Studies*, 2, 283 – 293.

Henggeler, S. W. , Schoenwald, S. K. , Borduin, C. M. , Rowland, M. D. and Cunningham, P. B. (1998) *Multisystemic Treatment of Antisocial Behavior in Children and Adolescents*. New York: Guilford.

Hope, T. (1995) Community crime prevention. In M. Tonry and D. P. Farrington (Eds.) *Building a Safer Society: Strategic Approaches to Crime Prevention* (pp. 21 - 89). Chicago: University of Chicago Press.

Kaplan, R. M. (2000) Two pathways to prevention. *American Psychologist*, 55, 382 - 396.

Kazdin, A. E. , Kraemer, H. C. , Kessler, R. C. , Kupfer, D. J. and Offord, D. R. (1997) Contributions of risk-factor research to developmental psychopathology. *Clinical Psychology Review*, 17, 375 - 406.

Leschied, A. and Cunningham, A. (2002) *Seeking Effective Interventions for Serious Young Offenders: Interim Results of a Four-Year Randomized Study of Multisystemic Therapy in Ontario, Canada*. London, Ontario, Canada: London Family Court Clinic.

Littell, J. H. (2005) Lessons from a systematic review of effects of multisystemic therapy. *Children and Youth Services Review*, 27, 445 - 463.

Manning, M. , Homel, R. and Smith, C. (2010) A meta-analysis of the effects of early developmental prevention programmes in at-risk populations on non-health outcomes in adolescence. *Children and Youth Services Review*, 32, 506 - 519.

O'Donnell, J. , Hawkins, J. D. , Catalano, R. F. , Abbott, R. D. and Day, L. E. (1995) Preventing school failure, drug use, and delinquency among low-income children: Long-term intervention in elementary schools. *American Journal of Orthopsychiatry*, 65, 87 - 100.

Olds, D. L. , Eckenrode, J. , Henderson, C. R. , Kitzman, H. , Powers, J. , Cole, R. , Sidora, K. , Morris, P. , Pettitt, L. M. and Luckey, D. (1997) Long-term effects of home visitation on maternal life course and child abuse and neglect: Fifteen-year follow-up of a randomized trial. *Journal of the American Medical Association*, 278, 637 - 643.

Olds, D. L. , Henderson, C. R. , Chamberlin, R. and Tatelbaum, R. (1986) Preventing child abuse and neglect: A randomized trial of nurse home visitation. *Pediatrics*, 78, 65 - 78.

Olds, D. L. , Henderson, C. R. , Cole, R. , Eckenrode, J. , Kitzman, H. , Luckey, D. , Pettitt, L. , Sidora, K. , Morris, P. and Powers, J. (1998) Long-term effects of nurse home visitation on children's criminal and antisocial behavior: 15-year follow-up of a randomized controlled trial. *Journal of the American Medical Association*, 280, 1238 – 1244.

Olweus, D. (1994) Bullying at school: Basic facts and effects of a school based intervention programme. *Journal of Child Psychology and Psychiatry*, 35, 1171 – 1190.

Patterson, G. R. (1982) *Coercive Family Process*. Eugene, Oregon: Castalia.

Patterson, G. R. , Reid, J. B. and Dishion, T. J. (1992) *Antisocial Boys.* Eugene, Oregon: Castalia.

Piquero, A. R. , Farrington, D. P. , Welsh, B. C. , Tremblay, R. E. andJennings, W. (2008) *Effects of Early Family/Parent Training Programmes on Antisocial Behaviour and Delinquency.* Campbell Systematic Reviews 2008:11.

Sanders, M. R. , Markie-Dadds, C. , Tully, L. A. and Bor, W. (2000) The Triple P-Positive Parenting Program: A comparison of enhanced, standard and self-directed behavioral family intervention for parents of children with early onset conduct problems. *Journal of Consulting and Clinical Psychology*, 68, 624 – 640.

Schweinhart, L. J. , Barnes, H. V. and Weikart, D. P. (1993) *Significant Benefits: The High/Scope Perry Preschool Study Through Age 27.* Ypsilanti, Michigan: High/Scope Press.

Schweinhart, L. J. , Montie, J. , Zongping, X. , Barnett, W. S. , Belfield, C. R. and Nores, M. (2005) *Lifetime Effects: The High/Scope Perry Preschool Study Through Age 40.* Ypsilanti, Michigan: High/Scope Press.

Schweinhart, L. J. and Weikart, D. P. (1980) *Young Children Grow Up: The Effects of the Perry Preschool Program on Youths Through Age 15.* Ypsilanti, Michigan: High/Scope Press.

Scott, S. , Spender, Q. , Doolan, M. , Jacobs, B. and Aspland, H. (2001) Multicentre controlled trial of parenting groups for child antisocial behaviour in clinical practice. *British Medical Journal*, 323, 194 – 196.

Sherman, L. W. , Farrington, D. P. , Welsh, B. C. , and MacKenzie, D. L. (2002, Eds.) *Evidence-Based Crime Prevention.* London: Routledge.

Smith, P. K. and Sharp, S. (1994) *School Bullying.* London: Routledge.

Thomas, R. and Zimmer-Gembeck, M. J. (2007) Behavioural outcomes of parent-child interaction therapy and Triple P-Positive Parenting programme: A review and meta-

analysis. Journal of Abnormal Child Psychology, 35, 475 – 495.

Tonry, M. and Farrington, D. P. (1995) Strategic approaches to crime prevention. In M. Tonry and D. P. Farrington (Eds.) *Building a Safer Society: Strategic Approaches to Crime Prevention* (pp. 1 – 20). Chicago: University of Chicago Press.

Tremblay, R. E. and Craig, W. M. (1995) Developmental crime prevention. In M. Tonry and D. P. Farrington (Eds.) *Building a Safer Society: Strategic Approaches to Crime Prevention* (pp. 151 – 236). Chicago: University of Chicago Press.

Tremblay, R. E. , Pagani-Kurtz, L. , Masse, L. C. , Vitaro, F. and Pihl, R. O. (1995) A bimodal preventive intervention for disruptive kindergarten boys: Its impact through mid-adolescence. *Journal of Consulting and Clinical Psychology*, 63, 560 – 568.

Webster-Stratton, C. (1998) Preventing conduct problems in Head Start children: Strengthening parenting competencies. *Journal of Consulting and Clinical Psychology*, 66, 715 – 730.

Webster-Stratton, C. and Hammond, M. (1997) Treating children with early-onset conduct problems: A comparison of child and parent training interventions. *Journal of Consulting and Clinical Psychology*, 65, 93 – 109.

Widom, C. S. (1989) The cycle of violence. *Science*, 244, 160 – 166.

Wilson, J. J. and Howell, J. C. (1993) *A Comprehensive Strategy for Serious, Violent, and Chronic Juvenile Offenders*. Washington, D. C. : Office of Juvenile Justice and Delinquency Prevention.

违法的风险因素和保护因素

大卫·P. 法林顿（David P. Farrington）

剑桥大学

罗尔夫·洛伯（Rolf Loeber）

匹兹堡大学

玛丽亚·M. 托菲（Maria M. Ttofi）

剑桥大学

在 20 世纪 90 年代，随着风险因素预防范式逐渐扩大影响力，犯罪学领域内发生了一场革命（Farrington, 2000）。这个范式的基本原理很简单：确定关键的犯罪风险因素，然后实施相应的、有针对性的预防措施。这一范式是从公共卫生领域引进而来的，一直被诸如霍金斯和加泰罗尼欧（Hawkins and Catalano, 1992）等先驱成功运用于治疗癌症和心脏病等疾病。这一风险因素预防范式将解释和预防，基础研究和应用研究，学者、政策制定者和实际工作者联系在一起。洛伯和法林顿（Loeber and Farrington）（1998）以青少年严重暴力犯罪为例就为这一范式作了详细的解释。

犯罪风险因素作为一项变量，可以用来预测将来的高犯罪概率。通常情况下，风险因素是两分的，它们可能存在也可能不存在。由于本书的重点，本章将着重于在干预下可能被改变的风险因素。因此，性别、种族、民族、有犯罪记录的父母和大家庭规模都将不会涉及，即使它们可能被解释为犯罪的可变因素。例如，费根等（Fagan *et al.*, 2007）得出了男孩犯罪会比女孩多的结论，这是由于男孩有更高的风险因素得分和较低的预防因素得分。为了确定风险因素是否是犯罪的预测值或可能诱因，需要在犯罪行为发生之前对风险因素进行测量。因此,开展风险因素的纵向研究是必要的。

通常这一范式也强调保护因素,这表明干预研究过程中有必要强化这方面因素。然而,在过去,保护因素是相当模糊的。一些研究人员认为,保护因素仅仅是量表上相对于风险因素的另外一端罢了(White, Moffitt, and Silva, 1989)。例如,如果缺乏父母监督是一项风险因素,那么良好的父母监督应该就是保护因素。然而,这看起来似乎是同一个变量用了两个术语。

其他研究人员建议在保护因素与风险因素相互作用下,以最大限度地减少或减缓风险因素影响(Rutter, 1985)。通常情况下,在研究风险因素的过程中也会涉及保护因素。洛伯等(Loeber *et al.*)(2008)提出一致的术语。西姆奥夫等(Sameroff *et al.*)(1998)作为其支持者,相对应风险因素,他们定义改善因素作为可预测低犯罪概率的变量,保护因素作为预测人群中低犯罪概率的变量。

为了区分风险因素和改善因素对犯罪的影响,将变量分为至少 3 种类别是非常重要的(改善作用、无影响、风险作用)。斯同瑟梅尔-洛伯等(Stouthamer-Loeber *et al.*)(2002)在美国匹兹堡青年研究中就做了类似的分类(详见后文)。他们通过比较改善因素和无影响因素对青少年犯罪发生的概率来研究改善因素的作用,而通过比较增加犯罪的风险因素和无影响因素对青少年犯罪发生概率的影响研究风险因素的效应。有些变量中含有改善因素但是不包含风险因素(例如,多动症和注意集中障碍),而有些则是只包含增加犯罪的风险因素(例如,青少年犯罪团伙)。在本章中会强调保护因素和改善因素,因为早前的犯罪预防措施是建立在提高保护因素和改善因素的作用而不是减少风险因素。波拉德、霍金斯、亚瑟(Pollard, Hawkins, and Arthur)(1999)认为将注意力放在保护因素和改善因素上,以及提高儿童的适应能力,相对于侧重解决麻烦和问题的减少风险因素方式而言,更加正面、积极,对于社区更有吸引力。

在一篇简短的文章内,要涵盖风险因素、改善因素和保护因素等所有方面是不太现实的(Lösel and Bender, 2003; Loeber, Slot, and Stouthamer-Loeber, 2006)。本文将只重点介绍最重要的易变因素:个体因素,如冲动程度和素养;家庭因素包括子女的抚养和家庭和谐程度;以及社会因素的影响,如社会经济地位,同伴和邻里影响等。本文将着重关注对犯罪进行纵向研究所获得的知识,研究对至少上百人从儿童时代起至青少年时期,直到成年,进行跟踪调查,这期间会不断对研究样本进行个人访谈和收集相关数据记录。研究的重点在于预测社区样本的犯罪状况,而不是侧重在预测社区中犯罪分子样本的持续犯罪或放弃犯罪(Loeber *et al.*, 2007)。

我们将特别关注两项纵向调查研究的结果:剑桥青少年犯罪的发展研究和匹兹堡青少年研究。在剑桥调查中对超过 400 名伦敦男性,从 8 岁至 48 岁进行长期跟踪研究(Farrington *et al.*, 2006;Farrington, Coid, and West, 2009)。在匹兹堡研究,对 1500 多名来自匹兹堡公立学校男学生进行了 12 年跟踪调查研究(Loeber *et al.*, 1998;Loeber *et al.*, 2008)。调查之初,500 名是一年级的(7 岁左右),500 名四年级的(10 岁左右),500 名七年级(13 岁左右),所有学生都是来自匹兹堡市公立学校。更多信息以及其他相关犯罪纵向研究请详见法林顿和威尔士(Farrington and Welsh)(2007, chapter 2)。

从中我们得出了以下主要结论:

1. 在犯罪干预研究中最值得关注的因素包括儿童的冲动程度、学习成绩、育儿方法、年轻母亲、虐待、父母冲突、不完整的家庭结构、贫穷、犯罪的同伴和贫穷的邻居。

2. 然而,我们对于以上变量最初扮演的是犯罪风险因素还是犯罪改善因素,又或者是两者兼而有之,知之甚少。

3. 同样地,对于这些变量是否是引发犯罪的起因,以及这些因素和诸如犯罪等输出之间的因果关系哪些是最重要的,我们也不得而知。

4. 另外,我们也不知道在不同的风险背景之下,哪些因素可以有效预防孩子成为犯罪分子。

5. 风险评估工具应该包括改善因素和保护因素。

6. 我们需要更多运用长期纵向调查,对社区样本通过频繁地面对面访谈方式,开展改善因素和保护因素的研究。

本文的结构是这样的:第一部分,介绍个体因素,包括多动性/冲动性和智商/学识。第二部分,介绍家庭因素,包括养育方法(专制和民主)、年轻母亲和虐待儿童、父母冲突和不完整的家庭。第三部分,回顾社会因素,包括社会经济地位、同伴的影响和邻里因素。第四部分,得出结论。自始至终,这都将是一次特殊的研究尝试,既是对于改善因素和保护因素的研究,也是对于风险因素的研究,当然后者的实验研究会更多一些。

一、个体因素

(一)多动性和冲动性

许多研究表明多动性或小儿多动症可以预测今后的犯罪行为(Pratt *et al.*,

2002）。在哥本哈根围产期项目中，11—13 岁年龄段少年表现出多动性（焦躁不安及注意力不集中）可以显著预测其到 22 岁后会由于暴力事件而被捕，特别是那些母亲经历过分娩并发症的男孩们（Brennan，Mednick，and Mednick，1993）。类似地，在瑞典奥雷博罗的纵向研究中，在 13 岁的时候多动性可以预测其 26 岁后的犯罪记录。暴力事件发生比例最高的是同时具有焦躁不安和注意力难以集中的男性（占 15%），而其他人的暴力事件发生率约为 3%（Klinteberg *et al.*，1993）。在西雅图社会发展项目中，多动性及青春期好冒险的特性可以预测青年时期的暴力行为（Herrenkohl *et al.*，2000）。

在剑桥调查中，那些被老师认为是注意力不集中或焦躁不安的男孩，那些被家长、老师、同龄人认为最敢于冒险的男孩，那些 8—10 岁时，精神运动性测量中最冲动的男孩，在其长大之后都有成为犯罪分子的倾向。鲁莽、注意力不集中以及焦躁不安都能预测官方的定罪和自我报告的犯罪行为，并且鲁莽一贯是最独立的预测因子之一。有趣的是，多动性可以单独预测行为问题的青少年犯罪（Farrington，Loeber，and Van Kammen，1990）。莱纳姆（Lynam）（1996）提出多动性并行为失常的男孩子最可能长期犯罪和精神变态，并且莱娜姆（Lynam）（1998）从匹兹堡青年研究中找到了支持上述假设的证据。

在匹兹堡青年研究中，怀特等（White *et al.*）（1994）用不同的测量方法对冲动性进行了最深入而广泛的研究。与自我报告的在 10—13 岁年龄段实施犯罪最强烈相关的测量有教师评估的冲动性（如行为不经过大脑思考），自我报告的冲动性，自我报告的失控（如无法接受延迟满足），神经兴奋（从录像观察），以及精神性冲动（运用追踪发展测试）等。一般来说，语言行为评估测试比神经运动绩效测试与犯罪行为有更强的相关性，这就意味着认知冲动性（如承认冲动行为）比行为冲动性（基于行为表现测试）与犯罪更相关。乔利夫和法林顿（Jolliffe and Farrington）（2009）的系统回顾表明早期对冲动的测量（尤其是鲁莽和冒险的测量）可以预测日后对暴力行为的测量结果。

洛伯等（Loeber *et al.*）（2008，chapter 7）在匹兹堡青年研究中，对改善因素预测和严重盗窃行为低概率发生做了最广泛的研究。他们在最年轻的群体中分成四个年龄阶段（7—9 岁，10—12 岁，13—16 岁和 17—19 岁），在最年长的群体中分成三个年龄阶段（13—16 岁，17—19 岁，20—25 岁）研究预测变量。预测变量被分为三种：风险因素，无作用因素及改善因素。他们发现，一贯地，作为改善因素，较低的多动症得分预示着低暴力行为，但是较高的多动症得分并不是一个风险因素。这些结论再现斯同瑟梅尔—洛伯等（Stouthamer-Loeber *et al.*）（2002）早先在相同项目中预测持续严重犯罪的结果。同样的,洛伯等(Loeber et al.)(2002)发现好的邻里环境是遏制冲动的保护因素,因为在良好的邻里关系下,冲动性不能预测犯罪。

(二)智商和学识

低智商和学习成绩差可以预测犯罪。在费城生物社会学项目中(Denno,1990),4—7岁时言语及行为方面智商低,13—14岁时加利福尼亚成绩测验分数低(词汇、理解、数学、语言、拼写),都能够预测22岁后因暴力行为被逮捕。在哥本哈根都市项目中,在12岁时低智商能够显著预测15—22岁期间记录在案的暴力行为。在低年级男孩中低智商与暴力之间的联系是最强的(Hogh and Wolf, 1983)。

在人生最初几年测量出低智商预示着日后的犯罪行为。在一个关于120人左右的斯德哥尔摩男孩的长期纵向调查中,3岁时被测量出低智商的男孩能够显著预测直到30岁的犯罪记录(Stattin and Klackenberg-Larsson, 1993)。惯犯(犯罪四次及四次以上)在3岁的时候平均智商是88,然而未犯罪者在3岁的时候平均智商是101。所有的这些结果在控制社会阶级因素情况下得到支持。相似地,在佩里学前教育项目中(Schweinhart et al. , 1993)4岁时低智商可以预测27岁前的被捕,在佩里合作项目中4岁低智商则可以预测17岁前被起诉(Lipsitt, Buka, and Lipsitt, 1990)。

在剑桥的研究中,8—10岁男孩在非语言智商测试(瑞文推理测验)中得分小于等于90的人在青少年时期犯罪的比例是其他人的两倍(West and Farrington, 1973)。然而,低智商很难与学校成绩差区分开来,因为两者存在显著的内在相关并且都能预测犯罪。非语言智商低预测自我报告的青少年犯罪,与青少年定罪几乎相同(Farrington, 1992b),意味着低智商与青少年犯罪之间的联系并不是由欠缺智慧的男孩子更有可能被捕引起的。同时,低智商和学校成绩差都能独立于其他变量来预测犯罪行为,所谓的其他变量如家庭收入低,家庭人数变化(Farrington, 1990)。

智商测试被设计用来预测今后学业成就(Barchard, 2005),而且低智商或许会通过介于学业挫败的因素而导致犯罪。学业挫败与青少年犯罪的联系在纵向研究中反复被论证过(Maguin and Loeber,1996)。在匹兹堡青年研究中,莱纳姆、莫菲特和斯同瑟梅尔–洛伯(Lynam, Moffitt, and Stouthamer-Loeber)(1993)总结语言方面的低智商会导致学业挫败,继而自我报告犯罪行为,但这仅仅只适用于非裔美籍男孩。另一种理论表明低智商与犯罪行为之间的联系受到去抑制(冲动、少儿多动症、缺乏罪恶感、不易移情)的中介作用,这些也在匹兹堡青年研究中进行过测试(Koolhof et al. , 2007)。费尔森和斯塔夫(Felson and Staff)(2006)认为自控力差在学业成绩差和犯罪之间起到中介作用。

学业成绩优秀通常被认为是改善或保护因素。在考艾岛，沃纳和史密斯（Werner and Smith）（1982）进行的经典纵向调查中，他们研究了那些在 2 岁前有四个或更多的风险因素（包括贫穷、缺乏母亲教育、离异家庭、围产期压力和低智商）的弱势儿童，并且把那些在 18 岁前成长过程中没有严重学习问题或行为问题的人与那些存在精神健康问题和承认严重犯罪的人相比较。所有的因素中最重要的保护因素包括：在 10 岁时候养成的良好的阅读能力、推理能力以及问题解决技巧（Werner and Smith, 1992, 2001）。同时，在匹兹堡青年研究分析（Loeber et al., 2008）中高学业成就常常是一个改善因素。

在纽卡斯尔千户家庭研究中（Kolvin et al., 1990）），对一群 5 岁左右，生活贫穷孩子进行追踪（贫穷的标准是基于对福利的依赖，过度拥挤的住房条件，缺乏生活照顾，缺乏母亲育儿，父母生病以及破碎家庭），发现在 32 岁前没有成为罪犯的人常常在 10—11 岁养成了良好的阅读、拼写及算数能力。同时，史密斯（Smith et al., 1994）在罗切斯特青少年发展研究中追踪了那些存在五个或五个以上家庭风险因素（包括社会救济家庭、年轻的母亲、虐待儿童、家庭成员中有罪犯、家庭里有吸毒的成员、父母失业以及父母受教育程度低）的孩子，发现没有犯下严重的罪行的人往往有较高的数学和阅读能力。几个另外的纵向研究报告高智商是高风险儿童预防犯罪的保护因素（Kandel et al., 1988；White, Moffitt, and Silva, 1989；Fergusson and Lynskey, 1996；Stattin, Romelsjo, and Stenbacka, 1997；Jaffee et al., 2007）。

解释连接低智商和犯罪行为之间关系有一个基本的、有一定道理的因素，即操控抽象概念的能力。在这方面能力缺乏的儿童往往智力测试和学业成绩表现不好，他们还有违法的趋势，主要因为他们预见自己犯罪后果的能力较差。犯罪者常常在非语言智商测试，比如物体聚合测验和积木设计，要比其语言智商测试表现更好，说明他们发现与抽象概念相比实物更容易处理。

易冲动、注意力问题、低智商以及学业挫败都能与位于大脑前脑叶部位特定功能区的不足相关。这些功能区包括了保持注意和集中，抽象推理，概念形成，目标制订，期望和计划，神经行为序列的程序和最初的目标，有效的行为自我控制和自我意识，抑制不当或冲动行为（Moffitt and Henry, 1991；Morgan and Lilienfeld, 2000）。有趣的是，在蒙特利尔纵向实验研究中，基于 14 岁孩子的测试表明，特定功能区测量是区分暴力和非暴力男孩的最高效的神经心理学鉴别途径（Seguin et al., 1995）。这个关系是独立于家庭逆境测量之外的（家庭逆境指父母生第一个孩子时的年龄、父母的受教育水平、破碎的家庭和较低的社会阶层等）。在匹兹堡青年研究中，生活经历不断的罪犯被认定为神经认知损伤（Raine et al., 2005）。

二、家庭因素

（一）养育方式

许多不同类型的育儿方法可以预测犯罪。最重要的养育方式维度有：监督或控制孩子，规则或是父母强化，温暖或是冷漠的情感关系，以及父母与孩子的互动。父母的监督指的是父母对孩子活动监控的程度，以及他们警戒性或警惕性的程度。在全部的养育方式中，父母监督的缺乏通常是犯罪行为最强有力且最能重现的预测值（Smith and Stern，1997）。在剑桥调查中，在 8 岁的时候缺乏父母监督的男孩子，在50 岁前他们中的 61% 会被判有罪，相比较而言，其他人则只有 36% 的犯罪率（Farrington *et al.*，2009）。

许多研究表明那些不知道孩子在哪里、什么时候出门的父母，以及任由孩子从小在街上闲逛疏于监督的父母，他们更有可能培养出犯罪的子女。比方说：麦科德（McCord）（1979）在波士顿实施的经典剑桥—萨默维尔研究中提及，童年时期父母监督的缺乏是在 45 岁前暴力和侵财型犯罪发生最好的预测值。莱斯切尔德等（Leschied *et al.*）（2008）发现在童年时代的中期，父母管理是强迫的、反复无常的，或者是缺乏监督、父母离异和婚姻状况都能有效地预测成人之后的犯罪。

父母规则指的是父母对孩子行为作出的反应。显而易见的，严厉或带有处罚性的规则（包括体罚）能预测犯罪（Haapasalo and Pokela，1999）。在随后对将近 700 名诺丁汉孩子的研究中，约翰和伊丽莎白（John and Elizabeth Newson）（1989）发现在 7岁和 11 岁的时候受到体罚能预测将来的犯罪行为，近 40% 的罪犯承认自己在 11 岁的时候曾被打脸或其他部位，而相比之下，未犯罪者中只有 14% 的人受到过体罚。不一致的或反复无常的规则也是犯罪的预测值。诸如其中一位家长的规则是无常的，有时候对坏习惯睁一只眼闭一只眼而有时候却严厉惩罚，或者父母双方意见和规则不统一，一方采取宽容放纵的方式，而另一方则强调严厉惩罚孩子。

正如麦科德（McCord）（1979）在剑桥—萨默维尔调查中所发现的，冷漠、漠不关心的父母有养育出犯罪儿童的倾向。她还得出结论：父母的温暖可以成为一个克服体罚影响的保护因素（McCord，1997）。鉴于在她的研究，遭受母亲冷漠对待和体罚的男孩，其中有 51% 会被判罪，而得到温暖同时又受到过母亲体罚的男孩中只有21% 会被判罪，与得到母亲温暖且无体罚的男孩中 23% 的犯罪率相近似。父亲给予的温暖也是一个克服父亲体罚的保护因素。

罗宾斯(Robins)(1979)在圣路易斯经典纵向研究表明,父母监督的缺乏,严厉的规则以及漠不关心的态度都能预测犯罪行为。同样的,在西雅图社会发展项目中,青春期家庭管理的贫乏(疏于监督、不一致的规则以及严厉的规则)能预测青少年时期的暴力行为(Herrenkohl *et al.*, 2000)。剑桥调查中也得到了相似的结论。8岁时测量的严厉或不稳定的父母规则,残酷、消极或忽略型的父母态度,以及父母监督的缺乏,都能预测将来青少年犯罪和自我报告的犯罪(West and Farrington,1973)。一般来说,任何这些不利的家庭背景特征的存在都会使青少年犯罪风险加倍。

德宗(Derzon)(2010)将家庭因素作为犯罪和暴力行为(与攻击性和问题行为一样)的预测值进行了元分析。该元分析是基于纵向研究的,但是许多的预测是在短期内的(55%的案例是少于四年的研究),许多结果变量在比较年轻的时候就被测量(40%的案例只跟踪到15岁进行预测了),而且许多研究规模较小(43%的案例少于200名参与者)。犯罪或暴力行为最强的预测因子是父母的教育程度(与犯罪行为的相关系数 $r=.30$),父母监督(暴力行为的相关系数 $r=.29$),养育技能(与犯罪行为的相关系数 $r=.26$),父母不和(与犯罪行为的相关系数 $r=.26$),家庭规模(与暴力行为的相关系数 $r=.24$)。明显的弱预测因子是年轻的父母、破裂的家庭以及社会经济地位。

在针对保护因素研究的罗切斯特青少年发展研究中,史密斯等(Smith *et al.*)(1994)发现可塑性强的(无犯罪行为的)高风险儿童倾向于有良好的父母监督以及良好的父母依恋关系。在纽卡斯尔千户家庭研究中,考尔文等(Kolvin *et al.*)(1990)对那些没有犯罪行为的贫穷儿童作了类似的调查,结果表明无犯罪行为的贫穷儿童倾向于有更好的父母监督。另外,在匹兹堡青年研究中(Loeber *et al.*, 2008),父母监督、被母亲体罚以及男孩在家庭活动中的参与状况有改善效应而不是风险影响。

对养育方式与犯罪行为的紧密关系的解释主要集中于依恋或社会学习理论。依恋理论受到鲍比尔(Bowlby)(1951)研究成果的启示,并强调情感上对温暖、充满爱并守法的父母存在依恋的孩子有成为罪犯的倾向。社会学习理论则认为孩子的行为取决于父母的奖惩及父母行为表现模式(Patterson,1995)。如果父母对孩子反社会的活动没有作出一致的、必要的反应,父母自己有反社会的行为,孩子有成为罪犯的倾向。

(二)年轻的母亲们和虐待儿童

至少在西方工业化国家,早生或者青春期少年怀孕,对孩子来说预示着许多无法预测的后果:包括学业成绩差、反社会的学校行为、毒品滥用以及早期的性行为。少女妈妈的孩子更有可能成为罪犯。比方说,莫那什(Morash)和拉克(Rucker)(1989)分析了美国和英国的四个调查(包括剑桥研究)的结果发现少女妈妈总是与低收入家庭、家庭救济和生父的缺失相联系,她们的养育方式不尽如人意,她们的孩子被归为学业成绩差和犯罪行为一类。但是,生父的出现可缓解诸多不利因素,并且通常看起来具有保护性效果。当然,需要记得的是这个年龄的母亲与这个年龄的父亲高度相关,年轻父亲与年轻母亲的问题一样重要。

在剑桥研究中,生育了多个孩子的少女妈妈们特别有可能养出犯罪儿童(Nagin,Pogarsky, and Farrington, 1997)。在纽卡斯尔千户家庭研究中,在孩子32岁前,少年时期结婚的妈妈们(与少年时期生育密切相关的因素),她们孩子的犯罪率是其他妈妈孩子的两倍(Kolvin et al., 1990)。并且,成为罪犯的失学孩子的母亲不太可能比为沦为罪犯的贫穷儿童的母亲年长(Kolvin et al., 1988a)。在匹兹堡青年研究中(Loeber et al., 2008),年长的母亲一直以来具有改善效应,而年轻的母亲则具有风险性。

一些学者们研究年轻母亲和儿童犯罪之间的中介因素。在新西兰的达尼丁研究中,杰夫等(Jaffee et al.)(2001)总结得到年轻母亲与暴力儿童的联系受到母性特征(如智力、犯罪行为)和家庭因素(如严厉的规则、家庭规模、父母离异)的中介作用。在罗切斯特青少年发展研究中,博格拉斯基(Pogarsky)、利扎特(Lizotte)和索佰里(Thornberry)(2003)发现最重要的中介因素是父母轮换的频率(照看者频繁的调换)。许多研究认为父母任务频繁改变能预测儿童的犯罪(Thornberry et al., 1999;Krohn, Hall, and Lizotte, 2009)

马克思菲尔德和卫东(Maxfield and Widom)(1996)在费城做的一项开创性的纵向调查发现,那些在11岁前身体上被虐待的儿童在接下来的15年里极有可能变成暴力罪犯。同样的,麦科德(McCord)(1983)在波士顿做的剑桥—萨默维尔市调查中也写道:大约有一半的被虐待或者是被忽视的男孩在他们35岁前被指控严重犯罪,或是成为酗酒者、精神病人,甚至死亡。2008年,罗伯尔等(Loeber et al.)(2008)在匹兹堡青少年研究中发现,在儿童12岁前对他们的虐待成为了他们将来成为暴力、严重盗窃犯的最一致的预测因素。史密斯和索恩伯里(Smith and Thornberry)(1995)在罗切斯特市青少年发展研究中指出,儿童在12岁前遭受的无论来自身体上、心理上还是性方面的虐待,都能够预测他们今后自我报告的犯罪和官方的定罪。此外,这些结果在控制了性别、种族、社会经济地位、家庭结构等因素后得到了支持。凯丽等(Keiley et al.)(2001)指出儿童在5岁以前受到虐待的危害性要大于在6至9岁受到虐待。马林斯基—拉梅尔(Malinosky-Rummell)和汉森(Hansen)(1993)承认童年遭受身体虐待可以预测今后的暴力或非暴力犯罪。

很少有关于父母虐待儿童的纵向研究试图测量那些改善或保护因素。然而,海伦科尔(Herrenkohl)(2005)宾夕法尼亚州儿童纵向调查中发现,在那些被虐待的儿童中,对学校有重要的承诺、父母和同伴对反社会行为的反对,这些因素将降低他们的暴力和犯罪行为发生的几率。杰夫(Jaffee)等(2007)环境风险研究中得出结论,那些没有反社会性的被虐待儿童中往往具有更高的智力,居住在有较高社会凝聚力和非正式社会控制的低犯罪社区。

卫东(Widom)(1994)总结了童年时期受害经历和青少年犯罪两者之间的一些可能的因果机制。第一,童年时期的受害经历可能产生直接但是长久的后果(比如对儿童的摇晃可能损坏儿童的大脑)。第二,童年时期的受害经历可能引起身体上的变化(比如对儿童对疼痛感知的减弱)从而引发后来行为的攻击性。第三,对儿童的虐待可能导致儿童模仿冲动或是分裂的行为方式,从而导致较差的问题解决能力和较差的学校表现。第四,童年时期的受害经历可能导致儿童自尊或是社会信息过程模式的改变,并且可能在未来刺激这些儿童在行为上变得更有攻击性。第五,儿童虐待可能会导致家庭环境的改变(比如儿童会被寄养在看护中心),这会产生相应的负面影响。第六,未成年人刑事司法实践可能会标签那些受害者,不仅会把他们和那些亲社会的同年龄人分离开来,还会促使他们和那些行为不良的同年龄人走在一起。

(三)父母冲突和破裂家庭

正如比勒(Buehler)(1997)元分析显示的,父母冲突和父母间暴力可以预测青少年期的反社会行为。剑桥调查指出父母之间的矛盾预测儿童在未来违法犯罪的可能(West and Farrington,1973)。新西兰柯莱斯特彻奇市的研究表明,根据自我报告那些目睹过父母之间家庭暴力的儿童更有可能会发生暴力和财产犯罪行为(Fergusson and Horwood,1998)。在控制诸如父母犯罪史、父母药物滥用、父母体罚、年轻母亲和低家庭收入等其他可能引发青少年犯罪的风险因素以后,目睹父亲引起的家庭暴力仍然具有上述的预测性。

很多研究发现破裂的家庭也能预测犯罪。在纽卡斯尔千户家庭调查中考尔文(Kolvin)(1988b)发现,在男孩出生后的最初五年,家庭婚姻的破裂(离婚或分居)能够预测其32岁前因为违法犯罪而被定罪。同样地,那些没有犯罪的失学儿童,极少是失去父亲的。相似地,亨利(Henry)(1993)在其新西兰达尼丁调查中也发现,那些父母不和及主要看护人多次变换的儿童更倾向于反社会和从事违法犯罪行为。德穆斯(Demuth)和布朗(Brown)于2004年发表的在全国青少年健康纵向调查中,德穆斯

（Demuth）和布朗（Brown）（2004）认为，单亲家庭能够预测犯罪的主要原因是他们处在低水平的父母监管、亲近和互动状态。

在英国健康和发展调查中，沃兹沃思（Wadsworth）（1979）阐述了家庭破裂原因的重要性。那些离异或分居家庭中的男孩与那些完整家庭或是因为父母死亡而破裂的家庭中的男孩相比，他们在21岁前更有可能被定罪或是被警告。男孩5岁前家庭破裂更能预测其今后犯罪的可能性，而在11岁至15岁之间家庭破裂的男孩则没有特别的犯罪基因。再婚（离婚或分居后的再婚比例远远高于死亡后的再婚比例）也可能增加儿童未来犯罪的风险，暗示出继父、继母也可能具有负面效应。韦尔斯（Wells）和兰金（Rankin）（1991）所做的元分析也表明那些由于父母分居或离异的破碎家庭相比于那些父母死亡而破碎的家庭，前者与犯罪具有较强的相关性。

很多关于破裂家庭的研究着重于对丧失父亲家庭的研究，原因很简单，就是因为家庭丧失父亲的现象更加普遍。麦科德（McCord）（1982）在波士顿作了一项缺少亲生父亲的破碎家庭和子女后来从事严重犯罪两者之间关系的有趣调查。她发现缺少慈爱母亲的离异家庭的男孩其犯罪普遍率很高（约为62%），而不管母亲是否慈爱，家庭完整但经常发生父母间冲突的男孩其犯罪普遍率达到52%。家庭完整且没有冲突家庭的孩子其犯罪率很低（只有26%），另外很重要的一点是，来自不完整家庭但是有母亲关爱的男孩，其犯罪普遍率也只有22%。这些结果说明引发青少年犯罪的原因不全是他们来自一个不完整的家庭，就像人们认为家庭矛盾常常会引发青少年的犯罪，这两者是不能等同的，其实从某种意义上来说一个富有爱心的母亲可以补偿失去父亲对孩子带来的影响。

剑桥研究中提到，儿童10岁以前无论是永久或暂时地与亲生父母分离（通常是和亲生父亲分离），都能预测其今后被定罪和自我报告的犯罪行为，当然这里所指的分离不包括由于父母死亡或是生病住院引起的分离（Farrington，1992）。然而，幼年（小于5岁）时期的家庭破裂则没有不同寻常的犯罪基因（West and Farrington，1973）。儿童10岁前父母分居能够同时预测青少年和成年期的定罪（Farrington，1992），并且这个因素对成年阶段犯罪的预测可以独立于低家庭收入、差的学校出勤率等因素之外独立作用的；在10岁生日前与父母中一位分离的男孩中，60%在其50岁前会因为从事违法犯罪行为而被定罪，而10岁生日时没有经历这种变故的男孩从事违法犯罪的只有36%（Farrington，2009）。

关于破碎家庭和青少年犯罪两者之间关系的解释有3个主要流派。创伤理论指出，丧失父亲或是母亲会给儿童造成一个破坏性的影响，这通常是由于孩子对父母的依恋。生命历程理论则关注父母的分离会带来一连串的压力体验，并且这些压力是来自多方面的,如父母之间的矛盾、父母的丧失、经济状况恶化、父母形象的改变和养育方式的贫乏。选择理论指出破碎家庭之所以会产生有违法行为的儿童是因为事先存在的风险因素就与其他家庭不同,如父母之间的矛盾、有犯罪前科或有反社会倾向的父母、低家庭收入或是养育方式的贫乏。

剑桥研究从三个理论中抽取假设,并在调查中进行了检验(Juby and Farrington,2001)。来自不完整家庭(永久破裂的家庭)的男孩比来自完整家庭的男孩更容易实施违法行为,但是没有高于来自完整却充满暴力家庭的男孩。总的来说,最重要的因素是家庭破坏后的轨迹。离异后仍然和他们的母亲在一起的男孩有着和来自低暴力完整家庭男孩相似的违法犯罪比例。与父亲、亲戚或者其他人(比如养父母)生活的男孩有着更高的违法犯罪比例。这样的生活安排更加不稳定,其他一些研究也显示父母的经常变换能预测孩子今后的犯罪。可以得出结论,事实相对于创伤理论和选择理论更加倾向于生命历程学说。

三、社会因素

(一)社会经济地位

剑桥研究测量了大量的社会经济地位(SES)的指标,不仅包括对男孩原来家庭也包括成人后的男孩本人,这些指标包括职业声望、家庭收入、住房和工作稳定性。大多职业声望的测量与儿童的犯罪没有显著的联系。孩子8—10岁时家庭社会经济地位差能显著预测后来自我报告的犯罪,但不是正式的定罪。最普遍的是,家庭收入低和住房条件差能预测官方记录和自我报告的青少年、成年时期的犯罪(Farrington,1992a,1992b)。

斯同瑟梅尔–洛伯(Stouthamer-Loeber)(2002)在匹兹堡青少年调查中指出,在最年长的群体中,孩子13岁时的家庭社会经济地位能够作为改善因素预测未来最长6年时间内孩子的长期严重违法行为。然而,在洛伯(Loeber)(2008)后续更加深入的分析中,社会经济地位同时具有风险和改善的效应。纽卡斯尔千户家庭调查发现,高的社会经济地位能帮助失学儿童克服违法行为起到保护性的作用(Kolvin,1990)。

许多研究者提出,低社会经济地位家庭和反社会行为之间的联系是受到家庭社会化实践中介作用的。举个例子,帕特森(Patterson)和拉兹利尔(Larzelere)(1990)在俄勒冈州青少年调查中得出结论,父母管理技巧在家庭社会经济地位预测违法行为中起着中介作用。换句话说,低社会经济地位预测违法行为是因为低社会经济地位家庭在教育管理孩子方面缺乏技术。弗格森、斯温-坎贝尔和霍伍德（Fergusson，Swain-Campbell，and Horwood）（2004）在克莱斯特切奇儿童健康和发展研究中写道，出生到 6 岁期间生活在一个低社会经济地位家庭里可以预测 15—21 岁间自我报告和官方记录在案的违法犯罪行为。然而，上述联系在控制了家庭因素（体罚、母亲的关爱、父母亲的变化等）行为问题、旷课逃学和不良的同伴之后就消失，意味着这些因素都是中介变量。

（二）同伴影响

有违法的朋友这个因素能预测今后的犯罪。巴汀等（Battin *et al.*）（1998）在西雅图社会发展项目中指出，同伴违法能预测自我报告的暴力犯罪。违法行为往往出现于小团体（通常情况下两个或三个人），而不是单独一人。与大团伙相比较少出现。在剑桥大学研究中，与他人犯罪的概率会随着年龄的增长而持续减少。17 岁之前，男孩们倾向于和他们年龄相仿、住处较近的同伴一起犯罪。17 岁之后，共同犯罪变得不那么普遍（Reiss and Farrington，1991）。

要解释的主要问题在于，是否年轻人在群体中比一个人的时候更有可能犯罪，或者是否共同犯罪普遍存在仅仅反映了一个事实，即如果年轻人出去，他们倾向于成群出去。是同伴们倾向于鼓励和促进犯罪，还是仅仅大多数离开家的活动（包括违法的和不违法的）都倾向于团体行动呢？另一种可能是，犯罪的实施鼓励相关人员的违法行为，也许是因为"物以类聚，人以群分"或由于法院的标签和制度化的指责和孤立效应。桑伯里等（Thornberry *et al.*）（1994）在罗彻斯特青少年发展研究中总结说，事实上存在一种相互效应，即违法同伴引发犯罪，犯罪吸引与之交往的同伴。

缺少违法的朋友，或拥有亲社会的朋友，可以作为一个保护因素。在剑桥研究中，没有成为罪犯的，来自犯罪基因背景的家庭（根据低家庭收入、大家庭规模、定罪的家长、低智商、养育方式不当）的男孩往往 8 岁的时候，只有很少或没有朋友（Farrington *et al.*，1988a，1988b）。新西兰克莱斯特彻奇的健康和发展研究，来自消极家庭背景的孩子没有犯罪记录、吸食毒品或学习问题，往往很少有违法的同伴（Fergusson and Lynskey，1996）。在罗彻斯特青少年发展研究中，没有严重犯罪的，来自风险家庭背景的孩子往往有亲社会的、传统价值观的同伴。最后，在蒙特利尔青少年调查中，弗格森等（Fergusson *et al.*）（2007）调查了使有犯罪同伴的儿童避免犯罪的保护因素，并得出结论，低冲动是一个主要的保护因素。

在匹兹堡青年研究中，对同伙犯罪和男孩个体犯罪之间的关系，从个体之间的（如比较同伙犯罪和某一特定年龄所有男孩的违法，然后将所有年龄段获得的两者之间的相关加以整合)和个体自身(例如比较同伙犯罪和某一男孩在他不同的年龄段的违法,然后将所有男孩的上述相关加以整合)进行了研究。同伙犯罪与个体间违法有最强的相关,但不能预测个体的犯罪(Farrington et al. , 2002)。相反的,父母监督差、父母强化差、男孩较少参与家庭活动,能预测个体间和个体自身的犯罪。结果表明,这三个家庭变量是最可能的原因,而犯罪同伴是男孩犯罪的最可能诱因。

很明显,年轻人在加入帮派之后增加了他们的犯罪。在西雅图社会发展项目中,巴汀等(Battin et al.)(1998)发现了这个规律,也表明帮派关系比有犯罪的同伴更能预测犯罪。在匹兹堡青少年研究中,戈登等(Gordon et al.)(2004)报告男孩在加入团伙之后不仅大大增加贩卖毒品、吸毒、暴力犯罪和侵财犯罪等违法行为,并且当他们离开帮派后犯罪频率降低到进入帮派前的水平。桑伯里等(Thornberry et al.)(2003)在罗彻斯特青少年发展研究和加蒂等(Gatti et al.)(2005)在蒙特利尔纵向实验研究中,还发现年轻人加入帮派后犯罪更多了。一部分这些研究对比了"选择"和"促进"假说,并得出结论说未来的帮派成员会越来越有犯罪倾向,并在加入帮派后变得更加行为不端。青春期少年的帮会关系是之后暴力行为的一个风险因素(Herrenkohl et al. , 2000),但这可能因为它们都是测量同样潜在组成的结果。

(三)邻里环境(社区)因素

许多研究表明,生活在城市与农村地区的犯罪行为预测截然相反(Derzon, 2010)。在美国国家青年调查中,自我报告袭击和抢劫的流行性显然是都市的年轻人比例更高(Elliott, Huizinga, and Menard, 1989)。在城市,生活在高犯罪率社区的男孩要比那些生活在低犯罪率社区的更暴力。罗彻斯特青少年发展研究中,生活在一个高犯罪率社区能够显著性预测自我报告的暴力(Thornberry, Huizinga, and Loeber, 1995)。同样,在匹兹堡青年研究中,生活在一个不良的邻里环境中(由母亲划分,或者是基于普查中贫穷、失业、女性持家的家庭)能够显著地预测自我报告的暴力(Farrington, 1998)以及谋杀罪行(Farrington et al. , 2008)。

在基于芝加哥邻里社区的人类发展项目中,桑普森,兰登布什和伊尔斯(Sampson, Raudenbush, and Earls)(1997)研究社区对暴力的影响。最重要的邻里社区预测值主要集中在经济劣势(用贫穷、女性持家的比例,以及非裔美国人的比例等来标注)、移民集中度(拉丁美洲人或外国出生的人的比例)、居住的不稳定性和低水平的非正式社会控制和社会凝聚力。他们提出邻里社区的集体效能,或居民干预和控制反社会的行为的意愿，可以作为控制犯罪的保护因素。的确，在环境风险研究中，欧吉尔等（Odgers et al.）（2009）发现集体效能防止反社会的行为，但只有在缺乏教育的邻里社区。桑普森、兰登布什和伊尔斯（Sampson, Morenoff, and Raudenbush）（2005），总结出非裔美国人和白人在暴力行为上最大的差别都可以解释为：面对风险因素而出现的种族差异，尤其是生活在一个不良的邻里环境中。类似的结论也出现在匹兹堡青年研究中（Farrington, Loeber and Stouthamer-Loeber, 2003）。

很明显，犯罪者不成比例地住在市中心附近，这些地区的典型特征是逐渐衰败，社区缺乏有机的组织，居民具有高度的流动性（Shaw and McKay, 1969）。但是，同样的，这很难确定这些地区在多大程度上影响了反社会行为，事实上有多大可能性具有反社会性的人生活在缺失教育的区域（例如，因为他们的贫穷或公有住房分配政策）。有趣的是，无论是邻里社区研究者如戈特弗雷德森、麦克尼尔（Gottfredson, McNeil, and Gottfredson）（1991），还是发展研究者如鲁特尔（Rutter）（1981）纷纷提出，邻里社区只能够通过作用于个体及其家庭间接影响反社会行为。在芝加哥青少年发展研究中，图兰、戈尔曼和亨利（Tolan, Gorman, and Henry）（2003）得出的结论是，父母养育实践、帮会关系和同伙暴力犯罪等在社区结构特性（集中的贫穷、种族异质性、经济资源、暴力犯罪率）个体暴力行为之间起到中介作用。

在匹兹堡青年研究中，维克斯乔姆和洛伯（Wikström and Loeber）（2000）发现不同类型的人对不同类型的区域之间一个有趣的相互作用。六个个体、家庭、同伴、学校变量三分为有风险性、一般的或保护性三类，然后将得分相加。获得最高风险评分的男孩趋于犯罪，这与他们居住在哪类区域无关。然而，高保护性得分的男孩如果他们生活在恶劣的公共住房区域则更容易犯罪。因此，当其他风险因素并不高的时候，地区风险则会变得重要，而且在高风险区域生活的男孩可以由家庭、同伴、学校保护因素来克服犯罪的风险。一般来说，在这项调查中恶劣的邻里社区是一个促进因素（Loeber et al., 2008）。

一个关键的问题是为什么社区犯罪率随时间发生改变，并且在何种程度上这是一个社区或者居于其中的个体变化的函数。回答这个问题需要对社区和个人进行跟踪的纵向研究来获得。建构环境影响的最好途径，是跟踪那些从一个地方搬到另一个地方的人们。例如，在剑桥研究中，搬离伦敦导致显著的官方定罪和自我报告的违法行为的降低（Osborn, 1980）。这种减少可能已经发生，因为迁移出去会导致与共同犯罪的群体分离，或因为在伦敦以外的城市犯罪机会较少。

四、讨论和结论

已经了解了很多关于犯罪风险因素,关于这个主题有许多系统的评论(Derzon, 2010;Jolliffe and Farrington, 2009)。相比之下,很少有针对在高危险群体犯罪的保护因素研究,关于改善因素的研究更少。运用前瞻性纵向调查,对社区样本频繁地进行面对面的访谈,开展对保护和改善因素的研究是十分迫切的。

关于改善和保护因素的知识对预防犯罪有着重要的暗示意义。聚焦风险的预防,致力于减少高风险孩子们的风险因素。如果目标因素真的扮演着风险因素的作用,这种努力可能是特别有效的,但是如果目标因素事实上是作为一种改善因素,那么努力的效果就相对减少了。例如,在匹兹堡青年研究的成人暴力预测中,有高犯罪同伴的男孩中40%有暴力行为,相比之下,暴力行为发生在有中等犯罪同伴的男孩中只占11%,低犯罪同伴的男孩中则只有9%(Loeber et al., 2008, p.227)。根据这样的结果,尽量减少有犯罪同伴的目标男孩与他们违法同伴的接触(如辅导制)是完全合乎逻辑的。

然而,聚焦风险的预防对于改善因素来说并不太明显。在匹兹堡青年研究中相同的预测分析,21%学业成绩低下的男孩实施暴力,相比之下,21%学业成绩一般的男孩和8%学业成绩较好的男孩有暴力行为。在这种情况下,指向的目标群体不仅仅是那些高危的孩子(例如,在学前知识充实项目:见斯科维哈特等(Schweinhart et al.)(2005),也包括那些中间群体,或换句话说有四分之三的孩子。为了减少暴力行为,试图让所有的孩子提高学业成绩并不是很合理。如前所述,强调优势就是一个更为积极和有吸引力的预防犯罪的途径,而不仅仅是只针对高犯罪风险的孩子,并尽量减少他们不足的部分。但是,风险和改善因素的研究非常有必要针对不同目标因素形成最有效的方法。

同样,更多关于保护因素的研究需要区分哪些项目对于哪些高风险孩子群体最有效。理想状态下,系统的回顾会标注哪些因素一直以来针对不同类型的高风险儿童都具有预防不同类型的犯罪的效能(例如有早期反社会行为,来自失学背景的、学习成绩差的等)。同样,在干预过程中,治疗师怎样定性风险与保护因素之间的相互作用,也是今后值得研究的领域。

改善和保护因素的研究对于风险评估工具具有重要的意义,它主要是关注风险因素。一些研究人员已经提出一个观点,即改善/保护因素的加入是否能够使评估工具具有更高的预测效果。洛伯等（Loeber et al.）（2008）尝试用组合风险—改善因素的得分来预测未来暴力犯罪和严重盗窃犯罪的效能。瑞尼和多兰（Rennie and Dolan）（2010）发现在 SAVRY 评估工具中，保护因素是年轻罪犯中断或持续犯罪的一个重要的预测指标。更多的关于风险评估工具中改善和保护因素的研究是很有价值的。

如今对违法犯罪的风险因素学界已有很多的研究和认识，但是，对其发生的原因，因果路径或机制却知之甚少。理论上，干预项目应该把犯罪的原因作为目标。确定原因的最好办法是进行实验或准实验研究。比如，一项干预实验如果能够成功减少冲动，并且由此导致违反行为的减少，那么可以预测冲动可能是违法行为的原因之一（Robins,1992）。同样的，如果个体本身在父母监管下发生了变化，继而改变了个体的违法行为，那么就能够证明父母监管可能是违法行为发生的原因（Farrington,1998）。

基于当前知识，下列因素应该成为干预的主要目标：冲动、学业成绩、子女养育方式、年轻母亲、虐待儿童、父母吵架和破裂家庭、贫困、犯罪的同伴、贫困的邻里社区。有效的干预应该减少冲动性和提高自我控制、提高学习成绩、改进子女养育方式、鼓励年轻人不要过早生育、阻止虐待儿童、促进家庭和睦、减少贫困、减少与反社会人员交往，增加与亲社会同伴相处，改善邻里环境。在本手册的这个部分的另外章节里，许多干预方式已经实施过，并经过严格的评估。以后，实证性研究会提供更多关于改善和保护因素的知识。

[参考文献见英文原作]

（丁靖艳　赵超颇　叶威明　译）

Risk and Protective Factors for Offending

David P. Farrington

University of Cambridge

Rolf Loeber

University of Pittsburgh

Maria M. Ttofi

University of Cambridge

During the 1990s, there was a revolution in criminology, as the risk factor prevention paradigm became influential (Farrington, 2000). The basic idea of this paradigm is very simple: identify the key risk factors for offending and implement prevention methods designed to counteract them. This paradigm was imported into criminology from public health, where it had been used successfully for many years to tackle illnesses such as cancer and heart disease, by pioneers such as Hawkins and Catalano (1992). The risk factor prevention paradigm links explanation and prevention, links fundamental and applied research, and links scholars, policy makers, and practitioners. Loeber and Farrington (1998) presented a detailed exposition of this paradigm as applied to serious and violent juvenile offenders.

A risk factor for offending is defined as a variable that predicts a high probability of later offending. Typically, risk factors are dichotomized, so that they are either present or absent. Because of the emphasis of this Handbook, this chapter focuses on risk factors that could possibly be changed in intervention studies. Therefore, gender, race/ethnicity, criminal parents, and large family size are not reviewed here, although their links with offending may be explained by changeable factors. For example, Fagan *et al.* (2007) concluded that boys committed more crimes than girls because boys had higher risk factor scores and lower protective factor scores. In order to determine whether a risk factor is a predictor or possible cause of offending, the risk factor needs to be measured before the offending. Therefore, prospective longitudinal surveys are needed to investigate risk factors.

This paradigm typically also emphasizes protective factors, suggesting that intervention methods to enhance them should also be implemented. However, in the past the term *protective factor* has been used ambiguously. Some researchers have suggested that a protective factor is merely the opposite end of the scale to a risk factor (e. g. White, Moffitt, and Silva, 1989). For example, if poor parental supervision is a risk factor, good parental supervision might be a protective factor. However, this seems to be using two terms for the same variable.

Other researchers have suggested that a protective factor interacts with a risk factor to minimize or buffer its effects (e. g. Rutter, 1985). Typically, the impact of a protective factor is then studied in the presence of a risk factor. Loeber *et al.* (2008) suggested a consistent terminology. Following Sameroff *et al.* (1998), they defined *promotive* factors as variables that predict a low probability of offending, and *protective* factors as variables that predict a low probability of offending among persons exposed to risk factors.

In order to disentangle risk and promotive effects, it is important to classify variables into at least three categories (the promotive end, the middle, and the risk end). Stouthamer-Loeber *et al.* (2002) did this in the Pittsburgh Youth Study (see later). They studied promotive effects by comparing the probability of delinquency in the promotive category versus the middle, and they studied risk effects by comparing the probability of delinquency in the risk category versus the middle. Some variables had promotive effects but not risk effects (e. g. Attention Deficit-Hyperactivity Disorder, or ADHD), while others had risk effects but not promotive effects (e. g. peer delinquency in the youngest cohort). There will be a special emphasis on promotive and protective factors in this chapter, because early crime prevention methods can be based on enhancing promotive and protective factors rather than reducing risk factors. Pollard, Hawkins, and Arthur (1999) argued that focusing on promotive and protective factors and on building resilience of children was a more positive approach, and more attractive to communities, than reducing risk factors, which emphasized deficits and problems.

Within one short chapter, it is impossible to review everything that is known about risk, promotive, and protective factors (see also Lösel and Bender, 2003; Loeber, Slot, and Stouthamer-Loeber, 2006). This chapter will review only the most important changeable factors: individual factors such as impulsivity and attainment, family influences such as child-rearing and disrupted families, and social influences such as socio-economic status, peer, and neighborhood factors. This chapter will focus especially on knowledge gained in major prospective longitudinal studies of offending, in which community samples of at least several hundred people are followed up from childhood into adolescence and adulthood, with repeated personal interviews as well as the collection of record data. The emphasis is on the prediction of offending in community samples, not on the prediction of persistence versus desistance in samples of offenders (see Loeber *et al.* , 2007).

There will be a special focus on results obtained in two prospective longitudinal surveys: the Cambridge Study in Delinquent Development and the Pittsburgh Youth Study. The Cambridge Study is a prospective longitudinal survey of over 400 London males from age 8 to age 48 (see Farrington *et al.* 2006; Farrington, Coid, and West, 2009). In the Pittsburgh Youth Study, over 1,500 boys from Pittsburgh public schools were followed up for 12 years (see Loeber *et al.* , 1998; Loeber *et al.* , 2008). Initially, 500 were in first grade (aged about 7), 500 were in fourth grade (aged about 10), and 500 were in seventh grade (aged about 13), of public schools in the City of Pittsburgh. See Farrington and Welsh (2007, chapter 2) for more information about these and other prospective longitudinal surveys of offending.

Our main conclusions are as follows:

● The most important factors that should be targeted in intervention research are impulsiveness, school achievement, child-rearing methods, young mothers, child abuse, parental conflict, disrupted families, poverty, delinquent peers, and deprived neighborhoods.

● However, little is known about whether these variables operate primarily as risk or promotive factors or both.

● Similarly, little is known about whether these variables act as causes or what are the important causal mechanisms linking these factors with outcomes such as offending.

- Similarly, little is known about what factors protect children from different types of risky backgrounds against becoming offenders.

- Risk assessment instruments should include promotive and protective factors.

- More research on promotive and protective factors is needed, using prospective longitudinal surveys of community samples with frequent face-to-face interviews.

The organization of this chapter is as follows. Section I reviews the individual factors of hyperactivity/impulsivity and intelligence/attainment. Section II assesses the family factors of child-rearing methods (supervision and discipline), young mothers and child abuse, and parental conflict and disrupted families. Section III reviews the social factors of socio-economic status, peer influence, and neighborhood factors. Section IV draws conclusions. Throughout, there is a special attempt to review research on promotive and protective factors as well as research on risk factors, although of course there are many more studies of risk factors.

INDIVIDUAL FACTORS

Hyperactivity and Impulsivity

Many studies show that hyperactivity or ADHD predicts later offending (see Pratt *et al.*, 2002). In the Copenhagen Perinatal project, hyperactivity (restlessness and poor concentration) at age 11—13 significantly predicted arrests for violence up to age 22, especially among boys whose mothers experienced delivery complications (Brennan, Mednick, and Mednick, 1993). Similarly, in theOrebro longitudinal study in Sweden, hyperactivity at age 13 predicted police-recorded violence up to age 26. The highest rate of violence was among males with both motor restlessness and concentration difficulties (15%), compared to 3% of the remainder (Klinteberg *et al.*, 1993). In the Seattle Social Development Project, hyperactivity and risk taking in adolescence predicted violence in young adulthood (Herrenkohl *et al.*, 2000).

In the Cambridge Study, boys nominated by teachers as lacking in concentration or restless, those nominated by parents, peers, or teachers as the most daring or taking most risks, and those who were the most impulsive on psychomotor tests at age 8—10, all tended to become offenders later in life. Daring, poor concentration, and restlessness all predicted both official convictions and self-reported delinquency, and daring was consistently one of the best independent predictors (Farrington, 1992b). Interestingly, hyperactivity predicted juvenile offending independently of conduct problems (Farrington, Loeber, and Van Kammen, 1990). Lynam (1996) proposed that boys with both hyperactivity and conduct disorder were most at risk of chronic offending and psychopathy, and Lynam (1998) presented evidence in favor of this hypothesis from the Pittsburgh Youth Study.

The most extensive research on different measures of impulsiveness was carried out in the Pittsburgh Youth Study by White *et al.* (1994). The measures that were most strongly related to self-reported delinquency at ages 10 and 13 were teacher-rated impulsiveness (e. g. acts without thinking) , self-reported impulsiveness, self-reported undercontrol (e. g. unable to delay gratification) , motor restlessness (from videotaped observations) , and psychomotor impulsiveness (on the Trail Making Test). Generally, the verbal behavior rating tests produced stronger relationships with offending than the psychomotor performance tests, suggesting that cognitive impulsiveness (e. g. admitting impulsive behavior) was more relevant than behavioral impulsiveness (based on test performance). A systematic review by Jolliffe and Farrington (2009) showed that early measures of impulsiveness (especially daring and risk-taking) predicted later measures of violence.

The most extensive research on promotive factors predicting a low probability of violence and serious theft was carried out in the Pittsburgh Youth Study by Loeber *et al.* (2008, chapter 7). They studied predictors over four age ranges in the youngest cohort (7—9, 10—12, 13—16, and 17—19) and over three age ranges in the oldest cohort (13—16, 17—19, 20—25). Predictor variables were trichotomized into the risk end, the middle, and the promotive end. They found that, consistently, low ADHD was a promotive factor for low violence, but high ADHD was not a risk factor. These results replicated the earlier findings of Stouthamer-Loeber *et al.* (2002) in the same project for predicting persistent serious delinquency. Also, Lynam *et al.* (2000) showed that a good neighborhood was a protective factor against impulsivity, since impulsivity did not predict offending in good neighborhoods.

Intelligence and Attainment

Low intelligence (IQ) and low school achievement also predict offending. In the Philadelphia Biosocial project (Denno 1990) , low verbal and performance IQ at ages 4 and 7, and low scores on the California Achievement test at age 13—14 (vocabulary, comprehension, maths, language, spelling) all predicted arrests for violence up to age 22. In Project Metropolitan inCopenhagen, low IQ at age 12 significantly predicted police-recorded violence between ages 15 and 22. The link between low IQ and violence was strongest among lower class boys (Hogh and Wolf, 1983).

Low IQ measured in the first few years of life predicts later delinquency. In a prospective longitudinal survey of about 120 Stockholm males, low IQ measured at age 3 significantly predicted officially recorded offending up to age 30 (Stattin and Klackenberg-Larsson 1993). Frequent offenders (with 4 or more offenses) had an average IQ of 88 at age 3, whereas nonoffenders had an average IQ of 101. All of these results held up after controlling for social class. Similarly, low IQ at age 4 predicted arrests up to age 27 in the Perry preschool project (Schweinhart *et al.*, 1993) and court delinquency up to age 17 in the Collaborative Perinatal Project (Lipsitt, Buka, and Lipsitt, 1990).

In the Cambridge Study, twice as many of the boys scoring 90 or less on a nonverbal IQ test (Raven's Progressive Matrices) at age 8—10 were convicted as juveniles as of the remainder (West and Farrington, 1973). However, it was difficult to disentangle low IQ from low school achievement, because they were highly intercorrelated and both predicted delinquency. Low nonverbal IQ predicted juvenile self-reported delinquency to almost exactly the same degree as juvenile convictions (Farrington, 1992b), suggesting that the link between low IQ and delinquency was not caused by the less intelligent boys having a greater probability of being caught. Also, low IQ and low school achievement predicted offending independently of other variables such as low family income and large family size (Farrington, 1990).

IQ tests are designed to predict later school success (Barchard, 2005), and low IQ may lead to delinquency through the intervening factor of school failure. The association between school failure and delinquency has been demonstrated repeatedly in longitudinal surveys (Maguin and Loeber, 1996). In the Pittsburgh Youth Study, Lynam, Moffitt, and Stouthamer-Loeber (1993) concluded that low verbal IQ led to school failure and subsequently to self-reported delinquency, but only for African American boys. An alternative theory is that the link between low IQ and delinquency is mediated by disinhibition (impulsiveness, ADHD, low guilt, low empathy), and this was also tested in the Pittsburgh Youth Study (Koolhof *et al.*, 2007). Felson and Staff (2006) argued that the link between low academic achievement and delinquency was mediated by low self-control.

High school achievement has often been identified as a promotive or protective factor. In the classic longitudinal survey of Werner and Smith (1982) in Kauai, they studied vulnerable children who had four or more risk factors by age 2 (including poverty, low maternal education, a disrupted family, perinatal stress, and low IQ) and compared those who did not develop any serious learning or behavioral problems by age 18 with those who had mental health problems or committed serious delinquencies. Among the most important protective factors were good reading, reasoning, and problem solving skills at age 10 (Werner and Smith, 1992, 2001). Also, high academic achievement was often a promotive factor in the Pittsburgh Youth Study analyses (Loeber et al. , 2008).

In the Newcastle Thousand Family Study, Kolvin et al. (1990) followed up children who were deprived at age 5 (based on welfare dependence, overcrowded housing, poor physical care, poor mothering, parental illness, and disrupted families) and found that those who became nonoffenders by age 32 tended to have good reading, spelling and arithmetic at age 10—11. Also, Smith et al. (1994) in the Rochester Youth Development Study followed up children with five or more family risk factors (including family on welfare, young mother, child abuse, criminal family member, drug problems of family member, parental unemployment, and poor parental education) and found that those who did not commit serious delinquency tended to have high math and reading ability. Several other longitudinal surveys report that high IQ is a protective factor against offending for high risk children (e. g. Kandel et al. , 1988; White, Moffitt, and Silva, 1989; Fergusson and Lynskey, 1996; Stattin, Romelsjo, and Stenbacka, 1997; Jaffee et al. , 2007).

A plausible explanatory factor underlying the link between low IQ and delinquency is the ability to manipulate abstract concepts. Children who are poor at this tend to do badly in IQ tests and in school achievement, and they also tend to commit offenses, mainly because of their poor ability to foresee the consequences of their offending. Delinquents often do better on nonverbal performance IQ tests, such as object assembly and block design, than on verbal IQ tests (Moffitt, 1993), suggesting that they find it easier to deal with concrete objects than with abstract concepts.

Impulsiveness, attention problems, low IQ, and low school achievement could all be linked to deficits in the executive functions of the brain, located in the frontal lobes. These executive functions include sustaining attention and concentration, abstract reasoning, concept formation, goal formulation, anticipation and planning, programming and initiation of purposive sequences of motor behavior, effective self-monitoring and self-awareness of behavior, and inhibition of inappropriate or impulsive behaviors (Moffitt and Henry, 1991; Morgan and Lilienfeld, 2000). Interestingly, in the Montreal longitudinal-experimental study, a measure of executive functioning based on tests at age 14 was the strongest neuropsychological discriminator between violent and nonviolent boys (Seguin *et al.*, 1995). This relationship held independently of a measure of family adversity (based on parental age at first birth, parental education level, broken family and low social class). In the Pittsburgh Youth Study, the life-course-persistent offenders had marked neurocognitive impairments (Raine *et al.*, 2005).

FAMILY FACTORS

Child-Rearing Methods

Many different types of child-rearing methods predict offending. The most important dimensions of child-rearing are supervision or monitoring of children, discipline or parental reinforcement, warmth or coldness of emotional relationships, and parental involvement with children. Parental supervision refers to the degree of monitoring by parents of the child's activities, and their degree of watchfulness or vigilance. Of all these child-rearing methods, poor parental supervision is usually the strongest and most replicable predictor of offending (Smith and Stern, 1997). In the Cambridge Study, 61% of boys who were poorly supervised at age 8 were convicted up to age 50, compared with 36% of the remainder (Farrington *et al.*, 2009).

Many studies show that parents who do not know where their children are when they are out, and parents who let their children roam the streets unsupervised from an early age, tend to have delinquent children. For example, in McCord's (1979) classic Cambridge-Somerville study in Boston, poor parental supervision in childhood was the best predictor of both violent and property crimes up to age 45. Leschied *et al.* (2008) found that parental management that was coercive, inconsistent, or lacking in supervision during mid-childhood was a strong predictor of adult criminality, as were parental separation and marital status.

Parental discipline refers to how parents react to a child's behavior. It is clear that harsh or punitive discipline (involving physical punishment) predicts offending (Haapasalo and Pokela, 1999). In their follow-up study of nearly 700 Nottingham children, John and Elizabeth Newson (1989) found that physical punishment at ages 7 and 11 predicted later convictions; 40% of offenders had been smacked or beaten at age 11, compared with 14% of non-offenders. Erratic or inconsistent discipline also predicts delinquency. This can involve either erratic discipline by one parent, sometimes turning a blind eye to bad behavior and sometimes punishing it severely, or inconsistency between two parents, with one parent being tolerant or indulgent and the other being harshly punitive.

Cold, rejecting parents tend to have delinquent children, as McCord (1979) found in the Cambridge-Somerville study. She also concluded that parental warmth could act as a protective factor against the effects of physical punishment (McCord, 1997). Whereas 51% of boys with cold physically punishing mothers were convicted in her study, only 21% of boys with warm physically punishing mothers were convicted, similar to the 23% of boys with warm non-punitive mothers who were convicted. The father's warmth was also a protective factor against the father's physical punishment.

The classic longitudinal study by Robins (1979) in St. Louis shows that poor parental supervision, harsh discipline and a rejecting attitude all predict delinquency. Also, in the Seattle Social Development Project, poor family management (poor supervision, inconsistent rules, and harsh discipline) in adolescence predicted violence in young adulthood (Herrenkohl et al. , 2000). Similar results were obtained in the Cambridge Study. Harsh or erratic parental discipline, cruel, passive or neglecting parental attitudes, and poor parental supervision, all measured at age 8, all predicted later juvenile convictions and self-reported delinquency (West and Farrington, 1973). Generally, the presence of any of these adverse family background features doubled the risk of a later juvenile conviction.

Derzon (2010) carried out a meta-analysis of family factors as predictors of criminal and violent behavior (as well as aggressive and problem behavior). The meta-analysis was based on longitudinal studies, but many predictions were over short time periods (less than four years in 55% of cases), many outcome variables were measured at relatively young ages (up to 15 in 40% of cases), and many studies were relatively small (less than 200 participants in 43% of cases). The strongest predictors of criminal or violent behavior were parental education ($r = .30$ for criminal behavior), parental supervision ($r = .29$ for violent behavior), child rearing skills (r = . 26 for criminal behavior), parental discord (r = . 26 for criminal behavior), and family size (r = . 24 for violent behavior). Notably weak predictors were young parents, broken homes, and socio-economic status.

In research on protective factors in the Rochester Youth Development Study, Smith *et al.* (1994) found that high-risk children who were resilient (nondelinquent) tended to have good parental supervision and good attachment to parents. In similar research on deprived children who became nondelinquents in the Newcastle Thousand Family Study, Kolvin *et al.* (1990) reported that the nondelinquent children tended to receive better parental supervision. Also, in the Pittsburgh Youth Study (Loeber *et al.*, 2008), parental supervision, physical punishment by the mother, and involvement of the boy in family activities tended to have promotive rather than risk effects.

Most explanations of the link between child-rearing methods and delinquency focus on attachment or social learning theories. Attachment theory was inspired by the work of Bowlby (1951), and suggests that children who are not emotionally attached to warm, loving and law-abiding parents tend to become offenders. Social learning theories suggest that children's behavior depends on parental rewards and punishments and on the models of behavior that parents represent (Patterson, 1995). Children will tend to become offenders if parents do not respond consistently and contingently to their antisocial behavior and if parents themselves behave in an antisocial manner.

Young Mothers and Child Abuse

At least in Western industrialized countries, early child-bearing, or teenage pregnancy, predicts many undesirable outcomes for the children, including low school attainment, antisocial school behavior, substance use and early sexual intercourse. The children of teenage mothers are also more likely to become offenders. For example, Morash and Rucker (1989) analyzed results from four surveys in the US and UK (including the Cambridge Study) and found that teenage mothers were associated with low income families, welfare support and absent biological fathers, that they used poor child-rearing methods, and that their children were characterized by low school attainment and delinquency. However, the presence of the biological father mitigated many of these adverse factors and generally seemed to have a protective effect. Of course, it must be remembered that the age of the mother is highly correlated with the age of the father, and that having a young father may be just as important as having a young mother.

In the Cambridge Study, teenage mothers who went on to have large numbers of children were especially likely to have convicted children (Nagin, Pogarsky, and Farrington, 1997). In the Newcastle Thousand-Family study mothers who married as teenagers (a factor strongly related to teenage childbearing) were twice as likely as others to have sons who became offenders by age 32 (Kolvin *et al.* , 1990). Also, the deprived children who became offenders were less likely to have older mothers than the deprived children who did not become offenders (Kolvin *et al.* , 1988a). In the Pittsburgh Youth Study (Loeber *et al.* ,2008), an older mother consistently had a promotive effect, rather than a younger mother having a risk effect.

Several researchers have investigated factors that might mediate the link between young mothers and child delinquency. In the Dunedin study in New Zealand, Jaffee *et al.* (2001) concluded that the link between teenage mothers and violent children was mediated by maternal characteristics (e. g. , intelligence, criminality) and family factors (e. g. , harsh discipline, family size, disrupted families). In the Rochester Youth Development Study, Pogarsky, Lizotte, and Thornberry (2003) found that the most important mediating factor was the number of parental transitions (frequent changes in care-givers). Much research suggests that frequent changes of parent figures predict offending by children (e. g. Thornberry *et al.* , 1999; Krohn, Hall, and Lizotte, 2009).

A pioneering longitudinal survey in Philadelphia by Maxfield and Widom (1996) found that children who were physically abused up to age 11 were significantly likely to become violent offenders in the next 15 years. Similarly, in the Cambridge-Somerville study in Boston, McCord (1983) reported that about half of the abused or neglected boys were convicted for serious crimes, became alcoholics or mentally ill, or died before age 35. Child maltreatment before age 12 was one of the most consistent predictors of violence and serious theft in the Pittsburgh Youth Study (Loeber *et al.* , 2008). In the Rochester Youth Development Study, child maltreatment under age 12 (physical, sexual or emotional abuse or neglect) predicted later self-reported and official offending (Smith and Thornberry 1995). Furthermore, these results held up after controlling for gender, race, socio-economic status and family structure. Keiley *et al.* (2001) reported that maltreatment under age 5 was more damaging than maltreatment between ages 6 and 9. The extensive review by Malinosky-Rummell and Hansen (1993) confirms that being physically abused as a child predicts later violent and nonviolent offending.

Few longitudinal studies on the effects of child abuse by parents have tried to measure promotive or protective factors. However, Herrenkohl et al. (2005), in a longitudinal survey of Pennsylvania children, found that a strong commitment to school, and having parents and peers who disapproved of antisocial behavior, predicted low rates of violence and delinquency among abused children. In the Environmental Risk Study, Jaffee et al. (2007) concluded that maltreated children who did not become antisocial tended to have high intelligence and to live in low crime neighborhoods with high social cohesion and informal social control.

Possible causal mechanisms linking childhood victimization and adolescent offending have been reviewed by Widom (1994). First, childhood victimization may have immediate but long-lasting consequences (e. g. shaking may cause brain injury). Second, childhood victimization may cause bodily changes (e. g. desensitization to pain) that encourage later aggression. Third, child abuse may lead to impulsive or dissociative coping styles that, in turn, lead to poor problem-solving skills or poor school performance. Fourth, victimization may cause changes in self-esteem or in social information-processing patterns that encourage later aggression. Fifth, child abuse may lead to changed family environments (e. g. being placed in foster care) that have harmful effects. Sixth, juvenile justice practices may label victims, isolate them from prosocial peers, and encourage them to associate with delinquent peers.

Parental Conflict and Disrupted Families

There is no doubt that parental conflict and interparental violence predict adolescent antisocial behavior, as the meta-analysis by Buehler et al. (1997) shows. In the Cambridge Study, parental conflict predicted delinquency (West and Farrington, 1973). In the Christchurch Study in New Zealand, children who witnessed violence between their parents were more likely to commit both violent and property offenses according to their self-reports (Fergusson and Horwood, 1998). Witnessing father-initiated violence was still predictive after controlling for other risk factors such as parental criminality, parental substance abuse, parental physical punishment, a young mother and low family income.

Many studies show that broken homes or disrupted families predict delinquency. In the Newcastle Thousand-Family Study, Kolvin et al. (1988b) reported that marital disruption (divorce or separation) in a boy's first five years predicted his later convictions up to age 32. Also, the deprived children who became nondelinquents were less likely to have lost their fathers. Similarly, in the Dunedin study in New Zealand, Henry *et al.* (1993) found that children who were exposed to parental discord and many changes of the primary caretaker tended to become antisocial and delinquent. In the National Longitudinal Survey of Adolescent Health, Demuth and Brown (2004) concluded that single-parent families predicted delinquency because of their lower levels of parental supervision, closeness, and involvement.

The importance of the cause of the broken home was demonstrated by Wadsworth (1979) in the UK National Survey of Health and Development. Boys from homes broken by divorce or separation had an increased likelihood of being convicted or officially cautioned up to age 21, in comparison with those from homes broken by death or from unbroken homes. Homes broken while the boy was under age 5 especially predicted offending, while homes broken while the boy was between ages 11 and 15 were not particularly criminogenic. Remarriage (which happened more often after divorce or separation than after death) was also associated with an increased risk of offending, suggesting a possible negative effect of step-parents. The meta-analysis by Wells and Rankin (1991) also indicates that broken homes are more strongly related to delinquency when they are caused by parental separation or divorce rather than by death.

Most studies of broken homes have focused on the loss of the father rather than the mother, simply because the loss of a father is much more common. McCord (1982) in Boston carried out an interesting study of the relationship between homes broken by loss of the natural father and later serious offending of the children. She found that the prevalence of offending was high for boys reared in broken homes without affectionate mothers (62%) and for those reared in united homes characterized by parental conflict (52%), irrespective of whether they had affectionate mothers. The prevalence of offending was low for those reared in united homes without conflict (26%) and-importantly-equally low for boys from broken homes with affectionate mothers (22%). These results suggest that it is not so much the broken home which is criminogenic as the parental conflict which often causes it, and that a loving mother might in some sense be able to compensate for the loss of a father.

In the Cambridge Study, both permanent and temporary separations from a biological parent before age 10 (usually from the father) predicted convictions and self-reported delinquency, providing that they were not caused by death or hospitalization (Farrington 1992b). However, homes broken at an early age (under age 5) were not unusually criminogenic (West and Farrington, 1973). Separation before age 10 predicted both juvenile and adult convictions (Farrington, 1992a), and it predicted adult convictions independently of other factors such as low family income or poor school attainment; 60% of boys who had been separated from a parent by their tenth birthday were convicted up to age 50, compared with 36% of the remainder (Farrington et al. , 2009).

Explanations of the relationship between disrupted families and delinquency fall into three major classes. Trauma theories suggest that the loss of a parent has a damaging effect on a child, most commonly because of the effect on attachment to the parent. Life course theories focus on separation as a sequence of stressful experiences, and on the effects of multiple stressors such as parental conflict, parental loss, reduced economic circumstances, changes in parent figures and poor child-rearing methods. Selection theories argue that disrupted families produce delinquent children because of pre-existing differences from other families in risk factors such as parental conflict, criminal or antisocial parents, low family income or poor child-rearing methods.

Hypotheses derived from the three theories were tested in the Cambridge Study (Juby and Farrington, 2001). While boys from broken homes (permanently disrupted families) were more delinquent than boys from intact homes, they were not more delinquent than boys from intact high conflict families. Overall, the most important factor was the post-disruption trajectory. Boys who remained with their mother after the separation had the same delinquency rate as boys from intact low conflict families. Boys who stayed with their father, with relatives or with others (e. g. foster parents) had high delinquency rates. These living arrangements were more unstable, and other research shows that frequent changes of parent figures predict offending. It was concluded that the results favored life course theories rather than trauma or selection theories.

SOCIAL FACTORS

Socio-economic Status

Numerous indicators of socio-economic status (SES) were measured in the Cambridge Study, both for the boy's family of origin and for the boy himself as an adult, including occupational prestige, family income, housing, and employment instability. Most of the measures of occupational prestige were not significantly related to offending. Low SES of the family when the boy was aged 8—10 significantly predicted his later self-reported but not his official delinquency. More consistently, low family income and poor housing predicted official and self-reported offending, juvenile and adult (Farrington, 1992a, 1992b).

In the Pittsburgh Youth Study, Stouthamer-Loeber *et al.* (2002) reported that socio-economic status at age 13 acted as a promotive factor in predicting persistent serious delinquency in the next six years in the oldest cohort. However, in more extensive later analyses by Loeber *et al.* (2008), socio-economic status had both risk and promotive effects. In the Newcastle Thousand Family Study, high socio-economic status was a protective factor against delinquency in the deprived children (Kolvin *et al.*, 1990).

Several researchers have suggested that the link between a low SES family and antisocial behavior is mediated by family socialization practices. For example, Larzelere and Patterson (1990) in the Oregon Youth Study concluded that the effect of SES on delinquency was entirely mediated by parent management skills. In other words, low SES predicted delinquency because low SES families used poor child-rearing practices. In the Christchurch Health and Development Study, Fergusson, Swain-Campbell, and Horwood (2004) reported that living in a low SES family between birth and age 6 predicted self-reported and official delinquency between ages 15 and 21. However, this association disappeared after controlling for family factors (physical punishment, maternal care, and parental changes), conduct problems, truancy, and deviant peers, suggesting that these may have been mediating factors.

Peer Influence

Having delinquent friends is an important predictor of later offending. Battin *et al.* (1998) showed that peer delinquency predicted self-reported violence in the Seattle Social Development Project. Delinquent acts tend to be committed in small groups (of two or three people, usually) rather than alone. Large gangs are comparatively unusual. In the Cambridge Study, the probability of committing offenses with others decreased steadily with age. Before age 17, boys tended to commit their crimes with other boys similar in age and living close by. After age 17, co-offending became less common (Reiss and Farrington, 1991).

The major problem of interpretation is whether young people are more likely to commit offenses while they are in groups than while they are alone, or whether the high prevalence of co-offending merely reflects the fact that, whenever young people go out, they tend to go out in groups. Do peers tend to encourage and facilitate offending, or is it just that most kinds of activities out of the home (both delinquent and non-delinquent) tend to be committed in groups? Another possibility is that the commission of offenses encourages association with other delinquents, perhaps because "birds of a feather flock together" or because of the stigmatizing and isolating effects of court appearances and institutionalization. Thornberry et al. (1994) in the Rochester Youth Development Study concluded that there were reciprocal effects, with delinquent peers causing delinquency and delinquency causing association with delinquent peers.

The absence of delinquent friends, or the presence of prosocial friends, may act as a protective factor. In the Cambridge Study, the boys from criminogenic backgrounds (defined by low family income, large family size, convicted parent, low IQ, and poor child-rearing) who did not become delinquents tended to have few or no friends at age 8 (Farrington et al. , 1988a, 1988b). In the Christchurch Health and Development Study in New Zealand, the children from adverse family backgrounds who did not show delinquency, substance use, or school problems tended to have low affiliations with delinquent peers (Fergusson and Lynskey, 1996). In the Rochester Youth Development Study, the children from risky family backgrounds who did not commit serious delinquency tended to have peers with prosocial, conventional values. Finally, in a survey of Montreal adolescents, Fergusson et al. (2007) investigated which factors protected children with delinquent peers from themselves becoming delinquents, and concluded that low impulsivity was a major protective factor.

In the Pittsburgh Youth Study, the relationship between peer delinquency and a boy's offending was studied both between individuals (e. g. comparing peer delinquency and offending over all boys at a particular age and then aggregating these correlations over all ages) and within individuals (e. g. comparing peer delinquency and offending of a boy at all his ages and then aggregating these correlations over all boys). Peer delinquency was the strongest correlate of offending in between-individual correlations but did not predict offending within individuals (Farrington et al. , 2002). In contrast, poor parental supervision, low parental reinforcement, and low involvement of the boy in family activities predicted offending both between and within individuals. It was concluded that these three family variables were the most likely to be causes, whereas having delinquent peers was most likely to be an indicator of the boy's offending.

It is clear that young people increase their offending after joining a gang. In the Seattle Social Development Project, Battin et al. (1998) found this, and also showed that gang membership predicted delinquency above and beyond having delinquent friends. In the Pittsburgh Youth Study, Gordon et al. (2004) reported not only a substantial increase in drug selling, drug use, violence, and property crime after a boy joined a gang, but also that the frequency of offending decreased to pre-gang levels after a boy left a gang. Thornberry et al. (2003) in the Rochester Youth Development Study and Gatti et al. (2005) in the Montreal longitudinal-experimental study also found that young people offended more after joining a gang. Several of these studies constrasted the "selection" and "facilitation" hypotheses and concluded that future gang members were more delinquent to start with but became even more delinquent after joining a gang. Gang membership in adolescence is a risk factor for later violence (Herrenkohl et al., 2000), but this may be because both are measuring the same underlying construct.

Neighborhood Factors

Many studies show that living in an urban as opposed to a rural area predicts criminal behavior (Derzon, 2010). In the U. S. National Youth Survey, the prevalence of self-reported assault and robbery was considerably higher among urban youth (Elliott, Huizinga, and Menard, 1989). Within urban areas, boys living in high crime neighborhoods are more violent than those living in low crime neighborhoods. In the Rochester Youth Development Study, living in a high crime neighborhood significantly predicted self-reported violence (Thornberry, Huizinga, and Loeber, 1995). Similarly, in the Pittsburgh Youth Study, living in a bad neighborhood (either as rated by the mother or based on census measures of poverty, unemployment, and female-headed households) significantly predicted official and reported violence (Farrington, 1998) and homicide offending (Farrington et al., 2008).

Sampson, Raudenbush, and Earls (1997) studied community influences on violence in the Project on Human Development in Chicago Neighborhoods. The most important community predictors were concentrated economic disadvantage (as indexed by poverty, the proportion of female-headed families, and the proportion of African Americans), immigrant concentration (the proportions of Latinos or foreign-born persons), residential instability, and low levels of informal social control and social cohesion. They suggested that the *collective efficacy* of a neighborhood, or the willingness of residents to intervene to prevent antisocial behavior, might act as a protective factor against crime. Indeed, in the Enviromental Risk Study, Odgers *et al.* (2009) found that collective efficacy protected against antisocial behavior, but only in deprived neighborhoods. Sampson, Morenoff, and Raudenbush (2005) concluded that most of the difference between African Americans and Caucasians in violence could be explained by racial differences in exposure to risk factors, especially living in a bad neighborhood. Similar conclusions were drawn in the Pittsburgh Youth Study (Farrington, Loeber, and Stouthamer-Loeber, 2003).

It is clear that offenders disproportionately live in inner-city areas characterized by physical deterioration, neighborhood disorganization, and high residential mobility (Shaw and McKay, 1969). However, again, it is difficult to determine to what extent the areas themselves influence antisocial behavior and to what extent it is merely the case that antisocial people tend to live in deprived areas (e. g. , because of their poverty or public housing allocation policies). Interestingly, both neighborhood researchers such as Gottfredson, McNeil, and Gottfredson (1991) and developmental researchers such as Rutter (1981) have argued that neighborhoods have only indirect effects on antisocial behavior through their effects on individuals and families. In the Chicago Youth Development Study, Tolan, Gorman-Smith, and Henry (2003) concluded that the relationship between community structural characteristics (concentrated poverty, racial heterogeneity, economic resources, violent crime rate) and individual violence was mediated by parenting practices, gang membership, and peer violence.

In the Pittsburgh Youth Study, Wikström and Loeber (2000) found an interesting interaction between types of people and types of areas. Six individual, family, peer, and school variables were trichotomized into risk, middle, or protective categories and added up. Boys with highest risk scores tended to be delinquent irrespective of the type of area in which they were living. However, boys with high protective scores were more likely to be delinquent if they were living in disadvantaged public housing areas. Hence, the area risk was only important when other risks were not high, and boys in high risk areas could be protected against delinquency by family, peer, and school factors. Generally, a bad neighborhood was a promotive factor in this survey (Loeber *et al.*, 2008).

One key question is why crime rates of communities change over time, and to what extent this is a function of changes in the communities or in the individuals living in them. Answering this question requires longitudinal research in which both communities and individuals are followed up. The best way of establishing the impact of the environment is to follow people who move from one area to another. For example, in the Cambridge Study, moving out of London led to a significant decrease in convictions and self-reported offending (Osborn, 1980). This decrease may have occurred because moving out led to a breaking up of co-offending groups, or because there were fewer opportunities for crime outside London.

DISCUSSION AND CONCLUSIONS

A great deal is known about risk factors for offending, and there are many systematic reviews on this topic (e. g. Derzon, 2010; Jolliffe and Farrington, 2009). In contrast, there are fewer studies of protective factors against offending in high risk groups, and very few studies of promotive factors. More research on protective and promotive factors is needed, using prospective longitudinal surveys of community samples with frequent face-to-face interviews.

Knowledge about promotive and protective factors would have important implications for crime prevention. In risk-focused prevention, efforts are made to reduce risk factors among high risk children. This is likely to be particularly effective if the targeted factor really acts as a risk factor, but less effective if the targeted factor really acts as a promotive factor. For example, in predicting adult violence in the Pittsburgh Youth Study, 40% of boys who were high on peer delinquency became violent, compared with 11% of the middle group and 9% of those who were low (Loeber *et al.*, 2008, p. 227). With this pattern of results, targeting boys who are high on peer delinquency and trying to reduce their association with delinquent peers (e. g., mentoring) is entirely logical.

Risk-focused prevention, however, seems less sensible with promotive factors. In the same prediction analysis in the Pittsburgh Youth Study, 21% of boys with low academic a-chievement became violent, compared with 21% of the middle group, and 8% of those with high academic achievement. In this case, it would be desirable to target not only the high risk boys (for example, in preschool intellectual enrichment programs: see

Schweinhart *et al.*, 2005) but also those in the middle group, or in other words three-quarters of all boys. In attempting to reduce violence, it would not be unreasonable to try to enhance the academic achievement of all boys. As mentioned, focusing on enhancing strengths is a more positive and attractive approach to crime prevention than targeting the high risk boys and trying to reduce their deficits. However, research on risk and promotive factors is needed to establish which approach is likely to be the most effective with different targeted factors.

Similarly, more research on protective factors is needed to indicate which programs are likely to be most effective with which groups of high risk children. Ideally, a systematic review would indicate which factors were consistently protective against different types of offending outcomes in different categories of high risk children (e. g. those showing early antisocial behavior, those from deprived backgrounds, those with low academic achievement, etc.). Also, more research is needed on how therapist characteristics interact with risk and protective factors in interventions.

Research on promotive and protective factors also has important implications forrisk assessment instruments, which overwhelmingly focus on risk factors. Several researchers have raised the issue of whether assessment instruments might have higher predictive efficiency if promotive/protective factors were added to them. Loeber *et al.* (2008) investigated the ability of combined risk-promotive factor scores to predict later violence and serious theft. Rennie and Dolan (2010) found that protective factors in the SAVRY assessment instrument were important predictors of later desistance versus persistence of young offenders. More research is needed on the usefulness of promotive/protective factors in risk assessment instruments.

While a great deal is known about risk factors for offending, less is known about causes, or about causal pathways or mechanisms. Ideally, intervention programs should target causes of offending. The best way of establishing causes is to carry out experimental or quasi-experimental analyses. For example, if an intervention experiment succeeded in reducing impulsivity and if there was a consequent reduction in offending, this would indicate that impulsivity might be a cause of offending (see Robins, 1992). Similarly, if changes within individuals in parental supervision were reliably followed by changes within individuals in offending, this would indicate that parental supervision might be a cause of offending (see Farrington, 1988).

Based on current knowledge, the following factors should be prime targets for intervention efforts: impulsiveness, school achievement, child-rearing methods, young mothers, child abuse, parental conflict and disrupted families, poverty, delinquent peers, and deprived neighborhoods. Efforts should be made to reduce impulsiveness and/or enhance self-control, to increase school achievement, to improve child-rearing, to encourage young people not to have children at an early age, to discourage child abuse, to increase parental harmony, to decrease poverty, to decrease association with antisocial peers and increase association with prosocial peers, and to improve bad neighborhoods. As other chapters in this section of the Handbook demonstrate, many of these types of interventions have already been implemented and rigorously evaluated. Further experimental research informed by more knowledge about promotive and protective factors needs to be conducted.

References

Barchard, Kimberly A. 2005. " Does Emotional Intelligence Assist in the Prediction of Academic Success?" *Educational and Psychological Measurement* 63: 840 – 858.

Battin, Sara R. , Karl G. Hill, Robert D. Abbott, Richard F. Catalano, and J. David Hawkins. 1998. " The Contribution of Gang Membership to Delinquency Beyond Delinquent Friends. " *Criminology* 36: 93 – 115.

Bowlby, John. 1951. *Maternal Care and Mental Health.* Geneva, Switzerland: World Health Organization.

Brennan, Patricia A. , Birgitte R. Mednick, and Sarnoff A. Mednick. 1993. "Parental Psychopathology, Congenital Factors, and Violence. " In *Mental Disorder and Crime*, edited by Sheilagh Hodgins. Newbury Park, CA: Sage.

Buehler, Cheryl, Christine Anthony, Ambika Krishnakumar, Gaye Stone, Jean Gerard, and Sharon Pemberton. 1997. "Interparental Conflict and Youth Problem Behaviors: A Meta-Analysis". *Journal of Child and Family Studies* 6: 233 – 247.

Demuth, Stephen, and Susan L. Brown. 2004. "Family Structure, Family Processes, and Adolescent Delinquency: The Significance of Parental Absence Versus Parental Gender". *Journal of Research in Crime and Delinquency* 41: 58 – 81.

Denno, Deborah W. 1990. *Biology and Violence: From Birth to Adulthood.* Cambridge, UK: Cambridge University Press.

Derzon, James H. 2009. "The Correspondence of Family Features with Problem, Aggressive, Criminal, and Violent Behavior: A Meta-Analysis". *Journal of Experimental Criminology* 6: 263 – 292.

Elliott, Delbert S. , David Huizinga, and Scott Menard. 1989. *Multiple Problem Youth: Delinquency, Substance Use, and Mental Health Problems.* New York: Springer-Verlag.

Fagan, Abigail A. , M. Lee Van Horn, J. David Hawkins, and Michael W. Arthur. 2007. "Gender Similarities and Differences in the Association between Risk and Protective Factors and Self-Reported Serious Delinquency". *Prevention Science* 8: 115 – 124.

Farrington, David P. 1988. "Studying Changes Within Individuals: The Causes of Offending. " In *Studies of Psychosocial Risk: The Power of Longitudinal Data*, edited by Michael Rutter. New York: Cambridge University Press.

Farrington, David P. 1990. "Implications of Criminal Career Research for the Prevention of Offending". *Journal of Adolescence* 13: 93 – 113.

Farrington, David P. 1992a. "Explaining the Beginning, Progress and Ending of Antisocial Behavior from Birth to Adulthood". In *Facts, Frameworks and Forecasts: Advances in Criminological Theory*, vol. 3, edited by Joan McCord. New Brunswick, NJ: Transaction.

Farrington, David P. 1992b. "Juvenile Delinquency". In *The School Years*, edited by John C. Coleman, 2nd ed. London: Routledge.

Farrington, David P. 1998. "Predictors, Causes, and Correlates of Youth Violence". In *Youth Violence*, edited by Michael Tonry and Mark H. Moore. Chicago: University of Chicago Press.

Farrington, David P. 2000. "Explaining and Preventing Crime: The Globalization of Knowledge-The American Society of Criminology 1999 Presidential Address ". *Criminology* 38: 1 – 24.

Farrington, David P. , Jeremy W. Coid, Louise Harnett, Darrick Jolliffe, Nadine Soteriou, Richard Turner, and Donald J. West. 2006. *Criminal Careers up to Age 50 and Life Success up to Age 48: New Findings from the Cambridge Study in Delinquent Development.* London: Home Office (Research Study No. 299).

Farrington, David P. , Jeremy W. Coid, and Donald J. West. 2009. "The Development of

Offending from Age 8 to Age 50: Recent Results from the Cambridge Study in Delinquent Development". *Monatsschrift fur Kriminologie und Strafrechtsreform (Journal of Criminology and Penal Reform)* 92: 160–173.

Farrington, David P. , Bernard Gallagher, Lynda Morley, Raymond J. St. Ledger, and Donald J. West. 1988a. "Are There any Successful Men from Criminogenic Backgrounds?" *Psychiatry* 51: 116–130.

Farrington, David P. , Bernard Gallagher, Lynda Morley, Raymond J. St Ledger, and Donald J. West. 1988b. A 24 Year Follow up of Men from Vulnerable Backgrounds. In *The Abandonment of Delinquent Behavior: Promoting the Turnaround*, edited by R. L. Jenkins and W. K. Brown. New York: Praeger.

Farrington, David P. , Rolf Loeber, Rebecca Stallings, and D. Lynn Homish. 2008. "Early Risk Factors for Homicide Offenders and Victims". In *Violent Offenders: Theory, Research, Public Policy and Practice*, edited by Matt Delisi and Peter J. Conis. Sudbury, MA: Jones and Bartlett.

Farrington, David P. , Rolf Loeber, and Magda Stouthamer-Loeber. 2003. "How Can the Relationship between Race and Violence be Explained?" In *Violent Crime: Assessing Race and Ethnic Differences*, edited by Darnell F. Hawkins. Cambridge, UK: Cambridge University Press.

Farrington, David P. , Rolf Loeber, and Welmoet Van Kammen. 1990b. "Long-term Criminal Outcomes of Hyperactivity-Impulsivity-Attention Deficit and Conduct Problems in Childhood". In *Straight and Devious Pathways from Childhood to Adulthood*, edited by Lee N. Robins and Michael Rutter. Cambridge, UK: Cambridge University Press.

Farrington, David P. , Rolf Loeber, Yanming Yin, and Stewart Anderson. 2002. "Are Within-Individual Causes of Delinquency the Same as Between-Individual Causes?" *Criminal Behavior and Mental Health* 12: 53–68.

Farrington, David P. , and Brandon C. Welsh. 2007. *Saving Children from a Life of Crime: Early Risk Factors and Effective Interventions.* New York: Oxford University Press.

Felson, Richard B. , and Jeremy Staff. 2006. "Explaining the Academic Performance-Delinquency Relationship". *Criminology* 44: 299–319.

Fergusson, David M. , and L. John Horwood. 1998. "Exposure to Interparental Violence in Childhood and Psychosocial Adjustment in Young Adulthood. "*Child Abuse and Neglect* 22: 339–357.

Fergusson, David M., and Michael T. Lynskey. 1996. "Adolescent Resiliency to Family Adversity". *Journal of Child Psychology and Psychiatry* 37: 281 – 292.

Fergusson, David M., Naomi Swain-Campbell, and L. John Horwood. 2004. "How does Childhood Economic Disadvantage Lead to Crime?" *Journal of Child Psychology and Psychiatry* 45: 956 – 966.

Fergusson, David M., Frank Vitaro, Brigitte Wanner, and Mara Brendgen. 2007. "Protective and Compensatory Factors Mitigating the Influence of Deviant Friends on Delinquent Behaviors during Early Adolescence". *Journal of Adolescence* 30: 33 – 50.

Gatti, Uberto, Richard E. Tremblay, Frank Vitaro, and Pierre McDuff. 2005. "Youth Gangs, Delinquency and Drug Use: A Test of the Selection, Facilitation and Enhancement Hypotheses." *Journal of Child Psychology and Psychiatry* 46: 1178 – 1190.

Gordon, Rachel A., Benjamin B. Lahey, Eriko Kawai, Rolf Loeber, Magda Stouthamer-Loeber, and David P. Farrington. 2004. "Antisocial Behavior and Youth Gang Membership: Selection and Socialization." *Criminology* 42: 55 – 87.

Gottfredson, Denise C., Richard J. McNeil, and Gary D. Gottfredson. 1991. "Social Area Influences on Delinquency: A Multilevel Analysis". *Journal of Research in Crime and Delinquency* 28: 197 – 226.

Haapasalo, Jaana, and Elina Pokela. 1999. "Child-Rearing and Child Abuse Antecedents of Criminality". *Aggression and Violent Behavior* 4: 107 – 127.

Hawkins, J. David, and Richard F. Catalano. 1992. *Communities That Care: Action for Drug Abuse Prevention*. San Francisco, CA: Jossey-Bass.

Henry, Bill, Terrie Moffitt, Lee Robins, Felton Earls, and Phil Silva. 1993. "Early Family Predictors of Child and Adolescent Antisocial Behavior: Who are the Mothers of Delinquents?" *Criminal Behavior and Mental Health* 3: 97 – 118.

Herrenkohl, Todd I., Eugene Maguin, Karl G. Hill, J. David Hawkins, Robert D. Abbott, and Richard F. Catalano. 2000. "Developmental Risk Factors for Youth Violence." *Journal of Adolescent Health* 26: 176 – 186.

Hogh, Erik, and Preben Wolf. 1983. "Violent Crime in a Birth Cohort: Copenhagen 1953—1977". In *Prospective Studies of Crime and Delinquency*, edited by Katherine T. Van Dusen and Sarnoff A. Mednick. Boston: Kluwer-Nijhoff.

Jaffee, Sara, Avshalom Caspi, Terrie E. Moffitt, Jay Belsky, and Phil A. Silva. 2001.

"Why are Children Born to Teen Mothers at Risk for Adverse Outcomes in Young Adulthood? Results from a 20-year Longitudinal Study." *Development and Psychopathology* 13: 377 – 397.

Jaffee, Sara R. , Avshalom Caspi, Terrie E. Moffitt, Monica Polo-Tomas, and Alan Taylor. 2007. "Individual, Family, and Neighborhood Factors Distinguish Resilient from Non-Resilient Maltreated Children: A Cumulative Stressors Model". *Child Abuse and Neglect* 31:231 – 253.

Jolliffe, Darrick and David P. Farrington. 2009. "A Systematic Review of the Relationship between Childhood Impulsiveness and Later Violence". In *Personality, Personality Disorder and Violence*, edited by Mary McMurran and Richard Howard. Chichester, UK: Wiley.

Juby, Heather, and David P. Farrington. 2001. "Disentangling the Link between Disrupted Families and Delinquency". *British Journal of Criminology* 41: 22 – 40.

Kandel, Elizabeth, Sarnoff A. Mednick, Lis Kirkegaard-Sorensen, Barry Hutchings, Joachim Knop, Raben Rosenberg, and Fini Schulsinger. 1988. "IQ as a Protective Factor for Subjects at High Risk for Antisocial Behavior". *Journal of Consulting and Clinical Psychology* 56: 224 – 226.

Keiley, Margaret K. , Tasha R. Howe, Kenneth A. Dodge, John E. Bates and Gregory S. Pettit. 2001. "The Timing of Child Physical Maltreatment: A Cross-Domain Growth Analysis of Impact on Adolescent Externalizing and Internalizing Problems ". *Development and Psychopathology* 13: 891 – 912.

Klinteberg, Britt af, Tommy Andersson, David Magnusson, and Hakan Stattin. 1993. "Hyperactive Behavior in Childhood as Related to Subsequent Alcohol Problems and Violent Offending: A Longitudinal Study of Male Subjects". *Personality and Individual Differences* 15: 381 – 388.

Kolvin, Israel, Frederick J. W. Miller, Mary Fleeting, and Philip A. Kolvin. 1988a. "Risk/Protective Factors for Offending with Particular Reference to Deprivation". In *Studies of Psychosocial Risk: The Power of Longitudinal Data*, edited by Michael Rutter. Cambridge, UK: Cambridge University Press.

Kolvin, Israel, Frederick J. W. Miller, Mary Fleeting, and Philip A. Kolvin. 1988b. "Social and Parenting Factors Affecting Criminal-Offence Rates: Findings from the Newcastle Thousand Family Study (1947—1980). "*British Journal of Psychiatry* 152:

80 - 90.

Kolvin, Israel, Frederick J. W. Miller, David M. Scott, S. R. M. Gatzanis, and Mary Fleeting. 1990. *Continuities of Deprivation? The Newcastle 1000 Family Study.* Aldershot, UK: Avebury.

Krohn, Marvin D. , Gina P. Hall, and Alan J. Lizotte. 2009. "Family Transitions and Later Delinquency and Drug Use". *Journal of Youth and Adolescence* 38: 466 - 480.

Larzelere, Robert E. , and Gerald R. Patterson. 1990. "Parental Management: Mediator of the Effect of Socioeconomic Status on Early Delinquency". *Criminology* 28: 301 - 324.

Leschied, Alan, Debbie Chiodo, Elizabeth Nowicki, and Susan Rodger. 2008. "Childhood Predictors of Adult Criminality: A Meta-Analysis Drawn from the Prospective Longitudinal Literature". *Canadian Journal of Criminology and Criminal Justice* 50: 435 - 467.

Lipsitt, Paul D. , Stephen L. Buka, and Lewis P. Lipsitt. 1990. "Early Intelligence Scores and Subsequent Delinquency: A Prospective Study". *American Journal of Family Therapy* 18: 197 - 208.

Loeber, Rolf, and David P. Farrington. 1998, Eds. *Serious and Violent Juvenile Offenders: Risk Factors and Successful Interventions.* Thousand Oaks, CA: Sage.

Loeber, Rolf, David P. Farrington, Magda Stouthamer-Loeber, and Welmoet Van Kammen. 1998. *Antisocial Behavior and Mental Health Problems: Explanatory Factors in Childhood and Adolescence.* Mahwah, NJ: Lawrence Erlbaum.

Loeber, Rolf, David P. Farrington, Magda Stouthamer-Loeber, and Helene R. White. 2008. *Violence and Serious Theft: Development and Prediction from Childhood to Adulthood.* New York: Routledge.

Loeber, Rolf, Dustin A. Pardini, Magda Stouthamer-Loeber, and Adrian Raine. 2007. "Do Cognitive, Physiological, and Psychosocial Risk and Promotive Factors Predict Desistance from Delinquency in Males?" *Development and Psychopathology* 19: 867 - 887.

Loeber, Rolf, Wim Slot, and Magda Stouthamer-Loeber. 2006. "A Three-Dimensional Cumulative Developmental Model of Serious Delinquency". In *The Explanation of Crime: Contexts and Mechanisms*, edited by Per-Olof H. Wikström and Robert J. Sampson. Cambridge, UK: Cambridge University Press.

Lösel, Friedrich, and Doris Bender. 2003. "Protective Factors and Resilience". In *Early Prevention of Adult Antisocial Behaviour*, edited by David P. Farrington and Jeremy W.

Coid. Cambridge, UK: Cambridge University Press.

Lynam, Donald R. 1996. "Early Identification of Chronic Offenders: Who is the Fledgling Psychopath?" *Psychological Bulletin* 120: 209 – 234.

Lynam, Donald R. 1998. "Early Identification of the Fledgling Psychopath: Locating the Psychopathic Child in the Current Nomenclature". *Journal of Abnormal Psychology* 107: 566 – 575.

Lynam, Donald R., Avshalom Caspi, Terrie E. Moffitt, Per-Olof H. Wikström, Rolf Loeber, and Scott Novak. 2000. "The Interaction between Impulsivity and Neighborhood Context on Offending: The Effects of Impulsivity are Stronger in Poorer Neighborhoods". *Journal of Abnormal Psychology* 109: 563 – 574.

Lynam, Donald R, Terrie E. Moffitt and Magda Stouthamer-Loeber. 1993. "Explaining the Relation between IQ and Delinquency: Class, Race, Test Motivation, School Failure or Self-Control?" *Journal of Abnormal Psychology* 102: 187 – 196.

McCord, Joan. 1979. "Some Child-Rearing Antecedents of Criminal Behavior in Adult Men." *Journal of Personality and Social Psychology* 37: 1477 – 1486.

McCord, Joan. 1982. "A Longitudinal View of the Relationship between Paternal Absence and Crime". In *Abnormal Offenders, Delinquency, and the Criminal Justice System*, edited by John Gunn and David P. Farrington. Chichester, UK: Wiley.

McCord, Joan. 1983. "A Forty Year Perspective on Effects of Child Abuse and Neglect." *Child Abuse and Neglect* 7: 265 – 270.

McCord, Joan. 1997. "On Discipline." *Psychological Inquiry* 8: 215 – 217.

Maguin, Eugene, and Rolf Loeber. 1996. "Academic Performance and Delinquency". In *Crime and Justice*, vol. 20, edited by Michael Tonry. Chicago: University of Chicago Press.

Malinosky-Rummell, Robin, and David J. Hansen. 1993. "Long-Term Consequences of Childhood Physical Abuse." *Psychological Bulletin* 114: 68 – 79.

Maxfield, Michael G., and Cathy S. Widom. 1996. "The Cycle of Violence Revisited 6 Years Later". *Archives of Pediatrics and Adolescent Medicine* 150: 390 – 395.

Moffitt, Terrie E. 1993. "Adolescence-Limited and Life-Course-Persistent Antisocial Behavior: A Developmental Taxonomy". *Psychological Review* 100: 674 – 701.

Moffitt, Terrie E., and Bill Henry. 1991. "Neuropsychological Studies of Juvenile Delinquency and Juvenile Violence". In *Neuropsychology of Aggression*, edited by J. S.

Milner. Boston: Kluwer.

Morash, Merry, and Lila Rucker. 1989. "An Exploratory Study of the Connection of Mother's Age at Childbearing to her Children's Delinquency in Four Data Sets". *Crime and Delinquency* 35: 45 - 93.

Morgan, Alex B. , and Scott O. Lilienfeld. 2000. "A Meta-Analytic Review of the Relation Between Antisocial Behavior and Neuropsychological Measures of Executive Function". *Clinical Psychology Review* 20: 113 - 136.

Nagin, Daniel S. , Greg Pogarsky, and David P. Farrington. 1997. "Adolescent Mothers and the Criminal Behavior of their Children". *Law and Society Review* 31: 137 - 162.

Newson, John, and Elizabeth Newson. 1989. *The Extent of Parental Physical Punishment in the UK*. London: Approach.

Odgers, Candice L. , Terrie E. Moffitt, Laura M. Tach, Robert J. Sampson, Alan Taylor, and Charlotte L. Matthews. 2009. "The Protective Effects of Neighborhood Collective Efficacy on British Children Growing up in the Deprivation: A Developmental Analysis". *Developmental Psychology* 45: 942 - 957.

Osborn, Stephen G. 1980. "Moving Home, LeavingLondon, and Delinquent Trends". *British Journal of Criminology* 20: 54 - 61.

Patterson, Gerald R. 1995. "Coercion as a Basis for Early Age of Onset for Arrest". In *Coercion and Punishment in Long-Term Perspectives*, edited by Joan McCord. Cambridge, UK: Cambridge University Press.

Pogarsky, Greg, Alan J. Lizotte, and Terence P. Thornberry. 2003. "The Delinquency of Children Born to Young Mothers: Results from theRochester Youth Development Study." *Criminology* 41: 1249 - 1286.

Pollard, John A. , J. David Hawkins and Michael W. Arthur. 1999. "Risk and Protection: Are Both Necesssary to Understand Diverse Behavioral Outcomes in Adolescence?" *Social Work Research* 23: 145 - 158.

Pratt, Travis C. , Francis T. Cullen, Kristie R. Blevins, Leah Daigle, and James D. Unnever. 2002. "The Relationship of Attention Deficit Hyperactivity Disorder to Crime and Delinquency: A Meta-Analysis". *International Journal of Police Science and Management* 4: 344 - 360.

Raine, Adrian, Terrie M. Moffitt, Avshalom Caspi, Rolf Loeber, Magda Stouthamer-Loeber, and Don Lynam. 2005. "Neurocognitive Impairments in Boys on the Life-course

Persistent Antisocial Path". *Journal of Abnormal Psychology* 114: 38 – 49.

Reiss, Albert J. , and David P. Farrington. 1991. "Advancing Knowledge about Co-offending: Results from a Prospective Longitudinal Survey of London Males". *Journal of Criminal Law and Criminology* 82: 360 – 395.

Rennie, Charlotte E. , and Mairead C. Dolan. 2010. "The Significance of Protective Factors in the Assessment of Risk". *Criminal Behavior and Mental Health* 20: 8 – 22.

Robins, Lee N. 1979. "Sturdy Childhood Predictors of Adult Outcomes: Replications from Longitudinal Studies." In *Stress and Mental Disorder*, edited by J. E. Barrett, R. M. Rose, and Gerald L. Klerman. New York: Raven Press.

Robins, Lee N. 1992. "The Role of Prevention Experiments in Discovering Causes of Children's Antisocial Behavior." In *Preventing Antisocial Behavior: Interventions from Birth through Adolescence*, edited by Joan McCord and Richard E. Tremblay. New York: Guilford.

Rutter, Michael. 1981. "The City and the Child". *American Journal of Orthopsychiatry* 51: 610 – 625.

Rutter, Michael. 1985. "Resilience in the Face of Adversity: Protective Factors and Resistance to Psychiatric Disorder". *British Journal of Psychiatry* 147: 598 – 611.

Sameroff, Arnold J. , W. Todd Bartko, Clare Baldwin, and Ronald Seifer. 1998. "Family and Social Influences on the Development of Child Competence". In *Families, Risk, and Competence*, edited by M. Lewis and C. Feiring. Mahwah, NJ: Lawrence Erlbaum.

Sampson, Robert J. , Jeffrey D. Morenoff, and Stephen W. Raudenbush. 2005. "Social Anatomy of Racial and Ethnic Disparities in Violence". *American Journal of Public Health* 95: 224 – 232.

Sampson, Robert J. , Stephen W. Raudenbush, and Felton Earls. 1997. "Neighborhoods and Violent Crime: A Multilevel Study of Collective Efficacy". *Science* 277: 918 – 924.

Schweinhart, Lawrence J. , Jeanne Montie, Xiang Zongping, W. Steven Barnett, Clive R. Belfield, and Milagros Nores. 2005. *Lifetime Effects: The High/Scope Perry Preschool Study Through Age 40*. Ypsilanti, MI: High/Scope Press.

Seguin, Jean, Robert O. Pihl, Philip W. Harden, Richard E. Tremblay, and Bernice Boulerice. 1995. "Cognitive and Neuropsychological Characteristics of Physically Aggressive Boys". *Journal of Abnormal Psychology* 104: 614 – 624.

Shaw, Clifford R. , and Henry D. McKay. 1969. *Juvenile Delinquency and Urban Areas*, rev. ed. Chicago: University of Chicago Press.

Smith, Carolyn A. , Alan J. Lizotte, Terence P. Thornberry, and Marvin D. Krohn. 1994. "Resilient Youth: Identifying Factors that Prevent High-Risk Youth from Engaging in Delinquency and Drug Use". In *Delinquency and Disrepute in the Life Course*, edited by John L. Hagan. Greenwich, CT: JAI Press.

Smith, Carolyn A. , and Susan B. Stern 1997. "Delinquency and Antisocial Behavior: A Review of Family Processes and Intervention Research". *Social Service Review* 71: 382 – 420.

Smith, Carolyn A. , and Terence P. Thornberry. 1995. "The Relationship Between Childhood Maltreatment and Adolescent Involvement in Delinquency". *Criminology* 33: 451 – 481.

Stattin, Hakan, and Ingrid Klackenberg-Larsson. 1993. "Early Language and Intelligence Development and their Relationship to Future Criminal Behavior". *Journal of Abnormal Psychology* 102: 369 – 378.

Stattin, Hakan, Anders Romelsjo, and Marlene Stenbacka. 1997. "Personal Resources as Modifiers of the Risk for Future Criminality: An Analysis of Protective Factors in Relation to 18-Year-old Boys". *British Journal of Criminology* 37: 198 – 223.

Stouthamer-Loeber, Magda, Rolf Loeber, Evelyn Wei, David P. Farrington, and Per-Olof H. Wikström. 2002. "Risk and Promotive Effects in the Explanation of Persistent Serious Delinquency in Boys". *Journal of Consulting and Clinical Psychology* 70: 111 – 123.

Thornberry, Terence P. , David Huizinga, and Rolf Loeber. 1995. "The Prevention of Serious Delinquency and Violence: Implications from the Program of Research on the Causes and Correlates of Delinquency". In *Sourcebook on Serious*, *Violent and Chronic Juvenile Offenders*, edited by James C. Howell, Barry Krisberg, J. David Hawkins, and John J. Wilson. Thousand Oaks, CA: Sage.

Thornberry, Terence P. , Marvin D. Krohn, Alan J. Lizotte, Carolyn A. Smith, and Kimberly Tobin. 2003. *Gangs and Delinquency in Developmental Perspective*. New York: Cambridge University Press.

Thornberry, Terence P. , Alan J. Lizotte, Marvin D. Krohn, Margaret Farnworth, and Soon J. Jang. 1994. "Delinquent Peers, Beliefs and Delinquent Behavior: A Longitudinal Test of Interactional Theory. "*Criminology* 32: 47 – 83.

Thornberry, Terence P. , Carolyn A. Smith, Craig Rivera, David Huizinga, and Magda

Stouthamer-Loeber. 1999. *Family Disruption and Delinquency*. Washington, DC: Office of Juvenile Justice and Delinquency Prevention.

Tolan, Patrick H., Deborah Gorman-Smith, and David B. Henry. 2003. "The Developmental Ecology of Urban Males' Youth Violence." *Developmental Psychology* 39: 274 – 291.

Wadsworth, Michael. 1979. *Roots of Delinquency*. London: Martin Robertson.

Wells, L. Edward, and Joseph H. Rankin. 1991. "Families and Delinquency: A Meta-Analysis of the Impact of Broken Homes". *Social Problems* 38: 71 – 93.

Werner, Emmy E., and Ruth S. Smith. 1982. *Vulnerable but Invincible: A Longitudinal Study of Resilient Children and Youth*. New York: McGraw-Hill.

Werner, Emmy E., and Ruth S. Smith. 1992. *Overcoming the Odds: High Risk Children from Birth to Adulthood*. Ithaca, NY: Cornell University Press.

Werner, Emmy E., and Ruth S. Smith. 2001. *Journeys from Childhood to Midlife*. Ithaca, NY: Cornell University Press.

West, Donald J., and David P. Farrington. 1973. *Who Becomes Delinquent?* London: Heinemann.

White, Jennifer L., Terrie E. Moffitt, Avshalom Caspi, Dawn J. Bartusch, Douglas J. Needles, and Magda Stouthamer-Loeber. 1994. "Measuring Impulsivity and Examining its Relationship to Delinquency". *Journal of Abnormal Psychology* 103: 192 – 205.

White, Jennifer L., Terrie E. Moffitt, and Phil A. Silva. 1989. "A Prospective Replication of the Protective Effects of IQ in Subjects at High Risk for Delinquency". *Journal of Consulting and Clinical Psychology* 37: 719 – 724.

Widom, Cathy S. 1994. "Childhood Victimization and Adolescent Problem Behaviors." In *Adolescent Problem Behaviors*, edited by Robert D. Ketterlinus and Michael E. Lamb. Hillsdale, NJ: Lawrence Erlbaum.

闭路电视监控系统

大卫·P. 法林顿（David P. Farrington）

剑桥大学

"闭路电视监控系统为警方办案提供了良好的技术支持,闭路电视监控系统的热点犯罪有助于识别不法分子并判定其罪行。闭路电视监控系统是一个真正的社会财富,是对犯罪的极大威慑力量,是公共安全的强大保障"（Michael Howard, Home Secretary, May 1995, quoted by Norris and Armstrong, 1998, p. 10）。

本文的主要目的是从实证的角度评估闭路电视监控系统的价值。

一、介　绍

闭路电视监控系统是指"将一个摄影机与一个封闭的电路或循环相连,并通过这一系统或循环将摄影机产生的图像发送到中央电视台的监视器或录影机的这样一个系统"（Goold, 2004, p. 12）。各个闭路电视监控系统的特征有很大的差异,而闭路电视监控系统这一技术也在不断地提高中。比如说,摄像机可以是静态的或是能被平移、倾斜与变焦的,可以是被固定或者是能被重新调试的,可以是公开性的也可以是隐蔽性的。由于闭路电视监控系统的形态各异,而且还往往会随着时间而更新,因此要总结出闭路电视监控系统的有效性十分不易。

所有的闭路电视监控系统都必须有一个监控室,而且各个监控室的操作方式大有不同。比如,监控器可以 24 小时全天候工作或者每周只工作一定时间,监控室与警方的互动可以是双向的或者是单向的(监控室可以听到警方的收音机,却不能通过拨打 999 直接与警方进行交流)。各个闭路电视监控系统的人员编制水平有很大的差异。根据吉尔(Gill)与斯普里格斯(Spriggs)2005 年对闭路电视监控系统的全国性评估,监控室的操作人员每个人管理的相机数量从 20—250 个各不相同。许多闭路电视监控系统还包括对街头照明的安装与改善。

二、历 史

2003 年,威廉姆斯(Williams)总结了英国石油闭路电视监控系统的历史。20 世纪 50 年代后期,警方(始于 1956 年,Durham)开始使用闭路电视监控系统以协助原本由单人操作的交通信号灯的运行。1960 年,在泰国王室家族对英国进行国事访问时英国警察局在特拉法尔广场树立了 2 个监视摄影机以检测广场上的人群。1964年,利物浦警方试图将闭路电视监控系统隐藏在各个场所的中心地点。这些摄影机被安装在中心商务区,并将拍到的图片发送给正在通过无线电联系便衣巡警的警官。然而,警方却声称"并没有因为安装了电视监控而逮捕到任何疑犯"。这样的电视监控是预防性的,更多的只能是心理层面上的,所以警方不得不不断移动相机的位置使电视监控的效果更佳(Williams, 2003, p. 15)。

根据威廉姆斯(Williams)的数据,到 1969 年为止一共有 14 个不同的警察部队使用了闭路电视监控系统,他们所使用的摄像头有 67 个。20 世纪 90 年代,闭路电视监控系统的使用量剧增。据阿米蒂奇(Armitage)统计,英格兰与威尔士的监视摄像机的数量在 1990 年时有 100 个,1994 年有 400 个,1997 年有 4200 个,2002 年有40000 个。根据麦卡希尔(McCahill)和诺里斯(Norris)在帕特尼所做的估计,2003 年伦敦至少有 50 万个摄像头,而英国至少有 420 万个摄像头。这样的增长比例或许并不是百分之百正确,但是这至少说明了英国引领了世界各国安装了成千上万的闭路电视监控系统。在 20 世纪 90 年代中后期和 21 世纪初,摄像机的数量大量增加,主要是因为中央与地方五亿多英镑的政府拨款。1996 年至 1999 年间,超过四分之三的家用办公室犯罪预防预算被用于闭路电视监控系统(Koch, 1998)。这笔资金反映了闭路电视监控系统的普及以及公众对闭路电视监控系统的需求,导致这一现象的原因大部分是因为闭路电视监控系统在诸如詹姆斯·巴尔杰案等大案中起到的作用:

"在1993年儿童詹姆斯·巴尔杰被谋杀一案中,闭路电视监控系统显示了其强大的作用,虽然杀手并不能通过镜头被直接确认或推定,但是闭路电视监控系统与犯罪控制之间的联系却是不可否认的"(Davies,1998,p.244)。

三、机　制

闭路电视监控系统能通过许多机制来有效预防犯罪(Gill and Spriggs,2005,pp.7-8)。震慑潜在犯罪是闭路电视监控系统最重要的作用。罪犯通常都觉得在有闭路电视监控系统监测的地方作案被抓的可能性会比较大,因此,他们通常会避免在有闭路电视监控系统监测的地方作案。这一机制的工作原理是让罪犯对是否犯罪进行选择,即罪犯对犯罪代价与犯罪获利的衡量。因此,闭路电视监控系统对于激情犯罪、强制性犯罪或在酒精与药物影响下的犯罪(如暴力犯罪或性犯罪)并没有震慑效果。

有闭路电视监控系统安装的场所也更加受人们的欢迎,也就是说如果在这些区域犯罪将会有更多的目击者,这也是闭路电视监控系统能震慑犯罪的另一个原因。闭路电视监控系统也有利于警察与安保人员阻止犯罪发生或逮捕疑犯。此外,闭路电视监控系统也能鼓励不同群众与雇员采取措施预防犯罪,干预罪犯的行为并阻止犯罪发生。

为了使闭路电视监控系统更好地起到预防犯罪的作用,我们必须让群众与想要实施犯罪行为的人知道摄像头所在的位置。如果摄像头的覆盖率低,就无法震慑潜在犯罪,因为想要实施犯罪行为的人可以选择在摄像头的覆盖范围之外作案。如果摄像头设在光线不足的地方,或者拍摄的图像质量很差,潜在的犯罪者或许会觉得他们将不会通过图像被辨认出来。在公共场所设闭路电视监控系统预防犯罪的效果最佳,在难以观测到的地方或在私人场所(如房屋等)设闭路电视监控系统预防犯罪的效果最差(如家庭暴力与虐待儿童)。

四、优点与缺点

除了能有效减少犯罪之外,闭路电视监控系统还有其他的优点。居民在有闭路电视监控系统检测的区域会减少对犯罪的恐慌。同时,闭路电视监控系统的安装

（例如安装在议会名下的房地产中）会让居民觉得议会在这一地区有投资,这一地区也在不断发展。这会让居民对社区更加具有认同感,更加会去积极阻止犯罪与混乱的发生。闭路电视监控系统也可以被用来获取情报,并能在公共场合监视那些众所周知的罪犯。此外,闭路电视监控系统还有许多别的用途,如控制拥挤的人群、控制交通、监测管制居住区、寻找走失儿童或帮助那些需要医疗救助的病人或伤患。

　　尽管闭路电视监控系统有上述的许多优点,但同时它也有许多的不足之处。闭路电视监控系统被认为是对人民自由权利特别是隐私权的一种威胁,它极易引发社会驱逐。适用闭路电视监控系统控制犯罪会引发一个潜在的犯罪转移的问题,罪犯会简单地将犯罪实施地转移到那些没有摄像头的地方,因此从总量上来说犯罪并没有减少。但同时与犯罪转移相对的则是对犯罪震慑效果的扩散（Weisburd *et al.*,2006）。闭路电视监控系统安装地区对于犯罪的震慑效果会扩散到邻近的区域,能震慑潜在犯罪或提高居民的社会认同感。此外,一旦人们对闭路电视监控系统预防犯罪的作用表示认同,那么他们将会因为周围装有闭路电视监控系统而对犯罪降低警觉,也会减少实施预防犯罪的措施。同时,如果人们因为讨厌被监视而转移到没有安装闭路电视监控系统的区域时,原本的区域就会因为人少而降低对犯罪的自然监视。更有甚者,安装闭路电视监控系统对一些居民来说就意味着该区域是危险的。

五、什么是证据?

　　英国对于闭路电视监控系统的效果最详尽的研究是 2005 年吉尔与斯普里格斯的全国性评估。他们在全国设有 14 个实验点,分别分布在城市中心、议会房地产、车站、公园与医院。许多试验点设有实验区域、相邻区域（用来测量犯罪转移）与不相邻控制区域。许多点对犯罪的测量不仅仅使用警方的数据,还使用在社会大众间进行调查所得的数据。由于闭路电视监控系统的安装,居民更加乐意向警方提供犯罪信息,因此这或许会给人们带来"闭路电视监控系统使得犯罪增加"的错觉,而要纠正人们这种错觉,调查研究是必不可少的。在剑桥大学对闭路电视监控系统功效的评估中,警方的数据显示在安装有闭路电视监控系统的地方犯罪率有所上升,但是对路人的调查结果显示两者的关系却并非如此。

　　全国性评估的结果是显而易见的。闭路电视监控系统能有效减少停车场的犯罪,但是对减少城市中心与市民区的犯罪则没什么效果（Farrington *et al.*,2007b）。没有证据能证明闭路电视监控系统在对犯罪的预防方面具有转移或扩散效应。闭路电视监控系统能有效预防车辆犯罪(这也是在停车场所作的唯一调查),同时在照明条件越好的地方预防犯罪的效果越佳。更重要的是,闭路电视监控系统的覆盖率直接决定了其能否有效预防犯罪。闭路电视监控系统之所以能有效地预防停车场的犯罪,或许得益于那里的摄像头的覆盖面积之大、照明条件之好或是安全设置之完善。此外,也有可能是因为对车辆犯罪的理性选择度比暴力犯罪与社会失序更高。

规模最大的评估闭路电视监控系统对于预防犯罪有效性的研究的操作者是威尔士与法林顿。他们的研究包含了闭路电视监控系统是否是唯一的干预因素,研究是否有至少一个实验组与对比组,是否在实验前后都对犯罪进行了测量等一系列的因素。他们最新的研究包含了 44 个评估结果。实验结果显示了闭路电视监控系统能大量减少(51%)停车场的犯罪,而在其他场所,闭路电视监控系统只能稍微(7%)减少一些犯罪。当然,大多数评估结果采用的都是警方的数据。

2003 年,在辛瓦拉加辛格姆对于医院、急救中心以及警方提供的相关受袭者的调查结果显示闭路电视监控系统对于减少犯罪具有更加积极的效果。他们比较了 20 世纪 90 年代安装有闭路电视监控系统的试验小镇与五个没有安装闭路电视监控系统的小镇的犯罪情况。实验结果显示,安装闭路电视监控系统的小镇上受袭者的数目比未安装的小镇少得多。但是警方的数据却显示前者比后者拥有更多的暴力犯罪数。研究者认为闭路电视监控系统事实上真的可以减少犯罪,只不过由于安装了闭路电视监控系统的缘故,被警方发现的犯罪数目反而增加了。

六、对闭路电视监控系统的态度

2005 年,吉尔(Gill)与斯普里格斯(Spriggs)在一些市中心与居住区开展了大量的调查,调查的内容是人们如何看待闭路电视监控系统。他们发现与控制组相比,有 2 个区域的居民在安装了闭路电视监控系统后减少了对于受害的忧虑,但是有 5 个区域的居民完全没有减少这种忧虑。他们还发现注意到该区域安装有闭路电视监控系统的人比未注意到的人更加担心犯罪的发生。事实上,闭路电视监控系统的安装反而会增加人们对于犯罪的担忧,同时也并不能为人们带去更多的安全感。

更令人不安的是,人们对闭路电视监控系统的信赖度在其被安装后会显著降低。吉尔与斯普里格斯调查了闭路电视监控系统是否会促使人们举报更多的案件,是否会缩短警察的反应时间,是否能够减少犯罪。在所有的 3 个案子中,居民在安装闭路电视监控系统前对其的信赖度更高。剑桥大学对于闭路电视监控系统效果的评估结果也与此类似(Farrington *et al.*,2007a)。与控制组的人相比,在安装了闭路电视监控系统之后,实验区的人们更加不会觉得安装闭路电视监控系统会给他们带去安全感,也不会更频繁地去安装了闭路电视监控系统的区域。

对于罪犯的调查结果显示,罪犯认为他们并不会特别担心会因为闭路电视监控系统而被抓。吉尔(Gill)与拉夫代(Loveday)对监狱中罪犯的调查结果显示,只有32%的人赞同"闭路电视监控系统是盗窃的障碍"这一观点。只有9%的罪犯因为闭路电视监控系统而被抓获。抢劫者与盗窃者的一个典型的观点是:"除非你倒霉至极或者警察正好在街上,否则当闭路电视监控系统的监测者看到犯罪行为并报警时,罪犯早就已经溜之大吉了";"即使路上安装有闭路电视监控系统,你只要沿着街道走,绕到房子背面进去,不要站在可以被看到的地方就可以了"。

总的来说,警察对于闭路电视监控系统的效用相当乐观。根据2004年刘易舍姆、吉尔以及海明的调查结果,大部分警察认为闭路电视监控系统有利于减少犯罪。比如说,87%的人认为街道抢劫会因为闭路电视监控系统的安装而减少。然而,只有17%的人不同意"镇中心安装的闭路电视监控系统只是让犯罪转移到摄像头拍不到的地方"这一说法。64%的人认为闭路电视监控系统具有震慑犯罪的作用,66%的人认为安装闭路电视监控系统后比安装前更安全。91%并不认为闭路电视监控系统对居民的隐私来说是一个不被接受的入侵物,75%的人认为花在镇中心闭路电视监控系统上的钱并不算太多。

半数以上的警察都使用过摄像头,不论是在访谈中出示给犯罪嫌疑人或者是在起诉时作为证据使用,他们认为摄影画面的使用使警察的努力事半功倍,特别是访问他们时他们所说的:"当镜头中的证据被摆在眼前时,大部分的疑犯都表示自己已经无话可说了"(Gill and Hemming,2004,p.65)。警察认为闭路电视监控系统中最重要的因素是操作者观看监控的程度以及他们和警方交流的程度。

七、反 恐

或许闭路电视监控系统在反恐怖工作上的作用尤其重要。1993年,在爱尔兰共和军对比肖普斯盖特的恐怖袭击中,闭路电视监控系统首次被投入使用于反恐怖斗争中去。这随后引起了1996年关于"钢戒"的讨论,90个摄像头被设于伦敦的各个入口,并相互联网对这些路口进行监测(Norris and McCahill,2006)。到20世纪90年代末期,每辆进入伦敦的车的汽车牌照都会被监测。

2005 年 7 月 7 日伦敦的炸弹自杀案使闭路电视监控系统参与反恐的角色进一步被强调。闭路电视监控系统的录影镜头中显示有 4 个背着大军包的青年男子于早晨的上下班高峰时段离开国王十字车站(Campbell and Laville, 2005)。调查显示闭路电视监控系统拍到的上述四名男子中的三个在爆炸案发生的九天前进行了犯罪预备。闭路电视监控系统让警方能够追踪他们的活动并在另外一个火车站找到了一个利兹出产的即将要爆炸的炸弹(Steele, 2005)。

尽管闭路电视监控系统能有效识别罪犯,但是找到正确的画面是十分费时的。比如说,闭路电视监控系统被成功用于解决布鲁克斯顿大卫科普兰的爆炸案,但是在这个案子中警方花了 4000 个小时看了 1100 盒闭路电视监控系统的录影带(Ford, 2009)。

八、结　论

实验的证据显示安装闭路电视监控系统有利于减少停车场的犯罪,但对于减少城市中心与居民区的犯罪的帮助不大。然而,如果只看警方的实验数据或许会造成人们的误解,因为安装了闭路电视监控系统的地方被发现的犯罪或许会增加。犯罪转移并不是一个严重的问题。闭路电视监控系统在警方询问犯罪嫌疑人与提起公诉时十分有用,也有利于反恐。我们还需要对闭路电视监控系统作更多的利弊分析。其中一个著名的调查是 1998 年斯金在唐卡斯特所作的研究,他得出的结论是每对闭路电视监控系统投入 1 英镑就能得到 3.5 英镑的回报。

调查中还需要更具随机性的实验来评估闭路电视监控系统的效果(Farrington and Painter, 2003)。在有或没有闭路电视监控系统覆盖的地方使用手机照相机看不同时段的犯罪率也是十分必要的。将来的研究应包含对潜在罪犯或潜在受害者的调查,不仅仅要调查他们对于闭路电视监控系统的看法,还要在警方提供的数据之外自行测量犯罪。将闭路电视监控系统与其他如街面照明情况这类的调查干扰因素的影响结果区分开来是十分重要的(Welsh and Farrington, 2004)。我们还需要对不同闭路电视监控系统特别是不同监控室都进行评估。

为了减少犯罪,政策上应做的调整是加大摄影机的拍摄面积,将摄影机安装在更好的位置,更好地宣传,提高监控室的效率(增加其与警方的交流),增加闭路电视监控系统与其他如街面照明情况等因素的契合度。闭路电视监控系统似乎更适合用来监测一些更需要理性选择的,如车辆盗窃这类犯罪。最理想的是,任何区域的犯罪都应该被仔细地分析，一系列的情景都应该被警察与其他人考虑与评估到。闭路电视监控系统并不能在每个案子中都发挥作用。我们必须吸取以前的教训，不要在评估到闭路电视监控系统具有很高作用前就花费 50 亿英镑来安装与更新闭路电视监控系统。

[主要来源和参考文献见英文原作]

（丁靖艳　沈宜嘉　译）

Closed Circuit Television

David P. Farrington

University of Cambridge

"CCTV is a wonderful technological supplement to the police··· CCTV spots crimes, identifies law breakers and helps convict the guilty··· CCTV is a real asset to communities, a great deterrent to crime, and a huge reassurance to the public" (Michael Howard, Home Secretary, May 1995, quoted by Norris and Armstrong, 1998, p. 10).

The main aim of this review is to assess the value of CCTV in light of empirical evidence.

INTRODUCTION

CCTV is "a system in which a number of video cameras are connected in a closed circuit or loop, with the images produced being sent to a central television monitor or recorder" (Goold, 2004, p. 12). CCTV systems can differ markedly, and the technology is always improving. For example, cameras can be static or can pan, tilt and zoom, they can be fixed or redeployable and they can be overt or covert. The variety of systems, and their changes over time, makes it difficult to draw conclusions about the effectiveness of CCTV.

No CCTV system can work without a control room, and there is wide variation in the way that these operate. For example, the monitors can be watched full-time or for a limited number of hours per week, and there could be two-way communication with the police or only one-way (operators can hear police radios but cannot communicate directly with the police except by dialling 999). Staffing levels vary greatly; the number of cameras per operator varied from 20 to 520 in the national evaluation of CCTV by Gill and Spriggs (2005). Many systems also include the installation or improvement of street lighting.

HISTORY

Williams (2003) has summarized the history of the use of CCTV in the UK. In the late 1950s, police forces (beginning with Durham in 1956) began to use CCTV to assist in the one-man operation of traffic lights. In 1960, the Metropolitan Police erected two cameras in Trafalgar Square to monitor the crowds at the state visit of the Thai royal family. In 1964, Liverpool police experimented with covert CCTV at various locations in their central area. The cameras were mounted on buildings in the central business district and fed images through to a police officer who was in radio contact with special plain-clothes patrols. However, the police concluded that "no arrests were made as a result of television surveillance. The effect was preventative but largely psychological and therefore the camera had to be moved around to be effective" (Williams, 2003, p. 15).

By 1969, according to Williams (2003), 14 different police forces were using CCTV, with a total of 67 cameras. There was a dramatic increase in the use of CCTV in the 1990s. According to Armitage (2002), the number of surveillance cameras in England and Wales increased from about 100 in 1990 to 400 in 1994, to 4,200 in 1997, and to 40,000 in 2002. Based on research in Putney, McCahill and Norris (2003) estimated that there were at least 500,000 cameras in London and hence 4,200,000 cameras in the UK. This scaling up may be dubious but it seems likely that the UK has led the world in installing hundreds of thousands of CCTV cameras. The massive increase in cameras in the late 1990s and early 2000s was driven by central and local government funding of at least £ 500 million. Between 1996 and 1999, over three-quarters of the Home Office crime prevention budget was spent on CCTV (Koch, 1998). This funding reflected the popularity of and public demand for CCTV, partly driven by its use in spectacular cases such as James Bulger:

"In 1993, hard on the heels of the murder of the toddler James Bulger, the symbolism that fuelled CCTV was extraordinarily powerful … Although the killers were not actually identified or apprehended as a result of this footage, the connection was irrevocably made between cameras and crime control" (Davies, 1998, p. 244).

MECHANISMS

There are many mechanisms through which CCTV is supposed to have an effect on crime (Gill and Spriggs, 2005, pp. 7 - 8), and deterrence of potential offenders is the most important. It is argued that offenders will think that they have an increased likelihood of being caught in CCTV-monitored areas, and therefore they will refrain from offending there. This mechanism will only work to the extent that crimes are committed rationally, with offenders weighing probable costs against probable benefits. To the extent that crimes are committed impulsively or compulsively or under the influence of drink or drugs (e. g. violent and sexual crimes), CCTV will not have a deterrent effect.

It is also argued that CCTV will encourage more people to use an area, and that the increased number of possible witnesses will have a deterrent effect on potential offenders. Another suggestion is that CCTV facilitates the effective deployment of police and security staff to intervene to prevent crimes and/or apprehend offenders. Also, it is argued that CCTV may encourage the general public and employees to take more precautions and to intervene to challenge offenders and prevent crimes.

In order for CCTV to be effective in preventing crimes, potential offenders and the general public need to be aware of the cameras. Also, potential offenders will not be deterred if the coverage of the cameras is low, since they can then choose to offend in places that are not covered by the cameras. Also, if places are poorly lit, or if the quality of images is poor, potential offenders may think that they will not be identified. It is likely that CCTV will be most effective in preventing crimes in public view and least effective in preventing crimes that are difficult to observe or that occur in private places such as houses (e. g. domestic violence or child abuse).

ADVANTAGES AND DISADVANTAGES

It is argued that CCTV has benefits beyond crime reduction. In particular, it is suggested that citizens will have a reduced fear of crime in CCTV-monitored areas. Also, the installation of CCTV (e. g. in a council housing estate) may suggest to the residents that the council is investing in the area and that the area is improving. In turn, this may lead residents to have increased community pride and hence an increased likelihood of intervening to prevent crime and disorder. Cameras can also be used to gather intelligence and to monitor the behaviour of known offenders in public places. They also have a variety of other uses, including crowd control, traffic control, monitoring custody areas, looking for lost children and identifying people who are suffering from illness or injury who need medical assistance. Arguably, CCTV evidence encourages offenders to plead guilty and helps the prosecution case.

Against these claimed advantages of CCTV, there are a number of claimed disadvantages. CCTV surveillance is allegedly a threat to civil liberties and more particularly to the right to privacy, and it may encourage social exclusion. There is a potential problem of displacement; offenders may simply move their offending to areas not covered by the cameras, so that no crimes are saved in total. The opposite of displacement is the diffusion of benefits (Weisburd et al., 2006); if CCTV is installed in an area, the benefits may spread to adjacent areas if potential offenders are deterred or if citizens have increased community pride. Another argument is that, to the extent that the general public believes in the effectiveness of CCTV, people may reduce their vigilance and take fewer precautions against crime. Also, the natural surveillance of an area may be reduced if fewer people use the area because they dislike being watched. Also, the cameras may signal to citizens that an area is dangerous.

WHAT IS THE EVIDENCE?

The most detailed study of the effects of CCTV in the UK was the national evaluation by Gill and Spriggs (2005), conducted in 14 sites, in city centres, council housing estates, station car parks and a hospital. Several sites had experimental (CCTV) areas, adjacent areas (to measure displacement) and non-adjacent control areas. Several sites measured crimes not only using police records but also using surveys of the general population. It is important to use surveys in case CCTV causes an increase in the probability of citizens reporting crimes to the police, which could create the false impression that CCTV caused an increase in crime. This may have happened in the Cambridge evaluation of the effects of CCTV; crimes increased in the CCTV area according to police records but did not change according to surveys of pedestrians.

The results of the national evaluation were quite conclusive. The bottom line was that CCTV caused a decrease in crimes in car parks but not in city centres or residential areas (Farrington et al., 2007b). There was no evidence of displacement or diffusion of benefits. CCTV was most effective in reducing vehicle crimes (which were the only types of crimes measured in the car park studies) and seemed to be most effective when combined with improved lighting. Importantly, the degree of coverage of the cameras predicted the success of the project in reducing crimes. CCTV may have been effective in station car parks because of the high degree of coverage there, or because CCTV was usually combined with improved lighting, fencing and security arrangements, or because vehicle crimes may be more rationally motivated than, say, violence or disorder.

The most extensive systematic reviews of the effectiveness of CCTV in preventing crimes were completed by Welsh and Farrington (2002, 2007). Studies were included in their reviews if CCTV was the main intervention, if there was at least one experimental area and one comparable control area, and if there were before and after measures of crimes. Their latest (2007) review covered 44 evaluations. The results showed that CCTV caused a significant (51%, on average) decrease in crimes in car parks. In general, CCTV schemes in other settings were followed by small (about 7%) but non-significant decreases in crimes. However, most of the evaluations measured crime using only police records.

More optimistic conclusions were drawn by Sivarajasingam et al. (2003) in a study of assault victims received by accident and emergency departments of hospitals, compared with police records of violent offences. They compared five experimental towns which had CCTV installed in the 1990s with five matched control towns which did not. They found that, after the installation of CCTV, the number of assault victims decreased in the experimental towns compared with the control towns, but police-recorded violence increased in the experimental towns compared with the control towns. They suggested that CCTV might have caused a true decrease in violence but an increased police detection of violence.

ATTITUDES TO CCTV

Gill and Spriggs (2005) carried out large-scale attitude surveys in city centres and housing estates before and after the installation of CCTV cameras. They found that there was a significant reduction in the worry about being a victim of crime in two areas but no reduction (compared to control areas) in five other cases. They also found that people who were aware of the cameras worried more about crime than those who were not, and concluded (p.48) that "the presence of CCTV in an area actually increases worry about crime". They also discovered that CCTV had no effect on feelings of safety (in 9 areas).

Most disturbingly, the belief in the effectiveness of CCTV decreased significantly after its installation. Gill and Spriggs (2005, p. 57) asked about whether CCTV would cause people to report more incidents, cause police to respond more quickly, and cause a decrease in crime. In all three cases, residents were more optimistic about the effectiveness of CCTV before the installation of cameras than afterwards. Similar results were found in the Cambridge evaluation of the effects of CCTV (Farrington et al. , 2007a). After the installation of CCTV, people in the experimental area (compared with those in the control area) were less likely to say that CCTV made them feel safer, and less likely to say that CCTV made them visit the area more frequently.

Surveys of offenders suggest that they are not particularly worried about being caught by CCTV. Gill and Loveday (2003) interviewed convicted offenders in prison and found that only 32% agreed that "Town-centre CCTV is a real impediment to coming into the area to steal". Only 9% of the offenders had actually been caught by CCTV. Typical views of robbers and burglars (pp. 83 − 84) were: "Unless you are unlucky and they have a team [police] working on the street, by the time they [CCTV operators] have found you and called for the police you are long gone. " "Even if there are cameras about, you're just walking along the street. Go round the back to get in, not stand at the front where you can be seen. "

In general, police officers seem to be quite positive about CCTV. In an evaluation in Lewisham, Gill and Hemming (2004) found that the majority of officers thought that CCTV had reduced crimes; for example, 87% thought that street robbery had been reduced. However, only 17% disagreed with the statement that "CCTV in town centres just moves crime out of the view of the cameras". Most thought that CCTV was a deterrent (64%) and that town centres with CCTV were safer than those without (66%). Most disagreed that CCTV was an unacceptable invasion of citizens' privacy (91%) or that too much money was spent on town centre CCTV (75%).

Almost half of the officers had made use of CCTV footage, either by showing it to suspects during interviews or by producing it as evidence in prosecutions, and they reported that the use of the images had generally resulted in positive effects, especially in interviews: "When the offender was presented with evidence on CCTV, he rolled his eyes and said 'What can I say?' (Gill and Hemming, 2004, p. 65). Officers thought that the most important factors in the success of CCTV were the quality of operators in the control room and the quality of their communication with the police.

TERRORISM

CCTV may be especially useful in the detection and prevention of terrorist acts. The IRA's terrorist attack on Bishopsgate in 1993 was said to be the original catalyst for the expansion of CCTV in London. This led to the introduction of the "Ring of Steel" in 1996, a network of 90 cameras used to monitor the many entrances to the City of London (Norris and McCahill, 2006). By the late 1990s, the licence plate of every car entering the City of London was being recorded.

The role of CCTV in counter-terrorism was further emphasized in the suicide bombings carried out in London on July 7, 2005. CCTV video footage, viewed days later, showed four young men with identical large military-style backpacks or rucksacks leaving Kings Cross station during the morning rush hour (Campbell and Laville, 2005). The investigation later revealed that CCTV cameras had filmed three of the four suicide bombers carrying out a "dry run" of their attack 9 days earlier. The CCTV images allowed police to trace their movements and discover a car at another railway station containing bomb-making equipment and a "ready-to-go" bomb, as well as a property in Leeds where the bombs were made (Steele, 2005).

While CCTV can be useful in identifying offenders, looking for the right image can be a very time-consuming exercise. For example, it has been argued that CCTV led to the capture of the Brixton nail bomber David Copeland. However, in this one case police spent 4,000 hours viewing 1,100 CCTV tapes (Ford, 2009).

CONCLUSIONS

The empirical evidence suggests that CCTV is very useful in reducing crimes in car parks, but less useful in reducing crimes in city centres or residential areas. However, misleading conclusions may be drawn if crimes are measured using only police records, because CCTV may increase the probability of reporting or recording crimes. Displacement does not seem to be a great problem. CCTV is useful to the police in interviewing offenders and in prosecutions, and it is useful in terrorism cases. More cost-benefit analyses of CCTV are needed. One of the most important studies was carried out by Skinns (1998) in Doncaster, who concluded that £ 3.50 was saved for every £ 1 expended on CCTV.

The main research implications are that randomized experiments should be carried out to evaluate the effectiveness of CCTV (Farrington and Painter, 2003). Using mobile cameras, crime rates during periods with or without CCTV coverage could be studied. Future evaluations should include interviews with potential offenders and potential victims, not only to find out their opinions about CCTV but also to have measures of crime other than those based on police records. It is important to try to disentangle the effects of CCTV from the effects of other interventions such as improved street lighting (Welsh and Farrington, 2004). Evaluations need to take account of different types of CCTV systems and especially the operation of the control room.

The main policy implications are that, in order to reduce crimes, there should be good coverage and positioning of the cameras, good publicity, improved operation of the control room (with good communication with the police), and the use of CCTV in combination with other interventions such as improved street lighting. It seems most sensible for CCTV to target more rational crimes such as theft of and from vehicles. Ideally, the crime problem in any area should be carefully analysed, and a range of possible solutions considered and evaluated, by police officers and others. In some cases, CCTV may be useful, but in other cases it may not. It is important to learn from the lessons of the past and not spend another £ 500 million installing or improving CCTV systems before high quality evaluations of the effectiveness of CCTV have been completed.

Key Sources

Gill, M. (Ed.) (2003) *CCTV*. Leicester: Perpetuity Press.

Gill, M. and Spriggs, A. (2005) *Assessing the Impact of CCTV*. London: Home Office (Research Study No. 292).

Available from: www. homeoffice. gov. uk/rds/pdfs05/hors292. pdf

Goold, B. J. (2004) *CCTV and Policing*. Oxford: Oxford University Press.

Ratcliffe, J (2006) *Video Surveillance of Public Places*. Washington, D. C. : Office of Community Oriented Policing Services (Problem-Oriented Guides for Police, Response Guides Series, No. 4). Available from: www. cops. usdoj. gov/RIC

Welsh, B. C. and Farrington, D. P. (2007) *Closed-Circuit Television surveillance and Crime Prevention*. Stockholm: Swedish National Council for Crime Prevention. Available from: www. bra. se (choose English).

References

Armitage, R. (2002) *To CCTV or not to CCTV? A Review of Current Research into the Effectiveness of CCTV Systems in Reducing Crime.* London: NACRO.

Campbell, D. and Laville, S. (2005) British suicide bombers carried outLondon attacks, say police. *The Guardian* (July 13). Available at: www. guardian. co. uk

Davies, S. (1998) CCTV: A new battleground for privacy. In Norris, C. , Moran, J. and Armstrong G. (Eds.) *Surveillance, Closed Circuit Television and Social Control.* Aldershot: Ashgate.

Farrington, D. P. , Bennett, T. H. and Welsh, B. C. (2007a) The Cambridge evaluation of the effects of CCTV on crime. In Farrell, G. , Bowers, K. J. , Johnson, S. D. and Townsley, M. (Eds.) *Imagination for Crime Prevention: Essays in Honour of Ken Pease.* (Crime Prevention Studies, vol. 21.) Monsey, N. Y. : Criminal Justice Press (pp. 187 – 201).

Farrington, D. P. , Gill, M. , Waples, S. J. and Argomaniz, J. (2007b) The effects of closed-circuit television on crime: Meta-analysis of an English national quasi-experimental multi-site evaluation. *Journal of Experimental Criminology*, 3, 21 – 38.

Farrington, D. P. and Painter, K. A. (2003) How to evaluate the impact of CCTV on crime. *Crime Prevention and Community Safety*, 5(3), 7 – 16.

Ford, R. (2009) Police mapping out mission to count every spy camera. *The Times* (March 7). Available at: www. timesonline. co. uk

Gill, M. (Ed.) (2003) *CCTV.* Leicester: Perpetuity Press.

Gill, M. and Hemming, M. (2004) *Evaluation of CCTV in the London Borough of Lewisham.* Leicester: PRCI.

Gill, M. and Loveday, K. (2003) What do offenders think about CCTV? In Gill, M. (Ed.) *CCTV.* Leicester: Perpetuity Press (pp. 81 – 92).

Gill, M. and Spriggs, A. (2005) *Assessing the Impact of CCTV.* London: Home Office (Research Study No. 292).

Available from: www. homeoffice. gov. uk/rds/pdfs05/hors292. pdf

Goold, B. J. (2004) *CCTV and Policing.* Oxford: Oxford University Press.

Koch, B. C. M. (1998) *The Politics of Crime Prevention.* Aldershot: Ashgate.

McCahill, M. and Norris, C. (2003) Estimating the extent, sophistication and legality of

CCTV in London. In Gill. M. (Ed.) *CCTV*. Leicester: Perpetuity Press (pp. 51 – 66).

Norris, C. and McCahill, M. (2006) CCTV: Beyond penal modernism. *British Journal of Criminology*, 46, 97 – 118.

Norris, C. , Moran, J. and Armstrong, G. (Eds.) (1998) *Surveillance, Closed Cirrcuit Television and Social Control*. Aldershot: Ashgate.

Ratcliffe, J (2006) *Video Surveillance of Public Places*. Washington, D. C. : Office of Community Oriented Policing Services (Problem-Oriented Guides for Police, Response Guides Series, No. 4). Available from: www. cops. usdoj. gov/RIC

Sivarajasingam, V. , Shepherd, J. P. and Matthews, K. (2003) Effect of urban closed circuit television on assault injury and violence detection. *Injury Prevention*, 9, 312 – 316.

Skinns, D. (1998) *Doncaster CCTV Surveillance System: Second Annual Report of the Independent Evaluation*. Doncaster: Faculty of Business and Professional Studies, Doncaster College.

Steele, J. (2005) With rucksacks on their backs, the suicide bombers go on a dummy run. *The Daily Telegraph* (September 21). Available at: www. telegraph. co. uk

Weisburd, D. ,Wyckoff, L. A. , Ready, J. , Eck, J. E. , Hinkle, J. C. and Gajewski, F. (2006) Does crime just move around the corner? A controlled study of spatial displacement and diffusion of crime control benefits. *Criminology*, 44, 549 – 591.

Welsh, B. C. and Farrington, D. P. (2002) *Crime Prevention Effects of Closed Circuit Television: A Systematic Review*. London: Home Office (Research Study No. 252). Available from www. homeoffice. gov. uk/rds/pdfs06/hors252. pdf

Welsh, B. C. and Farrington, D. P. (2004) Surveillance for crime prevention in public space: Results and policy choices inBritain and America. *Criminology and Public Policy*, 3, 497 – 525.

Welsh, B. C. and Farrington, D. P. (2007) *Closed-Circuit Television surveillance and Crime Prevention*. Stockholm: Swedish National Council for Crime Prevention. Available from: www. bra. se (choose English).

Williams, C. A. (2003) Police surveillance and the emergence of CCTV in the 1960s. In Gill, M. (Ed.) *CCTV*. Leicester: Perpetuity Press (pp. 9 – 22).

儿童和青年的严重暴力反社会行为的危险因素

菲德律·洛赛尔（Friedrich Lösel）

埃朗根·纽伦堡大学

道雷斯·班达（Doris Bender）

一、概　论

当前,很多国家都对日益严重的儿童和青少年侵略行为乃至暴力行为予以强烈关注。此类行为给家长、老师、同伴、邻里和社会公共服务都造成很多问题;而从长远角度来说,更是严重影响了孩子们的健康发展。随着新闻媒体高频率、高强度地报道和披露这些引发人身伤害乃至造成他人死亡的恶性案件,许多人都想知道,为什么孩子们在成长过程中会走上歧途,而这恰恰是本章尝试要回答的问题。为此,在基于文献回顾和实证研究发现的基础上,我们总结了当前导致儿童反社会行为和暴力行为发生、发展的危险因素。在此之前,我们还会简要介绍学界对此特定群体的定义和其各个发展阶段的基本情况。作为文章重点的第二部分从生物学、心理学和社会学的综合角度来阐释主要的危险因素。第三部分则运用实证研究量表对危险因素进行测试和调控。文章以对如何采取预防和干预措施来减少危险因素的讨论作结论(亦可参考本卷第六章)。

本文中尽管会讨论一些危险评估量表,但是不会将其作为重点。取而代之的是,本文会关注这些评估工具设计生成的基础,也就是说,在现有的实证知识的基础上,分析各种危险因素,从而使实践者们在各自的研究领域中,充分利用测评项目并建立有效的危险因素交流与整合模型。蒂芬(Tiffin)和理查森(Richardson)(附件一)也讨论了一些有益于实践者的评估工具。人们必须考虑的一个现实问题是,在日常生活中,如何预测并对行为控制进行基本的限制,而这些与行为发展的连续性和易变性原则都息息相关。将此牢记于心,亦有助于在解决这些儿童所存在问题的过程中,避免过度的悲观主义和羞耻感所造成的负面影响。

二、反社会行为发展中的基本问题

对于很多有严重侵犯行为的儿童而言,虽然他们有着相类似的背景和行为,但他们却来自不同群体;同时,他们也并非与那些有侵犯行为和行为不端的青年群体完全不同。在对青少年谋杀犯的研究中,上述情形在有较轻微的侵犯性行为的青少年中尤为普遍(Lempp, 1977; Traverso and Bianchi, 2002)。尽管没有明确分类,大约半数暴力犯罪的青少年同时也是习惯性的行为不端者(Loeber, Farrington and Waschbusch, 1988b)。这些个体往往显示出多种发生早、相对持久的、严重的反社会行为(Moffitt 1993; Patterson et al. 1988)。而这和人们普遍熟悉的典型犯罪行为曲线显然是不一样的,后者是与年龄曲线相关的,即犯罪行为在青少年时期随着年龄增长而增加,在一定年龄段到达顶峰,随后在成年早期,又随着年龄增长而减少(Farrington, 1989, Loeber et al., 1998a)。与年龄相关的青少年期犯罪行为模型是典型的青少年期过渡问题。相反的,严重的、持续性的群体不仅仅在成年期表现出频繁的侵犯行为、不端行为和其他犯罪问题,在儿童期也是如此(Farrington and Loeber, 2001; Patterson et al., 1998)。男孩中大约有 5% 会是这一类型(Moffitt and Caspi, 2001; Moffitt et al., 1996),而女孩的比例则远低于此(Loeber et al., 1998a; Moffitt et al., 2001)。在严重犯罪和暴力犯罪人中,此类个体的比例被过高地估计。在青少年期和成年期,超过一半的罪犯在此年龄阶段也都被归类于此(Loeber et al., 1998a; Wolfgang, Figlio and Sellin, 1972)。而且,早期开始的反社会行为和其他成年期的精神病症、社会问题一样,都是强烈的危险信号(Robins and Price, 1991)。

本质而言,上述两者的差别不包括在所有现实生活中的反社会行为的发展范围之内。比如说奈根(Nagin)和兰德(Land)(1993)发现了较轻微的、低阶段的、习惯性

程度较低的第三类群体;洛伯(Loeber)和海(Hay)(1994)发表文章表明,他们在行为上主要有三个不同体现:

- 直接的侵犯行为,如欺凌弱小、袭击、打架或者虐待动物而导致后来的攻击行为,如强奸或者故意杀人(蓄意反社会行为);
- 非直接的侵犯行为,如在商店里偷东西、习惯性撒谎、破坏公共财物或纵火而引发的入室盗窃、欺诈或者偷盗(蓄意反社会行为);
- 屡教不改的行为、反抗或不服从行为而导致的旷课、离家出走和夜不归宿(与权威反抗)。

在以上三种类型中,有此类问题行为的青少年人数比例随着年龄增长而下降,而问题行为的严重性则随着年龄增长而加重。有些孩子的问题行为在这三个方面都有体现,并且成为了发生早、程度严重且持续性强的犯罪行为类型的主要群体。

尽管此发展模型有很强的实证研究结论支持,我们却也不能忽略问题行为的延续性特点(Lösel and Bender, 2003;Tremblay, 2000)。在童年时期行为失常和侵犯行为多发的儿童中,大约有一半在青少年期没有表现出严重的犯罪行为(Moffitt *et al.*, 1996;Patterson *et al.*, 1998;Robins, 1978)。这种现象的成因,一部分是由个体生长发育的变化,成长过程中的保护机制和社会干预措施共同导致的(Laub and Sampson, 2003;Lösel and Bender, 2003)。当讨论危险因素时,我们必须也将其他的精神病理成因也考虑进去,毕竟问题行为的产生和发展不仅仅只有一个原因或源头,它是多种生理、心理和社会影响因素综合作用的结果。即使设计完美的研究也不是总能够清晰地阐明因果关系,但是只有危险因素会强化负面结果的可能性。不同的危险因素会引发特殊的行为结果(同效性),而同样的危险因素也有可能导致不同的结果(多效性),这都和导致反社会行为产生的相关原因和影响其持续或加剧的原因不同。而且,不同的儿童不仅是受生物社会学影响的被动对象,而且随着其年龄的增长,还是自身发展的积极构建者(通过他们对同伴和社会行为活动的选择而实现)。最后,当某个个体在特定的时间、特定的情境中呈现出暴力行为或其他问题行为时,不仅归因于个体发展的长期影响和心理倾向,也和环境因素有关。侵犯行为的环境因素是客观性和主观解释的产物。

三、引发严重反社会行为的危险因素

呈现出早发生的、严重的和持续性的反社会行为特征的青少年,在其童年时期就典型地表现出多种生理、心理和社会危险因素共存集聚的现象（Farrington and Loeber，2001；Hawkins *et al.*，1998；Loeber，1982；Lynam，1996）。这些因素的大量累积加强并激化了问题行为，使其发生连锁反应（Lösel，2001；Lösel and Bender，2003）。生物社会学方面的脆弱性理论、社会习得理论和神经心理学发展理论的综合构架能最清楚地解释这种高风险的连锁反应。图表1是一个关于对危险因素集群进行长期研究结果的综述。每一个单独的因素的影响力几乎很小（相关性在 r＝.10 至.20 之间），而随着产生严重问题行为的可能性的增加，我们知道，这是不同因素在不同领域积累的结果（Farrington，1997a；Loeber *et al.*，in press；Lösel and Bliesener，2003）。这种数量—回应关系在男女两性中都很显著。以下是对不同危险因素进行更细致的介绍：

表1　严重反社会行为的发展阶段的危险因素

危险领域	PB	EP	MC	AD	相关度
生理/生理社会因素					
男性	X	X	X	X	***
基因倾向（遗传因素）	X	X	X	X	***
母亲怀孕因素（怀孕并发症）	X	X	X	X	*
怀孕问题	X	X	X	X	*
较低的生理兴奋点	X	X	X	X	***
神经递质失常	X	X	X	X	**
荷尔蒙因素		X	X	X	*
青春期早期（尤指女孩）				X	*
家庭因素					
贫穷/低社会经济地位/依靠社会救济	X	X	X	X	***
父母教育程度低	X	X	X	X	**
种族背景（在某些国家）	X	X	X	X	***
青少年的母亲	X	X	X	X	**
单亲家庭	X	X	X	X	*
大家族	X	X	X	X	*
父母离婚/分居		X	X	X	*
养育者更换频繁		X	X	X	**
父母失业	X	X	X	X	*
父母犯罪	X	X	X	X	***
父母药物滥用	X	X	X	X	**

危险领域	PB	EP	MC	AD	相关度
父母精神失常	X	X	X	X	*
父母不和及争吵		X	X	X	**
疏忽子女/缺乏父母关怀		X	X	X	***
虐待儿童		X	X	X	***
体罚		X	X	X	**
缺少有效的管教和训导			X	X	***
家庭压力大		X	X	X	**
缺乏社会支持/社交孤立		X	X	X	**
鼓励异常行为的父母态度			X	X	**
兄弟姐妹的不端行为			X	X	**
早期儿童性格和行为因素					
低智能	X	X	X	X	**
语言障碍		X	X	X	*
低执行能力		X	X	X	***
发育迟缓		X	X	X	*
性情难相处/消极情绪	X	X	X	X	***
冲动		X	X	X	***
注意力不集中症		X	X	X	***
爱好冒险,寻求刺激		X	X	X	**
无内疚心		X	X	X	***
冷酷无情/缺乏同情心		X	X	X	***
缺少归属感		X	X	X	***
早期的反社会行为		X	X	X	***
多种环境下的问题行为		X	X	X	***
和学校相关的因素					
成就感问题			X	X	***
低动机/低义务感			X	X	**
旷课			X	X	**
辍学/经常转学			X	X	**
不足毕业资格				X	***
父母不关注学业			X	X	**
不良的学校风气和教室氛围			X	X	*
不良学生比例高			X	X	**

危险领域	PB	EP	MC	AD	相关度
同伴因素					
同伴拒绝		X	X	X	*
缺乏社会化前的接触		X	X	X	**
结交行为不端的群体			X	X	***
团伙成员				X	***
社会认知和态度因素					
偏爱侵略行为的社会信息		X	X	X	***
社会问题协作和解决能力的欠缺			X	X	***
不切实际的自尊			X	X	*
态度不端正/对异常亚文化的认同			X	X	***
生活方式因素					
毫无计划的休闲活动			X	X	**
大众媒体的暴力信息		X	X	X	**
酗酒			X	X	***
药物滥用				X	***
毒品贩卖				X	***
携带武器				X	***
其他有害健康的危险行为				X	**
职业培训困难/失业				X	**
社区/邻里因素					
贫困家庭/问题家庭集中			X	X	**
无秩序社区			X	X	*
易获得武器			X	X	*
暴力和毒品的环境			X	X	**

注:PB=产前/生育;EP=童年早期/学前(0—5 岁);MC=中学(6—12 岁);AD=青少年时期(13—18 岁)。

估计效量值: * 非常小,几乎无关; ** 较小有效性、有一些关系; *** 中度有效和中度相关。

四、生物学和生理社会学因素

虽然学者们在研究反社会行为理论时,经常忽视生物学因素产生的影响,但不可否认,它仍旧是问题行为产生发展过程中的基本因素(Raine,1993;Rowe,1994)。另外,基因因素也显然扮演着十分重要的角色。在大多数文化背景下,男性往往面临着更高危的严重侵犯性行为特征,而且只有一部分归因于社会习得理论(Hyde,1984;Miles and Carey, 1997;Moffitt *et al.* , 2001)。即使在同性的反社会行为程度上,基因因素也有着很大的影响(Harris, 1995;Mason and Frick, 1994)。基因在个体脾性和认知能力上发挥着重要的作用。这证明了基因与侵犯行为和不端行为密切相关(Plomin, 1994;Raine, 1997)。在稳定的反社会行为中,大约40%的个体内部差异的成因能追溯到基因。然而,基因组只是划分出了对可能行为所进行描绘的范围(显性)。基因是在生长环境、先天特征和后天养育的相互作用中对个人进行发展性的塑造的。比方说,社会家庭因素的遗传成分可以多种方式运行:(1)除了基因,孩子能从父母处遗传环境对个体的影响;(2)父母会对受遗传影响的孩子的品质有影响;(3)年长一点的孩子可能寻求适合其基因类型的工作(Pike *et al.* , 1996)。

在母亲怀孕期间,环境因素对胎儿的影响已经被研究人员们发现。婴儿的神经—心理发展会因为母亲酗酒而受到影响(胎儿酒精并发症;Conry and Fast, 2000;Steinhausen, Willms, and Spohr, 1993)。吸烟的孕妇也会使其后代暴露于中毒环境,从而影响其神经—生理发展和未来的反社会行为(Fergusson, Woodward, and Horwood, 1998;Koglin, 2003)。然而,这样的影响或多或少也是和家庭因素相关联的。比如说,在怀孕期间吸烟的母亲多来自于社会经济地位较低的家庭,所受教育程度也低,因此,在怀孕期间面临更多的危险(Koglin, 2003;Raine, 1993)。

生育时的并发症和产后缺乏情感支持、鼓励或营养,都会造成长远的生理危险(Hodgins, Kratzer, and McNeil, 2002;Koglin, 2003;Raine, Brennan, and Mednick, 1994)。同样的,这也不是唯一的成因,毕竟还要和社会因素联合起来考虑。比如说,结合社会因素,如父母遗弃、贫困或者家庭不稳定时,怀孕和生育并发症对儿童的社会行为也有影响(Brennan, Mednick, and Raine, 1997);反之亦然,缺少关爱等社会风险也与生理因素有关系(Plomin, 1994)。例如,和主要抚养者的分离会损害婴儿的大脑发育并减少其依赖行为(Kraemer, 1997)。

一些儿童过于冲动的性格以及不能从负面经历中吸取教训也和生理倾向有关。比如说,反社会行为突出的孩子的脉搏速率比常人低,神经刺激反应和脑电图速率则更慢(Farrington, 1997b;Raine, 1993)。低兴奋点表明对刺激的更大需求(如寻求刺激,敢于冒险等),对惩罚更不惧怕,事件规避能力更弱(Eysenck, 1977;Zuckerman, 1994)。

另一个因素可能是和雄性激素、荷尔蒙和睾酮的浓度有关。较高浓度的睾酮可能既是人类侵犯性行为的成因,也是结果(Archer, 1991)。虽然侵犯行为和睾酮浓度之间的关系在成年人中已经被广泛证实,但我们可以判断这种影响至少在青春期之前就已经有了（Tremblay et al.，1997）。青春期提前本身便是一个危险因素,尤其是对女孩子而言（Stattin and Magnusson,1990）。由于女孩们提前发育,她们与行为不端的男孩们和群体接触得更多,但她们也更早地摆脱问题行为的困扰。压力荷尔蒙皮质醇在生理脆弱性中扮演着长远的角色,并可能和睾酮一起在青少年期发挥作用（Tremblay et al.，1997）。鉴于焦虑的、孤僻的儿童体内有更高的皮质醇浓度,他们和反社会行为的关系便更加复杂（Lahey et al.，1999）。在我们自己的研究中,我们发现焦虑和孤僻儿童的唾液中,皮质醇浓度尤其高;相反的,在具有过度侵犯性行为和过度情感冷漠的儿童群体中,其浓度相对较低。

对于年轻人的反社会行为和荷尔蒙或神经递质活动的关系的相关研究比较少（Susman and Ponirakis, 1997；Tremblay et al.，1997）,比如说,有些研究表明,减少的或不平衡的神经递质血清素浓度在反社会行为中也有作用（af Klinteberg 1998，2002；Schalling et al.，1988；Virkkunen et al.，1994）。然而,这种遗传倾向与社会因素之间的相互影响一样,凯斯匹（Caspi）及其同事（2002）发现:特殊的基因因素在分解血清素中产生单胺氧化酶（MAO）,和一个孩子遭受家庭虐待有很强相关性。对这种先天—后天的相互影响的研究,可能为采取预防措施提供全新的方法,从而有效干预这些暴露在危险因素之下、尤为脆弱的孩子们。

（一）家庭特征与养育

尽管家庭因素在反社会行为的发展上的影响有时会受到质疑（Harris，1995）,但是这方面的危险因素在长久以来的研究中已被充分证实（Loeber and Farrington，1998,2001）。与普通家庭相比,有严重反社会行为儿童的家庭必须解决更多的家庭结构问题和多种缺失问题。他们更为穷困,社会经济地位低下,青春期恋母情结强,有单亲家庭经历和低学历的父母（Farrington，1998；Fergusson and Woodward，1999；Hawkins et al.，1998）。那些依靠社会福利救济,家庭组织相对庞大的被社会边缘化的少数群体,往往需要面对失业、被社会孤立和其他的压力（Elliott, Huizinga, and Menard, 1989；Farrington, 1989；Hill et al.，1994）。他们的父母会有更多的反社会行为、药物滥用行为乃至其他心理失常问题（Farrington et al.，1990；Hawkins et al.，1998；Tremblay et al.，2004）。上述因素多将儿童置于遭受虐待的危险环境之中（Jeyarajah-Dent, 1998；Hagell, 1998）。

家庭成员之间的互动交流和儿童抚养方式尤为重要。很多性格冲动的家长和儿童之间有着不和谐和争吵,这样就造成更多的离家出走、离婚和抚养权变更的情况（Elliott, 1994；Hawkins et al.，1998）。家长对儿童关爱不够,缺少情感投入（Kolvin et *al.*，1990；McCord，1979）。他们更多的是使用体罚或者其他或轻或重的不同惩罚方式教育子女（Farrington，1992，1998；Frick，1998；Lösel and Bliesener，2003；Loeber and Stouthamer-Loeber，1998；McCord，1979；Patterson，Reid，and Dishion，1992）。当然，从某种程度上而言，抚养期间的种种不足比其他次要问题所引发的后果更严重。举例来说，儿童受到虐待和被父母忽略对反社会行为的形成是非常危险的因素（Bender and Lösel，2005）。但是，严格来说，这种暴力的循环并不是密闭的（Oliver，1993；Widom，1989）。来自被虐待环境的儿童只有大约三分之一变得非常具有攻击性；同时，也有一些有攻击行为的儿童的家庭是没有家庭暴力背景的。

基于社会习得理论，具有上述特征的家庭对儿童攻击性行为的产生影响很大，并且有强化作用，这导致了个人认知意识对攻击性行为的偏好（Crickand Dodge，1994；Huesmann，1997；Lösel *et al.*，in press）。当外部控制缺少或者强化时，这些儿童的自我控制能力便会下降（Lösel，Toman，and Wustendorfer，1976）。当家长对儿童的管制力变弱时，他们对之前儿童所犯的错误的反应就会变成拒绝、缺乏耐心、有攻击性或是不能坚持（Patterson *et al.*，1992；Rutter，1990）。于是，儿童就会产生相应的行为，就会出现家长与儿童之间的强制互动（Patterson *et al.*，1992；Rutter，1990）。在这样的家庭环境中，儿童对家庭缺乏情感上的归属的风险就会比较大（Ainsworth，1991）。回避的、害怕的、强制的、紊乱的情感归属行为可能更为频繁（Fagot and Pears，1996），并对未来的社会关系和应对能力的发展也造成不利影响（Cassidy *et al.*，1996）。

很多单独的家庭特征在儿童问题行为方面只能解释无数可能中的一小部分及其相互之间的联系（Hawkins *et al.*，1998；Lipsey and Derzon，1998；Lösel，2002）。然而，这些影响累积在一起则最终引发了多重问题，并切实地增加了危险。

（二）儿童早期人格和行为问题

社会因素和生物因素影响儿童性格气质和认知能力的形成，并增加了儿童产生反社会行为的风险。这包括了冲动、亢奋、注意力问题、情绪不定、发育缓慢、语言障碍和相对低下的总体全低智力水平（Farrington，1992，1998；Hawkins *et al.*，1998；Lipsey and Derzon，1998；Moffitt，1993；Rutter，Giller and Hagell，1998）。神经心理学倾向于把问题归结于大脑在执行抽象思考、目标性指向行动和自我控制功能时出现了问题（Moffitt and Henry，1991；Seguin *et al.*，2004）。尽管如此，很多高危儿童并没有表现出主要功能损伤或是能力减弱、抑或智力缺陷等和正常人平均水平有显著区别的症状（Rutter *et al.*，1998）。注意力不集中症和反社会行为只有中度的关联性

（*Loeber et al.*，1998a）。这种病症有多种表现,不该将其与上面两种外化的问题过度结合（Seguin *et al.*，2004）,为此我们还是应把儿童的行为倾向放到他们与社会环境因素互动的背景中去检视。举个例子来说,家长们通常能处理儿童不易相处的性情,学习上遇到的困难和一些细微的反社会行为,但是一旦当他们自己出现了个人或社会的问题后,上述提到的在儿童抚养过程中的消极循环就很容易出现（Rutter，1990）。

同样,有必要假设不只是危险因素的累积,基于儿童个性特征的不同模式也发挥着作用。举例来说,弗里克（Frick）（1998）发现典型的社会化缺陷和认知功能形式只是不端行为演变的途径之一;还有第二种是对于麻木的、没有同情心的,而且成年后有精神分裂倾向的小部分儿童的行为演变解释（Lynam，1996）。还有一些有攻击性行为的个人看起来相对不冲动,不过度活跃,社会化程度更低且更加内向和孤僻。那些"过于控制的敌意"的人很有可能与神经过敏的群体有关（Blackburn，1993；White and Heilbrun，1995）。这些敌意只有当冲突升级时才会激发暴力从而导致严重后果。在社会环境中,由此引发的性质严重的暴力案例在其突然爆发之前,没有明显的攻击性征兆。

（三）与学校相关的危险因素

与学校相关的反社会人格的发展既有学生个人因素,也有社会环境因素。认知能力的缺陷、多动症、情绪易冲动等因素使得学生不能很好地适应学校的学习和生活。同样的,这些因素也会导致学业表现差、留级、辍学等情况的发生（Hawkins *et al.*，1998；McCord and Ensminger，1997；Moffitt *et al.*，1996）。而与此相伴的,便是学生对学校缺乏感情、没有学习动力、师生关系不好、逃课等反社会行为的重要体现（Hawkins *et al.*，1998）。与学校有关的风险因素还和家长的态度和行为有关。有反社会行为倾向的家长缺乏对学校教育的期待值,对子女的校园生活也没有兴趣（Farrington，1992；Stouthamer-Loeber *et al.*，1993）。

不过,与学校相关的形成反社会行为的风险因素,不仅仅源于个人和家庭特征,它同时也可能归结于学校本身。与人们普遍认同的观点相反,班级的平均规模、学校的规模和建筑风格对反社会行为的形成几乎没有影响（Lösel and Bliesener，2003；Olweus，1993）。反而是校园生活、学校和教室氛围等因素,对学生的影响更加显著。一个学校如果在组织方面、教学结构方面做得不好（如:对学校教学价值观的树立缺乏重视、学校教师没有模范作用、校园冲突多、学生的低参与度和低责任意识等等）,都会增加学生出现反社会行为的风险（Gottfredson，2001；Lösel and Bliesener，2003；

Mortimore，1995；Rutter *et al*.，1979）。在一个学校或一个班级里集聚了有喜欢攻击的、行为不端的学生也是一个重要的风险因素（kellam *et al*.，1998）。如果很多学生有相同的问题行为，这就有可能对学校的氛围产生负面影响，并强化学生的不良习惯。

（四）同伴群体因素

同伴群体对反社会行为的影响尤为重大（Harris，1995；Lösel，2003a；Thornberry，1998）。和其他的危险因素一样，对同伴群体的文献回顾表明，随着时间的变化，此因素和其他因素密切相关并且相互作用。有攻击性行为的儿童往往容易被他们表现正常的同伴所拒绝（Cairns and Cairns，1991；Parker *et al*.，1995；Patterson *et al*.，1992）。因为同伴拒绝，也因为其他原因，这些行为不端的儿童会频繁地参与到攻击性行为盛行、暴力活动普遍的团伙中去（Elliot，2004；Reiss and Farrington，1991；Thornberry，1998；Tremblay *et al*.，1995）。这样的青少年被同伴视作榜样，并常常地袭击他人、参与不良活动、滥用药品、贩卖毒品、态度不端，还会形成及时行乐、满足短期欲望的生活方式（Jessor，Donovan and Costa，1992；Lösel and Bliesener，1998；Tremblay *et al*.，1995）。更严重的情况是这些青少年加入了青少年团伙犯罪组织（Thornberry，1998）。一直以来，青少年犯罪团伙在北美十分普遍，并且近几年来不断地引起越来越多的关注（Klein，1995）。在欧洲，青少年团伙与移民和种族问题密切相关（BMI and BMJ，2001）。

参与到犯罪团伙的青少年不仅选择了这样的社会环境，而且深受影响。他们已经表现出对攻击性行为和不端行为的个人偏好，并很难再融入到其他群体中去（Lösel，2003b；Thornberry，1998；Tremblay *et al*.，1995）。另外，不良群体还有一个强化作用，即导致犯罪活动的严重性升级，特别是在团伙中。家庭压力巨大、家庭存在子女抚养问题、学业成绩不佳、呈现早期的反社会行为、同伴拒绝、所生活的社区秩序混乱且被边缘化、接触有类似成长背景的人的青少年更容易加入犯罪团体，并成为其中的一员（Thornberry，1998）。在这里，值得再次强调的是对不同领域的危险因素应该要综合起来分析，而不能孤立地对待。

（五）社会认知与态度

人们在家庭、朋友、学校和大众媒体中所经历的暴力会致使人们的观念和思维方式更倾向于暴力（Crick and Dodge，1994；Huesmann，1997；Lösel *et al*.，in press）。早在学龄前，有暴力行为倾向的孩子在处理社会信息的过程中，即表现出与其他正常同伴的不同之处。例如,他们更频繁地把与同伴之间的相互接触意图理解为有敌意的行为。他们更难站在他人的角度看待动机和体会感觉。相反,他们会以自我为中心。在他们的大脑里有着更多的具有攻击性的反应模式,他们倾向于乐观地估计暴力行为带来的后果,而他们却不具备相对高的、处理非攻击性行为的能力(Crick and Dodge, 1994;Lösel and Bliesener, 2003)。这种信息处理过程很大程度上导致了他们对外界环境主观的暴力反应结果。

社会信息处理机制也可以作为联系大众媒体暴力与暴力行为的机制。研究表明,媒体对已有暴力倾向或情感冷淡的儿童有不良影响(Bushman, 1995;Huesmann and Miller, 1994)。显然的,在一些情况严重的个案中,儿童或青少年会直接从视频或其他媒介中模仿严重的暴力行为(Glogauer, 1993)。然而,暴力的更深层因素和罪恶的根基在于他们对暴力行为的习惯、无人性主义的内化和对暴力倾向认知机制的巩固(Huesmann and Miller, 1994;Selg, 1990)。正因为这些潜在因素,儿童在遇到困难情况时更容易反应过激。

反社会的年青人们通过社会经验和自我强化认知过程,形成了那些能促进他们表现出不端行为的态度和价值观。例如,他们比常人更能够容忍不端行为,更支持暴力行为,对传统的成就价值观缺乏认同,对现有组织机构抱有更强的敌意(Gottfredson and Hirschi, 1990;Jessor et al., 1992;Lösel and Bliesener, 2003)。而群体氛围更是鼓励了这种态度。那些参与行为不端者派系和团伙的青少年逐渐地形成对亚文化的自我认同(Thornberry, 1998)。当然,青少年的不端态度也不能总被视作消极的,因为这也是他们个人成长过程中,从家庭中独立并形成自我认同感的必经阶段。攻击性行为轻微的青少年们也在父母家庭和同伴之间摇摆不定(Lösel and Bliesener, 2003)。尽管如此,如果青少年过度认同不良群体和亚文化,那显然还是过度了。

自我评价和反社会行为之间的关系也同样相对复杂。一些儿童和青少年尝试通过表现不端态度和行为来提高自尊心。然而,与普遍认同的观点相反,在实证研究中,低自尊心和反社会行为之间没有持续性的关系(Lösel and Schmucker, 2004)。尽管一些有侵犯行为的儿童面临着自我价值定位的问题,但其他一些亚群体也会具有消极的、不切实际且高估自我形象的问题(Baumeister, Smart, and Boden, 1996)。一旦这种脆弱的自我形象受到侮辱或破坏,很有可能导致倾向于接受侵略性信息和导致暴力的反应行为。

（六）异常的生活方式

异常的团体和亚文化促使了无组织的娱乐消遣活动的发展。酗酒、药品滥用、飙车、滥交等其他有害健康的活动都与反社会行为有关。在许多行为异常的青年中，上述的这些行为导致他们在很多方面出现问题（Jessor et al., 1992；Junger, Terlouw and van der Heijden, 1995；Lösel and Bliesener, 1998）。中庸地讲，这种情况对于一般青年而言也很典型，且不同的行为举止不一定在同一时间发生。然而，大多数情况严重的案例中，反社会行为往往伴随着药品滥用情况（Lösel and Bliesener, 1998）。毒品或酒精对人的影响，和在学习或工作中表现平平带来的压力产生影响一样，会增加犯重罪的几率。随着犯罪的进程，加上受到社会羞辱和排斥，这些都导致他们失去更多社会提供的机会，并强化了他们的犯罪动机（Hermann and Kerner, 1988）。

在青春期晚期和成人期早期，许多习惯性的反社会者们都面临着就业困难。他们不能完成职业培训或者在中途退出（Goppinger, 1997；Sampson and Laub, 1993）。因为教育程度低，有时甚至有阅读、写作和算术障碍，他们的就业机会就更少了。即使他们暂时获得工作，那些缺点也使他们只能胜任短期的、变动的且无需职业资格认证的工作。在一些案例中，失业引发了一些人的不良行为。但在大多数情况下，失业的影响也是相对的（Farrington, 2000）。因此，失业这一因素应该与青少年的动机结合起来分析。这一点从为具有反社会行为的青少年提供就业计划的低成功率可以看出（Lipsey and Wilson, 1998），他们对提供的就业岗位的拒绝态度更坚定。自然的，当全国或区域性失业率也居高不下时，他们的就业问题便更加突显了（Sherman et al., 1997）。

当一个青年具有如此典型的、长期的、严重的反社会行为时，问题会一直延续到成年时期。虽然犯罪生涯会随着时间逐渐结束，但其他问题将相继出现，如酗酒、长期失业、精神疾病以及家庭暴力等（Farrington, 1989）。这样的生活方式以及基因的遗传，反过来会成为对下一代的威胁。然而，同样的，这样的循环也不是封闭独立的（Bender and Lösel, 2005）。

（七）社区里存在的不良因素

在个人、家庭、学校和朋友圈内的危险因素会与更宽泛的社会环境因素相互作用，尤其是在那些彼此之间联系冷淡的邻里环境中（Catalano et al., 1998；Eisner, 2001）。在这样的社区中，很多人都穷困不堪，依靠社会救济生活，到处充满了暴力、酗酒、吸毒现象，并且很容易获得武器（Sampson and Lauritsen, 1994；Thornberry, 1998）。在这样的环境下，侵犯行为、暴力行为、不端行为和药物滥用行为十分普遍。

尽管将家庭特征和个人性格因素从这样的社区环境因素中剥离十分简单(Oberwittler et al. , 2001;Wikstrom and Loeber, 2000),但还是要综合考虑单独作用和相互作用的关系。有趣的是,和睦的家庭关系可以减弱暴力环境带来的不良影响(Richters and Martinez, 1993)。而一个良好的环境则可以提供一种缓冲,来降低那些有不良家庭背景的人们的犯罪几率(Kupersmidt, Burchinal, and Patterson, 1995)。由此可见,一个混乱的社会环境会滋生出反社会行为,尤其是对于那些没有家庭压力和个人问题的青年,他们多在青春期形成不良行为问题而非儿童时期(Wikstrom and Loeber, 2000)。而对于另一些来自边缘化的家庭并较早即表现出反社会行为的孩子来说,周围社区邻里对他们的影响便显得不是那么重要了。

五、结构化风险评估工具

以上总结的因素已被用于结构性危险评估量表的开发,目的是旨在提高临床预测的有效性。这些量表包含的评估项目大多来自对研究项目的总结、犯罪学理论和临床考虑(Farrington and Tarling, 1985;Le Blanc, 1998)。项目总结可以形成总危险指数,同时也可以揭示特定的危险模式(例如:主要是家庭或子女因素)。这些工具用于检查、深入评估和进行有关危险因素的管理(例如:决定儿童安置或设计具体的干预方案)。它们也可用于对干预项目作出不同的评价。测试者的年龄和性别、目标群体中的问题严重程度、理论和实证的基础、所遭受的危险因素的影响和数量、评估过程、评估所需时间、信息来源、评估机构环境和管理机制等等方面的不同,也会使评估工具随之调整(Hoge and Andrews, 1996;Le Blanc, 2002)。尽管许多评估工具已经设计好并应用于未成年人刑事司法领域(Achenbach, 1998;Barnoski, 2002;Borum, Bartel, and Forth, 2002;Hoge, Andrews, and Leschied, 1996),越来越多的则是运用于对社区和临床环境的早期评估(Augimeri et al. , 2001;Beuhring, 2002;Corrado, 2002;Doreleijers et al. , 2002)。一些量表重点关注特殊领域的风险。例如,早在50多年前,格卢克(Glueck)(1950)就已设计出研究小规模家庭危险因素的量表。其他量表,如重新修订之后的《精神病大全——儿童和青少年版》(Hare, 2001),就重点关注对青少年个性特征的分析(Forth, Kosson, and Hare, 2002;Frick, Bodin, and Barry, 2000)。大多数量表包含来自各方面的危险因素(如个人、家庭和邻里)。

风险评估工具必须符合一些方法和实践标准。为了满足客观性和可靠性标准,对项目内容和评分标准必须进行明确的阐述。在复杂量表的应用之前应该进行系统的培训。量表必须在信息的广度和经济之间找到契合点。当在大群体中筛选时,最好采用逐步门阶应用程序(Loeber, Dishion, and Patterson, 1984)。评估项目应该涉及多种情况下的行为表现和使用多个独立的信息来源(Achenbach, McConaughy, and Howell, 1987;Lösel et al., 2005)。他们不但要利用静态的危险因素,也要利用能通过干预措施改变的动态的危险因素。有关风险的信息应有防预因素和防预强度的数据作补充,然而这很少见(Borum et al., 2002)。虽然评估量表要特别根据目标群体的年龄和性别而制定,但同样也要能和不同群体在不同时间段里的评估结果进行系统比较。在许多国家,需要考虑文化上的差异(Cooke and Michie, 2002)。为避免羞辱、数据保护和其他问题的违规现象,法律和道德方面的问题也需要加以整合(Le Blanc, 1998)。最后,但也同样重要的是,评估量表在研究、使用过程中的有效性需要时时进行跟踪记录。下面,我们将介绍两份危险评估量表,它们创立的程序科学,并且也与临床有关。其余一些可能对实践人员有特殊用处的量表将会在 Tiffin 和 Richardson 一章中作介绍(附录1)。

(一)早期风险评估量表

男孩的早期风险评估量表(EARL-20B, Version 2;Augimeri et al., 2001)是在加拿大多伦多厄尔斯科特儿童和家庭中心对12岁以下男孩的外联项目(ORP)支持下发展的(Howell, 2001)。该项目包含了早期反社会儿童及其家庭的各种特征。开发、测试和修订 EARL-20B,来满足对高危儿童进行早期诊断和区别安置的需要。由于某些风险因素不为两性所同时适用,一个专门针对女孩的特定评估量表应运而生(EARL-21G; Levene et al., 2001)。两种列表都来源于有关对12岁以下儿童侵犯和暴力行为的实证研究文献及临床经验。它们关注6岁至12岁之间的风险因素,但也已尝试向更年幼和更年长组别进行扩展。量表的结构和这个研究小组其他有名的、用来分析暴力行为(HCR-20;Webster et al., 1997)和性暴力行为(SVR-20;Boer et al., 1997)的风险评估设计有相似之处。为了实现其透明度和客观性,每个项目都有准确的定义,并以三分制的形式进行计分。正如表2所显示的,项目结构可分为三个领域:家庭、儿童和响应度。各项试验研究表明,这一量表既可靠又有效(Webster et al., 2002)。然而,更多长期的、大规模的评估仍然是必需的。

表2　男孩早期风险评估量项目(Earl-20B, Augimeri et. al., 2001)

家庭(F)	儿童(C)	响应度(R)
F1 家庭环境	C1 生长发育问题	R1 家庭响应度

家庭（F）	儿童（C）	响应度（R）
F2 抚养者的固定性	C2 开始出现行为异常	R2 儿童响应度
F3 支持	C3 虐待/疏忽/创伤	
F4 压力	C4 多动症/冲动/注意力不集中	
F5 父母抚养方式	C5 喜欢程度	
F6 反社会的价值观和行为	C6 同伴社交影响	
	C7 学业表现	
	C8 邻里关系	
	C9 与权威力量的接触	
	C10 反社会态度	
	C11 反社会行为	
	C12 处理事务的能力	

（二）Krakow 风险评估量表

此量表是由加拿大温哥华市的西蒙佛斯大学的学者专家们设计的（Corrado，2002；Odgers，Vincent，and Corrado，2002），并在波兰克拉科夫市举行的 NATO 高级研讨会上最终被确定。这份量表涵盖的风险范围很广泛，其项目源自实证研究和临床实验结果。它的一个显著特征是区分了每个儿童不同的生长发育阶段特征，每个阶段都有不同的测量标准，分为出生、童年早期（0—5 岁）、童年中期（5—12 岁）和青少年期（13—18 岁）。以童年中期量表为例，除了有在此特定时期出现的危险因素，还包括出生阶段和童年早期阶段的危险因素。有时，一个评估项目的名称会随着年龄变化而变化（比如出生阶段涉及的是"亲生父母"，在随后的发展阶段则是"抚养者"）。所有的项目都描述清晰，并根据严重程度分成三个级别进行编码。而且，还应注明每个项目的信息和数据来源，并为其赋予一个具体的等级值。第二个编码表明每个案子中最重要的一些项目。情况最严重的儿童需要被最高强度的干预措施所关注。危险评估项目共分为五个部分：环境、个人、家庭、干预措施和外部行为。表 3 总结了该量表对不同年龄阶段儿童进行评估的内容。

表3　Krakow 危险评估量表（Corrado 2002；Odgers *et. al.*，2002）

环境	家庭
E1 助产混乱（PP→）	F1 青春期少女怀孕（PP→）
E2 母亲在怀孕时药物滥用（PP→）	F2 母亲/双亲处理事务能力（PP→）
E3 社区混乱（PP→）	F3 父母反社会行为/态度（PP→）
E4 家庭社会经济地位（PP→）	F4 家庭支持（PP→）
E5 住房稳定性（EC→）	F5 家庭冲突/家庭暴力（PP→）
E6 对暴力环境的接触（EC→）	F6 兄弟姐妹不端行为（EC→）
E7 同伴影响（EC→）	F7 无效的父母管教（EC→）
E8 学校环境（EC→）	F8 早期抚养者的分离和依附（EC→）
其他环境因素（PP→）	其他家庭因素父母教育背景和 IQ（PP→）
	家庭结构/单亲家庭（PP→）
个人	
I1 出生时缺陷（PP→）	干预措施
I2 父母精神病史（PP→）	IV1 前期干预措施（有针对性的）（PP→）
I3 执行力机能障碍（EC→）	IV2 干预措施的可介入性（PP→）
I4 习惯性的低兴奋点（EC→）	IV3 家庭对干预措施的反馈（PP→）
I5 认知能力障碍（EC→）	IV4 儿童对干预措施的反馈（EC→）
I6 个性障碍（EC→）	OtherIV 其他干预因素（PP→）
I7 其他精神病（EC→）	
I8 反社会态度（EC→）	外部行为
I9 处理事务能力障碍（EC→）	EB1 日常行为问题（EC→）
I10 学业表现（EC→）	EB2 暴力和侵略性行为（EC→）
其他个人因素（PP→）	EB3 药物滥用（MC→）
	EB4 日常违规行为（MC→）
	EB5 其他外部行为（EC→）

注：PP→Pre-Perinatal 及之后；EC→童年早期及之后；MC→童年中期及之后。

　　由于 Krakow 量表相对较新，其预测的有效性有待将来进一步的验证。根据我们对幼儿园儿童的发展和干预研究的初步数据（Lösel *et al.*，2004）显示，在母亲围产期之前的数值和童年早期的数值，和几年后的反社会行为之间都有着很强的相关性；并且童年早期的数值的相关性相对更高一些，大约在 0.20 至 0.40 之间变化（由调查持续性时间和结果评价决定）。

　　这样的效应值十分典型。除了先前的反社会行为，其他绝大多数单独项目的预测和行为结果之间的相关性很小（r=0.10 至 0.20 之间；Lösel，2002）。几乎所有的预测项多多少少都相互关联，而性质恶劣的案例的低发生率也限制了更进一步的预测。因此,0.40 至 0.50 或者大约20%变化率的相关性在早期对反社会行为和暴力行为预测中是典型的上限值域。毫无疑问,这样的效应值是不重要的,因为它们证明多于80%的案例是能被预测为有相关性的(Hawkins *et al.*,1998;Lipsey and Derzon,1998)。虽然有很大一部分结果被证明是假阳性和伪阴性的,但是早期的危险评估是不同的防预因素和干预措施得以实施的基础。

六、防预因素和干预措施

当然,上述提及的一系列相关的因素对反社会行为的发展无须在一个独立案例中全部显示。话虽如此,这些因素还在伴随着危险因素的增加而不断积累,并产生长期的负面影响(Farrington,1997a;Hawkins *et al.*,1998;Lösel and Bliesener,2003)。反过来说,正面的特征和经历在一些领域中也会破坏负面的系列反应。尽管这可能是长期干预措施造成的结果,但是这也可能在自然发展环境中产生。当年轻人接收到防预信息时,他们可能通过积极的社会发展来代替高危的反社会行为,或是在经历了一段艰难期之后改正了问题行为。这个原理表明,此类干预方法比危险评估更少为人们所研究(Lösel and Bliesener,1994;Sampson and Laub,2003;Werner and Smith,1992);而若要在这一领域开展充分的研究设计也更困难(Lösel and Bender,2003;Luthar,Cicchetti and Becker,2000)。当然,人们可以猜想在表1中,所罗列的危险变量的反面即是积极发展和改造的变量。然而,真正的防预作用需要抵消高危因素所发挥的作用(运用中和的方法;Rutter,1985)。现有的研究表明,有些因素能够防预反社会行为所带来的危害。表4罗列了一系列已经被证明有效的、源于个人力量或社会资源的防预措施(Lösel and Bender,2003):

表4　关于严重反社会行为防范措施的多方例子

生物的/生物—社会	没有行为异常的亲属、没有基因易损性倾向的、高生理兴奋点的、神经正常的和荷尔蒙功能正常
在怀孕及围产时期	母亲无酗酒习惯、母亲怀孕期间不吸烟、无出生并发症
孩子的个性	性格随和、自制力强、自我意识弹性强、智力正常、口头表达能力正常、规划未来、自我控制、具备解决社会问题的能力、受害人自我保护意识、情感依附安全、有罪恶感、有学习和工作动力、有特别的兴趣爱好、抵制毒品
认识能力和态度	没有敌意、没有攻击性行为、对攻击性行为持反对态度、在亲社会化中自我认同、无不正常的信仰、基于现实的自尊自信、具备一致性
家庭	没有贫困、收入稳定、家庭和睦、被家人认可、父母监督到位、具备连贯性、正面的学习榜样、关怀持续、无明显弱点、可以得到社会支持

生物的/生物—社会	没有行为异常的亲属、没有基因易损性倾向的、高生理兴奋点的、神经正常的和荷尔蒙功能正常
学校	成就感和团结,有侵犯性行为的学生数量少,有完善的接纳、体制和监管的校园氛围
同伴	无行为不端的同伴,有来自亲密的、亲社会的朋友的支持
社区	不被边缘化,生活在融合的、无暴力的社区环境,有专业人员援助
环境	保护目标强化、被害人援助服务、社会控制
法律	有效的枪支、毒品管理政策,有效的刑事司法干预措施
文化	低暴力、传统的道德价值认同、羞耻—负罪感指向、媒体暴力信息少

　　与危险因素一样,防预因素也有累积效果(Stattin, Romelsjo, and Stenbacka, 1997)。在和其他特征进行特殊的结合之后,一些因素可能既是一种风险,也具有防预因素的防范功能。比如说,班达(Bender)和洛赛尔(Lösel)(1997)发现尽管社会支持在保护有较低反社会倾向的高危青少年中发挥了作用,但是它也同时会加重那些已经有不端行为的青少年的问题。当审视危险因素和防预因素之间的相互影响时,进行不同方式的阐述,并质疑"是什么样的危险诱因,又是什么样的保护因素"总是必须的。比方说,焦虑和社会回避对于反社会行为是防预措施,但这可能增加焦虑症的风险和造成其他个人问题。

　　防预效果越低,则个人失范行为和社会混乱的影响持续越长,专业的防范和干预项目需要来弥补自然资源的缺陷。许多研究表明,在早期发育阶段实施防范和干预措施能够有效预防反社会行为的发生、发展(Farrington and Welsh, 2003;Kazdin, 1998;Lösel, 2005;Lösel and Beelmann, 2003, 2005;Tremblay and Japel, 2003;Utting, 2003;亦可参考本书第九章)。但是,整体的效果微弱或者适中,而所得的结果差异很大。由于存在很多不同的危险因素,针对多种危险因素进行防范的多模式干预项目是最有效的。以儿童技能培训项目为例,在解决非侵犯性社会问题过程中,我们发现社会认知项目所传授的认知思维和行为技能的效果最为明显(Lösel and Beelmann, 2005)。结合了父母—孩子共同培训的家庭导向型项目也相对成功(问题行为防范研究小组 2002;Tremblay et al., 1995),而具有多重目标定位的单亲母亲家访(Olds et al., 1998),学龄前儿童的学前强化项目和相关的父母咨询项目(Schweinhart, Barnes and Weikart, 1993),还有多系统化的治疗项目等也都有一定效果(Henggeler et al., 1998)。在儿童已经表现出问题行为时,儿童—家庭导向型的项目有更显著的实际运用效果(预见性的预防)。儿童的年龄对防预结果的影响不大(Farrington and Welsh, 2003;Lösel and Beelmann, 2003),这消除了太早或太迟采用保护性防预措施的顾虑,是鼓舞人心的。

因此,在青年治疗项目的文献回顾中我们反驳了"没什么措施是有效的"主义是不正确的(Lipsey and Wilson,1998;Lösel,1995;McGuire,2002)。理论上来说,构建好的、有良好的认知—行为体系的、社会性治疗的而且多种模式结合的家庭导向型项目有光明的应用前景。有效的治疗项目和防预项目的内容看起来十分相似(Lösel,2005)。因此,除了比较防预和治疗项目,我们还需要找到并整合出哪些方法在处理不同的发展阶段、在处理不同程度的违法行为上有效,这和对在儿童发育的不同年龄阶段出现的、多种危险因素的讨论一样,都是今后研究的重点。

七、结　论

许多有暴力行为或有其他严重反社会行为的青少年表现出问题行为发生早、持续性强的特点。许多因素加剧了这样的危险,同时也促进连锁反应并使反社会行为成为习惯。其中,尤为重要的是:生理易损性、脾性特点和神经心理缺陷;童年早期的问题行为、家庭结构性问题、家庭经济问题、家庭压力大、不和睦、被父母虐待/忽视、父母抚养方式不正确等;学业成绩差、逃学,校园氛围不佳;青少年对行为异常的团体的认同和依附,其反社会性的生活方式,还有便是生活在贫困和暴力社区等。虽然大多数的单一因素所造成的影响很小,但它们的积累则会增加问题的严重性。自然的保护因素和专业的干预措施可以通过减少特定的危险因素或抵消其带来的负面影响,从而阻断这样的连锁反应。系统的、和临床有关的评估量表可能有助于提高风险评估和问题行为管理实践的效果。防范和干预措施在帮助每一个个案时,应该全面地或有针对性地利用这些信息进行危险评估、分析个体需求和自我保护性潜质特征等。

致　谢

本章的写作得到了橡树基金和德国国家家庭事务部、老年人协会、女子协会和青少年协会的许可和大力支持。

[参考文献见英文原作]

（展万程　倪　彤　译）

Risk Factors for Serious and Violent Antisocial Behaviour in Children and Youth

Friedrich Lösel

University of Erlangen, Nuremberg

Doris Bender

INTRODUCTION

Many countries are experiencing strong concerns about seriously aggressive and violent children and youth. They cause a lot of problems for parents, relatives, teachers, peers, neighbours, social services and – in the long run – themselves as well. The most serious cases of physical injury or even death of others gain intensive coverage in the mass media, and many people want to know why children grow up and act in this way. The present chapter tries to answer this question. Specifically, we shall summarise the literature on empirically founded risk factors for the development of persistent antisocial and violent behaviour in children. Before we can do this, however, we need briefly to address some basic issues regarding the definition and development of this target group. The second part and core of the chapter presents the main risk factors within an integrated bio-psychosocial perspective. The third part then goes on to address structured instruments for risk assessment and management. The chapter closes with a brief discussion of protective factors and interventions that may help to reduce the impact of developmental risks (see also Chapter 6 in this volume).

Although some risk assessment instruments will be discussed, the chapter does not aim to review this literature comprehensively. Instead, if focuses on the foundations of such tools; that is, on the available empirical knowledge about a broad range of risk factors. This should enable practitioners to make adequate assessments and develop effective modes of risk communication and management in their own field. Tiffin and Richardson (Appendix 1) also discuss some tools to help practitioners. A realistic framework must take into account the basic limits of prediction and behavioural control in everyday life. These are related to the developmental principles of continuity and flexibility. Bearing these in mind should help to avoid the negative effects of undue pessimism and stigmatisation when working with such difficult children.

BASIC DEVELOPMENTAL ISSUES IN ANTISOCIAL BEHAVIOUR

Although there are similarities in the backgrounds and behaviour of many seriously aggressive children, they do not form a homogeneous group. They also do not stand out completely from other groups of aggressive and delinquent young people. Even studies of young murderers show that these have much in common with youth exhibiting less serious aggression (Lempp, 1977; Traverso and Bianchi, 2002). Despite the lack of a clear taxonomy, approximately half of the youngsters who have committed a violent offence are also 'chronic' delinquents (Loeber, Farrington, and Waschbusch, 1998b). These individuals show early-starting, relatively persistent, and serious antisocial behaviour in various forms (e. g. Moffit, 1993; Patterson et al., 1998). This developmental pathway can be distinguished from the much more prevalent adolescent-limited antisocial behaviour that leads to the typical age curve of criminality with its increase in adolescence and decline in early adulthood (Farrington, 1989; Loeber et al, 1998a). The adolescence-limited pathway is a typical youth transition problem. The serious and persistent group, in contrast, not only carry on offending into adulthood but also have already exhibited frequent aggression, delinquency and other conduct problems during childhood (e. g. Farrington and Loeber, 2001; Patterson et al. ,1998). More than 5 percent of boys follow this pathway (Moffitt and Caspi, 2001; Moffitt et al., 1996); while girls have a lower prevalence rate of serious antisociality (Loeber et al., 1998a; Moffitt et al., 2001). Individuals on this pathway are clearly overrepresented among serious and violent offenders. In adolescence and adulthood, more than one half of the offences in each age cohort can be attributed to this group (Loeber et al., 1998a; Wolfgang, Figlio, and Sellin, 1972). Moreover, such early-starting antisocial behaviour is also a strong risk market for other psychiatric and social problem in adulthood (Robins and Price, 1991).

Naturally, a differentiation into two types does not cover the whole range of antisocial developments in real life. For example, Nagin and Land (1993) found a third group of less serious low-level chronics. Loeber and Hay (1994) suggest three pathways that differ in their behaviour:

- directly aggressive behaviour such as bullying, hitting, fighting or cruelty to animals leading to later assault, rape or manslaughter(*overt antisocial behaviour*)
- more indirect forms of antisocial behaviour such as shoplifting, frequent lying, vandalism or fire setting leading to burglary, fraud or serious theft(*Covert antisocial behoviour*)
- stubborn behaviour, defiance or disobedience leading to truancy, running away or staying out late(*authority conflict*).

On all three pathways, the proportion of youngsters exhibiting such problem behaviour decreases with age, whereas the severity of the problem behaviour increases. Some children exhibit problem behaviour in all three areas (*versatile antisocial behaviour*), and these form the core group on the early-starting, serious and persistent pathway.

Although there is strong empirical support for this type of development, one should not overestimate the continuity of problem behaviour (Lösel and Bender, 2003; Tremblay, 2000). About one half of children with severe conduct disorders and intensive aggression in childhood do not progress to serious criminal behaviour in adolescence (e. g. Moffitt *et al.* , 1996; Patterson *et al.* , 1998; Robins, 1978). This is partly due to natural developmental changes, protective mechanisms and social interventions in the life course (Laub and Sampson, 2003; Lösel and Bender, 2003). When addressing risk factors, we must also take into account other principles of developmental psychopathology: problem behaviour rarely has a single cause or origin. It results from multiple bio-psychosocial influences. Even well-designed studies cannot always demonstrate clear causal relationships, but only risk factors that enhance the probability of a negative outcome. Specific behavioural outcomes may result from different risks (equifinality), but the same risk factors may lead to different outcomes (multifinality). Factors relevant for the onset of antisocial development may differ from those influencing its persistence or aggravation. Moreover, difficult children are not only a more or less passive object of biosocial influences but-with increasing age-also active constructors of their own development (e. g. through their choice of peers and social contexts). Finally, whether an individual exhibits violent or other problem behaviour at a specific time and in a specific context depends not only on these long-term influences and psychological dispositions but also on situational factors. The situational risks of aggressive behaviour are a product of both objective characteristics and their subjective interpretations.

RISK FACTORS FOR SERIOUS ANTISOCIALITY

Adolescents with early, serious and persistent antisocial behaviour typically reveal multiple bio-psychosocial risks that have been accumulating since childhood (Farrington and Loeber, 2001; Hawkins *et al.*, 1998; Loeber, 1982; Lynam, 1996). The accumulation of such factors consolidates and aggravates problem behaviour like a chain reaction (Lösel, 2001; Lösel and Bender, 2003). The high-risk chain reactions can best be understood within a theoretical framework of biosocial vulnerability, social learning and neuropsychological development (Bandura, 1979; Lösel and Bender, 2003; Moffitt, 1993). Table 1 gives an overview of factors that longitudinal research has shown to represent a risk in this process. Such single factors mostly have very small or small effects (correlatioan between r = 0. 10 and 0. 20). It is an accumulation of problems in various domains that is accompanied by a strong increase in the probability that serious problem behaviour will emerge (Farrington, 1997a; Loeber *et al.* in press; Lösel and Bliesener, 2003). This dosage-response relationship appears to be robust across both genders. We shall now address the various risk domains in more detail.

Table 1   Risk factors for the development of serious antisocial behaviour

Areas of risk	PB	EP	MC	AD	Effect
Biological/biosocial risks					
Male gender	×	×	×	×	***
Genetic disposition (hereditary factors)	×	×	×	×	***
Prenatal risks / pregnancy complications	×	×	×	×	*
Perinatal problems	×	×	×	×	*
Low level of physiological arousal	×	×	×	×	***
Neurotransmitter dysfunction	×	×	×	×	**
Hormonal factors		×	×	×	*
Early puberty (particularly in girls)				×	*

continued

Areas of risk	PB	EP	MC	AD	Effect
Family risks					
Poverty/ low SES/ living on welfare	×	×	×	×	* * *
Low parental education	×	×	×	×	* *
Ethnic background (in some countries)	×	×	×	×	* * *
Teenage motherhood	×	×	×	×	* *
Single parenthood	×	×	×	×	*
Large family size	×	×	×	×	*
Divorce/separation		×	×	×	*
Frequent change of caregiver		×	×	×	* *
Parental unemployment	×	×	×	×	*
Parental criminality	×	×	×	×	* * *
Parental substance abuse	×	×	×	×	* *
Parental mental disorder	×	×	×	×	*
Disharmony and conflict between parents		×	×	×	* *
Child neglect/ lack of parental warmth		×	×	×	* * *
Child abuse		×	×	×	* * *
Physical punishment		×	×	×	* *
Inadequate supervision and discipline			×	×	* * *
High family stress		×	×	×	* *
Lack of social support/ social isolation		×	×	×	* *
Parental attitudes that encourage deviance			×	×	* *
Sibling delinquency			×	×	* *
Early child personality and behavioural risks					
Low intelligence	×	×	×	×	* *
Language problems		×	×	×	*
Poor executive functioning		×	×	×	* * *
Developmental delays		×	×	×	*
Difficult temperament/negative emotionality	×	×	×	×	* * *
Impulsivity		×	×	×	* * *
Attention deficit hyperactivity disorder		×	×	×	* * *
Risk taking and need for stimulation		×	×	×	* *
Lack of guilt		×	×	×	* * *
Callousness/ lack of empathy		×	×	×	* * *

continued

Areas of risk	PB	EP	MC	AD	Effect
Attachment deficits		×	×	×	***
Early onset of antisocial behaviour		×	×	×	***
Problem behaviour in multiple contexts		×	×	×	***
School-related risks					
Achievement problems			×	×	***
Low motivation/ commitment to the school			×	×	**
Truancy			×	×	**
School dropout/ frequent change of school			×	×	**
Poor school-leaving qualifications				×	***
Low parental interest in school			×	×	**
Unfavourable school and classroom climate			×	×	*
High proportion of antisocial students			×	×	**
Peer group risks					
Peer rejection		×	×	×	*
Few prosocial contacts		×	×	×	**
Affiliation with delinquent cliques			×	×	***
Gang membership				×	***
Risks in social cognitions and attitudes					
Aggression-prone social information processing		×	×	×	***
Deficits in coping and social problem solving			×	×	***
Unrealistic self-esteem			×	×	*
Deviant attitudes/identification with deviant subcultures			×	×	***
Lifestyle risks					
Unstructured leisure-time activities			×	×	**
High consumption of violence in the mass media		×	×	×	**
Alcohol abuse			×	×	***
Use of illegal drugs				×	***
Drug dealing				×	***
Carrying of weapons				×	***
Other health risk behaviour				×	**
Difficulties with vocational training/ unemployment				×	**

continued

Areas of risk	PB	EP	MC	AD	Effect
Community/neighbourhood risks					
Concentration of poverty/problem families			×	×	**
Disorganised neighbourhood			×	×	*
Easy access to weapons			×	×	*
Context of violence and drugs			×	×	**

Presence of risk factors: PB = Prenatal/ Birth; EP = Early Childhood/ Preschool (age 0—5 years); MC = Middle Childhood (age 6—12 years); AD = Adolescence (age 13—18 years).

Approximate effect size ratings; * Very small effect and/ or not yet well replicated; ** Small effect and replicated; *** Up to medium effect and replicated.

BIOLOGICAL AND BIOSOCIAL FACTORS

Although biological influences are often neglected in theories of antisocial behaviour, they form a basis of vulnerability (Raine, 1993; Rowe, 1994). Genetic factors obviously play an important role. In most cultures, males face a higher risk for serious aggression and only a part of this risk can be attributed to social learning (Hyde, 1984; Miles and Carey, 1997; Moffitt *et al.*, 2001). Even within the same sex, genetic factors have a substantial impact on the degree of antisocial behaviour (Harris, 1995; Mason and Frick, 1994). They are responsible for significant differences in temperament and in cognitive functions that, in turn, relate to aggression and delinquency (Plomin, 1994; Raine, 1997). Approximately 40 percent of the inter-individual differences in stable antisocial behaviour can probably be traced back to genetic factors. Nonetheless, the genotype marks out only the boundaries delineating the breadth of possible behaviour (the phenotype). How this is actually shaped in individual development depends on the environment and nature-nurture interaction. For example, genetic components of social family factors can operate in various ways: (a) children may inherit environments along with genes from their parents; (b) parents may react to genetically influenced child traits; (c) older children may seek out environmental niches suited to their own genotype (Pike *et al.*, 1996).

Environmental influences can already be found during pregnancy. Neuropsychological development can be impaired through a mother's alcoholism (foetal alcohol syndrome; Conry and Fast, 2000; Steinhauesen, Willms and Spohr, 1993). Pregnant mothers who smoke expose their offspring to a prenatal intoxication that has an impact on the infant's neurobiology and future anti-social behaviour (Fergusson, Woodward and horwood, 1998;

Koglin, 2003). However, such an effect is related to a greater or lesser degree with family risks. For example, mothers who smoke during pregnancy more often have a low socio-economic status (SES), are less well educated and otherwise more at risk for deficits in parenting (Koglin, 2003; Raine, 1993).

Birth complications and a postnatal lack of emotional affection, stimulation or poor nutrition are further biological risks (Hodgins, Kratzer and McNeil, 2002; Koglin, 2003; Raine, Brennan and Mednick, 1994). Here as well, it does not seem to be isolated effects that are significant, but, above all, combinations with social factors. For example, pregnancy and birth complications impact on a child's social behaviour when they are accompanied by social risks such as parental rejection, poverty or family instability (Brennan, Mednick and Raine, 1997). Vice versa, social risks such as experiencing little affection also relate to biological factors (Plomin, 1994). For example, a deprived relation to the primary caregiver can impair an infant's brain development and attachment behaviour (Kraemer, 1997).

Biological predispositions are also involved when some children react more impulsively than others and are less able to learn from negative experiences. Antisocial children have, for example, lower pulse rates, reduced psycho-galvanic responses and slower electroen-cephalograms (e. g. Farrington, 1997b; Raine, 1993). Low arousal manifests in a greater need for stimulation (sensation seeking, thirst for adventure), less fear of punishment and poorer avoidance learning (Eysenck, 1977; Zuckerman, 1994).

Another risk may be related to the androgen hormone testosterone. Enhanced testosterone levels seem to be both causal and consequential factors of human aggression (Archer, 1991). Although relations between aggression and testosterone have been investigated more thoroughly in adults, we may expect an impact at least from puberty onwards (Tremblay et al. , 1997). Early puberty is in itself a risk factor, particularly for girls (Stattin and Magnusson, 1990). Due to their physical precocity, these girls have more contacts to deviant boys and groups; however, they also grow out of their behavioural problems earlier. The stress hormone cortisol plays a further role in biological vulnerability and may interact with testosterone in adolescence (Tremblay et al. , 1997). Whereas anxious and withdrawn children have higher cortisol levels, the relation to antisocial behaviour is more complex (Lahey et al. , 1999). In our own research (Lösel et al. , 2004), for example, we found particularly high salivary concentrations of cortisol in children who were both anxious and aggressive. In contrast, they were relatively low in the more proactively aggressive and 'cooler' children.

There is still little available research on the relation between antisocial behaviour of young people and hormonal or neurotransmitter activity (Susman and Ponirakis, 1997; Tremblay *et al.*, 1997). For example, some studies suggest that reduced levels or imbalances in the neurotransmitter serotonin play a role in antisocial behaviour (af Klinteberg, 1998, 2002; Schalling *et al.*, 1998; Virkkunen *et al.*, 1994). However, here as well genetic dispositions seem to interact with social influences. Caspi *et al.* (2002) found that specific genetic factors involved in decomposing serotonin in the monoamine oxidase (MAO) relate strongly to antisocial behaviour when a child had also experienced serious abuse in the family. Research on such nature-nurture interactions may open up new opportunities for measures of prevention that fit with the specific vulnerabilities of the child.

Family Characteristics And Upbringing

Although the impact of the family on the development of antisocial behaviour has sometimes been questioned (e. g. Harris, 1995), this area of risk factors is well confirmed in longitudinal research (e. g. Loeber and Farrington, 1998, 2001). Families of children who develop serious antisocial behaviour have to cope with significantly more structural problems and multiple deprivations than comparison groups. They reveal more poverty and low SES, teenage motherhood, single parenthood and low parental education (Farrington, 1998; Fergusson and Woodward, 1999; Hawkins *et al.*, 1998). The families more often live on social welfare, are relatively large, belong to deprived minorities and have to cope with unemployment, social isolation or other stressors (Elliott, Huizinga and Menard, 1989; Farrington, 1989; Hill *et al.*, 1994). Parents exhibit more antisocial behavior, substance abuse and other mental disorders (Farrington *et al.*, 1990; hawkins *et al.*, 1998; Tremblay *et al.*, 2004). Most of these factors are also risks for child maltreatment and abuse (Jeyarajah-Dent, 1998; Hagell, 1998).

The more proximal problems in family interaction and childrearing are particularly crucial. There is often disharmony and conflict between the parents of aggressive children and, as a consequence, more separation, divorce and change of caregivers over time (Elliott, 1994; Hawkins *et al.*, 1998). The parents do not treat their children lovingly and empathically (Kolvin *et al.* , 1990; McCord, 1979). They use more physical punishment and are either rigidly strict, too lax or inconsistent in their discipline (Farrington, 1992, 1998; Frick, 1998; Lösel and Bliesener, 2003; Loeber and Stouthamer- Loeber, 1998; McCord, 1979; Patterson, Reid and Dishion, 1992). Of course, extreme deficits in childrearing are more important than minor differences in degree. For example, Child abuse and neglect are particularly strong risk factors for antisocial child behaviour (Bender and Lösel, 2005). However, the ' cycle of violence ' is not closed (Oliver, 1993; Widom, 1989). ' Only ' approximately one-third of children from abusing families develop serious aggression, and aggressive children also come from families without domestic violence.

From the perspective of social learning theory, the above-mentioned features of family upbringing serve as models for aggressive behaviour and reinforce it. This leads to acquisition of cognitive schemes that favour aggression (Crick and Dodge, 1994; Huesmann 1997; Lösel *et al.* , in press). When external controls are either lacking or too rigid, deficits in self-control will develop or increase (Lösel, Toman and Wustendörfer, 1976). When parents are low in childrearing competence, their response to early behaviour problems in their child will tend to be rejecting, impatient, aggressive or inconsistent (Patterson *et al.* , 1992 ; Rutter, 1990). The child will then behave accordingly, and coercive interactions will emerge (Patterson *et al.* , 1992). In such a family climate, there is also a greater risk that children will not develop sound emotional attachments (Ainsworth, 1991). Avoidant, fearful, compulsive or disorganised attachment behaviour may be more frequent (Fagot and Pears, 1996), providing unfavourable preconditions for later social relationships and coping (Cassidy *et al.* , 1996).

Most individual family characteristics explain only a small amount of variance in child problem behaviour and many correlate with each other (see Hawkins *et al.* , 1998; Lipsey and Derzon, 1998; Lösel, 2002). However, their cumulative impact forms a multi-problem milieu with a clear increase in risk.

Early Child Personality And Behaviour Problems

Social and biological influences contribute to temperament characteristics and cognitive functions in a child that increase the risk of antisocial behaviour. These include impulsiveness, hyperactivity, attention problems, emotional instability, developmental delays, language deficits and relatively low overall intelligence (Farrington, 1992, 1998; Hawkins *et al.*, 1998; Lipsey and Derzon, 1998; Moffitt, 1993; Rutter, Giller and Hagell, 1998). Neuropsychological dispositions lead to problems in the executive brain functions responsible for abstract thinking, goal-directed actions and self-control (Moffitt and Henry, 1991; Séguin *et al.*, 2004). Nonetheless, many at-risk children do not have major functional impairments or diminished abilities, and the typical differences in intelligence between antisocial and well-adjusted groups average out at only a few IQ points (Rutter *et al.*, 1998). Attention deficit hyperactivity disorder (ADHD) also shows only moderate correlations with antisocial behaviour (Loeber *et al.*, 1998a). There are various facets of this syndrome, and both types of externalising problems should not be seen too much as combined (Seguin *et al.* 2004). The child's predispositions once again have to be viewed within the context of their interaction with factors in the social milieu. Whereas, for example, parents can often cope with a child's difficult temperament, learning problems and minor antisocial behaviour, the negative cycles in childrearing described above emerge more readily when parents have individual and social problems of their own (Rutter 1990).

It is also necessary to assume not only cumulative risks but also different patterns depending on a child's individual personality. For example, Frick (1998) found that the typical deficits in socialisation and cognitive functioning from just one of the pathways to deviance. There is also a second path for a smaller group of children who are particularly callous, non-emphatic and otherwise prone to psychopathic personality disorder in adulthood (Lynam, 1996). Some other aggressive individuals seem to be less impulsive, hyperactive and poorly socialised but more inhibited and withdrawn. Such 'over-controlled hostility' probably involves a more neurotic personality constellation (see Blackburn, 1993; White and Heilbrun, 1995). It triggers violence only when escalating conflicts lead to strong affect. These may well be those severe cases of violent outbursts in which no clear signs of aggressiveness have been noticed before by the social environment.

School-Related Risks

School-related risks for serious antisocial development are partially individual child factors and partially social context factors. The problematic cognitive competencies, hyperactivity and impulsivity sketched above are unfavourable preconditions for a successful school career. Correspondingly, there is an enhanced risk of low achievement, repetition of classes and early school dropout (Hawkins *et al.* , 1998; McCord and Ensminger, 1997; Moffitt *et al.* , 1996). In addition, and partially in interaction with a-chievement problems, such children also have poor bonds to their school. Low motivation, poor relations to teachers and truancy are significant predictors of antisocial behaviour (Hawkins *et al.* , 1998). Further school-related risks derive from parents' attitudes and be-haviour. Parents of children who develop antisocial behaviour have low school-oriented aspirations and values and show little interest in their child's school life (Farrington, 1992; Stouthamer-Loeber *et al.* , 1993)

However, school-oriented risks for antisocial behaviour are not just 'imported' from in-dividual and family characteristics. They are also due to the school itself. Contrary to popular stereotypes, the average size of classes, the sizes of schools or their architecture have little impact (Lösel and Bliesener, 2003; Olweus, 1993). It is factors related to the life and climate in the school and classroom that are more important. Schools with deficits in organisation and educational structure (i. e. low emphasis on school values, inconsistent teacher behaviour, many conflicts, low participation and responsibility) enhance the risk for antisocial behaviour (e. g. Gottftrdson, 2001; Lösel and Bliesener, 2003; Mortimore, 1995; Rutter *et al.* , 1979). A further risk factor is a concentration of aggressive and delinquent children in schools and classes (e. g. Kellam *et al.* , 1998). If a large proportion of children have similar behaviour problems, this may impact negatively on the school climate and enhance the risk of negative learning processes.

Peer Group

The peer group is a particularly important source of risk for antisocial behaviour (Harris, 1995; Lösel, 2003a; Thornberry, 1998). As with other risk factors, the literature suggests some change of relevant factors over time as well as relations to other areas of influence. Younger children who exhibit aggressive behaviour are often rejected by their more normal age-mates (Cairns and Cairns, 1991; Parker *et al.* , 1995; Patterson *et al.* , 1992). Partially as a consequence of such rejection and partially due to other factors, these deviant children frequently join cliques in which aggressive and delinquent activities prevail (Elliott, 2004; Reiss and Farrington, 1991; Thornberry, 1998; Tremblay *et al.* , 1995). Such peers serve as models and additionally reinforce aggression, delinquency, substance abuse, drug dealing, deviant attitudes and risky lifestyle focusing on immediate need gratification (Jessor, Donovan and Costa, 1992; Lösel and Bliesener, 1998; Tremblay *et al.*, 1995). A further enhancement of risk occurs when youngsters affiliate with organised youth gangs (Thornberry, 1998). Criminal youth gangs are a long-term issue in North American that has become increasingly topical in recent times (Klein, 1995). In Europe, this issue is closely related to problems of migration and ethnic conflict (BMI and BMI 2001).

Youngsters who join criminal cliques not only select this social context but are also influenced by it. They already show a personal disposition towards aggressive and delinquent behaviour and are less well integrated into other groups (Lösel, 2003b; Thornberry, 1998; Tremblay *et al.*, 1995). In addition, the deviant group has a reinforcing effect, leading to an increasing severity of offences-particularly in gangs. Adolescents more readily join gangs when they come from families with multiple stressors and childrearing deficits, have problems at school, exhibit early antisocial behaviour, are rejected by other peers, live in disorganised and deprived residential areas and have contacts to persons with similar difficulties (Thornberry, 1998). Once again, it becomes clear that risk factors in various domains should not be viewed in isolation.

Social Cognitions And Attitudes

Experiences of violence in the family, the peer group, school and in the mass media contribute to the development of perceptions and thinking patterns that encourage aggressive behaviour (Crick and Dodge, 1994; Huesmann, 1997; Lösel *et al.* in press). Already at preschool age, aggressive children exhibit schemes and scripts in their social information processing that differ significantly from their non-deviant peers. For example, they more frequently interpret the intentions of interaction partners as being hostile; they find it harder to view motives and feelings from the other person's perspective; they choose more egocentric goals; they have more aggressive reaction patterns stored in their memory; they evaluate the consequences of aggressive behaviour more positively; and they possess fewer skills for engaging in non-aggressive interaction (e.g. Crick and Dodge, 1994; Lösel and Bliesener, 2003). This type of information processing makes aggression a subjectively consequent reaction to their environment.

Schemes of social information processing can also serve as an 'interface' between a strong consumption of violence in the mass media and aggressive behaviour. Research has shown that mass media have an unfavourable influence when children are already predisposed to aggression or emotionally deprived (Bushman, 1995; Huesmann and Miller, 1994). Obviously, there are some serious single cases in which children or adolescents may have imitated serious acts of violence from videos or other mass media directly (Glogauer, 1993). However, the broader effects and the breeding ground for acts of violence come from a habituation to violent acts, the internalisation of dehumanisation, and a consolidation of aggression-prone cognitive schemes (Huesmann and miller, 1994; Selg, 1990). Given such potentials, children are more easily predisposed to react more aggressively when faced with difficult situations.

Through their social experiences and self-reinforcing cognitive processes, antisocial young persons acquire attitudes and values that encourage their deviant behaviour. For example, they tolerate more deviance than others, evaluate aggression more positively, place more value on autonomy, put less emphasis on traditional achievement norms and have more negative attitudes towards established institutions (Gottfredson and Hirschi, 1990; Jessor *et al.*, 1992; Lösel and Bliesener, 2003). Group processes encourage such attitudes. Adolescents who join delinquent cliques or gangs increasingly develop a subcultural identification (Thornberry, 1998). Of course, deviant attitudes in adolescents should not always be viewed as negative, because they are typical for the phase of separating from the family and developing one's own identity. Less aggressive adolescents are also torn between the influences of the parental home and the peer group (Lösel and Bliesener, 2003). Nonetheless, critical thresholds are crossed if adolescents identify exclusively with deviant groups and subcultures.

The relation between self-evaluation and antisocial behaviour is also relatively complex. Deviant attitudes and behaviours can be an attempt to increase self-esteem. However, in contrast to widespread opinions, there is no consistent empirical relationship between low self-esteem and antisocial behaviour (Lösel and Schmucker, 2004). Although some aggressive children suffer from problems of self-worth, another subgroup does not possess a negative but an unrealistically high self-image (Baumeister, Smart and Boden, 1996). Insulting this fragile self-image may well contribute to aggression-prone information processing and violent reactions.

Deviant Lifestyle

Deviant cliques and subcultures encourage unstructured leisure-time activities, alcohol and drug abuse, risk taking in road traffic, risky sexual behaviour and other health risks related to antisocial behaviour. In many deviant young persons, this leads to the emergence of a broad syndrome of adolescent problem behaviour (Jessor *et al.* , 1992; Jungerm Terlouw and van der Heijden 1995; Lösel and Bliesener, 1998). In a moderate form, this is also typical for normal youth, and the different problem behaviours do not necessarily coincide. However, in most high-intensity cases, antisocial behaviour goes along with substance abuse (Lösel and Bliesener, 1998). This in turn increases the risk of committing serious offences under the influence of drugs or alcohol as well as the threat of poor achievement at school or work. As criminality progresses, this is joined by social stigmatisation and exclusion, which further reduce social opportunities and strengthen the negative momentum of criminal career (Hermann and Kerner, 1988).

During late adolescence and early adulthood, many persistently antisocial individuals have difficulties with their work and employment. They more frequently fail to commence vocational training or drop out of it (Göppinger, 1997; Sampson and Laub, 1993). With relatively poor educational qualifications, and at times even basic deficits in reading, writing, and arithmetic skills, they have fewer chances on the labour market. Should they manager to start a career, this often develops a negative trajectory with fluctuating unqualified short-term jobs and periods of unemployment. There are some cases in which delinquency follows on from unemployment; but most cases tend to reveal the opposite causal direction (Farrington, 2000). Hence, unemployment should always be viewed within the context of a young person's motivation. This is illustrated by the low success rates of job creation schemes for antisocial juveniles (Lipsey and Wilson, 1998). Being able to hold down a job seems to be more decisive. Naturally, the problem of negative work careers is enhanced when national or regional unemployment rates are also high (Sherman *et al.* , 1997).

If a young person has gone through such a prototypical trajectory of long-term and serious antisocial behaviour, problems may often continue into adulthood. Although criminal careers tend to fade out as time goes by, other difficulties persist (e. g. alcoholism, chronic unemployment, psychiatric problems, and violence in the family; Farrington, 1989). Such lifestyles and the inheritance of genetic information are, in turn, a risk for the next generation. However, here as well, the cycle is not closed (Bender and Lösel, 2005).

Risk Factors In The Neighbourhood And Community

The risks in the individual, family, school and peer group interact with those in the broader social context. These particularly include socially disintegrated and deprived neighbourhoods (see Catalano *et al.* , 1998; Eisner, 2001). Such neighbourhoods contain a high rate of poverty; an accumulation of persons on welfare; high levels of violence, alcoholism and drug use; and easy access to weapons (Sampson and Lauritsen, 1994; Thornberry, 1998). In these contexts, it is easy to find models for aggression, violence, delinquency and substance abuse. Although it is easy to disentangle family and person characteristics from those of the neighbourhood, both independent effects and interactions have been described (Oberwittler *et al.* , 2001; Wikstrom and Loeber, 2000). Interestingly, intact family relations can act as a buffer against the negative effects of a violent environment (Richters and Martinez, 1993), and a favourable environment may lower the risks from a difficult family background (Kupersmidt, Burchinal and Patterson, 1995). However, a negative environment seems to encourage antisocial behaviour, particularly in young persons with no massive familial and personal risks who develop more behaviour problems in adolescence than in childhood (Wikstrom and Loeber, 2000). For children who already come from very deprived families and exhibit early antisocial behaviour, the additional influence of the neighbourhood environment seems to be less important.

Structured Risk Assessment Instruments

The factors summarized above have been used to develop structured risk assessment instruments that aim to increase the validity of clinical prediction. These scales typically contain a number of risk items selected from reviews of research, crime theories and clinical considerations (Farrington and Tarling, 1985; Le Blanc, 1998). Items are summed to form a total risk score and may also reveal specific risks patterns (e. g. mainly family or child factors). Such instruments are used for screening, in-depth assessment and related risk management (e. g. for decisions on the child's placement or specific interventions). They can also be applied in differentiated evaluations of intervention programs. Instruments vary with respect to the age and gender of their clients, problem intensity in the target groups, theoretical and empirical foundations, the number and domains of risks included, scoring procedures, time required for assessment, information sources, institutional contexts of administration and other issues (e. g. Hoge and Andrews, 1996; Le Blanc, 2002). Although many instruments have been designed for application in the juvenile justice system (e. g. Achenbach, 1998; Barnoski, 2002; Borum, Bartel and Forth, 2002; Hoge, Andrews and Leschied, 1996), an increasing number are available for earlier assessment in the community and in clinical contexts (Augimeri *et al.* , 2001; Beuhring, 2002; Corrado, 2002; Doreleijers *et al.* , 2000). Some instruments focus on specific areas of risks, for example, more than 50 years ago Glueck and Glueck (1950) had already developed short scales for screening family risks. Other scales such as the child and youth versions of the Psychopathy Checklist-Revised (Hare 2001) focus on individual characteristics of young people (Forth, Kosson and Hare, 2002; Frick, Bodin and Barry, 2000). Most instruments contain factors from various areas of risk (e. g. individual, family, neighbourhood).

Risk assessment instruments need to comply with a number of methodological and practical criteria. Item content and scoring must be clearly explicated in order to meet standards of objectivity and reliability. Systematic training should precede the application of a complex scale. Instruments must maintain a balance between broadness of information and economy. When screening large groups, it is best to apply a stepwise gating procedure (Loeber, Dishion and Patterson, 1984). Items should refer to multiple contexts of behaviour and use multiple sources of independent information (Achenbach, McConaughy and Howell, 1987; Lösel *et al.* , 2005). They should tap not only static risks but also dynamic factors that can be changed by interventions. Information on risks should be complemented by data on protective factors and strengths; however, this is rarely the case (e. g. Bornum *et al.* , 2002). Although scales need to be sufficiently specific to the target child's age and gender, they should also enable systematic comparisons across groups and time. In many countries, cultural differences will need to be taken into account (Cooke and Michie, 2002). Legal and ethical aspects also need to be integrated in order to avoid stigmatization, violations of data protection and other problems (Le Blanc, 1998). Last but not least, instruments need to be backed up with ongoing research on their validity. In the following, we shall sketch two examples of risk assessment devices that are both scientifically founded and clinically relevant. Several other tools that may be of particular use to practitioners are discussed in Tiffin and Richardson (Appendix 1).

The Early Assessment Risk List

The Early Assessment Risk List for Boys (EARL-20B, Version 2; Augimeri *et al.*, 2001) was developed in the Under 12 Outreach Project (ORP) of the Earlscourt Child and Family Centre in Toronto, Canada (Howell, 2001). The programme contains various components for early antisocial children and their families. The EARL-20B was developed, tested and revised to meet the need for early detection and differentiated placement of at-risk children within this framework. Because some risk factors are not equally relevant for both genders, a specific instrument was created for girls (EARL-21G; Levene *et al.*, 2001). Both scales were derived from the empirical literature and clinical experience on aggression and violence in children under 12 years of age. They focus on risk factor between ages 6 and 12. However, attempts have also been made to extend the assessment to younger and older age groups. The structure of the instrument is similar to other well-known risk assessment devices from this research group that address violent offenders (HCR-20; Webster *et al.*, 1997) and sexually violent offenders (SVR-20; Boer *et al.*, 1997). To attain transparency and objectivity, each item is defined precisely and scored on a three-point scale. As Table 3, 2 shows, items are structured into three domains; family, child and responsivity. Various pilot studies suggest that the scale is both reliable and valid (Webster *et al.*, 2002). However, more long-term and large-scale evaluations are still needed.

The Krakow Instrument of Risk Assessment

This tool has been developed at the Simon Fraser University, Vancouver, Canada (Corrado, 2002; Odgers, Vincent and Corrado, 2002). It is an outcome of a NATO Advanced Research Workshop held at Krakow, Poland. The instrument covers a particularly broad range of risks. Its items are derived from empirical studies and clinical experience. A specific feature of this tool is that it differentiates between the developmental stages of the respective child and thus has different scales covering Conception-Birth, Early Childhood (age 0—5), Middle Childhood (age 5—12), and Adolescence (age 13—18). The assessment of middle childhood, for example, covers those risk factors that were already present at birth and during early childhood plus factors that emerged later.

Sometimes, the content of an item varies with age (e. g. biological parents at birth and caregiver later). items are well described and coded on a three-point severity rating. Furthermore, each item requires notes on the kind of information or data sources on which the specific rating is based. A second coding addresses the most critical items in each case. The most critical issues for each child are those that must be targeted for the highest intensity of intervention. Risk items are grouped into five areas: environmental, individual, family, interventions and externalising behaviour. Table 3 summarises the contents of the tool for different child ages.

Table 2 Items in the Revised Early Assessment Risk List for Boys
(EARL-20B; Augimeri *et al.* , 2001)

Family (F) items	Child(C) items	Responsivity(R) items
F1 Household circumstances	C1 Developmental problems	R1 Family responsivity
F2 Caregiver continuity	C2 Onset of behavioural difficulties	R2 Child responsivity
F3 Supports	C3 Abuse/neglect/trauma	
F4 Stressors	C4 Hyperactivity/impulsivity/attention deficits	
F5 Parenting style	C5 Likeability	
F6 Antisocial values and conduct	C6 Peer socialisation	
	C7 Academic performance	
	C8 Neighbourhood	
	C9 Authority contact	
	C10 Antisocial attitudes	
	C11 Antisocial behaviour	
	C12 Coping abilities	

Because the Krakow Instrument is relatively new, its predictive validity needs further investigation. Preliminary data from our own developmental and prevention study on kindergarten children (Lösel *et al.* , 2004) have revealed significant correlations between both the Pre-Perinatal Score and the Early Childhood Score and antisocial behaviour several years later. Correlations for the Early Childhood Scale were higher, ranging from approximately 0. 20 to 0. 40 (depending on the length of follow-up and outcome criterion).

Such effect sizes are rather typical. With the exception of previous antisocial behaviour, most correlations between single predictors and outcome are small ($r = 0.10$ to 0.20;

Lösel, 2002). Nearly all predictors are more or less interrelated, and the low base rate of serious cases sets a further limit for prediction. As a consequence, a correlation of 0.40 to 0.50 or approximately 20 per cent explained variance is a typical upper threshold in the early prediction of antisocial behaviour and violence. Such effect sizes are by no means trivial because they confirm that more than 80 per cent of cases can be predicted correctly (Hawkins *et al.*, 1998; Lipsey and Derzon, 1998). Although there remains a substantial proportion of false positives and false negatives, careful early risk assessment is the cornerstone for a differentiated risk management through measure of prevention and intervention.

Table 3   contents of the Krakow Risk Assessment Instrument
(Corrado 2002; Odgers *et al.*, 2002)

Environmental	Family
E1 Obstetrical complications(PP→)	F1 Teenage pregnancy(PP→)
E2 Maternal substance use in pregnancy(PP→)	F2 Maternal/parental coping ability(PP→)
E3 Community disorganization(PP→)	F3 Parental antisocial practices/attitudes(PP→)
E4 Family socio-economic status (PP→)	F4 Family supports(PP→)
E5 Residential mobility(EC→)	F5 Family conflict/domestic violence(PP→)
E6 Exposure to violence (EC→)	F6 Sibling delinquency (EC→)
E7 Peer socialisation(EC→)	F7 Ineffective parenting(EC→)
E8 School environment (EC→)	F8 Early caregiver disruption and attachment
Other E (optional) (PP→)	(EC→)
	Other F (opt.) Parental education and IQ (PP→)
Individual	
11 Birth deficiencies (PP→)	Family structure/single parent family (PP→)
12 Parental history of mental illness (PP→)	**Interventions**
13 Executive dysfunction (EC→)	IV1 Previous interventions (specify) (PP→)
14 Chronic under-arousal (EC→)	IV2 Accessibility to interventions (PP→)
15 Cognitive delays/disorders (EC→)	IV3 Family responsivity to intervention (PP→)
16 Personality traits/disorders (EC→)	IV4 Child responsivity to intervention (EC→)
17 Other mental illnesses (EC→)	Other IV considerations (optional) (PP→)
18 Antisocial attitudes (EC→)	
19 Poor coping abilities (EC→)	
110 School functioning (EC→)	**Externalising behaviour**
Other 1(optional) (PP→)	EB1 General behavioural problems (EC→)
	EB2 Violence and aggression (EC→)

Environmental	Family
	EB3 Substance use(MC→)
	EB4 General offending (MC→)
	EB5 Considerations (optional) (MC→)

PP→=Pre-/Perinatal and later; EC→=Early Childhood and later; MC→=Middle Childhood and later.

PROTECTIVE FACTORS AND INTERVENTIONS

Naturally, all the links in the above-mentioned chain of development do not need to be present in the single case. Nonetheless, their accumulation is accompanied by a market increase in the risk of a serious and long-term negative development (Farrington, 1997a; Hawkins *et al.* , 1998; Lose and Bliesener, 2003). Vice versa, positive characteristics or experience in some domains may disrupt a negative chain reaction. Although this may be an outcome of deliberate interventions, it also occurs within the natural context of development. When protective factors are available to young people, they may show positive social development despite high risk of antisocial behaviour, or they may abandon their problem behaviour after a difficult phase. The mechanisms underlying such trajectories are less well investigated than the risks (e. g. Lösel and Bliesener, 1994; Sampson and Laub, 2003; Werner and Smith, 1992). It is also more difficult to implement adequate research designs in this field (Lösel and Bender, 2003; Luthar, Cicchetti and Becker, 2000). Of course, one can assume that the opposite to the risk value of the variables listed in Table 1 may promote positive development. However, truly protective effects need to compensate a given high-risk constellation (moderator approach; Rutter, 1985). The available research suggests a number of factors that may protect from the risks of antisocial behaviour. Table 4 reports a selection of such personal and social resources that have already been proven or may be promising (for a detailed review see Lösel and Bender 2003).

Table 4   multilevel examples for protective factors against serious antisocial behaviour (Lösel and Bender 2003)

Biological/biosocial	Non-deviant close relatives; no genetic vulnerabilities; high arousal; normal neurological and hormonal functioning
Pre-and perinatal	Non-alcoholic mother; no maternal smoking during pregnancy; no birth complications

Biological/biosocial	Non-deviant close relatives; no genetic vulnerabilities; high arousal; normal neurological and hormonal functioning
Child personality	easy temperament; inhibition; ego-resiliency; intelligence; verbal skills; planning for the future; self-control; social problem-solving skills; victim awareness, secure attachment; feelings of guilt; school and work motivation; special interests or hobbies; resistance to drugs
Cognitions/attitudes	Non-hostile attributions; non-aggressive response schemes; negative evaluation of aggression; self-efficacy in prosocial behaviour; non-deviant beliefs; realistic self-esteem; sense of coherence
Family	No poverty; income stability; harmony; acceptance; good supervision; consistency; positive role models; continuity of caretaking; no disadvantage; availability of social support
School	Achievement and bonding; low rate of aggressive students; climate of acceptance, structure, and supervision
Peer group	Non-delinquent peers; support from close, prosocial friends
Community	Non-deprived, integrated and non-violent neighbourhood; availability of professional help
Situational	Target hardening, victim assertiveness; social control
Legal	Effective firearm and drug control; effective criminal justice interventions
Cultural	low violence; tradition of moral values; shame-and guilt-orientation; low exposure to violence in the media

As with risks, protective factors also reveal cumulative effects (Stattin, Romelsjö and Stenbacka 1997). Depending on their specific combination with other characteristics, some factors may also serve both a risk and a protective function. For example, Bender and Lösel (1997) found that although satisfaction with social support protected high-risk youth with low antisociality from a negative development, it increased problem behaviour in those juveniles who were already deviant. When looking at the interplay of risk and protective factors, it is always necessary to phrase one's questions in a differentiated way and ask 'risk of what and protection against what?' For example, anxiety and social withdrawal are protective factors against antisocial development, but they may enhance the risk for depression and other internalising problem.

Because protective effects become increasingly rare the greater and more permanent the individual disorder and social disorganization, professional prevention and intervention programmes need to compensate for deficits in natural resources. Various reviews have shown that early developmental prevention and intervention can effectively counter antisocial behaviour (e. g. Farrington and Welsh, 2003; Kazdin, 1998; Lösel, 2005; Lösel and

Beelmann, 2003, 2005; Tremblay and Japel, 2003; Utting, 2003; see also Chapter 9 of this volume). However, overall effects are only small to medium and outcomes vary greatly. Because of the many different risk factors, multimodal programmes that address various areas of risk are most promising. In the field of child skills training, for example, we found the largest effects for social-cognitive programmes addressing both cognitive and behavioural skills in non-aggressive social problem solving (Lösel and Beelmann, 2005). Relatively successful family-oriented prevention programmes contain combinations of parent trainings and child trainings (Conduct Problems Prevention Research Group 2002; Tremblay et al. , 1995), multitargeted early home visits for single mothers (Olds et al. , 1998), intensive preschool programmes for children and related parent counseling (Schweinhart, Barnes and Weikart, 1993) or multisystemic therapy (Henggeler et al. , 1998). Both child- and family-oriented programmes reveal larger effects when they address children who already show behaviour problems (indicated prevention). The age of children does not relate significantly to outcome (Farrington and Welsh, 2003; Lösel and Beelmann, 2003). This is encouraging because it indicates that it may be neither too early nor too late to promote protective mechanisms.

Hence, the literature on young offender treatment also demonstrates the inappropriateness of the 'nothing works' doctrine (Lipsey and Wilson, 1998; Lösel, 1995; McGuire, 2002). Theoretically well-founded, structured cognitive-behavioural, social-therapeutic, multimodal and family-oriented programmes are particularly promising. The contents of effective treatment and prevention seem to be rather similar (Lösel, 2005). Therefore, instead of prevention versus treatment, we need integrated approaches to what works during different phases of development and at different degrees of deviance. This is in line with the discovery of a broad range of risk factors emerging at various ages in a child's development.

CONCLUSION

Many violent andotherwise seriously antisocial youngsters show early-starting and persistent problem behaviour. Numerous factors enhance the risk of such a development and facilitate chain reactions leading towards chronic problem. Particularly important are biological vulnerabilities; temperament characteristics, neuropsychological deficits, and early problem behaviour in the child; structural problems, economic disadvantage, multiple stressors, disharmony, abuse, neglect, and poor parenting in the family; school failure, truancy, and a problematic school context; affiliation with deviant peer groups or gangs; aggression-prone schemes of social information processing and deviant attitudes; antisocial lifestyle; and deprived and violent neighbourhoods. Although most single factors only reveal a small effect, their accumulation strongly increase the risk of serious problems. Natural protective factors or professional interventions can interrupt such chain reactions by reducing specific risks or compensating for their impact. Systematic and clinically relevant instruments may help to improve the practice of risk assessment and management. Prevention and intervention should use such information on the overall risk as well as on specific patterns of risks, needs and protective potentials in each individual case.

ACKNOWLEDGEMENT

Work on this chapter was supported by grants from the Oak Foundation and the German Ministry for Family Affairs, Seniors, Woman, and Youth.

References

Achenbach, T, M. (1998) 'Diagnosis, assessment, taxonomy, and case formulations.' In T. H. Ollendick and M. Hersen (eds) *Handbook of Child Psychology*. New York: Plenum Press.

Achenbach, T. M., McConaughy, S. H. and Howell, C. T. (1987) 'Child/adolescent behavioral and emotional problems: Implications of cross-informant correlations for situational specifity.' *Psychological Bulletin 101*, 213 – 232.

Ainsworth, M. D. S. (1991) 'Attachments and other affectional bonds across the life cycle.' In C. M. Parkes, J. Stevenson-Hinde and P. Marris (eds) *Attachment Across the Life Cycle*. London: Routledge.

Archer, J. (1991) 'The influence of testosterone on human aggression.' *British Journal of Psychology 82*, 1 – 28.

Augimeri, L. K., Koegl, C. J., Webster, C. D. and Levene, K. S. (2001) *Early assessment Risk List for boys (EARL-20B), Version 2*. Toronto: Earlscourt Child and

Family Centre.

Bandura, A. (1979) 'The social learning perspective: Mechanisms of aggression.' In H. Toch (ed) *Psychology of Crime and Criminal Justice*. New York: Holt, Rinehart and Winston.

Barnoski, R. (2002) 'Monitoring vital signs: Integrating a standardized assessment into Washington State's Juvenile Justice System.' In R. Corrado, R. Roesch, S. Hart and J. Gierowski (eds) *Multi-Problem Violent Youth: A Foundation for Comparative Research on Needs, Interventions and Outcomes*. Amsterdam: IOS Press/NATO Science Series.

Baumeister, R. F. , Smart, L. and Boden, J. M. (1996) 'Relation of threatened egotism to violence and aggression: The dark side of high self-esteem.' *Psychological Review 103*, 5 – 33.

Bender, D. and Lösel, F. (1997) 'Protective and risk effects of peer relations and social support on antisocial behaviour in adolescents from multi-problem milieus.' *Journal of Adolescence 20*, 260 – 271.

Bender, D. and Lösel, F. (2005) 'Risikofaktoren, Schutzafaktoren und Resilienz bei Misshandlung und Vernachlassigung' [Risk factors, protective factors and resilience in child abuse and neglect]. In U. T. Egle. S. O. Hoffmann and P. Joraschky (eds) *sexueller Missbrauch, Missbandlung. Vernachlassigung* [*Sexual Abuse, Physical Abuse, and Neglect*], 3 rd edn. Stuttgart: Schattauer.

Beuhring, T. (2002) 'The Risk Factor Profile Instrument: Identifying children at risk for serious and violent delinquency.' In R. Corrado, R. Roesch, S. Hart and J. Gierowski (eds) *Multi-problem Violent Youth*. Amsterdam: IOS Press/NATO Science Series.

Blackburn, R. (1993) *The Psychology of Criminal Conduct*. Chichester: Wiley.

BMI and BMJ (eds) (2001) *Erster Periodiscber Sicherheitsbericht* [*First Periodic Report on Public Safety*]. Berlin: Bundesministerium des Innern und Bundesministerium der Justiz.

Boer, D. P. , Hart, S. D. , Kropp, P. R. and Webster, C. (1997) *Manual for the Sexual Violence Risk-20. Professional Guidelines for Assessing Risk of Sexual Violence*. Burnaby, Canada: Mental Health, Law, and Policy Institute, Simon Fraser University.

Borum, R. , Bartel, P. and Forth, A. (2002) *Manual for the Structured Assessment of Violence Risk in Youth (SAVRY)*. Tampa, Fl: University of South Florida.

Brennan, P. A. , Mednick, S. A. and Raine, A. (1997) 'Biosocial interactions and violence: A focus on perinatal factors. ' In A. Raine, P. A. Brennan, D. P. Farrington and S. A. Mednick (eds) *Biosocial Bases of Violence*. New York: Pleum Press.

Bushman, B. J. (1995) 'Moderating role of trait aggressiveness in the effect of violent media on aggression. ' *Journal of Personality and Social Psychology 69*, 950 – 960.

Cairns, R. B. and Cairns, B. D. (1991) 'Social cognition and social networks: A developmental perspective. ' In D. J. Pepler and K. H. Rubin (eds) *The Development and Treatment of Childhood Aggression.* Hillsdale, NJ: Erlbaum.

Caspi, A. , McClay, J. , Moffitt, T. E. *et al.* (2002) 'Role of genotype in the cycle of violence in maltreated children. ' *Science 297*,851 – 854.

Cassidy, J. , Scolton, K. L. , Kirsh, S. J. and Parke, R. D. (1996) 'Attachments and representations of peer relationships. ' *Developmental Psychology 32*, 892 – 904.

Catalano, R. F. , Arthur, M. W. , Hawkins, J. D. , Berglund, L. and Olson, J. L. (1998) 'Comprehensive community and school-based interventions to prevent antisocial behavior. ' In R. Loeber and D. P. Farrington (eds) *Serious and Violent Juvenile Offenders*: ' *Risk Factors and Successful Interventions. '* Thousand Oaks, CA: Sage.

Conduct Problems Prevention Research Group (2002) 'Evaluation of the first three years of the fast track prevention trail with children at high-risk for adolescent conduct problems. ' *Journal of Abnormal Child Psychology 30*, 1 – 17.

Conry, J. and Fast, D. K (2000) *Fetal Alcohol Syndrome and the Criminal Justice System.* Vancouver: Law Foundation of British Columbia.

Cooke, D. J. and Michie, C. (2002) 'Towards valid cross-cultural measures of risk. ' In R. Corrado, R. Roesch, S. Hart and J. Gierowski (eds) *Multi-Problem Violent Youth.* Amsterdam: IOS Press/ NATO Science Series.

Corrado, R. (2002) 'An introduction to the risk/needs case management instrument for children and youth at risk for violence: The Cracow Instrument. ' In R. Corrado, R. Roesch, S. Hart and J. Gierowski (eds) *Multi-Problem Violent Youth*:*A foundation for Comparative Research on Needs*, *Interventions and Outcomes.* Amsterdam: IOS Press/NATO Science Series.

Crick, N. R. and Dodge, K. A. (1994) 'A review and reformulation of social information-processing mechanisms in children's social adjustment. ' *Psychological Bulletin 115*, 74 – 101.

Doreleijers, Th. A. H. , Moser, F. , Thijs, P. , van Engeland, H. and Beyaert, F. H. m.

(2000) 'Forensic assessment of juvenile delinquents: Prevalence of psychopathology and decision-making at court in the Netherlands.' *Journal of Adolescence* *23*, 263 – 275.

Eisner, M. (2001) 'Kriminalitat in der Stadt-Ist Desintegration das Problem?' [Crime in the city: Is disintegration the problem?] In J. M. Jehle (ed) *Raum und Kriminaliät* [*Space and Crime*]. Monchengladbach: Forum Verlag.

Elliott, D. S. (1994) 'Serious violent offenders: Onset, development course, and termination.' *Criminology 32*, 1 – 21.

Elliott, D. S., Huizinga, D. and Menard, S. (1989) *Multiple Problem Youth: Delinquely, Substance Use, and Mental Health Problem*. New York: Springer.

Eysenck, H. J. (1977) *Crime and Personality*. St Albans: Paladin Frogmore.

Fagot, B. I. and Pears, K. C. (1996) 'Changes in attachment during the third year: Consequences and predictions.' *Development and Psychopathology 8*, 325 – 344.

Farrington, D. P. (1989) 'Long-term prediction of offending and other life outcomes.' In H. Wegener, F. Lösel and J. Haisch (eds) *Criminal Behavior and the Justice System; Psychological Perspectives*. New York: Springer.

Farrington, D. P. (1992) 'Psychological contributions to the explanation, prevention, and treatment of offending.' In F. Lösel, D. Bender and T. Bliesener (eds) *Psychology and Law: International Perspective*. Berlin: De Gruyter.

Farrington, D. P (1997a) 'Early predictions of violent and nonviolent youthful offending.' *European Journal on Criminal Policy and Research 5*, 51 – 66.

Farrington, D. P. (1997b) 'The relationship between low resting heart rate and violence.' In A. Raine, P. A. Brennan, D. P. Farrington and S. A. Mednick (eds) *Biosocial Bases of Violence*, New York: Plenum Press/NATO ASI Series.

Farrington, D. P. (1998) 'Predictors, causes, and correlates of male youth violence.' In M. Tonry and M. H. Moore (eds) *Youth Violence. Crime and Justice*, Vol. 24. Chicago: University of Chicago Press.

Farrington, D. P. (2000) 'Explaining and Preventing crime: The globalization of knowledge.' *Criminology 38*, 801 – 824.

Farrington, D. P. (2005) 'The integrated cognitive antisocial potential (ICAP) theory.' In D. P. Farrington (ed) *Integrated Developmental and Life-Course Theories of Offending*. New Brunswick, NJ: Transaction Publishers.

Farrington, D. P. and Loeber, R. (2001) 'Summary of key conclusions.' In R. Loeber and D. P. Farrington (eds) *Child Delinquents*. Thousand Oaks, CA: Sage.

Farrington, D. P. and Tarling, R. (eds) (1985) *Prediction in Criminology*. Albany, NY: State University of New York Press.

Farrington, D. P. and Welsh, B. C. (2003) 'Family-based prevention of offending; A meta-analysis.' *Australian and New Zealand Journal of Criminology 36*, 127 – 151.

Farrington, D. P, Loeber, R., Elliot, D. S., Hawkins, J. D., Kandel, D. B., Klein, M. W., McCord, J., Rowe, D. C. and Tremblay, R. E. (1990) 'Advancing knowledge about the onset of delinquency and crime.' In B. Lahey and A. E. Kadzin (eds) *Advances in Clinical Child Psychology*, Vol. 5. New York: Plenum, pp. 283 – 342.

Fergusson, D. M. and Woodward, L. J. (1999) 'Maternal age and educational and psychosocial outcomes.' *Journal of Child Psychology and Psychiatry 40*, 479 – 489.

Fergusson, D. M. Woodward, L. J. and Horwood, L. J. (1998) 'Maternal smoking during pregnancy and psychiatric adjustment in late adolescence.' *Archives of General Psychiatry 55*, 71 – 77.

Forth, A., Kosson, D. and Hare, R. D. (2002) *The Hare Psychopathy Checklist: Youth Version (PCL-YV)*. Toronto: Multi-Health Systems.

Frick, P. J. (1998) *Conduct Disorders and Severe Antisocial Behavior*. New York: Plenum Press.

Frick, P. J., Bodin, S. and Barry, C. (2000) 'Psychopathic traits and conduct problems in community and clinic-referred samples of children: Further development of the psychopathy screening device.' *Psychological Assessment 12*, 382 – 393.

Glogauer, W. (1993) *Kriminalisierung von Kindern und Jugendichen durch Medien* [*The Mass Media and Crime in Children and Youth*]. Baden-Baden: Nomos.

Glueck, S. and Glueck, E. (1950) *Unraveling Juvenile Delinquency*. Cambridge, MA: Harvard University Press.

Göppinger, H. (1997) *Kriminologie* [*Criminology*], 5th edn. Munchen: Beck.

Gottfredson, D. (2001) *Schools and Delinquency*. Cambridge: Cambridge University Press.

Gottfredson, M. and Hirschi, T. M. (1990) *A General Theory of Crime*. Stanford, CA: Stanford University Press.

Hagell, A. (1998) *Dangerous Care*. London: Policy Studies Institute.

Hare, R. D. (2001) 'Psychopaths and their nature: Some implications for understanding human predatory violence.' In A. Raine and J. Sanmartin (eds) *Violence and Psychopathy*. New York: Kluwer Academic/ Plenum Publishers,

Harris, J. R. (1995) 'Where is the child's environment? A group socialization theory of development.' *Psychological Review 102*, 458 – 489.

Hawkins, J. D. , Herrenkohl, T. , Farrington, D. P. , Brewer, D. , Catalano, R. F. and Harachi, T. W. (1998) 'A review of predictors of youth violence.' In R. Loeber and D. P. Farrington (eds) *Serious and Violent Juvenile Offenders: Risk Factors and Successful Interventions*. Thousand Oaks, CA: Sage.

Henggeler, S. W. , Schoenwald, S. K. , Borduin, C. M. , Rowland, M. D. and Cunningham, P. B. (1998) *Multisystemic Treatment of Antisocial Behaviour in Children and Adolescents: Treatment Manuals for Practitioners*. New York: Guilford Press.

Hermann, D. and Kerner, H. J. (1988) 'Die Eigendynamik der Rückfallkriminalität' [The dynamics of reoffending.] *Kolner Zeitschrift fur Soziologic und Socialpsychologic 40*, 485 – 504.

Hill, H. M. , Soriano, F. L. , Chen, S. A. and LaFramboise, T. D. (1994) 'Sociocultural factors in the etiology and prevention of violence among ethnic minority youth.' In L. D. Eron and J. H. Gentry (eds) *Reason to Hope: A Psychosocial Perspective on Violence and Youth*. Washington, DC: American Psychological Association.

Hodgins, S. , Kratzer, L. and McNeil, T. F. (2002) 'Are pre and perinatal factors related to the development of criminal offending?' In R. R. Corrado, R. Roesch, S. D. Hart and J. K. Gierowski (eds) *Multi-Problem Violent Youth*. Amsterdam: IOS Press/NATO Science Series.

Hoge, R. D. and Andrews, D. A. (1996) *Assessing the Youthful Offender; Issues and Techniques*. New York: Plenum Press.

Hoge, R. D. , Andrews, D. A. and Leschied, A. W. (1996) 'An investigation of risk and protective factors in a sample of youthful offenders.' *Journal of Child Psychology and Psychiatry and Allied Disciplines 37*, 419 – 424.

Howell, J. C. (2001) 'Juvenile justice programs and strategies.' In R. Loeber and D. P. Farrington (eds) *Child Delinquents*. Thousand Oaks, CA: Sage.

Huesmann, L. R. (1997) 'Observational learning of violent behavior: Social and biosocial processes.' In A. Raine, D. P. Farrington, P. Brennan and S. A. Mednick (eds)

Biosocial Bases of Violence. New York: Plenum Press.

Huesmann, L. R. and Miller, L. S. (1994) 'Long-term effects of repeated exposure to media violence in childhood.' In L. R. Huesmann (ed) *Aggressive Behavior: Current Perspectives.* New York: Plenum.

Hyde, J. S. (1984) 'How large are gender differences in aggression? A developmental meta-analysis.' *Developmental Psychology 20*, 722 – 736.

Jeyarajah-Dent, R. (1998) *Dangerous Care: Working to Protect Children.* London: Bridge Child Care Development Service.

Jessor, R., Donocan, J. E. and Costa, F. M. (1992) *Beyond Adolescence: Problem Behavior and Young Adult Development.* Cambridge: Cambridge University Press.

Junger, M., Terlouw, G. J. and van der Heijden, P. G. M. (1995) 'Crime, accidents, and social support.' *Criminal Behaviour and Mental Health 5*, 386 – 410.

Kazdin, A. E. (1998) 'Psychosocial treatments for conduct disorder in children.' In P. E. Nathan and J. M. Gorman (eds) *A Guide to Treatments that Work.* New York: Oxford University Press.

Kellam. S. G., Ling, X., Merisca, R., Brown, C. H. and Ialongo, N. (1998) 'The effect of the level of aggression in the first grade classroom on the course and malleability of aggressive behavior into middle school.' *Development and Psychopathology 10*, 165 – 185.

Klein, M. W. (1995) *The American Street Gang: Its Nature, Prevalence and Control.* New York: Oxford University Press.

af Klinteberg, B. (1998) 'Biology and personality: Findings from a longitudinal project.' In D. J. Cooke, A. E. Forth and R. D. Hare (eds) *Psychopathy: Theory, Research and Implications for society.* Dordrecht, NL: Kluwer.

af Klinteberg, B. (2002) 'Underlying vulnerability influencing outcome factors/ behaviours in psychosocial disturbances.' In R. Corrado, R. Roesch, S. Hart and J. Gierowski (eds) *Multi-problem Violent Youth: A Foundation for Comparative Research on Needs, Interventions and Outcomes.* Amsterdam: IOS Press/ NATO Science Series.

Koglin, U. (2003) 'Die Soziale und Emotionale Entwicklung von Kindern mit Biologischen Risiken' [Social and Emotional Development of Children with Biological Risks]. Doctoral Dissertation. University of Erlangen-Nuremberg: Institute of Psychology.

Kolvin, I. , Miller, F. J, W. , Scott, D. McI. , Gatzanis, S. R. M. and Fleeting, M. (1990) *Continuities of Deprivation? The Newcastle 1000 Family Study*. Aldershot: Avebury.

Kraemer, G. W. (1997) 'Social attachment, brain function, aggression, and violence. ' In A. Raine, P. A. Brennan, D. P. Farrington and S. A. Mednick (eds) *Biosocial Bases of Violence*. New York: Plenum Press.

Kupersmidt, J. B. , Burchinal, M, and Patterson, C. J. (1995) 'Developmental patterns of childhood peer relations as predictors of externalizing behavior problems. ' *Development and Psychopathology 7*, 825 – 843.

Lahey, B. B. , Miller, T. L. , Gordon, R. A. and Riley, A. W. (1999) 'Developmental epidemiology of the disruptive behavior disorders. ' In H. C. Quay and A. E. Hogan (eds) *Handbook of Disruptive Behavior Disorder*. New York: Kluwer Academic/Plenum.

Laub, J. H. and Sampson, R. J. (2003) *Shared Beginnings, Divergent Lives: Delinquent Boys to Age 70*. Cambridge, MA: Harvard University Press.

Le Blanc, M. (1998) 'Screening of serious and violent juvenile offenders. ' In R. Loeber and D. P. Farrington (eds) *Serious and Violent Juvenile Offenders*. Thousand Oaks, CA: Sage.

Le Blanc, M. (2002) 'Review of clinical assessment strategies and instruments for adolescent offenders. ' In R. Corrado, R. Roesch, S. Hart and J. Gierowski (eds) *Multi-Problem Violent Youth*. Amsterdam: IOS Press/ NATO Science Series.

Lempp, R. (1977) *Jugendliche Mörder* [*Juvenile Murderers*]. Bern: Huber.

Levene, K. S. , Augimeri, L. K. , Pepler, D. , Walsh, M. , Webster, C. D. and Koegl, C. J. (2001) *Early Assessment Risk List for Girls, Version 1 (EARL-21G)*. Toronto: Earlscourt Child and Family Centre.

Lipsey, M. W. and Derzon, J. H. (1998) 'Predictors of violent or serious delinquency in adolescence and early adulthood. ' In R. Loeber and D. P. Farrington (eds) *Serious and Violent Juvenile Offenders: Risk Factors and Successful Interventions*. Thousand Oaks, CA: Sage.

Lipsey, M. W. and Wilson, D. B. (1998) 'Effective intervention for serious juvenile offenders: A synthesis of research. ' In R. Loeber and D. P. Farington (eds) *Serious and Violent Juvenile Offenders*. Thousand Oaks, CA: Sage.

Loeber, R. (1982) 'The stability of antisocial and delinquent child behavior. ' *Child De-*

velopment 53, 1431 – 1446.

Loeber, R. and Farrington, D. P. (eds) (1998) *Serious and Violent Juvenile Offenders*: *Risk Factors and Successful Interventions.* Thousand Oaks, CA: Sage.

Loeber, R. and Farrington, D. P. (eds) (2001) *Child Delinquents*: *Development*, *Intervention and Service Needs.* Thousand Oaks, CA: Sage.

Loeber, R. and Hay, D. H. (1994) ' Developmental approaches to aggression and conduct problems. ' In M. Rutter and D. H. Hay (eds) *Development Through Life*: *A Handbook for Clinicians.* Oxford: Blackwell.

Loeber, R. and Stouthamer-Loeber, M. (1998) ' Development of juvenile aggression and violence: Some common misconceptions and controversies. ' *American Psychologist 53*, 242 – 259.

Loeber, R. , Dishion, T. J. and Pattersion, G. R. (1984) ' Multiple gating: A multistage assessment procedure for identifying youths at risk for delinquency. ' *Journal of Research in Crime and Delinquency 21*, 7 – 32.

Loeber, R. , Farrington, D. P. , Stouthamer-Loeber, M. and van Kanmmern, W. B. (1998a) *Antisocial Behavior and Mental Health Problems.* Mahwah, NJ: Lawrence Erlbaum.

Loeber, R. , Farrington, D. P. and Waschbusch, D. A. (1998b) ' Serious and violent juvenile offenders. ' In R. Loeber and D. P. Farrington (eds) *Serious and Violent Juvenile Offenders*, Thousand Oaks, CA: Sage.

Loeber, R. , Homish, D. L. , Wei, E. H. *et al.* (2005) ' The prediction of Violence and homicide in young males. ' *Journal of Consulting and Clinical Psychology 73*, 1074 – 1088.

Lösel , F. (1995) ' The efficacy of correctional treatment: A review and synthesis of meta-evaluations. ' In J. McGuire (eds) *What Works*: *Reducing Reoffending. Guidelines Form Research and Practice.* Chichiester: Wiley.

Löesel, F. (2001) ' Nonviolence: Protective factors. ' In N. J. Smelser and P. B. Baltes (eds) *International Encyclopedia of the Social and Behavioral Science.* Oxford: Pergamon Press.

Lösel, F. (2002) ' Risk/need assessment and prevention of antisocial development in young people. ' In R. R. Corrado, R. Roesch, S. D. Hart and J. K. Gierowski (eds) *Multi-Problem Violent Youth.* Amsterdam: IOS Press/NATO Science Series.

Lösel, F. (2003a) 'The development of delinquent behavior. ' In D. Carson and R. Bull (eds) *Handbook of Psychology in Legal Contexts.* 2nd edn. Chichester: Wiley.

Lösel, F. (2003b) 'Grupprndelikte' [Group offending]. In R. Lempp, G. Schütze and G. Kohnken (eds) *Forensische Psychiatrie und Psychologie des Kindes-und Jugendalters* [*Forcnsic Psychiatry and Psychology in Childhood and Adolescence*]. 2nd edn. Darmstadt: Steinkopff.

Lösel, F. (2005) 'Evaluating developmental prevention of antisocial behavior: An example and a brief review. ' In A. Cerederecka, T. Jaskiewicz- Obdydzinska, R. Roesh and J. Wojcikiewicz (eds) *Forensic Psychology and Law.* Krakow: Forensic Research Publishers.

Lösel, F. and Beelmann, A. (2003) 'Effects of child skills training in preventing antisocial behavior: A systematic review of randomized evaluations. ' *Annals of the American Academy of Political and Social Science 587*, 84 - 109.

Lösel, F. and Beelmann, A. (2005) 'Social problem solving programs for preventing antisocial behavior in children and youth. ' In M. McMurran and J. McGuire (eds) *Social Problem Solving and Offending: Evidence and Evolution.* Chichester: Wiley.

Lösel, F. and Bender, D. (2003) 'Resilience and protective factors. ' In D. P. Farrington and J. Coid (eds) *Prevention of Adult Antisocial Behavior.* Cambridge: Cambridge University Press.

Lösel, F. and Bliesener, T. (1994) 'Some high-risk adolescents do not develop conduct problems: A study of protective factors. ' *International Journal of Behavioral Development 17*, 753 - 777.

Lösel, F. and Bliesener, T. (1998) 'Zum Einfluss des Familienklimas und der Gleichal- trigengruppe auf den Zusammenhang zwischen Substanzengebrauch und antisozialem Verhalten von Jugendlichen' [The impact of family climate and peer group on the relation between substance use and antisocial behaviour in youth]. *Kindheit und Entwicklung 7*, 208 - 220.

Lösel, F. and Bliesener, T. (2003) *Aggression und Delinquenz unter Jugendlichen: Unter- suchungen von kognitiven und sozialen Bedingungen* [*Aggression and Delinquency in Ad- olescence: Studies on Cognitive and Social Origins.*] Neuwied: Luchterhand.

Lösel, F. and Schmucker, M. (2004) 'Personlichkeit und Kriminalitat ' [Persönality and criminal behavior]. In K. Pawlik (eds) *Personlichkeitspsychologie* [*Personality*

Psychology], Vol. 5. Gottingen : Hogrefe.

Lösel, F. Toman, W. and Wustendorfer, W. (1976) 'Eine Untersuchung zum perzipierten elterlichen Erziehungsstil bei jugendlichen Delinquenten' [A study of perceived parental childrearing in juvenile delinquents]. *Zeitschrift für Experimentelle und Angewandte Psychologic 23*, 45 - 61.

Lösel, F. , Selg, H. , Müller-Luckmann, E. and Schneider, U. (1990) 'Ursachen, Prävention und Kontrolle von Gewalt aus psychologischer Sicht' [Origins, prevention, and control of violence from a psychological perspective]. In H. -D. Schwind and J. Baumann *et al.* (eds) *Ursachen, Pravention und Kontrolle von Gewalt. Analysen und Vorschlage der Unabhängigen Regierungskommission zur Verhinderung und Bekämpfung von Gewalt* [*Report of the German Federal Government's Commission on Origins. Prevention, and Control of Violence*]. Vol. 2. Berlin: Duncker and Humblot.

Lösel, F. , Beelman, A. , Jaursch, S. and Stemmler, M. (2004) *Soziale Kompetenz für Kinder und Familien* [*Social Competence for Children and Families*]. Berlin: Bundesministerium für Familie, Senioren, Frauen und Jugend.

Lösel, F. , Stemmler, M. , Beelmann, A. , and Jaursch, S. (2005) 'Aggressives Verhalten im Vorschulalter: Eine Untersuchung zum Problem verschiedener Informanten [Aggressive behaviour in preschool children: A study on the problem of different informants]. In I. Seiffge-Krenke (ed) *Aggressionsentwicklung zwischen Normalitat und Pathologie* [*The Development of Aggression Between Normality and Pathology*]. Göttingen: Vandenhoeck and Ruprecht.

Lösel, F. , Bliesener, T. and Bender, D. (in press) 'Social information processing, experiences of aggression in social contexts, and aggressive behavior in adolescents.' *Criminal Justice and Behavior.*

Luthar, S. S. , Cicchetti, D. and Becker, B. (2000) 'The construct of resilience: A critical evaluation and guidelines for future work.' *Child Development 71*, 543 - 562.

Lynam, D. R. (1996) 'Early identification of chronic offenders: Who is the fledgling psychopath?' *Psychological Bulletin 120*, 209 - 234.

McBurnett, K. , Lahey, B. B. and Pathouz, P. (2000) 'Low salivary cortisol and persistent aggression in boys referred for disruptive behavior.' *Archives of General Psychiatry 57*, 38 - 43.

McCord, J. (1979) 'Some Child-rearing antecedents of Criminal behavior in adult men. '

Journal of Persenality and Social Psychology 37, 1477 – 1486.

McCord, J. and Ensminger, M. E. (1997) 'Multiple risks and comorbidity in an African-American population.' *Criminal Behaviour and Mental Health 7*, 339 – 352.

McGuire, J. (2002) 'Integrating findings from research reviews.' In J. McGuire (ed) *Offender Rehabilitation and Treatment: Effective Programs and Policies to Reduce Reoffending.* Chichester: Wiley.

Mason, D. A. and Frick, P. J. (1994) 'The heritability of antisocial behavior: A meta-analysis of twin and adoption studies.' *Journal of Psychopathology and Behavioral Assessment 16*, 301 – 323.

Miles, D. R. and Carey, G. (1997) 'Genetic and environmental architecture of human aggression.' *Journal of Personality and Social Psychology 72*, 207 – 217.

Moffitt, T. E. (1993) 'Adolescence-limited and life-course-persistent antisocial behavior: A developmental taxonomy.' *Psychological Review 100*, 674 – 701.

Moffitt, T. E. and Caspi, A. (2001) 'Childhood predictors differentiate life-course persistent and adolescence-limited pathways among males and females.' *Development and Psychopathology 13*, 355 – 375.

Moffitt, T, E. and Henry, B, (1991) 'Neuropsychological studies of juvenile delinquency and juvenile violence.' In J. S. Milner (ed.) *Neurospsychology of Aggression.* Boston: Kluwer.

Moffitt, T. E. , Caspi, A. , Dickson, N. , Silva, P. and Stanton, W. (1996) 'Childhood-onset versus adolescent-onset antisocial conduct problems in males: Natural history from ages 3 to 18 years.' *Development and Psychopathology 8*, 399 – 424.

Moffitt, T. E. , Caspi, A. , Rutter, M. and Silva, P. A. (2001) *Sex Differences in Antisocial Behavior: Conduct Disorder, Delinquency, and Violence.* Cambridge: Cambridge University Press.

Mortimore, P. (1995) "The positive effects of schooling." In M. Rutter (ed) *Psychological Disturbances in Young People: Challenge for Prevention.* New York: Cambridge University Press.

Nagin, D. S. and Land, K. C. (1993) 'Age, criminal careers, and population heterogeneity: Specification and estimation of a nonparamateric, mixed Poisson model.' *Criminology 31*, 327 – 362.

Oberwittler, D. , Blank, T. , Köllisch, T. and Naplava, T. (2001) *Soziale Lebenslagen und Delinquenz von Jugendlichen* [*Social Conditions and Juvenile Delinquency*]. Freiburg: Max-Planck-Institut für ausländisches und internationals Strafrecht.

Odgers, C. , Vincent, G. M. and Corrado, R. R. (2002) 'A preliminary conceptual framework for the prevention and management of multi-problem youth. ' In R. R. Corrado, R. Roesch, S. D. Hart and J. K. Gierowski (eds) *Multi-Problem Violent Youth*. Amsterdam: IOS Press/NATO Science Series.

Olds, D. L. , Henderson, C. R. jr. , Cole, R. , *et al.* (1998) 'Long-term effects of nurse home visitation on children's criminal and antisocial behavior: 15-year follow-up of a randomized controlled trail. ' *Journal of the American Medical Association 280*, 1238 – 1244.

Oliver, J. (1993) 'Intergenerational transmission of child abuse: Rates, research, and clinical implications. '*American Journal of Psychiatry 150*, 1315 – 1324.

Olweus, D. (1993) *Bullying at School*. Oxford: Blackwell.

Parker, J. G. , Rubin, K. H. , Price, J. M. and DeRosier, M. E. (1995) 'Peer relationships, child development, and adaptation: A developmental psychopathology perspective. ' In D. Cicchetti and D. J. Cohen (eds) *Developmental Psychopathology*, *Vol.* 2: *Risk*, *Disorder*, *and Adaptation*. New York: Wiley.

Patterson, G. R. , Reid, J. B. and Dishion, T. J. (1992) *Antisocial Boys*. Eugence, OR: Oregon Social Learning Center.

Patterson, G. R. , Forgatch, M. S. , Yoerger, K. L. , and Stoolmiller, M. (1998) 'Variables that initiate and maintain an early-onset trajectory for juvenile offending. ' *Development and Psychopathology 10*, 531 – 547.

Pike, A. , McGuire, S. , Hetherington, E. M. , Reiss, D. and Plomin, R. (1996) 'Family environment and adolescent depressive symptoms and antisocial behavior: A multivariate genetic analysis. '*Developmental Psychology 32*, 590 – 603.

Plomin, R. (1994) *Genetics and Experience*. Newbury Park: Sage.

Raine, A. (1993) *The Psychopathology of Crime: Criminal Behavior as a Clinical Disorder*. San Diego: Academic Press.

Raine, A. (1997) 'Antisocial behavior and psychopathology: A biosocial perspective and a prefrontal dysfunction hypothesis. ' In D. M. Stoff, J. Breiling and J. D. Maser (eds) *Handbook of Antisocial Behavior*. New York: Wiley.

Raine, A. , Brennan, P. and Mednick, S. A. (1994) 'Birth complications combined with early maternal rejection at age 1 year predispose to violent crime at age 18 years. ' *Archives of General Psychiatry 94*, 984 – 988.

Reiss, A. J. and Farrington, D. P. (1991) 'Advancing knowledge about co-offending: Results from a prospective longitudinal survey of London males' *Journal of Criminal Law and Criminology* 82, 360 – 395.

Richters, J. E. and Martinez, P. E. (1993) 'Violent communities, family choices, and children's chances: An algorithm for improving the odds.' *Development and Psychopathology 5*, 609 – 627.

Robins, L. J. (1978) 'Sturdy childhood predictors of adult antisocial behavior: Replications from longitudinal studies.' *Psychological Medicine 8*, 611 – 622.

Robins, L. N. and Price, R. K. (1991) 'Adult disorders predicted by childhood conduct problems: Results from the NIMH epidemiologic catchment area project.' *Psychiatry 54*, 116 – 132.

Rowe, D. C. (1994) *The Limits of Family Influence: Genes, Experience, and Behavior.* New York: Guilford Press.

Rutter, M. (1985) 'Resilience in the face of adversity. Protective factors and resistance to psychiatric disorder.' *British Journal of Psychiatry 147*, 598 – 611.

Rutter, M. (1990) 'Psychosocial resilience and protective mechanisms.' In J. Rolf, A. Masten, D. Cicchetti, K. Nuechterlerin and S. Weintraub (eds) *Risk and Protective Factors in the Development of Psychopathology.* New York: Cambridge University Press.

Rutter, M. Maughan, B. , Mortimer. P. and Ouston, P. (1979) *Fifteen Thousand Hours. Secondary schools and their Effects on Children.* Somerset: Open Books.

Rutter, M. , Giller, H. and Hagell, A. (1998) *Antisocial Behavior by young people.* Cambridge: Cambridge Vniversity Press.

Sampson, R. J. and Laub, J. H. (1993) *Crime in the Marking: Pathways and Turning Points Through Life.* Cambridge. MA: Harvard University Press.

Sampson, R. J. and Laub, J. H (2003) 'Life-course desisters? Trajectories of crime among delinquent boys followed to age 70. ' *Criminology 41*, 319 – 339.

Sampson, R. and Lauritsen, J. (1994) 'Violent victimization and offending: Individual-situational, and community-level risk factors. ' In A. J. Reiss and J. A. Roth (eds) *Understanding and Preventing Violence, Vol. 3: Social Influences.* Washington, DC: National Academy Press.

Schalling, D, Edman. G. Asberg, M. and Oreland, L. (1988) 'Platelet MAO activity associated with impulsivity and aggressivity. ' *Personality and Individual Differences 9* , 597 - 605.

Schweinhart, L. L. Barnes, H. V. and Weikart, D. P. (1993) *Significant Benefits : The High/Scope Perry Preschool Study through age 27.* Ypsilanti, MI : High/Scope Press.

Seguin, J. R. Nagin, D. Assaad, J. -M. and Tremblay, R (2004) ' Cognitive-neuropsychological function in chronic physical aggression and hyperactivity. ' *Journal of Abnormal Psychology 113* ,603 - 613.

Selg, H, (1990) ' Gewaltdarstellungen in Medien und ihre Auswirkungen auf Kinder und Jugendliche' [Violence in the media and their impact on children and youth]. *Zeitscbrift für Kinder-und Jugendpaychiatrie 13* , 152 - 156.

Sherman, L. W. Gottfredson, D. Mackenzie, D. , Eck. J. , Reuter, P, and Bushway, S. (1997) *Preventing Crime : What Works, What Doesn ' t, What ' s Promsing.* Washington, DC : US Department of Justice.

Stattin, H, and Magnusson, D, (1990) *Pubertal Maturation in Female Development.* Hillsdale, NJ : Erlbaum.

Stattin, H, Romelsjö, A, and Stenbacka, M. (1997) ' Personal resources as modifiers of the risk for future criminality. ' *British Journal of Criminology 37* , 198 - 223.

Steinhausen, H-Ch. , Willms, J. , and Spohr, H. (1993) "Long-term psychopathological and cognitive outcome of children with fetal alcohol syndrome. " *Journal of the Academy of Child and Adolescent Psychiatry 32* ,990 - 994.

Stouthamer-Loeber, M. , Loeber, R, Farrington, D. P. Zhang, Q, van Kammen, W. and Maguin, E. (1993) ' The double edge of protective and risk factors for delinquency : Interrelations and developmental patterns. ' *Development and psychopathology 5* ,683 - 701.

Susman, E. J. and Ponirakis, A. (1997) ' Hormones-context interactions and antisocial behavior in youth. ' In A. Raine, P. A. Brennan. D. P. Farrington and S. A. Mednick (eds) *Biosocial Bases of Violence.* New York : Plenum.

Thornberry, T. P. (1998) ' Membership in youth gangs and involvement in serious and violent offending. ' In R. Loeber and D. P. Farrington (eds) *Serious and Violent Juvenile Offenders : Risk Factors and Successful Interventions.* Thousand Oaks, CA : Sage.

Traverso, G. B. and Bianchi, M. (2002) 'Adolescent murderers: A Genoa sample.' In R. Corrado, R. Roesch, S. Hart and J. Gierowski (eds) *Multi-problem Violent Youth*. Amsterdam: IOS Press/NATO Science Series.

Tremblay. R. E. (2000) "The development of aggressive behavior during childhood: What have we learned in the past century?" *International Journal of Behavioral Development* 24. 129 – 141.

Tremblay, R. E and Japel, C (2003) "Prevention during pregnancy, infancy, and the preschool years." In D. P Farrington and J. W. Coid (eds) *Early Prevention of Adult Antisocial Behavior*. Cambridge: Cambridge University Press.

Tremblay, R. E. Masse, L. C., Vitaro, F. and Dobkin, P. L. (1995) "The impact of friends' deviant behavior on early onset of delinquency: Longitudinal data from 6 to 13 years of age." *Development and psychopathology 7*, 649 – 667.

Tremblay, R. E. Schaal, B, Boulerice, B, Arseneault, L., Soussignan, R. and Perusse, D. (1997) 'Male physical aggression, social dominance and testosterone levels at puberty.' In A. Raine, D. P. Farrington, P. Brennan and S. A Mednick (eds) *Biosocial Bases of Violence*, New York: Plenum.

Tremblay, R. E. Nagin, D. S. Séguin, J. R. *et al.*, (2004) 'Physical aggression during early childhood: Trajectories and predictors.' *Pesiatrics 114*, 43 – 45.

Utting, D. (2003) 'Prevention through family and parenting programmes.' In D. P. Farrington and J. W Coid (eds) *Early prevention of Adult Antisocial behavior*. Cambridge: Cambridge University Press.

Virkkunen, M, Kallio, E. Rawlings, R. Tokala, R. Poland, R. E. Guidotti, A. *et al*, (1994) 'Personality profiles and state aggressiveness in Finnish alcoholic violent offenders, fire setters, and healthy volunteers.' *Archives of General Psychiatry 51*, 28 – 33.

Webster, C. D. Douglas, K. S, Eaves, D. and Hart, S, D. (1997) *HCR-20: Assessing Risk for Violence*, *Version 2*. Burnaby, BC: Mental Health, Law and Policy Institute; Simon Fraser University.

Weberster, C. D, Augimeri, L. K and Koegl, C. J. (2002) 'The Under 12 Outreach Project for antisocial boys: A research based clinical program.' In R. R. Corado, R. Roesch, S. D. Hart and J. K. Gierowski (eds) *Multi-problem Violent Youth*. IOS Press/ Nato Science Series. pp. 207 – 218.

Werner, E. E. and Smith, R. S. (1992) *Overcoming the Odds*. Ithaca: Cornell University Press.

White, A. J. and Heibrun, K. (1995) 'The classification of overcontrolled hostility: Comparison of two diagnostic methods.' *Criminal Behaviour and Mental Heath* 5, 106 – 123.

Widom, C. S. (1989) 'Does violence beget violence? A critical examination of the literature.' *Psychological Bulletin 106*, 3 – 28.

Wikström, P-O, and Loeber, R. (2000) 'Do disadvantaged neighbourhoods cause well-adjusted children to become adolescent delinquents? A study of male juvenile serious offending, risk and protective factors, and neighbourhood context,' *Criminology 38*, 1109 – 1142.

Wolfgang, M. E. Figlio, R. M. and Sellin, T. (1972) *Delinquency in a Birth Cobort* . Chicago, IL: Chicago University Press.

Zuckerman, M. (1994) *The Psychology of Sensation Seeking*. Cambridge: Cambridge University Press.

性犯罪干预的有效性:综合元分析

菲德律·洛赛尔(Friedrich Lösel)

马丁·斯马克(Martin Schmucker)

埃朗根·纽伦堡大学

在针对犯人的政策中,性罪犯的治疗方法是一个很重要的话题。媒体报告的很多以性动机驱动的严重犯罪包括谋杀、强奸、猥亵儿童等越来越受到人们的关注。而很多国家对此也制定出了大量惩罚和治疗并举的应对举措。由于大部分入狱的性犯罪者最终还是要回归社会,所以有效的治疗方法对未来性侵犯行为的预防有着举足轻重的地位。但当前已有的性犯罪治疗的经验还不足以预防未来性侵犯行为的发生。尽管最新的研究表明性犯罪人治疗有一些效果(Alexander, 1999;Aos et al., 2001;Gallagher et al., 2000;Hanson et al., 2002;Lösel, 2000;Polizzi et al., 1999),但是尚有瑕疵的研究方法、多种多样的研究结果以及质量不高的研究都让我们开始质疑是否真的存在有效处理性犯罪问题的对策(Lösel, 2000;Marques et al., 2005;Quinsey et al., 1993;Rice and Harris, 2003;White et al., 1998)。

实际上,与其他类型的犯罪治疗研究相比,高质量的关于评估性犯罪人疗效的研究并不多(Lipsey and Wilson, 1998;Lösel, 2001a;McGuire, 2002)。并且各种各样的设计与治疗方面的问题也混淆与掩盖了性犯罪人治疗是否真正有效的事实。

研究设计问题。相比较而言,案情较重的罪犯通常至少能接受某种治疗。这使得在研究中随机挑选没有治疗过的犯人作为对照组比较困难。官方相对较低机率的再犯率(Hanson and Bussiere, 1998)意味着我们需要大量的样本才能使研究取得显著效率。然而考虑到经济因素的局限性,评估性犯罪人治疗方法的研究经常只有一些小的样本。甚至在一些随机的研究设计中也有这样的现象存在。它大大减少了犯人被随机挑选的平等机率(Marques *et al.*, 2005)。进一步说,有选择性的放弃和其他的问题不仅使研究难以实施,也动摇了研究内部的可靠性(Barbaree, 1997; Marshall and McGuire, 2003)。除了总体上存在案件黑数问题之外,犯罪大都发生在有亲密关系的人之间。它大大削弱了官方数据的价值。

治疗方面的问题。对性犯罪的再犯情况的分析需要较长时间的后续跟踪调查(Prentky *et al.*, 1997),因此这方面的评估可能会涉及一些早期的研究项目,而这些项目已经不能准确反映现在性犯罪的情况了。此外,对性犯罪人的治疗研究还包括了大量的药物和心理治疗方面的研究,而且性犯罪人往往表现出群组上的异质性。因此,我们需要运用充分的差别化的评估和处理方法。并且性犯罪人通常不只接受一种治疗方案,而是接受大量因人而异的治疗"方案包"(比如说,心理和药物治疗;附加的酒精依赖治疗等)。而多种多样的治疗类型需要的评估方法也相对复杂。

相对于那些可以运用多种研究方法的研究领域,各种各样的问题使得我们对性犯罪治疗项目研究的系统性整合面临着更多的困难。因此,根据 Furby 在 1989 年的综合分析显示我们极少有良好设计的研究项目,并且得出"我们尚没有证据可以证明临床治疗可以降低性犯罪再犯率"的结论(第 27 页)。Cochrane 协会在九年后也得出了相类似的结论(White *et al.*, 1998)。由于把研究限制在随机评估,导致项目研究人员最终完成了三个项目的研究。其他近期的综合研究包括准实验研究也是如此。这也符合高质量的研究并非一维的"非全即无"的观念,我们能够从那些次优的研究中学到对实践有用的东西(Cronbach *et al.*, 1980; Lösel and Köferl, 1989; Shadish *et al.*, 2002)。

大多数的评估显示了治疗组平均性犯罪的再犯率较之对照组的要低。比如说 Hall 在 1995 年综合分析了 12 份的控制研究。治疗组平均性犯罪的再犯率是 19%,对照组是 27%(意味着影响范围:d = 0.24)。并且荷尔蒙治疗法和行为认知治疗比其他治疗方法成效更明显。然而,这些治疗效果的差别是建立在小样本的研究基础之上的,此外还发现单一的阉割治疗有显著的效果。亚历山大在 1999 年综合分析了 79 份关于心理治疗性犯罪人的研究。结果显示治疗过的性犯罪再犯率与对照组的相比相差约 5%(d = 0.12; Lösel and Schmucker, 2003)。但是还有大部分研究没有对照组(马里兰等级 1; Sherman *et al.*, 1997)。来自德语系国家的 20 份药物和心理治疗性犯罪人的综合分析也是如此。它的效果范围并不显著(d = 0.08; Lösel, 2000)。Gallagher 在 2000 年分析了 23 份质量相对较高的研究。治疗组比对照组的性犯罪再犯率低了大约 10%，并且其总体效果较好(d=0.47)。在近期研究中，汉森(Hanson)综合分析了 43 份关于性犯罪人心理治疗的研究。治疗组的性再犯率是 12.3%，对照组是 16.8%(d=0.13;Lösel and Schmucker, 2003)。过去的治疗大都收效甚微，目前的治疗项目，主要是行为认知治疗效果较好。

总体来说，过去十年性犯罪治疗评估的研究越来越多，前景越来越好。然而，这些综合研究在治疗效果、涉及的治疗类型、治疗主导方案的质量，项目的分类，实验环境以及综合分析的技巧方面都不一样。几乎所有的研究都来自北美的英语系国家。在这样背景的衬托下，一份全面的最新的独立的国际研究就具有了无与伦比的价值。这就是为什么康拜尔国际犯罪与司法合作组织要将对性犯罪人治疗研究项目的系统性调查纳入其议事范围的原因。这份研究也是我们综合分析的第一份研究材料。它包括 2003 年之前的英文以及其他语言版的心理和生理治疗的综合研究。

一、研究方法

(一)应包含的研究标准

主要的研究都必须符合以下的特征：

1. 对性犯罪人的研究。参与者必须曾经有性犯罪史或者曾经有过非法的性行为并经官方起诉定罪。

2. 对治疗的评估。只要是致力于减少再犯率的干预行为都不会受到限制(比如说心理和器质性的治疗模式，如荷尔蒙药物治疗，阉割手术)。然而，干预的举措必须结合治疗措施，单纯的威慑与惩罚措施不包括在内。治疗方案不一定要针对性犯罪人特别制定。如果研究项目涉及至少一个亚组的性犯罪人并且针对性犯罪人的治疗组和对照组各自形成研究结论，那么我们就应采取更多的常用治疗方法。

3. 再犯率的测量。再犯行为可以归类为因变量。我们将再犯采用广义的定义方法，再犯包括受到监禁或存在性侵犯方面的失误行为。而根据人格类型、荷尔蒙水平、医院的诊断结果以及其他结果来界定再犯的研究都不是我们的研究范围。

4. 对照组的设计。这项研究需要接受不同治疗方案的对照组产生与实验组相同的再犯率。因此对照组可以是未接受治疗的对照组，或者是一组接受常规治疗的性犯罪人，或者是其他项目内容与本项目内容、强度、特征。将中途退出的治疗人员作为对照组的研究将不符合我们的要求。

5. 样本大小。每个研究的最小样本量至少 10 人，其中至少有 5 位犯人。在特别小样本的研究中,哪怕是不同组重犯绝对数上的再少的差异,都可能导致极端的治疗效果,由此导致研究结果很不相同并且不可靠。

6. 足够的用于效果运算的数据。研究项目必须用可计算效果大小的方式形成研究报告。

7. 开展研究的国家。不限制研究的实施地。出于经济方面的考虑,我们的研究必须以英语、德语、法语、荷兰语或者是瑞士语形成研究成果。

8. 发布的时间。对发布时间没有严格的下限。所有发布于 2003 年 7 月之前的研究都符合标准。

(二)文献研究

我们计划搜集的研究评估可以是发表过的,也可以是未发表过的。为此,我们在各种各样的资料库中寻找相关研究。首先,通过对以前文献资料评论中的参考文献汇编了基本的研究库。其次,对那些已经明确的主要研究进行分析作为未来研究的参考。第三,我们分析了 14 个电子数据库(比如说 PsycInfo,MedLine,ERIC,Cochrane Library,Social Services Abstracts,NCJRS abstract and full-text databases,Dissertation Abstracts International,and UK National Health Service National Register)。第四,我们手工查找了一些与主题相关的杂志(Sexual Abuse,Journal of Sexual Aggression)。为了找到更多没有发布的文章,我们联系了性犯罪人治疗领域的专家了解是否有私下未发布的调查研究。最后,我们进行了网络搜集。因为网络的信息非常分散,我们无法全面地搜集。我们访问了相关的机构和监狱部门的网址,搜集了他们的相关信息,并找到了与他们相关的材料链接。

我们就用这种方法总共找到了 2039 份可供引用的文献资料。我们首先扫视了他们的标题。如果离题不是特别明显的话,我们还会查看摘要。如果这些只是表明材料可能相符或者文章没有摘要,我们会查看整篇报告以确保研究是符合条件的。报告中大约有 21 份(1%)研究报告无法找到(其中 18 份是没有摘要的)。总共 586 份引用是明确离题,242 份是关于一般犯人的研究,641 份并没有评价治疗项目。也就是说这些研究仅仅描述了治疗或者粗略地回顾了一下性犯罪人的治疗方法,没有深入评价治疗项目。最后还剩下 549 份引用文章是关于性犯罪人治疗评估的研究。而其中 189 份由于没有表明再犯的数据而被放弃,236 份没有完全使用对照组,56 份的评估是重复使用的,还有 2 份没有给出治疗效果的计算方法。最后 66 份报告符合具体的挑选标准。注意这里的一份报告其实包括了不止一项研究。针对这样的情况,我们把每个个体的研究作为一个分析单位。同时一些主要研究的结果适用在不同的次群体中(比如说不同的犯罪类型)。为了使差别显著化,同时又坚持作用范围的独立性的原则,我们还选择了次群体作为我们的研究单位。然而对次群体特征的说明必须跟整个样本一样的详细与清楚。根据这些原则,我们在69个研究中形成了80个比较组。

(三)给研究特征编码

编码遵循一份详细的操作守则。变量一块放在结果区(见于表1)。手册涉及了发表的一般特征(比如说发表年份,国家,发表的类型),样本描述(比如说样本的大小,犯人的类型,年龄,参与治疗的自愿度),研究方法的特征(比如说研究的设计,控制组的类型,跟踪研究的时间,再犯数据的来源)以及治疗的特征(比如说治疗的模式,治疗的环境,治疗的完整性,治疗的形式)。各种各样的性犯罪人治疗项目并不局限于某一治疗的范例而是中和了各种学派的治疗模式。因此,我们不仅把基本的治疗方法分类,而且把应用于个体干预的治疗因素分别归类到4个等级。

我们用综合评估体系整体评价每个研究方法的质量(比如说,做出了不同的选择,Farrington,2003)。我们根据自己的目标,改编了马里兰科学评估等级(Sherman *et al.*,1997)。它有5个等级。这5个等级综合了研究方法的特点,并根据因果分析来准确描述治疗效果。严格要求,随机挑选对象的研究编码为最高等级5,那些应用程序调整以确保每组之间的特征的相近(比如说,个体匹配、数据控制)或者是那些稍微有点瑕疵的随机设计编码为等级4。假定每组之间对象极为相近并随机挑选对象的研究等级编码为等级3(比如说已证明了相关变量的相似性的研究)。对照组被选中机率不同的研究则与编码2相对应。最后,编码1是用于表示那些失控的不符合我们综合分析标准的研究。在最原始的形态中,马里兰等级还涉及了样本的大小,数据测验充分度。然而,由于我们对治疗效果根据加权作用范围的方法对研究进行了整合,所以我们可以把相关性不大的方面在评价过程中舍弃了。

根据1989年的洛赛尔(Lösel)和考芬(Köferl)的研究,我们还对报告信息的完整度和准确率进行了评级。根据上述第四等的标准,这两个测量标准威胁到治疗概念,治疗实行,治疗目标的评测,以及治疗方法等领域"描述有效性"。

另一名作者对这些研究进行了编码。一位资深的评估员则对另外10份次样本进行编码。针对研究,评估员之间的一致性高达91%。对核心的变量比如说治疗类型,治疗设计的同一性达到了100%。对所有的变量评估,他们的一致性都不低于60%。

(四)对治疗效果的计算

在对治疗效果的计算上,我们采用优势比方法,这一方法广泛应用于二分类数据的运算(Fleiss,1994;Lipsey and Wilson,2001)。犯人治疗研究的主要结果是犯人的再犯率(p)或者治疗组和对照组的成功和失败人数的绝对数。其中 $TG_{Success}$,$TG_{Failure}$ 分别指治疗组中成功或失败人数的绝对数,$CG_{Success}$,$CG_{Failure}$ 分别指对照组中成功或失败人数的绝对数。在这样的条件下,我们应用了下列的公式来计算治疗效果:

$$OR = \frac{P_{CG} \times (1 - P_{TG})}{P_{TG} \times (1 - P_{CG})} \text{ 和 } OR = \frac{CG_{Failure} \times TG_{Success}}{TG_{Failure} \times CG_{Success}}$$

如果任何一组的 OR 值为 0,那么我们需要给每组 OR 值加上 0.5。一些研究里还出现了更为复杂的数据分析法。他们控制治疗组和控制组的数据差异。在这样的情况下,我们就不单一使用再犯率的数据,而是使用这些研究的结果。按照逻辑回归,这个系数与优势比的对数值(LOR)是相等的,如果作为 e 指数幂,也与优势比等值。这样有关治疗变量的结果就可以直接转换了。在回归分析过程中,研究结果以比值比的形式报告,比值比与优势比相似但不完全相同。我用比值比(RR)来评估对照组的再犯率以修正利用回归分析模型所造成的组别间的差异。(PCG = RR * PTG or PCG = RR/PTG,取决于主要研究中治疗项目变量的编码)。接着,我们运用了上述公式计算了优势比。极少有研究的实验数据不能转换成机会比率。如果有这样的情况的话,我们会使用正规的程序去计算 Cohen's d 值,(Lipsey and Wilson, 2001)。并且运用 $LOR = \frac{\pi}{\sqrt{3}} \times d$ 和 $OR = e^{LOR}$ 将它转换成优势比。

如果研究包括了许多独立的样本或次样本,我们则使用经比较后的具有内部最高可信度的样本(比如说一项研究中不仅有接受或未授受治疗的参与者再犯率的比较,或者附加了对这些组中子样本特征的匹配,那么我们会选择后一组的样本)。研究经常会出现多个结果变量。不同类型的再犯行为(比如说性犯罪、暴力犯罪、或者是一般再犯),会分别进行分析。如果研究使用了不同的失败指标(比如说再犯定义为犯人被指控了,被逮捕了,被定罪了,或者有过失的行为),治疗效果就需要分别编码,接着我们计算它们的平均数作为治疗效果的数据。

一些研究显示不同犯罪类型或者不同危险程度人群的研究结果不一样,但这并不符合以独立比较为标准的上述定义。此时,我们会分别计算经治疗后子群体的治疗效果,并运用加权平均数的方法以得出研究的治疗效果。

如果可能的话,我们也会把那些中途退出治疗的参与者也计算在治疗组内(包括那些想参加治疗的人)。然而我们还会拿他们与治疗和未经治疗的群体比较来评估治疗中止的人的治疗效果。

（五）数据整合与统计分析

数据的统计分析的对象是优势比的自然对数（Fleiss, 1994; Lipsey and Wilson, 2001）。为了整合治疗效果，我们在个体治疗效果的标准差基础上，运用了加权公式（Hedges and Olkin, 1985）。由于治疗效果的不同分布，我们采用了随机效果模式。在假定存在混合效果模式的情况下，我们运用了调节分析法对数据进行分析。

二、结　果

（一）描述性特征

表格 1 是分析中所要用到的各个研究与比较的特征的总体情况。大多数的研究来自北美。几乎三分之一的研究数据未被发布过。大多数还是最新的研究。几乎四分之三的研究发表于 1990 年之后。然而治疗这一栏显示，这些研究开始实施的时间更早。

几乎一半的比较研究涉及行为认知治疗项目。有两份研究，尽管采用了混合治疗的方法，但是非常地相似，所以我们把它们同样归类到这一子项目下。有 14 份比较研究是关于物理治疗，有 8 份是关于阉割手术的治疗。超过一半的研究表明，研究人跟项目之间都有密切的联系。大多数的治疗都是专门为性犯罪人设计的。然而，我们无法判断治疗实施是否可靠。只有四分之一的比较研究提供了一份证明治疗项目可靠与严谨的书面文稿。接近一半的治疗是在正规机构实行的。然而大多是集体接受治疗，还有近一半的治疗项目会包含一些个性化的治疗方法。其中仅有 15 个研究有治疗的延伸，会提供治疗后的照顾调养服务。

表1　综合分析中 80 个比较组的描述性特征

变量编码和分类	频数	比重（%）
一般研究的特征[a]		
发表的年份		
1980 年之前	7	10.1
1980s	11	15.9
1990s	29	42.0
2000 年后	22	31.9

变量编码和分类	频数	比重（%）
国家		
美国	31	44.9
加拿大	17	24.6
英国	8	11.6
德语系的国家	8	11.6
其他	5	7.2
发表的类型		
杂志论文	34	49.3
书，书中章节	10	14.5
未发布过	25	36.2
治疗的特征		
接受治疗的时间		
1970 年之前	14	17.5
1970s	17	21.3
1980s	30	37.5
1990s	19	23.8
治疗的模式		
认知行为模式	37	46.3
经典行为模式	7	17.5
认知导向模式	7	17.5
社区治疗	10	12.5
其他心理方面的模式或不明模式	5	6.3
荷尔蒙药物治疗	6	7.5
阉割手术	8	10.0
作者与治疗项目的联系		
有联系	42	52.5
没有联系	31	38.8
不清楚	7	8.8
有无提供因人而异的具体治疗		
有	64	80.0
没有	9	11.3
不清楚	7	8.8
实行治疗的公正性[b]		
可接受	18	25.0
有瑕疵	5	6.9
不清楚	49	68.1

变量编码和分类	频数	比重(%)
治疗环境		
监狱	25	31.3
医院	14	17.5
门诊部	29	36.3
混合型	10	12.5
不清楚	2	2.5
治疗的形式[b]		
只有集体的形式	18	22.5
主要是集体的形式	17	21.3
混合型	10	12.5
主要是个体的形式	8	10.0
只有个体的形式	7	8.8
不清楚	12	15.0
治疗后的照顾与调养		
必须	9	11.3
可选	6	7.5
没有提供或不清楚	65	81.3
犯人的特征		
按照年龄分类		
成年人	45	56.3
青少年	7	17.5
混合型	8	10.0
不清楚	20	25.0
年龄的均匀度		
高	7	17.5
中等	23	28.8
低	23	28.8
不清楚	27	33.8
犯罪类型[c]		
强奸	44	55.0
猥亵儿童	59	73.7
乱伦	38	47.5
露阴癖	24	30.0
摩擦癖,不是很具体	5	6.3
偷窥癖,不是很具体	5	6.3
不清楚	20	25.0

变量编码和分类	频数	比重（%）
参与治疗的情况		
自愿参与	37	46.3
非自愿参与	16	20.0
混合型	8	10.0
不清楚	19	23.8
研究方法的特点		
样本容量		
超过50	25	31.3
50—100	12	15.0
101—200	18	22.5
201—500	14	17.5
超过500	11	13.3
马里兰等级		
第二等级（挑选机率不同）	48	60.0
第三等级（假定相同的比例挑选）	19	23.8
第四等级（数据控制，相同比例的挑选）	7	8.8
第五等级（随机挑选）	6	7.5
不同组的相似性		
相似	20	25.0
不相似,治疗有更高的风险	14	17.5
不相似,对照组有更高的风险	4	5.0
不相似,但是方向不清楚	8	10.0
不相似,但是对数据进行了调控	5	6.3
不清楚	29	36.3
对照组的形成		
自愿接受治疗	13	16.3
没有提供治疗	14	17.5
没有治疗的义务	15	18.8
拒绝治疗	19	23.8
其他	10	12.5
不清楚	9	11.3
再犯的类型		
性犯罪	74	92.5
暴力犯罪	20	25.0
任何犯罪行为	49	61.3
跟踪的时间（月）		

变量编码和分类	频数	比重(%)
12—24	14	17.5
25—36	12	15.0
37—60	23	28.8
61—84	12	15.0
>84	19	23.8
再犯数据的来源		
仅以犯罪记录为准	64	80.0
自报案情	6	7.5
不清楚	10	12.5
再犯的定义		
逮捕	19	23.8
定罪	24	30.0
起诉	15	18.8
过失行为	3	3.8
复合结果	6	7.5
不清楚	13	16.3

备注：a. N=69。

　　b. K=72(无关于阉割治疗理由的合理分类)。

　　c. 对个体的比较可能涵盖多个分类。

　　7份比较研究的对象是专门针对青少年性犯罪人的治疗项目,也只有这7份研究的对象年龄最为相近。大多数的治疗项目结合了不同类型的性犯罪个体。猥亵儿童是继强奸之后,发生频率最高的。然而,没有哪个项目是专门针对强奸犯而设。有9个项目是专门治疗猥亵儿童的犯人,有四个是专门针对有露阴癖的人。接受治疗的大部分犯人都是自愿参与的。30%的比较研究项目所涉及的犯人,是基于义务而参与治疗项目的。

　　样本的容量(治疗组+控制组)从15到2557(Md=118)。大约三分之一到比较研究少于50名犯人。仅7份比较研究是按照随机抽样来设计的,但其中又有一份是采用了折中的方法,因此只有六份研究能够按照马里兰第五等级进行编码。60%的比较研究编码为马里兰等级二,那就意味着小组之间的平衡是不可能达到的。在测试和记录不同组别差异性的时候,我们会发现治疗组往往比对照组的区别更大。然而,有29份比较研究(包括所有随机抽样的试验),群体的差异性都不是很明显。这其中有接近四分之一研究的对照组由拒绝接受治疗的人组成。

　　几乎所有的研究都使用了性犯罪的再犯率这一衡量方法。再犯行为经常是在持续跟踪了平均至少5年之久才予以记录（治疗组均差：63.54个月，标准差：42.09个月；对照组均差：62.41个月，标准差：42.37个月）。这些都是根据官方犯罪记录得出来的结果，很少有研究的数据来自犯人自己主动报告的信息。大多数研究通常把治疗失败定义为重犯，即受到逮捕和新的指控。有三组比较研究将"不正当的"、"过失的"行为定义为治疗失败的标准，这样的标准显得相当宽松。

（二）总的效果

根据74份比较研究性再犯的数据，治疗组再犯平均率是12%，对照组的是24%（未加权平均数）。也就是接受治疗的人比没有接受治疗的人的再犯率整整少了一半。然而，当我们把74份比较研究中的治疗组和控制组的人数范围考虑进去再算他们的再犯率（比如说我们把治疗组和控制组进行了加权 n 平均数的计算），这两组再犯率的差异就完全消失了（每组的再犯率都变成了11%）。正是因为在一些主要的研究中组别之间的规模不一样，才产生了这些相矛盾的结论。有些研究的对照组规模较大，治疗组规模相对小，整体基本再犯率低。如果按加权平均数的方法计算，控制组再犯率就变得低多了，而治疗组的却变化不大。因此，我们仅从这些平均数来得出结论。治疗效果的整合可以避免因治疗组和控制组的规模带来的差异问题，因为我们可以先从个体水平来对再犯率进行评估，然后再将其整合起来，然后我们就可以用控制组再犯率的平均值来得出治疗效果的详细结论。以下图1给出了74组治疗效果（标记为 OR）的全貌。该图显示表明大多数的治疗效果都是积极的（k=53）。转化成 OR，治疗效果为0.17至33.33。

我们根据随机模型整合了个体治疗效果，以表2显示了整合后的效果。性犯罪再犯率的 OR 均值为1.70，表明治疗起到了显著的效果（z=4.96, P<0.001）。治疗组和控制组的再犯率绝对差值是6.4%，这表明控制组基础比例下降了37%。平均治疗效果与其他类型犯罪的数据相似。对于暴力犯罪而言，治疗效果的平均数为1.90（z=5.36, P<0.001）。治疗组的平均再犯率比未经治疗的人要低5.2%（少了44%）。对任一再犯而言，其平均效果为 OR=1.67（Z=4.52, P<0.001）。相应的一般治疗过的再犯率比没有治疗过的要少11.1%（减少了31%）。

除了暴力犯罪再犯外，其他类型的犯罪治疗效果分布相当的不均匀。对性再犯而言，Q(73)=237.14, P<0.001，对一般的再犯而言，Q(48)=159.80, P<0.001。因此，我们分析了一些对治疗的效果可能有影响的变量。我们主要分析性犯罪再犯的治疗效果，因为这是我们感兴趣的主要领域并且能获得最丰富的数据。

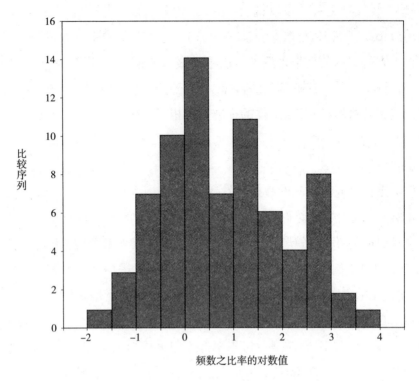

图 1　性犯罪再犯治疗效果分布（k＝74）

表 2　所有不同类型再犯治疗的总体平均效果

结果	k	OR	CI$_{95\%}$	Q	再犯率	
					TG^a	CG^b
性再犯	74	1.70＊＊＊	1.35—2.13	237.14＊＊＊	11.1	17.5
暴力再犯	20	1.90＊＊＊	1.49—2.33	19.68	6.6	11.8
其他再犯	49	1.67＊＊＊	1.33—2.08	159.80＊＊＊	22.4	32.5

备注:k 表示调查份数,OR 表示优势比,CI$_{95\%}$表示 95％ 的置信区间,Q 表示测试分布均匀程度(X^2,df＝k——1),TG
表示治疗组,CG 表示对照组,＊＊＊ P<0.001,a 表示加权平均数,b 表示再犯的估算值。

（三）调节分析

由于篇幅限制,在这里我们仅选择调节分析予以报告。表 3 报告了那些揭示了明显差异或与治疗实践相关的一些变量的结果。在整个分析过程中,我们还需考虑与其他一些变量的影响可能产生混淆的调节效应。

（四）治疗的特征

治疗方法之间的差别在于作用效果的不同。整体来说,物理治疗（OR＝7.37,

$CI_{95\%}$:4.14—13.11,z=6.80,P<0.001)比非物理治疗(比如说心理治疗)有更好的效果(OR=1.32,$CI_{95\%}$:1.07—1.62,z=2.60,P=0.01),Q(1,k=66)= 30.47,P<0.001。特别是平均作用幅度特别大的阉割手术,治疗结果更是如此。而荷尔蒙治疗也比其他的心理治疗法更有效。在所有的治疗方法中,行为认知治疗和经典行为治疗在性再犯的治疗上有更积极的效果。其他方法的优势比接近1,所以它们对再犯行为的影响不大。马里兰等级为4的个体治疗回归性分析更是确认了这一点。它的标准回归加权(β)显示了治疗了的显著性:认知导向疗法(0.36)、情境行为技巧(0.26)、荷尔蒙药物治疗(0.26),而且所有的 P<0.05。

在进一步的调节分析中,我们排除阉割手术的原因是:(a)这个方法与其他的方法大为不同。(b)现在几乎不使用这种治疗方法。(c)阉割手术作用效果极大且相似,Q(7)=1.32,P=0.99,因此它无疑会使结果产生偏差。

而剩下的 66 组对比研究,他们的平均效果也很明显(OR = 1.38,$CI_{95\%}$:1.13—1.69,z=3.16,P<0.01)。均质性检查也显示出治疗效果分布的高度均匀性,Q(65)= 163.92,P<0.001,因此适合做进一步的调节分析。

表 3 显示,近十年实施的治疗试验,其治疗的效果都比较显著。然而它们之间没有线性的关系。这一点,从相关性分析中可以得到确认(r=0.16,P=0.15)。因此,治疗试验并不是越现代化效果越好。从研究发表的年份也可看出相似的结果,由此显示的差距更不明显(r=0.08,P=0.51)。如果研究人员自己主动参与治疗项目的话,那它的效果更好。当研究人员与治疗项目没有联系的时候,OR 就接近于 1 了。

为性犯罪人专设治疗项目的效果最好。而其他的一些治疗项目甚至可能出现不良的后果。尽管我们发现治疗的环境对结果的影响不大,但是门诊治疗的效果比正式机构更好。而混合环境的效果居中。从正式机构到门诊部的线性变化顺序表明了治疗环境与治疗效果大小间的正相关关系(r=0.27,P=0.02)。

无论治疗是集体进行还是个体进行都对治疗效果影响不大。然而,按照这种分类方法,我们必须承受各种内在变量所造成的混淆。比如说荷尔蒙药物治疗和系统性的治疗都必须归纳到各个目录之下。

表3　调节分析

变量	k	Q_{bet}	OR	$CI_{95\%}$ 从低到高
治疗特征				
治疗方法		36.02 ***		

变量	k	Q_bet	OR	CI_{95%} 从低到高
行为认知治疗	35		1.45 **	1.12—1.86
经典行为治疗	7		2.19 **	1.22—3.92
认知主导治疗	5		0.98	0.51—1.89
社区治疗	8		0.86	0.54—1.35
其他心理治疗	5		0.94	0.53—1.65
荷尔蒙治疗	6		3.08 **	1.40—6.79
阉割手术	8		15.34 ***	7.34—32.05
治疗的时间		7.37 **		
1970 之前	5		0.56	0.32—0.98
1970s	14		2.03 ***	1.34—3.09
1980s	30		1.38 **	1.08—1.77
1990s	17		1.27	0.86—1.87
有无接受专设的性治疗方法		4.70 *		
有	56		1.56 ***	1.27—1.93
没有	5		0.76	0.41—1.41
治疗环境		5.10		
监狱	21		1.16	0.84—1.60
医院	8		1.10	0.62—1.94
门诊	27		1.93 ***	1.35—2.77
混合环境	10		1.37	0.78—2.41
治疗形式		6.74		
集体治疗	17		1.12	0.76—1.66
主要是集体治疗	17		1.57 *	1.02—2.42
混合治疗	8		2.45 *	1.36—4.40
主要是个体治疗	8		1.40	0.77—2.53
个体治疗	6		2.88 *	1.14—7.24
研究人员与研究有无联系		10.95 ***		
有	32		1.92 ***	1.44—2.56
没有	30		0.99	0.76—1.29
犯人的特征				
年龄		1.19		
只有青少年	7		2.35 *	1.01—5.43
只有成年人	36		1.43 *	1.08—1.90

变量	k	Q_{bet}	OR	CI$_{95\%}$ 从低到高
犯罪类型		9.04 *		
强奸	5		4.91 **	1.64—14.68
猥亵儿童（非家庭成员之间）	9		2.15 *	1.11—4.16
猥亵儿童（包括乱伦罪）	10		1.02	0.58—1.80
露阴癖	4		3.72 *	1.27—10.93
参与治疗人的意愿		2.22		
自愿	28		1.45 *	1.08—1.93
非自愿	15		1.05	0.70—1.58
混合型	7		1.01	0.57—1.77
治疗进程		−a		
完成治疗	44		1.58 ***	1.23—2.05
中途停止	14		0.51 ***	0.39—0.67
研究方法的特征				
样本容量		31.43 ***		
低于50	18		4.03 ***	2.50—6.50
51—100	10		1.32	0.76—2.27
101—200	16		1.65 **	1.13—2.41
201—500	12		1.00	0.72—1.38
超过500	10		0.88	0.64—1.21
马里兰等级		6.13		
等级2（机率不相同）	37		1.16	0.90—1.50
等级3（机率假定相同）	17		2.08 ***	1.40—3.08
等级4（匹配，控制数量）	6		1.19	0.67—2.12
等级5（随机）	6		1.48	0.74—2.96
对照组的构成		1.64		
拒绝治疗	11		1.96 **	1.20—3.20
其他	47		1.37 *	1.07—1.75
再犯的资料来源		4.56 *		
官方数据	57		1.28 *	1.04—1.57
自己上报形式	5		3.32 **	1.42—7.78

除了治疗方法的分析，其他都不包括阉割手术的数据分析。k 表示研究的份数，

Q_{bet}表示不同组别的差别测试(x^2-df表示类别的数量),OR表示机会比率,$CI_{95\%}$表示95%置信区间;CG表示控制组,比较的是对照组的相同部分,因此组别的差异用数据测试的方法获得。* $P<0.05$. ** $P<0.01$. *** $P<0.001$。

(五)犯人的特征

针对青少年犯人的治疗项目比成年人的治疗项目更有效果。然而这种差异并不明显。一份相关数据表明一组中实验对象的年龄越相近,试验就越可能成功。($k=48;r=0.23,P=0.10$)

尽管治疗对不同类型的犯人的效果究竟如何是研究中很重要的一个方面,但很少有研究会根据犯罪的类型分类治疗。除了对家庭内猥亵儿童的犯罪,其他类型犯人的治疗效果都不错。而家庭内部成员之间儿童猥亵犯人治疗不显著的结果可能是跟乱伦犯人基本再犯率比较低有关。根据5份相关的研究表明,对治疗强奸犯的成效显著。

在性犯罪人自愿参与治疗的时候,作用效果相当可观。强制参加和半自愿半强制参与情况下的效果并不好,但这两者的差别也不是很大。

是否正常完成治疗和过早结束治疗对性犯罪再犯治疗的效果也会产生影响。对正常完成治疗的犯人的治疗效果通常会好一些,中途退出治疗会导致重犯率翻番,这种负面效果在各个组中大致相同,$Q(13)=11.52,P=0.57$。相比较而言,对完成治疗犯人的治疗效果的分布明显地呈现不均衡性,$Q(43)=100.20,P<0.001$。

(六)研究方法的特征

样本大小与治疗效果之间有密切的联系($r=-0.26,P=0.03$)。这主要是由于样本大小间的差异极大。小样本($N\leqslant50$)的治疗效果明显,而相对较大样本治疗效果的平均数就低于1了。这种关系不仅仅归因于发表需要的偏见:尽管未出版的研究的治疗效果随着样本大小的变化而变化的幅度没有已发表的研究的明显,但与已经发表的研究相比,未发表研究的样本大小与治疗效果之间则存在明显的线性关系($r=0.34$vs. $r=0.20$)。

总的说来,高质量的研究设计并没有产生好的调节结果。等级相同的治疗组和对照组的比较研究(马里兰等级都处于3级或者3级以上)表明了平均作用幅度都处于1.69($CI_{95\%}:1.26—2.28$)。在$P=0.06$的时候,OR超过了马里兰等级2的1.16。然而表3表明,研究设计的质量与治疗效果之间并没有线性关系。随机试验结果也与其他研究结果相似,$Q(1,k=66)=0.07,P=0.79$。尽管包括拒绝治疗犯人的对照组的效果更为明显,但是这些结果与使用其他对照组的研究并没有明显的区别。

后续治疗时间长短与效果大小不相关($r=0.00$)。不同的再犯类型(比如说二次定罪,二次逮捕等等)与结果的变化没有影响,$Q(6, k=60)=3.45, P=0.49$。相比较而言,使用信息来源的渠道与效果大小有明显的关系,$Q(2, k=62)=7.91, P=0.02$。综合了官方数据和自报数据的研究,其治疗效果更为明显。然而因为所有有关荷尔蒙药物治疗的研究都包括自报告再犯状况,所以这个数据会与治疗方式相混淆。

我们可以预见,再犯基本比率高的研究其治疗效果也好,($r=0.30, P=0.01$)。因为非正式数据来源的基本再犯率要高。这种效果也是容易产生混淆的,因为非正式数据来源往往容易导致高的基本再犯率。在控制了这方面的影响后,基本再犯率与效果之间的关系就不明显了($ß=0.23, P=0.08$)。

描述的有效性并没有说明具体的治疗过程和对治疗效果的评估,却科学地报告了主要的过程。然而,我们的分析表明了这些与治疗效果相关。对治疗相关概念记载的质量($r=0.33, P<0.01$)和最后数据的报告都与治疗效果有较大的联系。

(七)研究的总体特征

在不同国家不同群体进行研究对治疗效果的影响不大,$Q(4, k=66)=2.46, P=0.65$。至于出版类型,我们仅发现已发表的比较研究之间存在明显的差异($k=40$, $OR=1.62, CI_{95\%}: 1.23—2.13, P<0.001$)。而未出版的比较研究的平均效果的优势比仅为$1.14$($k=26, CI_{95\%}: =0.84–1.54, P=0.42$)。然而,这种差异并不明显,$Q(1, k=66)=2.91, P=0.09$。

(八)灵敏度分析

调节效果可能受到大样本量研究的一些结果的影响(Lipsey and Wilson 2001)。因此,我们运用了两种不同的方法对灵敏度进行分析。首先,我们排除了样本量大于1000的研究($k=3$)。在第二种方法中,所有样本容量超过500的研究都被缩减为500。但有一项例外,灵敏度分析确认了表格3中调节效果的显著性。在排除容量超过1000的样本后,我们只发现了犯罪类型不清楚的治疗不符合标准。($P=0.08$)

(九)分层回归

以前的分析曾反复提到因调节变量混淆所带来的问题。因此,看看治疗效果在多大程度上与研究方法或评估的其他特征产生混淆就是与本研究特别相关的问题。

为了回答这一问题,我们进行了分层次回归分析以逐渐控制与减少治疗外对结果变化产生影响的因素。首先,我们把那些不具体的,关于研究方法方面的研究特征加入到研究模式中。紧接着,我们再加入犯人的特征、一般治疗方法的特征,最后则加入治疗的具体过程。我们把理论上或者实践意义上重要的变量输入到二元变量分析中($r \geq 0.20$)。分层的每一步中,那些无法用来解释变化的变量都予以排除($P > 0.10$)。由于相关研究的数量不多,同时为了减少模型中不相关变量影响,我们选择了这种方法。试验结果没有数据的,我们就用样本平均数替代,这样就降低了数据缺失对我们分析的影响(Cohen,1983)。与之前提到的双变量分析不同,因为我们希望进入分析的变量应能够大大减少样本间的异质性,因此我们分层回归分析建立在效果修正模型基础之上。结果可参见表4。

正如我们预期的那样,样本间的异质性得到有效减少从而变得不明显。$Q(55, k=66) = 65.40$,$P=0.16$。并且60%的数据表明这个模型能够解释大部分的效果变化,$Q(10, k=66) = 98.52$,$P<0.001$。然而,我们应该知道由于每群都逐步排除了一些变量,这个模型人为地变得"干净"了。现在每一群仅剩下一些变量作为独立指示变量。研究方法特征给实验结果也带来了巨大的变化(45%)。由于缺乏对样本的描述且样本之间存在差异性,犯人的特征仅能独立对治疗效果产生较小的影响。年龄的相近是唯一的相关变量,它使试验作用幅度变化的解释量增加了3%。治疗的共同性要重要一些。专为性犯罪人而设的治疗、有研究者参与的研究、接受治疗人员的群体性这三方面的因素使对实验效果变化的解释率增加了9%。尽管行为认知治疗是最后一步才加到模型中去的,但它对治疗效果变化的作用比前面几个集群中的变量要大。除此以外,就没有其他治疗变量再涉及模型分析。很明显,荷尔蒙药物治疗和行为条件反射方法的治疗结果更容易受到其他变量的干扰。总之,最后两个步骤表明治疗特征对治疗效果变化的影响至少有20%。在解读这个数据时,我们还应该注意这仅仅是在控制了其他变量的情况下得出的保守估计。

表4　分层回归分析

变量群	ΔR^2
研究方法的特征	0.45 ***
+汇报结果的质量(0.35 ***),描述治疗的质量(0.20 *),	
小样本,$N \leq 50$(0.42 ***),拒绝治疗的人作为控制组(0.16+)	
——中途退出的犯人也作为治疗组的成员(-0.24 **)	
不同类型的犯人	0.03 *

变量群	ΔR^2
+治疗组中年龄相近的人(0.16*)	
一般治疗的特征	0.10***
+作者参与项目(0.24**),集体接受治疗(0.18+)	
-没有专设给性犯罪人的治疗(-0.19ʳ)	
治疗内容	0.03*
+纠正认知(0.28*)	

指标的变化分别对应于效果幅度是更高(+)还是更低(—),(标准化 ß 的加权量体现在括号里)。总体而言,$R^2 = 0.06$,$Q(10) = 98.52$,$P<0.001$. $+P<0.10$。

*P<0.05。

**P<0.01。

***P<0.001。

三、讨 论

因为我们所涉及的研究有多种语言,而且这些研究最近一直在增加。从而使这份综合分析能够有 80 个对治疗组与对照组进行的比较研究,所包括的个体研究对象达到 22000 人。这是目前为止关于性犯罪治疗最为全面的数据库。有接近三分之一的研究发表于 2000 年之后,有三分之一的研究来自北美。这些研究表明的如何有效处理性犯罪问题已经引起了世界各国的兴趣。尽管我们排除了那些没有对照组,或者有中途退出的对照组的研究,但这些研究的研究方法的质量仍只处于中等水平。只有40%的研究达到了马里兰研究方法估量等级 3 或者之上的水平(Sherman *et al.*, 1997)。它表明我们对治疗组和对照组之间相似度的人为控制过强。只有七份评估所涉及的研究具有随机抽样的设计。我们之所以没有把本评估的研究限定在必须具备"黄金标准",其原因有以下几个方面:首先,如果研究仅局限于那些同种模式的治疗评估,那么它的分析结果将没有多大区别。其次,即使是具有随机抽样设计的研究也不能保证治疗组和对照组被挑中的机率相同(MarQues *et al.*, 2005)。第三,考虑到评估的差异性,我们往往保守估计治疗的效果(这一点对治疗组尤甚)。最后一点,随机研究的子样本效果不会随着研究设计质量的降低而发生明显变化(Lipsey and Wilson, 1998; Lösel, 1995)。

切记研究方法方面的问题,对我们的综合分析不要轻易地下结论。最为重要的是对性犯罪人治疗要全面、积极、有效。性犯罪再犯的平均优势比是1.70。d系数等于0.29处于对一般犯人治疗效果综合分析的正常范围之内（Lösel, 1995; McGuire, 2002）。性犯罪人治疗对一般再犯也同样有效（OR = 1.67）。很显然，有效的治疗项目不仅仅对因性引发的问题行为有效还对所有犯罪有广泛影响。这一点与许多性犯罪人并不专门从事性犯罪，而且还与从事与性无关的犯罪的事实相符（Hanson and Bussière, 1998）。但我们也发现，那些非特殊的治疗项目对性再犯治疗没有效果。

治疗组和对照组的性犯罪平均再犯率分别是11.1%和17.5%。乍看下来，6%多一点的绝对差数值似乎不大。但是如果把性再犯的低基本再犯率考虑进去，那就意味着性犯罪整整减少了37%。对一般的再犯而言，那就意味着减少了31%。特别是在性再犯研究中，我们还发现一般治疗效果比汉森等（Hanson et al.）（2002）的心理治疗综合分析得出的效果要好。这可能要归功于心理治疗和物理治疗并举的治疗项目。尽管荷尔蒙药物治疗效果也不错，但主要在于阉割手术的高效性。

尽管阉割手术良好的治疗效果经得住实践的反复考验（根据8份类似治疗效果的比较），但是这个疗法仍存在争议：没有一项阉割治疗的研究质量达到了马里兰等级3。因此我们不能确保治疗组和对照组在评估方面是处于同等地位的比较。参与阉割治疗的性犯罪人都是经过精心挑选并且有心理准备的人。他们自愿地参与这个疗程，而对照组的参与个体通常会拒绝治疗或者没有得到专家委员会的认可（Wille and Beier, 1989）。因此，治疗组比对照组更有可能不再犯。而出于道德、法律和医药的考量，阉割手术在现实中极少使用（Rosler and Witztum, 2000）。然而，低阉割性犯罪人再犯率也暗示着社会不应该对这种方法一票否决，而是需要一份不一样的肯定或者否定的评价体系去应对它。对高再犯率并因此可能要囚禁终身的一小部分性犯罪人而言，在确保公正和完全知情权的情况下，阉割治疗不失为一个选择。

大多男性犯罪人的雄性荷尔蒙都不是异常地高（Hucker and Bain, 1990; Fedoroff and Moran, 1997）。与阉割手术一样，荷尔蒙药物治疗想要取得良好的成果，这一点也不容忽视。尽管治疗中运用甲羟孕酮酸（比如说美国使用的安宫黄体酮）或者环丙孕酮酸（比如说欧洲使用的环丙氯地孕酮）并不能使非正常的雄性激素值正常化，但它或多或少降低了性欲（Rösler and Witztum, 2000）。此外，还有其他极为消极的副作用，这经常使一些人不配合或者直接中途退出我们的治疗（Langevin, 1979）。而中止药物治疗大大增加了再犯的风险（Meyer et al., 1992）。因此荷尔蒙药物治疗主要是针对因性欲引起的犯罪（Hall, 1996），此外它还应与心理治疗结合进行。心理治疗可以使参与人更好地配合试验，而从因果联系上来说它对防止性再犯有其独特的作用（Maletzky, 1991; Meyer and Cole, 1997）。

这也就解释了为什么我们在药物治疗研究综合分析的时候会包括对心理干预措施的研究。我们通过评估整体治疗方案中各个治疗措施来分析其对治疗效果的影响。一份回归分析表明只有三种治疗模式的效果比较显著:荷尔蒙药物治疗、行为治疗、行为认识治疗。与最后一项治疗相比,前两种治疗项目与研究方法和其他研究特征之间的混淆更为明显。在控制了这些变量后,我们发现只有认知行为疗法有单独的治疗效果(看表格4)。

认知行为疗法的积极作用是建立在35组独立的比较研究之上的。而经典行为疗法的数据库就小多了,它只有7份相关的研究。此外,对自知力导向治疗法、社区治疗以及其他的心理学治疗项目的运用也都一样没有产生明显效果。与对一般犯人治疗研究文献所显示的效果一样,设计良好的行为认知治疗的效果不错(Lösel,2001a;McGuire,2002)。它与早先关于性犯罪人治疗研究的发现相符(Gallagher *et al.*,2000;Hall,1995;Hanson,2002)。然而,我们针对行为认知疗法综合分析得出的治疗效果(OR = 1.45)与汉森等(Hason *et al.*)当下以行为认知疗法为主的研究有微小差别,(OR = 1.67,这个数据由我们转换出来)分析出来的效果度小些。

总之,我们最近还没有发现有什么效果更好的新治疗方法。尽管1970年代前的治疗没有取得很明显的效果,但是无论是1990年代的治疗项目还是2000年后发表的研究项目都没有比数十年前更为有效。甚至纯粹就行为认知疗这类方法来说,目前更多的新的治疗方法也没有比老的更为有效。一些最近实施的研究项目的评估效果更小甚至没有什么积极效果(Friendship *et al.*,2003;Hanson *et al.*,2004;Ruddijs and Timmerman,2000;Worling and Curwen,2000)。对一项被认为是最完善的治疗项目的跟踪评估也没有发现有什么积极的效果(MarQues *et al.*,2005)。

由于跟踪研究在时间上会出现一些必然的延迟,即使是新研究也无法完全代表当下对性犯罪人治疗方法的特征。我们必须时刻注意,当我们把实验中的治疗模式搬到实践中时,其效果往往被削弱。

类型相似的治疗项目之所以会出现不一样结果的部分原因可能在于其他因素影响了治疗效果。与治疗的内容相似,我们在进一步描述变量时必须格外留心:(a)一些效果只是建立在一小部分研究之上。(b)随机模型对变量的影响更为不明显(Overton,1998)。(c)对变量分析的多重显著性测试增加了出现α—错误率的风险。(d)变量之间相互混杂而且一些变量在多变量层次上没有影响。

尽管我们在项目设计质量与试验的结果之间没有找到任何线性关系,但是在机率相同的治疗组和对照组的研究(马里兰等级3)中有一种趋势,那就是设计质量好的研究效果更为明显。在性犯罪治疗研究领域,需要更多的相同类型治疗的随机性研究,采用与犯罪学其他领域相似的方式,来对这种趋势予以确认(Weisburd et al.,2001)。其他研究方法特征的影响表现得更为明显。比如说,包括官方数据和自我报告数据研究的效果更为明显。这一发现会在某种程度上与荷尔蒙药物治疗法产生混淆。描述可靠性方面的问题比如说对治疗描述的质量和结果汇报的质量都与效果有关。

就实际应用而言,样本大小和治疗效果的关系都尤为重要。小样本研究(N≤50)的治疗效果大些,而大研究(N>500)的治疗效果则较小。我们可以把这一结果理解为出于发表目的。样本大的研究更有利于揭示细微成效的重要意义(Weisburd et al.,2003)。由于作者或者编辑决定的影响,大研究可能发表,而小研究除非有更为明显的治疗效果来显示其重要的地位,否则就不会被发表。因此,发表过的研究比未发表研究的效果更显著。尽管这种差别也并不重要,但是我们还是发现了样本大小对未发表研究的影响,甚至这种影响有可能更为深远。当然,我们无法完全排除发表偏见的影响,因为否定性的结果很难在未发表的研究中发现(特别在遇到研究人员对成功治疗更为有兴趣的情况下)。然而我们也可以将其解释为:样本大的研究更难保证治疗与样本的完整和同一。这一点与治疗效果本身有关(Lösel and Wittmann,1989;Weisburd et al.,1993)。一份研究进一步支持了完整性对研究项目影响的解读:有项目设计者参与的研究,效果更为明显。由于对大多数治疗的测量超出了项目设计者的控制,本研究的发现表现这些项目得到了有效的贯彻和监督。在样本量比较小和(或)项目设计者参与的青少年犯罪治疗(Lipsey and Wilson,1998)、对反社会行为的发展性预防(Farrington and Welsh,2003;Lösel and Beelmann,2003)的效果方面,有与上述相似的结果。如果能得到更多的关于这种关系的证据支持,一些有关治疗完整性的比较研究就能得到确切评估。

治疗环境也与结果相关。移动性治疗比正式机构治疗效果好。因为我们只分析了对照组的治疗效果评估,所以这一发现不能降低不同组群犯人再犯的风险。犯人的特征对治疗效果也有一些影响。然而,通常情况下都缺乏关于实验样本的详细信息。在近一半的研究中,我们发现无法仅根据不同类型的性犯罪来区分样本。我们尽可能在结果中找到一些差异。只是由于家庭内猥亵儿童犯罪的基本再犯率非常低,所以没有治疗效果。次群体犯人的治疗评价则需要有坚实的实证基础来区别。

自愿型治疗比强制治疗效果更好,而青少年治疗比成年人治疗效果更好。尽管这一差别意义不大,并且会跟青少年高再犯率相混淆,但是相近年龄是分层回归研究的重要方面。而中途退出治疗的犯人再犯率更高也是我们的重要发现。因此,有中途退出治疗犯人的治疗组的治疗效果往往不大。中途退出治疗犯人的高再犯率也暗示着这样的群体是我们矫正、控制和评价的核心所在（Lösel，2001b）。我们不能把这种现象仅归因于个体的缺陷，而更应该把其看作是相互作用过程中犯人的需要、动机与项目的设置不相符的缘故（McMurran，2002）。加拿大、英格兰、威尔士和苏格兰等地项目鉴定过程的系统性和质量管理大大减少了治疗方面的各种问题。然而，从现实角度来说，我们不应在短期里期望得到太多。

总而言之，对性犯罪人的积极治疗效果是能够得到证据证明的。行为认知治疗、荷尔蒙治疗是眼下最有前景的治疗方式。此外，其他各种不同的调节因素对结果的好坏也会有影响。特别是研究方法因素也发挥了重要作用，并且似乎与治疗和犯人特征会产生混淆。变量间相互混杂的问题在研究中非常的普遍并且难以解决（Lipsey，2003）。我们初次尝试用分层回归分析解决性犯罪人治疗中的变量冲突问题。我们需要更多的阐述性罪犯这一亚群体的研究成果，也需要更详细的关于治疗特征和内容的过程评估。两个策略在研究和实践中的实施将进一步明确"什么样的措施在什么样的环境下对谁能够起作用"。

［附件及参考文献见英文原作］

（展万程　陈朦朦 译）

The Effectiveness of Treatment for Sexual Offenders: A Comprehensive Meta-analysis

Friedrich Lösel

Martin Schmucker

University of Erlangen, Nuremberg

Treatment for sexual offenders is a very important topic of criminal policy. Media reports on serious cases of sexually motivated murder, rape, and child abuse have made people particularly concerned about this area of crime. In various countries, policymakers have reacted by increasing measures of both punishment and treatment. Because most incarcerated sexual offenders return to the community, effective treatment is a cornerstone for preventing future offenses. However, the empirical basis of sex offender treatment is less solid than such a cornerstone should be. Although recent overviews suggest a moderately positive effect (e. g. , Alexander, 1999; Aos *et al.* , 2001; Gallagher *et al.* , 2000; Hanson *et al.* , 2002; Lösel, 2000; Polizzi *et al.* , 1999) , methodological problems, inconsistent results, and a lack of high quality studies question how far we know what works for sex offenders (e. g. , Lösel, 2000; Marques *et al.* , 2005; Quinsey *et al.* , 1993; Rice and Harris, 2003; White *et al.* , 1998).

Indeed, there is much less well-controlled research on the evaluation of programs for sex offenders than in the field of general offender treatment (Lipsey and Wilson, 1998; Lösel, 2001a; McGuire, 2002). Clear messages on the efficacy of programs for sex offenders are complicated by various problems that relate to issues of design and treatment.

Design issues. Serious offenders relatively often receive at least some kind of treatment. This makes it difficult to form randomized untreated control groups. The relatively low baserate of official sexual reoffending (e. g. , Hanson and Bussière, 1998) means that large samples are needed to reveal a significant effect. However, for economic reasons, evaluations of sex offender treatment often contain rather small samples. This enhances the risk of non-equivalent groups, even in randomized designs (Marques *et al.* , 2005). Furthermore, selective dropout and other problems make it difficult not only to implement but also to maintain internal validity (e. g. , Barbaree, 1997; Marshall and McGuire, 2003). In addition to the general problems of undetected crime, the registration of sexual offenses is influenced by the intimate nature of this kind of crime. This limits the value of official data.

Treatment issues. The analysis of sexual reoffending requires relatively long follow-up periods (Prentky *et al.* , 1997), so that evaluations may address old programs that do not represent the current ' state of the art. ' Furthermore, the treatment of sex offenders embraces a broad range of medical and psychosocial programs, and sex offenders are a rather heterogeneous group. As a result, adequate evaluations and replications need to be rather differentiated. Moreover, sex offenders often do not receive a single program but individualized 'packages' (e. g. , psychological and pharmacological treatment; additional programs for alcohol dependence). Disentangling the impact of specific modules would require relatively complex evaluations.

These and other problems make systematic research integrations more difficult than in those areas in which we can draw on a large number of methodologically sound evaluations. Accordingly, an early meta-analysis from Furby *et al.* (1989) found few well-designed studies and concluded that there is "as yet no evidence that clinical treatment reduces rates of sex reoffenses" (p. 27). Nine years later, a review for the Cochrane Collaboration came to a similar conclusion (White *et al.* , 1998). Restricting their analysis to randomized evaluations, the authors ended up with only three studies. Other recent meta-analyses included quasi-experimental studies as well. This is in line with the notion that methodological quality is not a unidimensional all-ornone category, and that practice can also learn from good but suboptimal studies (Cronbach *et al.* , 1980; Lösel and Köferl, 1989; Shadish *et al.* , 2002).

Most reviews report a lower average rate of sexual recidivism in treated groups than in control groups. For example, Hall (1995) integrated 12 controlled studies. The average rate of sexual recidivism was 19% in treated groups and 27% in controls (mean effect size (ES): $d = 0.24$). Hormonal and cognitive-behavioral treatments were more successful than other programs. However, such differential effects based on a small number of studies and a single evaluation of castration had a strong impact. Alexander (1999) integrated 79 studies on psychosocial sex offender treatment. The mean difference in recidivism was 5 percentage points in favor of treatment ($d = 0.12$; Lösel and Schmucker, 2003). However, the majority of studies contained no control group (Level 1 on the Maryland Scale of Methodological Rigor; Sherman et al., 1997). The same holds for a meta-analysis of 20 studies on medical and psychological treatment from German-speaking countries. This revealed a nonsignificant effect of $d = 0.08$ (Lösel, 2000). Gallagher et al. (2000) analyzed 23 studies of relatively good quality. Treated groups showed 10 percentage points less sexual recidivism than controls and the overall effect size was relatively large ($d = 0.47$). In the most comprehensive recent meta-analysis, Hanson et al. (2002) integrated 43 studies on psychological treatment. The average sexual offense recidivism was 12.3% for treatment groups and 16.8% for comparison groups (mean ES: $d = 0.13$; Lösel and Schmucker, 2003). Current, mainly cognitive-behavioral treatment revealed better outcomes whereas older programs appeared to have little effect.

Overall, the last decade has shown a strong increase and more positive outcomes in evaluations of sex offender treatment. However, research syntheses vary in effect size, type of treatment included, prevailing design quality, categorization of programs, treatment settings, and meta-analytical techniques (Lösel and Schmucker, 2003). Nearly all are restricted to English-language studies that mainly come from North America. Against this background, an updated, comprehensive, independent, and international review seems worthwhile. This is why the Campbell Collaboration Group on Crime and Justice (Farrington and Petrosino, 2001) has included a systematic review on sex offender treatment in its portfolio. The present study is a first report of our work on this synthesis. It contains a meta-analysis of studies on both psychological and biological treatment that were published up to 2003 in English and various other languages.

METHOD

Criteria for Inclusion of Studies

Primary studies had to have the following characteristics to be eligible:

1. *Study of sexual offenders.* Participants had to have been convicted of a sexual offense or to have committed acts of illegal sexual behavior that would have lead to a conviction if officially prosecuted.

2. *Evaluation of treatment.* No restrictions were made on the kind of intervention applied as long as it aimed to reduce recidivism (i. e. , psychosocial as well as organic treatment modes such as hormonal medication or surgical castration were included). However, interventions had to incorporate therapeutic measures; purely deterrent or punishing approaches were not included. Treatment did not have to be specifically tailored for sexual offenders. More general measures of offender treatment were included if the study addressed at least a subgroup of sexual offenders and reported separate results for sexual offenders in both the treated and control groups.

3. *Measure of recidivism as outcome.* Recidivist behavior had to be included as a dependent variable. We followed a broad definition of recidivism and included outcomes ranging from incarceration to lapse behavior. In contrast, primary studies focusing exclusively on changes in measures of personality or hormone levels, clinical ratings of improvement, and the like were not included.

4. *Control group design.* The study had to report the same recidivism outcome for a comparison group not receiving the same treatment. This could either be an untreated control group or a group of offenders receiving treatment 'as usual' or another kind of treatment that differed from the evaluated program in content, intensity and specificity. Studies using only treatment dropouts as a control group were not eligible.

5. *Sample size.* Studies had to contain a minimum total sample size of 10 persons with at least five offenders in each group. In very small samples, even minimal differences in absolute numbers of recidivism between groups may lead to extreme effect sizes, thus making results very heterogeneous while not being very reliable.

6. *Sufficient data for effect size computation.* Studies had to report outcomes in a way permitting the calculation of effect size estimates.

7. *Country of origin.* No restrictions were made as to where studies were conducted. For economic reasons, we restricted our analysis to studies reported in English, German, French, Dutch, or Swedish.

8. *Time of publication.* There were no restrictions regarding the time of publication. All studies reported up to June 2003 were eligible.

Literature Search

Searches were designed to tap published as well as unpublished evaluations. A wide range of sources was used to identify relevant studies. First, a basic study pool was compiled from the reference sections of previous reviews. Second, already identified primary studies were analyzed for further references. Third, 14 electronic databases were analyzed (e. g. , PsycInfo, MedLine, ERIC, Cochrane Library, Social Services Abstracts, NCJRS abstract and full-text databases, Dissertation Abstracts International, and UK National Health Service National Register). Fourth, we hand searched journals pertaining to the topic (e. g. , Sexual Abuse, Journal of Sexual Aggression). To identify more unpublished work, we contacted researchers in the field of sexual offender treatment and asked if they knew or had personally conducted further evaluations. Finally, an Internet search was conducted. Because the Internet constitutes a vast pool of rather loosely connected information, it cannot be searched in total. We visited the Internet sites of pertinent institutions and Departments of Corrections and searched them and their links for relevant material.

A total of 2,039 citations were identified in this way. These were scanned by their title first. If not obviously off-theme, we then examined the abstracts. If these indicated potential eligibility or if no abstract was available, we used the full reports to finally evaluate eligibility. Twenty-one (1%) of the reports could not be obtained (of which 18 also had no available abstract). A total of 586 citations were clearly off-topic; 242 referred to offenders in general; and 641 did not evaluate a program, that is, they either simply described a treatment or reviewed sex offender treatment more generally. This left 549 citations referring to primary studies evaluating sexual offender treatment. Of these, 189 were excluded because they did not report recidivism outcome, 236 did not employ an adequate comparison group, 56 duplicated evaluations already included, and two did not lend themselves to effect size calculation. In the end, 66 reports met the specified inclusion criteria. Some contained more than one eligible study. In such cases, we referred to the individual studies as the unit of analysis. Some primary studies presented results for different subgroups (e. g. , offense types). To allow for maximum differentiation while adhering to the principle of independency between effect sizes, we chose these subgroups as units of analysis. However, the characteristics of the subgroups had to be reported in just as much detail as the total sample. Following these rules, we formed a database of 80 comparisons from 69 studies.

Coding of Study Characteristics

Coding followed a detailed manual. A selection of variables is presented in the Results section (see Table 1). The manual covered general characteristics of the publication (e. g., year, country, type of publication), sample description (e. g., sample size, types of offender, age, voluntariness of treatment participation), methodological features (e. g., study design, type of control group, follow-up interval, source of recidivism data), and characteristics of the treatment (e. g., mode, setting, integrity, and format of treatment). Various programs for sex offenders are not restricted to a certain therapeutic paradigm but combine strategies from different 'schools' in an eclectic manner. Thus, as well as categorizing the basic therapeutic approach, we also rated the degree to which the different treatment elements were applied in an individual intervention on separate 4-point scales.

We evaluated the overall methodological quality of the individual study with an integrative rating scheme (see, for various options, Farrington, 2003). We adapted the Maryland Scale of Scientific Rigor (Sherman *et al.*, 1997) for our purposes. This is a 5-point scale integrating methodological features related to the validity of a causal interpretation of treatment effects. The highest level (5) is reserved for uncompromised random designs. Level 4 covers studies applying procedures to ensure group equivalence (e. g., individual matching, statistical control) or slightly compromised random designs. Designs based on incidental assignment are on Level 3 if group equivalence can be assumed (e. g., demonstrated equivalence on relevant variables). Studies incorporating a nonequivalent control group correspond to Level 2. Finally, Level 1 is reserved for uncontrolled studies that were not eligible for our meta-analysis. In its original form, the Maryland Scale also covers sample size and adequacy of statistical testing. However, because we integrated studies by means of weighted effect sizes, these aspects were not so relevant and we dropped them in our rating.

Following Lösel and Köferl (1989), we included ratings on the completeness and accuracy of information reported. On a 4-point scale, these measured threats to 'descriptive validity' in the domains of treatment concept, treatment implementation, assessment of treatment goals, and methods used.

Studies were coded by the second author. A subsample of 10 studies was additionally coded by an experienced rater. The average interrater agreement was 91%. Core variables such as treatment type or design showed full agreement. No variable fell below 60%.

Computation of Effect Size

As an effect size measure, we used odds ratios (OR). This is widely recommended for dichotomous data (Fleiss, 1994; Lipsey and Wilson, 2001). Results in primary studies on offender treatment are usually reported as simple recidivism rates (P) or as the absolute number of successes and failures in the treatment group ($TG_{Success}$, $TG_{Failure}$) and the comparison group ($CG_{Success}$, $CG_{Failure}$), respectively. In such cases, we applied the following formulas for effect size computation:

$$OR = \frac{P_{CG} \times (1 - P_{TG})}{P_{TG} \times (1 - P_{CG})} \quad \text{and} \quad OR = \frac{CG_{Failure} \times TG_{Success}}{TG_{Failure} \times CG_{Success}}$$

If any of these frequencies equaled zero, 0.5 was added to each frequency. Some studies reported more sophisticated statistical analyses that controlled for differences between treatment and control groups. In such cases, we used these results instead of the simple recidivism rates. In logistic regression, the coefficients equal the natural log of the odds ratio (LOR), and as an exponent to e this equals the odds ratio (see Fleiss, 1994). The result for the treatment variable could thus be transferred directly. In Cox regression, results are reported in the form of a rate ratio, which is similar but not identical to the odds ratio. We used the rate ratio (RR) to estimate a recidivism rate for the control group corrected for the group differences considered in the Cox regression model ($PCG = RR \times P_{TG}$ or $PCG = RR/P_{TG}$, depending on the coding of the treatment variable in the primary study). We then calculated the odds ratio with the above formula. Few studies reported other test statistics that could not be transformed readily into odds ratios. In these cases, we used standard procedures to calculate Cohen's d (see Lipsey and Wilson, 2001) and then converted these into odds ratios using $LOR = \frac{\pi}{\sqrt{3}} \times d$ (Hasselblad and Hedges, 1995, Formula 4, rearranged) and $OR = e^{LOR}$.

If a study contained multiple dependent (sub-) samples, we used the comparison with the highest internal validity (e. g., if a study compared recidivism rates for the total sample of treated/untreated participants and additionally matched a subsample of these groups on relevant characteristics, we would use the latter comparison). Studies often reported multiple outcome variables. Different domains of recidivist behavior (i. e. , sexual, violent, or general recidivism) were always analyzed separately. If a study used different indicators of failure (i. e. , charge, arrest, conviction, or lapse behavior), effect sizes were coded separately and then averaged to a single effect size.

Some studies reported separate results for different offender types or risk groups, but did not meet criteria for independent comparisons as defined above. Here, we calculated effect sizes separately for the subgroups and used the weighted average to obtain a study effect size (see Fleiss, 1994).

Whenever possible, participants who dropped out of treatment were included in the treatment group ('intent to treat'). However, we evaluated the effects of treatment dropout by additionally contrasting them with both treated and untreated groups.

Integration and Statistical Analyses

Statistical analyses were conducted on the natural log of the odds ratio (see Fleiss, 1994; Lipsey and Wilson, 2001). To integrate effect sizes, we applied the weighting procedures based on the standard error of individual effect sizes (Hedges and Olkin, 1985). Because of heterogeneous effect size distributions (according to the Q test of homogeneity; Hedges and Olkin, 1985), we applied a random effects model. Moderator analyses were carried out under the assumption of a mixed effects model (see, also, Lipsey and Wilson, 2001; Wilson, 2001).

RESULTS

Descriptive Characteristics

Table 1 gives an overview of some characteristics of the studies/comparisons included for analysis. Most studies came from North America. Approximately one-third contained unpublished data. Most were relatively recent. Nearly three quarters of the studies have been published since 1990. However, as the treatment section shows, the actual program implementation started much earlier.

Nearly one-half of the comparisons addressed cognitive-behavioral programs. Due to basic similarities, we also subsumed two studies of multisystemic treatment under this category. Fourteen comparisons addressed physical therapy, eight of which dealt with surgical castration. In more than one-half of the studies, authors were affiliated with the evaluated treatment. Most treatments were specifically designed for sex offenders. However, it was rarely possible to rate whether treatment was implemented reliably. Only one-quarter of the comparisons provided a documentation of adequate program integrity. Approximately one-half of the interventions took place in an institutional setting. Although a group format was most frequent, nearly one-half of the programs included at least some individualized treatment. An explicit extension of treatment through specific aftercare services was reported for only 15 comparisons.

Table 1   Descriptive characteristics of the 80 comparisons included in the meta-analysis

Coding variable and categories	Frequency	Percentage
General study characteristics[a]		
Publication year		
Before 1980	7	10. 1
1980s	11	15. 9
1990s	29	42. 0
Since 2000	22	31. 9
Country		
USA	31	44. 9
Canada	17	24. 6
Great Britain	8	11. 6
German-speaking countries	8	11. 6
Other	5	7. 2
Publication type		
Journal article	34	49. 3
Book, chapter	10	14. 5
Unpublished	25	36. 2
Treatment characteristics		
Time of treatment implementation		
Before 1970	14	17. 5
1970s	17	21. 3
1980s	30	37. 5
1990s	19	23. 8
Mode of treatment		
Cognitive-behavioral	37	46. 3
Classical behavioral	7	17. 5

Coding variable and categories	Frequency	Percentage
Insight-oriented	7	17.5
Therapeutic community	10	12.5
Other psychosocial, unclear	5	6.3
Hormonal medication	6	7.5
Surgical castration	8	10.0
Author affiliation to treatment program		
Yes	42	52.5
No	31	38.8
Unclear	7	8.8
Sex-offender-specific treatment		
Yes	64	80.0
No	9	11.3
No information available	7	8.8
Integrity of treatment implementation[b]		
Acceptable	18	25.0
Problematic	5	6.9
No information available	49	68.1
Setting of treatment		
Prison	25	31.3
Hospital	14	17.5
Outpatient	29	36.3
Mixed	10	12.5
No information available	2	2.5
Format of treatment[b]		
Only group treatment	18	22.5
Mainly group treatment	17	21.3
Mixed	10	12.5
Mainly individual treatment	8	10.0
Only individual treatment	7	8.8
No information available	12	15.0
Aftercare		
Obligatory	9	11.3
Optional	6	7.5
Not offered, not reported	65	81.3

Offender characteristics

Age group

Coding variable and categories	Frequency	Percentage
Adults	45	56. 3
Adolescents	7	17. 5
Mixed	8	10. 0
Unclear	20	25. 0
Homogeneity of age		
High	7	17. 5
Medium	23	28. 8
Low	23	28. 8
Unclear	27	33. 8
Offense type[c]		
Rape	44	55. 0
Child molestation	59	73. 7
Incest offenses	38	47. 5
Exhibitionism	24	30. 0
Other hands-on offenses, not specified	5	6. 3
Other hands-off offenses, not specified	5	6. 3
Not specified	20	25. 0
Treatment participation		
Voluntary	37	46. 3
Nonvoluntary	16	20. 0
Mixed	8	10. 0
Unclear	19	23. 8
Methodological characteristics		
Sample size		
Up to 50	25	31. 3
51-100	12	15. 0
101-200	18	22. 5
201-500	14	17. 5
More than 500	11	13. 3
Maryland scale		
Level 2 (nonequivalent)	48	60. 0
Level 3 (equivalence assumed)	19	23. 8
Level 4 (matching, statistical control)	7	8. 8
Level 5 (randomization)	6	7. 5
Initial group equivalence		
Yes	20	25. 0

continued

Coding variable and categories	Frequency	Percentage
No, TG at higher risk	14	17.5
No, CG at higher risk	4	5.0
No, direction unclear	8	10.0
No, but controlled for statistically	5	6.3
No information available	29	36.3
Control group formation		
Treatment volunteers	13	16.3
No treatment available	14	17.5
No treatment order	15	18.8
Treatment refused	19	23.8
Other	10	12.5
Unclear	9	11.3
Type of reoffense[c]		
Sexual	74	92.5
Violent	20	25.0
Any	49	61.3
Follow-up period (months)		
12-24	14	17.5
25-36	12	15.0
37-60	23	28.8
61-84	12	15.0
>84	19	23.8
Source of recidivism data		
Criminal records only	64	80.0
Self-report	6	7.5
Not indicated	10	12.5
Definition of recidivism		
Arrest	19	23.8
Conviction	24	30.0
Charge	15	18.8
Lapse behavior	3	3.8
Multiple outcomes	6	7.5
Not indicated	13	16.3

[a] $n = 69$.

[b] $k = 72$ (no reasonable categorization for surgical castration possible).

[c] Individual comparisons may cover multiple categories.

Seven comparisons referred to programs that targeted exclusively juvenile sexual offenders. Only these were very homogeneous in terms of age. Most treatment programs combined individuals with different types of sex offense. Child molestation was most frequent, followed by rape. However, no program referred exclusively to rapists. Nine programs addressed child molesters only, and four addressed exhibitionists only. Most frequently, treated offenders had participated voluntarily. Thirty percent of the comparisons referred to offenders who were at least partially obliged to attend treatment.

Sample sizes (TG + CG) varied from 15 to 2,557 (Md = 118). Roughly one-third of the comparisons contained less than 50 offenders. Only seven comparisons were based on a randomized design. One of these was compromised, so that only six could be coded on Level 5 of the Maryland Scale. Sixty percent of the comparisons were on Maryland Scale Level 2, that is, group equivalence could not be assumed. When group differences actually were tested and reported, the TG was more often at higher risk than the CG. However, for 29 comparisons (including all randomized trials), no information was available on group differences. In nearly one-quarter of the comparisons the CG consisted of treatment refusers.

Nearly all studies used a specific measure of sexual recidivism. Recidivism was recorded after an average follow-up period of more than 5 years (TG: $M = 63.54$ months, SD = 42.09; CG: $M = 62.41$, SD = 42.37). It was mainly based on entries in official criminal records. Few studies additionally used information from the offenders themselves. The most common definition of failure was reconviction, followed by rearrest and new charges. In three comparisons the criterion was defined rather loosely as 'inappropriate' or 'lapse' behavior. In six comparisons, outcomes were reported separately for different definitions.

Total Effects

The 74 comparisons reporting data on sexual recidivism revealed an average recidivism rate of 12% for treated groups and 24% for comparison groups (unweighted average). This is a 50% reduction. However, when we calculated the recidivism rates for treated and comparison participants taking the respective sizes of TG and CG in the 74 comparisons into account (i. e., when we calculated an *n*-weighted average for treated and comparison groups), the difference in recidivism rates vanished completely (11% each for treated and comparison participants). These conflicting results were due to great differences in the size of TG and CG in some primary studies. Studies with very large control groups and comparatively small treated groups and an overall low recidivism baserate reduced the n-weighted average of the CG recidivism rate considerably but not the TG average. Therefore, one should not draw conclusions from these averages. Effect-size integration avoids the problem of different TG/CG sizes, because the recidivism rates are first evaluated on the level of the individual comparisons and only then integrated. The mean effect size can then be used to estimate mean CG recidivism to illustrate results. Figure 1 gives an overview of the effect sizes (logged OR) of the 74 comparisons. It shows that the majority of effects were positive ($k = 53$). Converted to OR, the effects ranged from a minimum of 0. 17 to a maximum of 33. 33.

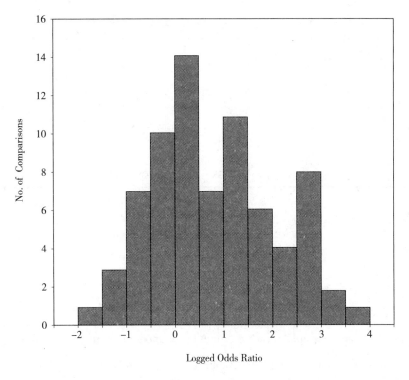

Figure 1 Distribution of effect sizes (logged odds ratios) for sexual recidivism ($k = 74$)

We integrated the individual effect sizes according to the random model. Results are shown in Table 2. The mean OR of 1. 70 for sexual recidivism was highly significant ($z = 4. 96$, $P<0. 001$). The absolute difference in sexual recidivism between TG and CG was 6. 4 percentage points. This is a 37% reduction from the base rate of the CG. Mean effects were similar for other areas of offending. For violent recidivism, the mean OR was 1. 90

$(z = 5.36, P < 0.001)$. The average recidivism rate for treated offenders was 5.2 percentage points lower than that for untreated offenders (44% reduction). For any recidivism, the mean effect size was $OR = 1.67$ ($z = 4.52, P < 0.001$). The corresponding rate of general recidivism for treated offenders was 11.1 percentage points lower than for untreated offenders (31% reduction).

Except for violent recidivism, the effect size distributions showed considerable heterogeneity, Q (73) = 237.14, $P < 0.001$ for sexual recidivism and Q (48) = 159.80, $P < 0.001$ for general recidivism. Therefore, we analyzed variables that may have influenced the treatment effects. We restricted our moderator analyses to sexual recidivism as an outcome because this is the main area of interest and provides the largest database.

Table 2   Total mean effects of treatment for different areas of recidivism

Outcome	k	OR	$CI_{95\%}$	Q	Recidivism (%)	
					TG[a]	CH[b]
Sexual recidivism	74	1.70 ***	1.35 − 2.13	237.14 ***	11.1	17.5
Violent recidivism	20	1.90 ***	1.49 − 2.33	19.68	6.6	11.8
Any recidivism	49	1.67 ***	1.33 − 2.08	159.80 ***	22.4	32.5

k = Number of comparisons, OR = mean odds ratio, $CI_{95\%}$ = 95% confidence interval, Q = test of homogeneity (x^2, $df = k-1$), TG = treated group; CG = comparison group.

*** P < 0.001.

[a] n-Weighted average.

[b] Estimated recidivism rate.

Moderator Analyses

For reasons of space, we only report a selection of moderator analyses. Table 3 reports the results on variables that revealed significant differences or are particularly relevant for treatment practice. In all analyses, we have to take into account that moderating effects may be confounded with the influence of other variables.

Treatment Characteristics

The various treatment approaches differed considerably in effect size. In total, physical treatment had higher effects ($OR = 7.37$, $CI_{95\%}$: 4.14 − 13.11, $z = 6.80$, $P < 0.001$) than did nonphysical (psychosocial) interventions ($OR = 1.32$, $CI_{95\%}$: 1.07 − 1.62, $z =$

2. 60, *P* = 0. 01), $Q(1, k = 66)$ = 30. 47, *P*<0. 001. This was particularly due to the very large mean ES for surgical castration. However, hormonal treatment also showed a higher effect than any of the psychosocial measures. Of these, only cognitive-behavioral treatments and classic behavior therapy had a significant impact on sexual recidivism. With OR close to 1, the other approaches did not influence recidivism significantly. A regression analysis entering the more differentiated 4-point scale ratings on the use of individual treatment elements confirmed these findings. It showed significant standardized regression weights (β) for a cognitive orientation (0. 36), behavioral conditioning techniques (0. 26), and hormonal medication (0. 26); all *P*<0. 05.

In the further moderator analyses, we excluded the studies on surgical castration for the following reasons: (a) This approach differs strongly from the others. (b) It is currently rarely used in practice. (c) The effect sizes for castration were extremely large and homogeneous, $Q(7)$ = 1. 32, *P* = 0. 99, and thus would have unduly biased the results.

For the remaining 66 comparisons, the mean effect remained significant (OR = 1. 38, $CI_{95\%}$: 1. 13 − 1. 69, *z*= 3. 16, *P*<0. 01). A test of homogeneity still indicated a highly heterogeneous effect size distribution, $Q(65)$ = 163. 92, *P*<0. 001, justifying further moderator analyses.

As Table 3 shows, the decade in which the program was implemented related significantly to effect size. However, there was no linear relationship. This was also confirmed in a correlation analysis (*r* = 0. 16, *P* = 0. 15). Thus, more 'modern' programs did not generally prove to be particularly successful. The year of publication as another indicator of recency showed a similar picture. Here, the differences were even less pronounced (*r* = 0. 08, *P* = 0. 51). When the study authors had been involved in the treatment program, there was a larger effect. When there was no such affiliation, the respective OR was close to 1.

Only programs designed specifically for sex offenders had a significant effect. The few others even showed a negative outcome. Although the setting variable revealed no significant difference, there was a strong tendency for relatively larger effects in outpatient treatment and smaller effects in institutions. Mixed settings had an intermediate ES. A linear order from institutional to outpatient treatment showed a significant correlation (*r* = 0. 27, *P* = 0. 02).

Whether the treatment was delivered in an individual or a group format did not result in significant outcome differences. However, in this category, we must assume confounding with various content variables. For example, both hormonal medication and systemic treatment had to be subsumed under the individual category.

Table 3　Moderator analyses

Variables	k	Q_{bet}	OR	$CI_{95\%}$ Lower-upper
Treatment characteristics				
Treatment approach		36. 02 ***		
Cognitive-behavioral	35		1. 45 **	1. 12 - 1. 86
Classic behavioral	7		2. 19 **	1. 22 - 3. 92
Insight oriented	5		0. 98	0. 51 - 1. 89
Therapeutic community	8		0. 86	0. 54 - 1. 35
Other psychosocial, un-clear	5		0. 94	0. 53 - 1. 65
Hormonal medication	6		3. 08 **	1. 40 - 6. 79
Surgical castration	8		15. 34 ***	7. 34 - 32. 05
Time of treatment imple-mentation		7. 37 **		
Before 1970	5		0. 56 *	0. 32 - 0. 98
1970s	14		2. 03 ***	1. 34 - 3. 09
1980s	30		1. 38 **	1. 08 - 1. 77
1990s	17		1. 27	0. 86 - 1. 87
Specific treatment sex of-fenders		4. 70 *		
Yes	56		1. 56 ***	1. 27 - 1. 93
No	5		0. 76	0. 41 - 1. 41
Setting of treatment		5. 10		
Prison	21		1. 16	0. 84 - 1. 60
Hospital	8		1. 10	0. 62 - 1. 94
Outpatient	27		1. 93 ***	1. 35 - 2. 77
Mixed	10		1. 37	0. 78 - 2. 41
Format of treatment		6. 74		
Only group treatment	17		1. 12	0. 76 - 1. 66
Mainly group treatment	17		1. 57 *	1. 02 - 2. 42
Mixed	8		2. 45 *	1. 36 - 4. 40
Mainly individual treat-ment	8		1. 40	0. 77 - 2. 53

continued

Variables	k	Q_{bet}	OR	CI$_{95\%}$ Lower-upper
Only individual treatment	6		2. 88 *	1. 14 - 7. 24
Author affiliation to treatment program		10. 95 ***		
Yes	32		1. 92 ***	1. 44 - 2. 56
No.	30		0. 99	0. 76 - 1. 29
Offender characteristics				
Age group		1. 19		
Adolescents only	7		2. 35 *	1. 01 - 5. 43
Adults only	36		1. 43 *	1. 08 - 1. 90
Offense type		9. 04 *		
Rape	5		4. 91 **	1. 64 - 14. 68
Child molestation (extrafam.)	9		2. 15 *	1. 11 - 4. 16
Child molestation (incl. incest)	10		1. 02	0. 58 - 1. 80
Exhibitionism	4		3. 72 *	1. 27 - 10. 93
Treatment participation		2. 22		
Voluntary	28		1. 45 *	1. 08 - 1. 93
Nonvoluntary	15		1. 05	0. 70 - 1. 58
Mixed	7		1. 01	0. 57 - 1. 77
Treatment termination		—a		
Treatment completed regularly	44		1. 58 ***	1. 23 - 2. 05
Dropped out of treatment	14		0. 51 ***	0. 39 - 0. 67
Methodological characteristics				
Sample size		31. 43 ***		
Up to 50	18		4. 03 ***	2. 50 - 6. 50
51 - 100	10		1. 32	0. 76 - 2. 27
101 - 200	16		1. 65 **	1. 13 - 2. 41
201 - 500	12		1. 00	0. 72 - 1. 38
More than 500	10		0. 88	0. 64 - 1. 21
Maryland Scale		6. 13		
Level 2 (nonequivalent)	37		1. 16	0. 90 - 1. 50
Level 3 (equivalence assumed)	17		2. 08 ***	1. 40 - 3. 08

continued

Variables	k	Q_{bet}	OR	CI$_{95\%}$ Lower-upper
Level 4 (matching, statistical control)	6		1. 19	0. 67 − 2. 12
Level 5 (randomization)	6		1. 48	0. 74 − 2. 96
Control group formation		1. 64		
Treatment refused	11		1. 96 **	1. 20 − 3. 20
Other	47		1. 37 *	1. 07 − 1. 75
Source of recidivism data		4. 56 *		
Criminal records only	57		1. 28 *	1. 04 − 1. 57
Also self-report	5		3. 32 **	1. 42 − 7. 78

Except for the analysis on treatment approaches, studies on surgical castration are not included in the moderator analyses.

k = number of comparisons, Q_{bet} = test of between group differences (X^2-distributed with df = number of categories −1), OR = odds ratio; CI$_{95\%}$ = 95% confidence interval; CG = comparison group.

[a] Comparisons are based on identical CG in part; between-group differences could thus not be tested statistically.

* $P < 0.05$.

** $P < 0.01$.

*** $P < 0.001$.

Offender Characteristics

Programs that specifically addressed juvenile sex offenders had a higher effect than those for adult offenders. However, this difference was not significant. A related analysis showed that treatment of agehomogeneous groups tended to be more successful ($k = 48$; $r = 0.23$, $P = 0.10$).

Although the impact on specific offender groups is highly important in treatment practice, only few studies differentiated offense categories. These comparisons showed significant effects for all categories except that of intra-familial child molesting. The latter finding is related to the low recidivism baserate for incest offenders. There was a relatively large effect for rapists, but this was based on only five studies.

When sexual offenders participated voluntarily in treatment, the average ES was significantly positive. Obligatory participation and mixed conditions resulted in no effect. However, these differences were not significant.

Whether treatment was terminated regularly or prematurely had an impact on sexual recidivism. Whereas regular completers showed better effects than the control groups, dropouts did significantly worse. Dropping out of treatment doubled the odds of relapse and this negative effect was even homogeneous, $Q(13) = 11.52$, $P = 0.57$. In contrast, effect sizes that referred to completers revealed considerable heterogeneity, $Q(43) = 100.20$, $P<0.001$.

Methodological Characteristics

Sample size correlated significantly with effect size ($r = -0.26$, $P = 0.03$). This was particularly due to the extreme poles of the sample sizes. Comparisons based on small samples ($N \leqslant 50$) showed very clear effects, whereas the mean OR for very large samples was slightly below 1. This relationship could not be attributed to a publication bias only: Although in unpublished studies, the effect was somewhat less pronounced at the extreme ends of the sample size distribution, there was an even clearer linear trend compared with published studies ($r = -0.34$ vs. r $= -0.20$).

Overall, design quality did not yield a significant moderator effect. Comparisons of equivalent TG and CG (Maryland Scale Level 3 and above) revealed an average OR of 1.69 ($CI_{95\%}$: 1.26 - 2.28). At $P = 0.06$, this exceeded the OR of 1.16 for Level 2 comparisons. However, as Table 3 shows, there was no linear relationship between design quality and ES. Randomized trials also did not differ from the other comparisons, $Q(1, k = 66) = 0.07$, $P = 0.79$. Control groups containing treatment refusers revealed relatively large effects, however, these effects did not differ significantly from studies using other control groups.

The length of follow-up did not correlate with ES ($r = 0.00$). Different indicators of re-offending (i.e., reconviction, rearrest, etc.) also did not relate systematically to outcome variation, $Q(6, k = 60) = 3.45$, $P = 0.49$. In contrast, the sources used to gather the respective information had a significant impact on ES, $Q(2, k = 62) = 7.91$, $P = 0.02$. Comparisons using not only official records but also self-reported data had larger effects. However, this variable was confounded with the type of treatment, because all studies on hormonal medication included self-reported recidivism.

As could be expected, a higher baserate of recidivism correlated with a larger ES ($r = 0.30$, $P = 0.01$). This effect was also confounded, because informal data sources produced higher baserates. After controlling for this aspect, the relationship between baserate and ES was weaker ($\beta = 0.23$, $P = 0.08$).

Features of descriptive validity do not address the process of treatment and its evaluation but primarily the process of scientific reporting. Nonetheless, our analysis showed that these also related to effect size. Both the quality of documenting the treatment concept ($r = 0.33$, $P<0.01$) and the reporting of outcome statistics ($r = 0.24$, $P = 0.03$) correlated significantly with ES.

General Study Characteristics

There were no significant ES differences between the various groups of countries in which the studies were performed, $Q(4, k = 66) = 2.46$, $P = 0.65$. Regarding publication type, we only found a significant effect for published comparisons ($k = 40$, OR $= 1.62$, $CI_{95\%}$: $1.23 - 2.13$, $P<0.001$). The mean effect for unpublished comparisons was only OR $= 1.14$ ($k = 26$, $CI_{95\%} := 0.84 - 1.54$, $P = 0.42$). However, this difference was not significant, $Q(1, k = 66) = 2.91$, $P = 0.09$.

Sensitivity Analysis

The effects of moderators may be influenced strongly by a few results from studies with very large sample size (Lipsey and Wilson 2001). Therefore, we conducted a sensitivity analysis by using two different procedures. First, we excluded all comparisons with sample sizes larger than 1,000 ($k = 3$). In a second approach, all comparisons with a sample size of more than 500 were truncated to $n = 500$. With one exception, the sensitivity analyses confirmed the significant moderator effects reported in Table 3. Only the effect of unspecific offender treatment failed to reach significance when we eliminated the comparisons with sample sizes larger than 1,000 ($P = 0.08$).

Hierarchical Regression

The previous analyses have repeatedly indicated problems of confounded moderators. Therefore, it is particularly relevant to see how far treatment effects are confounded with methodological and other characteristics of the evaluation. To answer this question, we computed a hierarchical regression analysis controlling sequentially for those proportions of outcome variance that could not be attributed to the treatment itself. At first, we entered unspecific and methodological study characteristics into the model. We then added offender characteristics, general treatment characteristics, and, finally, the treatment content. We entered variables that were theoretically important or empirically significant on the bivariate level ($r \geqslant 0.20$). At each hierarchical step, variables that did not contribute to the explanation of variance were excluded stepwise ($P>0.10$). Because only a relatively small number of comparisons were available for the analysis, we chose this procedure in order to not overload the model with insignificant variables. Missing values were plugged with the sample mean, and analyses controlled for the effects of missing values (see Cohen, 1983). In contrast to the previous bivariate analyses, the hierarchical regression was based on a fixed effects model because we expected that the variables included would reduce a considerable part of the observed heterogeneity. The results are presented in Table 4.

As expected, heterogeneity was of moderate magnitude and not significant, $Q(55, k = 66) = 65.40$, $P = 0.16$. With 60%, the model explained a large proportion of ES variance, $Q(10, k = 66) = 98.52$, $P<0.001$. However, one should bear in mind that due to the stepwise exclusion of variables on each cluster level, the model becomes artificially 'clean.' Only a few variables remained as independent predictors in each cluster. Methodological characteristics accounted for a considerable amount of variance (45%). Due to deficits in sample description and differentiation, offender characteristics only had a small independent impact on ES. Age homogeneity was the only relevant variable, and added 3% of explained variance. General characteristics of treatment were more important. Specificity of treatment for sex offenders, involvement of authors in the program, and a group format contributed to a 9 percentage points increase in explained ES variance. Although it was only entered in the final step, a cognitive treatment orientation still added significantly to the explanation of ES variance over and above the preceding clusters. None of the other treatment variables remained in the model. Obviously, the effects of hormonal medication and behavioral conditioning methods were highly confounded with other variables. Taken together, the last two steps suggest that at least one fifth of the explained ES variance could be attributed to treatment characteristics. When interpreting this figure, we should bear in mind that this is a very conservative estimate because all other variables had been controlled already.

Table 4   Hierarchical regression

Variable cluster	ΔR^2
Methodological characteristics	0.45 ***
+ Quality of outcome reporting (0.35 ***), Quality of treatment description (0.20 *),	

Variable cluster	ΔR^2
Small sample, $N \leqslant 50$ (0.42 ***), Treatment refusers as CG (0.16$^+$)	
$-$TG contains dropouts ($-$0.24 **)	
Offenders	0.03 *
$+$ Age homogeneity of TG (0.16 *)	
General treatment characteristics	0.10 ***
$+$ Involvement of authors (0.24 **), Group format (0.18$^+$)	
$-$Not specific for sexual offenders ($-$0.19$^+$)	
Content of treatment	0.03 *
$+$ Cognitive orientation (0.28 *)	

Changes in index direction correspond to higher ($+$) and lower ($-$) effect sizes respectively (standardized β weights are reported in brackets). Total $R^2 = 0.60$, $Q(10) = 98.52$, $P<0.001$.

$^+$P <0.10.

* P < 0.05.

** P< 0.01.

*** P < 0.001.

DISCUSSION

Due to a recent increase in research and the multilingual approach of our review, this meta-analysis contains 80 comparisons between treatment and control groups containing a total of more than 22,000 individuals. This is currently the most comprehensive database on the outcome of sex offender treatment. Nearly one-third of the studies have been published since 2000, and approximately one-third come from countries outside of North America. These are indicators of a strong international interest in 'what works' for sex offenders. However, even though we have excluded studies containing no control group or only a comparison with dropouts, the methodological quality of the studies still remains moderate. Only 40% of the comparisons reach a level of 3 or higher on the Maryland Scale of Methodological Rigor (Sherman *et al.* , 1997), indicating sufficient control of equivalence between TG and CG. Only seven evaluations contain a randomized design. We have not restricted our review to these 'gold-standard' studies for the following reasons: First, limitation to a few evaluations of heterogeneous modes of treatment would not allow a differentiated analysis. Second, even randomization does not guarantee full equivalence of TG and CG (see, e. g. , Marques *et al.* , 2005). Third, as far as nonequivalence can be assessed, it tends to promote a conservative estimate of treatment efficacy (more high-risk cases in the TGs). And last but not least, the effects of our subsample of randomized studies do not differ significantly from evaluations with lower design quality (see, also, Lipsey and Wilson, 1998; Lösel, 1995).

Bearing the methodological problems in mind, one should draw very cautious conclusions from our meta-analysis. The most important message is an overall positive and significant effect of sex offender treatment. The mean odds ratio is 1.70 for sexual recidivism. The e-quivalent d coefficient of 0.29 lies within the typical range found in meta-analyses of general offender treatment (Lösel, 1995; McGuire, 2002). Sexual offender treatment also has an effect on general recidivism (OR = 1.67). Obviously, effective programs do not just influence sexually motivated problem behavior but also have a broader impact on criminality. This is in accordance with the experience that many sex offenders are not 'specialized' but engage in nonsexual offenses as well (Hanson and Bussière, 1998). However, our analysis also shows that unspecific offender programs have no impact on sexual recidivism.

The mean rate of sexual recidivism is 11.1% in TGs and 17.5% in CGs. At first glance, this absolute difference of a little more than 6 percentage points may seem small. However, when the low baserate of sexual recidivism is taken into account, this is equivalent to a reduction of nearly 37%. For general recidivism, the reduction is 31%. Particularly in sexual recidivism, our general effect is larger than that found by Hanson *et al.* (2002) in their meta-analysis of psychological treatment (27%). Most probably, this is due to our inclusion of both psychological and medical modes of treatment. The average effect of physical treatment is much larger than that of psychosocial programs. The main source for this difference is a very strong effect of surgical castration, although hormonal medication also shows a relatively good outcome.

Although the very large effect of surgical castration seems to be well replicated (eight comparisons with homogeneous ES), it calls for further comment: None of the castration studies attain Level 3 on the Maryland Scale. Accordingly, we cannot assume equivalence between the TG and CG in these evaluations. Sex offenders receiving surgical castration are a highly selected and motivated group. They apply for this very intensive intervention voluntarily, whereas control individuals often refuse it or are not accepted by expert committees (e.g., Wille and Beier, 1989). Hence, the TGs probably are at lower risk of reoffending than the CGs. For ethical, legal, and medical reasons, surgical castration is also rarely used in practice (Rösler and Witztum, 2000). However, the very low rate of sexual recidivism in castrated offenders suggests that societies should not abandon this approach right away but perform a differentiated assessment of the pros and cons. Within an impartial and thorough process of informed consent, it may be an option for a subgroup of high-risk sex offenders who otherwise would receive very long or lifetime detention.

Most sex offenders do not have an abnormally high level of male sex hormones (Hucker and Bain, 1990; Fedoroff and Moran, 1997). As with surgical castration, we must take this into account when considering the relatively strong effect of hormonal medication. Treatment with medroxy-progesteronacetate (in the US; e. g., Provera) or cyproteronacetate (in Europe; e. g., Androcur) does not seem to work by normalizing extreme testosterone levels, but by strongly reducing more or less normal levels of sexual arousal (Rösler and Witztum, 2000). In addition, there are serious negative side effects that frequently lead to noncompliance and dropout (e. g., Langevin, 1979). The termination of medication may rapidly increase the risk of recidivism (Meyer et al., 1992). Therefore, hormonal medication is indicated primarily for cases in which sexual arousal plays a central role in offending (e. g., Hall, 1996) and should be accompanied by psychological treatment that supports compliance and has its own causal effect on sexual reoffending (Maletzky, 1991; Meyer and Cole, 1997).

This is why the pharmacological studies in our meta-analysis often contain psychosocial interventions as well. We have analyzed the impact of such 'treatment packages' by rating the various components separately. A regression analysis shows that only three modes of treatment have a significant impact: hormonal, behavioral, and cognitive-behavioral. The results of the first two types of program are more confounded with methodological and other study characteristics than those of the latter. After controlling for such variables, only the cognitive-behavioral orientation shows an independent treatment effect (see Table 4).

The significant positive effect of cognitive-behavioral programs is based on a solid number of 35 independent comparisons. With seven comparisons, the significant effect of classic behavior therapy has a much smaller database. The same applies to insight-oriented treatment, therapeutic communities, and other types of psychosocial programs that reveal no significant effect. That well-structured cognitive-behavioral programs work relatively well is in accordance with the literature on general offender treatment (e. g., Lösel, 2001a;

McGuire, 2002). It is also consistent with the findings of previous reviews of sex offender treatment (e. g. , Gallagher *et al.* , 2000; Hall, 1995; Hanson *et al.* , 2002). However, the effect size for cognitive-behavioral programs in our analysis (OR = 1.45) is slightly smaller than that reported by Hanson *et al.* , for 'current' programs that consist of mainly cognitive-behavioral approaches (OR = 1.67; direction converted by us).

Overall, we have not found that more recent programs are superior in outcome. Although treatment before the 1970s was clearly ineffective, neither programs from the 1990s nor publications after 2000 reveal stronger effects than in previous decades. Even within the cognitive-behavioral category, more current programs are not more effective than older ones. Some recent evaluations have revealed rather small or no positive effects (e. g. , Friendship *et al.* , 2003; Hanson *et al.* , 2004; Ruddijs and Timmerman, 2000; Worling and Curwen, 2000). A follow-up of one of the soundest evaluations has also found no positive effect (Marques *et al.* , 2005). Due to the necessary follow-up lags, even recent studies may not represent all the features of the current state of the art in sexual offender treatment. One must also bear in mind that outcomes of treatment often decline when model projects are transformed into routine practice (Lösel, 2001b).

The heterogeneity of outcomes within similar types of programs may be partially explained by the impact of other factors on effect size. Similar to the treatment content, these further moderators must be interpreted very cautiously: (a) Some effects are based on only a few studies. (b) The random model is less sensitive for moderator effects (Overton 1998). (c) Multiple significance testing in moderator analyses enhances the risk of an alpha error. (d) The moderators are confounded and some have no impact on the multivariate level.

Although we have found no linear relationship between design quality and outcome, there is a tendency of larger effects in studies containing equivalent treatment and control groups (at least Level 3 on the Maryland Scale). More randomized studies on the same types of treatment are needed to clarify this issue in the field of sexual offender treatmentin a similar wayas in other criminological areas (e. g. , Weisburd *et al.* , 2001). The impact of other methodological characteristics appears more clearly. For example, studies that include not only official recidivism data but also self-reports show larger effects. This finding is partially confounded with treatment by hormonal medication. Issues of descriptive validity such as quality of treatment description and outcome reporting are also related to larger effects.

In practical terms, the relation between sample size and treatment effectiveness is particularly important. Small studies ($N \leqslant 50$) reveal a large ES and large studies ($N > 500$) a small *ES*. One explanation of this result relates to publication bias. Larger samples are more likely to reveal the significance of a true small effect (Weisburd *et al.*, 2003). Due to author or editor decisions, such large studies may be published, whereas small studies, which would have needed a larger effect size to attain significance, remain unpublished. In accordance with such an interpretation, published studies have a larger effect than unpublished studies. However, this difference is not significant, and we have found a similar-even somewhat greater – impact of sample size among the unpublished studies. Of course, this does not fully rule out some kind of publication bias, because negative results may also be less likely to be reported in unpublished studies (particularly when the researcher has a strong vested interest in the success of the program). Nevertheless, we must take a second explanation into account: In large samples, it is more difficult to maintain integrity and homogeneity of treatments or samples, and this is related to the effect size itself (Lösel and Wittmann, 1989; Weisburd *et al.*, 1993). A further finding supports the interpretation in terms of integrity: Programs in which the study authors were involved have a larger effect. As most outcome measures are beyond the influence of authors, this finding may indicate a more thorough implementation and monitoring of the program. Similar results on the effect of small samples and/ or author involvement have been observed in juvenile offender treatment (Lipsey and Wilson, 1998) and developmental prevention of antisocial behavior (Farrington and Welsh, 2003; Lösel and Beelmann, 2003). The few comparisons for which treatment integrity can actually be rated provide further support for this relationship.

The context of treatment is also relevant for outcome. Ambulatory programs have larger effects than institutional treatment. Because we have analyzed only control group evaluations, this finding cannot be reduced to a different risk in the respective offender groups. Offender characteristics also have some impact on effect size. However, there is often a lack of detailed information on the samples. In nearly half of the studies, samples cannot even be differentiated according to the type of sexual offense. As far as this was possible, we found a significant difference in outcome. This is mainly due to a zero effect on incest child molesters resulting from the very low base rate of (official) recidivism in this group. More treatment evaluations on specific subgroups of offenders are needed to form a solid empirical basis for differential indication.

Voluntary treatment leads to a slightly better outcome than mandatory participation, and programs for adolescents are a little more effective than those for adults. Although, these differences are not significant and may be confounded with a larger baserate of recidivism in juveniles, age homogeneity is a significant moderator in the hierarchical regression. A more pronounced finding is the higher recidivism among treatment dropouts. As a consequence, studies that include dropouts in the treatment group have smaller effects. The high risk of recidivism in dropouts underlines that this group is a core problem in offender rehabilitation and controlled evaluation (Lösel, 2001b). It should not only be interpreted as an individual deficit of the offender but as an interactive process and lack of fit between the program and the offender's needs and motivations (McMurran, 2002). Systematic processes of program accreditation and quality management like those in Canada, England and Wales, or Scotland may help to reduce this and other problems in offender treatment. However, from a realistic perspective, we should not expect too much within a short time.

Overall, there is evidence for a positive effect of sexual offender treatment. Cognitive-behavioral and hormonal treatment are most promising. In addition, various other moderators are related to a better or worse outcome. In particular, methodological factors play an important role and seem to be confounded with treatment and offender characteristics. This problem of confounded moderators is rather general and difficult to solve (Lipsey, 2003). Our hierarchical regression is only a first attempt to disentangle such patterns in the field of sexual offender treatment. We need more high-quality outcome studies that address specific subgroups of sex offenders as well as more detailed process evaluations on various treatment characteristics and components. Implementing such strategies in research and practice will further clarify 'What works for whom under which circumstances?'

Appendix: Studies integrated into the meta-analysis

Allam, J. (1998). *Effective practice in work with sex offenders: A reconviction study comparing treated and untreated offenders*. Birmingham: West Midlands Probation Service Sex Offender Unit.

Bakker, L. , Hudson, S. M. ,Wales, D. S. & Riley, D. (1998). *"And there was Light"*: *Evaluating the Kia Marama Treatment Programme for New Zealand sex offenders against children*. Christchurch, NZ: Psychological Service, Department of Corrections.

Barbaree, H. E. & Seto, M. C. (1998). *The ongoing follow-up of sex offenders treated at the Warkworth Sexual Behaviour Clinic*. Toronto: Centre for Addiction and Mental Health.

Barnes, J. M. (2000). *Recidivism in sex offenders: A follow-up comparison of treated and untreated sex offenders released to the community in Kentucky*. Unpublished doctoral dissertation, University of Louisville, Louisville, KY.

Berner, W. & Karlick-Bolten, E. (1986). *Verlaufsformen der Sexualkriminalität. 5-Jahres-Katamnesen bei 326 Sexualdelinquenten unter Berücksichtigung von Frühsozialisation, vorausgegangener Delinquenz, psychiatrisch-psychologischer Diagnostik und Therapie* [Developmental courses of sexual criminality]. Stuttgart: Enke.

Bluglass, R. (1980). Indecent exposure in the West Midlands. In D. West (Ed.), *Sex offenders in the criminal justice system* (pp. 171 – 180). Cambridge: Cambridge Institute of Criminology.

Borduin, C. M. , Henggeler, S. W. , Blaske, D. M. & Stein, R. J. (1990). Multisystemic treatment of adolescent sexual offenders. *International Journal of Offender Therapy and Comparative Criminology* 34, 105 – 113.

Borduin, C. M. & Schaeffer, C. M. (2001). Multisystemic treatment of juvenile sexual offenders: A progress report. *Journal of Psychology and Human Sexuality* 13, 25 – 42.

Byrne, S. M. (1999). *Treatment efficacy of a juvenile sexual offender treatment program*. Unpublished doctoral dissertation, Memorial University of Newfoundland, St. Johns, Newfoundland, Canada.

Cornu, F. (1973). *Katamnesen bei kastrierten Sittlichkeitsdelinquenten aus forensisch-psychiatrischer Sicht* [Follow-ups with castrated sex offenders]. Basel: Karger.

Craissati, J. , Falla, S. , McClurg, G. & Beech, A. (2002). Risk, reconviction rates and pro-offending attitudes for child molesters in a complete geographical area of London. *Journal of Sexual Aggression* 8, 22 – 38.

Di Fazio, R. , Abracen, J. & Looman, J. (2001). Group versus individual treatment of sex offenders: A comparison. *Forum on Corrections Research* 13, 56 – 59.

Dünkel, F. & Geng, B. (1994). Rückfall und Bewährung von Karrieretätern nach

Entlassung aus dem sozialtherapeutischen Behandlungsvollzug und dem Regelvollzug [Relapse and non-relapse of career offenders after release from socialtherapeutic and standard prisons]. In M. Steller, K. -P. Dahle & M. Basqué (Eds.), *Straftä terbehandlung*: *Argumente für eine Revitalisierung in Forschung und Praxis* (pp. 35 – 74). Pfaffenweiler: Centaurus.

Fedoroff, J. P. , Wisner-Carlson, R. , Dean, S. & Berlin, F. S. (1992). Medroxy-progesterone acetate in the treatment of paraphilic sexual disorders: Rate of relapse in paraphilic men treated in long-term group psychotherapy with or without medroxy-progesterone acetate. *Journal of Offender Rehabilitation* 18, 109 – 123.

Friendship, C. , Mann, R. E. & Beech, A. R. (2003). Evaluation of a national prison-based treatment program for sexual offenders in England and Wales. *Journal of Interpersonal Violence* 18, 744 – 759.

Frisbie, L. V. (1969). *Another look at sex offenders in California* (Mental Health Research Monograph No. 12). Sacramento, CA: State of California, Department of Mental Hygiene.

Groth, N. A. (1983). Treatment of the sexual offender in a correctional institution. In J. G. Greer & I. R. Stewart (Eds.), *The sexual aggressor* (pp. 160 – 176). New York: Van Nostrand-Reinhold.

Guarino-Ghezzi, S. & Kimball, L. M. (1998). Juvenile sex offenders in treatment. *Corrections Management Quarterly* 2, 45 – 54.

Hall, G. C. N. (1995). The preliminary development of a theory-based community treatment for sexual offenders. *Professional Psychology*: *Research and Practice* 26, 478 – 483.

Hanson, R. K. , Steffy, R. A. & Gauthier, R. (1992). Long-term follow-up of child molesters: Risk predictors and treatment outcome.

Hanson, R. K. & Nicholaichuk, T. P. (2000). A cautionary note regarding Nicholaichuk *et al.* (2000). *Sexual Abuse*: *A Journal of Research and Treatment* 12, 289 – 293.

Hanson, R. K. , Broom, I. & Stephenson, M. (2004). Evaluating community sex offender treatment programs: A 12-year follow-up of 724 offenders. *Canadian Journal of Behavioural Sciences* 36, 87 – 96.

Hedderman, C. & Sugg, D. (1996). *Does treating sex offenders reduce offending?* (Research Findings No. 45). London: Home Office Research and Statistics Directorate.

Huot, S. J. (2002). *Recidivism, recidivism, recidivism! An update of several Minnesota recidivism studies*. Paper presented at the 21st Annual Research and Treatment Conference of the Association for the Treatment of Sexual Abusers on 'Best Practices: Clinical and Research Collaborations,' Montréal, Québec, Canada. October.

Janner, J. (1959). Über die Bedeutung psychiatrischer Betreuung verurteilter Sexualdelinquenten [About the importance of psychiatric care for convicted sexual offenders]. *Schweizerische Zeitschrift für Strafrecht* 74, 310 – 319.

Kansas Department of Corrections. (2000). *Offender programs evaluation: Volume IV*. Topeka: Kansas Department of Corrections.

Kaul, J., Huot, S. J., Epperson, D. & Dornfeld, M. (1994). *Sex offenders released in 1988* (Unpublished report). St. Paul, MN: Minnesota Department of Corrections.

Lab, S. P., Shields, G. & Schondel, C. (1993). Research note: An evaluation of juvenile sexual offender treatment. *Crime and Delinquency* 39, 543 – 553.

Langevin, R., Paitich, D., Hucker, S. J., Newman, S., Ramsay, G. & Pope, S., *et al.* (1979). The effect of assertiveness training, Provera, and sex of therapist in the treatment of genital exhibitionism. *Journal of Behavior Therapy and Experimental Psychiatry* 10, 275 – 282.

Looman, J., Abracen, J. & Nicholaichuk, T. P. (2000). Recidivism among treated sexual offenders and matched controls: Data from the Regional Treatment Centre (Ontario). *Journal of Interpersonal Violence* 15, 279 – 290.

Lowden, K., Hetz, N., Harrison, L., Patrick, D., English, K. & Pasini-Hill, D. (2003). *Evaluation of Colorado's prison therapeutic community for sex offenders: A report of findings*. Denver, CO: Office of Research and Statistics, Division of Criminal Justice.

Maletzky, B. M. (1991). The use of medroxyprogesterone acetate to assist in the treatment of sexual offenders. *Annals of Sex Research* 4, 117 – 129.

Maletzky, B. M. & Field, G. (2003). The biological treatment of dangerous sexual offenders. A review and preliminary report of the Oregon pilot depo-Provera program. *Aggression and Violent Behavior* 8, 391 – 412.

Marques, J. K. (1999). How to answer the question, "Does sex offender treatment work?" *Journal of Interpersonal Violence* 14, 437 – 451.

Marshall, W. L. & Barbaree, H. E. (1988). The long-term evaluation of a behavioral treatment program for child molesters. *Behaviour Research and Therapy* 26, 499 – 511.

Marshall, W. L. , Eccles, A. & Barbaree, H. E. (1991). The treatment of exhibitionists: A focus on sexual deviance versus cognitive and relationship features. *Behaviour Research and Therapy* 26, 129 – 135.

McConaghy, N. , Blaszczynski, A. & Kidson, W. (1988). Treatment of sex offenders with imaginal desensitization and/or medroxyprogesterone. *Acta Psychiatrica Scandinavica* 77, 199 – 206.

McGrath, R. J. , Hoke, S. E. & Vojtisek, J. E. (1998). Cognitive-behavioral treatment of sex offenders. A treatment comparison and long-term follow-up study. *Criminal Justice and Behavior* 25, 203 – 225.

McGrath, R. J. , Cumming, G. F. , Livingston, J. A. & Hoke, S. E. (2003). Outcome of a treatment program for adult sex offenders. From prison to community. *Journal of Interpersonal Violence* 18, 3 – 17.

McGuire, T. J. (2000). Correctional institution based sex offender treatment: A lapse behavior study. *Behavioral Sciences and the Law* 18, 57 – 71.

Meyer, W. J. , Cole, C. & Emory, E. (1992). Depo provera treatment for sex offending behavior: An evaluation of outcome. *Bulletin of the American Academy of Psychiatry and the Law* 20, 249 – 259.

Mulloy, R. & Smiley, W. C. (1996). *Recidivism and treated sexual offenders*. Paper presented at the International Congress of Psychology, August 16 – 21, Montréal, Canada.

Nicholaichuk, T. P. (1996). Sex offender treatment priority: An illustration of the risk/need principle. *Forum on Corrections Research* 8, 38 – 41.

Nutbrown, V. & Stasiak, E. (1987). Research monograph: A retrospective analysis of O. C. I. cost effectiveness 1977 – 1981. *Ontario Correctional Institute* 2, 1 – 16.

Ohio Department of Rehabilitation and Correction. (1996). *Five year recidivism follow-up of sex offender releases* (Unpublished Report). Columbus, OH: Ohio Department of Rehabilitation and Correction.

Oregon Department of Corrections. (1997). *Outcome evaluation of the Jackson County Sex Offender Supervision and Treatment Program*. Retrieved 5/29/01, from http:// www. doc. state. or. us/research/jackrpt2. pdf

Ortmann, R. (2002). *Sozialtherapie im Strafvollzug: Eine experimentelle Längsschnittstudie zu den Wirkungen von Strafvollzugsmaβnahmen auf Legal-und Sozialbewä hrung* [Social therapy in prison]. Freiburg: Edition iuscrim.

Perkins, D. (1987). A psychological treatment programme for sex offenders. In B. J. MacGurk & D. M. Thornton (Eds.), *Applying psychology to imprisonment: Theory and practice* (pp. 191 – 217). London: Her Majesty's Stationery Office Books.

Peters, J. J., Pedigo, J., Steg, J. & McKenna, J., Jr. (1968). Group psychotherapy of the sex offender. *Federal Probation* 32, 41 – 45.

Procter, E. (1996). A five-year outcome evaluation of a community-based treatment program for convicted sexual offenders run by the probation service. *Journal of Sexual Aggression* 2, 3 – 16.

Rasmussen, L. A. (1995). *Factors related to recidivism among juvenile sexual offenders.* Unpublished doctoral dissertation, University of Utah.

Rattenbury, F. R. (1985). *The outcomes of hospitalized and incarcerated sex offenders: A study of offender types, recidivism rates, and identifying characteristics of the repeat offender.* Unpublished doctoral dissertation, Loyola University of Chicago, Chicago, IL.

Rice, M. E., Harris, G. T. & Quinsey, V. L. (1993). Evaluating treatment programs for child molesters. In J. Hudson & J. V. Roberts (Eds.), *Evaluating justice: Canadian policies and programs* (pp. 189 – 203). Toronto: Thompson.

Robinson, D. (1995). *The impact of cognitive skills training on post-release recidivism among Canadian federal offenders* (Research Report No. R-41). Ottawa, Ontario, Canada: Correctional Service of Canada.

Romero, J. J. & Williams, L. M. (1983). Group psychotherapy and intensive probation supervision with sex offenders: A comparative study. *Federal Probation* 47, 36 – 42.

Ruddijs, F. & Timmerman, H. (2000). The Stichting ambulante preventie projecten method: A comparative study of recidivism in first offenders in a Dutch outpatient setting. *International Journal of Offender Therapy and Comparative Criminology* 44, 725 – 739.

Schmid, P. (1988). *Was geschieht mit den Sexualstraftätern in der Psychiatrie? Darstellung und Bewertung der psychiatrischen Behandlung von Sexualstraftätern im Psychiatrischen Landeskrankenhaus Bad Schussenried in den Jahren 1978 – 1987* [What happens to sexual offenders in psychiatric clinics]. Unpublished doctoral dissertation, Universität Tübingen, Tübingen.

Smith, M. A. (2000). *The impact of prison-based drug treatment on the timing and risk of reincarceration of sexual offenders*. Unpublished dissertation, Florida State University, Tallahassee, FL.

Song, L. & Lieb, R. (1995). *Washington State sex offenders: Overview of recidivism studies* (No. 95-02-1101). Olympia, WA: Washington State Institute for Public Policy.

Stalans, L. J., Seng, M., Yarnold, P., Lavery, T. & Swartz, J. (2001). *Process and initial impact evaluation of the Cook County Adult Probation Department's Sex Offender Program: Final and summary report for the period of June, 1997 to June, 2000*. Chicago, IL: Illinois Department of Corrections.

Stürup, G. K. (1953). Sexual offenders and their treatment in Denmark and other Scandinavian countries. *International Review of Criminal Policy* 4, 1 – 19.

Stürup, G. K. (1968). Treatment of sexual offenders in Herstedvester Denmark: The rapists. *Acta Psychiatrica Scandinavica Supplement* 204, 1 – 62.

Taylor, R. (2000). *A seven-year reconviction study of HMP Grendon Therapeutic Community* (Research Findings No. 115). London: Home Office Research and Statistics Directorate.

Wille, R. & Beier, K. M. (1989). Castration in Germany. *Annals of Sex Research* 2, 103 – 133.

Worling, J. R. & Curwen, T. (2000). Adolescent sexual offender recidivism: Success of specialized treatment and implications for risk prediction. *Child Abuse & Neglect* 24, 965 – 982.

Ziethen, F. (2002). Rückfallpräventive Effizienz der sozialtherapeutischen *Behandlung von Sexualstraftätern. Evaluation der Sozialtherapie in der JVA Berlin-Tegel* [Relapse preventive efficiency of socialtherapeutic treatment for sexual offenders]. Unpublished master thesis, Freie Universität Berlin.

References

Alexander, M. A. (1999). Sexual offender treatment efficacy revisited. *Sexual Abuse: A Journal of Research and Treatment* 11, 101 – 116.

Aos, S., Phipps, P., Barnoski, R. & Lieb, R. (2001). *The comparative costs and benefits of programs to reduce crime. Version 4. 0* (Report No. 01-05-1201). Washington: Washington State Institute for Public Policy.

Barbaree, H. (1997). Evaluating treatment efficacy with sexual offenders: The insensitivity of recidivism studies to treatment effects. *Sexual Abuse: Journal of Research and Treatment* 9, 111 – 128.

Cohen, J. & Cohen, P. (1983). *Applied multiple regression/correlation analysis for the behavioral sciences* (2nd ed.). Hillsdale, NJ: Erlbaum.

Cronbach, L. J. , Ambron, S. R. , Dornbusch, S. M. , Hess, R. D. , Hornik, R. C. & Phillips, D. C. , *et al.* (1980). *Toward a reform of program evaluation.* San Francisco, CA: Jossey Bass.

Farrington, D. P. (2003). Methodological quality standards for evaluation research. *Annals of the American Academy of Political and Social Science* 587, 49 – 68.

Farrington, D. P. & Petrosino, A. (2001). The Campbell Collaboration Crime and Justice Group. *Annals of the American Academy of Political and Social Science* 578, 35 – 49.

Farrington, D. P. & Welsh, B. C. (2003). Family-based prevention of offending: A meta-analysis. *Australian and New Zealand Journal of Criminology* 36, 127 – 151.

Fedoroff, J. P. & Moran, B. (1997). Myths and misconceptions about sex offenders. *Canadian Journal of Human Sexuality* 6, 263 – 276.

Fleiss, J. L. (1994). Measures of effect size for categorical data. In L. V. Hedges (Ed.), *The handbook of research synthesis* (pp. 245 – 260). New York: Russell Sage Foundation.

Friendship, C. , Mann, R. E. & Beech, A. R. (2003). Evaluation of a national prison-based treatment program for sexual offenders in England and Wales. *Journal of Interpersonal Violence* 18, 744 – 759.

Furby, L. , Weinrott, M. R. & Blackshaw, L. (1989). Sex offender recidivism: A review. *Psychological Bulletin* 105, 3 – 30.

Gallagher, C. A. , Wilson, D. B. & MacKenzie, D. L. (2000). *A meta-analysis of the effectiveness of sex offender treatment programs.* Retrieved 5/23/2001, from http:// www. wam. umd. edu/ ~ wilsondb/papers/sexoffender. pdf.

Hall, G. C. N. (1995). Sexual offender recidivism revisited: A meta-analysis of recent treatment studies. *Journal of Consulting and Clinical Psychology* 63, 802 – 809.

Hall, G. C. N. (1996). *Theory-based assessment, treatment, and prevention of sexual* aggression. New York: Oxford University Press.

Hanson, R. K. & Bussière, M. T. (1998). Predicting relapse: A meta-analysis of sexual offender recidivism studies. *Journal of Consulting and Clinical Psychology* 66, 348 – 362.

Hanson, R. K., Gordon, A., Harris, A. J. R, Marques, J. K., Murphy, W. D. & Quinsey, V. L., *et al.* (2002). First report of the collaborative outcome data project on the effectiveness of psychological treatment for sex offenders. *Sexual Abuse: A Journal of Research and Treatment* 14, 169 – 194.

Hanson, R. K., Broom, I. & Stephenson, M. (2004). Evaluating community sex offender treatment programs: A 12-year follow-up of 724 offenders. *Canadian Journal of Behavioural Sciences* 36, 87 – 96.

Hasselblad, V. & Hedges, L. V. (1995). Meta-analysis of screening and diagnostic tests. *Psychological Bulletin* 117, 167 – 178.

Hedges, L. V. & Olkin, I. (1985). *Statistical methods for meta-analysis*. Orlando: Academic Press.

Hucker, S. J. & Bain, J. (1990). Androgenic hormones and sexual assault. In W. L. Marshall, D. R. Laws & H. E. Barbaree (Eds.), *Handbook of sexual assault: Issues, theories, and treatment of the offender* (pp. 93 – 102). New York: Plenum Press.

Langevin, R., Paitich, D., Hucker, S. J., Newman, S., Ramsay, G., Pope, S., Geller, G. & Anderson, C. (1979). The effect of assertiveness training, Provera, and sex of therapist in the treatment of genital exhibitionism. *Journal of Behavior Therapy and Experimental Psychiatry* 10, 275 – 282.

Lipsey, M. W. (2003). Those confounded moderators in meta-analysis: Good, bad, and ugly. *Annals of the American Academy of Political and Social Science* 587, 69 – 81.

Lipsey, M. W. & Wilson, D. B. (1998). Effective intervention for serious juvenile offenders: A synthesis of research. In D. P. Farrington (Ed.), *Serious & violent juvenile offenders: Risk factors and successful interventions* (pp. 313 – 345). Thousand Oaks, CA: Sage.

Lipsey, M. W. & Wilson, D. B. (2001). *Practical meta-analysis*. Thousand Oaks: Sage.

Lösel, F. (1995). The efficacy of correctional treatment: A review and synthesis of metae-valuations. In J. McGuire (Ed.), *What works: Reducing reoffending. Guidelines from Practice and Research* (pp. 79 – 111). Chichester, UK: Wiley.

Lösel, F. (2000). The efficacy of sexual offender treatment: A brief review of German and international evaluations. In P. J. van Koppen & N. Roos (Eds.), *Rationality, information and progress in law and psychology. In honour of Hans Crombag* (pp. 145 – 170). Maastricht, NL: Metajuridica Publications.

Lösel, F. (2001a). Rehabilitation of the offender. In P. B. Baltes (Ed.), *International encyclopedia of the social & behavioral sciences* (Vol. 19, pp. 12988 – 12993). Amsterdam: Elsevier.

Lösel, F. (2001b). Evaluating the effectiveness of correctional programs: Bridging the gap between research and practice. In G. A. Bernfeld, D. P. Farrington & A. W. Leschied (Eds.), *Offender rehabilitation in practice. Implementing and evaluating effective programs* (pp. 67 – 92). Chichester, UK: Wiley.

Lösel, F. & Beelmann, A. (2003). Effects of child skills training in preventing antisocial behavior: A systematic review of randomized evaluations. *Annals of the American Academy of Political and Social Science* 587, 84 – 109.

Lösel, F. & Köferl, P. (1989). Evaluation research on correctional treatment in West Germany: A meta-analysis. In H. Wegener, F. Lösel & J. Haisch (Eds.), *Criminal behavior and the justice system* (pp. 334 – 355). New York: Springer.

Lösel, F. & Schmucker, M. (2003). *The efficacy of sex offender treatment: A brief synthesis of meta-analyses.* Report for the Campbell Crime and Justice Group (Updated). University of Erlangen-Nuremberg: Institute of Psychology.

Lösel, F. & Wittmann, W. W. (1989). The relationship of treatment integrity and intensity to outcome criteria. *New Directions for Program Evaluation* 42, 97 – 108.

Maletzky, B. M. (1991). *Treating the sexual offender.* Newbury Park, CA: Sage.

Marques, J. K., Wiederanders, M., Day, D. M., Nelson, C. & von Ommeren, A. (2005). Effects of a relapse prevention program on sexual recidivism: Final results from California's Sex Offender Treatment and Evaluation Project (SOTEP). *Sexual Abuse: A Journal of Research and Treatment* 17, 79 – 107.

Marshall, W. L. & McGuire, J. (2003). Effect sizes in the treatment of sexual offenders. *International Journal of Offender Therapy and Comparative Criminology* 47, 653 – 663.

McGuire, J. (2002). Integrating findings from research reviews. In J. McGuire (Ed.), *Offender rehabilitation and treatment: Effective programmes and policies to reduce re-offending* (pp. 3 – 38). Chichester, UK: Wiley.

McMurran, M. (Ed.). (2002). *Motivating offenders to change: A guide to enhancing engagement in therapy.* Chichester, UK: Wiley.

Meyer, W. J. & Cole, C. M. (1997). Physical and chemical castration of sex offenders: A review. *Journal of Offender Rehabilitation* 25, 1–8.

Meyer, W. J., Cole, C. & Emory, E. (1992). Depo provera treatment for sex offending behavior: An evaluation of outcome. *Bulletin of the American Academy of Psychiatry and the Law* 20, 249–259.

Overton, R. C. (1998). A comparison of fixed-effects and mixed (random-effects) models for meta-analysis tests of moderator variable effects. *Psychological Methods* 3, 354–379.

Polizzi, D. M., MacKenzie, D. L. & Hickman, L. J. (1999). What works in adult sex offender treatment? A review of prison-and non-prison-based treatment programs. *International Journal of Offender Therapy and Comparative Criminology* 43, 357–374.

Prentky, R. A., Lee, A. F. S., Knight, R. A. & Cerce, D. (1997). Recidivism rates among child molesters and rapists: A methodological analysis. *Law and Human Behavior* 21, 635–659.

Quinsey, V. L., Harris, G. T., Rice, M. E. & Lalumière, M. L. (1993). Assessing treatment efficacy in outcome studies of sex offenders. *Journal of Interpersonal Violence* 8, 512–523.

Rice, M. E. & Harris, G. T. (2003). The size and sign of treatment effects in sex offender therapy. In R. A. Prentky, E. S. Janus & M. C. Seto (Eds.). *Sexually coercive behavior: Understanding and management* (pp. 428–440). New York: New York Academy of Sciences.

Rösler, A. & Witztum, E. (2000). Pharmacotherapy of paraphilias in the next millennium. *Behavioral Sciences and the Law* 18, 43–56.

Ruddijs, F. & Timmerman, H. (2000). The Stichting ambulante preventie projecten method: A comparative study of recidivism in first offenders in a Dutch outpatient setting. *International Journal of Offender Therapy and Comparative Criminology* 44, 725–739.

Shadish, W. R., Cook, T. D. & Campbell, D. T. (2002). *Experimental and quasi-experimental designs for generalized causal inference.* Boston, MA: Houghton Mifflin.

Sherman, L., Gottfredson, D., MacKenzie, D., Eck, J., Reuter, P. & Bushway, S. (1997). *Preventing crime: What works, what doesn't, what's promising.* Report to the U.

S. Congress, Washington, DC.

Weisburd, D. , Petrosino, A. & Mason, G. (1993). Design sensitivity in criminal justice experiments. In M. Tonry (Ed.), *Crime and justice* (Vol. 17, pp. 337 – 379). Chicago: University of Chicago Press.

Weisburd, D. , Lum, C. M. & Petrosino, A. (2001). Does research design affect study outcomes in criminal justice? *Annals of the American Academy of Political and Social Science* 578, 50 – 70.

Weisburd, D. , Lum, C. M. & Yang, S. -M. (2003). When can we conclude that treatments or programs "don't work"? *Annals of the American Academy of Political and Social Science* 587, 31 – 48.

White, P. , Bradley, C. , Ferriter, M. & Hatzipetrou, L. (1998). Managements for people with disorders of sexual preference and for convicted sexual offenders. *The Cochrane Database of Systematic Reviews.* (1998, Issue 4).

Wille, R. & Beier, K. M. (1989). Castration inGermany. Annals of Sex Research 2, 103 – 133.

Wilson, D. B. (2001). Meta-analytic methods for criminology. *Annals of the American Academy of Political and Social Science* 578, 71 – 89.

Worling, J. R. & Curwen, T. (2000). Adolescent sexual offender recidivism: Success of specialized treatment and implications for risk prediction. *Child Abuse & Neglect* 24, 965 – 982.

反社会行为发展的一般预防：
儿童及父母导向项目的短期和长期效果

菲德律·洛赛尔（Friedrich Lösel）

埃朗根·纽伦堡大学

马克·施泰姆勒（Mark Stemmler）

斯蒂芬妮·乔斯（Stefanie Jaursch）

安德鲁斯·比尔曼（Andreas Beelmann）

一、导　论

　　之前的纵向研究已经为我们充分拓展了我们在以下几个方面研究方法的知识：反社会行为的发展，反社会行为的生理、心理和社会原因，反社会行为的风险因素以及阻止青少年违法犯罪的积极做法，尽管在最后一个方面的研究还比较少（Farrington and Welsh，2007；Loeber and Farrington，1998；Sampson and Laub，2003）。在这些研究基础上形成的发展性预防项目旨在探讨儿童反社会行为的早期干预措施，以防止促使儿童反社会行为发展成青少年和成人犯罪的连锁反应的出现。

　　虽然在西方国家，媒体公开报道的校园枪击案、刺刀杀人案或诸如此类的极端行为已引起了学者的广泛关注，政府和相关部门也提出了相应的预防性策略，这些方法的正确性也得到了其他一些理由的支持：

儿童的社会行为问题,例如品行不端、挑衅攻击甚至违法行为等都已十分普遍地存在。根据家长反映,在近期的"德国儿童和青少年健康调查"中,研究发现14.8%的社会行为问题存在于 0 到 17 岁的人群中(Holling, Erhart, Ravens-Sieberer and Schlack, 2007)。虽然临床诊断认为问题的比例要低一些(Ihle and Esser, 2002),但仍有近十分之一的儿童表现出品行不端行为和其他混乱状态(例如:多动症/注意力不集中、焦虑、抑郁和滥用药物)。当然,我们也没必要把此问题过度夸大,因为像挑衅攻击行为或违法行为等在儿童的成长转变中多属短期现象。然而值得关注的是,近三分之一的儿童在接触过不良行为后,开始逐渐形成相对持久和稳定的反社会行为(Loeber and Farrington, 2000)。这些现象不仅阻碍了儿童自身的成长发展,更是对受害者本人以及家庭造成了许多伤害,引发了诸多社会问题。儿童的反社会行为是他们身心成长过程中的一个风险性标记,是他们转变成持续性罪犯的一个风险性标记(Farrington, 1991;Robins and Price, 1991)。反社会性质严重的儿童一般很难被管制(Bender and Lösel, 2006),且对于其今后违法行为的提前治愈和调节效果也很不显著(Lösel, 1995;McGuire, 2002)。另外,对于反社会行为的早期预防,我们也可通过经济因素进行分析解释(Foster, Prinz, Sanders, and Shapiro, 2008)。在儿童成熟至 28 岁前,社会花费在有严重反社会性质的儿童上的费用高出普通无越轨行为儿童十倍多(Scott, Knapp, Henderson, and Maughan, 2001)。仅一个案例的花费就很容易超过一百万欧元或美元(Munoz, Hutchings, Edwards, Hounsome, and O' Ceilleachair, 2004)。

虽然在这些原因的影响下,关于预防措施的发展已有了大范围延伸,但许多国家在战略上还缺少协调的、长期的和合理的政策(Farrington and Welsh 2007;Junger et al., 2007)。控制良好的评估体制主要在北美洲地区得以实施。若系统性地回顾以学校、家庭或儿童为导向的研究项目,其总体效果表现出较强的积极性,但若平均到长期计划中,其效应则不十分明显(Farrington and Welsh, 2003,2007;Lösel and Beelmann, 2003;Wilson, Gottfredson and Najaka, 2001;Lipsey, Wilson and Derzon, 2003;Lundahl, Risser and Lovejoy, 2006;Tremblay and Japel, 2003)。因此,我们通过给两个项目进行分类,精心挑选被试对象并将其分组,合理设计研究方案,科学运用数据的结果观察指标,讨论决定被试者的跟踪调查时长、样本数量大小以及研究者的介入程度等,最后综合分析后得出调查结果。虽然一些著名的项目如"High / Scope Perry 学前教育计划"(Schweinhart et al., 2005)或是"家庭照料计划"(Olds et al., 1998)等显示出长期的效应,但也有些项目表现出零效应(Henggeler et al., 1998;Littell, 2005)甚至些微负效应(McCord, 2003)。但许多有前途的计划,更应当致力于解决高危儿童的问题,为儿童的日常生活需求提供宽广环境(Farrington and Welsh,2007;Lösel,2005)。

在除了北美洲以外的其余地区外,尤其是在以德语为官方语言的国家,实证研究存在明显不足。据德国联邦家庭事务部调查结果表明,德国每年有近20万的家庭导向型研究项目(Lösel,Schmucker,Plankensteiner,and Weiss,2006)。但相比较发现,其中只有27组项目设立了对照组进行实验,只有4组具有高水平的研究方法。大部分低水平的项目效果都非根据系统科学的实证调查得出。直到最近,一些合理有效的项目才逐渐产生。显而易见,这些非科学的项目所显示的调查结果,其结论较为错综复杂。与无相应对照组的实验项目相比,有些项目的结果具有积极效应(Heinrichs et al.,2006),有些项目的结果则没有积极效应(Schmid et al.,2007;Eisner,Ribeaud,Junger,and Meidert,2007),有的只在内部产生积极效应(Schick and Cierpka,2003)。总体而言,一些出于经济目的的实验项目比高质量的实证研究项目要多很多(Lösel,2004;Eisner et al.,2007)。

当前在以德语为官方语言的国家,研究预防措施发展的课题时间跨度最长的,莫过于"Erlangen-Nuremberg 研究"(Lösel,Beelmann,Jaursch,and Stemmler,2004;Lösel,Beelmann,Stemmler and Jaursch,2006)。该课题是结合实证研究和纵向研究来调查分析儿童反社会行为的。而本文中,我们希望评估和验证其课题的预防部分,即"预防措施在家庭中对父母和孩子产生的效应"部分。该部分专门为预防学前儿童的反社会行为发展而设计。本文中的项目研究主要包括三部分:针对儿童如何解决社会问题(Shure,1992)而制定的儿童社会技能培训,根据 Oregon 模型编制的父母如何积极家教行为(Fisher et al.,1997)的培训,以及两种培训的结合型。

在之前的出版文章中,我们发现,经幼儿园老师评估认为,预防措施在控制儿童社会行为中能产生显著的短期积极效应(Lösel et al.,2006)。虽然总体上看效应不是很大,但当父母与孩子同时参与该项目时效应则十分显著。尤其是在接受项目培训前曾表现出行为问题的那些儿童,他们在项目中尤为受益。在接受项目培训一两年后,仍能看到一些积极效应(Lösel et al.,2006),对于父母的行为则能间接产生更多的特殊效果(Stemmler,Beelmann,Jaursch,and Lösel,2007)。当然,这些鼓舞人心的研究结果也存在一定的欠缺之处。第一,本研究未比较其余信息渠道对儿童行为的影响;第二,对于课题评估,作者只着重研究了参与一半以上课程的那些人员,而未能一一针对个体进行分析;第三,数据分析只做到了宏观角度的随机广泛性,而未能解决组内样本的差异性。因此,本研究主要验证了项目效果在儿童反社会行为变化的因果关系上是否准确有效。

二、研究方法

（一）样本

本文有关"Erlangen-Nuremberg 预防和发展课题"的核心内容,该处要申明的是,先前在关于高危儿童调查研究或种族家庭因素调查研究中报告展示的数据,并未在本文中得以采用。本研究的核心被试者由来自于 609 个家庭的 675 名幼儿园儿童组成(其中 336 名男孩,339 名女孩)。经三次年度测量验证后,该样本的损耗率只在5% 左右,即数据有效率为 95%。在最新运行的第六次评估后,我们已测量出 85% 的家庭的数据具有效度。在第一次测量结果中,儿童的平均年龄为 56.4 个月(标准差=9.3)。近 99% 的母亲和 96% 的父亲为被试儿童的亲生父母,86% 的父母为第一次婚姻,近 10% 的母亲为单身母亲。被试对象中,属于第一次婚姻的母亲的平均年龄为 34.5 岁(标准差=4.3),父亲的平均年龄为 37.1 岁(标准差=5.2)。其中,约12% 的家庭为移民家庭。根据计算家庭收入、家庭成员受教育程度、家庭成员职业和房屋条件而得出的一项综合性社会经济地位指数报告,结果表明,13.3% 的家庭为低层阶级,32.3% 的家庭为中下层阶级,30.6% 为中层阶级,15.4% 为中上层阶级,3.0% 为上层阶级。该比例分布与"Erlangen and Nuremberg 样本人群"的分布情况十分相似(Beelmann, Lösel, Stemmler, and Jaursch, 2006)。

（二）小组安排

经过第一次人员评估后,全部的被试者被分配到四组中,分别为:1. 不接受培训组(对照组);2. 儿童接受培训组;3. 父母接受培训组;4. 父母和儿童均接受培训的结合组。所有培训均始于第一次婚姻后,终于第二次评估的二到三个月前。对接受培训的父母或儿童的安排以及对实验对照组的安排都考虑和兼顾了方法论的科学性和实际操作的有效性。若是对个体被试者进行随机安排,则会对研究结果的信效度产生多种不利影响。例如,控制组中未接受培训的家庭可能会产生消极反映或中途退出;当控制组中的儿童或家庭彼此间发生接触时可能会产生实验性的竞争或治疗上的扩散。此外,从时间、空间和分组情况等方面考虑,并非所有幼儿园都适于接受培训。因此,我们按以下步骤对实验对象进行了分组:第一步,运用组织性标准,选择适合培训的幼儿园;第二步,以小组为单位对幼儿园进行随机选择;第三步,根据儿童年龄、性别、家庭社会经济地位、学前行为问题等因素(由学前老师评估产生),在其他幼儿园中招收相配对的实验对象。儿童与幼儿园的一一对应在实验中尤为重要,因为总样本数量大、范围广,若不对应培训,则会影响实验效果。此外,我们通过统计学分析(详见下文)样本内部的不均匀现象。

(三)培训项目

儿童培训

培训项目以"我能解决问题"为主题,作者将被试儿童平均分成 21 个小组,每组 6—10 人次。培训课程主要以教导儿童如何解决社会问题为重点,培训项目则依托培训手册开展课程(Beelmann, Jaursch, and Lösel, 2004)。该课程改编自 SHURE (1992),并根据德国的情况作了修订。培训项目由两部分组成:第一部分阐明基本情况,包括基本概念、情感的鉴定识别、因果关系的逻辑思考以及行为举止的产生原因等;第二部分包括对社会认知问题的培训,如在面对冲突时如何选择解决对策、对行为的预测及对行为后果的评估等。在培训中,作者运用了一系列教学方法,如看图解析、问答环节、角色扮演、猜谜游戏、画图学识以及唱歌游戏等。儿童共需接受 15 节课的培训,平均每周 3 到 4 节课,每节课时为半小时或一小时时长。在两位技术人员的指导协助下,幼儿园设定于每天早上在独立教室分别开始培训课程。190 名儿童及其家庭参与了该项目培训,12 名儿童因相关原因无法完成整个培训,因此,共有来自 157 个家庭的 178 名儿童顺利完成了儿童培训。这是个参与率高达 93.7% 的培训项目,有 96% 的儿童听取了一半以上的培训课程。

家长培训

家长培训课程由 12 门课组成,8 门开设在晚上,4 门课安排在下午进行。培训项目旨在提高和增强家长积极家教的技能(Beelmann and Lösel, 2004)。因此,课程内容包括如何照顾子女以及单身母亲的家教方式等。该培训项目以"Oregon 社会学习中心"(Dishion and Patterson 1996; Fisher et al., 1997)的项目理念为基础,该理念曾被作为试点项目广泛地在德国范围内推广使用。为了保证家长的参与度,减少中途退出的现象,培训课程以短而精为主。家长共需接受 5 节课的培训,每周一节课,每课时为 90 分钟到两小时。培训项目专门请到"EFFEKT"团队的两名资深成员进行授课。每组参与的家长为 6 到 15 人次不等。培训内容包括积极家教的基本要领、需求关系的处理、如何设定儿童的忍耐限度、处理家教遇到的困境、处理家庭压力以及强化家庭内外与社会的联系等。培训同样运用了一系列教学方式,如培训讲师演示文稿、家长间开设专题研会、小组讨论、角色扮演、自我意识的训练、有组织的对应帮教以及布置作业等。255 个家庭参与了该项目培训,其中,170(67%)的家庭至少听取了其中一节课。许多情况下,母亲代表家庭参与培训(共 163 人次),但也有 48 位父亲参与了培训。四分之三的家庭参加了两课时以上的培训。

(四)结果测量

"学前社会行为调查问卷"

作者运用德语版的"学前社会行为调查问卷"(Tremblay *et al.*,1992)来对儿童的行为问题进行观察测量。该测量工具包含 46 项测量项目,使用"三点度量表",分别为"完全不正确"(标记为 0),"有时正确"(标记为 1)和"非常正确"(标记为 2)。在调查问卷中,我们还搜集了来自学前班老师和儿童母亲对儿童的独立信息。在匹配程序训练的预培训的程序中,我们也运用了来自学前班老师提供的信息。德语版"学前社会行为调查问卷"(Lösel,Beelmann,and Stemmler,2002)。在本研究中,我们将"学前社会行为调查问卷总分"(内部一致性 $\alpha = .90$)以及问卷的次量表运用于观察测量"外化问题"(身体攻击、违法行为、破坏公共物品以及过度活跃等)和"内化问题"(焦虑现象、情绪错乱和社会性自闭症)。外化量表包括 20 项测量项目,如"他/她经常打、踢或咬其他儿童","他/她经常在家或幼儿园偷东西","他/她易冲动,经常做事不考虑后果"($\alpha = .89$)。由于"学前社会行为调查问卷"着重于测量反社会行为问题,内化量表所测内容则相对较少,只包括 8 项,如"他/她太胆小或焦虑"或者"他/她不像其他儿童那样快乐"($\alpha = .75$)。在第一次评估后和培训 2—3 个月后,我们还进行了对学前班老师和儿童母亲的"学前社会行为调查问卷"的信息搜集。关于儿童母亲的问卷回答信息,还被运用于评估培训两年以上的项目所具有的潜在长期效应。由于多数学生都已在当时离开幼儿园,我们通过搜集学校相关信息来进行未来独立结果的测量。

学校成绩单

作者通过内容分析法,分析学校成绩单(期中成绩和期末成绩;Stemmler *et al.*,2005)来评估小学一、二年级儿童的行为问题。在德国,一、二年级学生的成绩并非用标准的分数等级进行评定,取而代之的是老师关于学生课堂表现的一个主观评价报告。老师根据儿童是否有攻击行为/违法行为、注意力是否过度活跃、儿童的交流情况、儿童的合作表现和冲突行为、是否团结友爱、是否遵守纪律、儿童的情感基调、自我信赖度以及社会融入度等方面综合评估学生,奖惩分明。评分者间的认同度较高,卡帕值在 .71 到 1 之间。老师在学生一、二年级教学中强调鼓励儿童,因此,他们在学校成绩单上的评语也以褒义词居多,如"优秀"、"良好"、"没有不良行为",而像"差"、"不好"或"有不良行为"(一般只有 1%—15% 的成绩单中有提及)等贬义词则出现较少。平均算来,每份成绩单中只有 .72 内容关于行为问题。基于这样的低报告率,作者只选取了三种及以上行为问题作为儿童严重问题的恰当测量内容。

(五)统计分析

为分析"学前社会行为调查问卷"的效果,我们采取因果性回归分析模型(Steyer et al. , 2000)。我们在进行方差分析或协方差分析时,可能会对实验和培训的真实效应分析有误,如"辛普森悖论"(Novick, 1980)就是其中一例。而我们运用因果性回归模型进行分析,则可避免这方面的不足。在这种情况下,这样的实验培训效应被称之为情景效应,即根据调查每组差异后而体现出差异性。情景性回归分析以调查时的差异而采取不同分析方式,区别于此的因果性回归模型,则以计算因果关系间的平均效应来分析数据。治疗的预期结果根据以下公式(1)计算所得:

$$E(Y|X,Z) = g_0(Z) + g_1(Z)X \tag{1}$$

Y 代表 time 2(t_2)计算后的实验结果,Z 一般为 time 1(t_1)计算后的协方差。X 作为虚变数有两种价值,一是作为对照组(X=0),一是作为实验组(X=1)。而公式(2)则主要计算截距,因为在公式(1)中 $g_0(Z)$ 代表截距。这描述了在无实验情况下(X=0),协方差(Z)和实验结果(Y)之间的关系。该公式的作用就类似于发展的作用。它描述了在无实验进行时,Y 随时间的变化。

$$g_0(Z) = \gamma_{00} + \gamma_{01}(Z) \tag{2}$$

公式(3)主要计算斜率。因为在公式(1)中,$g_1(Z)$ 代表回归方程的斜率。

$$g_1(Z) = (\gamma_{10} + \gamma_{11}(Z))X \tag{3}$$

通过计算效应的公式,可得出在实验组影响下的发展过程。根据公式(1)的计算,我们可对三项原假设进行验证:1. 区别于 $E(g_1(Z))$ 和 $E(g_0(Z))$ 为 0 的结果,该实验没有平均实验效应。实验的结果效应称之为"平均因果效应",因为它是未经处理过的最初实验效应。2. 实验中没有所谓的协方差效应;比如 $g_0(Z)$ 是一个常数,($\gamma_{01}=0$)。3. 实验没有情景效应,例如,实验和协方差之间没有其相互作用($\gamma_{11}=0$)。以上结论通过"EffectLite 2.05 软件"(Steyer and Parchev, 2006)获取。下列在成绩单中的结果则是通过频率比较和卡方检验分析得到的。统计结果的显著性因样本数量而显现差异,标准的效应数量则被输入电脑系统进行结果分析。

由于在进行培训和结果测量时,都有中途退出项目的人员,因此我们采取保守策略来评估计划的效果。那些参加了但未完成整项项目的儿童和家长一律被视为实验组成员。为了避免接下来的短期效应和长期效应的检测无效,我们也删除了其一一对应的信息。这两种方法都控制了对结果评估的选择。

三、结　果

（一）短期评估

学前老师的信息反馈

老师在接受过2—3个月培训后填写了"学前社会行为调查问卷"，表1则包含了问卷中他们信息反馈后的平均数、标准差以及对平均因果效应的分析。由于按组随机抽样，相互间具有对应性，因此实验组（TG）和对照组（CG）预测前的分数在总体上十分相似。

大部分平均因果效应都十分显著。在"学前社会行为调查问卷"中可发现，无论是整体计划（d=.23），还是儿童培训方面（d=.25），或是儿童和父母结合的培训（d=.36），都表现出积极效应。结果模式与外化量表相似，但效应程度则略显薄弱（最大值为结合培训所得，d=.25）。对以上三项的内化量表，则体现出显著的下降。再者，后者的效应最大（d=.33）。单由家长接受培训的一组，其实也体现出直接预期的效果，但在统计方面未能体现出其显著性。

表1　"学前社会行为调查问卷"中（短期评估、培训结束2—3月后）的学前老师对
儿童行为的评价的描述性统计资料及其平均因果性效应

PSBQ-Scales	问题总分			外化问题			内化问题		
	实验前	实验后	平均效应	实验前	实验后	平均效应	实验前	实验后	平均效应
	平均数（标准差）	平均数（标准差）	效应（标准错误）效应程度	平均数（标准差）	平均数（标准差）	效应（标准错误）效应程度	平均数（标准差）	平均数（标准差）	效应（标准错误）效应程度
全部培训									
实验组（n=239）	11.56（8.96）	9.97（8.26）	-2.31 *** （0.59）	6.10（6.48）	5.21（5.83）	-1.28 *** （0.38）	2.82（2.53）	2.20（2.31）	-0.44 * （0.19）
对照组（n=239）	11.77（8.12）	12.44（10.00）	0.23	6.74（6.33）	6.98（7.42）	0.17	2.42（2.16）	2.46（2.41）	0.19
儿童培训									
实验组（n=89）	11.29（9.33）	9.82（8.14）	-2.47 * （0.98）	5.98（6.82）	5.20（5.76）	-1.06+ （0.63）	2.75（2.58）	2.14（2.48）	-0.64 * （0.31）
对照组（n=89）	11.58（8.27）	11.51（9.91）	0.25	6.67（6.50）	6.79（7.13）	0.14	2.45（2.12）	2.61（2.49）	0.26
家长培训									

PSBQ-Scales	问题总分			外化问题			内化问题		
	实验前	实验后	平均效应	实验前	实验后	平均效应	实验前	实验后	平均效应
	平均数（标准差）	平均数（标准差）	效应（标准错误）效应程度	平均数（标准差）	平均数（标准差）	效应（标准错误）效应程度	平均数（标准差）	平均数（标准差）	效应（标准错误）效应程度
实验组（n=77）	11.78（7.75）	10.82（8.41）	−0.90（0.98）	5.84（6.01）	5.18（5.90）	−0.81（0.65）	3.25（2.60）	2.79（2.41）	0.20（0.33）
对照组（n=77）	11.81（8.11）	11.74（10.19）	0.09	6.40（6.01）	6.49（7.43）	0.11	2.64（2.38）	2.33（2.13）	0.09
结合培训									
实验组（n=73）	11.66（9.78）	9.25（8.28）	−3.62＊＊（1.09）	6.52（7.13）	5.28（5.92）	−1.94＊＊（0.69）	2.44（2.35）	1.64（1.80）	−0.79＊（0.35）
对照组（n=73）	11.97（8.08）	13.10（9.94）	0.36	7.16（6.52）	7.71（7.78）	0.25	2.16（1.97）	2.41（2.61）	0.33

效应程度的记录有助于解释积极相关性对所设计方向上的效应的预示作用。

+p（显著性）<.10；＊p<.05；＊＊p<.01；＊＊＊p<.001。

表 2 显示了对协方差和情景性效应的分析。所有协变量的回归系统都明显很高。这预示着儿童的行为问题相当稳定，并未随时间而变化。外化问题的相关性总体上高于内化问题（如对总体样本而言：$\gamma_{01}=.91$ vs. .42）。从外化问题的量表来看，在总体 EFFEKT 计划、家长培训和结合培训方面，项目都出现了情景性效应。这表明，培训对于预测之前问题较严重的儿童更为受益。

表 2 "学前社会行为调查问卷"（短期评估，培训结束 2—3 月后）中的学前老师对儿童行为评估的协方差实验的情景性效应

PSBQ-Scales					
问题总分		外化问题		内化问题	
协方差（标准错误）	情景性效应（标准错误）	协方差（标准错误）	情景性效应（标准错误）	协方差（标准错误）	情景性效应（标准错误）
全部培训（实验组和对照组：n=239）					
0.84＊＊＊（0.06）	−0.14+（0.07）	0.91＊＊＊（0.05）	−0.19＊＊（0.06）	0.42＊＊＊（0.07）	0.12（0.08）
儿童培训（实验组和对照组：n=89）					
0.77＊＊＊（0.10）	−0.09（0.11）	0.81＊＊＊（0.08）	−0.13（0.10）	0.45＊＊＊（0.12）	0.22（0.14）
家长培训（实验组和对照组：n=77）					

			PSBQ-Scales		
问题总分		外化问题		内化问题	
协方差（标准错误）	情景性效应（标准错误）	协方差（标准错误）	情景性效应（标准错误）	协方差（标准错误）	情景性效应（标准错误）
0.97 * * * (0.09)	−0.14 (0.12)	1.00 * * * (0.08)	−0.20⁺ (0.11)	0.37 * * * (0.09)	0.14 (0.13)
结合培训（实验组和对照组：n=73）					
0.82 * * (0.11)	−0.15 (0.13)	0.95 * * * (0.09)	−0.23 * (0.10)	0.45 * * (0.15)	−0.16 (0.17)

+p（显著性）<.10；* p<.05；* * p<.01；* * * p<.001。

母亲的信息反馈

母亲在接受过 2—3 个月培训后填写了"学前社会行为调查问卷"，表 3 则包含了问卷中她们信息反馈后的平均数、标准差以及对平均因果效应的分析。由于测量方式是与第一次评估中关于学前老师信息反馈的分数计算相对应的，相比于"学前社会行为问卷调查"对学前老师的数据分析，实验组和对照组的预测方式相对不均匀。母亲的信息反馈中，对儿童问题的反映也体现出略高的分数。

无论是在"学前社会行为调查问卷"的总量表还是分量表中，儿童问题的分数在培训后都比培训前低。然而，这不仅体现在问题组中，也反映在对照组中。有两组平均因果性效应与预期表现出显著的差异：整个问题组和结合型培训组中的母亲，比对照组的母亲更多地报告了其孩子的内化问题（d=.22 和−.35，p<.05）。

表 3 "学前社会行为调查问卷"中（短期评估、培训结束 2—3 月后）的母亲
对儿童行为的评价的描述性统计资料及其平均因果性效应

PSBQ-Scales	问题总分			外化问题			内化问题		
	实验前	实验后	平均效应	实验前	实验后	平均效应	实验前	实验后	平均效应
	平均数（标准差）	平均数（标准差）	效应（标准错误）效应程度	平均数（标准差）	平均数（标准差）	效应（标准错误）效应程度	平均数（标准差）	平均数（标准差）	效应（标准错误）效应程度
全部培训									
实验组（n=203）	13.98 (6.84)	12.43 (6.89)	0.76⁺ (0.43⁺)	7.97 (5.03)	7.33 (4.77)	0.23 (0.30)	3.24 (2.04)	2.88 (2.08)	0.41 * (0.16)
对照组（n=203）	12.86 (6.57)	11.28 (6.35)	−0.11	7.79 (5.34)	6.96 (4.93)	−0.05	3.11 (2.10)	2.40 (1.86)	−0.22
儿童培训									

PSBQ-Scales	问题总分			外化问题			内化问题		
	实验前	实验后	平均效应	实验前	实验后	平均效应	实验前	实验后	平均效应
	平均数(标准差)	平均数(标准差)	效应(标准错误)效应程度	平均数(标准差)	平均数(标准差)	效应(标准错误)效应程度	平均数(标准差)	平均数(标准差)	效应(标准错误)效应程度
实验组(n=70)	12.29(6.68)	11.30(5.91)	0.26(0.73)	7.27(4.82)	6.67(4.31)	0.14(0.54)	3.06(2.04)	2.64(2.03)	0.17(0.29)
对照组(n=70)	13.65(6.76)	11.91(6.26)	-0.04	8.06(5.18)	7.04(4.78)	-0.02	3.49(2.44)	2.66(1.86)	-0.09
家长培训									
实验组(n=68)	14.47(6.88)	13.12(7.68)	0.53(0.75)	8.19(5.27)	7.31(4.99)	-0.03(0.51)	3.72(2.06)	3.18(2.11)	0.36(0.28)
对照组(n=68)	12.47(5.24)	10.93(5.90)	-0.09	7.29(4.95)	6.63(4.86)	-0.00	3.03(2.14)	2.40(1.97)	0.18
结合培训									
实验组(n=65)	13.42(6.22)	12.94(6.95)	1.15(0.74)	8.49(4.98)	8.05(4.96)	0.47(0.53)	2.92(1.96)	2.82(2.11)	0.61*(0.29)
对照组(n=65)	12.42(7.18)	10.95(6.91)	-0.17	8.02(5.93)	7.22(5.21)	-0.09	2.80(1.58)	2.14(1.74)	-0.35

效应程度的记录有助于解释积极相关性对所设计方向上的效应的预示作用。

+p(显著性)<.10；*p<.05。

表4显示了关于母亲报告的协方差和情景性效应的分析。协方差的相关性从.45到.78不等,均表现出显著性。这再一次充分预示了行为问题在第一次评估和第二次评估后所体现的稳定性,虽然在外化问题($\gamma_{01}=.67$)和内化问题($\gamma_{01}=.49$)上的差异性均比学前老师的报告不明显。在情景性效应上,则未表现出显著性。

表4 "学前社会行为调查问卷"(短期评估,培训结束2—3月后)中的学前老师对儿童行为评估的协方差实验的情景性效应

PSBQ-Scales					
问题总分		外化问题		内化问题	
协方差(标准错误)	情景性效应(标准错误)	协方差(标准错误)	情景性效应(标准错误)	协方差(标准错误)	情景性效应(标准错误)
全部培训					
0.66***(0.08)	-0.02(0.12)	0.67***(0.08)	-0.05(0.11)	0.41***(0.08)	0.03(0.13)

PSBQ-Scales					
问题总分		外化问题		内化问题	
协方差 （标准错误）	情景性效应 （标准错误）	协方差 （标准错误）	情景性效应 （标准错误）	协方差 （标准错误）	情景性效应 （标准错误）
儿童培训					
0.73 *** （0.04）	0.07 （0.07）	0.72 *** （0.04）	−0.02 （0.05）	0.49 *** （0.05）	0.07 （0.08）
家长培训					
0.77 ** （0.07）	0.12 （0.11）	0.72 *** （0.06）	0.09 （0.10）	0.45 *** （0.13）	0.24 （0.16）
结合培训					
0.78 *** （0.08）	0.10 （0.12）	0.76 *** （0.08）	0.01 （0.10）	0.62 *** （0.08）	−0.03 （0.13）

** p<.01；*** p<.001。

（二）长期评估

母亲的信息反馈

培训计划结束的两年多后，对计划的跟踪评估再次展开。由于被试儿童大部分已从幼儿园毕业，因此我们对"学前社会行为调查问卷"的信息只能从儿童的母亲中搜集获取，而不能从学前老师中了解。平均数、标准差以及对平均因果性效应的分析等都如表5所示。

然而，没有任何种类的项目及其结果表现出显著的效应。通过对协方差的效应分析，我们可发现其从培训前到跟进评估后都有高度显著的预测作用（"学前社会行为调查问卷"：g＝.74；p<.001）。再次，外化问题（γ_{01}＝.71；p<.001）比内化问题（γ_{01}＝.57）更具稳定性。我们未发现情景性效应的显著性。

老师对成绩单的信息反馈

本研究中，我们将先前对成绩单（Lösel *et al.*，2006）的分析从一年级学生扩展到了二年级学生（在计划实施后三年内）。和以前一样，我们选取了其中能预示儿童严重行为问题的三个或三个以上典型问题。表6显示的就是一、二年级学生有以上问题的所占据的比例。

表5　"学前社会行为调查问卷"中（长期评估、培训结束2年后）的母亲
对儿童行为的评价的描述性统计资料及其平均因果性效应

PSBQ-Scales	问题总分			外化问题			内化问题		
	实验前	实验后	平均效应	实验前	实验后	平均效应	实验前	实验后	平均效应
	平均数（标准差）	平均数（标准差）	效应（标准错误）效应程度	平均数（标准差）	平均数（标准差）	效应（标准错误）效应程度	平均数（标准差）	平均数（标准差）	效应（标准错误）效应程度
全部培训									
实验组（n=179）	13.14（6.61）	11.79（6.60）	0.39（0.49）	7.57（5.00）	6.73（4.77）	0.23（0.34）	3.43（2.15）	2.83（1.93）	0.11（0.19）
对照组（n=179）	12.08（5.75）	10.63（6.28）	−0.06	7.25（4.60）	6.28（4.49）	−0.05	2.93（1.85）	2.46（1.93）	−0.06
儿童培训									
实验组（n=59）	12.02（6.48）	11.03（6.48）	0.09（0.90）	7.03（4.84）	6.12（4.45）	−0.04（0.63）	3.19（1.91）	2.97（2.72）	0.32（0.34）
对照组（n=59）	13.02（6.36）	11.66（6.84）	0.01	7.83（5.08）	6.68（4.99）	−0.019	3.15（2.02）	2.63（2.13）	−0.15
家长培训									
实验组（n=66）	14.12（6.69）	12.23（6.82）	0.17（0.80）	7.68（5.11）	6.79（4.97）	0.21（0.53）	3.94（2.38）	3.11（2.34）	−0.08（0.34）
对照组（n=66）	11.14（5.11）	10.39（5.89）	0.03	6.94（4.30）	6.03（4.16）	−0.05	2.88（1.78）	2.59（2.05）	0.04
结合培训									
实验组（n=54）	13.17（6.57）	12.07（6.52）	0.97（0.92）	8.02（5.08）	7.33（4.86）	0.48（0.64）	3.06（2.00）	2.35（2.00）	0.11（0.32）
对照组（n=54）	11.22（5.73）	9.78（6.05）	−0.16	6.98（4.42）	6.15（4.37）	−0.11	2.74（1.75）	2.13（1.49）	0.07

效应程度的记录有助于解释积极相关性对所设计方向上的效应的预示作用。

正如预期的，只有小部分儿童的老师在其成绩单上提及他们长期具有多种行为问题。基于这样的低比例，项目中实验组与对照组的差异显著性在5%以下。然而，在项目实验组中，仍有四分之三的儿童存在多种行为问题。对于与项目相结合的培训而言，其观察到的差异性可能为 $p < .10$。

表6 一、二年级学生成绩单中有多种(3个及以上)行为问题的
儿童所具的比例(长期评估,培训结束后3年内)

	行为问题			
	实验组	对照组		
	%	%	χ^2	ES
所有培训 (TG=162/CG=162)	1.2	4.3	2.83[+]	0.20
儿童培训 (TG=58/CG=58)	1.7	1.7	0.00	0.00
父母培训 (TG=56/CG=56)	1.8	5.4	1.04	0.20
结合培训 (TG=48/CG=48)	0.0	6.1	3.03[+]	0.50

TG=实验组;CG=对照组;M=平均数;SD=标准差;SE=标准错误;ES=效应程度(Cohen系数);效应程度的记录有助于解释积极相关性对所设计方向上的效应的预示作用。
+p(显著性)<.10。

四、讨 论

本研究评估了预防反社会行为发展的一个项目的结果效应,分别评估了其在项目培训结束2—3月后的短期效应和长达3年的一个长期效应。比起以前的评估,本次评估在时间上更持久(Beelmann et al.,2006;Lösel et al.,2006;Stemmler et al.,2007),在研究方法论上更严密。第一,我们运用了更精确的统计模型来分析项目中的因果性效应和情景性效应。第二,我们通过不同的信息渠道来对儿童行为作出评估。第三,我们针对中途退出项目的儿童实施了意向培训分析,例如,无论儿童还是父母,只要参加过项目中的一节课,就在评估中被视为有"意向"。结合样本广泛和个体对应等问题,意向培训分析更能保证其对潜在效应的一个精确估测。

结果表明,无论是"EFFEKT计划"本身还是其各部分都具有明显的积极效应。然而在国际研究中(Beelmann and Lösel,2007;Bernazzani and Tremblay,2006;Farrington and Welsh,2007;Lösel and Beelmann,2003,2005),学者的结论随时间计算方式和结果评估标准的不同而不同。我们曾进行过只对参加了一半以上计划的儿童和家长进行的预调查,其效应与本次学前老师在成绩单上对儿童评估的短期效应相似(Lösel et al.,2006)。无论是项目的整体效应还是项目各分组中的大部分效应

都表现出统计学上的显著性。最一般的(整个项目组和"学前社会行为调查问卷"总分)效应为d=.23(p<.001),而在总体问题分数中,结合培训表现出最大效应,为d=.36。只有单纯父母培训的组别未能体现出显著效应。我们发现,父母在其中体现出了较好的合作性以及对培训的较高满意度(Lösel et al. ,2004),因此,我们觉得这可能不是培训实施方面的问题。有人猜测,父母培训未能体现出显著效应,可能是培训时间持续相对较短的原因。然而,从系统上说来,项目的强度是效应程度体现的一项缓和剂,在一些短期计划中,也曾有过积极效应的结果(Beelmann and Lösel,2007;Nowak and Heinrichs,2008;Wilson et al. ,2001)。我们的父母培训对其被试个体自身,即那些家教行为的参与者而言也有显著效应(Stemmler et al. ,2007)。值得注意的是,家长对其家教行为的自我报告,与学前老师对儿童行为问题的评估之间具有较少的相关性(Lösel,Stemmler,Beelmann,and Jaursch,2005)。因此,我们无法预测在干预方面是否有显著效应。虽然家教效应不明显,但家长还是能要求儿童对有关行为进行转变。然而,调节儿童行为最关键的,还是要通过社会信息途径和解决社会问题,来解决儿童行为问题。

在结合培训的结果中可以得出,家长培训并非毫无效应。家长与儿童结合组的效应为本研究中最有效的短期效应。效应也在内化问题和外化问题上体现出一致性。本研究中,外化问题相对更稳定并难以被改变(详见表2中的协方差效应)。

虽然学前老师对儿童行为问题的短期结果评估具有积极效应,但效应显著性不大(d=.17-.36)。这是对一个重要的短期项目的真实发现。外化问题的效应程度为d=.25,这表明实验组中有13%的儿童比对照组更不暴力。而通过对儿童社会技能培训的元分析而得出的平均效应,则与测量那些每天接受培训的儿童行为的结果相似(Lösel and Beelmann,2003,2005)。在对威尔逊等(Wilson et al.)(2001)的元分析中,9所基于认知行为计划的学校表现出显著性,但效应程度只为d=.10。在对儿童行为进行跟踪调查和独立测量,而非评估父母态度和行为时,父母培训的效应也不大(Beelmann,2008;Lösel et al. ,2006;Lundahl et al. ,2006;Nowak and Heinrichs,2008)。这是普遍性预防措施研究中的一则典型。必须明确的是,本研究属于该范畴之一,例如,本项目是由各儿童和家庭参与完成的。总体而言,对于那些已表现出行为问题或有反社会倾向的儿童,基于诊所的预防项目会比基于普通学校或普通幼儿园的预防项目更有效应(Beelmann,2008;Farrington and Welsh,2003,2007;Lösel and Beelmann,2003,2005;Nowack and Heinrichs,2008)。这看似有理,因为大部分儿童即使不参与普遍项目,也不会有行为问题。因此,实验组人员和对照组人员的区分,主要是根据儿童是否具有反社会倾向以及是否需要培训计划进行的。同样的,研究发现,关于少年犯的培训对有危险的儿童的影响也较小(Lipsey and Landenberger, 2006;Lösel and Schmucker, 2005)。

普遍性预防项目的效应较小这一发现并非意味着我们要着重关注那些高危儿童以及一些具体的预防。普遍性预防项目避免了潜在问题的一些早期征兆,因此可推广普及到普通学校进行运用(Le Blanc, 1998;Lösel, 2002)。到底是普遍性预防或是具体预防计划更有效,其实是关于被试目标的问题和支出收益的问题(Swisher, Scherer and Yin, 2004;Welsh and Farrington, 2001)。普遍性项目由于参与人数多,则必须短期进行以减少开支,但这样对于那些需要高强度培训的高危儿童而言,则成效不明显。因此,采取不同策略来干预行为发展则更为恰当(Lösel, 2007a)。但是,普遍项目的效应不显著不代表高危儿童不受益其中。例如在公共健康方面,就曾因低程度的普遍性效应降低了总体危险分布,同时也降低了分组高危人群的问题普遍度(Coid, 2003)。因此,本研究发现了许多不同的情景性效应(表2)。这些效应暗示着,那些预测前有更多行为问题的儿童比那些危险性较低的儿童在项目培训中受益更多。

这不仅仅存在于短期效应评估中的外化问题,在通过学校成绩单所评估的长期效应中也表现了这样的现象。在研究孩子的日常行为时,学校的证书是相当难使用的数据,因为它不是在研究项目的背景下产生的。我们的研究结果显示,在所有项目组(d=.20)和在组合型项目组(d=.50)中,有多种行为问题的孩子比较少。在美国的"快速跟踪预防实验"中,另一个较重要的发现就是严重行为问题案例在减少(Conduct Problems Prevention Research Group, 2002)。当然,在我们的研究中,必须牢记于心的是这些效果都是产生于少量样本的基础上的,因此只有在 p<. 10 时才有显著效果。然而,在经过培训3年后,有多重长期性行为问题的孩子少了3个百分点,这也是一个不小的发现。如果这样的效果能够在孩子进入青春期后仍然发生作用,这将能显著地减少社会为有严重反社会倾向的孩子所付出的代价(Munoz et al. , 2004;Scott et al. , 2001)。

在对于这个项目的潜在效益作出太多猜测之前,我们需要强调一下我们的研究中一个并不是十分鼓舞人心的结果:不管是短期评估,还是长期评估,在母亲对于孩子的行为问题报告中,计划都没有展示出一个积极的效果。更甚者,在内化问题范围里,还有两个消极的短期效果存在着。

在不同的成果测试中,部分不一致的研究结果并不罕见,这在预防项目评估中反而是相当正常的。在大范围个例研究和元分析中都存在着这样的问题。例如,洛赛尔(Lösel)和比尔曼(Beelmann)(2006)发现,在通过使用教师和家长的报告的研究中,儿童技能训练的效果更好;自我报告和官方数据中,效果就会差一些。长期效果只对于教师信息比较显著。一个在"Triple-P-Program"计划中的元分析则揭示了在父母评分中的效果,但是如果这个儿童的行为是通过独立专家或是自我汇报评估的,那效果就会很小或者没有严重影响。数据来源之间的差异性不完全是由于可信性与真实性上的不同。通过不同信息对儿童行为问题进行的评估,结果显示了一个很小的大约 r=.30 的关联性。当两个提供信息的人在相同的背景下观察儿童行为时,一致性才比较强。在"Erlangen-Nuremberg 研究"中,我们也发现了相似的被调查者之间的差别。

在本研究中,我们没有对结果的差异性做确切解释,但是我们可以假设多种原因:我们的配对工作不仅仅是在个人相关数据的基础上(年龄、性别、社会经济地位),也是在"学前社会行为问卷调查"中学前老师的报告的基础之上的。因此,相对于来自于母亲报告的数据,评估过程能够在使用这些数据之下被更好地控制。相对于学前班和学校老师的数据,母亲的报告可能更容易受到来自研究项目的影响。为了在纵向研究中,避免学生辍学,我们为所有可以用电话、信件联系到的父母亲,组织了一个大型的年度会议。这些必要的措施可能会对一些对照组的父母行为或他们对于孩子的看法有一定影响。此外,在项目组中那些改变了自己行为的家长,可能会造成他们孩子短时间内无法适应这种改变的问题。这种培训还可能导致对他们孩子的问题更敏感的观察。以上两种原因都可能可以解释外化问题范围中存在的消极的短期效应。

有时,零效应可能会随着时间慢慢消失,因为适应和学习的过程会在接下来导致一个更积极的研究结果。然而,这样一个"休眠效应"在我们的研究中是不会特别显著的。在培训两年之后,父母对他们孩子的报告没有显示任何太明显的效果。因此,我们必须假设在母亲的报告中,这是没有效应的。

为了更好地理解这个研究发现,我们必须注意以下几点:尽管家长与孩子的关系比老师与孩子的关系更紧密,但是老师比家长有更多的机会将孩子与其他孩子进行对比(尤其是在独生子女家庭)。学前班和学校老师或是一些其他专家都对儿童问题有了一个更规范、更专业的观点。许多的研究表明,对于评估和预测儿童的行为问题,这样的信息有很高的可靠性(Bank, Duncan, Patterson, and Reid, 1993; Brown *et al.*, 2006; Hinshaw, Han, Erhardt, and Huber, 1992; Ronning *et al.*, 2009)。利用同样的信息来对儿童行为打分,结果还是不随时间改变而相对稳定的。在我们的研究中,比如在第一次评估中母亲的"学前社会行为问卷调查"报告与他们几年后的打分有很大的相关性。这样长期研究的相关性比代表性评分数据更大(Lösel, 2002)。这样的相关性可能不仅仅反映了儿童行为的稳定性,还能反映相对固定的认知图式。因此,对同样的几个人做重复的评估的干预效果会比从独立观察者那里得来的信息更不敏感(Hacker et al. , 2007)。相应的,在我们这个项目里的另一个评估显示,如果实验前和试验后的老师不是同一个人的话,这个针对小学生的项目会有更好的效果。当学前班老师短期评估以及在这之后通过学校成绩单做的完全不同的评估中,数据波动不大,我们就能在目前的研究中,假设一个相似的过程。对接下来所得的数据分析结果将会揭开这是否只是一个看似合理的假设。

归结起来,这个研究显示了儿童成长过程中不良行为的儿童导向型和家长导向型预防项目的一个令人欣喜的效果。然而,这个效果并不大,并且随着时间推移或根据不同的成果评测的手段,这个效果只能是部分的一致。母亲评分中的零效应不应该被当作一个例外而低估,而应该被看作一个重要的信号。人们提到的一个反复出现的现象就是:项目的发起者所进行的研究效果往往比独立评估的效果要更积极一些(Eisner et al. , 2007;Lipsey and Landenberger, 2006;Lösel and Beelmann, 2003)。在其他的干预领域中,我们不能将这个在北美的示范项目简单地应用到其他的国家以及日常的实践中(Lösel, 2007b)。我们应该将一件事牢记于心,非常对口的预防项目是很难实现的,不能一刀切。比如我们研究一个针对学龄儿童加压项目和一个移民家庭以及情感压抑母亲适应项目,就应采取不同的项目预防。本文中初步的发现,向我们展示了一些前景光明的成果(Lösel, 2008)。然而总的来说,我们讨论并建议在今后的研究中,要以更谨慎而乐观的态度进行研究。关于暴力犯罪发展的预防,我们需要更多的以证据为依托的培训项目来支撑,并以一个更长期的政策来作为财政支持(Farrington and Welsh, 2007;Junger et al. , 2007)。

[参考文献见英文原作]

(展万程　刘可忻　译)

Universal Prevention of Antisocial Development : Short-and Long-Term Effects of a Child-and Parent-Oriented Program

Friedrich Lösel

University of Erlangen , Nuremberg

Mark Stemmler

Stefanie Jaursch

Andreas Beelmann

INTRODUCTION

Prospective longitudinal studies have substantially increased our knowledge about pathways of antisocial development, bio-psycho-social origins and risk factors and-still less investigated-positive processes of abstaining and desistance from delinquency (Farrington and Welsh, 2007; Loeber and Farrington, 1998; Sampson and Laub, 2003). These findings form the basis for programs of developmental prevention which aim for an early interruption of chain reactions towards juvenile and adult offending. Although spectacular media reports on school shootings, knife murder, and similarly extreme cases triggered more preventive policies in Western countries, such approaches are also well justified by other reasons:

Problems of social behavior such as conduct disorders, aggression and delinquency are particularly frequent. Based on parent reports, the recent Child and Youth Health Survey in Germany found 14. 8 % social behavior problems in the population at age 0 – 17 years

(Hölling, Erhart, Ravens-Sieberer and Schlack, 2007). Clinical assessments reveal lower prevalence rates (Ihle and Esser, 2002), but still suggest that one out of ten youngsters exhibits conduct problems and many have other disorders as well (e. g. hyperactivity/ attention deficits, anxiety, depression, and substance abuse). Of course, one should not dramatize this too much because aggressive or delinquent behavior is often a short-term manifestation in de velopmental transitions. However, approximately one third of the »early starters« enter a pathway of relatively persistent antisocial behavior (Loeber and Farrington, 2000). These youngsters do not only cut off chances in their own life but also cause many problems for victims, the family and the society. Their antisocial behavior is a risk marker for persistent criminality and other mental health problems in youth and adulthood (Farrington, 1991; Robins and Price, 1991). Seriously antisocial youngsters are very difficult to place and manage (Bender and Lösel, 2006) and the typical effects of later offender treatment are only small to moderate (Lösel, 1995; McGuire, 2002). Early prevention of antisocial behavior is also attractive for economic reasons (Foster, Prinz, Sanders and Shapiro, 2008). Up to age 28, the society's costs for a seriously antisocial person are nearly ten times higher than those for a non-deviant youngster (Scott, Knapp, Henderson and Maughan, 2001). The costs for only one case easily amount to more than 1 Million Euro or US Dollar (Muñoz, Hutchings, Edwards, Hounsome and O'Ceilleachair, 2004).

Although such good reasons have led to a strong expansion of developmental prevention, most countries show a lack of coordinated, long-term and evidence-based strategies (Farrington and Welsh, 2007; Junger et al., 2007). Well-controlled evaluations have mainly been carried out in North America. Systematic reviews of child-, family-and school-oriented programs show overall positive outcomes, however, average effect sizes in »hard «and long-term outcome measurement are small (e. g. Farrington and Welsh, 2003, 2007; Lösel and Beelmann, 2003; Wilson, Gottfredson and Najaka, 2001; Lipsey, Wilson and Derzon, 2003; Lundahl, Risser and Lovejoy, 2006; Tremblay and Japel, 2003). Findings depend on the type of program, selection of target groups, research design, outcome measures, length of follow up, sample size, involvement of researchers, and many other moderators. Although some famous programs such as the High Scope/Perry Preschool Program (Schweinhart et al., 2005) or the Family-Nurse-Partnership Program (Olds et al., 1998) revealed long-term positive findings, others showed positive and zero effects

(Henggeler et al., 1998; Littell, 2005) or even slightly negative outcomes (McCord, 2003). Most promising are multimodal programs for high-risk groups that address a broad range of needs in the child's daily environment (Farrington and Welsh, 2007; Lösel, 2005).

Outside North America and, in particular, in the German-speaking countries there is a clear deficit of sound empirical evaluations. For example, a systematic survey of the German Family Ministry revealed approximately 200, 000 deliveries of family-oriented group programs per annum (Lösel, Schmucker, Plankensteiner, and Weiss, 2006). In comparison, there are only 27 evaluation studies with control groups, of which no more than four had good methodological quality. The majority of the mainly low-structured programs were not based on any systematic empirical investigation. Only recently, more sound evaluations are carried out. The findings of these studies are mixed. Some show positive outcomes in comparison to obviously non-equivalent control groups (e. g. Heinrichs et al., 2006), others reveal no significant effects (e. g. Schmid et al., 2007; Eisner, Ribeaud, Jünger and Meidert, 2007) or positive effects in internalizing problems only (Schick and Cierpka, 2003). Overall, there is more marketing of prevention programs than sound empirical research (Lösel, 2004; Eisner et al., 2007).

The currently longest-running research project on developmental prevention in German-speaking countries is the Erlangen-Nuremberg Study (e. g. Lösel, Beelmann, Jaursch and Stemmler, 2004; Lösel, Beelmann, Stemmler and Jaursch, 2006). It is a combined experimental and longitudinal study on antisocial child behavior. In its preventive part we evaluate the program »Entwicklungsförderung in Familien: Eltern-und Kindertraining« (EFFEKT; Development Promotion in Families: Parent and Child Training). The package was designed for universal prevention at preschool age. It contains a child social·skills training that is based on concepts of social problem solving (Shure, 1992) and a parent training that is derived from the Oregon Model of positive parenting (Fisher et al., 1997). We also implemented a combination of both programs.

In previous publications we found that the prevention program had significant short-term effects on the social behavior of the children as assessed by the preschool teachers (Lösel et al., 2006). Effect sizes were mainly small, but more pronounced when both children and parents participated in a program. Children who already showed some behavioral problems before the training benefitted most. There were also some positive outcomes a year and two years after the training (Lösel et al., 2006) and more specific effects on mediating constructs such as parenting behavior (Stemmler, Beelmann, Jaursch, and Lösel, 2007). Although these findings were encouraging, they had various limitations. First, we did not compare multiple sources of information on the child behavior. Second, the evaluation focused on participants of at least half of the programs and did not apply an intent-to-treat analysis. Third, the statistical analyses did not control for intra-group heterogeneity in the group-wise randomization. Therefore, the present study investigates whether the outcomes are robust in more sophisticated causal analyses.

METHOD

Sample

The present article refers to the core study of the Erlangen-Nuremberg Development and Prevention Project. Data from smaller studies on high-risk and ethnic minority families are not reported here. The sample of the core study consisted of 675 kindergarten children (336 boys, 339 girls) from 609 families. The attrition rate after three annual waves of measurement was 5%. In the currently running 6th assessment we already have at least some measures for over 85% of the families. The average age of the children at the first measurement was $M = 56.4$ months ($SD = 9.3$). Approximately 99% of the mothers and 96% of the fathers were the biological parents and 86% were married at Time 1. About 10% of the mothers were single. The age of the mothers at T_1 was $M = 34.5$ years ($SD = 4.3$) and the age of the fathers $M = 37.1$ years ($SD = 5.2$). About 12% of the families were migrants. According to an index of the socioeconomic status (SES; Geißler, 1994) which included income, education, profession, and housing conditions, 13.3% of the families were lower class, 32.3% lower middle class, 30.6% middle class, 15.4% upper middle class, and 3.0% upper class. This is very similar to the population of Erlangen and Nuremberg (Beelmann, Lösel, Stemmler, and Jaursch, 2006).

Group Assignment

After the first assessment, the total sample was divided into four parts: 1. no training (developmental study/control group); 2. child training; 3. parent training; 4. combination of child and parent training. All training took place after T_1 and ended between two to three months before the second assessment. The assignment of families/children to the training and control groups followed both methodological and practical considerations. A random assignment on the individual level would have caused various threats to validity, for example negative reactions and selective dropout of the control group families who did not get a training program, experimental rivalry of control group parents or diffusion of treatment when trained children/parents of the same kindergarten get in contact with the control individuals. Furthermore not all kindergartens were suitable for the training with regard to location, space and or group size. Therefore, groups were assigned in several steps: First, organizational criteria were used to select kindergartens suitable for training. Second, the training kindergartens were selected randomly on the group level. Third, matched pairs were recruited from the other kindergartens with regard to age, gender, SES, and pre-training behavioral problems (as assessed by the preschool teachers). The matching seemed to be necessary because group-wise randomization does not guarantee full equivalence if there is not a large number of units. Furthermore, we controlled for heterogeneity by statistical analysis (see below).

Training Programs

child training

The program "I can problem solve" was delivered to 21 groups of six to ten children. The course is a manual-based group training in social problem solving (Beelmann, Jaursch, and Lösel, 2004). It was adapted from *Shure* (1992) and modified for the German context. The program consists of two parts: The first part addresses basics such as elementary verbal concepts, identification of emotions, and reflection on causality and reasons for behavior. The second part contains the training of social cognitive problem-solving skills such as providing alternative solutions in conflicts, anticipation of actions and evaluation of consequences. The training uses a range of didactical methods, e. g. analyses of pictures, question-and-answer rounds, role-plays, quizzes, drawing and singing games. Each of the 15 sessions lasted 30 to 60 minutes and there were three to five sessions per week. Guided by two skilled facilitators, all sessions were performed in the morning in separate rooms of the kindergarten. The program was offered to 190 children and their families. Twelve children were not able to participate, resulting in 178 children from 157 families who took part in the child training. This is a high attendance rate of 93. 7 %. Of the participating children 96 % were present for at least half of the sessions.

parent training

The parenting program was delivered in 12 courses. Eight courses were held in the evening, four in the afternoon, including child care to enable single mothers to attend. The training aims for an enhancement of positive parenting skills (Beelmann and Lösel, 2004). It is partly based on the programs of the Oregon Social Learning Center (Dishion and Patterson, 1996; Fisher *et al.*, 1997) and was adapted to the German context over various pilot studies. It was kept short to increase participation and reduce dropout. The training consisted of five sessions distributed over five weeks and lasting 90—120 minutes each. The courses were delivered by two experienced facilitators from the EFFEKT team. The group size varied between six and 15 participants. The training included basic rules for positive parenting, requests and demands, setting limits, dealing with difficult parenting situations, coping with stress, and enhancing social relationships within and outside the family. Presentations by the trainers, workshops, group discussions, role-playing, self-awareness exercises, structured teaching aids, and some homework were used as didactic measures. The training was offered to 255 families, of which 170 (67 %) participated in at least one session. In most cases the mothers represented the family (n = 163), but there were also 48 fathers in the courses. Three quarters of the parents attended more than half of the program.

Outcome Measures

preschool social behavior questionnaire.

German adaptations of the PSBQ (Tremblay *et al.*, 1992) were used to measure children's behavior problems. The instrument contains 46 items which are rated on a three point scale ranging from »never or not true« (rating: 0) over »sometimes or somewhat true« (rating: 1) to »often or very true« (rating: 2). We gathered independent information in the PSBQ from preschool teachers and the children's mothers. The information from the preschool teachers was also applied in the pre-training matching procedure. For details of the German version of the PSBQ see Lösel, Beelmann and Stemmler(2002). In the present study we used the *PSBQ-Total Score* (internal consistency d =. 90) and subscales on *Externalizing Problems* (physical aggression, delinquency, damage of objects and hyperactivity) and *Internalizing Problems* (anxiety, emotional disorder and social withdrawal). The *Externalizing Scale* contains 20 items such as »He/she kicks, bites and hits other children«, » He/she steals at home/in the kindergarten «, » He/she is impulsive and acts without thinking« (d = . 89). As the main focus of the PSBQ is on antisocial problems, the *Internalizing Scale* is shorter and consists of 8 items such as » He/she is too fearful or anxious« or »He/she is not as happy as other children« (d=. 75). The PSBQ for preschool teachers and mothers was applied in the first wave of assessment and 2—3 months after the training. The mothers' version was also used for the assessment of potential long-term effects more than two years after the training. As most of the students had left the kindergarten at this time, we used information from the school as a further independent outcome measure:

school report cards

Behavioral problems in the first and second grade of elementary school were assessed by a content analysis of the school report cards (mid-term record and final record; *Stemmler et al.* , 2005). In Germany, in first and second school classes no standardized grades are given. Instead, teachers write a report on the child' s achievement and behavior in the class-room. Praise as well as critique was assessed for the following behaviors: aggression/delinquency, attention/hyperactivity, communication, cooperation, conflict behavior, contact with others, emotional tone, obeying rules, self-reliance, and social integration. Inter-rater agreement was good and varied between Kappa = . 71 and 1. 00. Teacher reports in the first two grades aim at encouraging the children, therefore positive remarks like»excellent«, »good«, »has no problems with« were much more frequent than negative remarks such as » bad«, » not very well«, and» has problems with« (typically mentioned in only 1—15 % of the cases). On average teachers mentioned only. 72 behavioral problems in each report card. Due to this low base rate, three or more reported behavior problems were chosen as an appropriate indicator of serious difficulties in a child.

Statistical Analyses

For the analyses of treatment effects in the PSBQ scales we applied causal regression models (Steyer *et al.* , 2000). These methods avoid shortcomings of repeated measures analysis of variance or analysis of covariance which can deceive the actual treatment effect as in the case of Simpson' s Paradox (Novick, 1980). In such a case, the treatment effects are so called conditional effects, which differ depending on the group under investigation. Causal regression models (Steyer, 2003) calculate an average (causal) effect which is the difference between the expected means of the conditional regressions under investigation (e. g. , one for the control group and one for the treatment group). The expected outcome of the treatment variable is calculated using the following equation (1):

$$E(Y|X, Z) = g_0(Z) + g_1(Z)X \qquad (1)$$

Y is the treatment outcome measured at time 2 (t_2). Z is the covariate, usually measured at time 1 (t_1). X is a dummy variable with two values, one for the control group (X = 0) and one for the treatment (X = 1). Equation (2) is the so called intercept function, because in equation (1) $g_0(Z)$ represents the intercept. It describes the relationship between the covariate (Z) and the treatment outcome (Y) under the condition of no treatment (X = 0). This function is similar to a developmental function. It describes the change of Y over time if no treatment takes place.

$$g_0(Z) = \gamma_{00} + \gamma_{01}(Z) \qquad (2)$$

Equation (3) is the so called slope of effect function, because in equation (1) $g_1(Z)$ represents the slope of the regression equation.

$$g_1(Z) = (\gamma_{10} + \gamma_{11}(Z))X \qquad (3)$$

The effect function describes the development under treatment. Based on equation (1) three null hypotheses may be tested: 1. There is no average treatment effect, that is the difference between $E(g_1(Z))$ and $E(g_0(Z))$ is zero. The resulting effect is called »average causal effect« because it is undiluted, and represents the pure treatment effect. 2. There is no covariate effect; i. e. $g_0(Z)$ is a constant ($\gamma_{01} = 0$). 3. There is no conditional effect, i. e. there is no interaction between the treatment and the covariate ($\gamma_{11} = 0$). For these analyses the software EffectLite 2. 05 (Steyer and Parchev, 2006) was used.

The follow-up outcome in the school report cards was analyzed by frequency comparisons and Chi^2-tests. As statistical significance depends on sample size, standardized effect sizes d were computed for all analyses.

As there was some dropout in the training as well as in the outcome measurement, we used a conservative strategy of evaluating effectiveness. Children or parents who had started but not completed the programs were assigned to the experimental group. In cases where no short-or long-term follow-up measures were available, the respective matched partner was also deleted from the analysis. Both approaches control for selection effects in the outcome evaluation.

RESULTS

Short-Term Evaluation

preschool teachers' information

Table 1 contains means, standard deviations and the analyses of average causal effects in the PSBQ for preschool teachers 2—3 months after the training. Due to the group-wise randomization and matching procedure, the pretest scores of the treatment groups (TGs) and control groups (CGs) were very similar in all scales. At post-test, all mean scores of the program groups decreased, whereas the Total and Externalizing problem scores in the control groups slightly increased.

The majority of average causal effects were significant. In the PSBQ Total scale there was a positive effect for the whole program (d = .23) as well as for the child training (d = .25) and the combination of the child and parent training (d = .36). The outcome pattern was similar in the Externalizing scale, but the effect sizes were a little smaller (maximum: d = .25 for the combined program). There was also a significant reduction of Internalizing problems for the training in total, the child program and the combined training. Again, the effect was largest for the latter (d = .33). The effects for the parent program alone went in the expected directed but were too small for reaching statistical significance.

Table 1 **Descriptive statistics and average causal effects in preschool teachers' ratings of child behavior in the PSBQ (short-term evaluation, 2—3 months after the program)**

PSBQ-Scales	Total Problem Score			Externalizing Problems			Internalizing Problems		
	Pre	Post	Average Effects	Pre	Post	Average Effects	Pre	Post	Average Effects
	M (SD)	M (SD)	Effect (SE) ES	M (SD)	M (SD)	Effect (SE) ES	M (SD)	M (SD)	Effect (SE) ES
All Trainings									
TG (n=239)	11.56 (8.96)	9.97 (8.26)	−2.31 ***	6.10 (6.48)	5.21 (5.83)	−1.28 ***	2.82 (2.53)	2.20 (2.31)	−0.44 *
CG (n=239)	11.77 (8.12)	12.44 (10.00)	(0.59) 0.23	6.74 (6.33)	6.98 (7.42)	(0.38) 0.17	2.42 (2.16)	2.46 (2.41)	(0.19) 0.19
Child Training									
TG (n=89)	11.29 (9.33)	9.82 (8.14)	−2.47 * (0.98)	5.98 (6.82)	5.20 (5.76)	−1.06^{+} (0.63)	2.75 (2.58)	2.14 (2.48)	−0.64 * (0.31)

PSBQ-Scales	Total Problem Score			Externalizing Problems			Internalizing Problems		
	Pre	Post	Average Effects	Pre	Post	Average Effects	Pre	Post	Average Effects
	M (SD)	M (SD)	Effect (SE) ES	M (SD)	M (SD)	Effect (SE) ES	M (SD)	M (SD)	Effect (SE) ES
CG (n=89)	11.58 (8.27)	12.51 (9.91)	0.25	6.67 (6.50)	6.79 (7.13)	0.14	2.45 (2.12)	2.61 (2.49)	0.26
Parent Training									
TG (n=77)	11.78 (7.75)	10.82 (8.41)	−0.90 (0.98)	5.84 (6.01)	5.18 (5.90)	−0.81 (0.65)	3.25 (2.60)	2.79 (2.41)	0.20 (0.33)
CG (n=77)	11.81 (8.11)	11.74 (10.19)	0.09	6.40 (6.01)	6.49 (7.43)	0.11	2.64 (2.38)	2.33 (2.13)	0.09
Combined Training									
TG (n=73)	11.66 (9.78)	9.25 (8.28)	−3.62 ** (1.09)	6.52 (7.13)	5.28 (5.92)	−1.94 ** (0.69)	2.44 (2.35)	1.64 (1.80)	−0.79 * (0.35)
CG (n=73)	11.97 (8.08)	13.10 (9.94)	0.36	7.16 (6.52)	7.71 (7.78)	0.25	2.16 (1.97)	2.41 (2.61)	0.33

TG = Training Group; CG = Control Group; M = Mean; SD = Standard Deviation; SE = Standard Error; ES = Effect Size (Cohen's d); effect sizes recoded so that positive coefficients indicate effects in the desired direction.

+ p<.10 * p<.05 ** p<.01 *** p<.001.

Table 2 shows the analyses of the covariate and conditional effects. All regression coefficients for the covariates were highly significant. This indicates relatively stable problem scores over time. Coefficients for Externalizing problems were generally higher than those for Internalizing problems (e. g. for the total sample: $\gamma_{01} = .91$ vs. .42). There were several conditional effects, i. e. for the whole EFFEKT program, the parent training, and the combined program in the scale on Externalizing problems. This shows that children with larger problem scores in the pretest benefitted more from the program than other children.

Table 2 Conditional effects of treatment by covariate in preschool teachers' ratings of child behavior in the PSBQ (short-term evaluation, 2—3 months after the program)

PSBQ-Scales					
Total Problem Score		Externalizing Problems		Internalizing Problems	
Covariate (SE)	Conditional Effects (SE)	Covariate (SE)	Conditional Effects (SE)	Covariate (SE)	Conditional Effects (SE)
All Trainings (TG and CG: n = 239)					
0. 84 *** (0. 06)	−0. 14+ (0. 07)	0. 91 *** (0. 05)	−0. 19 ** (0. 06)	0. 42 *** (0. 07)	0. 12 (0. 08)
Child Training (TG and CG: n = 89)					
0. 77 *** (0. 10)	−0. 09 (0. 11)	0. 81 *** (0. 08)	−0. 13 (0. 10)	0. 45 *** (0. 12)	0. 22 (0. 14)
Parent Training (TG and CG: n = 77)					
0. 97 *** (0. 09)	−0. 14 (0. 12)	1. 00 *** (0. 08)	−0. 20^{+} (0. 11)	0. 37 *** (0. 09)	0. 14 (0. 13)
Combined Training (TG and CG: n = 73)					
0. 82 ** (0. 11)	−0. 15 (0. 13)	0. 95 *** (0. 09)	−0. 23 * (0. 10)	0. 45 ** (0. 15)	−0. 16 (0. 17)

TG = Training Group; CG = Control Group; SE = Standard Error.

+$p <$. 10 * $p <$. 05 ** $p <$. 01 *** $p <$. 001.

mothers' information

Table 3 contains the means, standard deviations and the analyses of average causal effects in the PSBQ for mothers 2—3 months after the training. Because the matching was based on the preschool teachers' scores in the first assessment, the pretest means in the treatment and control groups were less homogeneous than in the analyses of the preschool teachers' PSBQ data. The mothers' scores on the child problems were also slightly higher.

In all subgroups and all PSBQ scales the problem scores decreased from pretest to post-test measurement. However, this was not only the case in the program groups but also in the control groups. There were two significant average causal effects which did not go in the expected direction: In the whole program group and in the combined training group the mothers reported more Internalizing problems of their children than the mothers of the respective control groups (d = −. 22 and −. 35, $p <$. 05).

Table 3 **Descriptive statistics and average causal effects in mothers' ratings of child behavior in the PSBQ (short-term evaluation, 2—3 months after the program)**

PSBQ-Scales	Total Score			Externalizing Problems			Internalizing Problems		
	Pre	Post	Average Effects	Pre	Post	Average Effects	Pre	Post	Average Effects
	M (SD)	M (SD)	Effect (SE) ES	M (SD)	M (SD)	Effect (SE) ES	M (SD)	M (SD)	Effect (SE) ES
All Trainings									
TG (n=203)	13.98 (6.84)	12.43 (6.89)	0.76[+] (0.43[+])	7.97 (5.03)	7.33 (4.77)	0.23 (0.30)	3.24 (2.04)	2.88 (2.08)	0.41 * (0.16)
CG (n=203)	12.86 (6.57)	11.28 (6.35)	−0.11	7.79 (5.34)	6.96 (4.93)	−0.05	3.11 (2.10)	2.40 (1.86)	−0.22
Child Training									
TG (n=70)	12.29 (6.68)	11.30 (5.91)	0.26 (0.73)	7.27 (4.82)	6.67 (4.31)	0.14 (0.54)	3.06 (2.04)	2.64 (2.03)	0.17 (0.29)
CG (n=70)	13.65 (6.76)	11.91 (6.26)	−0.04	8.06 (5.18)	7.04 (4.78)	−0.02	3.49 (2.44)	2.66 (1.86)	−0.09
Parent Training									
TG (n=68)	14.47 (6.88)	13.12 (7.68)	0.53 (0.75)	8.19 (5.27)	7.31 (4.99)	−0.03 (0.51)	3.72 (2.06)	3.18 (2.11)	0.36 (0.28)
CG (n=68)	12.47 (5.24)	10.93 (5.90)	−0.09	7.29 (4.95)	6.63 (4.86)	−0.00	3.03 (2.14)	2.40 (1.97)	0.18
Combined Training									
TG (n=65)	13.42 (6.22)	12.94 (6.95)	1.15 (0.74)	8.49 (4.98)	8.05 (4.96)	0.47 (0.53)	2.92 (1.96)	2.82 (2.11)	0.61 * (0.29)
CG (n=65)	12.42 (7.18)	10.95 (6.91)	−0.17	8.02 (5.93)	7.22 (5.21)	−0.09	2.80 (1.58)	2.14 (1.74)	−0.35

TG = Training Group; CG = Control Group; M = Mean; SD = Standard Deviation; SE = Standard Error; ES = Effect Size (Cohen's d); effect sizes recoded so that positive coefficients indicate effects in the desired direction.
+p<.10 * p<.05.

Table 4 shows the analyses of covariate and conditional effects in the mothers' reports. The covariate coefficients ranged between .45 and .78 and were all significant. This once more indicated substantial stability of the behavior problems from the first to the second assessment, although the difference in stability between Externalizing (γ_{01} = .67) and Internalizing problems(γ_{01} = .49) was less pronounced than in the preschool teachers' reports. There was no significant conditional effect.

Table 4 Conditional effects of treatment by covariate in mothers' ratings of child behavior in the PSBQ (short-term evaluation, 2—3 months after the program)

PSBQ-Scales					
Total Score		Externalizing Problems		Internalizing Problems	
Covariate (SE)	Conditional Effects (SE)	Covariate (SE)	Conditional Effects (SE)	Covariate (SE)	Conditional Effects (SE)
All Trainings					
0. 66 *** (0. 08)	−0. 02 (0. 12)	0. 67 *** (0. 08)	−0. 05 (0. 11)	0. 41 *** (0. 08)	0. 03 (0. 13)
Child Training					
0. 73 *** (0. 04)	0. 07 (0. 07)	0. 72 *** (0. 04)	−0. 02 (0. 05)	0. 49 *** (0. 05)	0. 07 (0. 08)
Parent Training					
0. 77 ** (0. 07)	0. 12 (0. 11)	0. 72 *** (0. 06)	0. 09 (0. 10)	0. 45 *** (0. 13)	0. 24 (0. 16)
Combined Training					
0. 78 *** (0. 08)	0. 10 (0. 12)	0. 76 *** (0. 08)	0. 01 (0. 10)	0. 62 *** (0. 08)	−0. 03 (0. 13)

TG = Training Group; CG = Control Group. SE = Standard Error.
** p < . 01 *** p <. 001.

Long-Term Evaluation

mothers' information

More than two years after the end of the program a follow-up evaluation was carried out. Because the majority of children had left the kindergarten, we could not gather PSBQ information from the preschool teachers but from the mothers only. The means, standard deviations and analyses of the average causal effects are presented in Table 5.

There was no significant effect for any type of program and outcome scale. The analysis of covariate effects (not reported in detail) revealed highly significant predictions from the pre-training to the follow-up assessment (PSBQ Total: g = . 74; p < . 001). Once more, the Externalizing problems (γ_{01} = . 71; p < . 001) were more stable than the Internalizing problems (γ_{01} = . 57). No significant conditional effect could be found.

Teachers' information in the school report cards. The present study expands our previous analysis of the school report cards (Lösel *et al.* , 2006) from the first to the second grade (up to three years after the programs). As previously, three or more problems were chosen as an indicator of serious behavior problems in a child. *Table 6* contains the percentages of children who had such a number of problems in both the first and second grade.

Table 5 **Descriptive statistics and average causal effects in mothers' ratings of child behavior in the PSBQ (long-term evaluation, 2 years after the program)**

PSBQ-Scales	Total Score			Externalizing Problems			Internalizing Problems		
	Pre	FU	Average Effects	Pre	FU	Average Effects	Pre	FU	Average Effects
	M (SD)	M (SD)	Effect (SE) ES	M (SD)	M (SD)	Effect (SE) ES	M (SD)	M (SD)	Effect (SE) ES
All Trainings									
TG (n=179)	13. 14 (6. 61)	11. 79 (6. 60)	0. 39 (0. 49)	7. 57 (5. 00)	6. 73 (4. 77)	0. 23 (0. 34)	3. 43 (2. 15)	2. 83 (1. 93)	0. 11 (0. 19)
CG (n=179)	12. 08 (5. 75)	10. 63 (6. 28)	−0. 06	7. 25 (4. 60)	6. 28 (4. 49)	−0. 05	2. 93 (1. 85)	2. 46 (1. 93)	−0. 06
Child Training									
TG (n=59)	12. 02 (6. 48)	11. 03 (6. 48)	0. 09 (0. 90)	7. 03 (4. 84)	6. 12 (4. 45)	−0. 04 (0. 63)	3. 19 (1. 91)	2. 97 (2. 27)	0. 32 (0. 34)
CG (n=59)	13. 02 (6. 36)	11. 66 (6. 84)	0. 01	7. 83 (5. 08)	6. 68 (4. 99)	−0. 019	3. 15 (2. 02)	2. 63 (2. 13)	−0. 15
Parent Training									
TG (n=66)	14. 12 (6. 69)	12. 23 (6. 82)	0. 17 (0. 80)	7. 68 (5. 11)	6. 79 (4. 97)	0. 21 (0. 53)	3. 94 (2. 38)	3. 11 (2. 34)	−0. 08 (0. 34)
CG (n=66)	11. 14 (5. 11)	10. 39 (5. 89)	0. 03	6. 94 (4. 30)	6. 03 (4. 16)	−0. 05	2. 88 (1. 78)	2. 59 (2. 05)	0. 04
Combined Training									
TG (n=54)	13. 17 (6. 57)	12. 07 (6. 52)	0. 97 (0. 92)	8. 02 (5. 08)	7. 33 (4. 86)	0. 48 (0. 64)	3. 06 (2. 00)	2. 35 (2. 00)	0. 11 (0. 32)
CG (n=54)	11. 22 (5. 73)	9. 78 (6. 05)	−0. 16	6. 98 (4. 42)	6. 15 (4. 37)	−0. 11	2. 74 (1. 75)	2. 13 (1. 49)	0. 07

TG = Training Group; CG = Control Group; M = Mean; SD = Standard Deviation; SE = Standard Error; ES = Effect Size (Cohen's d); effect sizes recoded so that positive coefficients indicate effects in the desired direction; no significances.

As expected, there were only a small number of children for whom the teachers mentioned stable multiple behavior problems in the school report cards. Due to the low base rate, no difference between the program and control group was below the 5 %-level of significance. However, in three out of four comparisons there were fewer multi-problem children in the program group and for the whole program and the combined training the probability of the observed differences was p < . 10.

Table 6 Percentage of children with multiple behavioral problems (three or more) recorded in their first and second grade reports (long-term evaluation; up to 3 years after the program)

	Behavioral Probems			
	Training Group	Control Group		
	%	%	χ^2	ES
All Trainings (TG = 162/CG = 162)	1. 2	4. 3	2. 83[+]	0. 20
Child Training (TG = 58/CG = 58)	1. 7	1. 7	0. 00	0. 00
Parent Training (TG = 56/CG = 56)	1. 8	5. 4	1. 04	0. 20
Combined Trainings (TG = 48/CG = 48)	0. 0	6. 1	3. 03[+]	0. 50

TG = Training Group; CG = Control Group; ES = Effect Size = arcus(P_{TG}) - arcus(P_{CG}); effect sizes recoded so that positive coefficients indicate effects in the desired direction.
[+]p< . 10.

DISCUSSION

Our study evaluated outcomes of a prevention program against antisocial development over a period from 2—3 months up to 3 years after the training. The analyses cover a longer followup period than in our previous evaluations (Beelmann et al. , 2006; Lösel et al. , 2006; Stemmler et al. , 2007) and are also methodologically more rigorous. Firstly, we applied more sophisticated statistical models for the analysis of causal and conditional effects. Secondly, we used different informants for the assessment of child behavior. And thirdly, we carried out an intent-to-treat analysis with regard to dropouts; i. e. all children and parents who had attended at least one program session were regarded as »treated« in the evaluation. Together with the group-wise randomization and individual matching, these procedures ensure a very strict estimate of potential effects.

The results showed a number of positive effects of the EFFEKT program as a whole and of its components. However, as in international research (e. g. Beelmann and Lösel, 2007; Bernazzani and Tremblay, 2006; Farrington and Welsh, 2007; Lösel and Beelmann, 2003; 2005), the findings are mixed with regard to outcome criteria and time of measurement.

The short-term findings in the preschool teachers' PSBQ ratings were similar to our previous study in which we included only children and parents who had received at least half of the training (Lösel et al. , 2006). All effects of the whole program and the majority of the effects in the various subgroups were statistically significant. The most general effect (whole program group and PSBQ total problem score) was d = . 23 (p < . 001) and the largest effect size was d = . 36 for the combined program in the Total problem score. Only the parent training alone did not reveal a significant effect. This was probably not due to implementation problems because we found good cooperation and consumer satisfaction (Lösel *et al.* , 2004) . One may assume that the non-significant findings for the stand-alone parent training are a consequence of its relatively short duration. However, although program intensity is a moderator of effect size in some systematic reviews, there are positive outcomes of short programs as well (e. g. Beelmann and Lösel, 2007; Nowak and Heinrichs, 2008; Wilson *et al.* , 2001) . Our parent program also had significant effects on its main target, the participants' parenting behavior (Stemmler *et al.* , 2007) . It is noteworthy that self-reported parenting behavior showed very low correlations to child behavior problems as assessed by the preschool teachers (Lösel, Stemmler, Beelmann and Jaursch, 2005) . Therefore, one cannot expect larger effects of interventions. Although there was a small program effect on parenting, this requires a further transfer to change the child's behavior. In contrast, the key mediating constructs of the child program, social information processing and problem solving, are more proximal to behavioral outcomes in the child.

That the parent training was not without any impact is indicated by the results on the combined program. This multimodal approach showed the largest short-term effects in our study. The effects were also consistent with regard to both Internalizing and Externalizing problems. The latter are normally more difficult to change and were also more stable in our study (see the covariate effects in *Table 2*) .

Although the short-term outcomes in the preschool teachers' ratings of the child problems are positive, the significant effect sizes are small (d = . 17 - . 36) . This is a realistic finding for a rather short program and by no means trivial. An effect size of d = . 25 in Externalizing problems indicates that there is ca. 13 % less aggression and delinquency in the program group than in the control group. The mean effects sizes of meta-analyses on child social skills trainings are in a similar range when outcome measures refer to everyday child behavior and not to intermediate constructs that are closer to the content of the training (Lösel and Beelmann, 2003, 2005) . In the meta-analysis of *Wilson et al.* , (2001) , the mean effect of nine school-based cognitive-behavioral programs was significant, but only d = . 10 in effect size. Effects of parent group trainings are also small when the outcomes are not parental attitudes or behavior, but independent measures of child behavior in follow-up studies (Beelmann, 2008; Lösel *et al.*, 2006; Lundahl *et al.*, 2006; Nowak and Heinrichs, 2008). This is particularly the case for studies of universal prevention. It is important to bear in mind that our study belongs to this category, i. e. the program was delivered to a representative sample of children and families. In general, universal school-or preschool-based prevention programs have much smaller effects than indicated or clinic-based programs for children who already exhibit some problem behavior and are at risk for an antisocial development (e. g. Beelmann, 2008; Farrington and Welsh, 2003, 2007; Lösel and Beelmann, 2003, 2005; Nowack and Heinrichs, 2008). This is plausible because the majority of children in a universal program would not develop behavior problems even without a program. Accordingly, differences between treatment and control groups are mainly due to the small fraction of youngsters who are at risk and in need of a program. Similarly, studies on offender treatment also found no or only very small effects for low-risk individuals (e. g. Lipsey and Landenberger, 2006; Lösel and Schmucker, 2005).

The finding of small effects in universal prevention does not imply that one should concentrate on indicated prevention and high-risk children only. Universal prevention programs avoid potential problems of early stigmatization and can reach whole populations when delivered in schools etc. (Le Blanc, 1998; Lösel, 2002). Whether a universal or indicated prevention strategy is preferable is a matter of target and cost-benefit (Swisher, Scherer and Yin, 2004; Welsh and Farrington, 2001). Universal programs for large populations must be short for financial reasons and may not be sufficient for high-risk children who need more intensive programs. Therefore, a differentiated strategy of developmental intervention is most appropriate (Lösel, 2007a). However, a small universal effect does not mean that the risk-cases can not benefit. As in public health, a small general effect shifts the overall risk distribution to the lower end and will also reduce the prevalence of problems in subgroups at the upper risk end (e. g. Coid, 2003). Accordingly, the present study revealed various significant conditional effects (see *Table 2*). These effects suggest that children with more behavioral problems at pretest benefitted more from the program than children at lower risk.

This was not only the case for Externalizing problems in the short-term evaluation but is also indicated by the long-term effects as assessed via the school report cards. The school certificates are rather hard data on the child's everyday behavior which were not produced within the context of the research project. Our findings showed a lower number of children with multiple behavior problems in the whole program group (d = . 20) and in the combined program group (d = . 50). A reduction in cases with serious behavior problems was also the most important finding in the Fast Track Prevention Trial in theUnited States (Conduct Problems Prevention Research Group, 2002). Certainly, in our study one must bear in mind that these effects are based on small numbers and therefore only significant at p < . 10. However, three percentage points less of the few children with multiple and stable behavior problems three years after the training are not a trivial finding. If such an effect would last into adolescence, it would substantially reduce the society's costs for seriously antisocial children (Munoz et al. , 2004; Scott et al. , 2001).

Before speculating too much about such potential benefits of the program, we need to emphasize the less encouraging results of our study: Neither the short-term nor the long-term evaluation revealed any positive effect in the mothers' reports on child behavior problems. Furthermore, there were even two negative short-term effects in the scale on Internalizing problems.

Partially inconsistent findings in different outcome measures are not a rarity but rather normal in evaluations of prevention programs. This is the case in large-scale single studies (e. g. Conduct Problems Prevention Research Group, 1999, 2002; Sanders, Markie-Dadds, Tully and Bor, 2000) as well as in meta-analyses. For example, Lösel and Beelmann (2006) found larger effects of child skills trainings in studies that used teacher or parent reports and weaker effects in self reports and official data. Long-term effects were only significant for teacher information. A meta-analysis on the Triple-P-Program revealed positive effects in parent ratings but very small or no significant effects if the children's behavior was assessed by independent experts or in self reports (Nowak and Heinrichs, 2008). Such discrepancies between data sources are not necessarily due to differences in reliability or validity. Assessments of child behavior problems by different informants (e. g. parents and teachers) normally show small correlations of approximately r = . 30 (Achenbach, McConaughy and Howell, 1987). Agreement is only stronger (r ca . 60) when the two informants observe the child in the same context (e. g. mother and father in the family). Similar differences between informants were also found in the Erlangen-Nuremberg Study (Lösel et al. , 2005).

There is no definite explanation for the outcome discrepancies in our study, but we assume various reasons: Our matching was not only based on biographic data (age, gender and SES) but also on the preschool teachers' reports in the PSBQ. Therefore, the evaluation is better controlled with regard to these data than with regard to the mothers' reports. The mothers' reports may also have been more influenced by the research project than the data from the preschool and school teachers. To avoid dropouts from the longitudinal study we organized large annual meetings with all parents, were available for questions by phone, and sent out a newsletter for the parents. These necessary measures of panel care may have influenced some control group parents' behavior or their view on their children. In addition, parents in the program group who changed their behavior may have caused temporary problems of adaptation in their children. The training could also have triggered a more sensitive observation of their child's problems. Both reasons may explain the negative short-term effects in the scale on Internalizing problems.

Sometimes, zero effects may disappear over time because adaptation and learning processes lead to more positive findings at follow-up (e. g. Tremblay et al., 1995). However, such a »sleeper effect« was not apparent in our study. The parents' reports on their children two years after the training did not reveal any significant effect. Therefore, we must assume that the non-effect in the mothers' reports is robust.

For a better understanding of this finding one should take the following into account: Although parents are more in contact with their children than teachers, they have less opportunity to compare the child's behavior with that of other children (particularly in the case of a single child). Preschool and school teachers or neutral experts have a more normative and professional view on children (Doncker, 2004). Various studies suggest that such information is more valid with regard to the assessment and prediction of child behavior problems (e. g. Bank, Duncan, Patterson and Reid, 1993; Brown et al., 2006; Hinshaw, Han, Erhardt and Huber, 1992; Ronning et al., 2009). Behavior ratings of children by the same informant are also rather stable over time. In our study, for example, the mothers PBSQ reports in the first assessment correlated strongly with their ratings several years later. Such longitudinal correlations are larger than cross-sectional ratings by different informants (Lösel, 2002). They may not only reflect stability in the child's behavior but also relatively fixed cognitive schemata about the child. As a consequence, repeated assessments by the same persons would be less sensitive for intervention effects than information from independent observers. Accordingly, another evaluation in our project showed much stronger effects of a program for elementary school children when the teachers at pretest and follow up were not the same (Hacker *et al.* , 2007). A similar process can be assumed in the present study as there was some fluctuation of preschool teachers in the short-term evaluation and a totally different assessment via the school report cards at the follow up. The analyses of further follow-up data will reveal whether this is a plausible hypothesis or not.

In conclusion, this study showed some encouraging effects of a child-and parent-oriented program on developmental prevention. However, the effect sizes are small and only partially consistent across outcome measures and time. The zero effects in the mothers' ratings should not be downplayed as an exception but viewed as a critical signal. They refer to the repeated finding that the effects of programs in independent evaluations are less positive than in studies which have been carried out by the original program developers (Eisner *et al.* , 2007; Lipsey and Landenberger, 2006; Lösel and Beelmann, 2003). As in other fields of intervention, one cannot simply generalize the findings of demonstration projects in North America to other countries and routine practice (Lösel, 2007b). One should also bear in mind that one punctual prevention program is often not enough and one size does not fit all. Therefore, for example, we investigate a booster program for elementary school age and program adaptations for migrant families and emotionally stressed mothers. Preliminary findings show some further promising effects (Lösel, 2008). However, in general we recommend realistic expectations and a cautionary optimism. Successful developmental prevention of violence and crime requires more evidence-based programs and a more long-term investment at the policy level (Farrington and Welsh, 2007; Junger *et al.* , 2007).

References

Achenbach, T. M. , McConaughy, S. H. & Howell, C. T. (1987). *Child/adolescent behavioral and emotional problems: Implications of cross-informant correlations for situational specifity.* Psychological Bulletin 101, 213 – 232.

Bank, L. , Duncan, T. , Patterson, G. R. & Reid, J. (1993). *Parent and teacher ratings in the assessment and prediction of antisocial and delinquent behavior.* Journal of Personality 61, 693 – 709.

Beelmann, A. (2008). *The effect of parent training programs in the prevention and treatment of antisocial behavior in childhood and adolescence.* Paper presented at the 18th Conference of the European Association of Psychology and Law, 2—5 July 2008, Maastricht/NL.

Beelmann, A., Jaursch, S. & Lösel, F. (2004). Ich kann Probleme lösen: *Soziales Trainingsprogramm für Vorschulkinder.* Universität Erlangen-Nürnberg: Institut für Psychologie.

Beelmann, A, Jaursch, S., Lösel, F. & Stemmler, M. (2006). Frühe universelle Pravention von dissozialen Entwicklungsproblemen: *Implementation und Wirksamkeit eines verhaltensorientierten Elterntrainings.* Praxis der Rechtspsychologie 16, 120 – 143.

Beelmann, A. & Lösel, F. (2004). *Elterntraining zur Förderung der Erziehungskompetenz.* Universität Erlangen-Nürnberg: Institut für Psychologie.

Beelmann, A. & Lösel, F. (2006). *Child social skills training in developmental crime prevention: Effects on antisocial behavior and social competence.* Psicothema, 18, 603 – 610.

Beelmann, A. & Lösel, F. (2007). *Pravention von externalisierendem Problemverhalten,* in: B. Röhrle (Hrsg.), Prävention und Gesundheitsförderung, Bd. 3: Kinder und Jugendliche, 557 – 595. Tübingen.

Beelmann, A., Lösel, F., Stemmler, M. & Jaursch, S. (2006). *Beurteilung von sozialen Verhaltensproblemen und Erziehungsschwierigkeiten im Vorschulalter.* Eine Untersuchung zur deutschen Adaptation des Eyberg Child Behavior Inventory (ECBI). Diagnostica 52, 189 – 198.

Bender, D. & Lösel, F. (2006). *Working with violent children in German youth services*: Results of a survey, in: A. Hagell & R. Jeyarah Dent (eds.), Children Who Commit Acts of Serious Interpersonal Violence: Messages for Practice, 167 – 185. London.

Bernazzani, O. & Tremblay, R. E. (2006). *Early parent training*, in: B. C. Welsh & D. P. Farrington (eds.), Preventing Crime: What Works for Children, Offenders, Victims, and Places, 21 – 32. Dordrecht.

Brown, J. D., Wissow, L. S., Gadomski, A., Zachary, C., Bartlett, E. & Horn, I. (2006). *Parent and teacher mental health ratings of children using primary-care services: Interrater agreement and implications for mental health screening*. Ambulatory Pediatrics 6, 347 – 351. *Coid, J. W.* (2003). Formulating strategies for the primary prevention of adult antisocial behaviour: »High risk« or »population« strategies?, in: D. P. Farrington & J. W. Coid (eds.), Early Prevention of Adult Antisocial Behaviour, 32 – 78. Cambridge.

Conduct Problems Prevention Research Group (1999). *Initial impact of the Fast Track Prevention Trial for conduct problems: II. Classroom effects*. Journal of Consulting and Clinical Psychology 67, 648 – 657.

Conduct Problems Prevention Research Group (2002). *Evaluation of the first 3 years of the Fast Track Prevention Trial with children at high risk for adolescent conduct problems*. Journal of Abnormal Child Psychology 19, 553 – 567.

Dishion, T. J. & Patterson, S. G. (1996). *Preventive Parenting with Love, Encouragement, and Limits*. The Preschool Years. Eugene/OR.

Donker, A. (2004). *Precursors and Prevalence of Young-Adult and Adult Delinquency*. Diss. Leiden/NL.

Eisner, M. , Ribeaud, D. , Jünger, R. & Meidert, U. (2007). *Fruhpravention von Gewalt und Aggression*. Zurich.

Farrington, D. P. (1991). *Antisocial personality from childhood to adulthood*. The Psychologist 4, 389 – 394.

Farrington, D. P. & Welsh, B. C. (2003). *Family based prevention of offending: A meta-analysis*. The Australian and New Zealand Journal of Criminology 36, 127 – 151.

Farrington, D. P. & Welsh, B. C. (2007). *Saving Children from a Life of Crime*. Oxford/UK.

Fisher, P. A. , Ramsay, E. , Antoine, K. , Kavanagh, K. , Winebarger, A. , Eddy, J. M. & Reid, J. B. (1997). *Success in Parenting: A Curriculum for Parents with Challenging Children*. Eugene/OR.

Foster, E. M. , Prinz, R. J. , Sanders, M. R. & Shapiro, C. J. (2008). *The costs of a public health infrastructure for delivering parenting and family support*. Children and Youth Services Review 30, 493 – 501.

Geißler, R. (Hrsg.) (1994). *Soziale Schichtung und Lebenschancen in Deutschland*. Stuttgart. Hacker, S. , Lösel, F. , Stemmler, M. , Jaursch, S. , Runkel, D. & Beelmann, A. (2007). *Training im Problemlosen (TIP): Implementation und*

Evaluation eines sozial-kognitiven Kompetenztrainings für Kinder. Heilpädagogische Forschung 23, 11–21.

Heinrichs, N., Hahlweg, K., Bertram, H., Kuschel, A., Naumann, S. & Harstick, S. (2006). *Die langfristige Wirksamkeit eines Elterntrainings zur universellen Pravention kindlicher Verhaltensstorungen: Ergebnisse aus Sicht der Mutter und Vater*. Zeitschrift fur Klinische Psychologie und Psychotherapie 35, 82–96.

Henggeler, S. W., Schoenwald, S. K., Borduin, C. M., Rowland, M. D. & Cunningham, P. B. (1998). *Multisystemic Treatment of Antisocial Behavior in Children and Adolescents*. New York.

Hinshaw, S. P., Han, S. S., Erhardt, D. & Huber, A. (1992). *Internalizing and externalizing behavior in preschool children: Correspondence among parent and teacher ratings and behavior observations*. Journal of Clinical Child Psychology 21, 143–150.

Hölling, H., Erhart, M., Ravens-Sieberer, U. & Schlack, R. (2007). *Verhaltensauffälligkeiten bei Kindern und Jugendlichen*. Erste Ergebnisse aus dem Kinderund Jugendgesundheitssurvey. Bundesgesundheitsblatt, Gesundheitsforschung, Gesundheitsschutz, 784–793.

Ihle, W. & Esser, G. (2002). *Epidemiologie psychischer Störungen im Kindes-und Jugendalter*: Prävalenz, Verlauf, Komorbidität und Geschlechtsunterschiede. Psychologische Rundschau 53, 159–169.

Junger, M., Feder, L., Clay, J., Coté, S., Farrington, D. P., Freiberg, K., Garrido, V., Homel, R., Lösel, F., Manning, M., Mazerolle, P., Santos, R., Schmucker, M., Sullivan, C., Sutton, C., Tremblay, R. E. & van Yperen, T. (2007). *Preventing violence in seven countries: Global convergence in policy*. European Journal on Criminal Policy and Research 13, 327–356.

LeBlanc, M. (1998). *Screening of serious and violent juvenile offenders: Identification, classification, and prediction*, in: R. Loeber & D. P. Farrington (eds.), Serious and Violent Juvenile Offenders: Risk Factors and Successful Interventions, 167–193. Thousand Oaks. *Lipsey, M. W. & Landenberger, N. A. (2006)*. Cognitive-behavioral interventions, in: B. C. Welsh & D. P. Farrington (eds.), Preventing Crime: What Works for Children, Offenders, Victims, and Places, 57–71. Dordrecht.

Littell, J. H. (2005). *Lessons from a systematic review of effects of multisystemic therapy*. Children and Youth Services Review 27, 445–463.

Loeber, R. & Farrington, D. P. (eds.) (1998). *Serious & Violent Juvenile Offenders*. Risk Factors and Successful Interventions. Thousand Oaks.

Loeber, R. & Farrington, D. P. (2000). *Young children who commit crime: Epidemiology, developmental origins, risk factors, early interventions, and policy implications*. Development and Psychopathology 12, 737 – 762.

Loeber, R., Farrington, D. P., Stouthamer-Loeber, M. & White, H. R. (2008). *Violence and Serious Theft: Development and Prediction from Childhood to Adulthood*. New York.

Lösel, F. (1995). *The efficacy of correctional treatment: A review and synthesis of meta-evaluations*, in: J. McGuire (ed.), What Works: Reducing Reoffending. Guidelines from Research and Practice, 79 – 111. Chichester.

Lösel, F. (2002). *Risk/need assessment and prevention of antisocial development in young people: Basic issues from a perspective of cautionary optimism*, in: R. Corrado, R. Roesch, S. D. Hart & J. Gierowski (eds.), Multi-Problem Violent Youth, 35 – 57. Amsterdam.

Lösel, F. (2004). *Multimodale Gewaltprävention bei Kindern und Jugendlichen: Familie, Kindergarten und Schule*, in: W. Melzer & H. -D. Schwind (Hrsg.), Gewaltprävention in der Schule, 326 – 348. Baden-Baden.

Lösel, F. (2005). *Evaluating developmental prevention of antisocial behavior: An example and a brief review*, in: A. Cerederecka, T. Jaskiewicz-Obdydzinska, R. Roesch & J. Wojcikiewicz (eds.), Forensic Psychology and Law, 389 – 408. Cracow.

Lösel, F. (2007a). *It's never too early and never too late: Towards an integrated science of developmental intervention in criminology*. Criminologist 35/2, 1 – 8.

Lösel, F. (2007b). *Doing evaluation in criminology: Balancing scientific and practical demands*, in: R. D. King & E. Wincup (eds.), Doing Research on Crime and Justice, 141 – 170. 2nd ed. Oxford.

Lösel, F. (2008). *What works in saving children from a life of crime?* Evaluating developmental prevention programs. Invited plenary lecture at the 28th Congress of the Australian and New Zealand Association of Psychiatry, Psychology and Law, 23 – 26 October, Sydney, Australia.

Lösel, F. & Beelmann, A. (2003). *Effects of child skills training in preventing antisocial behavior: A systematic review of randomized evaluations*. The Annals of the American Academy of Political and Social Science 587, 84 – 109.

Lösel, F. & Beelmann, A. (2005). *Social problem-solving programmes for preventing antisocial behaviour in children and youth*, in: M. MacMurran & J. McGuire (eds.), Social Problem Solving and Offending: Evidence, Evaluation, and Evolution, 127 – 143. Chichester.

Lösel, F. & Beelmann, A. (2006). *Child skills training*, in: B. C. Welsh & D. P. Farrington (eds.), Preventing Crime: What Works for Children, Offenders, Victims, and Places, 33 – 54. Dordrecht.

Lösel, F., Beelmann, A., Jaursch, S., Koglin, U. & Stemmler, M. (2005). *Entwicklung und Prävention früher Probleme des Sozialverhaltens*: Die Erlangen-Nürnberger Studie, in: M. Cierpka (Hrsg.), Möglichkeiten der Gewaltprävention, 201 – 249. Göttingen.

Lösel, F., Beelmann, A., Jaursch, S. & Stemmler, M. (2004). *Soziale Kompetenz für Kinder und Familien*: Ergebnisse der Erlangen-Nurnberger Entwicklungs-und Präventionsstudie. Berlin: Bundesministerium für Familie, Senioren, Frauen und Jugend.

Lösel, F., Beelmann, A. & Stemmler, M. (2002). *Skalen zur Messung sozialen Problemverhaltens bei Vorschul-und Grundschulkindern*. Universitut Erlangen-Nurnberg: Institut fur Psychologie.

Lösel, F., Beelmann, A., Stemmler, M. & Jaursch, S. (2006). *Prävention von Problemen des Sozialverhaltens im Vorschulalter*: Evaluation des Eltern-und Kindertrainings EFFEKT. Zeitschrift für Klinische Psychologie und Psychotherapie 35, 127 – 139.

Lösel, F. & Bender, D. (2003). *Protective factors and resilience, in*: D. P. Farrington & J. W. Coid (eds.), Early Prevention of Adult Antisocial Behaviour, 130 – 204. Cambridge.

Lösel, F. & Schmucker, M. (2005). *The effectiveness of treatment for sexual offenders*: A comprehensive meta-analysis. Journal of Experimental Criminology 1, 117 – 146.

Lösel, F., Schmucker, M., Plankensteiner, B. & Weiss, M. (2006). *Bestandsaufnahme und Evaluation der Elternbildung*. Berlin: Bundesministerium für Familie, Senioren, Frauen und Jugend.

Lösel, F., Stemmler, M., Beelmann, A. & Jaursch, S. (2005). *Aggressives Verhalten im Vorschulalter*: Eine Untersuchung zum Problem verschiedener Informanten, in: I.

Seiffge-Krenke (Hrsg.), Aggressionsentwicklung zwischen Normalitut und Pathologie, 141 – 167. *Gattingen. -Lundahl, B. , Risser, H. J. & Lovejoy, M. C. (2006)*. A meta-analysis of parent training: Moderators and follow-up effects. Clinical Psychology Review 26, 86 – 104.

McCord, J. (2003). *Cures that harm: Unanticipated outcomes of crime prevention programs*. The Annals of the American Academy of Political and Social Science 587, 16 – 30.

McGuire, J. (2002). *Integrating findings from research reviews*, in: J. McGuire (ed.), Offender Rehabilitation and Treatment: Effective Practice and Policies to Reduce Re-offending, 1 – 35. Chichester.

MuRoz, R. , Hutchings, J. , Edwards, R. T. , Hounsome, B. & O' Ceilleachair, A. (2004). *Economic evaluation of treatments for children with severe behavioural problems*. Journal of Mental Health Policy Economics 7, 177 – 189.

Novick, M. R. (1980). *Statistics as psychometrics*. Psychometrika 45, 411 – 424.

Nowak, C. & Heinrichs, N. (2008). *A comprehensive metaanalysis of Triple P-Positive Parenting Program using hierarchical linear modeling: Effectiveness and moderating variables*. Clinical Child and Family Psychology Review 11, 114 – 144.

Olds, D. L. , Henderson, C. R. , Cole, R. , Eckenrode, J. , Kitzman, H. , Luckey, D. , Pettitt, L. , Sidora, K. , Morris, P. & Powers, J. (1998). *Long-term effects of nurse home visitation on children's criminal and antisocial behavior*. Journal of the American Medical Association 280, 1238 – 1244.

Robins, L. N. & Price, R. K. (1991). *Adult disorders by childhood conduct problems*. Results from the NIMH Epidemiologic Catchmemt Area Project. Psychiatry: Journal of the Study of Interpersonal Processes 54, 116 – 132.

Ronning, J. A. , Sourander, A. , Kumpulainen, K. , Tamminen, T. , Niemelu, S. , Moilanen, I. , Helenius, H. , Piha, J. & Almquist, F. (2009). *Cross-informant agreement about bullying and victimization among eightyear-olds: Whose information best predicts psychiatric caseness 10 – 15 years later?* Social Psychiatry and Psychiatric Epidemiolgoy 44, 15 – 22.

Sampson, R. J. & Laub, J. H. (2003). *Life-course desisters? Trajectories of crime among delinquent boys followed to age 70*. Criminology 41, 555 – 592.

Sanders, M. R. , Markie-Dadds, C. , Tully, L. A. & Bor, W. (2000). *The Triple P-*

Positive Parenting Program: A comparison of enhanced, standard, and self-directed behavioral family intervention for parents of children with early onset conduct problems. Journal of Consulting and Clinical Psychology 68, 624 – 640.

Schick, A. & Cierpka, M. (2003). *Faustlos: Evaluation eines Curriculums zur Fürderung sozial-emotionaler Kompetenzen und zur Gewaltpravention in der Grundschule.* Kindheit und Entwicklung 12, 100 – 110.

Schmid, H., Anliker, S., Bodenmann, G., Cina, A., Fäh, B., Kern, W., Lattmann, U. P. & Schönenberger, M. (2007). *Empowerment in family and schools: A randomized controlled trial.* Research report. Lausanne: Schweizer Institut für die Pravention von Alkohol-und Drogenproblemen.

Schweinhart, L. J., Montie, J., Xiang, Z., Barnett, W. S., Belfield, C. R. & Nores, M. (2005). *Lifetime Effects: The High/Scope Perry Preschool Study through Age 40.* Ypsilanti.

Scott, S., Knapp, M., Henderson, J. & Maughan, B. (2001). *Financial cost of social exclusion: Follow up study of antisocial children into adulthood.* British Medical Journal 323, 191 – 191.

Serketich, W. J. & Dumas, J. E. (1996). *The effectiveness of behavioral parent training to modify antisocial behavior in children: A meta-analysis.* Behavior Therapy 27, 171 – 186.

Shure, M. B. (1992). *I Can Problem Solve: An Interpersonal Cognitive Problem-Solving Program: Kindergarten & Primary Grades.* Champaign/IL.

Stemmler, M., Beelmann, A., Jaursch, S. & Lösel, F. (2007). *Improving the family environment to prevent child behavior problems: A study on the parent training of the EFFEKT program.* International Journal of Hygiene and Environmental Health 210, 563 – 570.

Stemmler, M., Lösel, F., Beelmann, A., Jaursch, S. & Zenkert, B. (2005). *Child problem behavior in kindergarten and in primary school: A comparison between prediction configural frequency analysis and multiple regression.* Psychology Science 47, 467 – 478.

Steyer, R. (2003). *Wahrscheinlichkeit und Regression.* Berlin.

Steyer, R., Gabler, S., von Davier, A., Nachtigall, C. & Buhl, T. (2000). *Causal regression models I: Individual and average causal effects.* Methods of Psychological

Research Online 5, 39 - 71.

Steyer, R. & Partchev, I. (2006). *Effect-Lite 2. 05*. Software. -Swisher, J., Scherer, J. & Yin, R. (2004). Cost-benefit estimates in prevention research. Journal of Primary Prevention 25, 137 - 145.

Tremblay, R. E. & Japel, C. (2003). *Prevention during pregnancy, infancy, and the preschool years*, in: D. P. Farrington & J. W. Coid (eds.), Early Prevention of Adult Antisocial Behaviour, 205 - 242. Cambridge.

Tremblay, R. E., Pagani-Kurtz, L., Vitaro, F., Masse, L. C. & Pihl, R. O. (1995). *A bimodal preventive intervention for disruptive kindergarten boys: Its impact through mid-adolescence*. Journal of Consulting and Clinical Psychology 63, 560 - 568.

Tremblay, R. E., Vitaro, F., Gagnon, C., Piché, C. & Royer, N. (1992). *A prosocial scale for the preschool behavior questionnaire: Concurrent and predictive correlates*. International Journal of Behavioral Development 15, 227 - 245.

Welsh, B. C. & Farrington, D. P. (2001). *A review of research on the monetary value of preventing crime*, in: B. C. Welsh, D. P. Farrington & L. W. Sherman (eds.), Cost and Benefits of Preventing Crime, 87 - 122. Oxford.

Wilson, D. B., Gottfredson, D. C. & Najaka, S. S. (2001). *School-based prevention of problem behaviors: A meta-analysis*. Journal of Quantitative Criminology 17, 247 - 272.

Wilson, S. J., Lipsey, M. W. & Derzon, J. H. (2003). *The effects of school-based intervention programs on aggressive behavior: A meta-analysis*. Journal of Consulting and Clinical Psychology 71, 136 - 149.

正是时候：对犯罪学发展性干预的整合

菲德律·洛赛尔（Friedrich Lösel）

剑桥大学

犯罪学历来不仅关注热门理论的发展趋势及舆论走向，也很关注由此得出的一些与犯罪相关的政策。罪犯治疗和改造就是其中一个典型例子。在 20 世纪 60 年代和 20 世纪 70 年代初期，犯罪学这个领域备受瞩目，有许多创新性项目在美国以及其他西方国家实施。不久之后，一个关于对矫正性措施的全面审查评估研究揭露出其严重的方法论上的缺陷以及结果上的不一致（Lipton et al. , 1975）。因此，"没有什么措施是有效的"成为反对犯罪矫正的各个不同派别的有力论据，说它缺乏实证研究的支持。举例来说，他们认为犯罪是一个社会问题而非个人问题，担心司法太不正式了，并主张罪犯受到应有的惩罚，想以此省去治疗罪犯所需的花费，或者说他们主要是想严惩罪犯。尽管在实践过程中也有许多实证研究的结果是支持犯罪改造的，也有许多犯罪矫正的尝试，但在 20 世纪 80 年代时，罪犯治疗就从主流犯罪相关政策列表中消失了。与此相反，曾经支持犯罪矫正的先驱者们，例如加利福尼亚州开始实行严格的监禁政策（例如："三次犯罪后将失去假释机会"）。

鼓舞人心的系统性综合研究成果以及公众对性犯罪、暴力犯罪和青少年犯罪的担心引发了 20 世纪 90 年代罪犯改造的复兴（Lösel，1993；Palmer，1992）。探索"什么措施管用"的运动则使得人们将新的工作重点落在了对犯罪行为的研究项目上（MacKenzie，2006；McGuire，1995，2002，Sherman et al. , 2002）。加拿大、英国和威尔斯等国家则实施了资格认证和质量管理政策，并大规模推出了证据导向型治疗项目。然而,这些努力并没得到高质量的评估效果,有些研究不但没有取得期望中的积极结果,反而在一些日常实践中出现了一些问题(Harper and Chitty,2005;Maguire,2004)。这样,目前这种以惩罚性的政策趋势、很多国家不断增加的监禁率和资金压力,都有可能减少基于证据的犯罪矫正项目的开展。

矫正性治疗措施也受到了生命历程理论中的早期干预论点的挑战(Tremblay and Craig,1995)。基于影响行为人之后犯罪的风险因素和保护性因素的长期研究结果,对儿童或青少年犯罪社会行为的发展性预防措施无论是在研究上还是实践中都有所增加(Farrington and Welsh,2007;Loeber and Farrington,1998)。有很多项目已经发展并被运用到家庭、幼儿园、学校、社会服务部门、临床运用以及青少年刑事司法当中。许多系统性的检验都显示出令人鼓舞的结果(Farrington and Welsh,2003,2007;Lösel and Beelmann,2003;Wilson *et al.*,2003)。他们都支持一个直观且让人信服的观点,那就是,对犯罪生涯开始和加剧的预防比致力于减少再犯和改造更好。这个推论在提及改变罪犯长期反社会发展所需花的高费用和改变犯罪行为上的困难时,就显得特别合理了。

尽管如此,当我们再仔细观察如今急速扩大的发展性预防项目的"市场"时,它提醒着年长的观察者们数十年前在罪犯治疗方面发生的事:一方面,当时有很多项目、好的意图以及成功的预期。另一方面,只有很少一部分的项目从方法论上来看会有较好的效果,而且用"严格"的衡量标准来看,其积极性的结果是可以复制的,具有持续的结果的。许多项目都不是以实证研究为基础的,或者是通过很不牢靠的评论标准来检验的,因而会得出前后矛盾的结果。在这一背景下,我们应该谨记早期在犯罪矫正方面的乐观主义很容易偏向没什么管用"主义"。因此,只有一个现实的、长期的和证据导向的政策才可能避免发展性预防中相类似的认识和做法上的摇摆不定。

发展性预防和治疗在讨论时通常被看作理论和实践方面相互独立的两个领域。研究其中一个领域的专家极少跨越这个边界而去研究另一个领域。有时候,人们甚至主张有必要加大发展性预防,因为治疗失败了。然而有诸多理由促使我们对于这两者在政策概念方面采取更加综合的观点:预防和治疗之间的边界并不清晰。有许多预防性项目都是面向那些已经显现出或多或少的严重的行为问题的年轻人的。各种其他项目都可以以同样的方式应用于有风险案件、未被判决的反社会的年轻人或是正式的罪犯中。就算是最好的预防项目都可能无法覆盖所有的有风险案件,或者说无法获得普遍的成功。尽管"处于违法犯罪初期的人"是特别重要的干涉对象,其他方法也可用于对严重犯罪的治疗。由于这样或那样的原因,在发展性预防和治疗中用一个更加综合、循序渐进的策略显得更加适合。正因为如此,这篇文章将比对两个领域的实验和结果。本文将重点放在评估性研究并将阐述以下几个议题:1. 总体效果;2. 两个项目结果上的变化;3. 方法论因素的影响;4. 目标组的特征;5. 入学和退学;6. 项目以外的因素。

一、总体效果

过去的二十年里出现了许多系统性的检验和元分析(指对研究结果的定量综合分析,译者注),综合了数以百计的相对来说受到控制的罪犯治疗研究。虽然该项目的类型、目标组、方法论质量、环境、结果的衡量和其他入选标准大相径庭,但其传递的主要信息呈现积极效果。总体效果的最好评价的相关度 r = 0. 10(±. 05)(Lösel,1995)。虽然从统计学的角度看来这仅仅是一个很小的效果,但其却有着实践和政治上的双重相关性。举例来说,对于不同实验组的再犯率而言,可以由实验组的55%降到治疗组的45%。再犯率降低 10 或 18 个百分点不仅对于潜在的受害人很重要,而且还有利于财务预算的平衡(Welsh et al. , 2003)。在改造性治疗的某些特殊领域,其效果更佳。例如,一个关于性犯罪者的元分析显示其累犯率下降了 37%(Lösel and Schmucker, 2005)。而一个关于一般犯罪的认知行为项目的元分析表明其累犯率下降了 27%(Lipsey and Landenberger, 2006)。

一些研究评论表明,发展性预防项目的平均效应值看起来比罪犯治疗项目要大。但是,很多预防研究都缺乏严格的对照设计,或者是没有后续的结果衡量。效果的评价标准也常常与项目的内容密切相关(例如,对儿童社会认知能力或者父母的态度的测试)。这些包含了大量的后续阶段和日常攻击行为、违法犯罪或是其他反社会行为的面向儿童的、家庭的以及学校的评估项目,其结果是平均效应值和罪犯治疗项目处在同一个幅度(Farrington and Welsh, 2003; Lösel and Beelmann, 2003, Tremblay and Japel, 2003; Wilson et al. , 2001, 2003)。

虽然发展性预防和罪犯治疗项目的平均效应值看起来相似,但前者有一个优势,那就是它可以避免在实施后者前可能会发生的大量犯罪行为。这是应该在成功预防方面投入的一个有力论据。尽管如此,我们也不能减少在犯罪改造方面的努力。因为考虑到发展性项目无法避免的失败率以及治疗项目效果评估的困难性,从基于证据的角度来看,后者也是有其合理性的。

二、项目间的差异

总的说来,平均效应展现的实证研究证据太模糊了。在两个领域的干预中,所有系统性的研究都表明它们各自都有着截然不同的结果。这是通过两个有着最长的后续阶段的预防研究所体现的:高范围的佩里学前班项目在智力能力、收入、房产拥有、一生中被捕次数之少以及其他直至研究对象中年时期的指标都显现出积极的效应。相反,剑桥—萨默维尔青年研究(McCord, 2003)的研究对象在 40 岁时却显示出负面效果。项目组比控制组表现出更多的累犯率、酗酒、家庭问题、精神病和早逝。这就提醒我们,尽管有些项目的初衷是好的,它却可能带来伤害。

项目发起者总是推荐他们自己的项目,这并不令人感到惊讶,有些还具有实证基础。然而,目前的文献并没有揭示在罪犯治疗或发展性预防项目上有着独一无二的黄金标准。相反,研究表明,有效研究方法的基本特征往往被视作项目资格认证的标准(Correctional Services Accreditation Panel, 2007)。例如,在通常的罪犯治疗中,基于理论的、多模式的认知行为性项目和结构化的治疗性社区在累犯率上有着相对来说比较一致的积极效应(Lösel, 1995;MacKenzie, 2006;McGuire, 2002)。该项目必须阐明罪犯身上特殊的易引发犯罪的需求和学习方式(Andrews *et al.*, 1990)。其强度要匹配罪犯本身的风险程度,并且要有足够的持续关怀。对于某些亚组的罪犯的额外医学治疗可能是合适的(Lösel and Schmucker, 2005)。相比于这些项目,心理动力学和其他一些非特定的方法不如它有效。没有改造成分的威慑性干预则没有任何效果(boot camps;MacKenzie *et al.*, 2001)。

发展性预防方面的成功项目其核心标准和罪犯治疗相类似。例如,这些项目有很好的社会学习理论的理论基础,运用行为认识理论的方法,有其结构体系并且阐述了多重的风险因素和保护性因素(Farrington and Welsh, 2003;Lösel and Beelmann, 2005;Tremblay and Craig, 1995;Webster-Stratton and Taylor, 2001)。结构化较低,带有指导和咨询性质的项目往往显现较小的效果(Lösel *et al.*, 2006b;Wilson *et al.*, 2001)。合适的多模式预防项目可能包括儿童社会问题解决方面的训练以及父母积极的教养方法训练(Lösel *et al.*, 2006a;Tremblay *et al.*, 1995)。更综合的方法是,他们会阐述学校和其他社会情境下的风险因素和保护性因素(Conduct Problems Prevention Research Group, 2002;Hawkins *et al.*, 1992;Henggeler *et al.*, 1998)。早期的干预措施比如孕期的家访项目和童年早期家访项目(Olds *et al.*, 1998)丰富了社会学习方法的内容。与罪犯治疗相类似,有效的发展性预防项目根据年龄、危险水平、问题的复杂度和强度等阐述了目标组的特殊需求。

然而,这两个领域有一个共同的发现,那就是,就算是最有希望的项目,当放在不同的实施和结果衡量标准当中时,就可能总是成功的。例如,"说服和改造"罪犯治疗项目的有些发现就不如其他项目的那样令人满意(Tong and Farrington,2007)。尽管一些研究证明了多系统疗法的有效性,但其结果却并不总能通过高质量研究的检验(Littell,2006)。早期家访项目通常在加强对孩子的照顾、防治虐待和忽视方面有着积极的效果,但如果以孩子攻击性行为作为衡量标准的话,其并不总能体现出积极的效果(Bilukha et al.,2005)。这些发现目前来说是合理的,因为大部分的元分析都表明项目本身仅仅是其结果的其中一个来源,而其结果还受其他诸多因素的影响。

三、方法论研究的特征

不论是治疗还是预防,评估研究的方法论特征对其结果有着尤其强烈的影响,而这似乎与这些研究使用的是随机对照试验(RCT)还是较弱的准实验研究设计无关。尽管威斯勃德(Weisburd)等人(2001)发现 RCT 试验的效应较小,但他们的分析却综合了较大范围的刑事司法项目。在罪犯治疗或发展性预防方面比较同种的领域研究中,RCT 试验和准实验研究的结果与实验组的差异并不明显(Lipsey and Wilson,1998;Lösel,1995;Lösel and Beelmann,2003),只是 RCT 试验似乎正趋向于更加同质化,并且其效应也更加小了,这可能与元分析里面的设计质量的范围有关。然而,设计质量经常会和其他能影响结果的方法论的特征混淆。

例如,处理那些拒绝参与或者要求退出的项目参与者,是与上述两个领域均相关密切。如果单单把试验组和完成项目者相比较,其效果通常情况下会比在更合适的"意向治疗"分析中的大。另一个方法论特征是结果衡量。预防和治疗研究通常都包含了相对来说较临近的起媒介作用的衡量方法,比如问卷调查和测验,它们都直指涉及项目内容。在这些例子中,记忆、社会期待和印象管理都可能导致更强的效应,但与日常行为指向(比如正式犯罪、老师或自首的反社会行为)的关系却很弱。这种结果间的不一致性不仅在看起来较完善的单个研究中很明显(Conduct Problems Prevention Research Group,2002),而且在大规模的元分析中也很明显(Lipsey,1992;Lösel and Beelmann,2005)。

同样重要的是后续工作的长度。有少部分的研究,尤其在发展性预防研究中曾观察到睡眠效应。这或许是由于参加者需要回顾和练习所学知识这一阶段。然而，在这两个领域中，后续阶段时间越长，所显现的效果也就越小，这成了一个大体的趋势（Lösel，1995；Lösel and Beelmann，2003）。

样本大小则是另一个重要的问题。关于罪犯治疗的各种元分析发现在样本较小的研究中效果更强（Lipsey and Wilson，1998；Lipsey and Landenberger，2005；Lösel and Schmucker，2005）。以家庭和儿童为导向的预防项目的综合研究表明，样本大小和效应值之间在一些主要研究方面呈负相关关系（Farrington and Welsh，2003；Lösel and Beelmann，2003）。这种关系的形成可能由多种原因导致：比如，这可能是出于发表的需要，因为样本越大就越可能表明真实研究效果越低。从作者或编辑的角度考虑，在小样本研究中，有显著效果的研究往往比效果相同但却不显著的研究发表的频率更大。相比之下，那些样本较小的研究可能只有在其揭示的效应值相对较大时才会被发表。然而，在一些未发表的元分析研究中，也发现了样本大小和效应值之间的负相关关系。另一个原因则与项目的实施有关。在大的研究中，保持项目的真实和样本的同质性可能会减少设计的敏感性，从而会导致效应值偏低（Lösel and Wittmann，1989；Weisburd et al.，1993）。其他的一些发现也强调了诚实的重要性。当研究的主持者和项目参与人员参与到预防或治疗项目的实施中去，效应值就更大（Lipsey and Landenberger，2005；Lipsey and Wilson，1998；Lösel and Beelmann，2003；Lösel and Schmucker，2005）。在这些示范或是模范项目中，研究者对于项目高质量的监督和管理有着真正的兴趣。因此，这些结果比在例行实践中更加可靠。

这些结果所表明的含义超出了方法论的范围，并且有着清晰的政策方面的深意：当大范围地推行预防或罪犯治疗项目时，我们应当期待的是比在理想状态下的示范研究更小的效应值。为了缩小最初的研究成果估算和日常实践的差距，充当充分应用质量管理和审查方面的一些好的方法。

四、目标组的特性

关于发展性预防和罪犯治疗的元分析都表明项目参与者的特征是研究结果差异的一个重要来源。然而，从这些发现中得出一个结论比从其他研究中更难。在很多研究中，或者缺少参与者的详细数据，或者样本太小了以至于无法和其他亚组进行比对。

在这两个干预研究方面，年龄和效应值都并不一致。在发展性预防项目中，这两者之间的相关性特别明显，因为人们总是希望在对年龄更小的儿童的研究方面获得明显的效果(在任何严重问题尚未开始之前)。然而,各种元分析都表明儿童年龄(Farrington and Welsh, 2003)和结果之间并无多大关系。而其他一些研究则显示负相关或者曲线相关(Lösel and Beelmann, 2003; Wilson *et al.*, 2003)。这些发现必须放在风险和基准率的框架内来认识。

从总体上看,风险性较高的研究效果往往比低风险的要强。例如,以儿童和家庭为导向的,针对具有较高风险的反社会发展的预防项目(指预防或临床实验项目)所得出的效应值,要比面向所有人的或样本未经过选择的普通项目的效应值(Farrington and Welsh, 2003; Lösel and Beelmann, 2003; Wilson *et al.*, 2003)更大。而罪犯治疗方面的研究在高风险或高累犯率案例上则显示出一种相类似的趋势(Lipsey and Wilson, 1998)。浅眼看来,这些结果似乎与直觉相反,因为我们会料想改变低危险度或犯错较少的人的行为会更容易些。然而,从方法论的角度看,这些发现也是合理的:在评估低危险度罪犯的治疗或者普通的预防项目时,有很大比例的项目参与者在没有受到干预之前就已经没有更多的问题了。到目前为止,未经处理的控制组之间的差异还是很小,因为它仅仅是面向那些确实需要项目帮助的人(高危险度案例)。

尽管这些发现表明控制组对于高危险度样本的评估其效应值预计会更高,我们不应该由此简单地得出政策方面的结论。例如,该预防项目的高效应值并不和普通预防项目相矛盾。如果普通项目成功的话,它们将降低总体的危险程度,尤其是高危险案例的反社会发展。由于普通项目避免了早期选择和潜在偏见所带来的问题,因此其优势远不止于研究的效应值。在罪犯治疗领域,低风险、高投资似乎并不值得。然而,在发展性预防领域,我们也不可以把在高危险度样本中发现的高效应值过于普遍化。对于未来犯罪危险度非常高的案例(比如患精神病的),要想有一个好的效果是相当困难的。因此,控制组里危险程度和效应值之间的关系应该呈倒 U 型函数关系(Lösel, 1996)。

五、不愿参加与中途退出

如前所述,如果想取得好的实验效果,实验对象不愿参加或中途退出都是一个问题。从方法论的角度看,它们至少可以通过意向治疗分析和差异化统计分析得以部分解决。然而,已加入的和已完成的实验对象同样存在严重的实践和政策问题。例如,在发展性预防中,要帮助那些很需要服务的家庭要付出很大的努力(Le Blanc, 1998)。通常情况下,不到半数的目标人群愿意参与实验,而且,在为期更长的项目中,更多的人不愿按规定完成这种干预,这就是为什么以儿童为重点的项目通常情况下更容易得以实施的原因。罪犯治疗领域也有类似问题,尤其在与基于社区的常规犯罪行为项目,参与率和退出率通常比基于监狱的项目以及特殊群体(比如性犯罪者)更令人满意(Harper and Chitty, 2005)。

实验对象的不愿参加和中途退出引发了各种实践问题,在发展性预防和罪犯治疗中,我们在动机说明、资料步骤、处理暂时的中止和退出管理方面还需要更多的系统性研究。参加者的动机作为一个基本的需要,是不应该被概念化为稳定的个人特征,而应该作为各个参与其中的当事者相互作用的结果。对动机的访谈或步骤改变的分析或许有助于解决这些问题(McMurran, 2002)。在这两个干预领域,我们还需要更好地研究合适的人选标准以及这些标准是否被可靠地运用于日常实践中。在很多研究中,实验对象中途退出产生的实验结果不仅会比定期完成的更差,而且也比控制组的差。尽管退出通常是对困难案例的消极选择,这种失败或许还将增加自我效能和评价方面的问题。到目前为止,一个正在试验期的以及错误的政策在道德上和法律上都是不合理的。

六、项目之外的影响因素

与罪犯治疗和发展性预防十分类似的更深层的问题是项目内容以外的因素所带来的影响。正如之前所提到的,各种说服、改造及多系统的治疗措施的实施的结果有着很大的不同(Littell, 2006;Tong and Farrington, 2007)。对性犯罪者的行为认知治疗的效果范围甚至在很强的积极作用和没有作用或者有时候是消极作用之间变动(Schmucker and Lösel, 2006)。在发展性预防中对于特定的家长培训,比如父母教养课程(Tiple-P)(Eisner and Ribeaud, 2007)或者儿童技能行为认知训练的实验结果也有大范围的变化(Lösel and Beelmann, 2005)。

这种结果上的差异可以部分地解释成是由于方法上的差异、样本的不同以及其他的研究特性。然而,这些差异甚至在其他比较类似的研究中也出现,而且,几乎所有的关于发展性预防和罪犯治疗的元分析都显示出无法解释的多样性。因此,对于那些影响结果却在评估中并没有进行充分阐述的重要因素我们还需要更多的知识来研究。

例如,项目进行的质量和诚实性似乎是取得成功的关键特征(Gendreau *et al.*, 1999)。就像在临床药理学那样,与其他项目的结合可能也很重要。然而,项目的实施和评估常常遵循着"筒仓方式"(即各自为政的方式),没有根据项目需要对项目的模式和配置进行细化。精神疗法的研究表明,相比于治疗项目的内容或技术,客户和医生的关系和人际关系模式对结果更有影响力（Orlinsky *et al.*，1994）。然而，罪犯治疗和发展性预防领域都缺乏对员工—客户关系以及类似过程的特征的数据。在机构矫正计划中，其所处的社会风气和社会制度的特征对于某个项目是否起作用有着重要的影响。对于基于社区的干预项目，社会环境和服务网络都会产生重要作用，这和先天的保护性因素，比如积极的家庭关系和邻居的帮助（Lösel and Bender，2003；Sampson and Laub，1993）有关。复杂的多模式预防和治疗项目试图解决这些问题。然而，对它们的过程评估比那些相对来说较狭窄、受到限制的干预项目更加困难。要分析到底发生了什么，我们不应该仅仅限于实验条件（Lösel，2002）。控制组并不是生活在真空中的，"没有治疗"或者"通常疗法"之类的条件包含了大范围自然的积极或消极影响。近期对于某些罪犯治疗项目的效果和之前的研究（Lipsey and Landenberger，2006；Lösel and Schmucker，2005；Tong and Farrington，2007）相比变小了，这或许是由于对条件的控制有了提高的缘故。

七、结　论

对反社会行为的发展性预防以及罪犯治疗在过去十年中无论是在研究还是在实践上都有很大的进步。这两个领域有着类似的发现和问题，如果在概念上和资源配置上把它们看作是竞争对手，那是不合适的。无论是理论上、实证上、被害人导向上、经济上还是其他方面，我们都有理由增加在发展性预防和早期干预上的投入。但是，我们应该避免不现实的预期，避免一个重在允诺却忽视评估的"预防市场"。这很容易会引发在改造领域发生过的摇摆运动。相比之下，本文建议从整个人生发展的角度，采用的是更综合的犯罪学干预科学。这种途径需要长期的研究策略、广泛的项目实施、实践中的有效评估以及非官方机构的科学指导和质量管理。这也需要来自政府的可靠的经济投资。然而，对发展性预防和罪犯治疗的花费—收益分析表明，好的项目和评估可以为社会省钱。一个综合性的政策也有助于将各种不同的服务联系起来，共同对付犯罪和反社会行为问题（比如，刑事司法、教育、社会福利、医疗保障和社区建设等）。它倡导一种以证据为导向的、人本主义的犯罪干预政策："（对付犯罪问题）永远不会太早，也不会太迟。"

[参考文献见英文原作]

（展万程　张　雪译）

It's Never Too Early and Never Too Late: Towards an Integrated Science of Developmental Intervention in Criminology

Friedrich Lösel

University of Cambridge

The history of criminology has not only seen fashion trends and pendulum swings in popular theories but also in its recommended crime policies. A typical example is offender treatment and rehabilitation. In the 1960s and early 1970s there was much enthusiasm in this field and a lot of innovative programs were implemented in theU. S. and other Western countries. Some time later, a comprehensive review of the evaluation research on correctional treatment stated serious methodological weaknesses and inconsistent outcomes (Lipton *et al.* , 1975). As a consequence, 'nothing works' became a strong argument for very different parties who opposed rehabilitation for non-empirical reasons. For example, they saw crime as a social and not an individual problem, feared that justice becomes too informal, were advocates of just-deserts punishment, wanted to avoid the financial costs of treatment or were more basically in favor of getting tough on crime. Although there were also various positive empirical findings and many rehabilitative approaches continued in practice, treatment disappeared from the list of popular crime policies during the 1980s. In contrast, former pioneers in offender rehabilitation such as the State of California took the lead in tough incarceration policies (e. g. , 'Three strikes and you are out').

Triggered by encouraging findings of systematic research integrations and supported by public concern over sexual offending, violence, and youth crime, the 1990s showed a revitalization of offender rehabilitation (e. g., Lösel, 1993; Palmer, 1992). The "what works" movement led to new emphasis on offending behavior programs (e. g., MacKenzie, 2006; McGuire, 1995, 2002; Sherman *et al.*, 2002). Countries such as Canada, England and Wales implemented policies of program accreditation and quality management and rolled out evidence-led treatment programs on a large scale. However, these efforts were insufficiently accompanied by high-quality evaluation and some studies did not show the expected positive findings but problems of program implementation in routine practice (Harper and Chitty, 2005; Maguire, 2004). As a consequence, current punitive trends, increased incarceration rates and financial pressures in many countries may once more reduce the potential of evidence-based programs in correction.

Correctional treatment is also challenged by arguments for an earlier intervention in the life course (e. g., Tremblay and Craig, 1995). Based on the longitudinal findings on risk and protective factors for later crime, there is an increase in research and practice in the developmental prevention of antisocial behavior in childhood and youth (Farrington and Welsh, 2007; Loeber and Farrington, 1998). Many programs have been developed and implemented in families, preschools, schools, social services, clinical settings and youth criminal justice. A number of systematic reviews show encouraging results (e. g., Farrington and Welsh, 2003, 2007; Lösel and Beelmann, 2003; Wilson *et al.*, 2003). They support the intuitively convincing view that it is better to prevent the onset and aggravation of a criminal career than to focus on reducing re-offending and correctional rehabilitation. This reasoning is particularly plausible when one refers to the high costs of a long-term antisocial development and the difficulties in changing offending behaviors.

However, a closer look at the rapidly expanding "market" of developmental prevention reminds older observers of what happened in offender treatment some decades ago: On the one hand, there are many programs, good intentions and promises of success. On the other hand, only a few programs seem to be based on methodologically sound evaluations with well-replicated positive findings in lasting outcomes on "hard" behavioral measures. Many programs have no empirical basis or are tested in weak evaluations and with inconsistent results. Against this background, one should not forget how easily the early optimism about offender treatment tilted towards the nothing works doctrine. Therefore, only a realistic, longer-term and evidence-driven policy may avoid similar pendulum movements in developmental prevention.

Developmental prevention and treatment are normally discussed as two separate areas of research and practice. Experts working in one field rarely cross the border to the other. Sometimes, it is even argued that more developmental prevention is necessary because treatment failed. However, there are reasons for a more integrated view on both policy concepts: The borders between prevention and treatment are not clear-cut. Many prevention programs follow an indicated approach that addresses youngsters who already reveal more or less serious behavioral problems. Various programs can be applied to at-risk cases, non-adjudicated antisocial youngsters or official offenders in a similar manner. Even the best prevention programs will neither reach all risk cases nor lead to a general success. Although "early starters" are a particularly important target for intervention, there are also other pathways into serious criminality. For these and other reasons, a more integrated and stepwise strategy for developmental prevention and treatment is appropriate. Therefore, this article will compare experiences and findings in both areas. It will focus on evaluation research and address the following issues: 1. overall effects; 2. outcome variation between programs; 3. impact of methodological factors; 4. characteristics of target groups; 5. recruitment and dropout; 6. factors beyond programs.

OVERALL EFFECTS

In the last two decades, numerous systematic reviews and meta-analyses integrated hundreds of relatively controlled studies on offender treatment. Although the program types, the target groups, methodological quality, settings, outcome measurement and other inclusion criteria vary substantially across the reviews, the general message is a positive effect. The best estimate of this overall effect is a correlation of $r = .10$ plus/minus $.05$ (Lösel, 1995). Although this is only a small effect in statistical terms, it has practical and political relevance. Dependent on the respective recidivism rates this is, for example, a reduction from 55% in the control group to 45% in the treatment group. A reduction of 10 percentage points or 18% in re-offending is not only important for potential victims but can well pay off in financial terms (e. g. , Welsh *et al.* , 2003). In specific fields of correctional treatment effects can even be more beneficial. For example, a meta-analysis of sex offender treatment revealed a 37% decrease in the recidivism rate (Lösel and

Schmucker, 2005) and a meta-analysis of cognitive-behavioral programs for general offenders showed a 27% reduction (Lipsey and Landenberger, 2006).

According to some research reviews the mean effect sizes of developmental prevention programs seem to be larger than those in offender treatment. However, many prevention studies have no well-controlled design or contain no follow-up outcome measures. Effect criteria are also often closely related to the program content (e. g. , tests on social-cognitive child competences or parental attitudes). For those evaluations of child-, family- and school-oriented programs that contain a substantial follow-up period and measure of everyday aggression, delinquency or other antisocial behavior as outcome the mean effect sizes are in the same range as in offender treatment (e. g. , Farrington and Welsh, 2003; Lösel and Beelmann, 2003, Tremblay and Japel, 2003; Wilson *et al.* , 2001, 2003).

Although the mean effect size of developmental prevention and offender treatment seems to be similar, the former has the advantage of avoiding a substantial proportion of those offenses that would have happened before implementation of the latter. This is a strong argument for investing in successful prevention. However, it is no argument to do this by reducing efforts in correctional programs. Taking the unavoidable failure rates of developmental programs and the overall " harder " outcome measures of treatment evaluations into account, the latter are also justified from an evidence-based perspective.

DIFFERENCES BETWEEN PROGRAMS

Overall mean effects give a too rough picture of the empirical evidence. In both areas of intervention all systematic reviews show a large variation of outcomes around the respective means. This is illustrated by the two prevention studies with the longest follow-up period: The High/Scope Perry Preschool Project showed positive effects on intellectual competencies, income, home ownership, low lifetime number of arrests, and other indicators up to middle adulthood. In contrast, the Cambridge-Somerville Youth Study (McCord, 2003) revealed a negative outcome at age 40. The program group showed more criminal recidivism, alcohol abuse, family problems, mental illnesses, and early deaths than the control group. This reminds us that in spite of good intentions some programs may even harm.

It is no surprise that developers often recommend their own program, and some have an empirical basis for this. However, the current literature does not reveal that there is a one and only gold standard program of offender treatment or of developmental prevention. Instead, research suggests basic characteristics of effective approaches that are used as criteria for program accreditation (e. g. , Correctional Services Accreditation Panel, 2007). For example, in general offender treatment theory-based, multi-modal, cognitive-behavioral programs and structured therapeutic communities have relatively consistent positive effects on recidivism (Lösel, 1995; MacKenzie, 2006; McGuire, 2002). The program must address the offender's specific criminogenic needs and learning style (Andrews et al. , 1990). Its intensity must match the offender's risk level and there should be sufficient continuity of care. For specific subgroups of offenders additional pharmacological treatment may be appropriate (e. g. , Lösel and Schmucker, 2005). In contrast to such programs, psychodynamic and unspecified approaches are less effective. Deterrent interventions with no rehabilitative component seem to have no effect (e. g. , boot camps; MacKenzie et al. , 2001).

The core criteria of successful programs in developmental prevention are similar to those in offender treatment. For example, such programs have a sound theoretical basis in social learning theory, follow a cognitive-behavioral approach, are well structured and address multiple risk and protective factors (Farrington and Welsh, 2003; Lösel and Beelmann, 2005; Tremblay and Craig, 1995; Webster-Stratton and Taylor, 2001). Low-structured programs, mentoring and counseling reveal smaller effect sizes (e. g. , Lösel et al. , 2006b; Wilson et al. , 2001). Appropriate multi-modal prevention programs may contain child trainings in social problem solving and trainings of positive parenting (e. g. , Lösel et al. , 2006a; Tremblay et al. , 1995). In more comprehensive approaches they will also address risk and protective factors at school and in other social contexts (e. g. , Conduct Problems Prevention Research Group, 2002; Hawkins et al. , 1992; Henggeler et al. , 1998). Very early interventions such as home visiting programs during pregnancy and early childhood (Olds et al. , 1998) add a bonding component to the social learning approach. Similarly to offender treatment, effective developmental prevention addresses the specific needs of the target groups according to age, risk level, intensity and complexity of problems.

However, it is also a common finding in both areas that even the most promising programs are not consistently successful in different implementations and outcome measures. For example, some findings for the 'Reasoning and Rehabilitation' offender treatment program are less favorable than others (Tong and Farrington, 2007). Although several studies prove the effectiveness of Multisystemic Therapy, the findings are not yet consistent across high-quality studies (Littell, 2006). Early home visiting programs generally show positive effects on child-care, abuse and neglect, but less consistent outcomes in criteria of the child's aggressive behavior (Bilukha et al., 2005). These findings are insofar plausible as most meta-analyses reveal that the program itself is only one source of outcome among other influences.

METHODOLOGICAL STUDY CHARACTERISTICS

In both treatment and prevention methodological characteristics of the evaluation studies have a particularly strong impact on the outcome. This seems not to be primarily an issue of whether the studies use a randomized control trial (RCT) or a weaker quasi-experimental design. Although Weisburd et al. (2001) found smaller effects of RCTs, their analysis integrates a very broad range of criminal justice programs. In the more homogeneous domains of offender treatment or developmental prevention, outcome differences between RCTs and quasi-experiments with control groups are not yet so clear (e. g., Lipsey and Wilson, 1998; Lösel, 1995; Lösel and Beelmann, 2003). There only seems to be a tendency towards more homogeneous and smaller effects in RCTs. This may have to do with the range of design quality included in meta-analyses. However, design quality is often confounded with other methodological features that have an impact on outcome.

For example, a particularly relevant issue in both fields is the handling of program persons who refuse to participate or drop out of the program. If only completers are compared with the control group, effects are normally larger than in a more appropriate intent-to-treat analysis. Another methodological feature is outcome measurement. Both prevention and treatment studies often contain relatively proximal intermediate measures such as questionnaires and tests that more or less directly refer to the program content. In these cases memory, social desirability, and impression management may lead to larger effects that are only weakly related to indicators of everyday behavior (e. g., official offending, teacher or self-reports of antisocial behavior). Such inconsistencies between outcomes are not only obvious in sound single studies (e. g., Conduct Problems Prevention Research Group, 2002) but also in large-scale meta-analyses (Lipsey, 1992; Lösel and Beelmann, 2005).

Similarly important is the length of follow-up. There are a few studies, particularly in prevention, in which sleeper effects have been observed. This may be due to periods during which the participants need to reflect and exercise the acquired knowledge. However, as a general trend, longer follow-up periods reveal smaller effects in both areas (Lösel, 1995; Lösel and Beelmann, 2003).

Another important issue is sample size. Various meta-analyses on offender treatment found larger effects in studies with smaller samples (e. g. , Lipsey and Wilson, 1998; Lipsey and Landenberger, 2005; Lösel and Schmucker, 2005). Research syntheses on family- and child-oriented prevention programs revealed a similar negative correlation between effect size and sample size in primary studies (Farrington and Welsh, 2003; Lösel and Beelmann, 2003). This relationship may be due to various reasons: For example, it could reflect a publication bias. Larger samples are more likely to reveal the significance of a true low effect. Due to author or editor decisions, this significant result may be published more frequently than the same, but nonsignificant, effect in a smaller sample. In contrast, studies with small samples may only be published when they have relatively large effects. Some meta-analyses, however, also found a negative relation between sample size and effect size in unpublished studies. Another reason for the moderating effect of sample size relates to program implementation. In large studies, difficulties in maintaining program integrity and homogeneity of samples may reduce design sensitivity and thus lead to smaller effects (Lösel and Wittmann, 1989; Weisburd et al. , 1993). Other findings also underline the importance of integrity. When the study authors and their staff are involved in the implementation of prevention or treatment programs, effect sizes tend to be larger (e. g. , Lipsey and Landenberger, 2005; Lipsey and Wilson, 1998; Lösel and Beelmann, 2003; Lösel and Schmucker, 2005). In these demonstration or model projects, the researchers have genuine interest to monitor and manage a high quality program delivery. Accordingly, outcomes are better than in routine practice.

The implications of such results go beyond methodology and have clear policy implications: When prevention or offender treatment programs are rolled out on a large scale we should expect smaller effects than under the optimal conditions of demonstration studies. To reduce this difference between initial research evaluations and daily practice, sound measures of quality management and audit need to be implemented.

CHARACTERISTICS OF THE TARGET GROUPS

Both meta-analyses on developmental prevention and on offender treatment show that characteristics of the program participants are a further important source for differences in outcome. However, it is more difficult to draw general conclusions from these findings than from those on other study features. In many studies there is a lack of detailed data on the participants or sample sizes are too small to compare various subgroups.

In both areas of intervention the relation between age and effect size is not yet consistent. This is particularly relevant for developmental prevention because one would expect a stronger program impact in younger children (before the onset of any serious problems). However, various meta-analyses show no significant correlation between outcome and child age (e. g. , Farrington and Welsh, 2003) and others reveal an opposite or curvilinear tendency (e. g. , Lösel and Beelmann, 2003; Wilson et al. , 2003). Such findings must be put into the framework of risk and base-rates:

As a general trend effects are larger for higher risk than for lower risk cases. For example, child-and family-oriented prevention programs that target higher risks for antisocial development (indicated prevention or clinic-based programs) reveal larger effect sizes than universal programs that address the whole population or unselected samples (e. g. , Farrington and Welsh, 2003; Lösel and Beelmann, 2003; Wilson et al. , 2003). In reviews of offender treatment a similar tendency has been shown for cases of higher risk of re-offending (e. g. , Lipsey and Wilson, 1998). At first glance, these results seem to be counter-intuitive because one would expect it to be easier to change the behavior of low risk or less deviant cases. However, from a methodological viewpoint the findings are plausible: In evaluations of the treatment of low-risk offenders or universal prevention programs there is a high proportion of program participants who would already show no further problems without an intervention. Insofar, the overall difference of an untreated control group remains small because it is only based on the minority of those who are really in need of a program (higher risk cases).

Although these findings suggest that one can expect higher effect sizes in control group e-valuations for high-risk samples, one should not derive too simple policy conclusions from them. For example, the larger effects of targeted prevention programs do not contradict universal prevention. If universal programs are successful they will reduce the overall risk level and in particular the antisocial development of high-risk cases. As universal programs avoid problems of early selection and potential stigmatization, they have additional advantages that go beyond the mere study effect size. In the area of offender treatment a high investment in low risk cases seems to be less worthwhile. However, as in developmental prevention one should not over-generalize the finding of larger effect sizes in samples of higher risk. In cases of very high risk for future offending (e. g. , psychopathy) it is particularly difficult to have a strong program impact. Therefore, the relation between risk level and effect size in control group studies may follow an inverted U-shaped function (Lösel, 1996).

NON-PARTICIPATION AND DROPOUT

As mentioned above, non-participation and program dropout are problems for a sound e-valuation. From a methodological perspective, they can at least partially be solved by intent-to-treat-analyses and differentiated statistical analyses. However, recruitment and completion are also serious practical and policy problems. For example, in developmental prevention it requires very strong efforts to reach those families who are particularly in need of a service (e ,g. , Le Blanc, 1998). Often less than half of the target population can be recruited and particularly in longer programs a further proportion does not complete the intervention regularly. This is why child-focused programs are normally easier to implement. In offender treatment problems are similar, in particular in community-based general offending behavior programs. Recruitment and dropout rates are normally more favorable in prison-based programs and for specific groups such as sexual offenders (e. g. , Harper and Chitty, 2005).

Non-participation and non-completion raise various practical issues. In both developmental prevention and offender treatment we need more systematic research on motivational strategies, information procedures, coping with temporary stagnation, and management of dropout. As a basic requirement participant motivation should not be conceptualized as a stable individual characteristic but as an outcome of the interaction between all parties involved. Motivational interviewing or analyses of the change process may be helpful approaches to these problems (e. g. , McMurran, 2002). In both areas of intervention we also need more research on appropriate inclusion criteria and on the reliable application of such criteria in daily routine delivery. In many studies, program dropouts show not only worse outcomes than regular completers but also than control groups. Although dropouts often are a negative selection of difficult cases, the failure may also increase problems of self-efficacy and stigmatization. Insofar, a trial and error policy is not justifiable for ethical and legal reasons.

FACTORS BEYOND PROGRAMS

A further issue that is very similar in both offender treatment and developmental prevention is the impact of those factors that go beyond the content of a program. As mentioned above, various implementations of Reasoning and Rehabilitation or Multisystemic Therapy vary substantially in their outcomes (Littell, 2006; Tong and Farrington, 2007). The range of effects of cognitive-behavioral sex offender treatment even varies between very strong positive and null or sometimes even negative outcomes (Schmucker and Lösel, 2006). In developmental prevention there is also a broad range of findings for specific parent trainings such as Triple-P (e. g., Eisner and Ribeaud, 2007) or cognitive-behavioral child skills training (Lösel and Beelmann, 2005).

Such outcome differences can be explained partially by variations in methods, sample and other study characteristics. However, they even appear in rather similar studies and nearly all meta-analyses on developmental prevention and offender treatment show a large proportion of unexplained variance. Therefore, we need more knowledge about factors that are important for outcomes but often not sufficiently addressed in evaluations.

For example, quality of program delivery and integrity seem to be key features for success (Gendreau et al., 1999). As in clinical pharmacology, the combination with other programs may also be important. However, program implementation and evaluation often follow a "silo approach" that does not specify patterns or configurations of various services. From research on psychotherapy we know that the client-therapist relationship and interpersonal style often has a stronger impact on outcome than the content of specific therapeutic programs or techniques (Orlinsky et al., 1994). However, in both offender treatment and developmental prevention we have a lack of data on staff-client relationships and similar process characteristics. In institutional programs characteristics of the broader social climate and regime (Liebling and Arnold, 2002) can play an important role for whether a specific program works or does not work. For community-based interventions the wider social context and network of services is relevant. This relates to the role of natural protective factors such as positive family relations and neighborhood support (Lösel and

Bender, 2003; Sampson and Laub, 1993). Complex multi-modal programs of prevention and treatment try to address these issues. However, their process evaluation is more difficult than that of relatively narrow, circumscribed interventions. The analysis of what really happens should not be restricted to the experimental condition alone (Lösel, 2002). Control groups are not living in a vacuum and conditions such as 'no treatment' or 'treatment as usual' can contain a broad range of natural positive or negative impacts. That some recent evaluations of specific offender treatment programs show smaller effects than older studies (Lipsey and Landenberger, 2006; Lösel and Schmucker, 2005; Tong and Farrington, 2007) may be due to improvements in the control conditions.

CONCLUSIONS

During the last decade, there is substantial progress in research and practice in developmental prevention of antisocial behavior and offender treatment. Both fields have so many similarities in findings and problems that it is inappropriate to see them as rivals in concept and resource allocation. There are theoretical, empirical, victim-oriented, monetary, and other good reasons for a particular increase of our efforts in developmental prevention and early intervention. However, we should avoid unrealistic expectancies and a 'prevention market' that is based more on promises than on sound evaluations. This could easily lead to similar pendulum movements as we have seen in correctional rehabilitation. In contrast, this article proposes a more integrated science of criminological intervention that follows a life-span developmental perspective. Such an approach requires long-term strategies in research, broad program implementation and sound evaluation in practice, and non-bureaucratic institutions for scientific guidance and quality management. It will also require a solid financial investment from the governments. However, cost-benefit analyses for both developmental prevention and offender treatment have demonstrated that sound programs and evaluations will save money for society. An integrated policy will also help to connect the many different services that are involved in problems of crime and antisocial behavior (e. g. criminal justice, education, social welfare, health care, community development etc.). It would suggest an intervention policy that is both evidence-led and humane: 'It's never too early and never too late'.

References

Andrews, D. A. , Zinger, I. , Hoge, R. D. , Bonta, J. , Gendreau, P. , & Cullen, F. T. (1990). Does correctional treatment work? A clinically relevant and psychologically informed meta-analysis. *Criminology*, 28, 369 – 404.

Bernazzani, O. , & Tremblay, R. E. (2006). Early parent training. In B. C. Welsh and D. P. Farrington (Eds.), *Preventing crime: What works for children, offenders, victims, and places* (pp. 21 – 32). Dordrecht, NL: Springer.

Bilukha, O. , Hahn, R. A. , Crosby, A. , Fullilove, M. T. , Liberman, A. , Moscicki, E. , Snyder, S. , Tuma, F. , Corso, P. , Scholfield, A. , & Briss, P. A. , (2005). The effectiveness of early childhood home visitation in preventing violence: a systematic review. *American Journal of Preventive Medicine*, 28, 11 – 39.

Conduct Problems Prevention Research Group (2002). Evaluation of the first 3 years of the Fast Track Prevention Trial with children at high risk for adolescent conduct problems. *Journal of Abnormal Child Psychology*, 19, 553 – 567.

Correctional Services Accreditation Panel (2007). *The Correctional Services Accreditation Panel Report* 2005 – 06. London: NOMS/Home Office.

Eisner, M. , & Ribeaud, D. (2007). Effects of a combined family and school-based universal early prevention trial: Findings from the Zurich Project on the Social Development of Children. *Paper presented at the Stockholm Criminology Symposium* 2007.

Farrington, D. P. , & Welsh, B. C. (2003). Family-based prevention of offending: A meta-analysis. *Australian and New Zealand Journal of Criminology*, 36, 127 – 151.

Farrington, D. P. , & Welsh, B. C. (2007). *Saving children from a life of crime*. Oxford, UK: Oxford University Press.

Gendreau, P. , Goggin, C. , & Smith, P. (1999). The forgotten issue in effective correctional treatment: Program implementation. *International Journal of Offender Therapy and Comparative Criminology*, 43, 180 – 187.

Harper, G. , & Chitty, C. (Eds.) (2005). *The impact of corrections on re-offending: a review of 'what works'*. Home Office Research Study 291. London: Home Office.

Hawkins, J. D. , Catalano, R. F. , Morrison, D, M. , O'Donnell, J. , Abbott, R. D. , & Day, L. E. (1992). The Seattle Social Development Project: Effects of the first four years on protective factors and problem behaviors. In J. McCord and R. Tremblay (Eds.) , *Preventing antisocial behavior* (pp. 139 – 161). New York: Guilford.

Henggeler, S. W. , Schoenwald, S. K. , Borduin, C. M. , Rowland, M. D. , & Cunningham, P. B. (1998). *Multisystemic treatment of antisocial behavior in children and adolescents*. New York: Guilford.

LeBlanc, M. (1998). Screening of serious and violent juvenile offenders: Identification, classification, and prediction. In R. Loeber & D. P. Farrington (eds.) , *Serious and violent juvenile offenders: Risk factors and successful interventions* (pp. 167 – 193). Thousand Oaks: Sage.

Liebling, A. , & Arnold, H. (2002). Measuring the quality of prison life. *Research Findings 174.* London: Home Office.

Lipsey, M. W. (1992). The effect of treatment on juvenile delinquents: Results from meta-analysis. In F. Lösel, D. Bender and T. Bliesener (Eds.) , *Psychology and law: International perspectives* (pp. 131 – 143). Berlin: de Gruyter.

Lipsey, M. W. , & Landenberger, N. A. (2006). Cognitive-behavioral interventions. In B. C. Welsh and D. P. Farrington (Eds.) , *Preventing crime: What works for children, offenders, victims, and places* (pp. 57 – 71). Dordrecht, NL: Springer.

Lipsey, M. W. , &Wilson, D. B. (1998). Effective intervention for serious juvenile offenders. In R. Loeber and D. P. Farrington (Eds.) , *Serious & violent juvenile offenders* (pp. 313 – 345). Thousand Oaks, CA: Sage.

Lipton, D. S. , Martinson, R. & Wilks, J. (1975). *The effectiveness of correctional treatment*. New York: Praeger.

Littell, J. H. (2006). The case for Multisystemic Therapy: Evidence or orthodoxy? *Children and Youth Services Review*, 28, 458 – 472.

Loeber, R. & Farrington, D. P. (Eds.) , *Serious and violent juvenile offenders*. Thousand Oaks, CA: Sage.

Lösel, F. (1993). The effectiveness of treatment in institutional and community settings. *Criminal Behaviour and Mental Health*, 3, 416 – 437.

Lösel, F. (1995). The efficacy of correctional treatment: A review and synthesis of meta-evaluations. In J. McGuire (Ed.) , *What works: Reducing reoffending* (pp. 79 – 111). Chichester, UK: Wiley.

Lösel, F. (1996). Changing patterns in the use of prisons: An evidence-based perspective. *European Journal on Criminal Policy and Research*, 4, 108 – 127.

Lösel, F. (2001). Evaluating the effectiveness of correctional programs: Bridging the gap between research and practice. In G. A. Bernfeld, D. P. Farrington and A. W. Leschied (Eds.), *Offender rehabilitation in practice* (pp. 67 – 92). Chichester, UK: Wiley.

Lösel, F., & Beelmann, A. (2003). Effects of child skills training in preventing antisocial behavior: A systematic review of randomized experiments. *The Annals of the American Academy of Political and Social Science*, 587, 84 – 109.

Lösel, F., & Beelmann, A. (2005). Social problem solving programs for preventing antisocial behavior in children and youth. In M. McMurran and J. McGuire (Eds.), *Social problem solving and offending: Evidence, evaluation and evolution* (pp. 127 – 144). Chichester, UK: Wiley.

Lösel, F., Beelmann, A., Stemmler, M., & Jaursch, S. (2006). Prävention von Problemen des Sozialverhaltens im Vorschulalter: Evaluation des Eltern-und Kindertrainings EFFEKT. [Prevention of conduct problems in preschool age: Evaluation of the parent-and child-oriented program EFFEKT]. *Zeitschrift für Klinische Psychologie und Psychotherapie*, 35, 127 – 139.

Lösel, F., & Bender, D. (2003). Protective factors and resilience. In D. P. Farrington and J. Coid (Eds.), *Prevention of adult antisocial behaviour* (pp. 130 – 204). Cambridge, UK: Cambridge University Press.

Lösel, F., & Schmucker, M. (2005). The effectiveness of treatment for sexual offenders: A comprehensive meta-analysis. *Journal of Experimental Criminology*, 1, 117 – 146.

Lösel, F., Schmucker, M., Plankensteiner, B., & Weiss, M. (2006). Bestandsaufnahme und Evaluation der Elternbildung [Survey and evaluation of parent education]. Berlin: German Federal Ministry for Family Affairs, Seniors, Women and Youth.

Lösel, F., & Wittmann, W. W. (1989). The relationship of treatment integrity and intensity to outcome criteria. *New Directions for Program Evaluation*, 42, 97 – 108.

MacKenzie, D. L. (2006). *What works in corrections*. Cambridge, UK: Cambridge University Press.

MacKenzie, D. L. , Wilson, D. B. , & Kider, S. B. (2001). Effects of correctional boot camps on offending. *The Annals of the American Academy of Political and Social Science*, 578, 126 – 143.

Maguire, M. (2004). The Crime Reduction Programme in England and Wales: reflections on the vision and the reality. *Criminal Justice*, 4, 231 – 237.

McCord, J. (2003). Cures that harm: Unanticipated outcomes of crime prevention programs. *The Annals of the American Academy of Political and Social Science*, 587, 16 – 30.

McGuire, J. (Ed.) (1995). *What works: Reducing reoffending-guidelines for research and practice*. Chichester: Wiley.

McGuire, J. (Ed.) (2002). *Offender rehabilitation and treatment: Effective programmes and policies to reduce re-offending*. Chichester, UK: Wiley.

McMurran, M. (2002). Motivation to change: selection criterion or treatment need? In M. McMurran (Ed.), *Motivating offenders to change* (pp. 3 – 13). Chichester, UK: Wiley.

Olds, D. L. , Henderson, C. R. , Cole, R. , Eckenrode, J. , Kitzman, H. , Luckey, D. , Pettitt, L. , Sidora, K. , Morris, P. , & Powers, J. (1998). Long-term effects of nurse home visitation on children's criminal and antisocial behavior. *Journal of the American Medical Association*, 280, 1238 – 1244.

Orlinsky, D. E. , Grawe, K. , & Parks, B. K. (1994). Process and outcome in psychotherapy. In A. E. Bergin and S. L. Garfield (Eds.), *Handbook of psychotherapy and behavior change*, 4th ed. (pp. 270 – 376). New York: Wiley.

Palmer, T. (1992). *The re-emergence of correctional intervention*. Newbury Park, CA: Sage.

Sampson, R. J. , & Laub, J. H. (1993). *Crime in the making: Pathways and turning points through life*. Cambridge: Harvard University Press.

Schmucker, M. , & Lösel, F. (2006). Beyond programs: Outcome differences between cognitive-behavioral programs of sex offender treatment. *Paper presented at the 58th Annual Meeting of the American Society of Criminology*, November 2005, Los Angeles.

Schweinhart, L. J. , Montie, J. , Xiang, Z. , Barnett, W. S. , Belfield, C. R. & Nores, M. (2005). *Lifetime effects: The High/Scope Perry Preschool Study through age* 40. Ypsilanti: High/Scope Press.

Sherman, L. W. , Farrington, D. P. , Welsh, B. C. , & MacKenzie, D. L. (Eds.) (2002). *Evidence-based crime prevention*. New York: Routledge.

Tremblay, R. E. , & Craig, W. M. (1995). Developmental crime prevention. In M. Tonry and D. P. Farrington (Eds.), *Building a safer society: Strategic approaches to crime prevention*, vol. 19 (pp. 151－236). Chicago: The University of Chicago Press.

Tremblay, R. E., & Japel, C. (2003). Prevention during pregnancy, infancy, and the preschool years. In D. P. Farrington and J. W. Coid (Eds.), *Early prevention of adult antisocial behaviour* (pp. 205－242). Cambridge, UK: Cambridge University Press.

Tremblay, R. E., Pagani-Kurtz, L., Vitaro, F, Masse, L. C., & Pihl, R. O. (1995). A bimodal preventive intervention for disruptive kindergarten boys: Its impact through mid-adolescence. *Journal of Consulting and Clinical Psychology*, 63, 560－568..

Tong, L. R. J., & Farrington, D. P. (2007). *Effectiveness of 'Reasoning and Rehabilitation' in reducing reoffending*. Unpublished paper. Institute of Criminology, University of Cambridge, UK.

Utting, D. (2003). Prevention through family and parenting programmes. In D. P. Farrington and J. W. Coid (Eds.), *Early prevention of adult antisocial behaviour* (pp. 243－264). Cambridge, UK: Cambridge University Press.

Webster-Stratton, C., & Taylor, T. (2001). Nipping early risk factors in the bud: Preventing substance abuse, delinquency, and violence in adolescence through intervention targeted at young children (0－8 years). *Prevention Science*, 2, 165－192.

Weisburd, D., Lum, C. M., & Petrosino, A. (2001). Does research design affect study outcomes in criminal justice? *The Annals of the American Academy of Political and Social Science*, 578, 50－70.

Weisburd, D., Petrosino, A., & Mason, G. (1993). Design sensitivity in criminal justice experiments: Reassessing the relationship between sample size and statistical power. In M. Tonry and N. Morris (Eds.), *Crime and Justice*, vol. 17. Chicago: University of Chicago Press.

Welsh, B. C., Farrington, D. P., &Sherman, L. W. (Eds.) (2001), *Costs and benefits of preventing crime*. Oxford, UK: Westview Press.

Wilson, D. B., Gottfredson, D. C., & Najaka, S. S. (2001). School-based prevention of problem behaviors: A meta-analysis. *Journal of Quantitative Criminology, Consulting and Clinical Psychology*, 17, 247－272.

Wilson, S. J., Lipsey, M. W., & Derzon, J. H. (2003). The effects of school-based intervention programs on aggressive behavior: A meta-analysis. *Journal of Consulting and Clinical Psychology*, 71, 136－149.

国际犯罪学大师系列
GUOJI FANZUIXUE DASHI XILIE

国际犯罪学大师论

犯罪控制科学 2

Master Criminologists on the
Science of Crime Control（Volume 2）

主编◉刘建宏　　副主编◉金诚

人民出版社

刘建宏　博士

Jianhong Liu

　　刘建宏教授 1988 年取得南开大学硕士学位后赴美留学，于 1993 年春获美国纽约州立大学博士学位，之后在美国任教多年，2002 年获终身正教授。2007 年起任澳门大学教授。现任亚洲犯罪学学会会长，西南政法大学讲席教授，博士生导师，博士后导师。主要研究领域为刑事司法、犯罪学、毒品犯罪、社会科学方法论与社会统计学等。刘建宏教授应邀担任《定量犯罪学》（SSCI）编委，《犯罪、法律与社会变迁》（SSCI）编委，《国际罪犯矫治与比较犯罪学》（SSCI）专刊特邀编辑及副编辑，《澳大利亚与新西兰犯罪学杂志》（SSCI）专刊特邀编辑。2005 年起任《亚洲犯罪学》总顾问编辑，2009 年起任《亚洲犯罪学》主编。

　　刘建宏教授曾获国际犯罪学会青年学者奖。曾与美国犯罪学学会副会长史蒂文·F. 梅斯纳教授等共获美国国家科学研究基金奖在中国进行犯罪学研究。2006 年获美国国务院福布莱特学者奖。自 2009 年起当选为世界著名学术组织"康拜尔合作组织犯罪和司法领导委员会"委员。2011 年 6 月、2012 年 6 月两次应邀在"斯德哥尔摩犯罪学奖"学术大会上做主题发言。

　　刘建宏教授长期活跃在国际前沿学术领域，并在努力消除西方社会对中国的偏颇认识、积极促进中外学者合作交流方面做出了有益的贡献。

金 诚 教授
Cheng Jin

　　金诚，浙江警察学院教授、治安系副主任，澳门大学博士候选人。现任亚洲犯罪学学会理事、中国预防青少年犯罪研究会理事、浙江省青少年犯罪研究会秘书长、《预防青少年犯罪研究》杂志编委。2004 年，澳大利亚新南威尔士州警察学院访问学者；2006 至 2007 年，美国山姆·休斯敦州立大学刑事司法学院访问教授。先后被授予全国公安模范教育训练工作者、浙江省高校中青年学科带头人、浙江省高校优秀留学回国人员等称号；主持国家社科基金项目、教育部人文社科研究规划基金项目、浙江省社科规划课题等项目。曾在国内外学术刊物上发表论文 40 余篇，多篇论文被《人大复印资料》、《高等学校文科学报文摘》（CUPA）全文转载。曾组织"中美青少年团伙犯罪问题研究"研讨会、公安部引智项目"犯罪控制与警务战略"国际高峰论坛等国际学术会议。

作者简介

大卫·威斯勃德 博士

David Weisburd, Ph.D

　　现为美国乔治梅森大学犯罪学、法律和社会学、以色列希伯来大学法律和刑事司法学院杰出教授，华盛顿警察基金会高级研究员及研究咨询委员会主席。2010 犯罪学斯德哥尔摩奖获得者。除刑事司法干预领域的实验和评价等研究领域外，他的重点研究兴趣还包括地点犯罪学、警务、统计方法和白领犯罪。担任康拜尔合作组织犯罪和司法领导委员会联席主席，美国刑事法律和司法国家研究理事会委员会和国家司法研究所／哈佛大学警察学执行委员会委员。出版学术著作及编著 15 部，发表学术论文 80 多篇。任《实验犯罪学》杂志主编，《犯罪学》、《犯罪和司法》《犯罪和违法》及《定量犯罪学》杂志的编委。

Dr. David Weisburd holds a joint appointment as a Distinguished Professor in the Department of Criminology, Law and Society at George Mason University and also as the Walter E. Meyer Professor of Law and Criminal Justice at the Hebrew University Law School in Jerusalem. He is also a Senior Fellow at the Police Foundation in Washington, DC, and Chair of their Research Advisory Committee. He is the 2010 recipient of the Stockholm Prize in Criminology. In addition to his experimental and evaluation work on criminal justice interventions, Dr. Weisburd's key research interests include the criminology of places, policing, statistical methodology, and white collar crime. He also serves as the Co−Chair of the steering committee of the Campbell Crime and Justice Group. Professor Weisburd is also a member of the National Research Council Committee on Crime Law and Justice, and of the National Institute of Justice/Harvard University Executive Session in Policing. Professor Weisburd is author or editor of fifteen books and more than eighty scientific articles. He is editor of the Journal of Experimental Criminology and serves on a number of journal editorial boards including Criminology, Crime and Justice, the Journal of Research in Crime and Delinquency, and the Journal of Quantitative Criminology.

史蒂文·F. 梅斯纳　博士

Steven F. Messner, Ph.D

作者简介

　　现为美国纽约州立大学奥尔巴尼分校杰出社会学教授。现任美国犯罪学会会长。任《国际冲突与暴力》主编,《美国社会学评论》副主编。还担任《英国社会学杂志》国际顾问委员会委员,《国际刑事司法评论》、《亚洲犯罪学》、《凶杀案研究》、《刑事法律和犯罪学》等期刊的编委。同时担任德国比勒费尔德大学" 冲突和暴力行为 "跨学科研究所国际学术顾问委员会主席。

Dr. Steven F. Messner is the Distinguished Teaching Professor of Sociology, University at Albany, State University of New York. He is the President of American Society of Criminology in 2010—2011 and was the President—Elect in 2009—2010. He is the Co—Editor of International Journal of Conflict and Violence (2006—present) and was the Deputy Editor of American Sociological Review (2006—2009). He is the member of the International Advisory Board of British Journal of Sociology, the member of the Editorial Board of International Criminal Justice Review, the Editorial Board of Asian Journal of Criminology, the Editorial Board of Homicide Studies, and the Editorial Advisory Board of Journal of Criminal Law and Criminology. He also serves as the Chair of International Academic Advisory Board of the Institute for Interdisciplinary Research on Conflict and Violence, Bielefeld University, Bielefeld, Germany.

目　　录

"地点"在警务活动中的重要性：实证性证据与对策建议

大卫·威斯勃德（David Weisburd）

希伯来大学

科迪·W. 特勒普（Cody W. Telep）

乔治梅森大学

安东尼·布拉加（Anthony A. Braga）

哈佛大学

携同

伊丽莎白·R. 格勒夫（Elizabeth R. Groff）

坦普尔大学

约书亚·C. 欣克尔（Joshua C. Hinkle）

乔治亚州立大学

辛西娅绥·露穆（Cynthia Lum）

乔治梅森大学

南希·A. 莫里斯（Nancy A. Morris）

南伊利诺伊大学

劳拉·A. 怀科夫（Laura A. Wyckoff）

马里兰大学

苏铭·杨（Sue-Ming Yang）

佐治亚州立大学

前　言

在当今社会警察的角色涉及不同任务。这些任务包括维持治安秩序和保护公众安全,为公民提供保护和援助,调查犯罪和逮捕罪犯。警方在预防犯罪领域也发挥着关键作用。

后一方面的警察角色,即犯罪预防工作,有时被忽视,这不仅仅是因为它既不会导致数量较多的罪犯被检控及定罪,也不会有任何可见的破案率提高。不过,警方预防犯罪工作的重要性,从犯罪受害者和犯罪的社会成本两个角度可以看出来。警方有效的犯罪预防工作将意味着减少犯罪受害者,同时也将大大减少犯罪的社会成本。

研究工作可以提供警方如何提高预防犯罪效率的知识,研究也就显得非常重要。同样重要的是,将这些研究结果分发给警察服务体系内外的群体参考学习。

在这份受瑞典国家预防犯罪委员会委托报告中,大卫·威斯勃德(David Weisburd)教授和他的同事对这一可能改善警方犯罪预防工作成效、崭新而又令人兴奋的研究领域进行了总结。作者从实践和理论两个角度展示了他的研究:警方如何通过直接地将注意力放到很小的、明确的犯罪高发点上来,实质性地提高犯罪预防工作的成效。这份报告的研究发现,强有力地表明:相比传统警务方式,这种基于地点警务在犯罪预防上投入的资源相对更少。

让警察部门这样的大机构接受新的理念有时会很难。报告的作者也意识到,推行这样一种新的警务模式需要进行相关的、深远的警务变革,例如,如何让警察看待警务工作中心目标。对其他方面来说,变革意味着对警务工作成绩衡量不仅仅体现在警察逮捕了多少人,而且要求警务工作是不是使得这个地区对生活、旅游和工作在那里的人们更加安全了。

因此,该报告可以被看作不仅是对警察部门能更有效地进行犯罪预防工作的策略描述,对警察而言,也是接纳新理念并将警察角色定位到犯罪预防这一机遇的一种挑战。

扬·安德森(*Jan Andersson*)总干事

2010 年 5 月于斯德哥尔摩

一、简　介

预防犯罪的研究和政策的重点历来侧重在罪犯或潜在可能的罪犯上（Weisburd，1997，2002）。研究人员已通过研究制定出对策，以阻止个体参与犯罪或改造罪犯，这样他们就不会再想犯罪。近年来犯罪预防工作往往侧重于让高危罪犯失去犯罪能力，从而使他们不能自由地伤害守法公民。在对犯罪预防政策的公开辩论中，这些战略常被认为颇具竞争性。然而，有关犯罪的预防研究和对策，他们有一个共同的假设：即对犯罪的理解和控制必须从罪犯开始。在所有这些路径中，预防犯罪的重点是人和他们的犯罪行为。

警方的做法也主要侧重于人。他们的工作通常从应对公民的报警开始。他们的工作重点是在确定谁犯罪，并在逮捕这些罪犯和走完刑事司法程序后结束。警方同时也关注更广泛的社区问题以及"社区服务"（Kahan and Meares，1998；Mastrofski，1999）。此外，警察还被赋予在紧急情况下确保社区安全、紧近以来应对国土安全威胁等角色（Waddington and Neyroud，2007）。但是，不论警方的任务如何广泛地扩展，警务活动的核心仍然是建立在无论是受害者还是罪犯都是警务工作的重点这一假设上。

在这本专著中，我们将阐明，如果警方能将警务工作的基点从人转移到地点上，那么警务更有效率。这种转变已经在美国警务实践中展开，地点已经成为警方犯罪预防工作的重点（Koper，2008；Weisburd and Lum，2005）。但即使在美国，人仍然是警务的焦点，而不是地点。我们这里说的地点，并不是指很大的地理单元，如街坊和社区等犯罪学家在预防犯罪时通常所关注的重点（Bursik and Webb，1982；Sampson，Raudenbush，and Earls，1997；Shaw and McKay，1942［1969］），也不是警务组织中的重要单位即巡区和辖区。地点在本文中指的是社区和邻里等较大社会环境下具体的位置（Eck and Weisburd，1995）。他们可以被定义为某个大楼或地址（Green，1996；Sherman，Gartin，and Buerger，1989），或者是街面或路段（Sherman and Weisburd，1995；Taylor，1997），也可以是具有相同犯罪问题的地址群、街面群或路段群（Block，Dabdoub，and Fregly，1995；Weisburd and Green，1995a）。

基于地点警务战略，就如"热点"巡逻一样简单，正如在明尼阿波利斯的热点警务实验一样（Sherman and Weisburd，1995），在实验中，警察干预将更多的巡逻资源集中到犯罪聚集的地点。但是，基于地点警务还可以采取更多综合手段缓解犯罪问题。在泽西市毒品市场分析报告中（Weisburd and Green，1995a），比如，减少毒品热点区域犯罪问题的一个三步方案(包括确定和分析问题,制定专门的反应,维持犯罪控制的收益)。在泽西市的问题导向警务项目中(Braga, Weisburd, Waring, Mazerolle, Spelman, and Gajewski, 1999),问题导向警务模式运用于发展应对每个小型区域,即暴力犯罪热点区域犯罪问题的具体战略。

警方为什么要重新调整警务战略和组织机构,以更多地关注于地点?为什么基于地点警务成为警方控制犯罪和违法的核心方法?在这本专著中,我们就基于地点警务模式基本轮廓阐述案例,并运用证据来支持地点警务模式是有效和高效的。我们在下一部分中追踪20世纪80年代犯罪预防中出现的犯罪地点,然后在第三部分中,我们将开展对犯罪和地点的基础性研究,以证实犯罪集中城市的犯罪热点区域。这是评判地点警务的一个关键性发现,因为它提供了一个逻辑:将警察资源专注于一块小地区要比将他们广泛地分散在整个城市里强。但是,即使犯罪集中在几个地方,如果它简单地从一个地方转移到了城市的另一个地方,将使警察的犯罪预防工作失去稳定的焦点。专著的第四部分描述了犯罪在地点上具有较强的稳定性,而相比之下,罪犯个体的犯罪行为具有不稳定性。在第五部分,我们展示了有关犯罪地理分布基础研究,是如何强烈支持警方需要把重点放在犯罪热点上,而不是放在像邻里、社区等更大的地理单元上。最后,在第六部分,我们将呈现犯罪地点相关性这一新兴的研究,以支持基于地点的干预模式的这些特点。

值得一提的是,这个地点警务的案例不仅仅取之于基础研究,还包括明显的证据证明基于地点警务模式能得到应用。我们的专著的第七部分回顾了基于地点或热点警务的实证文献,这些文献表明警察干预微观地点目标,可以减少地点上的犯罪和违法。但是,是否一个地方犯罪减少,会导致犯罪转移到城市中的其他地方去?当这种犯罪位移的观点为过去一直阻碍基于地点警务的发展(Reppetto, 1976),第八部分中所阐述的近来实证证据表明,犯罪位移对基于地点项目带来的犯罪预防效益并不构成主要威胁。事实上,研究表明基于地点警务更有可能带来“犯罪预防效益的扩散”(Clark and Weisburd, 1994),而不是犯罪位移。在接下来的两个部分中,我们讨论了以地点而不是以罪犯为中心的警务模式有巨大的潜在法律和社会效益,但警方必须开始更加重视针对某一地点实施警务干预的合法性。最后,我们认识到简单地热衷于基于地点警务是不够的,我们建议在实际工作中,警方必须转而高效地执行基于地点这一途径。当然,在推进新的路径之前,在实务中警察遇到困难和机会时,要不断适应和勇于创新。过去二十年中,警方已经显示对创新的深度兴趣,这也推进实践能力的提升(National Research Council [NRC], 2004; Weisburd and Braga, 2006a)。在这种推动警务改进的努力下,基于地点警务展现了一个自然的发展过程。

二、犯罪预防中犯罪地点的呈现

当传统的犯罪学研究与理论把焦点集中到个人与社区的时候（Nettler，1978；Sherman，1995），犯罪学家们一开始就认识到，从特定场所和所提供的情景机会可能会导致犯罪的发生。例如，爱得威·萨瑟兰（Edwin Sutherland），他的研究重点放在犯罪的学习过程，认为学习过程致使违法者习得犯罪行为，他在自己的经典犯罪学著作中提到了即时情景可对犯罪产生多重影响。再有，当商贩不在视野中的时候，盗窃犯就可能对一个水果摊实施盗窃，而当他在商贩的视野中时就不会实施盗窃；银行入室盗窃犯会对保护措施薄弱的银行实施攻击，而一个银行有警卫和防盗报警器的时候他就不会采取行动（Sutherland，1947：5）。尽管如此，和其他犯罪学家一样，萨瑟兰（Sutherland）并不认为犯罪地点是犯罪学研究的相关重点。如果这是事实的话，部分原因是因为地点提供的犯罪机会很多并在特定地点聚集这一现象对理论和对策并无太大的帮助。于是，犯罪学家们传统地认为，相比"犯罪倾向的驱动力"，情景因素在解释犯罪的时候并不重要（Clarke and Felson，1993：4；Trasler，1993），将犯罪机会大量存在的假设和罪犯自认为积极实施犯罪的观点结合起来，就容易理解为什么犯罪学家很少注意犯罪发生的地点。

随着基于罪犯的犯罪预防对策的发展，将地点中潜在的利益作为犯罪预防的重点，给理论与实务界带来不少失落感。这种失落被部分归咎于基础研究难以解释犯罪行为的起因及发展。20世纪80年代的一系列研究表明，我们很难确定今后谁将会成为重罪案犯，或者预言重犯可能会实施犯罪的时间与手法（Albrecht and Moitra，1988；Barnett and Lofaso，1985；Blumstein and Cohen，1979；Elliot，Dunford，and Huizinga，1987；Estrich，Moore，McGillis，and Spelman，1983；Gottfredson and Gottfredson，1990）[①]。这也导致我们得出这样一个结论：基础研究既无法提供一个清晰的方案或挑选适合实施犯罪预防干预的个人，也不能提升旨在告诫犯罪嫌疑人的犯罪预防策略的有效性（Earls，1991；Earls and Carlson，1995）。即便已经有充分的证据来预测某些犯罪类型，比如一些成人犯的特有犯罪类型（Blumstein，Cohen，Das，and Moitra，1988；Kempf，1986），但法律和道德的两难问题阻挡了实践中犯罪预防策

---

① 最近的一项检验犯罪学理论定量测试解释能力的研究，说明这一状况在过去的二十年几乎没有得到改进（Weisburd and Piquero，2008）。

略的发展（Moore，1986）。本书将在后半部分中提出基于地点犯罪预防可以避免很多法律和道德的两难问题。

鉴于犯罪预测的困难，我们并不惊讶20世纪70、80年代以罪犯为中心的应用性研究无法阐明影响成功犯罪干预项目发展的主要障碍到底是什么。始于1974年年初罗伯特·马丁森（Robert Martinson）对犯罪改造项目的批判（Lipton，Martinson，and Wilks，1975），一系列的研究印证了传统犯罪预防措施的失败（Sechrest，White，and Brown 1979；Whitehead and Lab，1989）。很多学者认为，诸多失败的症结是在于方案设计的研发不够（Farrington，Ohlin and Wilson，1986；Goldstein，1990）。此外，一些评论强调，以罪犯为重点的犯罪预防，有一些成功的案例，这些案例为提升犯罪预防政策的有效性提供了指引（Farrington，1983；Lipsey，1992）。然而，即便那些寄希望提升该犯罪预防政策有效性的学者，也逐渐认识针对犯罪行为的犯罪预防工作所存在的固有困难（Visher and Weisburd，1997）。总结所谓传统"罪犯为中心的"预防犯罪的整体地位，帕曲克（Patricia）和保罗·布兰廷厄姆（Paul Brantingham）在1990年写道："如果传统的办法行之有效，寻找新的犯罪预防途径会有一点压力。如果传统的方法效果很好，那么很少有人会有犯罪的动机，真正实施犯罪的则会更少"（1990:19）。

对于许多学者和决策者而言，以人为中心的犯罪预防的危机意味着不得不重新思考犯罪性和如何来使罪犯不参与到犯罪中的命题。事实上在过去二十年里，人们对罪犯改造方案重新产生了兴趣，与早期的研究相比，如今许多研究证明了罪犯改造是有积极效果的（Andrews，Zinger，Hoge，Bonta，Gendreau，and Cullen，1990；Cullen，2005；Lipsey and Cullen，2007）①。但也有人建议，积极调整预防犯罪的方向是必要的。他们认为，这种转变肯定不是出自于曾经运用过的战略和理论，而是基于形成犯罪预防工作基础的单位分析上。这种新方法引导的重点不在于人，即到底是谁犯了罪，而是在于犯罪发生的环境上。

科恩（Cohen）和费尔森（Felson）（1979）对传统性理解犯罪的犯罪学方法提出了颇有影响力的批评，这一批评激发起人们对犯罪地点的兴趣并产生了较大的影响。他们认为将预防犯罪的重点放在犯罪学理论中个人动机上，就无法认识到犯罪等式中其他因素的重要性。他们认为犯罪事件的发生，不仅需要一个罪犯的存在，一个合适的犯罪目标，同时缺失有技能的保安。他们表示犯罪率会受犯罪目标的性质及该目标受保护的程度的改变，而不管该犯罪的动机是什么。1979年，科恩（Cohen）和费

---

① 然而，在警务研究领域，以犯罪人为中心的项目研究证据还很薄弱，最多是结论不明（Weisburd and Eck，2004）。

尔森(Felson)在犯罪学学术圈提出了一个激进的观点:即便在没有罪犯个体作案动机的影响下,犯罪也会产生变化。他们所提出的日常活动的观点,将犯罪环境建构为犯罪学研究的重点。

相似研究还有,以罗纳德·克拉克为带头人的英国学者们开始探索情景犯罪预防的理论价值和实践可能性(Brantingham and Brantingham, 1990; Clarke, 1980, 1983, 1992, 1995; Cornish and Clarke, 1986)。通过这一思路,并借助于对物质、组织以及社会环境等诱发犯罪因素的考量,似乎让我们加深了对犯罪和犯罪预防战略有效性的理解。以情景为路径的考量并没有忽略罪犯,只是将他们置于与犯罪环境相关联的、广义犯罪预防方程中的一个要素。它需要我们转变对犯罪预防路径的认识,从首先考虑人们为什么会犯罪到首先关注犯罪为什么会在特定环境下发生。这一认识上的转变,使犯罪环境转而成为犯罪的中心,而传统意义上犯罪的中心——罪犯,则成为影响犯罪的众多因素中的一个。

情境预防理论的拥护者认为,犯罪环境对改进传统基于罪犯的犯罪预防政策提供了一种很好的可选路径。他们认为相对于人而言,在绝大部分情况下情境更具有稳定性,犯罪预防工作的重点也更容易预测。在某种程度上,这一假设是从机会与犯罪关系的常识中发展而来。例如,从定义上讲,商店行窃发生在商店而非住所,在工业区家庭纠纷不可能成为一个问题。相对高危人群,高犯罪地区就不可能避开刑事司法的干预。从具有一定特征的市场或组织发展形成的犯罪不可能轻易转移到符合其他组织特征的情境中(Goldstock, 1991)。

这种强调犯罪情景尤其对警方及基于地点警务带来较为明晰的启示。什么是基于地点警务? 它的核心就是要关注犯罪聚集的地点,它始于这么一种假设:犯罪之所以在那里发生是因为那个地方存在某种导致犯罪的因素。如此说来,地点警务是以常规行为理论为理论依据的(Cohen and Felson, 1979; Felson, 1994),即将犯罪定义为一种聚合:合适目标(例如:受害人),保卫缺失(例如:警察)和存在犯罪的动机或潜在罪犯等因素综合的结果。当然,这些要素都应是在一定的地点或场景下出现的,相应的,基于地点警务认识到存在某些特定的场所会导致这些因素的聚合(Brantingham and Brantingham, 1981 [1991], 1984)。

三、地点上犯罪的聚集

对于采用基于地点警务的一个重要条件是,犯罪很大程度上会集中某个被称之为"犯罪热点"的区域(Sherman *et al.*, 1989；Sherman and Weisburd, 1995；Weisburd and Green, 1995a)。如果缺少犯罪在地点聚集这一条件,集中在某地开展犯罪预防工作就缺乏理由。还有,如果一个城市犯罪的分布是随机的,那么基于地点警务的效益就很低。

始于20世纪80年代末的大量研究表明,不管特定的分析单位如何确定,犯罪在某些地点明显的聚集性是存在的(Brantingham and Brantingham, 1999；Crow and Bull, 1975；Pierce, Spaar, and Briggs, 1986；Roncek, 2000；Sherman *et al.*, 1989；Weisburd and Green, 1994；Weisburd, Maher, and Sherman, 1992, Weisburd, Bushway, Lum, and Yang, 2004；Weisburd, Morris, and Groff, 2009)。其中最有影响的研究,也许就是谢尔曼(Sherman)、嘉定(Gartin)和布泽尔(Buerger)在1989这一年的时间里对那些报警信息中街道地址的分析研究。谢尔曼(Sherman)和他的团队发现,人们在明尼苏达州明尼阿波利斯3.5%的街道地址上拨出了全市50%的报警电话。他们对这样一个结果感到分外吃惊,并由此开拓了一个崭新的研究领域,即"地点犯罪学"。

其他的研究也获得了犯罪在犯罪热点聚集的相似证据。威斯勃德(Weisburd)和马泽罗勒(Mazerolle)在2000年做的研究中发现,将近20%的破坏公共秩序的犯罪和14%的侵犯人身权利的犯罪都集中在新泽西州泽西市56个毒品犯罪热点,而这些地区只占这个城市所有街头段和十字路口的4.4%。埃克(Eck)、盖什(Gersh)和泰勒(Taylor)在2000年也发现相似的情况,在布朗克斯和巴尔的摩最活跃的那10%的地点(就犯罪而言),发生了全市近32%的抢劫、殴打他人、入室盗窃、巨额盗窃和机动车盗窃。

威斯勃德(Weisburd)、布什威(Bushway)、鲁姆(Lum)和杨(Yang)在2004年做的一项研究,不仅有力地支持了犯罪的聚集性,同时也证实了该犯罪聚集会在一段较长的时间内保持稳定。威斯勃德(Weisburd)和他的团队分析了1989年到2002年期间西雅图市街段上的案件情况。他们发现在过去14年间50%的犯罪案件,只发生在4.5%的街段上。如图1所示,这些犯罪聚集年年都非常稳定。这些数据还得出了一种犯罪的"聚集规律",证实犯罪在城市的高度集中性。

当我们关注犯罪的特定类型时,犯罪聚集规律中所蕴含的犯罪预防机会就变得更加清晰起来。在西雅图所做的另一个研究,威斯勃德(Weisburd)、莫里斯(Morris)和格罗夫(Groff)(2009)检验了青少年逮捕地的犯罪聚集规律。他们发现在14年间,所有被正式逮捕青少年案件中的三分之一,发生在西雅图市全部25000多个街段中的86个街段里。就在更多的研究试图发现有多少犯罪聚集现象是因警察巡逻的

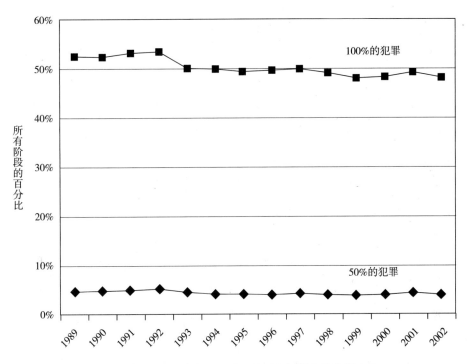

图 1　1989 至 2002 年间 50% 和 100% 犯罪报告的街段之比

资料来源：威斯勃德等（2004）。

密度所引起的时候，本研究则认为应将研究重点拓展到警察在城市的犯罪热点地区如何开展犯罪预防工作。

劳伦斯·谢尔曼（Lawrence Sherman）（1995）认为，地点上犯罪的聚集性要比个体的犯罪聚集性高得多。他用了他在明尼阿波利斯的研究数据，并与费城研究中的违法聚集行为做了比较（Wolfgang，Figlio，and Sellin，1972），他认为通过犯罪发生地的地址来预测犯罪可靠性要比通过罪犯的身份来预测犯罪高出 6 倍（1995：36-37）。谢尔曼（Sherman）问："我们为什么不在这方面做得更多一些？我们为什么不去更多地追查犯罪地，而不仅仅是追查犯罪人呢？"

根据在西雅图收集的纵向数据，威斯勃德（Weisburd）（2008：5）持相类似的观点。当使用犯罪目标作为尺度时，关注犯罪地点确实要比关注罪犯有效。在那个时间段内平均计算，每年西雅图 50% 的犯罪案件发生在 1500 个街段上。而在同时期，每年西雅图 50% 的犯罪案件则由 6108 个罪犯所为。简而言之，就确定相同的犯罪目标及身份而言，如果警察关注的是人而不是地区，那么他们的工作量将增加四倍。

四、热点的稳定性作为犯罪预防的目标

犯罪在地点的聚集性支持了将警察热点巡逻勤务作为一种犯罪预防的有效战略（Sherman and Weisburd, 1995; Weisburd and Braga, 2006b），即将犯罪预防的资源集中到犯罪高发的特定区域。然而，犯罪的聚集性本身既不能为重新调整犯罪预防资源，或作出有关"为什么犯罪会聚集"这一重大理论突破提供实证基础。举例来说，如果"犯罪热点"很快地从一个地方转移到另一个地方，那么我们采取集中犯罪控制资源的努力就没有多大的意义了，因为那个区域的犯罪活动即便没有刑事司法的干预，也会自然而然地削减（Spelman, 1995）。类似的，如果犯罪聚集点可以很快地在城市间转移，那样我们费心去理解那些具有地点特征的犯罪活动就没有多大的意义。

我们所收集的数据表明，对基于地点警务持有异议的观点缺乏实证依据。举个例子，斯皮尔曼（Spelman）（1995）分析了波士顿市来自学校的、公共住房的、地铁站、公园和运动场的报警电话。他发现的有关证据证明，在过去 3 年里，在这些地方的"治安最差"区域产生的犯罪具有相当高的稳定性。斯皮尔曼（Spelman）总结道："要让那些生活和工作在高风险地方的人们明白这个道理，也要让服务这些民众的警官和政府官员明白这个道理，以便花时间去发现、分析并解决这些顽症（1995:131）。"泰勒（Taylor）（1999）运用 1981 年到 1994 年收集的数据所开展的小组研究设计，调查了马里兰州巴尔的摩市 90 多个街区上的犯罪和犯罪的恐惧感，找到了犯罪在地点上具有长期高度稳定性的证据。有关犯罪在地点的长期稳定性最为全面的研究，是由威斯勃德等人在 2004 年完成的（Weisburd），他们对西雅图街区发生的犯罪事件进行研究。他们运用集群轨迹分析法（Nagin, 1999, 2005; Nagin and Land, 1993），并采用一种被用于研究犯罪职业生涯的方法，发现了与发展轨迹相似的群。

威斯勃德（Weisburd）和他的同事（2004）在他们的数据中找出了 18 种独特的轨迹模式。在他们的研究中最重要的发现是犯罪会长时间在某一个区域保持稳定。相比这种犯罪在地点上的高度稳定性，有关个体的发展犯罪学研究认为罪犯个体的犯罪行为会在相对较短的时间内发生较大的变化，尤其是对高危犯而言更是如此。（Horney, Osgood, and Marshall, 1995; Nagin, 1999; Nagin and Tremblay, 1999）一个有关年轻人的犯罪职业生涯典型轨迹分析与西雅图研究结果的比较，更证明了这一结论。我们也注意到西雅图数据中那些长期罪犯群体的相对稳定性，纳金（Nagin）（1999）在图 3 中对这些惯犯作了对比。

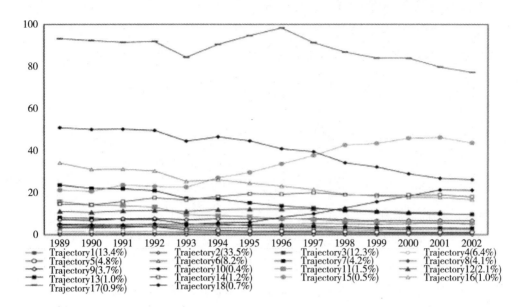

图2　18种西雅图犯罪事件轨迹图

注意:括号内的百分比代表了每种的轨迹占西雅图全城的比例。

资料来源:威斯勃德等人(Weisburd *et al.* , 2004)。

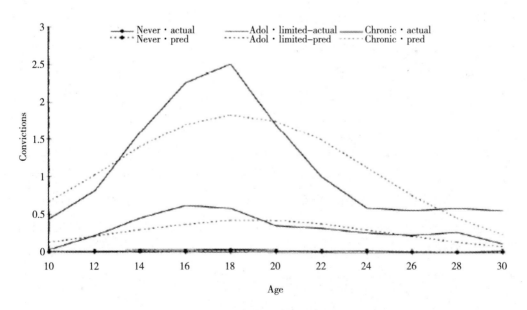

图3　个人犯罪的轨迹图

Adol. =adolescent(青少年),pred. =predicted(可预测)。

总数为411。长期:7%,仅在青少年时期:22%,从未犯罪:71%。

资料来源:纳金(Nagin,1999)。

毋庸质疑的是,犯罪热点在一定时期内有着非常高的稳定性的观点已经被证实。相比而言,犯罪学中目前尚无发现比犯罪职业生涯中违法行为更具可变性和不稳定性的事实。这些变化性的一个重要因素是事实上罪犯在浪子回头的时候,其年龄都相对较轻(Blumstein, Cohen, Roth, and Visher, 1986;Gottfredson and Hirschi, 1990;Laub and Sampson, 2003;Tracy and Kempf-Leonard, 1996;Wolfgang, Thornberry, and Figlio, 1987)。但是也有证据显示对于大多数违法者而言,甚至在很短的时间内,其犯罪行为都具有很强的不稳定性(Bushway, Thornberry, and Krohn, 2003;Horney et al., 1995;Nagin, 1999)。

以上数据证明,基于地点的犯罪预防对于城市中犯罪和公共安全具有长效的潜在影响。地点上"均值回归"模式表明,区域犯罪往往一开始"很热",之后便自然"冷却"了。在此模式中我们得出,如果我们将精力都放在犯罪率最高的热点区域,那么犯罪预防的效益并不高,因为即便警察没有采取任何犯罪预防措施,这些区域的犯罪也会变得"更冷"。从某些角度来讲,这就是个体违法的主导模式,因为我们知道很多人很快就超过了犯罪高发的年龄。相反,犯罪热点会保持并持续很长一段时间。

回到我们感兴趣的地点犯罪的理论基础,我们可以推测这些犯罪热点的所处情境中,存在着一些能让犯罪聚集的因素。这些因素就能够解释为什么犯罪会长期在某个地点聚集。同时,这也能够解释犯罪在犯罪低发地点的较高稳定性。通过对西雅图长达 14 年的考察发现,将近 2/3 的街区没有或是很少有犯罪活动(Weisburd et al., 2004)。为什么这些街区通常没有犯罪活动出现呢? 我们也能够推测或许是这些区域的某些特征和人们的日常活动影响着这里的犯罪机会。在第六章我们会用实证研究所得出的结论,更详细回答这些问题。

在我们上述的讨论中,我们已经强调了在某一段时期内地点上犯罪的稳定性。西雅图研究还在验证过的数据中确定了有关犯罪发展趋势性的研究兴趣。举例而言,在该项目研究期间,西雅图的犯罪率整体下降了 20%,这与美国的其他城市的犯罪变动趋势接近(Blumstein and Wallman, 2000)。但是在威斯勃德等人(Weisburd et al.)(2004)的研究中,只有 14% 的街区显示有这样的下降趋势。这就意味着,在西雅图犯罪的减少只是限定在这个城市的一小部分区域。也许,最有意思的是,在这个城市超过 500 个街区见证了在这段时间里出现的犯罪浪潮,犯罪在这个受到影响的街区内以一个平均超过 40% 的速度增长。以上事实说明,将警务的重点放在具体的地点要比放在更大的地理单位如一个城市更为重要。对犯罪趋势的总体回顾,会让警察错误地认为整个西雅图的犯罪已经均匀地减少了。事实上,大部分街区难有任何改变,并且在此期间许多街区还经历了一场犯罪浪潮。

五、基于地点的犯罪预防比基于社区更为重要

以上讨论中的证据构建了犯罪在地点上的聚集性和稳定性,但我们到目前为止还没探究犯罪热点是如何地理分布的。这个问题很值得探究,因为它关系到使用微小的地点而不是更大地理意义上的区域单位作为分析单位,是否会影响我们对犯罪和罪犯预防对策的理解(Weisburd, Bruinsma, and Bernasco, 2009)。将犯罪预防的重点置于地点是重要的,但如果我们将工作重点置于巡逻辖区、社区或邻里,是否会对犯罪产生同样的影响? 如果犯罪热点主要仅仅集中在城市的一个或两个街区,是否意味着不管犯罪在热点的聚集性如何,我们都应将犯罪预防的重点从社区撤出?

截止目前的证据表明,一个城市到处都能发现犯罪热点。以威斯勃德(Weisburd)和马泽罗勒(Mazerolle)(2000)为例,他们在新泽西州泽西市确定了56个毒品市场。如图4所示,毒品市场遍布泽西市。令参与这项研究的警察惊讶的是,虽然毒品市场更集中在社会底层地区,但这些市场也在一般被认为富人区中发现。威斯勃德(Weisburd)和马泽罗勒(Mazerolle)解释道,好的邻里也有坏的死角。重要的是,大多数地方,即使是很差的邻里相对来说反而没有很严重的毒品问题。这一发现在六十年前就有回应,亨利·麦凯(Heney McKay)指出在犯罪率高的邻里内的有些街区缺少罪犯(Albert J. Reiss, Jr., Sherman and Weisburd, 1995)。

使用更复杂的地理分析,威斯勃德(Weisburd)和同事(2004)创造了用核密度地图来检验地点犯罪轨迹趋势分布(见图5)。这些地图再次证实了前面的研究发现:犯罪的热点遍及整个城市。他们也发表了一些耐人寻味的初步研究发现,并由此得出如下结论:同一街段往往具有较稳定的犯罪率,这样的街段分布于整个城市,但是集中于低密度居住率和高收入地区(见图5)。他们注意到犯罪增长和下降集中地区重叠分布于市中心地区。这是一个特别有趣的发现,因为这表明要么是犯罪高潮和犯罪下降两者相似过程,要么是街段层次的特性(而不是更大面积的层次),对人们认识犯罪趋势有着重大的影响。

在对86个最热街段上的青少年逮捕事件所作的纵向性研究中,威斯勃德(Weisburd)、莫里斯(Morris)和格勒夫(Groff)(2009)又发现了犯罪热点是全城分布的(见图6)。但是就像在威斯勃德等人(Weisburd et al.)(2004)的研究中提及的,在中央商务区有一个比较大的热点聚集。威斯勃德(Weisburd)、莫里斯(Morris)

图 4　泽西市毒品市场的位置

资料来源：威斯勃德（Weisburd）和马泽罗勒（Mazerolle）（2000）。

和格勒夫（Groff）（2009）进一步检验了青少年逮捕热点的聚集现象，并质疑道：这种热点聚集是否表明存在着重要的地区性趋势影响该地点上的青少年犯罪，并且是较大地区性趋势还是街段性趋势正在影响犯罪形态。

在检验街段空间因素时，他们在街段形态轨迹中发现街段的街与街之间巨大的差异性。他们总结道"大量的'行动'确实是在微观地点发生的，如街区"（Groff *et*

a. 稳定的犯罪轨迹群　　b. 犯罪上升的轨迹群　　c. 犯罪下降的轨迹群

图5　核密度估算街段类别层面上,显示出了犯罪稳定,增长和下降的轨迹

资料来源:威斯勃德(Weisburd)等人。

al. ,2009:84)。这说明如果将注意力集中在类似邻里和人口普查单位等较大的单位将会错失很多关于犯罪的信息。

有关犯罪热点分布最复杂地理信息研究,是由格勒夫(Groff),威斯勃德(Weisburd)和杨(Yang)采用16年(1989—2004)的西雅图犯罪事件数据完成的(2010;也可参见Weisburd,Groff and Yang正在进一步研究的课题)。有关微观地理层面上街道之间变化这一重要的问题,在先前的研究并没有回答。为了解决这个问题,他们探索了西雅图街面犯罪在时间和空间上的变化。格勒夫等人(Groff *et al.*)采用了威斯勃德等人(Weisburd *et al.*)分类出来的轨迹群特征(还在进一步研究中)。然后他们采用了多种定量空间统计数据来从空间上对每一个模式的成员排列,从而证明街道在空间上分布是否具有相同的时间轨迹特征,或者在时间特征上街面与街面之间的不同特性。

虽然大部分地区呈现无犯罪和低且稳定犯罪等主流特征(所提供的压倒性数量并不奇怪,分别有12033和7696个街段),但呈现高犯罪率轨迹群的街段还是分散在这些地区里的。进一步检视时间轨迹特征,揭示了西雅图部分地区不同的犯罪轨迹。在图7,呈现了西雅图中心街面之间轨迹群的分布图。尽管这张地图不能为已经呈现出的空间关联显著性提供定量化的实质证据,但是它为街面层面上犯罪形态的不均匀性和均匀性提供一个有力佐证,同时也强有力地证明了街段之间犯罪率的差异。格勒夫等人(Groff *et al.*)(2010)也指出了西雅图市区对城市西部犯罪形态的影响。

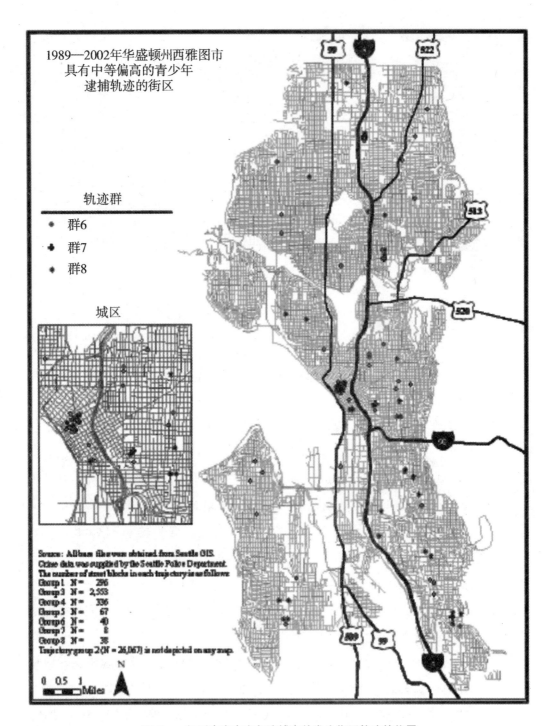

图6 一般到高发青少年逮捕事件发生街区轨迹的位置

资料来源：威斯勃德（Weisburd）、莫里斯（Morris）和格勒夫（Groff）（2009）。

就在这里，他们观察到了街面之间时间轨迹形态的巨大差异性，以及高犯罪率在街道集中的现象。在市中心东面的老住宅区，这种显著的变化也存在着。他们由此指得出,不能通过对大范围的犯罪趋势和简单推测,来理解犯罪活动。

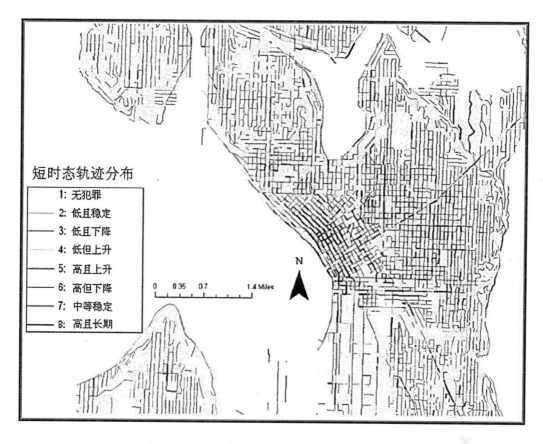

图7　西雅图市中心时间轨迹上的犯罪空间分布图

资料来源:格勒夫(Groff),威斯勃德(Weisburd)和杨(Yang)(即将出版)。

　　格勒夫(Groff)和他的同事们应用统计分析补充了描述性分析,该分析呈现出了令人惊讶的街段间犯罪时间轨迹形态的高度非均匀性。换言之,街段之间的犯罪时间轨迹形态往往会发生变化。犯罪低稳定街段不容易与犯罪中等稳定、高增长、高下降的街区相邻,这一形态不仅呈现在地图上,同时也呈现在他们的研究发现之中,这同时也表明了最相近的街段具有扩散性的犯罪时间轨迹。街段之间犯罪特性的不同,并不是因为非均匀性现象,而是与特定犯罪时间轨迹有关。在城市的某个区域会出现犯罪从没有到低稳定性的趋势。有时候,这种变化是由低稳定到另一个较高轨迹状态。在其他区域,犯罪形态的转变是缓慢长期的,不仅仅因为街段之间变化,也是因为犯罪时间轨迹的层次和特征上的变化。这些研究结果表明,地点层次上的分析意在捕捉趋势上的重要变化,如果我们仍然关注于那些犯罪学家和警察们传统上关注的大型地理单位上，这种变化将会被蒙蔽[①]。

六、我们能够解释犯罪为什么在地点上聚集？

当已经了解到犯罪在热点上的聚集性及在时间上的稳定性、大部分的犯罪行为发生在地点层面上这一事实后，我们就会引向另一个问题，即能否解释发生在地点层面的犯罪。这样的解释是重要的，因为它可以为警察所作的犯罪预防工作提供理论基础。如果我们认识了为什么有些地方会成为犯罪热点的原因，我们就会比较容易地采取专门犯罪预防战略，以减少犯罪及解决在那些地点上呈现的相关问题。

正如我们先前注意到的，绝大多数的犯罪热点研究是以常规行为理论（Cohen and Felson，1979）作为解释地点层面犯罪趋势变化的依据，同时这也是构建犯罪预防实务对策的依据（Eck and Weisburd，1995；Sherman et al.，1989）。这个观点的主要假设是那个特定场所的特征，比如：监护的性质，有动机罪犯的出现，有无合适的目标，均强烈影响着犯罪发生的可能性（also Felson，1994）。检验这些因素在微观地点上预测犯罪的研究，基本上肯定了以上犯罪的成因关系（Roncek and Bell，1981；Roncek and Maier，1991；Smith，Frazee，and Davison，2000；Weisburd et al.，2009；Weisburd et al.，正在进一步深入研究）。

例如，假定青少年被吸引到特定类型的活动中，这些活动反过来就会影响他们的"活动空间"（Felson，2006）。众所周知，商场和电影院是青年人经常去玩的地方，事实上，上述行业也在试图吸引年轻人成为其客户。此外，因为这样的活动空间不仅能吸引大量的潜在犯罪人，也吸引了大量潜在的受害目标，由此我们可以预期到青少年犯罪会大量地在此聚集。例如，一些研究人员发现，青少年犯罪与其经过和不正派的同龄人一起参加无组织的社交活动紧密相关（Agnew and Peterson，1989；Osgood，Wilson，O'Malley，Bachman，and Johnston，1996；Wallace and Bachman，1991）。青少年往往会欺负其他青少年这一事实（Snyder，2003），进一步强化了在青少年犯罪发展过程中该活动空间的重要性。

[①] 格勒夫等人（Groff et al.）（2010，也可参见格勒夫等人（Groff et al.）（2009））发现较大区域会影响地点犯罪的证据感到并不意外。他们在适度距离位置上发现在相同时间轨迹特征内的街段有较强的空间依赖性。他们还发现，部分街段呈现的时间犯罪轨迹特征代表了某些地区的总体特征。这些现象较多地发生在低犯罪率的轨迹阶段，即使这些区域有其他的轨迹交叉分布。然而，在犯罪长期高发的街段附近也观察了这一现象：一种由高犯罪率主导但又与低犯罪率交织在一起的区域。

威斯勃德等人（Weisburd *et al.*）（2009）在西雅图研究青少年犯罪的数据有力地证实了青少年活动空间与日常行为理论的相关性，以理解青少年逮捕事件在某些地点的高度集中性。威斯勃德等人（Weisburd *et al.*）能够识别那些犯罪事件会发生在哪儿，并由此描述出活动空间和青少年犯罪热点的相关性（见表1）。青少年犯罪热点发生率最高的轨迹（见6—8组的轨迹），相比低发生率轨迹，极有可能发生在学校或青年中心，商场、商店或餐馆的逮捕事件。在每一组低发生率轨迹中（1—4组）发生在学校或者青年中心的逮捕事件不到4%。然而，在轨迹8组中发生在学校或青年中心的逮捕事件超过30%。在轨迹7组中的逮捕事件为12.7%和在轨迹6组中发生在学校或青年中心的逮捕事件为17.1%。当分析发生在商店、百货商场、餐馆逮捕事件所占的比例时，低和高发生率组之间的差异更加明显。在每个低发生率轨迹群组（1—4）中，发生在上述类型的地点逮捕事件低于15%，但是在轨迹群组6组和8组中，发生在商店、商场或者餐厅的逮捕事件占34.3%和75.4%。

表1 以事件发生的地点划分少年犯罪轨迹群组成员（总数=30,004）

			事件位置				
	学校、青年中心	商店、商场、餐馆	街、胡同、公共空间	私人住宅	酒吧、俱乐部、酒馆	其他	总数
群组							
1	1.9%	10.2%	32.1%	47.3%	.2%	8.3%	100.0%
2	1.8%	2.1%	53.7%	34.3%	.1%	8.0%	100.0%
3	2.9%	4.8%	43.3%	40.1%	.3%	8.6%	100.0%
4	3.9%	14.3%	42.5%	29.8%	.2%	9.3%	100.0%
5	6.5%	26.0%	40.7%	14.3%	.4%	12.2%	100.0%
6	17.1%	34.3%	32.5%	5.2%	2.5%	8.4%	100.0%
7	12.7%	75.4%	8.8%	.2%	.1%	2.9%	100.0%
8	30.7%	38.9%	21.5%	.7%	.0%	8.0%	100.0%

资料来源：威斯勃德（Weisburd）、莫里斯（Morris）和格勒夫（Groff）（2009）。

这些数据为青少年犯罪集中是因为青少年活动空间的集中的假设提供了重要支持。发生率最高的轨迹中的事件，最有可能在学校和青年中心，或商店、百货商场、餐馆的周围或附近被发现。这意味研究青少年犯罪热点，就逮捕事件发生情况来看，很有可能在青少年聚集的地方。毫不奇怪，在威斯勃德等人（Weisburd *et al.*）（2009）的青少年犯罪研究中，逮捕事件很少在酒吧、俱乐部和小酒馆里面发现。成年人热衷的活动场所，经常也是犯罪热点（Roncek and Bell,1981；Roncek and Maier, 1991），但它们并不属于青少年活动的空间。

当日常行为理论已成为当下在犯罪热点研究兴趣的中心问题时,其他理论也可能是理解地点犯罪和预防犯罪有效对策的途径,关注这一点也非常重要。比如,过去常常用于解释社区犯罪形态的社会失范生态理论(Schmid,1960a,1960b;Shaw and McKay,1942〔1969〕),也可以运用到犯罪热点研究中(Smith *et al.*,2000)。最近的一项由格勒夫(Groff),威斯勃德(Weisburd)和杨(Yang)(即将出版)主持的研究表明,社会失范理论可能与地点犯罪预防具有较强的相关性。

例如,学者们最近也突出强调的社区中的"集体效能",作为社区实现共同的价值观和规范行为的一种能力指标(Sampson *et al.*,1997;Sampson,2004)。将街段层面上的投票行为作为集体效能的一项指标,威斯勃德等人(Weisburd *et al.*)发现集体效能与犯罪特征之间有直接的联系。正如预期的那样,无和低发生率犯罪街区通过积极投票行为反应出来的集体效能指标最高。长期的犯罪轨迹街段的投票参与性是最低的(见表2)。这些发现很重要,因为它们暗示着并预示着警察除了将目标对准犯罪热点之外,也应该关注这个地点的社会生活状况。当许多热点警务项目主要依靠集中的执法活动来缓解犯罪问题时(例如 Braga *et al.*,1999;Sherman and Rogan,1995a,1995b),这些数据却强调运用社区警务和其他警务策略来提升地点上居民们非正式的社会控制能力的重要性。

表 2　集体效能(积极的投票者)与轨迹特征的关系

轨迹的分类	积极的投票者初始值	与无犯罪形态的对比值
无犯罪(总数=12033)	0.3534	N/A
低且稳定(总数=7696)	0.4238	↑
低且下降(总数=2212)	0.4164	↑
低但上升(总数=903)	0.3151	↓
中等稳定(总数=292)	0.2472	↓
高但下降(总数=574)	0.2388	↓
高且上升(总数=221)	0.2089	↓
长期(总数=247)	0.1741	↓

↑指:该特征比无犯罪中的特征有明显高的集体效能水平。
↓指:该特征比无犯罪中的特征有明显低的集体效能水平。
资料来源:威斯勃德(Weisburd)、格勒夫(Groff)和杨(Yang)(即将出版)。

威斯勃德等人(Weisburd *et al.*)甚至找到了直接衡量社会失范程度和街段层面犯罪之间更强的关系。用非法倾倒作为衡量街段层面社会规范的直觉现象,他们发现了轨迹形态之间存在很强的关系(见表3)。在观察的第一年,非法倾倒事件随着罪犯轨迹特征增长而增长。这种关系在各个轨迹群组里面都很显著。到目前为止,最低数量的非法倾倒事件是在无犯罪区发现的。和无犯罪群组的轨迹特征相比,在低发生率群组中有高出 4 倍,在高发生率轨迹特征群组里有高于 10 倍的非法倾倒事件发生。对长期热点群组里这种增长则更高。

观察随时间推移的变化,这种关系依然很强。对高且增长和中等稳定的轨迹特征群组里,非法倾倒事件不断增长,虽然只有在稳定群组里这种变化有统计学意义上的显著性。与之对比的是,在最后的一段观察期,在高但下降的轨迹特征群组里面的非法倾倒事件显示出了统计学意义上的下降趋势。这种特征在观察低发生率的群组里也可见。在低但上升特征的群组里面,非法倾倒事件有 1/3 的增长率,这是非常显著的增长率。在低且下降特征群组里,有明显的统计学上下降但幅度更小一些。低且稳定的特征群组在观察期间几乎没有显示出变化。这些数据显示,在一定时期内社会失范行为的变化和街段层面的犯罪变化之间有直接关系。

表3　非法倾倒事件数量和轨迹特征之间的关系

轨迹	非法倾倒的初始值	和无犯罪形态对比值	非法倾倒结束值	街区随时间而变化	街区成对样本试验显著性	组平均值的变化
无犯罪(总数=12033)	0.0373	N/A	0.0425	.0052	.012 *	13.94%
低且稳定(总数=7696)	0.1455	↑	0.1507	.0052	.307	3.57%
低且下降(总数=2212)	0.1534	↑	0.1308	−.0226	.013 *	−14.73%
低但上升(总数=903)	0.1694	↑	0.2410	.0716	.000 ***	42.27%
中等稳定(总数=292)	0.3870	↑	0.4840	.0970	.032 *	25.06%
高但下降(总数=574)	0.4344	↑	0.3333	−.1011	.008 *	−23.27%
高且上升(总数=221)	0.4736	↑	0.5279	.0543	.383	11.47%
长期(总数=247)	0.6221	↑	0.6923	.0702	.366	11.28%

↑指:该特征比无犯罪中的特征有明显高的集体效能水平。
↓指:该特征比无犯罪中的特征有明显低的集体效能水平。
*** p<.001,** p<.01,* p<.05 是表示街区成对样品 t 值检验。
资料来源:威斯勃德(Weisburd)、格勒夫(Groff)和杨(Yang)(即将出版)。

目前为止,我们的讨论揭示了犯罪学家和警察们可以确定与犯罪有关的地点特征。但是,我们对地点上犯罪的解释并确定犯罪成因的能力,是不是比在解释个体犯罪和确定个体犯罪成因的能力要强一些呢? 这个问题不太容易马上回答。我们还需要对犯罪地点做更多的研究,才能将其和我们在个体层面上众多的研究进行对比。

另外,威斯勃德(Weisburd)、格勒夫(Groff)和杨(Yang)(即将出版)最近的研究成果显示,尽管该研究还处在起步阶段,但目前所付诸的努力已经对这一问题有了深层的解释。在对街段组的轨迹特征的预测研究中,他们发现该地点犯罪模型能够解释2/3 的犯罪趋势变化。对比发现,个体犯罪模型只能平均解释出30%的犯罪趋势变化(Weisburd and Piquero,2008)。

七、热点警务的实证性证据

目前为止的基础研究,为基于地点警务的发展构筑了强大的基础。犯罪总是集中城市数量相对较少的几个地方的现象表明,采用基于地点警务或者热点警务,为警察更加有效地处置犯罪问题提供了一个机会。而且这些地点代表着长期持续的犯罪方位,并且不会随着时间单纯发生改变。如果警察能成功地改善这些地点犯罪问题,这将意味着长期的犯罪控制收益。此外,地点上的犯罪不能简单地认为是社区犯罪。关于地点犯罪基础研究表明,很多的犯罪行为发生在这些我们称之为犯罪地点的地理小单元上,而将注意力集中在巡逻区块、辖区或者社区等较大的地区,我们的犯罪预防工作就会失去效率和效能。最后,我们拥有的强大知识体系,既说明了影响犯罪和地点的因素,也成为警方针对犯罪热点开展犯罪预防工作的理论基础。

重要的是,这一基础研究,进一步地被警方有效应对地点犯罪的能力所印证并得以强化。一系列的随机实地试验表明,针对犯罪热点的警务能够有效地减少犯罪与治安混乱(Braga,2001,2005,2007)。其中的第一个实验,是明尼阿波利斯热点巡逻实验(Sherman and Weisburd,1995),用电脑绘制了报警电话地图,从而确定了大致街区般长度的110 处热点。10 个月的实验期间,警方在试验点平均增加了一倍多的巡逻警力。实验研究发现,与对照组相比,实验区的犯罪报警和可观察的治安混乱现象在统计学意义上显著下降。在另一项随机试验中,堪萨斯城毒品窝点打击实验(Sherman and Rogan,1995a),对毒品窝点的严打行动,被发现试验地区治安相对显著地改善,虽然这个影响(测量公民报警和犯罪报告)比较温和并在短时期内消退了。然而,在另一项随机试验中,埃克(Eck)和沃特尔(Wartell)(1996)发现,如果在专项行动之后,警方随即与业主接触,预防犯罪的收益可以得到加强,并会持续较长时间。

更多的常态犯罪和治安混乱效应在3 个其他随机的,为了解决犯罪热点的,更有针对性的,运用问题导向警务策略的测试实验中被报道出来。泽西市问题导向警务中关于暴力地方的试验中(Braga et al.,1999),相对于控制的热点,在干预的热点地区犯罪总数和报警电话数出现了具有统计学意义上的显著性下降。重要的是，所有犯罪的种类都减少了，同时观测到的数据显示，在社会治安秩序混乱程度方面也出现统计学意义上的显著下降。在泽西市毒品市场分析实验项目中（Weisburd and Green，1995a），热点警务战术在减低毒品犯罪热点地区的治安混乱方面比整体的执法行动更加有效。在奥克兰辖区健康研究中，马泽罗尔（Mazerolle）和罗尔（Rohl）（1998）也发现在针对特定涉毒地点开展民事责任赔偿性干涉项目的实验评估中，犯罪和治安混乱状况有较大的下降。

非实验性研究也提供了类似的结论。例如，堪萨斯城枪支项目评估（Sherman and Rogan，1995b）中发现热点警务模式有很强的犯罪控制收益。在由十个街区组成的八块区域内密集执法，包括交通拦截和搜查，谢尔曼（Sherman）和罗根（Rogan）（1995）发现与控制的对照组相比，实验组警方枪支查获率上升了65%，而涉枪犯罪减少了49%。侯博（Hope）（1994）检验了在密西西比州圣路易斯城（St. Louis，Missouri）内的三个毒品热点内依赖于传统的执法策略、依赖于电话求助的问题导向警务策略的效果。该评估对比实验区所在位置和街区相邻近地址上报警电话数和目标犯罪热点区域的全部报警电话数。侯博（Hope）（1994）发现，与对照组相比，实验区出现显著的犯罪下降。

这种严格的评估实验致使国家研究院委员会于2004年根据《警方政策和实践回顾研究》报告得出如下结论：

> 在过去二十年的警务实践中，研究者对打击具体的犯罪类型，罪犯和犯罪地点的研究已经有越来越多的兴趣。尤其是，犯罪热点警务已经成为减少犯罪和治安混乱问题的一种常用警务策略。虽然只有初步的证据支持针对罪犯特定类型的警务模式的成效，但是强大的证据体表明，采用聚焦地理方式应对犯罪问题，可以提高警务工作的效能（2004：35）。

对热点警务成效的进一步证据来自于由安东尼·布拉加（Anthony Braga）（2001，2005，2007）主持的康拜尔合作组织系统性评论。当适当地使用元分析方法提供对文献综述的统计学摘要（Lipsey and Wilson，2001）时，一项康拜尔评论要比一般陈述性评论涉及更为系统。为保持康拜尔的标准，只有那些分析比较了实施热点警务干预的地点和开展传统常规警务服务地点的研究，才算合格。

九项合格的研究被确定并列入康拜尔评论中，分别罗列如下：

1. 明尼阿波利斯同一地址重复呼叫警务项目（Sherman，Buerger，and Gartin，1989）*

2. 明尼阿波利斯热点巡逻项目（Sherman and Weisburd，1995）*

3. 泽西市毒品市场的分析项目（DMAP）（Weisburd and Green，1995a）*

4. 泽西市暴力地点的问题导向警务项目（（Braga *et al.*，1999）*

5. 圣路易斯三个毒品市场位置的问题导向警务研究（Hope，1994）

6. 堪萨斯城枪支项目（Sherman and Rogan，1995b）

7. 堪萨斯城警方毒品窝点专项行动项目（Sherman andRogan，1995a）*

8. 休斯敦目标性巡逻项目（Caeti,1999）

9. 澳大利亚宾利市服务电话项目（Criminal Justice Commission，1998）

　　这九项研究是在美国五个大城市和澳大利亚的一个郊区进行的。五个选定的研究采用了随机实验设计（在上面的清单中用星号表示出来的），四个使用非等效控制群的准实验设计。预防犯罪的干预措施通常有三种类型：问题导向警务的干预性执法，直接和积极的巡逻方案以及警方严打和专项行动（Braga，2001，2005，2007）。

　　康拜尔评论，着重报告了九个选中的研究中有七个出现犯罪和治安混乱的下降。由于准实验研究中项目效果报告的不一致性，只有随机试验被列入了康拜尔评论元分析中（Braga，2005，2007）。由于所有的热点警务实验都将公民的报警电话作为一种结果衡量，每项研究主要的效应大小均基于报警电话的统计报告计算得出。这些效果大小详见表4。

　　在泽西市暴力地点上问题导向警务实验中，与控制对照组相比，实验组中针对热点的警务干预效应量明显（2.05），同时具有统计学上的显著性。尽管该研究报告称有很大的效应量，但因为其样本量小、相应小的异方差而对整体元分析的影响一般。泽西市 DMAP 的实验干预也有很大的效应量（0.689），同时明尼阿波利斯热点巡逻实验干预有一定统计学意义上的显著效应量（0.322）。在商贸区的堪萨斯城警方毒品窝点专项行动项目和明尼阿波利斯同一地址重复呼叫警务项目有较小的非统计学意义上的显著效应，实验组的效应比控制对照组更大些（分别为2.19 和0.89）。在住宅区的明尼阿波利斯同一地址重复呼叫警务项目有着很微小的，不具有统计意义上的显著性差异，控制组的效应比实验组略高。

　　由于效应量被证实为不均分布，康拜尔评论采用随机效应元分析模型来计算所有研究中效应量的均值。总体而言，康拜尔评论发现，相对于控制对照组而言，热点警务干预减少了公民的报警求助电话（Braga，2005，2007）。六项热点警务干预研究的效应量平均值居于中等（0.345），呈现统计学意义的显著性。基于方法论的原因，当元分析中不包括明尼阿波利斯同一地址重复呼叫警务项目时，平均效应量变大（0.632），呈现统计学上的显著性。

表4　热点试验效应量元分析的主要结果

实验名称	效应量	标准差	异方差（%总比重）	95%置信区间
泽西市问题警务实验	2.05*	.504	3.93（1.8%）	高于3.04 低于1.06
泽西市毒品市场的分析项目	.689*	.275	13.21（6.0%）	高于1.23 低于.15
明尼阿波利斯热点巡逻项目	.322*	.142	27.15（12.3%）	高于.60 低于.044
堪萨斯城警方毒品窝点专项行动项目	.219	.139	51.32（23.3%）	高于.492 低于-.054
商务区明尼阿波利斯同一地址重复呼叫警务	.089	.127	62.49（28.3%）	高于.337 低于-.159
居民区明尼阿波利斯同一地址重复呼叫警务	-.009	.127	62.49（28.3%）	高于.238 低于-.256
所有研究的元分析	.345*	.150	总比重=220.59	高于.640 低于.058
除去明尼阿波利斯同一地址重复呼叫警务的所有研究的分析	.632*	.253	除去明尼阿波利斯同一地址重复呼叫警务的所有研究的分析的比重=95.61	高于1.13 低于.138

* $p < 0.05$。

随着康拜尔评论最新述评的出版,另一项有关热点警务犯罪预防效益评估的随机对照实验也已完成。在马萨诸塞州的洛威尔,一项随机对照实验评估了问题导向警务模式对治安混乱治理的效应。3/4的热点被匹配为17对,每对中的一个被分配到一个随机的街区试验中。效应影响评价结果显示,与控制对照组相比,在实验组中犯罪和治安混乱的求助报警电话在统计学意义上显著地减少20%。系统的观测数据分析还显示,与控制对照组相比,在社会治安混乱及环境混乱程度方面,实验组有显著的下降。

总之,热点警务得到了实证研究的广泛支持。一些实验和准实验的研究表明,对小而犯罪高发的地理区域重点布置警力,对犯罪和治安混乱状况的改善会产生积极和显著的影响。虽然热点警务得到了实证研究的强力支持,但是如果犯罪会简单地位移到邻近地区,该地点警务方式的有效性将大打折扣。有关犯罪位移效应问题,将在下一章中予以讨论。

八、犯罪是否只是转移了?

犯罪转移,是指在特定地域内打击特定种类犯罪会导致犯罪活动简单地转移到其他区域,或者以转换另一种作案方式,或者转换为另一种犯罪类型,从而使犯罪控制效益大大地减弱（Reppetto，1976）。这种关于警方解决地点犯罪的犯罪预防效能的观点，源于犯罪动机倾向理论，这些质疑被"机会减少对策"早期研究所证实（Clarke，1980；Gabor，1990）。比如，虽然纽约公交严格的票务制度减少了公交车上抢劫数量，但是相应的在地铁上的抢劫数量上升了（Chaiken，Lawless and Steveson，1974）。另外，警方对街面毒品市场传统的控制策略已被认为，在这种策略下犯罪易于在空间上、时间上及策略上发生位移（Caulkins，1992；Eck，1993；Sherman，1990）。

1990年以来，有关犯罪位移的报告见于四项重要的实证研究评论：即巴尔（Barr）和皮斯（Pease）（1990）；艾克（Eck）（1993）和何塞林（Hesseling）（1994）；以及固瑞特（Guerrtte）和博尔（Bower）（2009）等研究。该四项研究评论的区别在于其综合性方面。巴尔和皮斯将他们的研究限定在英国，艾克评述了美国、加拿大、英国及其他一些国家共33份英文版的研究。何塞林（Hesseling）检索了来自北美、欧洲还有一些其他地区共55份用英文及荷兰文版本的研究。固瑞特（Guerrtte）和博尔（Bower）系统评论了102份有关情境犯罪预防的研究。所有的这四项研究评论得出三个基本结论：第一，很少有证据证实犯罪预防措施会导致转移犯罪与被预防的犯罪一样多；第二，当犯罪转移发生时，其规模往往要小于被预防的犯罪；第三，在有关犯罪转移的犯罪控制评估报告中，常见的发现就是，所谓的犯罪转移并无证据支持。总的来说，大部分的研究没有或者很少发现犯罪转移。

但是，我们在考虑以上这些结果的时候，一定要在同时考虑以下几个重要的附加条件：第一，犯罪转移的数量，一定程度上取决于我们使用的犯罪干预手段。比如，何塞林指出目标的固化比途径控制将转移更多的犯罪。第二，犯罪转移的数量，一定程度上取决于被预防的犯罪和违法行为。比如艾克（Eck）指出，贩毒相对于其他类型的犯罪要更容易转移（尽管威斯勃德（Weisburd）和格林（Green）在1995年得出相反的结论）并且几种特定的毒品市场对于犯罪转移特别敏感。第三，也是最重要的，因这些研究并没有着手去检测犯罪转移，所以这些评估专家很少采用有研究设计的方法论去检测这些犯罪转移（Weisburd and Green 1995）。对这一相对生僻的研究，研究人员必须要善于分配研究基金和资源。如果研究者对一项研究的犯罪控制直接效益不明确的话，那么把研究资金放在评估目标的直接效益要比仅仅评估目标是否有效更为合理。

犯罪在空间上的转移对于地点警务而言是一种直接而重大的威胁。假如犯罪会因为警方在一个热点上打击犯罪而转移，那么实施热点警务也就显得没什么意义了。本次研究中针对热点警务的证据是十分充足和强大的。仅有少量的证据证明犯罪会转移到附近的热点去。确实，一系列的研究表明，克拉克和威斯勃德(Clarke and Weisburd)所描述的"犯罪预防收益扩散"会延伸到附近的热点区域。在这样的情况下，我们在犯罪控制上取得的收益看起来似乎是扩散到了热点所在的周边区域了。

比如在泽西市毒品市场分析研究中(Weisburd and Green,1995a)，测量了每一个热点周边两个街区之内的毒品市场的犯罪转移，并没有发现明显的犯罪或者治安违法行为的报警发生转移。更重要的是，调查者发现在转移区域跟毒品有关的或者公共道德有关的报警数量明显减少了。像这样类似的"犯罪预防收益的扩散"在新泽西暴力犯罪地点实验(Braga,1999)和堪萨斯城枪支计划(Sherman and Rogan,1995b)中也同样被发现了。在每项研究中，都没有报告发现犯罪的转移，相反，在附近区域内发现了治安情况好转的现象。只有侯博(Hope,1994)的研究报告了直接的犯罪转移，尽管这一现象仅仅出现在直接实验地点并且转移的效应在总体上要比犯罪预防效应小很多。名为"康拜尔"的系统评论，描述了九个研究中五个研究的犯罪转移数据，没有发现犯罪在空间上从目标区域大量快速地转移到附近区域(Braga,2001，2005,2007)的现象。

随着更多的注意力被转移到了犯罪转移上，方法论上的问题及其度量方法也被不断地重新审视(Weisburd and Green,1995,特例请见 Barr and Pease,1990 和 Pease,1991)。这并不是说犯罪转移未被研究，只是说对犯罪转移或犯罪效益扩散的实证检测已经成为其他研究的副产品。通常，对有关犯罪转移或效益扩散的认识，往往从以创新性犯罪预防项目效果为出发点的研究中得到。问题是，用于直接衡量项目效应的研究设计在度量犯罪转移或效益扩散时，通常会遇到比较重大的方法论问题(Weisburd and Green,1995b)。

威斯勃德(Weisburd)和他的同事在最近的一份针对贩毒和卖淫市场进行热点警务干预的研究中，将犯罪的空间转移和扩散作为首要的研究目标，并有力地揭示了针对警察的打击犯罪为什么不会简单地转移的本质。为了准确地衡量转移和扩散效应，采集了实验地区和下游区域，大约目标区域周边两个街区范围里大量数据。本次实验使用了超过6000 的 20 分钟的对实验地点社会观察，并以实验地段被逮捕者的访谈及人类学田野观察作为补充。

大量旨在检验犯罪热点的定量研究表明，警方在本地区形式严厉的打击并不会导致犯罪简单的转移。实际上，该研究认为在一个地区如此集中的犯罪预防工作很可能会给周边地区带来犯罪效益扩散。这一观点在图 8 里得到说明，图 8 展示了在研究时间段内实验区域以及下游转移区域内卖淫现象的动态监测数据。在此，同威斯勃德(Weisburd)在其他研究中发现的结论一样，在目标区域内实施高强度的犯罪预防措施后,其周边区域的犯罪数量并没有提高。反而是下游区域的犯罪变化呈现出了与目标区域相似的趋势,即表现为犯罪控制收益的扩散效应。

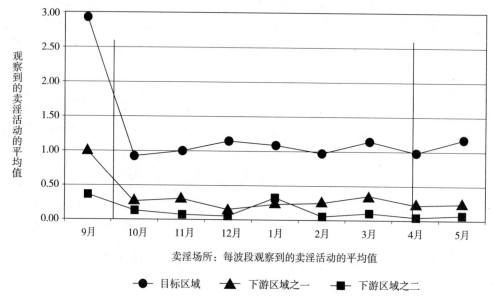

图8　在目标区域以及下游转移区域观察卖淫事件

注:黑色的垂直线表明警方干预的开始和结束的区段。
来源:Weisburd *et al.*,(2006)。

　　一项有关人类学田野研究及对被逮捕者的访谈,重新强化了常规行为和理性选择的观点,并用于解释为什么犯罪空间转移的证据是少之又少。理性选择理论,即就犯罪活动的效益而言,强调努力、风险、机会之间平衡关系(Clarke and Cornish,1985,2001)。威斯勃德等人(Weisburd *et al.*)在2006年收集的定性数据,又进一步表明了犯罪的空间移动会使违法者增加付出和风险。

　　一些被访谈的犯罪人抱怨说被警方干预之后,要重建他们的犯罪王国是多么的困难。比如,一个在毒品犯罪现场被抓住的人就曾解释说,犯罪其实是很难转移的,因为"钱是不一样的"。或者说他"若再从摸爬滚打开始",那样的话就会"需要很长的时间去积累客户群"。此外,害怕被害也是防止犯罪空间转移的重要因素。套用一位卖淫女浅显的话来讲,处于安全的考虑,"常规"是很重要的。

　　"如果这是反常规的,我会尝试去弄清楚,我会采取预防措施。我从不和两个男人上一部车。我每次都会提前检查客户的门锁确保在必要的时候能顺利逃出,比如发生紧急情况的时候或者说某个男人想要伤害我的时候。我总是去我熟悉的地方,这样假如我在需要帮助的时候我就会知道如何寻求帮助。但是,同样,我从来不去那些会暴露并使我被捕的地方。简单的讲,我不让男人们带着我去他们想去的地方。假如他们坚持,我就会要他们在拉下拉链之前先付钱(Brisgone,2004:129)。"

另一个受访者解释说,去镇上其他地方卖淫也很困难的,因为其他妓女会生气,并且告诉她,"这是我们的地盘,请你离开"。类似的拒绝犯罪转移的证据,在采访抓获的毒品犯也有所见。贩毒者与他们做交易的地方紧密联系,也是防止犯罪转移的重要机制之一。许多贩毒者解释说,你做生意的地方就在你住的附近,因为那是你的"地盘"。一位被抓住的人还解释说,"你真不能在不是你居住的地方做交易,因为那儿不是你的地盘"。那也是他们为什么会在那儿被杀死(Weisburd *et al.*,2006:578)。

理性选择理论的另一个重要观点是:影响犯罪人和非犯罪人的因素往往是相似的(Cornish and Clarke,1986)。这一观点已经是成为许多重要的犯罪学观点(Akers,1973;Sutherland,1947),但是在识别犯罪个体和将犯罪人从非犯罪人中区分出来时,该理论观点常常被人忘记(Weisburd and Waring,2001)。犯罪人不情愿犯罪位移的重要原因,和正常人一样,他们总是觉得在自己的地盘和熟悉的人打交道更为舒适。对常人而言,搬房子或调工作,是对人们生活环境重要而艰难的改变。例如,一位妓女曾解释道:

"我路过(墓地或公墓),我没想赚钱。这对我来说是陌生的。就像,就像……我不熟悉的地方。我不认识这些家伙(客户们)。你认不出这些人。我知道在外面的每一天(陌生环境中),那些汽车,那些张脸,都是不同的。我在自己的地盘上,我认识他们。而当我在这'小山坡上'——我真的不认识镇上那头的人(Brisgone,2004:199)。"

虽然这些数据强化了常规活动与理性选择理论的观点,帮助我们理解了为什么威斯勃德等人(Weisburd *et al.*)在他们的研究很少观察到犯罪位移,但是他们并没有解释在卖淫和毒品犯罪地区为什么出现明显的犯罪控制效益扩散现象。即使有很好的理由解释若犯罪人不会转移其他地方作案,比如类似的犯罪机会不会出现,而反会使犯罪风险增加,但是为什么这些地点上的犯罪和违法活动在逐渐下降呢?

威斯勃德等人(Weisburd *et al.*)认为,他们观察到威慑在犯罪控制效益扩散中起着关键作用(Clarke and Weisburd,1994)①。在采访那些在特定目标区域被捕的犯罪

① 对邻近区域犯罪控制效益的另外一种解释是"无能力"。在目标地区的很多犯罪者都被逮捕了,如果说他们与邻近区域的犯罪有关的话,那么我们也许能观察到这些地区的犯罪和违法在下降。然而,尽管目标区域内执法活动密集,但在整个研究时间段中,很多的犯罪人还是一直活跃着。妓女们很少会被延长监禁,很多被逮捕后只会离开街区一至两天。在毒品热点区域进行的"暴力犯罪清除项目",旨在通过建立长效机制清除毒品热点上暴力犯罪,然而只有很少一部分犯罪人在该项目中会被起诉。

人时,他们发现这些人对警察活动的地域范围并不清楚。他们的这种认知,可以从一个称之为"学习曲线"的术语中认识到(Brisgone,2004)。尽管如此,定性数据表明,犯罪人在作案时是基于一种被理性选择理论称之为"固定理性"(Johnson and Payne,1986),他们对警方采取行动的判断往往受制于有限或不正确的信息。在这种情形下,他们通常认为警方的严打行动不仅仅针对有限的目标区域的,而只是警方大规模执法活动的一部分而已。

在史密斯(Smith)、克拉克(Clarke)和皮斯(Pease)(2002)主持的情境犯罪预防研究述评中,也发现了支持该论点的证据。在分析了"预期性犯罪预防效益"现象后,他们发现在研究评述中约40%报告犯罪在警方干预行动开始前就已经下降了。史密斯(Smith)和她的同事们认为,犯罪预防收益首先源于警方干预行动的"宣传"或"假情报"影响。他们推测,媒体对警务干预行动的前期报道,警务干预行动的准备工作(如,安装闭路电视),或者对警察干预行动的道听途说,使得潜在犯罪人认为犯罪的风险和代价上升了。在威斯勃德等人(Weisburd *et al.*)(2006)的研究中,可能存在着相似"假情报"过程,这些"假情报"有些来自那些目标区域犯罪人自己对警方行动的观察,有些源自于被警方打击的犯罪人,而有些则出自社区中其他人员。

现在证据强有力地反驳了所谓集中打击犯罪地点的行动会因犯罪位移而收效甚微的认识。事实上,与地点警务紧密相关的有关犯罪空间位移的证据,有力地支持了热点警务有助于犯罪预防效益扩散到犯罪热点邻近区域。

九、减少法律的束缚,减少对犯罪人的逮捕和监禁

警察经常抱怨在与罪犯的斗争中,他们被困住了手脚。虽然法律对警务工作的不断约束备受争议(Bittner,1967;Ohlin and Remington,1993;NRC,2004;Vollmer,1933;Wickersham Commission,1931;Wilson,1950),但可以肯定的是,地点警务为警务干预活动提供了新的路径,可以较少地受制于传统法律的限制。普通法和法律传统更关注于个人权利的而不是地点上的权利保护。但并不是说警察在地点上就可以为所欲为了,确切地说,就地点的权利保护而言,宪法和程序保障就不那么严格了。

当地点被视作犯罪目标或投入特殊保护时,由于开展的合法化执法行动要比针对个体犯罪人容易得多。例如,丹·可汗(Dan Kahan)和特雷西·马尔斯(Tracey Meares)(1998:1172)提到,执法官员们"不必获得搜查证或合理的怀疑……就可执行停车检查或对所有进入机场或者政府大楼的人员进行搜身"。这就意味着,在公

共安全作为核心问题的某些地点,警方可以开展一些在其他一些地方个体所不能接受的警务活动。犯罪聚集之地经常被视为符合这一标准的,例如许多城市将毒品市场设定为公众应特别小心的区域。还有学校安全区域,警方可以被允许实施特别的行动,因为这里有潜在的、脆弱的受害者。宪法问题十分复杂,警方对每个案件不能在任何情况下简单地介入。尽管如此,政治家、法官,事实上包括普通市民均直觉地认为,警察在应对一些具体问题时,如犯罪聚集之处,同时又获得居民的支持的时候,应当被赋予适当的自由裁量权。

相应的,地点警务为警方开展犯罪预防策略时减少了执法的约束(Weisburd,2008)。但更重要的是,它还为警方提供了威胁更少,长期来说更人性化的一种犯罪预防策略。为使地点警务模式更为成功,警务人员有必要意识到他们的工作目标是地点而不是个人。民事法律要比执法活动更能成功地对地点犯罪进行干预。(Mazerolle and Roehl,1998)正如切赫(Cheh)已经观察到的(1991:1329),"警察、检察官多采用民事策略,不仅因为他们认为扩张武力可以制止反社会行为,官员还认为,民事救济能提供快速的解决方案——这些方案不受与刑事审判相关的宪法保护的限制。无论是因为何种原因,犯罪预防的战术将从那些依靠刑法转移到那些依靠民事或行政法律上来,最终的结果是,当今犯罪预防将减少依靠逮捕和监禁罪犯的传统执法方式"。

美国在过去的三十年中,监禁的比例一直在急速扩展,并有证据表明,监禁率在其他西方国家也正在上升(Walmsley,2009)。美国监狱的支出增长率超过教育和医疗支出增长速度的两倍。道德成本是指总共230万美国人关在监狱或拘留所(West and Sabol,2008),牢房内都是没有人性和堕落的。地点警务强调减少地点的犯罪机会,而不是在等罪行发生,然后逮捕他们。在地点上成功的犯罪预防项目,不会导致大量的逮捕行动,特别是在方法得当的时候,例如,通过"第三方警务"使得犯罪人不想犯罪(Mazerolle and Ransley,2005)。这样一来,地点警务为犯罪预防提供了一种策略:既可以提高公众的安全感,又可以降低监禁人数和经济成本。

如果地点警务成为警务活动的重点,而不是逮捕和拘留罪犯,我们将同时看到监禁人员的减少和预防犯罪效能的增加。

十、认识地点警务中警察合法性的重要性

基础研究和应用研究支持基于地点警务在预防犯罪上的潜力和机会。基于地点

警务还为警察进行预防犯罪减少了法律约束。然而,警务的效果又有赖于公众对警察行为合法性的感知(NRC, 2004; Tyler, 1990, 2004)。即使警察可以降低犯罪率,如果警方的行动在社区难以被接受的话,那么就很难说地点警务是成功的。

众所周知,有关地点警务对警民关系的影响缺乏研究评估。这种认识上的差距对地点警务尝试者而言意义重大,因为许多观察家认为热点警务所开展的卓有成效的犯罪预防努力会造成警民关系的潜在伤害(Meares, 2006; Rosenbaum, 2006; Taylor, 2006; Weisburd and Braga, 2006b)。如果公众对警察的信任和信心正在减弱,那么警察预防犯罪的能力就会因法律诉讼而弱化,服从法律意愿也会降低,还有失去现有的合作伙伴关系的可能(Tyler, 1990, 2004)。非法的警务活动所导致的政治后果将极大妨碍警察部门在犯罪控制策略上的创新。

有一些证据表明,居住在引起警方关注区域内的民众欢迎警方在治安乱点开展重点治乱行动(McGarrell, Chermak, Weiss, and Wilson, 2001; Shaw, 1995)。在对堪萨斯城枪支项目的单独检查(Sherman and Rogan, 1995b)中发现,社区坚决支持加强巡逻,并感受到了通过邻里的治理生活质量得到了改善。然而,该研究并没有试图度量那些被警察拦下并搜查的人对该干预项目的感受。

丹尼斯·罗生鲍姆(Dennis Rosenbaum)(2006)认为,热点警务因其在操作层面常被定义为在特殊区域开展咄咄逼人的执法活动,而存在弱化警民关系的风险。罗生鲍姆(Rosenbaum)(2006)认为热点警务可以很容易被当作"零容忍"警务来操作,因为这种方法对警察来说很容易采用。不加区分的咄咄逼人的策略会使警察与社区关系受到损害,社区会开始感觉自己像目标而非伙伴:

> 因为警察已经决定先将铲除"坏蛋"作为警务战略的重点,将自己置身于"好"与"坏"之间的"淡蓝色线",这些策略会使社区的一些成员对抗另一些成员,就像"好"的居民被要求成为"线人",做警察的"耳目"。父母、兄弟姐妹及帮派成员的弟兄们会感觉到忠诚不在,仿佛被夹在交火之中(Rosenbaum, 2006:253)。

罗生鲍姆(Rosenbaum)(2006)提出了一个问题,即在少数民族社区持续的执法是否将有助于纠正少数民族偏高的监禁率。不考虑采用什么样具体的途径或者战术,热点警务将增加小区域内警民接触的机会。在这些区域里,警方行动将会极大地影响居住在犯罪热点地区成员对犯罪预防的支持度和参与性。最大限度地提高警方在这些地区应对犯罪问题的能力,警察管理者应致力于确保公平的警民互动、加强社区成员之间合作关系,该策略成功应用于推杆警务(Braga and Winship, 2006; Kennedy, 2006)当中。尽管困难重重,但是促使社区参与犯罪预防的长期努力,对改进警民关系、加强犯罪预防的合作将大有裨益。

对特定犯罪热点街区开展集中整治,为警察与社区内那些易受害的、曾经感到过犯罪恐惧、因严峻的犯罪或治安问题使得生活质量严重下降的成员们建立良好关系,提供了良好契机。令人遗憾的是,这些社区民众往往就是那些用怀疑眼光看待警察,质疑警方在他们居住的社区所实施犯罪控制行为合法性的人。从这个意义上讲,犯罪率高的区域内的居民和企业主代表了社区中对警务人员不满和不信任的"热点"。如果警方希望改善他们与社区成员关系,从"热点"中的居民和企业主着手,似乎合乎逻辑。就像犯罪、糟糕的警民关系,并非充斥于城市的每一个角落。如果警察能赢得热点地区长期遭受犯罪居民的民心和支持,比起在更多的治安稳定的邻里社区搞好警务关系,对城市警察执法的总体合法性会产生更大的影响,因为在治安相对稳定的社区里人们更可能普遍地对警察服务有好感了。

以理解警方策略的有效性为例,在问题地区预防犯罪工作中,警察对公民如何看待警察执法合法性的潜在影响力,很大程度上取决于警务策略的选择和热点地区的具体环境。泛泛的以及不加区分的执法行动似乎会恶化警察和热点地区居民之间的关系。我们相信,警察应采取综合治理的措施来控制犯罪热点,而不仅仅是依赖一种密集的打击活动。当然,逮捕犯罪分子是警察职责的核心,仍然应当作为处置犯罪热点的一个非常重要的手段。但是将社区警务和问题导向警务的原则融入到地点警务当中,我们相信能够使那些饱受犯罪和治安混乱之苦的民众提升对警察合法性的认识(Braga and Weisburd,2010;Mastrofski,Braga,and Weisburd,2010;Taylor,2006)。

十一、基于地点警务的意图

是什么让我们必须转而实施全面的基于地点警务战略?一个重要认识是,事实上警方一直在关注着地点。卡罗林·布鲁克(Carolyn Block)(1998:28)谈及警方对于犯罪地图的兴趣时说:"犯罪地图并不是什么新鲜事。自从标针被发明之后它就安在了警察局长桌子后边的墙壁上。"此外,在过去的十年里,热点警务也成为美国警务中的一种常见模式。威斯勃德(Weisburd)和鲁姆(Lum)(2005)在最近的一项研究中发现,调查样本中的125个配置100名或以上警员的警察局中,有62%已运用计算机犯罪地图这项技术。其中,有80%的警察局声称已经开展犯罪热点分析,有三分之二的警察局将热点警务作为巡逻策略。2007年"警察执行研究论坛(PERF,

2008）"的一项研究发现,192个警察局中有74%将"打击犯罪热点"作为应对暴力犯罪的一项战略。在过去十年间,计算机统计战略(Compstat)已被美国的一些大规模警察机构所普遍采用(Weisburd, Mas-trofski, McNally, and Greenspan, 2001; Weisburd, Mastrofski, McNally, Greenspan, and Willis, 2003)。计算机统计战略不仅仅是针对集中警力打击特定目标和提高组织控制力及职责的一项创新,同时也是激发犯罪地理分析的一项创新。

然而,推进基于地点警务战略,需要一些更激进的措施,而不是简单地主张警方向警务干预篮子里添加一项新战略。若要使基于地点警务战略取得成功,警察必须从认识犯罪和预防犯罪的高度改变犯罪分析单位。当下的警务,仍然是将人视为警务工作的中心。这反映在警察是如何收集数据,如何组织警务活动。基于地点警务战略要求在警力结构上作出根本性改革以解决犯罪和其他社区问题。

例如,警方数据历来关注于罪犯及其特征上。事实上,基于地点的标识并非主要来源于事件、逮捕,或者报警电话数据库。在80年代后期,研究者试图用警方数据库分析犯罪地点,但常常无力查明犯罪会在哪儿发生。通常存在着类似的地址有多个名称的现象,有的根据实际地址命名,而有些则是以该地址上的商店或其他机构的一些名称来命名的。这种名称标识往往包括可能的地址排列,但这些地址标识符经常不能确定该地址城市的具体方位。在过去的十年间,警方已能够更精确地查明犯罪地点,一方面是因为记录管理系统的重大改进,另一方面得益于地理信息系统的发展。但令人不解的是,大多数警局的警察们只能从数据库中识别非常简单的地址信息。

就逮捕数据库而言,很容易收集到罪犯年龄、性别、教育程度和其他人口统计方面的特征。但这种数据库很少能用来提供警务活动背景性质的信息。成功的基于地点警务项目需要警察经常掌握有关地点的丰富数据。我们需要像了解罪犯一样了解犯罪热点地区。这种资料应定期提供给警察用于开展对特定地点集中警务干预。若不能定期收集这些数据,或从其他机构获得该数据,将限制警方开展有效的地点警务战略的能力。布鲁克(Block)和格林(Green)(1994)强调了诸如地理档案(GEORCHIVE)等数据库的重要性。伊利诺伊州刑事司法信息管理局将地理档案库(GEORCHIVE)发展成为一个全面的社区地理数据库和执法数据。这些收集的数据包括:街道地图数据,官方犯罪数据(求助、逮捕、罪犯特点,受害者特点),监狱数据(犯人执行缓刑或假释的地址),地标性数据(例如:公园,学校,公交车站,酒类专卖店,废弃的建筑物),以及人口信息(Block,1998)。

用传统的以人为中心的警务模式去收集用于基于地点警务战略数据的失败在

于,警官们对掌握他们的警员身在何处缺乏兴趣。虽然追踪警察巡逻方位的技术,如机动车自动定位技术已有数十年了,但是在美国很少有警察局使用该技术来提高警务效能。例如,有关犯罪会在哪儿发生和警察应在哪儿巡逻的认识可为提升特别警务战略效益提供重要基础。追踪警察出警的能力也可用来确保将稀缺的警力资源派到需要的地方。目前警务基金会正在与美国得克萨斯州达拉斯警察局合作,开展创新项目以达到这些目标。在一定程度上,警方推进地点警务战略之所以失败,原因在于这项技术直到现在才开始被应用到犯罪预防的实务之中。

如今,警务地理机构还没认识到地点在警务策略发展中的重要性。向大辖区和巡区布置警力,警方的假设是犯罪通常在大范围地理层面上被发现的。

辖区和巡区很少能够匹配像社区这般大的地理单位这一现象已经饱受争议,这种划分肯定不太适合作为地点警务的地理单位。也许,警方应考虑根据一定时期内在微观地点上具有相似犯罪水平和犯罪趋势来划分巡逻力量。如此地点上的警力重组,应将重点放在战略思维和调动资源上以解决普遍性问题。以地点为基础的警务中重组警力还可以采取其他不同的形式,但有一点是很清楚的,如今的辖区或巡区与我们所了解的犯罪地理分布以及犯罪集中在相对比较小的犯罪地点上这一情形并不匹配。

针对地点开展警务,我们应从以逮捕和起诉犯罪者为重心向减少地点上犯罪机会转变。警察过于专注于执法并非是个新主意,赫尔曼·戈尔茨坦(Herman Goldstein)在1979年在介绍问题导向警务时就提出了该中心思想。过去三十年里,戈尔茨坦(Goldstein)和其他人试图让警察少侧重于逮捕和对犯罪人的起诉而是更关注于解决犯罪问题。但是这些呼吁充其量只能是部分地被警方听取了,而且有证据表明执法、逮捕罪犯仍然是警务工作中的首要手段,甚至在某些警务创新项目中也是如此(Braga and Weisburd,2006)。在警察文化中,以人为基础的警务仍然占据主导,警官们也很自然地继续把工作重点放在罪犯和逮捕罪犯上。

基于地点警务为警务重点的转移创造了机遇,因为该战略将犯罪预防程式的中心置于犯罪地点而不是犯罪人。它将警方工作中心由简单的处理犯罪人转移到了改善地点。在此背景下,对成功犯罪预防工作的评价不在于警察逮捕多少犯罪,而是是否让人们在这些地方生活、参观或工作更加安全了。地点警务要求警方扩展传统警务执法的手段。在此背景下,地点警务不仅要求警方关注犯罪地点、罪犯人、受害者,而且还要关注潜在的非警力型保安力量。如果警察的目标是提高地点的安全,那么对地点的警务活动将很自然地关注埃克(Eck)等人所提出的"地点管理者"概念(Eck,1994;Eck and Wartell,1996)。"第三方警务"(Mazerolle and Ransley,2005)也自然而然地成为地点警务的一部分。但从更广义上讲,地点警务让警察将其注意力扩展到了全体公众以及作为犯罪问题一部分的具体环境。

在倡导地点警务的同时,很重要的一点是,警察不应该放弃对犯罪活动中人的关注。人不应该被忽视,但应该将其置于犯罪发生的具体环境之中。说人不应该成为犯罪方程的中心并不意味着它们不是犯罪方程的一部分。不同在于如何让警方更好地收集整理信息并做好犯罪预防工作。此外,可能会有一些犯罪行为,以关注个体为中心可能会比关注地点更好地理解犯罪,这也应是我们在理解地点警务时候的一个重要考量。尽管对累犯和重复被害人的犯罪预防工作的有效性尚缺乏有力的科学证据,但是有一点很清楚,高频犯罪人和受害人群体应成为警方特别关注的对象。

十二、结　论

基本的研究表明,犯罪活动发生在非常小的地理分析单位上,如街段或小的街段群。相对于不断变动的刑事犯罪人,地点为警方干预提供了稳定的目标。地点上的犯罪并不是简单地指大区域或社区的犯罪;事实上,基本的研究证据表明许多犯罪活动发生在非常小的地理单位上。基本的研究还强化了这么一种观念:地点特征会受到警务活动的影响,并与地点上的犯罪紧密相关。但基于地点的警务并不仅仅来自于基础研究。有强有力的实验证据证明基于地点警务的有效性。此外,研究还表明,基于地点警务不会简单地导致犯罪位移。事实上,现有证据表明,这种警务干预措施更有可能导致附近地区的犯罪控制效益扩散。

研究还表明,现在已到了从基于人的警务向基于地点的警务模式转变的时候了。尽管这种战略转变在很大程度上是过去十几年以来战略趋势的一种演进,它会彻底改变警务活动中对数据采集的要求、警察活动组织,尤其彻底转变警察的整体世界观。在如今,缉拿罪犯仍然成为警察们眼中警务工作的真正重点。现在是时候来改变这种世界观的时候了,要让警方意识到预防犯罪的关键是对地点上的犯罪实施改造。

[参考文献见英文原作]

（金　诚　吴胜淼　译）

The Importance of Place in Policing Empirical Evidence and Policy Recommendations

David Weisburd

Hebrew University

Cody W. Telep

George Mason University

Anthony A. Braga

Harvard University

with

Elizabeth R. Groff

Temple University

Joshua C. Hinkle

Georgia State University

Cynthia Lum

George Mason University

Nancy A. Morris

Southern Illinois University

Laura A. Wyckoff

University of Maryland

Sue-Ming Yang

Georgia State University

FOREWORD

The role of the police in today's society involves a range of different tasks. These include maintaining public order and public safety, providing citizens with protection and assistance, investigating crimes and arresting offenders. The police also have a central role to play in the field of crime prevention.

This latter aspect of the police's role, i. e. the work of crime prevention, is sometimes neglected, not least because it leads neither to larger numbers of offenders being prosecuted and convicted, nor to any visible improvements in the clearance rate. However, the police's crime prevention role is important from the perspective of both crime victims and the cost of crime to society. More effective crime prevention work on the part of the police would mean fewer crime victims and would also greatly reduce the social costs of crime.

Research that can provide new knowledge about how the police can improve their effectiveness in the field of crime prevention is therefore very important. It is also important that the results of this research are disseminated to relevant groups both within and outside the police service.

In this report, which has been commissioned by the Swedish National Council for Crime Prevention (Brå), Professor David Weisburd and his colleagues summarise the results from an exciting and still relatively new field of research with great potential to improve the effectiveness of the police's crime prevention work. The authors present research which describes from both empirical and theoretical perspectives how the police can produce substantial crime prevention effects by directing their focus at small, well-defined locations with high levels of crime. The research findings presented in this report also strongly indicate that place-based policing of this kind can prevent crime using considerably less resources than more traditional policing methods.

It can sometimes be difficult however to get large organisations such as the police to adopt new ways of thinking. The authors of the report note for example that this new approach to policing may require relatively extensive changes to how the police view the central goals of police work. Amongst other things, it would mean measuring success not only in terms of how many people are arrested by the police but also in terms of whether places become safer for the people who visit, live or work in them.

The report can thus be viewed not only as a description of a strategy for more effective crime prevention work within the police service, but also as a challenge to the police to open up to the opportunities that may result from adopting new ways of thinking about and structuring their role as a central actor in the field of crime prevention.

Stockholm in May 2010

Jan Andersson

Director General

INTRODUCTION

Crime prevention research and policy have traditionally been focused on offenders or potential offenders (Weisburd, 1997, 2002). Researchers have looked to define strategies that would deter individuals from involvement in crime or rehabilitate them so they would no longer want to commit criminal acts. In recent years crime prevention efforts have often focused on the incapacitation of high-rate or dangerous offenders so they are not free to victimize law-abiding citizens. In the public debate over crime prevention policies, these strategies are usually defined as competing approaches. However, they have in common a central assumption about crime prevention research and policy: that efforts to understand and control crime must begin with the offender. In all of these approaches, the focus of crime prevention is on people and their involvement in criminality.

Police practices are also focused primarily on people. They often begin with a response to citizens who call the police. They are focused on identifying offenders who commit crimes, and end with the arrests of those offenders and their processing through the criminal justice system. Police attention is also directed at times to broader community problems and "community caretaking" (Kahan and Meares, 1998; Mastrofski, 1999), and the police are expected to play a role in securing communities in emergencies and more recently in response to homeland security threats (Waddington and Neyroud, 2007). But despite the broader mandate of the police, the core practices of policing assume that people, whether victims or offenders, are the key units of police work.

In this monograph we will argue that the police can be more effective if they shift the primary concerns of policing from people to places. Such a shift is already underway in American policing where place has begun to be seen as an important focus of police crime prevention efforts (Koper, 2008; Weisburd and Lum, 2005). But even in the U. S. , people and not places remain the central concern of policing. By place, we do not mean large geographic units such as neighborhoods or communities that have commonly been the focus of criminologists concerned with crime prevention (see Bursik and Webb, 1982; Sampson, Raudenbush, and Earls, 1997; Shaw and McKay, 1942 [1969]), or the beats and precincts that have been key to the organization of policing. Places in this context are specific locations within the larger social environments of communities and neighborhoods (Eck and Weisburd, 1995). They may be defined as buildings or addresses (see Green, 1996; Sherman, Gartin, and Buerger, 1989), as block faces or street segments (see Sherman and Weisburd, 1995; Taylor, 1997), or as clusters of addresses, block faces or street segments that have common crime problems (see Block, Dabdoub, and Fregly, 1995; Weisburd and Green, 1995a).

The strategies of place-based policing can be as simple as hot spots patrol, as was the case in the Minneapolis Hot Spots Policing Experiment (Sherman and Weisburd, 1995), where the police intervention involved placing more patrol resources at places where crime was concentrated. But place-based policing can also take a much more complex approach to the amelioration of crime problems. In the Jersey City Drug Market Analysis Project (Weisburd and Green, 1995a), for example, a three-step program (including identifying and analyzing problems, developing tailored responses, and maintaining crime control gains) was used to reduce problems at drug hot spots. In the Jersey City Problem-Oriented Policing Project (Braga, Weisburd, Waring, Mazerolle, Spelman, and Gajewski, 1999), a problem-oriented policing approach was taken in developing a specific strategy for each of the small areas defined as violent crime hot spots.

Why should police reorient the strategies and organization of policing to be more concerned with place? Why should place-based policing become a core approach in police efforts to control crime and disorder? In this monograph we present the case for place-based policing drawing from an emerging body of basic and applied evidence that suggests that policing places is efficient and effective. We begin in the next section by tracing the emergence of crime places in crime prevention in the 1980s, and then in the third section, we present basic research on crime and place that shows that crime is concentrated in cities in crime hot spots. This is a key finding in the justification of place-based policing, because it provides a logic for focusing police resources on small areas, rather than spreading them widely across the city. But even if crime is concentrated at place, if it simply shifts from place to place in a city it would not present a stable focus for police crime prevention efforts. The fourth section of our monograph describes the strong stability of crime at place, as contrasted with the instability of criminal offending. We then show in the fifth section how basic research on the geographic distribution of crime places supports strongly the need to focus in on hot spots of crime, rather than larger geographic units such as neighborhoods or communities. Finally, in section six we present emerging research on the correlates of crime at place that suggests the salience of place-based interventions.

Importantly, the case for policing places is not simply derived from basic research, but also includes strong applied evidence of the effectiveness of place-based policing. The seventh section of our monograph reviews the empirical literature on place-based or hot spots policing and shows that police interventions targeted at micro places can reduce crime and disorder at places. But doesn't the reduction of crime at one place simply lead to the shifting of crime to other places in a city? While this idea of displacement of crime has in the past been a strong barrier to the development of place-based policing (see Reppetto, 1976), recent empirical evidence described in section eight shows that it is not a major threat to the crime prevention benefits of place-based programs. Indeed, the research suggests just the opposite-that place-based policing is more likely to lead to a "diffusion of crime prevention benefits" (Clark and Weisburd, 1994) than displacement of crime. In the following two sections we argue that there are strong potential legal and societal benefits of focusing on places as opposed to offenders, but that police must begin to pay greater attention to the "legitimacy" of police interventions at places. Finally, recognizing that it is not enough to simply argue in favor of place-based policing, we conclude by suggesting practical ways in which the police must change to effectively implement place-based approaches. Of course, in advancing new approaches, the police in the field will adopt and innovate as they identify new problems and opportunities. Police over the last two decades have shown a remarkable degree of interest in innovation to advance police practices (National Research Council [NRC], 2004; Weisburd and Braga, 2006a). Place-based policing represents a natural progression in such efforts to improve policing.

THE EMERGENCE OF CRIME PLACES IN CRIME PREVENTION

While the traditional focus of research and theory in criminology has been on individuals and communities (Nettler, 1978; Sherman, 1995), criminologists recognized from the outset that the situational opportunities provided by specific places or contexts can impact upon the occurrence of crime. Edwin Sutherland, for example, whose main focus was upon the learning processes that bring offenders to participate in criminal behavior, noted in his classic criminology textbook that the immediate situation influences crime in many ways. For example, "a thief may steal from a fruit stand when the owner is not in sight but refrain when the owner is in sight; a bank burglar may attack a bank which is poorly protected but refrain from attacking a bank protected by watchmen and burglar alarms" (Sutherland, 1947:5). Nonetheless, Sutherland, much like other criminologists, did not see crime places as a relevant focus of criminological study. This was the case, in part, because crime opportunities provided by places were assumed to be so numerous as to make concentration on specific places of little utility for theory or policy. In turn, criminologists traditionally assumed that situational factors played a relatively minor role in explaining crime as compared with the "driving force of criminal dispositions" (Clarke and Felson, 1993:4; Trasler, 1993). Combining an assumption of a wide array of criminal opportunities, and a view of offenders that saw them as highly motivated to commit crime, it is understandable that criminologists paid little attention to crime at places.

Interest in the potential of places as a focus of crime prevention can be traced to a growing frustration both among scholars and practitioners with the development of effective offender-based crime prevention policies. This frustration was due in part to basic research, which suggested the difficulty of explaining the causes and development of criminality. A series of studies in the 1980s concluded that it is difficult to identify who is likely to become a serious offender, or to predict the timing and types of offenses that repeat offenders are likely to commit in the future (e. g. Albrecht and Moitra, 1988; Barnett and Lofaso, 1985; Blumstein and Cohen, 1979; Elliot, Dunford, and Huizinga, 1987; Estrich, Moore, McGillis, and Spelman, 1983; Gottfredson and Gottfredson, 1990).[1] This led to a conclusion that basic research did not offer a clear program either for selecting individuals who would be amenable to crime prevention interventions or for development of effective crime prevention strategies that would alter the patterns of criminality among offenders (Earls, 1991; Earls and Carlson, 1995). Even where there was stronger

---

[1]   A more recent study examining the explanatory power of quantitative tests of criminological theories suggests that the situation has improved little in the last two decades (see Weisburd and Piquero, 2008).

evidence of prediction, for example in the case of specialization for some types of adult offenders (e. g. Blumstein, Cohen, Das, and Moitra, 1988; Kempf, 1986), legal and ethical dilemmas were seen as preventing the development of practical crime prevention policies (Moore, 1986). Later in this monograph we will argue that place-based prevention avoids many of these legal and ethical dilemmas.

Given the difficulty of predicting criminality, it is not surprising that applied research in offender-centered crime prevention in the 1970s and 1980s more often than not illustrated the significant barriers that are faced in the development of successful interventions. Beginning with Robert Martinson's critique of rehabilitation programs in 1974 (see also Lipton, Martinson, and Wilks, 1975), a series of studies documented the failures of traditional crime prevention initiatives (e. g. Sechrest, White, and Brown, 1979; Whitehead and Lab, 1989). A number of scholars argued that many such failures were due to inadequacies in program development and research design (e. g. Farrington, Ohlin and Wilson, 1986; Goldstein, 1990). Moreover, some reviews stressed that there were examples of successful offender-focused crime prevention efforts, which could provide guidance for the development of more effective prevention policies (Farrington, 1983; Lipsey, 1992). Nonetheless, even those scholars that looked to improve such policies came to recognize the difficulties inherent in trying to do something about criminality (Visher and Weisburd, 1997). Summarizing the overall standing of what they defined as traditional "offender-centred" crime prevention, Patricia and Paul Brantingham wrote in 1990: "If traditional approaches worked well, of course, there would be little pressure to find new forms of crime prevention. If traditional approaches worked well, few people would possess criminal motivation and fewer still would actually commit crimes" (1990:19).

For many scholars and policymakers, the crisis in person-centered crime prevention meant having to rethink assumptions about criminality and how offenders might be prevented from participating in crime. And indeed the last two decades have seen a resurgence of interest in rehabilitation programs for offenders (e. g. see Andrews, Zinger, Hoge, Bonta, Gendreau, and Cullen, 1990; Cullen, 2005; Lipsey and Cullen, 2007), many achieving much more positive results than the earlier studies noted above. [1] But

---

[1] Nonetheless, in the area of policing, the evidence for offender-based programs continues to be weak or at best inconclusive (Weisburd and Eck, 2004).

others suggested that a more radical reorientation of crime prevention efforts was warranted. They argued that the shift must come not in terms of the specific strategies or theories that were used but in terms of the unit of analysis that formed the basis of crime prevention efforts. This new approach called for a focus not on people who commit crime but on the context in which crime occurs.

One influential critique of traditional criminological approaches to understanding crime that was to have strong influence on the development of interest in crime places was brought by Cohen and Felson (1979). They argued that the emphasis placed on individual motivation in criminological theory failed to recognize the importance of other elements of the crime equation. They argued that for criminal events to occur there is a need for not only a criminal, but also a suitable target and the absence of a capable guardian. They showed that crime rates could be affected by changing the nature of targets or of guardianship, irrespective of the nature of criminal motivations. That Cohen and Felson suggested that crime could be affected without reference to the motivations of individual offenders was a truly radical idea in criminological circles in 1979. The routine activities perspective they presented established the context of crime as an important focus of study.

Drawing upon similar themes, British scholars led by Ronald Clarke began to explore the theoretical and practical possibilities of situational crime prevention (Brantingham and Brantingham, 1990; Clarke, 1980, 1983, 1992, 1995; Cornish and Clarke, 1986). This approach looks to develop greater understanding of crime and more effective crime prevention strategies through concern with the physical, organizational, and social environments that make crime possible. The situational approach does not ignore offenders; it merely places them as one part of a broader crime prevention equation that is centered on the context of crime. It demands a shift in the approach to crime prevention, from one that is concerned primarily with why people commit crime to one that looks primarily at why crime occurs in specific settings. It moves the context of crime into central focus and places the traditional focus of crime-the offender-as just one of a number of factors that affect it.

Situational prevention advocates argue that the context of crime provides a promising alternative to traditional offender-based crime prevention policies. They assume for the most part that situations are a more stable and predictable focus for crime prevention efforts than are persons. In part this assumption develops from commonsense notions of the relationship between opportunities and crime. For example, shoplifting is by definition clustered in stores and not residences, and family disputes are unlikely to be a problem in industrial areas. High-crime places, in contrast to high-crime people, cannot flee to avoid criminal justice intervention. Crime that develops from the specific characteristics of certain marketplaces or organizations cannot be easily transferred to other organizational contexts (Goldstock, 1991).

This emphasis on the context of crime has clear implications for the police and place-based policing in particular. What is meant by place-based policing? At its core is a concern with focusing in on places where crimes are concentrated, and it begins with an assumption that there is something about a place that leads to crimes occurring there. In this sense, place-based policing is theoretically based on routine activities theory (Cohen and Felson, 1979; Felson, 1994), which identifies crime as a matter of the convergence of suitable targets (e. g. , victims), an absence of capable guardians (e. g. , police), and the presence of motivated or potential offenders. Of course, this all must occur in the context of a place or situation, and accordingly place-based policing recognizes that there is something about specific places that leads to the convergence of these elements (Brantingham and Brantingham, 1981 [1991], 1984).

THE CONCENTRATION OF CRIME AT PLACE

A key requirement for the adoption of place-based policing is that crime is heavily concentrated in what some have termed "crime hot spots" (Sherman et al. , 1989; Sherman and Weisburd, 1995; Weisburd and Green, 1995a). Absent a concentration of crime at place there seems little reason to refocus crime prevention efforts. Indeed, if crime were spread randomly across a city place-based policing would provide little benefit.

A number of studies, beginning in the late 1980s suggest that significant clustering of crime at place exists, regardless of the specific unit of analysis defined (see Brantingham and Brantingham, 1999; Crow and Bull, 1975; Pierce, Spaar, and Briggs, 1986; Roncek, 2000; Sherman et al. , 1989; Weisburd and Green, 1994; Weisburd, Maher, and Sherman, 1992, Weisburd, Bushway, Lum, and Yang, 2004; Weisburd, Morris, and Groff, 2009). Perhaps the most influential of these was Sherman, Gartin and Buerger's (1989) analysis of emergency calls to street addresses over a single year. Sherman et al. , found that only $3\frac{1}{2}$ percent of the addresses in Minneapolis, Minnesota produced 50 percent of all calls to the police. They regarded these results as so startling that they called for a new area of study which they termed the "criminology of place."

Other studies produced similar evidence of the concentration of crime in crime hot spots. Weisburd and Mazerolle (2000), for example, found that approximately 20 percent of all disorder crimes and 14 percent of crimes against persons were concentrated in just 56 drug crime hot spots in Jersey City, New Jersey, an area that comprised only 4.4 percent of street segments and intersections in the city. Similarly, Eck, Gersh, and Taylor (2000) found that the most active 10 percent of places (in terms of crime) in the Bronx and Baltimore accounted for approximately 32 percent of a combination of robberies, assaults, burglaries, grand larcenies and auto thefts.

A study conducted by Weisburd, Bushway, Lum and Yang (2004) not only confirms the concentration of crime, but also the stability of such concentrations across a long time span. Weisburd et al., examined street segments in the city of Seattle from 1989 through 2002. They found that 50 percent of crime incidents over the 14 year period occurred at only $4\frac{1}{2}$ percent of the street segments. As illustrated by Figure 1, this concentration is very stable year to year. These data overall illustrate a kind of "law of concentration" for crime, suggesting that crime is heavily clustered in urban areas.

The crime prevention opportunities of this law of concentration are even clearer when focusing on specific types of crime. In another study in Seattle, Weisburd, Morris and Groff (2009) examine the concentration of crime incidents in which a juvenile is arrested. They found that only 86 street segments out of more than 25,000 account for 1/3 of all official juvenile arrest incidents over a 14 year period. While more research will have to be done to establish how much of such crime concentrations are due to concentrations of police patrol, this study suggests the extent to which police efforts should be focused on hot spots in a city.

Lawrence Sherman (1995) argues that such clustering of crime at places is even greater than the concentration of crime among individuals. Using his Minneapolis data and comparing these to the concentration of offending in the Philadelphia cohort study (see Wolfgang, Figlio, and Sellin, 1972), he notes that future crime is "six times more predictable by the address of the occurrence than by the identity of the offender" (1995:36 37). Sherman asks, "why aren't we doing more about it? Why aren't we thinking more about wheredunit, rather than just whodunit?"

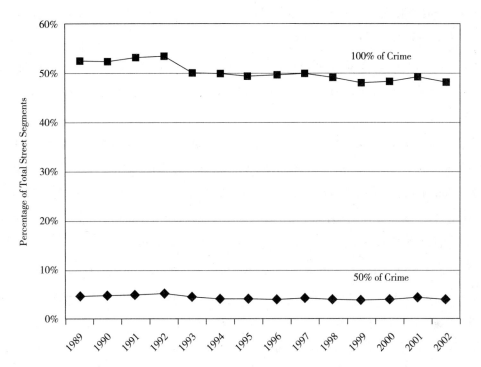

Figure 1   Percentage of Street Segments with 50% and 100% of Incident Reports from 1989 to 2002
Source: Weisburd *et al.* , (2004) .

Weisburd (2008:5) argues similarly regarding longitudinal data in Seattle. When using "targets" as a criterion, places were indeed found to be a more efficient focus than offenders. On average about 1,500 street segments accounted for 50 percent of the crime each year during this period. During the same period about 6, 108 offenders were responsible for 50 percent of the crime each year. Simply stated, the police would have to approach four times as many targets to identify the same level of overall crime when they focus on people as opposed to places.

THE STABILITY OF HOT SPOTS AS CRIME PREVENTION TARGETS

The concentration of crime at place suggests significant crime prevention potential for such strategies as hot spots patrol (Sherman and Weisburd, 1995; Weisburd and Braga, 2006b), which focus crime prevention resources at specific locations with large numbers of crimes. However, concentration itself does not provide a solid empirical basis for either re-focusing crime prevention resources or calling for significant theorizing about why crime is concentrated at places. For example, if "hot spots of crime" shift rapidly from place to place it makes little sense to focus crime control resources at such locations, because they would naturally become free of crime without any criminal justice intervention (Spelman, 1995). Similarly, if crime concentrations can move rapidly across the city landscape, it may not make much sense to focus our understanding of crime on the characteristics of places.

The data we have suggests that these possible objections to place-based policing have little empirical basis. Spelman (1995) for example, examined calls for service at schools, public housing projects, subway stations, and parks and playgrounds in Boston. He found evidence of a very high degree of stability of crime at the "worst" of these places over a three year period. Spelman concluded that it "makes sense for the people who live and work in high-risk locations, and the police officers and other government officials who serve them, to spend the time they need to identify, analyze and solve their recurring problems" (1995:131). Taylor (1999) also reported evidence of a high degree of stability of crime at place over time, examining crime and fear of crime at 90 street blocks in Baltimore, Maryland using a panel design with data collected in 1981 and 1994 (see also Taylor, 2001).

The most comprehensive examination of the stability of crime at place over time was conducted by Weisburd et al. (2004) in their study of crime incidents at street segments in the city of Seattle. Using group-based trajectory analysis (Nagin, 1999, 2005; Nagin and Land, 1993) they identified clusters of similar developmental trajectories, adopting an approach that has been used extensively to study patterns of change in offending and aggression as people age (see Nagin, 1999; Nagin and Tremblay, 1999).

Weisburd and colleagues (2004) identified 18 specific trajectory patterns in their data (see Figure 2). The most important finding in their study was that crime remained fairly stable at places over time. This can be contrasted with developmental studies of individual offending where there is often tremendous change across relatively short periods, especially for high rate offenders (Horney, Osgood, and Marshall, 1995; Nagin, 1999; Nagin and Tremblay, 1999). A comparison of a typical trajectory analysis of developmental patterns of crime among young people (see Figure 3) with the results of the Seattle study emphasizes this point. Note the relative stability of the most chronic offending group in the Seattle data (trajectory group 17), as contrasted with the chronic offenders identified by Nagin (1999) in Figure 3.

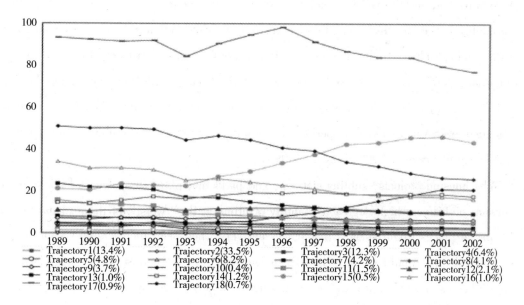

Figure 2   18 Trajectories of Crime Incidents inSeattle

Note: The percentages in parentheses represent the proportion of street segments that each trajectory accounts for in the city of Seattle.

Source: Weisburd *et al.* , (2004) .

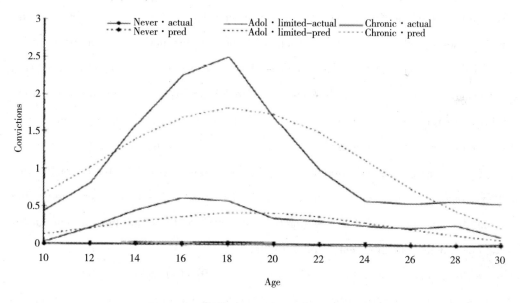

Figure 3   Trajectories of Individual Offending

Adol. = adolescent, pred. = predicted.

Total N=411. Chronic:7% ,Adolescent Limited:22% and Never Offend:71% .

Source: Nagin (1999).

What is clear is that hot spots of crime evidence tremendous stability across the period examined. In contrast, there is perhaps no more established fact in criminology than the variability and instability of offending across the life course. A primary factor in this variability is the fact that most offenders age out of crime, often at a relatively young age (Blumstein, Cohen, Roth, and Visher, 1986; Gottfredson and Hirschi, 1990; Laub and Sampson, 2003; Tracy and Kempf-Leonard, 1996; Wolfgang, Thornberry, and Figlio, 1987). But there is also evidence of strong instability in criminal behavior for most offenders even when short time periods are observed (Bushway, Thornberry, and Krohn, 2003; Horney et al. , 1995; Nagin, 1999).

What these data suggest is that crime prevention at places has the potential for long term impacts on crime and public safety more generally in cities. A model of "regression to the mean" at places would suggest that places get very "hot" and then naturally cool off. In this model there would be little benefit in focusing on the "hottest spots" because they would become cooler even if the police did not bring any crime prevention to those places. In some sense, this is the predominant model of individual offending, since we know that most people will age out of crime relatively quickly. In contrast hot spots of crime appear to remain hot over longer periods of time.

Returning to the theoretical roots of interest in crime at place, we can speculate that there is something about the specific context of these crime hot spots that makes them places of crime concentrations. That would explain why crime is so concentrated at such places over long periods of time. It would also provide an explanation for the very strong stability of very low crime places. In Seattle, about two-thirds of the street segments had little or no crime across the entire 14 years examined (Weisburd et al. , 2004). Why are these street segments generally free of crime? Again we might speculate that characteristics of these places or the people whose routine activities bring them there affect the opportunities for crime at place. In section 6 we will examine these questions in more detail basing our conclusions on recent empirical data.

In our discussion so far we have emphasized the stability of crime across place over time. But the Seattle study also identifies interesting developmental trends in the data examined. For example, the city of Seattle experienced an overall crime drop of more than 20 percent during the period of study, following trends in many other American cities (Blumstein and Wallman, 2000). But only 14 percent of the street segments in the Weisburd et al. , (2004) study showed evidence of such decreasing trends. This means that the crime drop in Seattle was restricted to only a small part of the city. Perhaps even more interesting is the fact that more than 500 street segments in the city evidenced a crime wave during this period, with an average of more than a 40 percent increase across the affected street segments. This suggests the importance of focusing in on policing places rather than larger geographic units such as cities. An overall review of crime trends would have led the police to mistakenly assume that crime was declining uniformly across Seattle. In fact, most street segments changed hardly at all, and many experienced a crime wave during this period.

THE IMPORTANCE OF PLACE-BASED RATHER THAN COMMUNITY-BASED CRIME PREVENTION

While the evidence discussed above establishes the concentration and stability of crime at place, we have so far not examined how hot spots of crime are distributed geographically. This question is important to explore, because it gets at the issue of whether using micro places as the unit of analysis as opposed to larger areas of geography affects our understanding of crime and our approach to crime prevention (see Weisburd, Bruinsma, and Bernasco, 2009). Is it important to focus on crime places, or would we have about the same impact on crime if we focused on beats, communities or neighborhoods? Are crime hot spots concentrated in only one or two neighborhoods in a city, suggesting that despite the concentration of crime in hot spots we would be better off focusing crime prevention on communities?

Evidence to date suggests that crime hot spots can be found throughout a city. Weisburd and Mazerolle (2000) for example, identified 56 drug markets in Jersey City, New Jersey. As Figure 4 illustrates the drug markets were spread across Jersey City. To the surprise of police involved in the study, though the drug markets were more concentrated in socially disadvantaged areas, they could even be found in areas that were generally seen as more established and better off. Weisburd and Mazerolle argued that even good neighborhoods can have bad places. Importantly, most places even in very disadvantaged neighborhoods were relatively free of serious drug problems. Echoing this finding nearly sixty years ago, Henry McKay noted the lack of offenders on some blocks within high crime neighborhoods (Albert J. Reiss, Jr., personal communication as cited in Sherman and Weisburd, 1995).

Using more sophisticated geographic analyses, Weisburd and colleagues (2004) created kernel density maps to examine the distribution of developmental trajectories of crime at

N

Figure 4　Jersey City Drug Market Locations

Source: Weisburd and Mazerolle(2000).

place (see Figure 5). These maps reinforced findings from prior studies showing a spread of hot spots of crime across the city. They also presented some intriguing preliminary findings which led them to conclude that street segments with a fairly stable crime rate tended to be diffused throughout the city but concentrated in areas with less residential density and higher income (see Figure 5). They noted that the areas with the highest concentrations of increasing crime and decreasing crime overlapped in the downtown area. This was a particularly interesting finding since it suggests either that similar processes underlie both crime waves and crime declines, or that street segment level characteristics (and not large area characteristics) are the primary influence in understanding crime trends at places.

a. Stable Trajectory Groups   b. Increasing Trajectory Groups   c. Decreasing Trajectory Groups

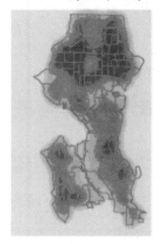  

**Figure 5   Kernel Density Estimations of Segments Classified as Exhibiting Stable,
Increasing or Decreasing Crime Trajectories**

Source: Weisburd *et al.*, (2004).

Mapping the 86 hottest street segments in their longitudinal study of juvenile arrest incidents, Weisburd, Morris and Groff (2009) show again that hot spots of crime are spread throughout the city (see Figure 6). But as in the Weisburd *et al.*, (2004) study, there is a relatively large clustering of such hot spots in the central business area. Groff, Weisburd, and Morris (2009) further examined the clustering of juvenile arrest hot spots by asking whether that clustering suggests that there are important area trends that are influencing juvenile crime at place, and to what extent large area trends versus trends at the street segment level appear to be influencing crime patterns. Examining spatial dependence of street segments, they found tremendous street by street variability in the trajectory patterns of street segments. They conclude that "a great deal of the 'action' is indeed at micro places such as street blocks" (Groff *et al.*, 2009: 84) indicating that much information about crime would be missed by focusing on larger units such as neighborhoods or census tracts.

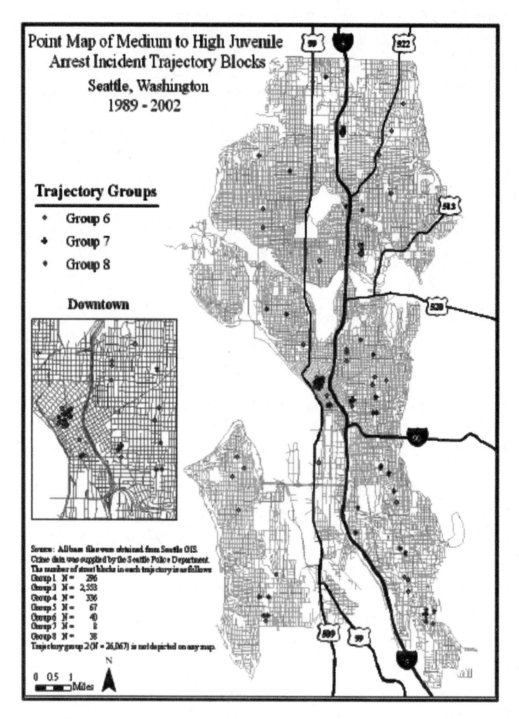

Figure 6 Location of Medium to High Juvenile Arrest Incident Trajectory Blocks

Source: Weisburd, Morris, and Groff (2009).

Perhaps the most comprehensive geographic study of the distribution of hot spots of crime was conducted by Groff, Weisburd, and Yang (2010; see also Weisburd, Groff and Yang, in progress) using 16 years of crime incident data in Seattle (1989—2004). A major question that has not been answered in prior research concerns the form and the degree of street to street variability at micro levels of geography. To answer this question, they explored both temporal and spatial variation in crime across Seattle streets. Groff *et al.*, drew upon trajectory group patterns identified by Weisburd *et al.* (In progress). They then applied a variety of quantitative spatial statistics to the spatial arrangement of each pattern's members to establish whether streets having the same temporal trajectory pattern are collocated spatially or whether there is street to street variation in the temporal patterns of crime.

While there were large areas consisting of predominantly crime free and low stable crime patterns (not surprising given their overwhelming numbers, 12,033 and 7,696 street segments respectively), street segments from higher rate trajectory groups were interspersed within those areas. A closer examination of the pattern of temporal trajectories reveals differences by section of Seattle. In Figure 7, a map of street by street trajectory group assignment in central Seattle is presented. While this map does not provide quantitative substantiation for the significance of the spatial associations revealed, it does offer a strong indication of heterogeneity as well as homogeneity in crime patterns at the street segment level and provides striking evidence of street segment to street segment variation in crime rates. Groff *et al.* (2010) point out the influence of the downtown area of Seattle on the western portion of the city. It is here they observed the greatest magnitude of variation of the temporal trajectory patterns from street to street and the greatest concentration of streets with high crime. A high level of variability was also present in the older residential sections east of downtown. Thus, they point out that one cannot understand the action of crime by simply extrapolating from large area trends.

Groff and colleagues supplemented this descriptive analysis with a statistical analysis that revealed a surprisingly high degree of heterogeneity in the temporal crime trajectory patterns of street segments. In other words, the temporal crime trajectory pattern often changes from street segment to street segment. This was apparent in both the descriptive map and in their finding that low stable street segments were "weakly attracted" to moderate stable, high increasing, and high decreasing street segments, suggesting proximal places can have very divergent temporal crime trajectories. What varied from place to place was not the phenomenon of heterogeneity but rather the specific temporal trajectory pattern involved. In certain areas of the city, the tendency was to see changes from crime

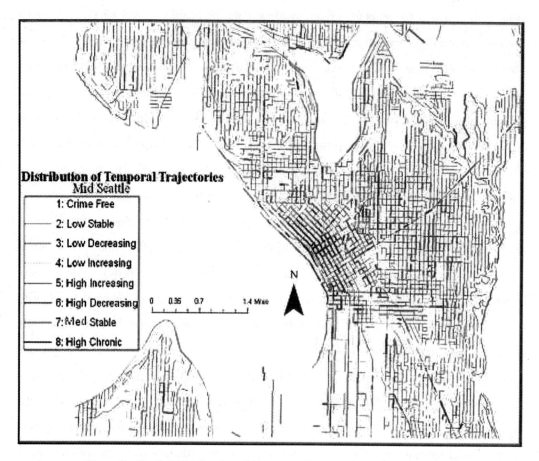

Figure 7   Spatial Distribution of Temporal Trajectories in Central Seattle

Source: Groff. Weisburd, and Yang(Forthcoming).

free to low stable. Sometimes the change was from low stable to another higher rate trajectory pattern. In other areas, the pattern of change was extremely chaotic varying not only from street to street but also by both level and pattern of temporal crime trajectory pattern. These findings demonstrate that the place level of analysis is capturing important variability in trends, and that this variability would be masked if we focused our interest on the larger geographic units that criminologists and the police have traditionally directed attention. [1]

---

[1] Groff *et al.* , (2010; see also Groff *et al.* , 2009) not surprisingly also find evidence of possible larger area influences on crime at place. They found, for example, significant spatial dependence among street segments within the same temporal trajectory pattern at moderate distances. They also found street segments representing certain temporal crime trajectory patterns tended to dominate in certain areas. This occurred more frequently among low rate trajectory patterns but even these areas had other trajectories interspersed within them. However, they also saw this phenomenon in the vicinity of high chronic street segments: a dominant trend of higher rate places with low rate places intermingled.

CAN WE EXPLAIN WHY CRIME IS CONCENTRATED AT PLACE?

Having established the concentration of crime at hot spots and its stability across time, and the fact that much of the action for crime occurs at the local level of crime places, we are led to the question of whether we can explain crime at place. Such explanation is important because it can form the basis for police crime prevention efforts. If we know why some places become hot spots it is easier to develop specific crime prevention strategies to reduce crime and other problems at those places.

As we noted earlier, most study of crime hot spots has relied on routine activities theory (see Cohen and Felson, 1979) as an explanation for why crime trends vary at places and as a basis for constructing practical crime prevention approaches (see Eck and Weisburd, 1995; Sherman *et al.*, 1989). The main assumptions of this perspective are that specific characteristics of places such as the nature of guardianship, the presence of motivated offenders, and the availability of suitable targets will strongly influence the likelihood of criminal events (see also Felson, 1994). Studies examining the factors that predict crime at micro places generally confirm this relationship (see Roncek and Bell, 1981; Roncek and Maier, 1991; Smith, Frazee, and Davison, 2000; Weisburd *et al.*, 2009; Weisburd *et al.*, In progress).

For example, juveniles are assumed to be attracted to very specific types of activities which in turn influence their "activity spaces" (Felson, 2006). Malls and movie theatres are well known "hang outs" for youth, and indeed such businesses seek to draw young people as customers. Moreover, because such activity spaces will attract large numbers of not only potential offenders, but also potential targets, we might expect large concentrations of juvenile crime in such places. For example, several researchers have found that juvenile delinquency is strongly associated with time spent socializing in unstructured activities with peers in the absence of authority figures (Agnew and Peterson, 1989; Osgood, Wilson, O'Malley, Bachman, and Johnston, 1996; Wallace and Bachman, 1991). The fact that juveniles are most likely to victimize other juveniles (Snyder, 2003) reinforces the importance of such activity spaces in the development of juvenile crime.

Data from Weisburd *et al.*, 's (2009) study of juvenile crime in Seattle provide strong confirmation of the relevance of juvenile activity spaces and routine activity theory for understanding the very high concentration of juvenile arrest incidents at places. Weisburd *et al.* , were able to identify where crime events occurred and thus they were able to describe the activity spaces most associated with hot spots of juvenile crime (see Table 1). The highest rate trajectories of juvenile crime hot spots (see trajectories 6—8) were much more likely to have arrest incidents committed at schools and/or youth centers, and shops/malls and restaurants, as compared to low rate trajectory groups. In each of the low rate trajectory groups (1—4) fewer than four percent of the arrest incidents occurred at schools or youth centers. However, more than 30 percent of the arrest incidents in trajectory group 8 occurred at a school or youth center. 12. 7 percent of the incidents in trajectory group 7 and 17. 1 percent of the incidents in trajectory group 6 occurred at a school or youth center. The differences between the high rate and low rate groups were even more pronounced when examining the proportion of arrest incidents found at shops, malls and restaurants. While fewer than 15 percent of incidents in each low rate trajectory group (1—4) occurred at these types of locations, between 34. 3 percent and 75. 4 percent of arrest incidents in trajectories 6 through 8 occurred at shops, malls and restaurants.

Table 1　Juvenile Trajectory Group Membership by Location of Incident(N = 30,004)

	School, Youth Center	Shops, Malls, Restaurants	Street, Alley, Public Spaces	Private Dwelling	Bars, Clubs, Taverns	Other	Total
Group							
1	1. 9%	10. 2%	32. 1%	47. 3%	. 2%	8. 3%	100. 0%
2	1. 8%	2. 1%	53. 7%	34. 3%	. 1%	8. 0%	100. 0%
3	2. 9%	4. 8%	43. 3%	40. 1%	. 3%	8. 6%	100. 0%
4	3. 9%	14. 3%	42. 5%	29. 8%	. 2%	9. 3%	100. 0%
5	6. 5%	26. 0%	40. 7%	14. 3%	. 4%	12. 2%	100. 0%
6	17. 1%	34. 3%	32. 5%	5. 2%	2. 5%	8. 4%	100. 0%
7	12. 7%	75. 4%	8. 8%	. 2%	. 1%	2. 9%	100. 0%
8	30. 7%	38. 9%	21. 5%	. 7%	. 0%	8. 0%	100. 0%

Source: Weisburd, Morris, and Groff (2009).

These data provide important support for the assumption that juvenile crime is concentrated because of the concentration of juveniles in juvenile activity spaces. Incidents in the highest rate trajectories were most likely to be found at and around schools and youth centers, or shops, malls and restaurants. This means that hot spots of juvenile crime, as evidenced by arrest incidents, are likely to be located in places where juvenile congregate. Not surprisingly, given Weisburd *et al.*, 's (2009) focus on juvenile crime, very few arrest incidents are found at bars, clubs and taverns. While prominent activity places for adults, and often crime hot spots (Roncek and Bell, 1981; Roncek and Maier, 1991), they are not part of the activity spaces of juveniles.

While routine activities theory has been a central feature of recent interest in crime hot spots, it is important to note that other theoretical approaches might also be important in understanding crime at place and developing effective crime prevention approaches. Ecological theories of social disorganization used to explain crime patterns in communities (see Schmid, 1960a, 1960b; Shaw and McKay, 1942 [1969]), for example, might also be applied to crime hot spots (see Smith *et al.*, 2000). Recent research by Weisburd, Groff and Yang (In progress) suggests that social disorganization theories may have strong relevance for crime prevention at place.

For example, scholars have recently emphasized the importance of "collective efficacy" in communities as an indicator of a community's ability to realize common values and regulate behavior (see Sampson *et al.*, 1997; Sampson, 2004). Using voting behavior at the street segment level as an indicator of collective efficacy, Weisburd *et al.*, find a direct relationship between collective efficacy and crime patterns. As expected, the crime free and low activity segments have the highest rates of collective efficacy as reflected by active voting patterns. The chronic crime trajectory segments have the lowest evidence of voting participation (see Table 2). These findings are particularly important, because they suggest that in targeting hot spots of crime the police should also consider the social features of life at places. While many hot spots policing programs have relied largely upon intensive enforcement to ameliorate crime problems (e. g. Braga *et al.*, 1999; Sherman and Rogan, 1995a, 1995b), these data emphasize the importance of applying community policing and other strategies that might reinforce the ability of residents of places to bring to force informal social controls.

Table 2 Relationship Between Collective Efficacy (Active Voters) and Trajectory Patterns

Classification of Trajectories	% Active Voters Initial Value (1999)	Pairwise Comparison To Crime Free Pattern
Crime Free (n=12,033)	0. 3534	N/A

continued

Classification of Trajectories	% Active Voters Initial Value (1999)	Pairwise Comparison To Crime Free Pattern
Low Stable (n=7,696)	0. 4238	↑
Low Decreasing (n=2,212)	0. 4164	↑
Low Increasing (n=903)	0. 3151	↓
Moderate Stable (n=292)	0. 2472	↓
High Decreasing (n=574)	0. 2388	↓
High Increasing (n=221)	0. 2089	↓
Chronic (n=247)	0. 1741	↓

↑ Pattern has Significantly Higher Level of Collective Efficacy than Crime Free Pattern.
↓ Pattern has Significantly Lower Level of Collective Efficacy than Crime Free Pattern.
Source: Weisburd, Groff, and Yang (in progress).

Weisburd *et al.*, find even stronger relationships between direct measures of social disorganization and crime at the street segment level. Using illegal dumping as an immediate and visceral indication of the social order of street segments they find a strong relationship with the trajectory patterns (see Table 3). The number of illegal dumping incidents increase as the levels of crime in trajectory patterns increase in the first year of observations. This relationship is significant and strong across the trajectory groupings. By far the lowest number of illegal dumping incidents is found in the crime free trajectory pattern. In the low rate trajectory groupings there are about four times as many illegal dumping incidents, and in the high rate trajectory patterns this increase is more than tenfold as compared with the crime free trajectory pattern. For the chronic hot spots group the increase is higher still.

Looking at change over time, the relationships are also strong. For the high increasing and moderate stable trajectory patterns the number of illegal dumping incidents increases, though the change is statistically significant only for the stable grouping. In contrast, in the high decreasing trajectory pattern there is a statistically significant decline in the number of illegal dumping incidents in the final observation period. The same pattern emerges looking at the low rate trajectory patterns. In the low increasing pattern there is about a one third increase in the number of illegal dumping incidents, and the change is highly significant. There is a statistically significant though much smaller decline in the low decreasing pattern. The low stable pattern shows almost no change during the period. These data suggest a direct relationship between changes over time in social disorder and changes in crime at the street segment level.

Table 3 Relationship Between Number of Illegal Dumping Incidents and Trajectory Patterns

Trajectories	Illegal Dumping Initial Value (93–95)	Pairwise Comparison To Crime Free Pattern	Illegal Dumping Ending Value (02–04)	Block Change Over Time	Sig. of Paired Sample test for Blocks	Group Mean Change
Crime Free (n = 12,033)	0. 0373	N/A	0. 0425	. 0052	. 012 *	13. 94%
Low Stable (n = 7,696)	0. 1455	↑	0. 1507	. 0052	. 307	3. 57%
Low Decreasing (n=2,212)	0. 1534	↑	0. 1308	−. 0226	. 013 *	−14. 73%
Low Increasing (n=903)	0. 1694	↑	0. 2410	. 0716	. 000 ***	42. 27%
Moderate Stable (n=292)	0. 3870	↑	0. 4840	. 0970	. 032 *	25. 06%
High Decreasing (n=574)	0. 4344	↑	0. 3333	−. 1011	. 008 **	−23. 27%
High Increasing (n=221)	0. 4736	↑	0. 5279	. 0543	. 383	11. 47%
Chronic (n=247)	0. 6221	↑	0. 6923	. 0702	. 366	11. 28%

↑ Pattern has Significantly Higher Number of Illegal Dumping Incidents Than Crime Free Pattern.

↓ Pattern has Significantly Lower Number of Illegal Dumping Incidents Than Crime Free Pattern.

*** p<. 001 , ** p<. 01 , * p<. 05 for paired sample t-test for blocks.

Source: Weisburd, Groff, and Yang(in rogress).

Our discussion so far illustrates that criminologists and the police can identify characteristics of places that are associated with crime. But is our ability to explain and thus identify causes of crime at place greater than our ability to explain crime among people? There is no hard and fast way to answer this question, and much additional research will be needed on crime places before we can compare our knowledge to the large number of studies that have been conducted with individuals. Nonetheless, recent work by Weisburd, Groff and Yang (In progress) suggests that even in this early stage of development of this research agenda, efforts can yield very high levels of explanation. In predicting trajectory pattern membership of street segments they find that the models developed explain about two thirds of variability in crime trends. This may be contrasted with models of individual criminality which have average variance explained levels of about 30 percent (Weisburd and Piquero, 2008).

THE EMPIRICAL EVIDENCE FOR HOT SPOTS POLICING

The basic research we have examined so far establishes a strong basis for the development of place-based policing. Crime is concentrated at a relatively small number of places in the city suggesting that place-based or hot spots policing provides an opportunity for the police to be efficient in tackling crime problems. Those places moreover represent long term chronic crime locations, and do not simply shift from year to year. If the police can be successful at ameliorating crime problems at places this suggests that there will be long term crime benefits. Additionally, crime at place is not simply a proxy for crime in communities. The basic research on crime at place suggests that much of the action of crime is occurring at these small geographic units we have termed crime places, and that focus on larger areas such as beats, precincts or communities would lead to a loss of efficiency and effectiveness in crime prevention efforts. Finally, we have already a strong body of knowledge suggesting the factors that influence crime and place, and thus a basis for identifying crime prevention practices for police at crime hot spots.

Importantly, this basic research is reinforced by strong scientific evidence of the ability of the police to effectively respond to crime at place. A series of randomized field trials show that policing that is focused on hot spots can result in meaningful reductions in crime and disorder (see Braga, 2001, 2005, 2007). The first of these, the Minneapolis Hot Spots Patrol Experiment (Sherman and Weisburd, 1995), used computerized mapping of crime calls to identify 110 hot spots of roughly street-block length. Police patrol was doubled on average for the experimental sites over a ten-month period. The study found that the experimental as compared with the control hot spots experienced statistically significant reductions in crime calls and observed disorder. In another randomized experiment, the Kansas City Crack House Raids Experiment (Sherman and Rogan, 1995a), crackdowns on drug locations were also found to lead to significant relative improvements in the experimental sites, although the effects (measured by citizen calls and offense reports) were modest and decayed in a short period. In yet another randomized trial, however, Eck and Wartell (1996) found that if the raids were immediately followed by police contacts with landlords, crime prevention benefits could be reinforced and would be sustained for longer periods.

More general crime and disorder effects are also reported in three other randomized controlled experiments that tested a more tailored, problem-oriented approach to dealing with crime hot spots. In the Jersey City Problem-Oriented Policing in Violent Places experiment (Braga *et al.*, 1999), strong statistically significant reductions in total crime incidents and total crime calls were found in the treatment hot spots relative to the control hot spots. Importantly, all crime categories experienced reductions and observational data revealed statistically significant declines in social and physical disorder as well. In the Jersey City Drug Market Analysis Program experiment (Weisburd and Green, 1995a), hot spots policing tactics were found to be more effective at reducing disorder at drug hot spots than generalized enforcement. In the Oakland Beat Health study, Mazerolle and Roehl (1998) also reported strong reductions in crime and disorder in an experimental evaluation of civil remedy interventions at specific drug-involved locations.

Nonexperimental studies provide similar findings. For instance, the Kansas City Gun Project evaluation (Sherman and Rogan, 1995b) found strong crime control gains for hot spots policing approaches. Using intensive enforcement in an eight by ten block area, including traffic stops and searches, Sherman and Rogan (1995b) reported a 65 percent increase in guns seized by the police and a 49 percent decrease in gun crimes in the treatment area relative to a matched control area. Hope (1994) examined the effects of a problem-oriented policing strategy, which relied primarily on traditional law enforcement tactics, on total calls for service in three drug hot spot locations in St. Louis, Missouri. The evaluation compared total calls in the targeted drug hot spots to addresses proximate to the treatment locations and blocks in the surrounding areas. Hope (1994) reported significant crime reductions in the treatment locations when compared to the control locations.

This strong body of rigorous evaluations led the National Research Council Committee to Review Research on Police Policy and Practices to conclude in 2004:

> *There has been increasing interest over the past two decades in police practices that target very specific types of crimes, criminals, and crime places. In particular, policing crime hot spots has become a common police strategy for reducing crime and disorder problems. While there is only preliminary evidence suggesting the effectiveness of targeting specific types of offenders, a strong body of evidence suggests that taking a focused geographic approach to crime problems can increase the effectiveness of policing (2004:35).*

Further evidence of the effectiveness of hot spots comes from a Campbell Collaboration systematic review conducted by Anthony Braga (2001, 2005, 2007). A Campbell review involves a more systematic review of the literature than a narrative review and, when appropriate, uses meta-analysis to provide a statistical summary of the literature (Lipsey and Wilson, 2001). In keeping with Campbell standards, eligible studies included only those that examined crime places that received the hot spots policing intervention compared to places that experienced routine levels of traditional police service. Nine eligible studies were identified and included in the Campbell review, several of which were described above:

1. Minneapolis Repeat Call Address Policing (RECAP) Program (Sherman, Buerger, and Gartin, 1989) *

2. Minneapolis Hot Spots Patrol Program (Sherman and Weisburd, 1995) *

3. Jersey City Drug Markets Analysis Program (DMAP) (Weisburd and Green, 1995a) *

4. Jersey City Problem-Oriented Policing at Violent Places Project (Braga et al., 1999) *

5. St. Louis Problem-Oriented Policing in Three Drug Market Locations Study (Hope, 1994)

6. Kansas City Gun Project (Sherman and Rogan, 1995b)

7. Kansas City Crack House Police Raids Program (Sherman and Rogan, 1995a) *

8. Houston Targeted Beat Program (Caeti, 1999)

9. Beenleigh, Australia Calls for Service Project (Criminal Justice Commission, 1998)

These nine evaluations were conducted in five large cities in the United States and one suburb in Australia. Five of the selected studies used randomized experimental designs (indicated with an asterisk in the list above) and four used non-equivalent control group quasi-experimental designs. The treatments used to prevent crime at hot spots fell into three broad categories: enforcement problem-oriented policing interventions, directed and aggressive patrol programs, and police crackdowns and raids (see Braga, 2001, 2005, 2007 for more information on each study).

The Campbell review reported noteworthy crime and disorder reductions in seven of the nine selected studies. Due to inconsistent reporting of program effects in the quasi-experimental studies, only randomized trials were included in the Campbell review meta-analysis (Braga, 2005, 2007). Since all hot spots policing experiments used citizen calls for service as an outcome measure, the main effect size for each study was calculated based on the statistics reported for key calls for service findings. These effect sizes are reported in Table 4.

The effect size of the hot spots policing intervention on the treatment places relative to control places was very large (2.05) and statistically significant in the Jersey City Problem-Oriented Policing at Violent Places experiment. While the study reported a very large effect size, its influence on the overall meta-analysis was moderated by its small sample size and correspondingly small inverse variance weight. The Jersey City DMAP experiment intervention also had a large statistically significant effect size (.689) and the Minneapolis Hot Spots Patrol experiment intervention had a moderate statistically significant effect size (.322). The Kansas City Crack House Raid experiment and the Minneapolis RECAP experiment at commercial addresses had smaller non-statistically significant effect sizes that favored the treatment places relative to the controls (.219 and .089, respectively). The Minneapolis RECAP experiment at residential addresses had a very small, non-statistically significant effect size that slightly favored the control places relative to the treatment places.

Since the distribution of effect sizes was found to be heterogeneous, the Campbell review used a random-effects meta-analytic model to calculate the mean effect size for all studies. Overall, the Campbell review found that hot spots policing interventions reduced citizen calls for service in the treatment places relative to the control places (Braga, 2005, 2007). The mean effect size for the hot spots policing intervention for the six studies was moderate (.345) and statistically significant. When the RECAP study was not included in the meta-analysis due to methodological concerns, the mean effect size was large (.632) and statistically significant.

Table 4   Meta-Analysis of Hot Spots Experiment Effect Sizes for Main Outcomes

Experiment	Effect Size	Standard Error	Inv. Var. Weight (% Total Weight)	95% C. I.
Jersey City POP	2.05 *	.504	3.93(1.8%)	Upper 3.04 Lower 1.06

continued

Experiment	Effect Size	Standard Error	Inv. Var. Weight (% Total Weight)	95% C.I.
Jersey City DMAP	.689 *	.275	13.21(6.0%)	Upper 1.23 Lower .15
Minneapolis Patrol	.322 *	.142	27.15(12.3%)	Upper .60 Lower .044
Kansas City Crack	.219	.139	51.32(23.3%)	Upper .492 Lower −.054
Minneapolis RECAP Commercial	.089	.127	62.49(28.3%)	Upper .337 Lower −.159
Minneapolis RECAP Residential	−.009	.127	62.49(28.3%)	Upper .238 Lower −.256
Meta-Analysis All Studies	.345 *	.150	Total Weight = 220.59	Upper .640 Lower .058
Meta-Analysis w/o RECAP	.632 *	.253	Total Weight w/o RECAP=95.61	Upper 1.13 Lower .138

* p<.05.

Since the publication of the most recent iteration of the Campbell review, an additional randomized controlled experiment evaluating the crime prevention benefits of hot spots policing has been completed. In Lowell, Massachusetts, a randomized controlled experiment evaluated the effects of policing disorder, within a problem-oriented policing framework, at crime and disorder hot spots (Braga and Bond, 2008). Thirty-four hot spots were matched into 17 pairs and one member of each pair was allocated to treatment conditions in a randomized block field experiment. The impact evaluation revealed a statistically significant 20 percent reduction in crime and disorder calls for service at the treatment places relative to the control places. Analyses of systematic observation data also revealed significant reductions in social and physical disorder at the treatment places relative to the control places.

In sum, the empirical research is highly supportive of hot spots policing. Several experimental and quasi-experimental studies have demonstrated that a focus on small high crime geographic areas can have a positive and statistically significant impact on crime and disorder. While empirical support for hot spots policing is strong, such approaches would be much less useful if they simply displaced crime to other nearby places. The issue of displacement effects is reviewed in the next section.

DOES CRIME JUST MOVE AROUND THE CORNER?

Crime displacement is the notion that efforts to eliminate specific crimes at a place will simply cause criminal activity to move elsewhere, be committed in another way, or even be manifested as another type of crime, thus negating any crime control gains (Reppetto, 1976). This perspective on the crime prevention effectiveness of police efforts to control problem places developed from dispositional theories of criminal motivations, and the views of these skeptics were supported by early studies of opportunity-reducing measures (Clarke, 1980; Gabor, 1990). For instance, although exact fare systems reduced the number of robberies on New York City buses, a corresponding increase in robberies occurred in the subways (Chaiken, Lawless, and Stevenson, 1974). In addition, traditional police efforts to control street level drug markets have been assumed to be quite susceptible to spatial, temporal, and tactical displacement (see Caulkins, 1992; Eck, 1993; Sherman, 1990).

Since 1990 there have been four main reviews of empirical studies that report on displacement: Barr and Pease (1990); Eck (1993); Hesseling (1994); and Guerette and Bowers (2009). The four reviews vary in their comprehensiveness. Barr and Pease restricted their review to studies from the United Kingdom. Eck reviewed 33 studies from the United States, Canada, the United Kingdom, and other countries printed in English. Hesseling examined 55 studies from North America, Europe and other areas printed in English or Dutch. Guerette and Bowers's systematic review examined 102 studies of situational crime prevention. All four reviews arrived at three basic conclusions. First, there is little evidence of crime prevention strategies that displaced as much crime as was prevented. Second, displacement, when it occurs, is usually less than the amount of crime prevented. And third, for crime prevention evaluations that reported on displacement, the most common finding was that there was no evidence of displacement. In sum, most studies found no, or negligible, displacement of crime.

These results must be taken with three important caveats. First, the amount of displacement depends, in part, on the type of intervention being used. For example, Hesseling (1994) suggests that target hardening may displace more crime than access control. Second, the amount of displacement also depends, in part, on the crime or disorder being prevented. Eck (1993) suggests that drug dealing may be more likely to displace than other forms of crime (though see Weisburd and Green, 1995b for the opposite view) and that certain forms of drug markets are particularly susceptible to displacement. Third, and most importantly, because the studies did not set out to examine displacement, it was rare that evaluators were able to use a methodologically sound research design for detecting it (see Weisburd and Green, 1995b). This is the case in part because researchers must make decisions about the allocation of scarce research funds and resources. If, for example, a researcher is unsure about the direct crime control benefits of a program, it makes sense to invest in assessing the direct target effects rather than outcomes that are important only if a target effect is found.

Spatial displacement represents a direct and significant threat to place-based policing. If crime will simply move around the corner as a response to targeted police programs at hot spots, there is little point in carrying out hot spots policing programs. The research evidence regarding displacement in hot spots policing is particularly strong and consistent. There is little evidence of displacement of crime to areas nearby targeted hot spots. Indeed, a series of studies suggest that there is likely to be what Clarke and Weisburd (1994) have termed a "diffusion of crime prevention benefits" to areas near to hot spots policing targets. In this sense, the crime prevention gains for hot spots policing seem to spread out from targeted locations.

In the Jersey City Drug Market Analysis Experiment (Weisburd and Green, 1995a), for example, displacement within two block areas around each hot spot was measured. No significant displacement of crime or disorder calls was found. Importantly, however, the investigators found that drug-related and public-morals calls actually declined in the displacement areas. This "diffusion of crime control benefits" was also reported in the Jersey City Violent Crime Places experiment (Braga et al., 1999), the Beat Health study (Mazerolle and Roehl, 1998), and the Kansas City Gun Project (Sherman and Rogan, 1995b). In each of these studies, no displacement of crime was reported, and some improvement in the surrounding areas was found. Only Hope (1994) reports direct displacement of crime, although this occurred only in the area immediate to the treated locations and the displacement effect was much smaller overall than the crime prevention effect. The Campbell systematic review described above examined displacement data for five of the nine studies, finding that none reported substantial immediate spatial displacement of crime into areas surrounding the targeted locations (Braga, 2001, 2005, 2007).

While much attention has been paid to the idea of displacement, methodological problems associated with its measurement have often been overlooked (Weisburd and Green, 1995b; for exceptions see Barr and Pease, 1990 and Pease, 1991). This is not to say that displacement has not been studied; only that empirical examinations of displacement or diffusion have been a byproduct of the study of something else. Typically, knowledge of displacement or diffusion has been gained from a study that was primarily about the effects of an innovative crime prevention program. The problem is that a study that is designed to measure direct program effects will likely face significant methodological problems in measuring displacement or diffusion (Weisburd and Green, 1995b).

A recent study by Weisburd and colleagues (2006) of hot spots policing interventions at drug and prostitution markets explicitly examined spatial displacement and diffusion as a primary outcome and presents important insights about why crime does not simply move around the corner as a response to targeted policing efforts at crime hot spots. To examine displacement and diffusion effects, a wealth of data was collected in the intervention target areas and surrounding catchment areas, approximately two blocks surrounding each target area. The study employed analyses of more than 6,000 20-minute social observations at the research sites, supplemented by interviews with arrestees from the target areas and ethnographic field observations.

Quantitative findings indicated that for the crime hot spots examined, crime did not simply move around the corner in response to intensive police crime prevention efforts at places. Indeed, the study supported the position that the most likely outcome of such focused crime prevention efforts is a diffusion of crime control benefits to nearby areas. This is illustrated in Figure 8, which documents observed prostitution events in the target and displacement catchment areas during the period of the study. Here, as in other analyses conducted by Weisburd *et al.* (2006), crime did not go up in the catchment areas after there were strong crime prevention gains at the target site. Indeed, the catchment areas followed a similar pattern to the target site, suggesting a diffusion of crime control benefits.

An examination of the ethnographic field work and arrestee interviews reinforce routine activities and rational choice perspectives as a means to help understand why there was little evidence of spatial displacement. Rational choice theories emphasize the importance of the balancing of effort, risks and opportunities with the benefits that will be gained from criminal activities (Clarke and Cornish, 1985, 2001). The qualitative data collected by

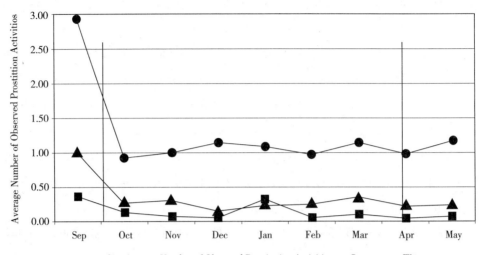

Prostitution Site Average Number of Observed Prostitution Activities per Segment per Wave

—●— Target Area　—▲— Catehmant Srea 1　—■— Catehment Area 2

Figure 8　Obserued Prostitution Events in the Target and Displacement Catchment Aneas

Note: Black vertical lines indicate the beginning and end of the police intervention period.

Source: Weisburd *et al.*, (2006).

Weisburd et al., (2006), in turn, suggest that spatial movement from crime sites involves substantial effort and risk by offenders.

A number of the offenders they spoke to complained about the time and effort it would take to reestablish their activities in other areas as a reaction to the police intervention. One respondent arrested at the drug crime site, for example, explained that it is difficult to move because the "money won't be the same," that he "would have to start from scratch," and that it "takes time to build up customers." Fear of victimization was also an important factor in preventing spatial displacement. One prostitute provided a keen sense of why, for safety reasons, it is important to have "regulars".

> "If they aren't regulars, I try to feel them out. I use precautions. I never will get
> into a car with two men. I always check the doors to make sure I can get out if I
> need to, like if an emergency arises, like a guy trying to hurt me. I will always go
> into an area I know. This way, if I need help, I know that somehow I can find
> someone or get someone's attention. But, in the same way, I don't go into an area
> that would give away what I am doing and get me arrested. I basically don't let
> the guys take me where they want to go. If they insist on this, then I make them

pay me up front, before the zipper goes down. " (Brisgone , 2004:129)

Another respondent explained that going to a different area of town was difficult because other prostitutes got angry and told her "this is our turf, stay away". Similar resistance to displacement was evident in interviews with offenders arrested in the drug crime site. The drug dealers' intimacy with the area in which they worked was one of the primary mechanisms preventing spatial displacement. A number of dealers explained that you work near where you live because that is your "turf. " One arrestee elaborates, "you really can' t deal in areas you aren' t living in, it ain' t your turf. That's how people get themselves killed" (Weisburd *et al.* , 2006:578)

Another emphasis of rational choice theorists is that the factors influencing offender choices are often very similar to those of non-offenders (Cornish and Clarke, 1986). This insight has been part of a number of important criminological perspectives (e. g. see Akers, 1973; Sutherland, 1947) , but it is sometimes lost in the identification of individuals as criminals and the criminological focus on what distinguishes them from non-criminals (Weisburd and Waring, 2001). One important explanation for the resistance to spatial displacement is simply that offenders, like non-offenders, come to feel comfortable with their home turf and the people that they encounter. As with non-offenders, moving jobs or homes can be seen as an important and difficult change in life circumstances. One prostitute explained, for example:

> "*I walked over (to the graveyard cemetery) and I didn' t think I' d make money. It was unfamiliar to me. It was like, It was like . . . unfamiliar to me. I didn' t know the guys (clients). On Cornelison you recognize the guys. I know from being out there every day (on Cornelison), the cars, the faces. It's different. In my area, I know the people. Up on ' the hill' —I don' t really know the people at that end of town. " (Brisgone, 2004:199)*

While these data reinforce routine activities and rational choice perspectives, and help us understand why Weisburd *et al.* , observe little evidence of spatial displacement in their data, they do not explain why there is a significant diffusion of crime control benefits both in the prostitution and drug crime sites. Even if there is good reason not to move to other sites either because they do not offer similar opportunities, or increase the risks for offenders, why should observed crime and disorder go down in those areas?

Weisburd *et al.*, argue that deterrence played a central role in the diffusion processes they observed (see Clarke and Weisburd, 1994). [1]In interviews with offenders arrested in the target areas, they found that they often did not have a clearly defined understanding of the geographic scope of police activities. Such understanding often improved in what might be termed a "learning curve" over time (Brisgone, 2004). Nonetheless, the qualitative data suggest that offenders acted in a context of what rational choice theorists call "bounded rationality" (Johnson and Payne, 1986) in which they made assumptions about police behavior that were based on limited or incorrect information. In this context, they often assumed that the crackdowns were not limited to the target areas but were part of a more general increase in police enforcement.

Support for this argument is found in a review of situational crime prevention studies conducted by Smith, Clarke and Pease (2002). Examining a phenomenon they describe as "anticipatory crime prevention benefits," they find that in about 40 percent of studies reviewed, crime declined before the intervention had begun. Smith and her colleagues argue that the crime prevention benefit in such cases can be traced primarily to "publicity" or "disinformation." They speculate that such factors as pre-program media reports about interventions, the visibility of preparations for interventions (e. g. the installation of CCTV), or "hearsay" regarding impending police actions, lead potential offenders to assume that the risks or efforts associated with offending have increased. It may be that a similar process of "disinformation" occurred in the Weisburd *et al.*, (2006) study, based on offender observations of police activities in the target areas, information from offenders who had been the subject of police actions, or from other members of the community.

The evidence to date challenges strongly the assumption that targeted crime prevention at places will have little overall benefit because of displacement of crime. Indeed, the

---

① Another possible explanation for diffusion of crime control benefits in the catchment areas is "incapacitation." Many offenders were arrested in the target areas, and if these individuals were also responsible for crime in the catchment areas, we might expect observed crime and disorder to have declined in the catchment areas. However, despite the intensive enforcement activities at the target sites, many offenders remained active in these areas throughout the study period. Few prostitutes studied were imprisoned for extended periods, and most arrests led to just one or a few days off the street. Though a Violent Offender Removal Program in the drug site was intended to remove offenders from the drug site for longer periods, only a small proportion of active offenders were actually prosecuted in the program.

evidence regarding spatial displacement, which is most relevant to place-based policing, strongly supports the conclusion that hot spots policing will lead to a diffusion of crime prevention benefits to nearby areas.

REDUCING LEGAL CONSTRAINTS WHILE DECREASING ARRESTS AND IN-CARCERATION OF OFFENDERS

Police often complain that their hands are tied in doing something about criminals. While the extent of legal constraints on policing are the source of much debate (Bittner, 1967; Ohlin and Remington, 1993; NRC, 2004; Vollmer, 1933; Wickersham Commission, 1931; Wilson, 1950), it is clear that place-based policing offers a target for police interventions that is less protected by traditional legal guarantees. The common law and our legal traditions have placed less concern over the rights of places than the rights of individuals. It is not that police can do what they like at places. Rather, the extent of constitutional and procedural guarantees has at times been relaxed where places are targeted.

When it is established that places are crime targets or deserve special protection, it becomes easier to legally justify enforcement in regard to individual offenders. For example, Dan Kahan and Tracey Meares (1998:1172) note that law enforcement officials "needn't obtain a warrant or even have probable cause ... to stop motorists at sobriety checkpoints or to search all individuals entering airports or government buildings." This means that at certain places, where issues of public safety are a central concern, it is possible to justify policing activities that would be unacceptable if carried out against individuals in other places. Places where crime is concentrated are often seen to meet this criterion, as is the case in many cities that have designated drug market areas for special attention. Safe school zones are another example of the identification of places that allow special activities by the police, in this case because of the vulnerability of potential victims. The constitutional issues here are complex and do not simply justify intrusion in every case. Nonetheless, politicians, judges, and, indeed, ordinary citizens have an intuition that police should be allowed appropriate discretion to police certain places that exhibit specific problems, such as concentrated crime, when there is the support of residents.

Place-based policing, accordingly, provides a target for police that may lead to fewer constraints in terms of the development of crime prevention strategies (Weisburd, 2008).

But, importantly, it also suggests an approach to policing that may lead to less coercive and, in the long term, more humane crime prevention practices. To be successful in place-based policing, it is often necessary for police to expand their toolbox to take into account the fact that their targets are places and not people. The civil law rather than law enforcement is often the most successful method for interrupting crime at place (Mazerolle and Roehl, 1998). As Cheh has observed (1991:1329), "Police and prosecutors have embraced civil strategies not only because they expand the arsenal of weapons available to reach antisocial behavior, but also because officials believe that civil remedies offer speedy solutions that are unencumbered by the rigorous constitutional protections associated with criminal trials." Whatever the reason for the shift in tactics from ones that rely on the criminal law to ones that rely on civil or administrative law, the end result is crime prevention strategies that are less reliant on traditional law enforcement practices that often lead to the arrest and imprisonment of offenders.

Over the last three decades in the U. S. , rates of imprisonment have dramatically expanded, and there is evidence that imprisonment rates are also rising in other Western countries (Walmsley, 2009). Spending on prisons in the U. S. has increased at more than double the rate of spending on education and health care (Hughes, 2006). The moral cost is that fully 2. 3 million Americans everyday are in prisons or jails (West and Sabol, 2008), institutions that are often dehumanizing and degrading. Policing places puts emphasis on reducing opportunities for crime at places, not on waiting for crimes to occur and then arresting offenders. Successful crime prevention programs at places need not lead to high numbers of arrests, especially if methods are developed that discourage offenders, for example through "third party policing" (Mazerolle and Ransley, 2005). In this sense, place-based policing offers an approach to crime prevention that can increase public safety while decreasing the human and financial costs of imprisonment. If place-based policing was to become the central focus of police, rather than the arrest and apprehension of offenders, we would likely see at the same time a reduction of prison populations and an increase in the crime prevention effectiveness of the police.

RECOGNIZING THE IMPORTANCE OF POLICE LEGITIMACY IN POLICING PLACES

Basic and applied research supports the potential and actual crime prevention opportunities of place-based policing. Place-based policing moreover offers opportunities for police to carry out crime prevention with fewer legal constraints. However, the effectiveness of policing is also dependent on public perceptions of the legitimacy of police actions (NRC, 2004; Tyler, 1990, 2004). Even if the police can lower crime, if they alienate the community in carrying out their efforts it is difficult to identify place-based policing as successful.

There is a noteworthy lack of research assessing the effects of place-based policing on police-community relations. This gap in knowledge is significant for hot spots policing initiatives as many observers suggest a tension between the crime prevention effectiveness of focused police efforts and their potential harmful effects on police-community relations (Meares, 2006; Rosenbaum, 2006; Taylor, 2006; Weisburd and Braga, 2006b). If the public's trust and confidence in the police is undermined, the ability of the police to prevent crime will be weakened by lawsuits, declining willingness to obey the law, and withdrawal from existing partnerships (Tyler, 1990, 2004). The political fallout from illegitimate police actions can seriously impede the ability of police departments to engage in innovative crime control tactics.

There is some evidence that residents of areas that are subject to focused police attention welcome the concentration of police efforts in problem places (McGarrell, Chermak, Weiss, and Wilson, 2001; Shaw, 1995). A separate examination of the Kansas City Gun Project (Sherman and Rogan, 1995b) found that the community strongly supported the intensive patrols and perceived an improvement in the quality of life in the treatment neighborhood (Shaw, 1995). The study did not, however, attempt to measure how the individuals who were stopped and searched by the police felt about the program.

Dennis Rosenbaum (2006) suggests that hot spots policing, because it has often been operationally defined as aggressive enforcement in specific areas, runs the risk of weakening police-community relations. Rosenbaum (2006) argues that hot spots policing can easily become "zero tolerance" policing because this approach is easy for the police to adopt. Indiscriminate aggressive tactics can drive a wedge between the police and communities, as the latter can begin to feel like targets rather than partners:

> *Because the police have chosen to focus on removing the "bad element" and*
> *serving as the "thin blue line" between "good" and "bad" residents, these*

strategies can pit one segment of the community against another, as the "good"
residents are asked to serve as the informants and the "eyes and ears" of the
police. Parents, siblings, and friends of gang members can feel a divided loyalty
and be caught in the crossfire (Rosenbaum, 2006:253).

Rosenbaum (2006) also raises the question of whether sustained enforcement efforts in minority communities will contribute to disproportionate minority confinement. Regardless of the specific approach employed or tactics engaged, hot spots policing will generate an increased amount of police-citizen contacts in very small areas. Police behavior in these areas will greatly influence the amount of support and involvement from community members residing in crime hot spot areas. To maximize their ability to manage crime problems in these places, police managers should strive to ensure fair police-citizen interactions and the development of strong partnerships with community members, an approach used successfully in pulling-levers policing (Braga and Winship, 2006; Kennedy, 2006). While the work is difficult, long-term community engagement efforts can pay large dividends in improving the quality of police-community relationships and collaborative crime prevention efforts.

The concentration of crime at specific hot spot locations within neighborhoods provides an important opportunity for police to make connections with community members who are most vulnerable to victimization and experience fear and diminished quality of life as a result of ongoing and intense crime and disorder problems. Regrettably, these community members are often the same people who view the police with suspicion and question the legitimacy of police efforts to control crime in their neighborhoods. In this sense, residents and business owners in high-activity crime places represent "hot spots" of community dissatisfaction with and mistrust of the police. If police departments are concerned with improving their relationships with community members, the residents and business owners in hot spot locations seem like a logical place to start. Like crime, poor police-community relationships are not evenly spread throughout city environments. If the police can win the hearts and minds of long suffering community members in hot spot areas, it seems likely to produce larger impacts on the overall legitimacy of police departments in the city than developing stronger relationships with community members in more stable neighborhoods, who are more likely to already have generally positive perceptions of police services.

As in the case of understanding the effectiveness of police strategies, the potential impact of police crime prevention efforts in problem places on citizen perceptions of legitimacy may depend in good part on the types of strategies used and the context of the hot spots affected. Unfocused and indiscriminate enforcement actions seem likely to produce poor relationships between the police and community members residing in hot spot areas. We believe that the police should adopt alternative approaches to controlling hot spots that do not rely solely on one-dimensional intensive enforcement. Of course, arresting criminal offenders is a central part of the police function and should remain an important tool in an array of responses to crime hot spots. But place-based policing programs infused with community and problem-oriented policing principles hold great promise in improving police legitimacy in the eyes of community members living in places suffering from crime and disorder problems (Braga and Weisburd, 2010; Mastrofski, Braga, and Weisburd, 2010; Taylor, 2006).

AN AGENDA FOR PLACE-BASED POLICING

What must change to implement a broad program of place-based policing? It is important to start out by recognizing that places have indeed always been a concern for the police. As Carolyn Block (1998:28) has noted in discussing interest in crime mapping among police, "Crime maps are nothing new. Pin maps have graced walls behind police chiefs' desks since pins were invented." Moreover, over the last decade, hot spots policing approaches have become a common staple of American policing. In a recent study, Weisburd and Lum (2005) found that 62 percent of a sample of 125 departments with 100 or more sworn officers claimed to have adopted computerized crime mapping. Of these, 80 percent claimed to conduct hot spots analysis and two thirds used hot spots policing as a patrol strategy. A 2007 Police Executive Research Forum (PERF, 2008) study found that 74 percent of police departments surveyed in 192 jurisdictions used "hot spots enforcement" as a strategy to address violent crime. Compstat has also been adopted widely by larger American police agencies over the last decade (Weisburd, Mastrofski, McNally, and Greenspan, 2001; Weisburd, Mastrofski, McNally, Greenspan, and Willis, 2003). And though Compstat is an innovation that seeks to concentrate police efforts on specific goals and increase organizational control and accountability, it has encouraged geographic analysis of crime as one of its innovations.

Place-based policing, however, requires something more radical than simply advocating that police add a new strategy to the basket of police interventions. For place-based policing to succeed, police must change their unit of analysis for understanding and doing something about crime. Policing today continues to place people at the center of police practices. This is reflected in how data are collected, as well as how the police are organized. Place-based policing demands a fundamental change in the structure of police efforts to do something about crime and other community problems.

Police data, for example, has developed historically out of a system that was focused on offenders and their characteristics. Indeed, the addition of a place-based identifier was not initially a source of much concern in incident, arrest, or police call databases. In the late 1980s, researchers who tried to analyze the locations of crime using police databases were often frustrated by an inability to identify where a crime occurred. There were often multiple names given to similar addresses, some based on the actual address and some on the names given to stores or other institutions at that address. Such name identifiers often included scores of possible permutations, and address identifiers often failed to identify whether the address was in the south, north, east, or west of cities with such designations. Over the last decade, police have become much better at identifying where the crime is located, in part because of significant advances in records management systems and in part because of advances in geographic information systems. But it is striking how police in most jurisdictions have failed to go very much beyond the simple identification of an address in their data systems.

In the case of arrest databases, it is common to collect data on age, gender, and often education and other demographic characteristics of offenders. But it is rare for such databases to tell us much about the nature of the places that are the context of police activities. A successful program of place-based policing would require that the police routinely capture rich data about places. We should know as much about the places that are hot spots of crime as we do about offenders who commit crimes. Such data should be regularly available to police when they decide to focus interventions on specific places. The failure to collect such data routinely, or to gain such data from other agencies, limits the ability of police to develop effective place-based policing strategies. Block and Green (1994) have already suggested the importance of such databases in what they have called a GeoArchive. The Illinois Criminal Justice Information Authority developed the GeoArchive as an extensive geographic database of community and law enforcement data. A variety of data are collected including: street map data, official crime data (calls for service, arrests, offender characteristics, victim characteristics), corrections data (the addresses of persons released on probation or parole), landmark data (parks, schools, public transportation, liquor stores, abandoned buildings), and population information (Block, 1998).

The failures of traditional person-centered policing to develop data sources relevant for place-based policing is also evidenced in the lack of interest of police executives in knowing where the police are. While technologies for tracking the whereabouts of police, often termed automated vehicle locator technologies, have been available for decades, very few U. S. police agencies have used these technologies to improve the effectiveness of policing. For example, knowledge about where crime is and where police patrol could provide important insights into the benefits of specific police strategies. Ability to track police presence could also be used to make sure that scarce patrol resources are actually being sent to where they are needed. The Police Foundation is currently working on an innovative program in collaboration with the Dallas, Texas Police Department with these aims in mind. But it is in some sense indicative of the failure of police to take a place-based approach that this technology has only now begun to be applied to practical crime prevention.

The geographic organization of policing today also fails to recognize the importance of places in developing police strategies. By arranging police in large precincts and beats, the police have assumed that the common denominator of crime is found at large geographic levels.

While it might be argued that precincts and beats are seldom fit for even larger geographic units such as communities, they are particularly ill fit for place-based policing. Perhaps police should consider dividing patrol according to micro places that have similar crime levels and developmental trends over time. Such a reorganization of police around places would focus strategic thinking and resources on solving common problems. The reorganization of police for place-based policing might also take other forms, but it is clear that today's precincts or beats do not take into account what we know about the geographic distribution of crime and its concentration at relatively small crime places.

In policing places, there must also be a shift from arresting and prosecuting offenders to reducing the opportunities for crime at place. The idea that police were too focused on law enforcement is not a new one, and indeed was a central concern of Herman Gold-stein when he introduced the idea of problem-oriented policing in 1979. For three decades Goldstein and others have tried to influence the police to be less focused on arrest and prosecution of individual offenders and more focused on solving crime problems. But these calls have at best been only partially heeded by the police, and there is much evidence that law enforcement and arrest of offenders remains the primary tool of policing even in innovative programs (Braga and Weisburd, 2006). In a police culture in which person-based policing is predominant, it is natural for police officers to continue to focus on offenders and their arrest.

Place-based policing provides an opportunity to finally shift this emphasis, because it places the crime place rather than the offender at the center of the crime prevention equation. It changes the central concern of police to improving places rather than simply processing offenders. Success in this context must be measured not in terms of how many arrests the police make but in terms of whether places become safer for the people who live, visit, or work in such places. Policing places requires the expansion of the toolbox of policing far beyond traditional law enforcement. In this context, place-based policing requires that police be concerned not only about places, offenders, and victims but also about potential non-police guardians. If the goal of the police is to improve safety at places, then it is natural in policing places to be concerned with what Eck and others have termed "place managers" (Eck, 1994; Eck and Wartell, 1996). "Third party policing" (Mazerolle and Ransley, 2005) is also a natural part of place-based policing. But, more generally, place-based policing brings the attention of the police to the full range of people and contexts that are part of the crime problem.

In advocating place-based policing, it is important to note that police should not abandon concern with people involved in crimes. People should not be ignored, but rather they should be seen in the context of where crime occurs. Saying that people should not be at the center of the crime equation does not mean that they are not an integral part of that equation. The difference is in good part how the police should organize information and crime prevention efforts. Moreover, there may be some crimes that are better understood by focusing on people rather than places, and this should also be a central component of our understanding of place-based policing. Though there is as yet little solid scientific evidence that repeat offender or victim crime prevention programs are effective (Weisburd and Eck, 2004), it is clear that very high-rate criminals or victims should be the subjects of special police attention.

CONCLUSIONS

Basic research suggests that the action of crime is at very small geographic units of analysis, such as street segments or small groups of street segments. Such places also offer a stable target for police interventions, as contrasted with the constantly moving targets of criminal offenders. Crime at place is not simply a proxy for larger area or community effects; indeed the basic research evidence suggests that much of the action of crime occurs at very small geographic units of place. Basic research also reinforces the idea that characteristics of places that can be affected by policing are strongly related to crime at place. But the case for place-based policing does not come only from basic research. There is a strong body of experimental evidence for the effectiveness of place-based policing. Moreover, studies today suggest that place-based policing will not simply move " crime around the corner. " Indeed, the evidence available suggests that such interventions are much more likely to lead to a diffusion of crime control benefits to areas nearby.

Research accordingly suggests that it is time for police to shift from person-based policing to place-based policing. While such a shift is largely an evolution in trends that have begun over the last few decades, it will nonetheless demand radical changes in data collection in policing, in the organization of police activities, and particularly in the overall world view of the police. It remains true today that police officers see the key work of policing as catching criminals. It is time to change that world view so that police understand that the key to crime prevention is in ameliorating crime at place.

References

Agnew R. , & Peterson D. M. (1989). Leisure and delinquency. *Social Problems*, 36, 332 – 350.

Akers, R. L. (1973). *Deviant behavior: A social learning approach.* Belmont, CA: Wadsworth Publishing.

Albrecht, H. J., & Moitra, S. (1988). Escalation and specialization - A comparative analysis of patterns in criminal careers. In G. Kiser &I. Geissler (eds.), *Crime and criminal justice*. Freiburg: Max Planck Institute.

Andrews, D. A., Zinger,I., Hoge, R. D., Bonta, J., Gendreau, P., & Cullen, F. T. (1990). Does correctional treatment work? A clinically relevant and psychologically informed meta-analysis. *Criminology*, 28(3), 369 – 404.

Barnett, A., & Lofaso, A . J. (1985). Selective incapacitation and the Philadelphia cohort data. *Journal of Quantitative Criminology*, 1, 3 – 36.

Barr, R., & Pease, K. (1990). Crime placement, displacement, and deflection. In M. Tonry & N. Morris (eds.), *Crime and Justice: A Review of Research*, vol. 12. Chicago: University of Chicago Press.

Bittner, E. (1967). The police on skid-row: A study of peacekeeping. *American Sociological Review*, 32, 699 – 715.

Block, C. R. (1998). The GeoArchive: An information foundation for community policing. In D. Weisburd & T. McEwen (eds.), *Crime mapping & crime prevention*, *Crime Prevention Studies*, vol. 8 (pp. 27 – 81). Monsey, NY: Criminal Justice Press.

Block, C. R., & Green, L. A. (1994). *The GeoArchive handbook: A guide for developing a geographic database as an information foundation for community policing*. Chicago: Illinois Criminal Justice Information Authority.

Block, C., Dabdoub, M., & Fregly, S. (eds.) (1995). *Crime analysis through computer mapping*. Washington, DC: Police Executive Research Forum.

Blumstein, A., & Cohen, J. (1979). Estimation of individual crime rates from arrest records. *Journal of Criminal Law and Criminology*, 70, 561 – 585.

Blumstein, A., & Wallman, J. (eds.). (2000). *The crime drop in America*. New York: Cambridge University Press.

Blumstein, A., Cohen, J., Roth, J. A., & Visher, C. B. (eds.). (1986). *Criminal careers and "career criminals"*. Washington, DC: National Academies Press.

Blumstein, A., Cohen, J., Das, S., & Moitra, S. D. (1988). Specialization and seriousness during adult criminal careers. *Journal of Quantitative Criminology*, 4, 303 – 345.

Braga, A. A. (2001). The effects of hot spots policing on crime. *The Annals of the American Academy of Political and Social Science*, 578, 104 – 115.

Braga, A. A. (2005). Hot spots policing and crime prevention: A systematic review of randomized controlled trials. *Journal of Experimental Criminology*, 1, 317–342.

Braga, A. A. (2007). *Effects of hot spots policing on crime.* A Campbell Collaboration systematic review, Available online at: http://campbellcollaboration. org/lib/download/118/

Braga, A. A., & Weisburd, D. (2006). Problem-oriented policing: The disconnect between principles and practice. In D. Weisburd & A. A. Braga (eds.), *Police innovation: Contrasting perspectives* (pp. 27–43). New York: Cambridge University Press.

Braga, A. A., & Winship, C. (2006). Partnership, accountability, and innovation: Clarifying Boston's experience with pulling levers. In D. Weisburd & A. A. Braga (eds.), *Police innovation: Contrasting perspectives.* New York: Cambridge University Press.

Braga, A. A., & Bond, B. J. (2008). Policing crime and disorder hot spots: A randomized controlled trial. *Criminology*, 46, 577–608.

Braga, A. A., & Weisburd, D. (2010). *Policing problem places: Crime hot spots and effective prevention.* Oxford University Press.

Braga, A. A., Weisburd, D. L., Waring, E. J., Mazerolle, L. G., Spelman, W., & Gajewski, F. (1999). Problem-oriented policing in violent crime places: A randomized controlled experiment. *Criminology*, 37, 541–580.

Brantingham, P. J., & Brantingham, P. L. (1981 [1991]). The dimensions of crime. In P. J. Brantingham & P. L. Brantingham (eds.), *Environmental criminology* (pp. 7–26). Beverly Hills, CA: Sage Publications.

Brantingham, P. J., & Brantingham, P. L. (1984). *Patterns in crime.* New York: Macmillan.

Brantingham, P. J., & Brantingham, P. L. (1990). Situational crime prevention in practice. *Canadian Journal of Criminology*, 32(1), 17–40.

Brantingham, P. L., & Brantingham, P. J. (1999). Theoretical model of crime hot spot generation. *Studies on Crime and Crime Prevention*, 8, 7–26.

Brisgone, R. (2004). Report on qualitative analysis of displacement in a prostitution site. In *Does crime just move around the corner? A study of displacement and diffusion in Jersey City, NJ*, D. Weisburd, L. A. Wyckoff, J. Ready, J. E. Eck, J. C. Hinkle, & F.

Gajewski (eds.). Report submitted to National Institute of Justice. Grant No. 97-IJ-CX-0055. Washington, DC: U. S. Department of Justice.

Bursik, R. J. Jr. , & Webb, J. (1982). Community change and patterns of delinquency. *American Journal of Sociology*, 88(1), 24 – 42.

Bushway, S. D. , Thornberry, T. P. , & Krohn M. D. (2003). Desistance as a developmental process: A comparison of static and dynamic approaches. *Journal of Quantitative Criminology*, 19(2), 129 – 153.

Caeti, T. (1999). *Houston's targeted beat program: A quasi-experimental test of patrol strategies.* Doctoral dissertation, Sam Houston State University. Ann Arbor, MI: University Microfilms International.

Caulkins, J. (1992). Thinking about displacement in drug markets: Why observing change of venue isn't enough. *Journal of Drug Issues*, 22, 17 – 30.

Chaiken, J. , Lawless, M. , & Stevenson, K. (1974). *The impact of police activity on crime: Robberies on the New York City subway system.* Santa Monica, CA: Rand Corporation.

Cheh, M. (1991). Constitutional limits on using civil remedies to achieve criminal law objectives: Understanding and transcending the criminal-civil law distinction. *Hastings Law Journal*, 42, 1325 – 1413.

Clarke, R. V. (1980). "Situational" crime prevention: Theory and practice. *British Journal of Criminology*, 20(2), 136 – 147.

Clarke, R. V. (1983). Situational crime prevention: Its theoretical basis and practical scope. In M. Tonry & N. Morris (eds.), *Crime and Justice: A Review of Research*, vol. 14. Chicago: University of Chicago Press.

Clarke, R. V. (1992). *Situational crime prevention: Successful case studies.* Albany, NY: Harrow and Heston.

Clarke, R. V. (1995). Situational crime prevention. In M. Tonry & D. Farrington (eds.), *Building a safer society: Strategic approaches to crime prevention. Crime and Justice: A Review of Research*, vol. 19 (pp. 91 – 150). Chicago: University of Chicago Press.

Clarke, R. V. , & Cornish, D. B. (1985). Modeling offender's decisions: A framework for research and policy. In M. Tonry & N. Morris (eds.), *Crime and Justice: A Review of Research*, vol. 6. Chicago: University of Chicago Press.

Clarke, R. V. , & Felson, M. (1993). Introduction: Criminology, routine activity, and rational choice. In R. V. Clarke & M. Felson (eds.) , *Routine activity and rational choice. Advances in Criminological Theory*, vol. 5. New Brunswick, NJ: Transaction Press.

Clarke, R. V. , & Weisburd, D. (1994). Diffusion of crime control benefits: Observations on the reverse of displacement. In R. V. Clarke (ed.) , *Crime Prevention Studies*, vol. 2 (pp. 165 – 184). Monsey, NY: Criminal Justice Press.

Clarke, R. V. , & Cornish, D. B. (2001). Rational choice. In R. Paternoster & R. Bachman (eds.) , *Explaining criminals and crime*. Los Angeles: Roxbury Publishing.

Cohen, L. E. , & Felson, M. (1979). Social change and crime rate trends: A routine activity approach. *American Sociological Review*, 44(4), 588 – 605.

Cornish, D. , & Clarke, R. V. (eds.). (1986). *The reasoning criminal: Rational choice perspectives on offending*. New York: Springer-Verlag.

Criminal Justice Commission (1998). *Beenleigh calls for service project: Evaluation report*. Brisbane, Queensland: Author.

Crow, W. , & Bull, J. (1975). *Robbery deterrence: An applied behavioral science demonstration – Final report*. La Jolla, CA: Western Behavioral Science Institute.

Cullen, F. T. (2005). Twelve people who saved rehabilitation: How the science of criminology made a difference. *Criminology*, 43(1), 1 – 42.

Earls, F. (1991). Not fear, nor quarantine, but science: Preparation for a decade of research to advance knowledge about causes and control of violence in youths. *Journal of Adolescent Health* 12, 619 – 629.

Earls, F. , & Carlson, M. (1995). Promoting human capability as an alternative to early crime prevention. In P. O. Wikström, R. V. Clarke & J. McCord (eds.) , *Integrating crime prevention strategies: Propensity and opportunity*. Stockholm, Sweden: National Council for Crime Prevention.

Eck, J. E. (1993). The threat of crime displacement. *Criminal Justice Abstracts*, 25, 527 – 546.

Eck, J. E. (1994). *Drug markets and drug places: A case-control study of the spatial structure of illicit dealing*. Doctoral dissertation, University of Maryland, College Park. Ann Arbor, MI: University Microfilms International.

Eck, J. E. , & Weisburd, D. (1995). Crime places in crime theory. In J. E. Eck & D. Weisburd (eds.) , *Crime and place, Crime Prevention Studies*, vol. 4 (pp. 1 – 33).

Monsey, NY: Willow Tree Press.

Eck, J. E. , & Wartell, J. (1996). *Reducing crime and drug dealing by improving place management: A randomized experiment.* Report to the San Diego Police Department. Washington, DC: Crime Control Institute.

Eck, J. E. , Gersh, J. S. , & Taylor, C. (2000). Finding crime hot spots through repeat address mapping. In V. Goldsmith, P. G. McGuire, J. H. Mollenkopf & T. A. Ross (eds.) ,*Analyzing crime patterns: Frontiers of practice* (pp. 49 – 64). Thousand Oaks, CA: Sage Publications.

Elliott, D. S. , Dunford, F. W. , & Huizinga, D. (1987). Identification and prediction of career offenders utilizing self – reported and official data. In J. D. Burchard & S. N. Burchard (eds.) , *Prevention of delinquent behavior.* Newbury Park, CA: Sage Publications.

Estricht, S. , Moore, M. H. , McGillis, D. , & Spelman, W. (1983). *Dealing with dangerous offenders – Executive summary.* Washington, DC: National Institute of Justice, U. S. Department of Justice.

Farrington, D. P. (1983). Randomized experiments on crime and justice. In M. Tonry & N. Morris (eds.) ,*Crime and Justice: A Review of Research.* vol. 4. Chicago: University of Chicago Press.

Farrington, D. P. , Ohlin, L. E. , & Wilson, J. Q. (1986). *Understanding and controlling crime.* New York: Springer-Verlag.

Felson, M. (1994). *Crime and everyday life: Insight and implications for society.* Thousand Oaks, CA: Pine Forge Press.

Felson, M. (2006). *Crime and nature.* Thousand Oaks, CA: Sage Publications.

Gabor, T. (1990). Crime displacement and situational prevention: Toward the development of some principles. *Canadian Journal of Criminology, 32,* 41 – 74.

Goldstein, H. (1979). Improving policing: A problem-oriented approach. *Crime & Delinquency,* 25, 236 – 258.

Goldstein, H. (1990). *Problem-oriented policing.* New York: McGraw-Hill.

Goldstock, R. (1991). *The prosecutor as problem solver.* New York: New York University Center for Research in Crime and Justice.

Gottfredson, S. D. , & Gottfredson, D. M. (1990). *Classification, prediction and criminal justice policy.* Washington, DC: National Institute of Justice, U. S. Department of Justice.

Gottfredson, M. , & Hirschi, T. (1990). *A general theory of crime.* Stanford, CA: Stanford University Press.

Green, L. (1996). *Policing places with drug problems.* Thousand Oaks, CA: Sage Publications.

Groff, E. R. , Weisburd, D. , & Morris, N. (2009). Where the action is at places: Examining spatio-temporal patterns of juvenile crime at places using trajectory analysis and GIS. In D. Weisburd, W. Bernasco & G. J. N. Bruinsma (eds.), *Putting crime in its place: Units of analysis in spatial crime research.* New York: Springer-Verlag.

Groff, E. R. , Weisburd, D. , & Yang, S. -M. (2010). Is it important to examine crime trends at a local "micro" level?: A longitudinal analysis of street to street variability in crime trajectories. *Journal of Quantitative Criminology*, 26(1), 7 – 32.

Guerette, R. T. , & Bowers, K. J. (2009). Assessing the extent of crime displacement and diffusion of benefits: A review of situational crime prevention evaluations. *Criminology*, 47(4), 1331 – 1368.

Hesseling, R. B. P. (1994). Displacement: A review of the empirical literature. In R. V. Clarke (ed.), *Crime Prevention Studies*, vol. 3 (pp. 197 – 230). Monsey, NY: Criminal Justice Press.

Hope, T. (1994). Problem-oriented policing and drug market locations: Three case studies. In R. V. Clarke (ed.), *Crime Prevention Studies*, vol. 2 (pp. 5 – 32). Monsey, NY: Criminal Justice Press.

Horney, J. , Osgood, D. W. , & Marshall, I. H. (1995). Criminal careers in the short-term: Intra-individual variability in crime and its relation to local life circumstances. *American Sociological Review*, 60(5), 655 – 673.

Hughes, K. A. (2006). *Justice expenditure and employment in the United States, 2003.* Washington, DC: Bureau of Justice Statistics, U. S. Department of Justice.

Johnson, E. , & Payne, J. (1986). The decision to commit a crime: An information-processing analysis. In D. B. Cornish & R. V. Clarke (eds.), *The reasoning criminal: Rational choice perspectives on offending.* New York. Springer-Verlag.

Kahan, D. M. , & Meares, T. L. (1998). The coming crisis of criminal procedure. *Georgetown Law Journal*, 86, 1153 – 1184.

Kempf, K. (1986). Offense specialization – Does it exist? In D. B. Cornish & R. V. Clarke

(eds.) , *The reasoning criminal*: *Rational choice perspectives on offending*. New York: Springer-Verlag.

Kennedy, D. M. (2006). Old wine in new bottles: Policing and the lessons of pulling levers. In D. Weisburd & A. A. Braga (eds.), *Police innovation*: *Contrasting perspectives*. New York: Cambridge University Press.

Koper, C. (2008). The varieties and effectiveness of hot spots policing: Results from a national survey of police agencies and a reassessment of prior research. Paper presented at the Annual Meeting of the American Society of Criminology, November 14, St. Louis, MO.

Laub, J. H. , & Sampson, R. J. (2003). *Shared beginnings*, *divergent lives*: *Delinquent boys to age* 70. Cambridge, MA: Harvard University Press.

Lipsey, M. W. (1992). Juvenile delinquency treatment: A metaanalytic inquiry into the variability of effects. In T. D. Cook *et al.* , (eds.), *Meta-analysis for explanation*: *A casebook*. New York: Russell Sage.

Lipsey, M. W. , & Wilson, D. B. (2001). *Practical meta-analysis*. Thousand Oaks, CA: Sage Publications.

Lipsey, M. W. , & Cullen, F. T. (2007). The effectiveness of correctional rehabilitation: A review of systematic reviews. *Annual Review of Law & Social Science*, 3, 297 – 320.

Lipton, D. , Martinson, R. , & Wilks, J. (1975). *The effectiveness of correctional treatment*. New York: Praeger.

Martinson, R. (1974). What works? Questions and answers about prison reform. *Public Interest*, 35, 22 – 54.

Mastrofski, S. (1999). Policing for people. *Ideas in American Policing*. Washington, DC: Police Foundation.

Mastrofski, S. M. , Weisburd, D. , &Braga, A. A. (2010). Rethinking policing: The policy implications of hot spots of crime. In N. A. Frost, J. D. Freilich, & T. R. Clear (eds.), *Contemporary issues in criminal justice policy*: *Policy proposals from the American Society of Criminology conference* (pp. 251 – 264). Belmont, CA: Cengage/Wadsworth.

Mazerolle, L. , & Roehl, J. (1998). Civil remedies and crime prevention. In L. Mazerolle & J. Roehl (eds.), *Civil remedies and crime prevention*, *Crime Prevention Studies*, vol. 9. Monsey, NY: Criminal Justice Press.

Mazerolle, L., & Ransley, J. (2005). *Third party policing*. New York: Cambridge University Press.

McGarrell, E. F., Chermak, S. Weiss, A., & Wilson, J. (2001). Reducing firearms violence through directed police patrol. *Criminology and Public Policy*, 1, 119 – 148.

Meares, T. L. (2006). Third-party policing: A critical view. In D. Weisburd & A. A. Braga (eds.), *Police innovation: Contrasting perspectives*. New York: Cambridge University Press.

Moore, M. H. (1986). Purblind justice-Normative issues in the use of prediction in the criminal justice system. In A. Blumstein, J. Cohen, J. A. Roth & C. A. Visher (eds.), *Criminal careers and career criminals*, vol. 2. Washington DC: National Academies Press.

Nagin, D. S. (1999). Analyzing developmental trajectories: A semiparametric group-based approach. *Psychological Methods*, 4, 139 – 157.

Nagin, D. (2005). *Group-based modeling of development over the life course*. Cambridge, MA: Harvard University Press.

Nagin, D. S., & Land, K. C. (1993). Age, criminal careers, and population heterogeneity: Specification and estimation of a nonparametric, mixed Poisson model. *Criminology*, 31(3), 327 – 362.

Nagin, D., & Tremblay, R. E. (1999). Trajectories of boys' physical aggression, opposition, and hyperactivity on the path to physically violent and nonviolent juvenile delinquency. *Child Development* 70, 1181 – 1196.

National Research Council. (2004). *Fairness and effectiveness in policing: The evidence*. Committee to Review Research on Police Policy and Practices. W. Skogan & K. Frydl (eds.). Committee on Law and Justice, Division of Behavioral and Social Sciences and Education. Washington, DC: National Academies Press.

Nettler, G. (1978). *Explaining crime*. 2nd edition. New York: McGraw-Hill.

Ohlin, L., & Remington, F. (eds.). (1993). *Discretion in criminal justice: The tension between individualization and uniformity*. Albany: State University of New York Press.

Osgood D. W., Wilson, J. K., O'Malley, P. M., Bachman, J. G., Johnston, L. D. (1996). Routine activities and individual deviant behavior. *American Sociological Review*, 61, 635 – 655.

Pease, K. (1991). The Kirkholt Project: Preventing burglary on a British public housing *estate. Security Journal*, 2, 73 – 77.

Pierce, G. , Spaar, S. , & Briggs, L. R. (1986). *The character of police work: Strategic and tactical implications.* Boston, MA: Center for Applied Social Research, Northeastern University.

Police Executive Research Forum (2008). Violent crime in America: What we know about hot spots enforcement. *Critical Issues in Policing Series.* Washington, DC: Author.

Reppetto, T. (1976). Crime prevention and the displacement phenomenon. *Crime & Delinquency*, 22, 166 – 177.

Roncek, D. W. (2000). Schools and crime. In V. Goldsmith, P. G. McGuire, J. H. Mollenkopf, & T. A. Ross (eds.), *Analyzing crime patterns: Frontiers of practice* (pp. 153 – 165). Thousand Oaks, CA: Sage Publications.

Roncek, D. W. , &Bell, R. (1981) Bars, blocks and crimes. *Journal of Environmental Systems*, 11, 35 – 47.

Roncek, D. W. , & Maier, P. A. (1991). Bars, blocks, and crimes revisited: Linking the theory of routine activities to the empiricism of " hot spots ". *Criminology*, 29, 725 – 753.

Rosenbaum, D. (2006). The limits of hot spots policing. In D. Weisburd & A. A. Braga (eds.), *Police innovation: Contrasting perspectives.* New York: Cambridge University Press.

Sampson, R. J. (2004). Neighborhood and community: Collective efficacy and community safety. *New Economy*, 11, 106 – 113.

Sampson, R. J. , Raudenbush, S. W. , & Earls, F. (1997). Neighborhoods and violent crime: A multilevel study of collective efficacy. *Science*, 277, 918 – 924.

Schmid, C. F. (1960a). Urban crime areas: Part I. *American Sociological Review*, 25(4), 527 – 542.

Schmid, C. F. (1960b). Urban crime areas: Part II. *American Sociological Review*, 25 (5), 655 – 678.

Sechrest, L. , White, S. O. , & Brown, E. D. (1979). *The rehabilitation of criminal offenders: Problems and prospects.* Washington, D. C. : National Academies Press.

Shaw, J. (1995). Community policing against guns: Public opinion of the Kansas City Gun Experiment. *Justice Quarterly*, 12, 695 – 710.

Shaw, C. R. , & McKay, H. D. (1942 [1969]). *Juvenile delinquency and urban areas. A study of rates of delinquency in relation to differential characteristics of local communities in American cities*, Chicago: University of Chicago Press (Revised ed.).

Sherman, L. W. (1990). Police crackdowns: Initial and residual deterrence. In M. Tonry & N. Morris (eds.), *Crime and Justice: A Review of Research*, vol. 12. Chicago: University of Chicago Press.

Sherman, L. W. (1995). Hot spots of crime and criminal careers of places. In J. E. Eck & D. Weisburd (eds.), *Crime and place*, *Crime Prevention Studies*, vol. 4 (pp. 35 - 52). Monsey, NY: Criminal Justice Press.

Sherman, L. W., & Rogan, D. P. (1995a). Deterrent effects of police raids on crack houses: A randomized controlled experiment. *Justice Quarterly*, 12, 755 - 782.

Sherman, L. W., and Rogan, D. P. (1995b). Effects of gun seizures on gun violence: 'Hot spots' patrol in Kansas City." *Justice Quarterly*, 12, 673 - 694.

Sherman, L. W., & Weisburd, D. (1995). General deterrent effects of police patrol in crime hot spots: A randomized controlled trial. *Justice Quarterly*, 12, 625 - 648.

Sherman, L. W., Buerger, M. E. & Gartin, P. R. (1989). *Repeat call address policing: The Minneapolis RECAP experiment*. Final Report to the U. S. Department of Justice, National Institute of Justice. Washington, DC: Crime Control Institute.

Sherman, L. W., Gartin, P. R., & Buerger, M. E. (1989). Hot spots of predatory crime: Routine activities and the criminology of place. *Criminology*, 27, 27 - 56.

Smith, W. R., Frazee, S. G., & Davison, E. L. (2000). Furthering the integration of routine activity and social disorganization theories: Small units of analysis and the study of street robbery as a diffusion process. *Criminology*, 38(2), 489 - 523.

Smith, M. J., Clarke, R. V., & Pease, K. (2002). Anticipatory benefits in crime prevention. In N. Tilley (ed.), *Analysis for crime prevention*, *Crime Prevention Studies*, vol. 13. Monsey, NY: Criminal Justice Press.

Snyder, H. N. (2003). *Juvenile arrests* 2001. *Juvenile justice bulletin*. Washington, DC: Office of Juvenile Justice and Delinquency Prevention.

Spelman, W. (1995). Criminal careers of public places. In J. E. Eck & D. Weisburd (eds.), *Crime and place*, *Crime Prevention Studies*, vol. 4. Monsey, NY: Willow Tree Press.

Sutherland, E. H. (1947). *Principles of criminology*. 4th ed. Chicago: JB Lippincott Company.

Taylor, R. B. (1997). Social order and disorder of street blocks and neighborhoods: Ecology, microecology, and the systemic model of social disorganization. *Journal of Research in Crime and Delinquency*, 34, 113 – 155.

Taylor, R. B. (1999). *Crime, grime, fear, and decline: A longitudinal look*. Research in Brief. Washington, DC: National Institute of Justice, U. S. Department of Justice.

Taylor, R. B. (2001). *Breaking away from broken windows: Baltimore neighborhoods and the nationwide fight against crime, grime, fear, and decline*. Boulder, CO: Westview Press.

Taylor, R. B. (2006). Incivilities reduction policing, zero tolerance, and the retreat from coproduction. In D. Weisburd & A. A. Braga (eds.), *Police innovation: Contrasting perspectives*. New York: Cambridge University Press.

Tracy, P. E., & Kempf-Leonard, K. (1996). *Continuity and discontinuity in criminal careers*. New York: Plenum Press.

Trasler, G. (1993). Conscience, opportunity, rational choice, and crime. In R. V. Clarke & M. Felson (eds.), *Routine activity and rational choice. Advances in Criminological Theory*, vol. 5. New Brunswick, NJ: Transaction Publishers.

Tyler, T. R. (1990). *Why people obey the law: Procedural justice, legitimacy, and compliance*. New Haven, CT: Yale University Press.

Tyler, T. R. (2004). Enhancing police legitimacy. *The Annals of the American Academy of Political and Social Science*, 593, 84 – 99.

Visher, C. A., & Weisburd, D. (1997). Identifying what works: Recent trends in crime prevention strategies. *Crime, Law and Social Change*, 28, 223 – 242.

Vollmer, A. (1933). Police progress in the past twenty-five years. *Journal of Criminal Law and Criminology*, 24, 161 – 175.

Waddington, P. J., & Neyroud, P. (eds.). (2007). Policing terrorism. *Policing: A Journal of Policy and Practice*, 1(1).

Wallace, J. M., & Bachman, J. G. (1991). Explaining racial/ethnic differences in adolescent drug use: The impact of background and lifestyle. *Social Problems*, 38, 333 – 357.

Walmsley, R. (2009). World prisoner population list. 8th edition. London: Kings College International Centre for Prison Studies.

Weisburd, D. (1997). *Reorienting crime prevention research and policy: From causes of crime to the context of crime*. National Institute of Justice Research Report. Washington, DC: U. S. Government Printing Office.

Weisburd, D. (2002). From criminals to criminal contexts: Reorienting criminal justice research and policy. In E. Waring & D. Weisburd (eds.), *Crime and social organization*, *Advances in Criminological Theory*, vol. 10 (pp. 197 – 216). New Brunswick, NJ: Transaction Publishers.

Weisburd, D. (2008). Place-based policing. *Ideas in American Policing*. Washington, DC: Police Foundation.

Weisburd, D., & Green, L. (1994). Defining the street level drug market. In D. MacKenzie &C. Uchida (eds.), *Drugs and crime: Evaluating public policy initiatives* (pp. 61 – 76). Thousand Oaks, CA: Sage Publications.

Weisburd, D., & Green, L. (1995a). Policing drug hot spots: The Jersey City Drug Market Analysis Experiment. *Justice Quarterly*, 12, 711 – 36.

Weisburd, D., & Green, L. (1995b). Measuring immediate spatial displacement: Methodological issues and problems. In J. E. Eck & D. Weisburd (eds.), *Crime and place*, *CrimePrevention Studies*, vol. 4. Monsey, NY: Willow Tree Press.

Weisburd, D., & Mazerolle, L. G. (2000). Crime and disorder in drug hot spots: Implications for theory and practice in policing. *Police Quarterly*, 3(3), 331 – 349.

Weisburd, D., & Waring, E. (2001). *White-collar crime and criminal careers*. New York: Cambridge University Press.

Weisburd, D., & Eck, J. E. (2004). What can the police do to reduce crime, disorder, and fear? *The Annals of the American Academy of Political and Social Science*, 593, 42 – 65.

Weisburd, D., & Lum, C. (2005). The diffusion of computerized crime mapping policing: Linking research and practice. *Police Practice and Research*, 6, 419 – 434.

Weisburd, D., &Braga, A. A. (2006a). Introduction: Understanding police innovation. In D. Weisburd & A. A. Braga (eds.), *Police innovation: Contrasting perspectives* (pp. 1 – 23). New York: Cambridge University Press.

Weisburd, D., & Braga, A. A. (2006b). Hot spots policing as a model for police innovation. In D. Weisburd & A. A. Braga (eds.), *Police Innovation: Contrasting perspectives* (pp. 225 – 244). New York: Cambridge University Press.

Weisburd, D., & Piquero, A. R. (2008). How well do criminologists explain crime?

Statistical modeling in published studies. In M. Tonry (ed.), *Crime and Justice: A Review of Research*, vol. 37 (pp. 453 – 502). Chicago: University of Chicago Press.

Weisburd, D., Maher, L., & Sherman, L. (1992). Contrasting crime general and crime specific theory: The case of hot spots of crime. In F. Adler & W. Laufer (eds.), *New Directions in criminological theory*, *Advances in Criminological Theory*, vol. 4 (pp. 45 – 69). New Brunswick, NJ: Transaction Press.

Weisburd, D., Bernasco, W., & Bruinsma, G. J. N. (eds.). (2009). *Putting crime in its place: Units of analysis in geographic criminology*. New York: Springer.

Weisburd, D., Morris, N. A., & Groff, E. R. (2009). Hot spots of juvenile crime: A longitudinal study of arrest incidents at street segments in Seattle, Washington. *Journal of Quantitative Criminology*, 25(4), 443 – 467.

Weisburd, D., Groff, E. R., & Yang, S. -M. (In progress). *The criminology of place: Developmental patterns and risk and preventive factors*.

Weisburd, D., Mastrofski, S. D., McNally, A. M., & Greenspan, R. (2001). *Compstat and organizational change: Findings from a national survey*. Washington, DC: National Institute of Justice, Police Foundation.

Weisburd, D., Bushway, S., Lum, C., & Yang, S-M. (2004). Trajectories of crime at places: A longitudinal study of street segments in the city of Seattle. *Criminology*, 42 (2), 283 – 321.

Weisburd, D., Mastrofski, S. D., McNally, A. M., Greenspan, R., and Willis, J. J. (2003). Reforming to preserve: Compstat and strategic problem solving in American policing. *Criminology and Public Policy*, 2, 421 – 456.

Weisburd, D., Wyckoff, L. A., Ready, J., Eck, J. E., Hinkle, J. C., & Gajewski, F. (2006). Does crime just move around the corner? A controlled study of spatial displacement and diffusion of crime control benefits. *Criminology*, 44(3), 549 – 592.

West, H. C., & Sabol, W. (2008). *Prisoners in 2007*. Washington, DC: Bureau of Justice Statistics, U. S. Department of Justice.

Whitehead, J. T., & Lab, S. P. (1989). A meta-analysis of juvenile correctional treatment. *Journal of Research in Crime and Delinquency*, 26, 276 – 295.

Wickersham Commission. (1931). Wickersham report on police. *American Journal of Police Science*, 2, 337 – 348.

Wilson, O. W. (1950). *Police administration*. New York: McGraw-Hill.

Wolfgang, M. E., Figlio, R., & Sellin, T. (1972). *Delinquency in a birth cohort.* Chicago: University of Chicago Press.

Wolfgang, M., Thornberry, T. P., & Figlio, R. M. (1987). *From boy to man, from delinquency to crime.* Chicago: University of Chicago Press.

地点导向警务模式的效率性

大卫·威斯勃德（David Weisburd）

希伯来大学

科迪·W.特勒普（Cody W. Telep）

乔治梅森大学

越来越多的证据表明，警方针对地理概念下小单元打击犯罪所付诸的努力，为提升控制犯罪策略的效率创造了机会。我们确定了提高基于地点警务效率的三方面原因。第一，通过在多个城市的研究调查表明，犯罪率在地点分布上有很强的集中性，这使警方以某些犯罪高发地点为目标打击犯罪的活动，远比在整个城市范围内散布警力和资源更高效。第二，在犯罪热点地区，犯罪在长时间内处于相对稳定状态，并且从证据而言，长期犯罪行为要比单个犯罪行为要稳定得多。在此意义上，"地点"对于警方而言，是一个高效"目标"。另外，由于地点的地理位置是固定的，因而相比违法者，更易被警方进行长期掌控。第三，犯罪移转研究表明，在热点区域集中警力并不是简单地"将犯罪挤到角落里"。实际上，基于地点的干预模式反而更可能促成犯罪控制效益的扩散，而不是犯罪移转。

一、引　言

大量证据表明，警察能够有效打击小范围地理区域即通常被称作"热点区域"内的犯罪。一系列随机的现场实验证明,在热点区域集中投入精力能够有效地减少犯罪和扰乱秩序(Braga and Bond, 2008; Braga, Weisburd, Waring, Mazerolle, Spelman, and Gajewski, 1999; Sherman and Weisburd, 1995; Weisburd and Green, 1995)。我们还可以从安东尼·布拉加(Anthony Braga)(2001,2005,2007)做的一份康拜尔合作组织系统性评述中得到热点警务有效性的进一步证据。Braga 发现在热点警务的 9 个实验或准实验评估中,有 7 个实验结果为犯罪或者扰乱秩序显著减少。大量强有力及严密的评估使得国家研究委员会理事会做了有关警察政策与实务评述研究(2004,p.35),结论如下:

> 在过去的二十年里,警方针对有关特定犯罪类型、罪犯以及犯罪地点的警务实践兴趣不断提升。特别是在犯罪热点警务,已经成为减少犯罪和扰乱秩序的一种普遍的警务战略。相比只是少量证据可以证明以特定类型违法者为目标的警务活动的有效性,大量强有力的证据却表明,专注于地理的路径来应对犯罪问题可以提高警务效率(Weisburd and Eck, 2004)。

由此,大量严密的实证研究证明了针对犯罪热点的警察干预是有效的。然而,对警方而言,对这一路径有效性的讨论却很少。有效不仅与要达到特定目标有关,而效率更侧重于资源的投入。正如斯考根(Skogan)(1976,p.278)所提到的,"无论其效果如何,有效率的警察机构带给我们更多的价值"。例如,即便热点区域警务对特定地点减少犯罪是有效的,如果警方对某个地点的干预仅仅是将犯罪挤到邻近社区(即空间移位),那么警方针对犯罪热点的警务并不是真正有效率的。按此逻辑,警方仅仅是简单地将犯罪从这个地方赶到其他地方。同样,如果犯罪热点每年都是无规律地在城市内变动(即一地的犯罪率不存在长期稳定的情况),那么警方就不需要将精力浪费在这些地方,因为热点区域的犯罪率会随着时间的推移而自然下降。在理想的状态下,警方应该通过战术和战略的改进,实现警务效率和有效性的最大化。

在本文中,我们主要阐述的观点是地点导向的警务不仅是有效的,而且对警方而言,这也是一种有效的解决问题的路径。我们可以不断提供证据证明,在小范围地点内投入警力打击犯罪,为警方提高控制违法犯罪战略的有效性创造了机会。我们将在接下来的两个部分里来定义"地点"和"基于地点警务"这两个概念。然后,我们再讨论基于地点警务之所以高效的三个关键原因。第一,关于许多城市的横向和纵向研究都表明,犯罪率在地点分布上有很强的集中性,因此警方若以某些犯罪高发地点为目标远比在整个城市范围内散布警力和资源高效。第二,长期来看,犯罪热点的犯罪相当稳定,且与个体的犯罪相比,证据要稳定得多。在这种意义上,"地点"对于警方而言,是一个高效"目标"。另外,由于地点的地理位置是固定的,相比违法个体而言,更易被警方进行长期追踪。最后,犯罪移转研究表明,有关地点警务的批评,认为在热点区域集中警力的效率性不高,只是简单地"将犯罪挤到角落里",是不正确的。实际上,基于地点的干预模式反而更宜促成犯罪控制效益的扩散。

二、什么是"地点"?

首先申明,我们在本文中提到的"地点"与传统意义上基于地理区位警务的概念并不相同。所谓地点,我们并不是指大范围的地理单位,如常被犯罪学家用于犯罪预防研究的邻里和社区(Bursik and Webb, 1982;Sampson, Raudenbush, and Earls,1997;Shaw and McKay, 1942[1969]),又非警察组织体制中关键的巡区和辖区。在本文中,"地点"是指在社区和邻里等较大的社会环境中的某些特定地理位置(Eck and Weisburd,1995)。这些非常小的"微型"分析单位,可以是建筑物或住址(Green,1996;Sherman, Gartin, and Buerger, 1989),可以是街面或路段(Sherman and Weisburd, 1995;Taylor,1997),也可以是具有相同犯罪问题的地址群、街面群或路段群(Block, Dabdoub, and Fregly, 1995;Weisburd and Green, 1995;Oberwittler and Wikström, 2009)。

我们将用到有关犯罪地点的两个例证,因为他们分别从不同方面证明了地点对理解警务干预模式的重要性。谢尔曼(Sherman)和威斯勃德(Weisburd)(1995)在"明尼阿波里斯市热点区域巡逻实验"中,将路段或街道作为增加巡逻队出现率的分析单位(见图1)。我们将街区的部分作为用于分析的单位,因为它们容易被警方识别并且为警务干预提供自然环境。而学者们也发现,这些小区域,比如路段,与城市生活结构有着一定的关联性(Appleyard, 1981;Jacobs, 1961;Smith, Frazee, and Davison, 2000;Taylor, 1997)。例如泰勒(Taylor)(1998)提出,街区居民之间的视觉接触、相互的角色义务、对特定公共道德规范和行为的认可度、常见的规律性的活动、街道的物理界限和路段的历史演变都使得街区成为地点分析中非常有价值的单位(Hunter and Baumer, 1982;Taylor, Gottfredson, and Brower,1984)。

在泽西市犯罪空间移位和扩散项目中,威斯勃德(Weisburd)、威科夫(Wyckoff)、雷迪(Ready)、埃克(Eck)、欣克尔(Hinkle)和加耶夫斯基(Gajewski)(2006)认为应当定义一个不相关联的地点以引起警察注意。但是这个研究也仅仅只是关注特定类型的犯罪市场。而这样的市场,就大范围的犯罪活动而言,往往遍布整个街区。图2

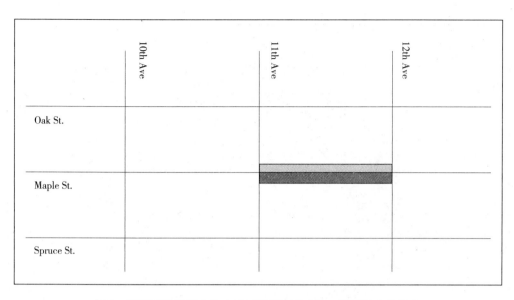

图1 明尼阿波里斯市热点区域巡逻实验中的一个试验点的样本

资料来源：Weisburd（2008）。

描绘了在泽西市警务干预过程中确定的一个毒品市场的边界范围。这个市场虽然包括了一组城市街道，但重要的是，这个地理单位比警务干预和犯罪科学研究中常涉及的邻里和辖区要小得多。有关犯罪空间位移的项目以及明尼阿波里斯市实验说明，依据警方利益以及犯罪问题深层结构的不同，所用于分析的地点单位也不同。

三、什么是"基于地点警务"？

"基于地点警务"到底是指什么呢？其起始于"一地的犯罪是因该地点的某些因素而导致"这一假设，其核心是关注于犯罪聚焦的地点。就此意义而言，基于地点警务模式的理论基础是日常活动理论之上的（Cohen and Felson, 1979; Felson, 1994）。该理论认为，犯罪是由具备合适的目标（如受害者）、缺少有能力的守卫者（如警察）和存在潜在的违法者这三个因素聚合、共同作用而导致的。当然，这三者必须在一个地点或一个场景的背景下发生，于是基于地点警务认为，在这些特定的地点上存在着某些事物导致以上因素的聚合（Brantingham and Brantingham, 1981 ［1991］, 1984）。值得一提的是，基于地点警务并不是简单地将警务策略应用到地理单位上。在这种意义上，传统警务也可以被看作是基于地点的警务，因为警方通过从较大的范围来确定组织实践单位，比如警察辖区和巡区等。如上所述，本文中的地点，是指比传统警

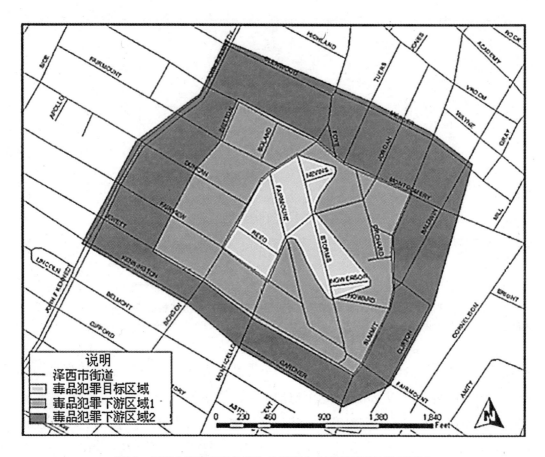

图 2　泽西市犯罪空间位移和扩散研究中毒品犯罪的目标区域

资料来源：Weisburd *et al.*，（2006）。

方行政和策划部门所感兴趣的区域小得多的地理聚合。

基于地点警务的策略可以像热点区域巡逻那么简单，比如明尼阿波里斯市热点区域巡逻实验（Sherman and Weisburd，1995）中，在犯罪集中的地点，警务干预投入更多的巡逻资源。但是，基于地点警务也可以采用更为综合的途径来改善犯罪问题。例如在泽西市毒品市场分析项目（Weisburd and Green，1995）中，采用了一个三步骤程序（包括识别和分析问题，开发定制的应对机制和维护犯罪控制收益）来减少毒品热点区域的问题。在泽西市暴力犯罪地点实验（Braga，Weisburd，Waring，Mazerolle，Spelman，and Gajewski，1999）中，采取了以问题为导向的警务途径，为每个被认为是暴力犯罪热点的小区域制定特定的策略。

简单回顾表明，运用于基于地点警务的具体策略可以是多样的，但是这些策略均关注犯罪活动高发的小范围地理单位。

四、基于地点警务之所以高效是因为犯罪在地点分布上高度集中

基于地点警务有效性的一个重要条件,就是犯罪高度集中在被称为"犯罪热点"的区域(Sherman *et al.*, 1989;Sherman and Weisburd, 1995;Weisburd and Green, 1995)。如果缺少犯罪在地点上高度集中这一条件,那么集中力量投入犯罪预防的努力就缺乏依据了。实际上,如果犯罪只是在整个城市里随机分布,那么基于地点警务就几乎没有效益。

始于20世纪80年代末期的诸多研究证明,无论分析单位如何确定,犯罪在地点的存在具有很强的群聚性(Brantingham and Brantingham, 1999;Crow and Bull, 1975;Pierce, Spaar, and Briggs, 1986;Roncek, 2000;Sherman *et al.*, 1989;Weisburd and Green, 1994;Weisburd, Maher, and Sherman, 1992;Weisburd, Bushway, Lum, and Yang, 2004;Weisburd, Morris, and Groff, 2009)。其中,最具有影响力的可能是谢尔曼(Sherman),加廷(Gartin)和伯格(Buerger)(1989)关于一年内报警电话的街道地址分析。谢尔曼(Sherman)等发现,在美国明尼苏达州明尼阿波里斯市,所有报警电话中的50%来自仅占全市3.5%的街道地址。他们认为这一发现令人震惊,并由此开展了被他们称为是"地点犯罪学"的崭新研究领域。

其他研究也得到了有关犯罪在犯罪热点聚集的类似证据。例如威斯勃德(Weisburd)和马哲罗(Mazerolle)(2000)发现,大约20%的扰乱社会秩序的犯罪和14%的侵犯人身的犯罪仅集中在新泽西州泽西市的56个毒品犯罪热点,面积仅占全市路段和交叉口的4.4%。同样的,埃克(Eck)、格什(Gersh)和泰勒(Taylor)(2000)发现,布朗克斯市、纽约市和马里兰州的巴尔的摩市中最为活跃的10%的地点(以犯罪率为依据),占据了抢劫、人身攻击、入室盗窃、大金额盗窃以及汽车盗窃等一系列犯罪活动数量的32%。

威斯勃德等人(Weisburd *et al.*)(2004)的研究不仅确认了犯罪的聚集性,还证明了在一段较长的时间里,这种聚集具有稳定性。威斯勃德等人(Weisburd *et al.*)研究了西雅图市所有城市路段自1989年至2002年的犯罪数据。他们发现在这14年间,50%的犯罪案件发生地仅占了全市路段总面积的4.5%。如图3所示,这种聚集性年年都很稳定。

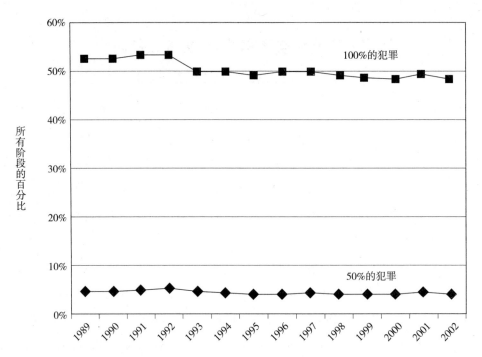

图 3　1989—2002 年西雅图市 50% 和 100% 的犯罪案件报告在路段上分布的比例

资料来源：Weisburd *et al.*，（2004）。

　　这些研究总体上阐明了犯罪现象存在着一种"集中法则"，认为从每年一个城市的大部分犯罪，高度聚集在 5%—10% 以内的住址、街区路段，或者小范围的住址群和路段群。

　　当针对特定犯罪类型的时候，"集中法则"所蕴含的犯罪预防机会就愈加明显。威斯勃德（Weisburd）、米雷斯（Mirris）和格罗夫（Groff）（2009）在西雅图进行的另一项研究中调查了青少年被捕的犯罪事件的聚集性。他们发现，在过去的 14 年里，官方所提供的青少年被捕事件总数的三分之一仅来自几乎全部 30000 个街区中的 86 个街区路段。就在许多研究还在构建到底有多少犯罪聚集是因警察巡逻力量之聚焦而引起之时，本研究已经拓展到警方可以通过关注城市中的热点区域以提高效率这一命题。

　　劳伦斯·谢尔曼（Lawrence Sherman）（1995）提出，这种在地点上出现的犯罪群聚现象甚至比在个人身上的犯罪集中现象更为明显。他运用明尼阿波里斯的数据，并与费城出生组研究中的犯罪集中数据（Wolfgang，Figlio，and Sellin，1972）相比较，提出"通过发生地点预测未来犯罪的准确性是通过识别违法者预测的六倍"（1995，pp. 36 - 37）。谢尔曼（Sherman）质疑："为什么我们不在这方面做得更多？为什么我们不是更多思考发生在哪里，而只是考虑谁做的？"

威斯勃德（Weisburd）（2008, p. 5）提出类似的西雅图市关于纵向研究的数据。当我们使用"目标"作为一个标准，相对于违法者而言，地点具有更高的精度。采用这种方法，他发现在过去的 14 年里每年平均 50% 的犯罪总量分布在约 1500 个街区路段。在同样的时间跨度内，每年 50% 的犯罪总量是由约 6108 名违法者实施。简而言之，若警方专注于违法者，那么面对相同犯罪总量，确定犯罪目标的工作量将是专注于地点工作量的四倍。

五、基于地点警务之所以高效是因为从时间 跨度看犯罪在地点上是稳定的

犯罪在地点上的聚集性，为犯罪预防策略提供了一个很大的可能，例如犯罪热点巡逻（Sherman and Weisburd, 1995；Weisburd and Braga, 2006）。然而犯罪聚集性本身并不能为重新调整犯罪预防资源提供坚固的实证基础。比如，若犯罪的热点区域迅速地从一个地点转移到另一个地点，那么在这样的位置投入犯罪控制资源就鲜有意义了，因为即便没有刑事司法干预，犯罪也会自然而然地在这些地点消失，警务干预将不具有效率（Spelman, 1995）。

现有的数据证明犯罪热点的迅速转移，还缺少实证基础。例如斯佩尔曼（Spelman）（1995）研究了波士顿市有关学校、公有住宅、地铁站以及公园和游乐园的报警电话。他发现了在这些地点中"最差地点"的犯罪在三年的时间里具有高度稳定的证据。斯佩尔曼（Spelman）从而指出，"可以理解那些生活和工作在高危区域的人们，以及为他们服务的警察和其他政府官员，需要花费大量的时间确定、分析和解决他们反复出现的问题"（1995, p. 131）。通过使用 1981 年和 1994 年收集的数据进行的专门小组设计，研究了巴尔的摩市 90 个街区的犯罪以及人们对犯罪的恐惧感，泰勒（Taylor）（1999）提出随着时间的推移犯罪在地点上保持高度的稳定性的相关证据（Taylor, 2001）。

关于随着时间的推移犯罪在地点上保持高度稳定性的最全面研究，是威斯勃德（Weisburd）等人（2004）关于西雅图市街段犯罪事件的研究。通过采用基于团体的轨迹分析（Nagin, 1999, 2005；Nagin and Land, 1993），他们识别出了一群有着相似犯罪发展趋势的地点，并采用了曾被广泛用于研究人的攻击性和侵犯性随年龄变化的研究方法（Nagin, 1999；Nagin and Tremblay, 1999）。

Weisburd 和他的同事在 2004 年从他们的数据中确定了 18 个特定轨迹模式（见

图4）。在他们的研究中最重要的发现是,随着时间的推移犯罪在地点上保持相对稳定。这可与个体违法行为的发展研究进行对比,个体违法往往在相对较短的时间内就有巨大的变化,尤其是对高频率违法者而言,更是如此（Horney, Osgood, and Marshall, 1995；Nagin, 1999；Nagin and Tremblay, 1999）。

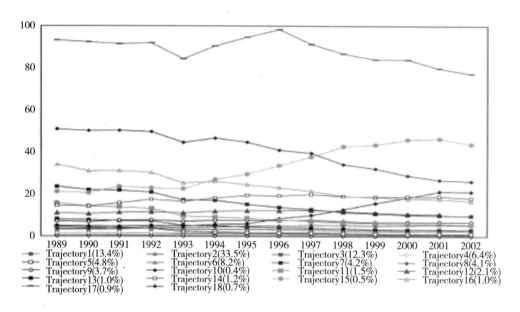

图4 西雅图市 18 个犯罪事件轨迹（1989–2002）

备注：圆括号里面的百分比代表了每个轨迹涉及的街段所占西雅图市街段的比例。
资料来源：Weisburd *et al.*，（2004）。

非常清楚的是,犯罪热点为犯罪在时间跨度上的稳定性提供了重要的证据。相对而言,在犯罪学中,可能只有犯罪生涯当中的违法犯罪具有可变性和不稳定性。这种可变性的首要因素是,大多数违法者随着年龄的增长,逐渐脱离了犯罪,而且通常是在相对年轻的年龄（Blumstein, Cohen, Roth, and Visher, 1986；Gottfredson and Hirschi, 1990；Laub and Sampson, 2003；Tracy and Kempf-Leonard, 1996；Wolfgang, Thornberry, and Figlio, 1987）。但是,我们同样可以找到证据证明大多数违法者的犯罪行为即使是在很短的时间内观察到的,也具有很强的不稳定性（Bushway, Thornberry, and Krohn, 2003；Horney *et al.*，1995；Nagin, 1999）。

这些数据证明了通过在特定地点上进行犯罪预防,能够对犯罪和公共安全产生长期的影响,尤其是对城市而言。一种在地点上"均数回归趋势"模式说明,地点上的犯罪会由高而后自然降低。在这种模式中,通过关注最高热点区域警务干预效益很低,因为即使没有警务干预该地点的犯罪也会自然而然地降低。在某种意义上,这是个体违法的主要模式,因为我们知道大多数人会在相对较快的时间内随着年龄的增长而停止犯罪。相反的,犯罪热点在一段较长的时间内保持着高犯罪率。在这种意义上,热点区域警务似乎比传统警务策略的效率更高。

此外,在这种背景下,违法者(通常指人)是会移动的目标,极少只停留在一个地点。2010 年美国人口统计局关于人口在地理上的移动数据显示 2009 年有 3700 万美国人(约占总人口的 12.5%)迁移了他们的居所。那些居住在高犯罪率同时也是贫困地区的人们,更可能迁移。2009 年,有超过 23% 的生活水平低于贫困线的美国人搬了家。许多研究常常提出在进行调查研究的过程中,往往很难对违法者进行追踪(Wolfgang *et al.*,1987;Laub and Sampson,2003)。这也是警方常有的经历,常常在寻找一个罪犯的时候却发现他或她不再居住在之前知晓的地点。例如,美国全国失踪和受剥削儿童中心估计,16% 的性犯罪者(总数超过 100000 人)不符合注册条件或无法确定其居所(Levenson,Letourneau,Armstrong,and Zgoba,2010)。

相反的,重要的意义在于,地点不像违法者,不是会移动的目标,它们通常保持不变的物理位置。纵向上,警方对一个街区进行追踪并不难,因为地点是不会移动的。当考虑在地点上投入警力资源开展犯罪防控时,这并不是一个毫无意义的问题。一个地点见证了发生在那里的活动,在时间上的相对稳定性。例如,一个居民住宅区不大可能在短时间内转变为一个工业中心。当非居民住宅区和混合型街区随着时间的推移产生了分区上的变化,居民住宅区往往还保留着住宅状态(McMillan and McDonald,1991)。在威斯勃德(Weisburd)、格罗夫(Groff)和杨(Yang)(即将出版)的关于西雅图市土地使用数据分析中,他们发现在 14 年的时间里,混合型街区的比例及其地理位置几乎没有变化。

六、基于地点警务之所以高效是因为犯罪空间位移通常是有限的

正如前言所述,即使越来越多的证据证明对特定区域集中警力能够对犯罪起到震慑作用,但是这样的方法仍存在风险,它促使犯罪从一个地点转移到另一个没有警务干预项目的地点。这个现象常被称为"犯罪空间位移",同时也是传统研究质疑基于地点预防模式的效益性的主要原因(Reppetto,1976)。

基于当今社会存在大量犯罪机遇和积极动机性的违法者的假设,犯罪预防学者在传统上总是认为大多数情境预防策略的犯罪控制效益会因犯罪的空间位移而表

失。然而,从 20 世纪 80 年代开始一系列综述已经得到普遍认同,犯罪的空间位移总的来说很少能够计算出来而且通常是无关紧要的(Barr and Pease, 1990;Clarke, 1992;Eck, 1993;Gabor, 1990;Hesseling, 1994;Guerette and Bowers, 2009; Teichman, 2005)。

推翻即时空间位移假说最有力证据,源自于近期有关犯罪热点干预研究(Braga, 2001, 2005, 2007)。例如在泽西市毒品市场分析实验(Weisburd and Green, 1995)中,检测了两个街区范围内每个犯罪热点的犯罪空间位移情况。没有发现显著的犯罪或违法现象空间位移的情况。在一系列其他犯罪热点的实验中,包括泽西市暴力犯罪地点实验(Braga *et al.* , 1999)、奥克兰 SMART 项目(Green, 1995)、堪萨斯市枪支项目(Sherman and Rogan, 1995)以及洛厄尔治理热点区域扰乱社会秩序的实验(Braga and Bond, 2008)等,也得到了相同的发现。只有霍普(Hope)(1994)报告在集中热点区域进行警务干预时导致了直接犯罪空间位移,即使这仅仅发生在随后立即开展警务干预的地点,而且总体而言犯罪空间位移的负面效果要比犯罪预防的效果小很多。

最近的研究对犯罪空间位移假说提出了进一步的质疑,认为针对地点的犯罪预防还产生了意想不到的积极效果。在这些案例里,研究者发现邻近的、非犯罪预防干预的目标区域的犯罪现象也得到了改善(Green, 1995;Weisburd and Green, 1995)。克拉克(Clarke)和威斯勃德(Weisburd)(1994)指出,这种现象已足以赢得一个标准术语——"犯罪控制的扩散效应"。在其他研究中研究者也称之为"搭便车效应"(Miethe, 1991)、"红利效应"(Sherman, 1990)、"晕轮效应"(Scherdin, 1992)或者"乘数效应"(Chaiken, Lawless, and Stevenson, 1974)。在本质上,扩散效应与犯罪的空间位移相对立。扩散效应指的是犯罪控制效益扩散到了原先没有加强犯罪预防的区域。犯罪预防策略中关于扩散效应的记录多种多样,如警方严打(Sherman, 1990; Weisburd and Green, 1995)、登记保护系统(Scherdin, 1992)和在令人厌恶的地点执行民事法规(Green, 1995, 1996)。

最近的关于犯罪空间位移以及扩散效应的对照研究是由威斯勃德(Weisburd)和他的同事(2006)进行的,在警方针对新泽西州泽西市的卖淫和毒品犯罪热点的严打过程中,他们的研究将空间位移和扩散效应作为首要结果进行明确地检验。为了检验犯罪空间位移和扩散效应,他们收集了大量关于干预目标区域以及周边"下游区域"(大约每个目标区域附近的两个街区)的数据,包括社会观察、对被逮捕者的采访以及人种学方面的实地观察。

定量的调查结果表明,警方针对地点开展有目的的犯罪预防,犯罪并不会简单地在街角附近移动。而实际上,努力集中犯罪预防所带来的最可能的结果是给周边区域带来犯罪控制效益的扩散的观点,得到了研究支持。威斯勃德等人(Weisburd *et al.*)(2006)进行的分析中指出,在目标地点获得巨大的犯罪预防收益的情况下,下游区域的犯罪和违法行为并没有增长。下游区域沿袭了目标地点有相似的态势,体现了犯罪控制效益的扩散效应。定性数据揭示了违法者在移动其活动中会遇到各种各样的障碍,包括因担心转移到不熟悉或不舒服的地点所产生的犹豫,以及对竞争的地盘的考虑。

在后续的研究中,谷口(Taniguchi)、雷吉特(Rengert)和麦考德(McCord)(2009)探究了为什么以非法毒品市场为目标能够导致犯罪控制效益的扩散。将"聚集经济"理论运用于费城,他们发现,从非法毒品市场里除掉最大的、获利最多的卖点,并通过降低周边区域毒品交易的盈利性,能够缩小整个市场的范围。这其中的逻辑借鉴了合法零售业的经济学原理,就如大型购物中心主要的百货商店倒闭后,可能会给周边较小商店的盈利带来负面影响。

七、总 结

从本文开始,我们就简要探讨了主张以基于地点为途径来提高警务活动的效率的实证研究。尽管这个研究主张在地点上集中警务干预的效益,但是这种途径是否能够高效运用警力资源也是需要考虑的问题。我们的探讨认为这种模式基于诸多理由。首先,犯罪在地点上是高度集中的,而且这种犯罪集中度高于个体犯罪的集中度。在这种意义上,基于地点警务模式是高效的,警方能够通过专注于相对少量的地点从而获得相对大的犯罪预防收益。重要的是,犯罪不仅仅只在地点高度集中,在纵向上,犯罪热点保持高度的稳定性。与经常因年龄增长而脱离违法行为的慢性违法者相比,犯罪热点似乎长时间持续"高温"。在这种背景下,地点对警方来说是一个高效的关注点,因为警方可以避免在证明随时间推移犯罪率会自然下降的目标上浪费资源。对警方而言,犯罪热点就是一个简便的关节点。不像到处移动的违法者那样难以追踪,从最基本的常识来说,地点是固定不变的。最后,基于地点的犯罪预防不是简单地促使犯罪的空间位移。事实上,当前有强有力的证据证明犯罪热点警务模式更能给周边区域带来犯罪预防效益上的扩散效应。这反而加固了关于基于地点警务效率性的论点。

相应的研究表明,现在到了让警察从关注人转向更多地关注地点的时候了。这种转移作为一种演化趋势,早在过去的几十年里就已经开始。尽管如此,它依旧需要在警务数据收集,警务活动组织,尤其是警察的整体世界观等方面进行彻底的变革(Weisburd, 2008)。为了使有效性与效率性两者同时最大化,是时候改变警方的世界观,使他们明白犯罪预防的关键在于减轻地点上的犯罪。

[参考文献见英文原作]

（**金 诚 陈韵汝 译**）

The Efficiency of Place-Based Policing

David Weisburd

Hebrew University

Cody W. Telep

George Mason University

We present a growing body of evidence suggesting that police efforts to combat crime at small units of geography represent an opportunity to increase the efficiency of police strategies to control crime. We identify three reasons for the efficiency of place-based policing. First, research in multiple cities indicates a strong concentration of crime at place, which makes it more efficient for police to target specific high crime locations than to spread their resources broadly within cities. Second, crime is fairly stable over time at hot spots and evidences much greater stability longitudinally than individual offending. Places are in this sense an efficient "target" for the police. Additionally, places stay in the same place, making them far easier for the police to track over time than offenders. Finally, crime displacement research shows that a focus on hot spots does not simply "push crime around the corner." Indeed, place-based interventions are more likely to lead to a diffusion of crime control benefits than to a displacement of crime.

INTRODUCTION

There is substantial evidence that police have the ability to be effective in combating crime at small geographic units, commonly termed "hot spots." A series of randomized field trials demonstrate that police efforts focused on hot spots can result in meaningful reductions in crime and disorder (see e. g. Braga and Bond, 2008; Braga, Weisburd, Waring, Mazerolle, Spelman, and Gajewski, 1999; Sherman and Weisburd, 1995; Weisburd and Green, 1995). Further evidence of the effectiveness of hot spots policing comes from a Campbell Collaboration systematic review conducted by Anthony Braga (2001, 2005, 2007). Braga found that seven of nine experimental or quasi-experimental evaluations of hot spots policing reported noteworthy crime or disorder reductions. This strong body of rigorous evaluations led the National Research Council Committee to Review Research on Police Policy and Practices (2004, p. 35) to conclude:

> There has been increasing interest over the past two decades in police practices that target very specific types of crimes, criminals, and crime places. In particular, policing crime hot spots has become a common police strategy for reducing crime and disorder problems. While there is only preliminary evidence suggesting the effectiveness of targeting specific types of offenders, a strong body of evidence suggests that taking a focused geographic approach to crime problems can increase the effectiveness of policing (see also Weisburd and Eck, 2004).

Thus, a sizable body of rigorous empirical research demonstrates the *effectiveness* of police interventions that focus on crime hot spots. Much less discussion exists, however, on the *efficiency* of such an approach for the police. While effectiveness is concerned with achieving specific goals, efficiency focuses on the resources used. As Skogan (1976, p. 278) notes "whatever their effectiveness, efficient agencies give us 'more for our money.'" For example, even if hot spots policing is effective in reducing crime at specific places, if police interventions in one place just push crime to a neighboring community (i. e. spatial displacement), then a police focus on crime hot spots would not be very efficient. The police in this context would simply be chasing crime from place to place. Similarly, if crime hot spots jumped around the city randomly from year to year (i. e. there was no long term stability of crime at place), then police need not focus their efforts at these places because crime would naturally decline over time at crime hot spots. Ideally, police agencies should focus on tactics and strategies that maximize both effectiveness and efficiency.

In this article we argue that place-based policing is not only effective but is also an efficient approach for the police. We present a growing body of evidence that suggests that police efforts to combat crime at small places represent an opportunity to increase the efficiency of police strategies to control crime and disorder. We begin by defining "place" and "place-based policing" in the next two sections. We then identify three key reasons why a place-based approach is efficient for policing. First, both cross-sectional and longitudinal research in multiple cities indicate a strong concentration of crime at place, which makes it more efficient for police to target specific high crime locations than to spread their resources across the landscape of a city. Second, crime is fairly stable over time at crime hot spots and evidences much greater stability than individual offending over time. Places are in this sense an efficient "target" for the police. Additionally, places stay in the same place, making them far easier for the police to track over time than offenders. Finally, research on crime displacement shows that critiques of place-based policing are incorrect in suggesting that a focus on hot spots is inefficient because crime will simply "move around the corner." Indeed, place-based interventions are more likely to lead to a diffusion of crime control benefits.

WHAT IS A "PLACE"?

It is important at the outset to note that our definition of place departs from traditional geographic-based approaches for policing. By place, we do not mean large geographic units such as neighborhoods or communities that have commonly been the focus of criminologists concerned with crime prevention (see Bursik and Webb, 1982; Sampson, Raudenbush, and Earls, 1997; Shaw and McKay, 1942 [1969]), or the beats and precincts that have been key to the organization of policing. Places in this context are specific locations within the larger social environments of communities and neighborhoods (Eck and Weisburd, 1995). These very small "micro" units of analysis may be defined as buildings or addresses (see Green, 1996; Sherman, Gartin, and Buerger, 1989), as block faces or street segments (see Sherman and Weisburd, 1995; Taylor, 1997), or as clusters of addresses, block faces or street segments that have common crime problems (see Block, Dabdoub, and Fregly, 1995; Weisburd and Green, 1995; Oberwittler and Wikström, 2009).

Two illustrations of crime places are useful since they point to the different ways that place may be important in understanding police interventions. In the Minneapolis Hot Spots Patrol Experiment Sherman and Weisburd (1995) identified street segments or street blocks for increased patrol presence (see Figure 1). They used street blocks in part because they represented a unit of analysis that was easily identified by police and could provide a natural setting for police interventions. But scholars have also recognized the relevance of small areas such as street segments in organizing life in the city (Appleyard, 1981; Jacobs, 1961; Smith, Frazee, and Davison, 2000; Taylor, 1997). Taylor (1998), for example, argues that the visual closeness of block residents, interrelated role obligations, acceptance of certain common norms and behavior, common regularly recurring rhythms of activity, the physical boundaries of the street, and the historical evolution of the street segment make the street block a particularly useful unit for analysis of place (Hunter and Baumer, 1982; Taylor, Gottfredson, and Brower,1984).

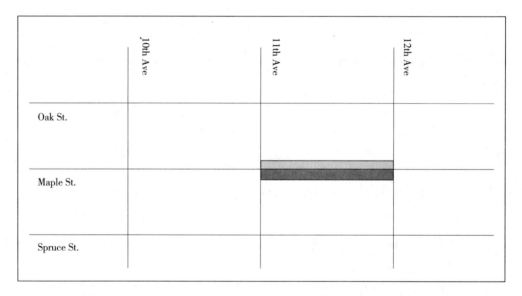

Figure 1   Example of a Hot Spot in theMinneapolis Hot Spots Experiment
Source: Weisburd (2008).

In the Jersey City Displacement and Diffusion Project Weisburd, Wyckoff, Ready, Eck, Hinkle, and Gajewski (2006) also sought to identify a discrete place for police attention. But in this study the focus was on specific types of criminal markets. Such markets often spread across street segments in a larger area of criminal activity. Figure 2 illustrates the boundaries of a drug market identified for intervention in Jersey City. Included in this market is a group of city blocks but, importantly, this geographic unit is still much smaller than the neighborhoods or police precincts that have often been the focus of police interventions and scientific study of crime. The displacement project and the Minneapolis experiment illustrate more generally the ways in which units of place might differ depending on the interests of the police and the underlying structure of crime problems.

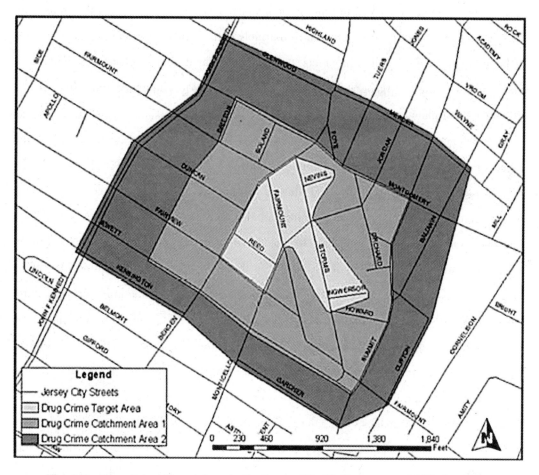

Figure 2 Drug Crime Target Area in the Jersey City Displacement and Diffusion Study
Source: Weisburd *et al.*, (2006).

WHAT IS PLACE-BASED POLICING?

What is meant by place-based policing? At its core is a concern with focusing in on places where crime is concentrated, and it begins with an assumption that there is something about a place that leads to crimes occurring there. In this sense, place-based policing is theoretically based on routine activities theory (Cohen and Felson, 1979; Felson, 1994), which identifies crime as a matter of the convergence of suitable targets

(e. g. , victims) , an absence of capable guardians (e. g. , police) , and the presence of motivated or potential offenders. Of course, this all must occur in the context of a place or situation, and accordingly place-based policing recognizes that there is something about specific places that leads to the convergence of these elements (Brantingham and Brantingham, 1981 [1991] , 1984). Importantly, place-based policing is not simply the application of police strategies to units of geography. Traditional policing in this sense can be seen as place-based, since police have routinely defined their units of operation in terms of large areas, such as police precincts and beats. As noted above, place here refers to a much smaller level of geographic aggregation than has traditionally interested police executives and planners.

The strategies of place-based policing can be as simple as hot spots patrol, as was the case in the Minneapolis Hot Spots Policing Experiment (Sherman and Weisburd, 1995) , where the police intervention involved placing more patrol resources at places where crime was concentrated. But place-based policing can also take a much more complex approach to the amelioration of crime problems. In the Jersey City Drug Market Analysis Project (Weisburd and Green, 1995) , for example, a three-step program (including identifying and analyzing problems, developing tailored responses, and maintaining crime control gains) was used to reduce problems at drug hot spots. In the Jersey City Violent Crime Places Experiment (Braga, Weisburd, Waring, Mazerolle, Spelman, and Gajewski, 1999) , a problem-oriented policing approach was taken in developing a specific strategy for each of the small areas defined as violent crime hot spots.

As this brief review makes clear, the exact tactics employed in place-based policing can vary, but they share a common focus on small units of geography that are high in criminal activity. We turn now to a wide body of empirical evidence suggesting the efficiency of a place-based approach to policing.

PLACE-BASED POLICING IS EFFICIENT BECAUSE CRIME IS VERY STRONGLY CONCENTRATED AT PLACES

A key requirement for the efficiency of place-based policing is that crime is heavily concentrated in what some have termed "crime hot spots" (Sherman et al. , 1989; Sherman and Weisburd, 1995; Weisburd and Green, 1995). Absent a concentration of crime at place there seems little reason to refocus crime prevention efforts. Indeed, if crime were spread randomly across a city, place-based policing would provide little benefit.

A number of studies, beginning in the late 1980s, suggest that significant clustering of crime at place exists, regardless of the specific unit of analysis defined (see Brantingham and Brantingham, 1999; Crow and Bull, 1975; Pierce, Spaar, and Briggs, 1986; Roncek, 2000; Sherman et al., 1989; Weisburd and Green, 1994; Weisburd, Maher, and Sherman, 1992, Weisburd, Bushway, Lum, and Yang, 2004; Weisburd, Morris, and Groff, 2009). Perhaps the most influential of these was Sherman, Gartin and Buerger's (1989) analysis of emergency calls to street addresses over a single year. Sherman et al., found that only $3\frac{1}{2}$ percent of the addresses in Minneapolis, Minnesota produced 50 percent of all calls to the police. They regarded these results as so startling that they called for a new area of study, which they termed the "criminology of place."

Other studies produced similar evidence of the concentration of crime in crime hot spots. Weisburd and Mazerolle (2000), for example, found that approximately 20 percent of all disorder crimes and 14 percent of crimes against persons were concentrated in just 56 drug crime hot spots in Jersey City, New Jersey, an area that comprised only $4\frac{1}{2}$ percent of street segments and intersections in the city. Similarly, Eck, Gersh, and Taylor (2000) found that the most active 10 percent of places (in terms of crime) in the Bronx, New York and Baltimore, Maryland accounted for approximately 32 percent of a combination of robberies, assaults, burglaries, grand larcenies and auto thefts.

A study conducted by Weisburd et al., (2004) not only confirms the concentration of crime, but also the stability of such concentrations across a long time span. Weisburd et al., examined street segments in the city of Seattle from 1989 through 2002. They found that 50 percent of crime incidents over the 14 year period occurred at only 4.4 percent of the street segments. As illustrated by Figure 3, this concentration is very stable year to year.

These studies overall illustrate a kind of "law of concentrations" for crime suggesting that crime is heavily clustered in cities with fewer than five or ten percent of addresses, street segments, or small clusters of addresses and street segments accounting for a majority of crime in a city each year.

The crime prevention opportunities of this law of concentration are even clearer when focusing on specific types of crime. In another study in Seattle, Weisburd, Morris and Groff (2009) examined the concentration of crime incidents in which a juvenile was

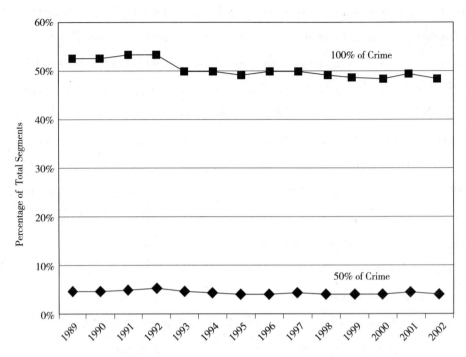

**Figure 3　Percentage of Seattle Street Segments with 50% and 100%
of Incident Reports from 1989 to 2002**

Source: Weisburd *et al.* , (2004).

arrested. They found that only 86 street segments out of almost 30,000 accounted for 1/3 of all official juvenile arrest incidents over a 14 year period. While more research will have to be done to establish how much of such crime concentrations are due to concentrations of police patrol, this study suggests the extent to which police can increase efficiency by focusing on hot spots in a city.

Lawrence Sherman (1995) argues that such clustering of crime at places is even greater than the concentration of crime among individuals. Using his Minneapolis data and comparing these to the concentration of offending in the Philadelphia birth cohort study (see Wolfgang, Figlio, and Sellin, 1972), he notes that future crime is "six times more predictable by the address of the occurrence than by the identity of the offender" (1995, p. 36-37). Sherman asks, "why aren't we doing more about it? Why aren't we thinking more about wheredunit, rather than just whodunit?"

Weisburd (2008, p. 5) argues similarly regarding longitudinal data in Seattle. When using "targets" as a criterion, places were indeed found to be a more efficient focus than offenders. Using this approach, he found that on average about 1,500 street segments accounted for 50 percent of the crime each year over a 14 year period. During the same period about 6,108 offenders were responsible for 50 percent of the crime each year. Simply stated, the police would have to approach four times as many targets to identify the same level of overall crime when they focus on people as opposed to places.

PLACE-BASED POLICING IS EFFICIENT BECAUSE CRIME IS STABLE AT PLACES ACROSS TIME

The concentration of crime at place suggests significant crime prevention potential for such strategies as hot spots patrol (Sherman and Weisburd, 1995; Weisburd and Braga, 2006). However, concentration itself does not provide a solid empirical basis for refocusing crime prevention resources. For example, if "hot spots of crime" shift rapidly from place to place it makes little sense to focus crime control resources at such locations, because they would naturally become free of crime without any criminal justice intervention and hence police intervention would be inefficient (Spelman, 1995).

The available data suggest that the possibility of crime shifting rapidly has little empirical basis. Spelman (1995) for example, examined calls for service at schools, public housing projects, subway stations, and parks and playgrounds in Boston. He found evidence of a very high degree of stability of crime at the "worst" of these places over a three year period. Spelman concluded that it "makes sense for the people who live and work in high-risk locations, and the police officers and other government officials who serve them, to spend the time they need to identify, analyze and solve their recurring problems" (1995, p. 131). Taylor (1999) also reported evidence of a high degree of stability of crime at place over time, examining crime and fear of crime at 90 street blocks in Baltimore using a panel design with data collected in 1981 and 1994 (see also Taylor, 2001).

The most comprehensive examination of the stability of crime at place over time was conducted by Weisburd et al., (2004) in their study of crime incidents at street segments in the city of Seattle. Using group-based trajectory analysis (Nagin, 1999, 2005; Nagin and Land, 1993) they identified clusters of places with similar developmental crime trends, adopting an approach that has been used extensively to study patterns of change in offending and aggression as people age (see Nagin, 1999; Nagin and Tremblay, 1999).

Weisburd and colleagues (2004) identified 18 specific trajectory patterns in their data (see Figure 4). The most important finding in their study was that crime remained fairly stable at places over time. This can be contrasted with developmental studies of individual offending where there is often tremendous change across relatively short periods, especially for high rate offenders (Horney, Osgood, and Marshall, 1995; Nagin, 1999; Nagin and Tremblay, 1999).

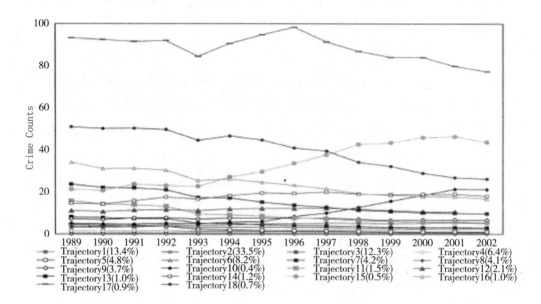

Figure 4　Eighteen Trajectories of Crime Incidents in Seattle (1989—2002)

Note: The percentages in parentheses represent the proportion of street segments that each trajectory accounts for in the city of Seattle.

Source: Weisburd et al., (2004).

What is clear is that hot spots of crime evidence a remarkable degree of stability across time. In contrast, there is perhaps no more established fact in criminology than the variability and instability of offending across the life course. A primary factor in this variability is the fact that most offenders age out of crime, often at a relatively young age (Blumstein, Cohen, Roth, and Visher, 1986; Gottfredson and Hirschi, 1990; Laub and Sampson, 2003; Tracy and Kempf-Leonard, 1996; Wolfgang, Thornberry, and Figlio, 1987). But there is also evidence of strong instability in criminal behavior for most offenders even when short time periods are observed (Bushway, Thornberry, and Krohn, 2003; Horney et al., 1995; Nagin, 1999).

What these data suggest is that crime prevention at places has the potential for long term impacts on crime and public safety more generally in cities. A model of "regression to the mean" at places would suggest that places get very "hot" and then naturally cool off. In this model there would be little benefit in efficiency by focusing on the "hottest spots" because they would become cooler even without police intervention. In some sense, this is the predominant model of individual offending, since we know that most people will age out of crime relatively quickly. In contrast hot spots of crime appear to remain hot over longer periods of time. In this sense, hot spots policing is likely to be more efficient than traditional policing tactics.

Additionally, offenders (like people more generally) are a moving target in the sense that they rarely just stay in one place. U. S. Census Bureau (2010) data on geographic mobility show that over 37 million Americans changed residences in 2009 (about 12. 5 percent of the population). Those who live in high crime areas, which are often disadvantaged areas as well, are even more likely to move. Over 23 percent of Americans below the poverty line moved in 2009. Studies have often noted the difficulty of tracking offenders for survey research (Wolfgang *et al.*, 1987; Laub and Sampson, 2003), and it is a common experience of the police to look for an offender and find that he or she no longer lives at the last known address. For example, the National Center for Missing and Exploited Children estimates that 16 percent of sex offenders (over100, 000 in total) are not compliant with registration requirements and cannot be located (Levenson, Letourneau, Armstrong, and Zgoba, 2010).

In contrast, places are not moving targets in the important sense that, unlike offenders, they remain at the same physical place. The police will have no difficulty tracking a street block longitudinally; the place will not move. This is not an insignificant issue when considering the investment of police resources in crime prevention. A place also evidences relative stability over time in the nature of activities that occur there. For example, a residential street block is unlikely to shift to an industrial center in a short period of time. While nonresidential blocks and mixed use blocks show some change longitudinally in zoning, residential blocks typically remain residential over time (McMillan and McDonald, 1991). In their analysis of land use data from Seattle, Weisburd, Groff, and Yang (Forthcoming) found little change over 14 years both in the percentage of street blocks with mixed land use and in the geographic location of these blocks.

PLACE-BASED POLICING IS EFFICIENT BECAUSE CRIME DISPLACEMENT IS USUALLY LIMITED

As noted in the introduction, although there is growing evidence that police can have an impact on crime at the specific areas where they focus their efforts, such approaches risk shifting crime or disorder to other places where programs are not in place. This phenomenon is usually termed displacement, and it has been a major reason for traditional skepticism about the overall crime prevention benefits and efficiency of place-based prevention efforts (Reppetto, 1976).

Based on assumptions about the large number of crime opportunities available in modern societies, and the highly motivated nature of offenders, crime prevention scholars have traditionally assumed that most of the crime control benefits of situational prevention strategies would be lost due to displacement. A series of reviews since the 1980s have led to general agreement, however, that displacement of crime is seldom total and often inconsequential (Barr and Pease, 1990; Clarke, 1992; Eck, 1993; Gabor, 1990; Hesseling, 1994; Guerette and Bowers, 2009; for an opposing view, see Teichman, 2005).

The strongest evidence against the assumption of immediate spatial displacement has come from recent studies of focused interventions at crime hot spots (see Braga, 2001, 2005, 2007). In the Jersey City Drug Market Analysis Experiment (Weisburd and Green, 1995), for example, displacement within two block areas around each hot spot was measured. No significant displacement of crime or disorder calls was found. These findings were replicated in a series of other hot spots experiments including the Jersey City Violent Crime Places Experiment (Braga et al., 1999), the Oakland SMART Project (Green, 1995), the Kansas City Gun Project (Sherman and Rogan, 1995) and the Lowell policing disorder at hot spots experiment (Braga and Bond, 2008). Only Hope (1994) reports direct displacement of crime as a result of a focused hot spots intervention, though this occurred only in the area immediate to the treated locations and was much smaller overall than the crime prevention effect.

Further challenge to the displacement hypothesis is found in recent studies that suggest a positive though unanticipated consequence of crime prevention at place. In these cases, investigators found improvement in areas close to but not targeted by crime prevention efforts (see Green, 1995; Weisburd and Green, 1995). Clarke and Weisburd (1994) argue that this phenomenon is general enough to deserve a standard term—"diffusion of crime control benefits. " It has been described elsewhere by investigators as the free rider effect (Miethe, 1991), the bonus effect (Sherman, 1990), the halo effect (Scherdin, 1992), or the multiplier effect (Chaiken, Lawless, and Stevenson, 1974). In essence, diffusion is the reverse of displacement. It refers to the diffusion of crime control benefits to contexts that were not the primary focus of crime prevention initiatives. Diffusion has been documented in crime prevention strategies as diverse as police crackdowns (Sherman, 1990; Weisburd and Green, 1995), book protection systems (Scherdin, 1992), and enforcement of civil regulations at nuisance locations (Green, 1995, 1996).

A recent controlled study of displacement and diffusion effects by Weisburd and colleagues (2006) explicitly examined spatial displacement and diffusion as primary outcomes during an intensive police crackdown in a prostitution hot spot and a drug hot spot in Jersey City, New Jersey. To examine displacement and diffusion effects, a wealth of data was collected in the intervention target areas and surrounding catchment areas, approximately two blocks surrounding each target area, including social observations, arrestee interviews, and ethnographic field observations.

Quantitative findings indicated that crime did not simply move around the corner in response to intensive police crime prevention efforts at places. Indeed, the study supported the position that the most likely outcome of such focused crime prevention efforts is a diffusion of crime control benefits to nearby areas. In analyses conducted by Weisburd *et al.*, (2006) crime and disorder did not go up in the catchment areas after there were strong crime prevention gains at the target site. The catchment areas followed a similar pattern to the target site, suggesting a diffusion of crime control benefits. The qualitative data revealed there were various barriers to offenders moving their activity elsewhere, including a hesitancy to move to other areas that were unfamiliar, uncomfortable, or considered rival turf.

In an extension of these findings, Taniguchi, Rengert, and McCord (2009) explored why targeting illegal drug markets may lead to a diffusion of crime control benefits. Applying the theory of "agglomeration economies" to Philadelphia they found that removing the largest and most profitable site from an illegal drug market will reduce the size of the overall market by making drug dealing in the surrounding area less lucrative. The logic here follows the economics of the legitimate retail sector, where closing a major department store in a mall may negatively impact the profits of smaller surrounding stores.

CONCLUSIONS

We began this article with a brief review of the empirical research supporting a place-based approach to improve police effectiveness. While this research suggests the benefits of focusing police interventions on places, it is also necessary to consider whether such a focused approach is an efficient use of police resources. Our review suggests that it is for multiple reasons. First, crime is highly concentrated at places and such crime concentrations are greater than the concentration of crime among individuals. In this sense, place-based policing is efficient because the police can focus on a relatively small number of places and gain relatively larger crime prevention benefits. Importantly, crime is not only concentrated at place, there is also strong stability in crime hot spots over time. In contrast to chronic offenders who often age out of crime quickly, hot spots of crime seem to continue to be "hot" over long periods. In this context places are an efficient focus for the police, because the police do not risk wasting resources on targets that would evidence lower crime naturally over time. And crime hot spots represent an easy to "find" focus for police. Unlike offenders who move from place to place and are difficult to track, in the most basic sense crime places stay in the same place. Finally, crime prevention at places does not simply lead to crime displacement. Indeed, there is strong evidence today that hot spots policing is more likely to lead to a diffusion of crime prevention benefits to areas nearby. This only strengthens the argument for the efficiency of place-based policing.

Research accordingly suggests that it is time for police to shift from concentrating primarily on people to focusing more on places. While such a shift is largely an evolution in trends that have begun over the last few decades, it will nonetheless demand radical changes in data collection in policing, in the organization of police activities, and particularly in the overall world view of the police (see Weisburd, 2008). To maximize both effectiveness and efficiency, it is time to change the world view of police so that they recognize the key to crime prevention is in ameliorating crime at place.

References

Ap Pleyard, D. (1981). *Livable streets*, Berkley, University of California Press.

Barr, R. , & Pease, K. (1990). "Crime placement, displacement, and deflection," In

Tonry, M. & Morris, N. (eds.), *Crime and Justice: A Review of Research*, vol. 12. Chicago, University of Chicago Press.

Block, C., Dabdoub, M., & Fregly, S. (eds.) (1995). *Crime analysis through computer mapping*, Washington, DC, Police Executive Research Forum.

Blumstein, A., Cohen, J., Roth, J. A., & Visher, C. B. (eds.). (1986). *Criminal careers and "career criminals"*, Washington, DC, National Academies Press.

Braga, A. A. (2001). "The effects of hot spots policing on crime," *The Annals of the American Academy of Political and Social Science*, 578, 104–115.

Braga, A. A. (2005). "Hot spots policing and crime prevention: A systematic review of randomized controlled trials," *Journal of Experimental Criminology*, 1, 317–342.

Braga, A. A. (2007). *Effects of hot spots policing on crime*, Campbell Collaboration systematic review, Available online at: http://campbellcollaboration. org/lib/download/118/.

Braga, A. A., & Bond, B. J. (2008). "Policing crime and disorder hot spots: A randomized controlled trial," *Criminology*, 46, 577–608.

Braga, A. A., Weisburd, D. L., Waring, E. J., Mazerolle, L. G., Spelman, W., & Gajewski, F. (1999). "Problem-oriented policing in violent crime places: A randomized controlled experiment," *Criminology*, 37, 541–580.

Brantingham, P. J., & Brantingham, P. L. (1981 [1991]). "The dimensions of crime," In Brantingham, P. J. & Brantingham, P. L. (eds.), *Environmental criminology* Beverly Hills, CA, Sage Publications, 7–26.

Brantingham, P. J., & Brantingham, P. L. (1984). *Patterns in crime*, New York, Macmillan.

Brantingham, P. L., & Brantingham, P. J. (1999). "Theoretical model of crime hot spot generation," *Studies on Crime and Crime Prevention*, 8, 7–26.

Bursik, R. J. JR., & Webb, J. (1982). "Community change and patterns of delinquency," *American Journal of Sociology*, 88, 24–42.

Bushway, S. D., Thornberry, T. P., & Krohn M. D. (2003). "Desistance as a developmental process: A comparison of static and dynamic approaches," *Journal of Quantitative Criminology*, 19, 129–153.

Chaiken, J., Lawless, M., & Stevenson, K. (1974). *The impact of police activity on crime: Robberies on the New York City subway system*, Santa Monica, CA, Rand Corporation.

Clarke, R. V. (1992). *Situational crime prevention: Successful case studies*, Albany, NY, Harrow and Heston.

Clarke, R. V. , & Weisburd, D. (1994). Diffusion of crime control benefits: Observations on the reverse of displacement. In CLARKE, R. V. (ed.) , *Crime Prevention Studies*, vol. 2 Monsey, NY: Criminal Justice Press, 165 – 184.

Cohen, L. E. , & Felson, M. (1979). "Social change and crime rate trends: A routine activity approach," *American Sociological Review*, 44, 588 – 605.

Crow, W. , & Bull, J. (1975). *Robbery deterrence: An applied behavioral science demonstration – Final report*, La Jolla, CA, Western Behavioral Science Institute.

Eck, J. E. (1993). "The threat of crime displacement," *Criminal Justice Abstracts*, 25, 527 – 546.

Eck, J. E. , & Weisburd, D. (1995). "Crime places in crime theory," In Eck, J. E. & Weisburd, D. (eds.), *Crime and place*, *Crime Prevention Studies*, vol. 4, Monsey, NY, Willow Tree Press, 1 – 33.

Eck, J. E. , Gersh, J. S. , & Taylor, C. (2000). "Finding crime hot spots through repeat address mapping," In Goldsmith, V. , Mcguire, P. G. , Mollenkopf, J. H. & Ross, T. A. (eds.) , *Analyzing crime patterns: Frontiers of practice*, Thousand Oaks, CA, Sage Publications, 49 – 64.

Felson, M. (1994). *Crime and everyday life: Insight and implications for society*, Thousand Oaks, CA, Pine Forge Press.

Gabor, T. (1990). "Crime displacement and situational prevention: Toward the development of some principles," *Canadian Journal of Criminology*, 32, 41 – 74.

Gottfredson, M. , & Hirschi, T. (1990). *A general theory of crime*, Stanford, CA, Stanford University Press.

Green, L. (1995). "Cleaning up drug hot spots in Oakland, California: The displacement and diffusion effects," *Justice Quarterly*, 12, 737 – 754.

Green, L. (1996). *Policing places with drug problems*, Thousand Oaks, CA, Sage Publications.

Guerette, R. T. , & Bowers, K. J. (2009). "Assessing the extent of crime displacement and diffusion of benefits: A review of situational crime prevention evaluations," *Criminology*, 47, 1331 – 1368.

Hesseling, R. B. P. (1994). "Displacement: A review of the empirical literature," In Clarke, R. V. (ed.), *Crime Prevention Studies*, vol. 3, Monsey, NY: Criminal Justice Press, 197–230.

Hope, T. (1994). "Problem-oriented policing and drug market locations: Three case studies," In Clarke, R. V. (ed.), *Crime Prevention Studies*, vol. 2, Monsey, NY, Criminal Justice Press, 5–32.

Horney, J., Osgood, D. W., & Marshall, I. H. (1995). "Criminal careers in the short-term: Intra-individual variability in crime and its relation to local life circumstances," *American Sociological Review*, 60, 655–673.

Hunter, A. J., & Baumer, T. L. (1982). "Street traffic, social integration, and fear of crime," *Sociological Inquiry*, 52, 122–131.

Jacobs, J. (1961). *The death and life of great American cities*, New York, Vintage Books.

Laub, J. H., & Sampson, R. J. (2003). *Shared beginnings, divergent lives: Delinquent boys to age 70*, Cambridge, MA, Harvard University Press.

Levenson, J., Letourneau, E., Armstrong, K., & Zgoba, K. M. (2010). "Failure to register as a sex offender: Is it associated with recidivism?" *Justice Quarterly*, 27, 305–331.

Mcmillan, D. P., & Mcdonald, J. F. (1991). "A Markov Chain model of zoning change," *Journal of Urban Economics*, 30, 257–270.

Miethe, T. D. (1991). "Citizen based crime control activity and victimization risks: An examination of displacement and free-rider effects," *Criminology*, 29, 419–440.

Nagin, D. S. (1999). "Analyzing developmental trajectories: A semiparametric group-based approach," *Psychological Methods*, 4, 139–157.

Nagin, D. (2005). *Group-based modeling of development over the life course*, Cambridge, MA, Harvard University Press.

Nagin, D. S., & Land, K. C. (1993). "Age, criminal careers, and population heterogeneity: Specification and estimation of a nonparametric, mixed Poisson model," *Criminology*, 31, 327–362.

Nagin, D., & Tremblay, R. E. (1999). "Trajectories of boys' physical aggression, opposition, and hyperactivity on the path to physically violent and nonviolent juvenile delinquency," *Child Development*, 70, 1181–1196.

National Research Council. (2004). *Fairness and effectiveness in policing: The evidence,*

Committee to Review Research on Police Policy and Practices, Skogan, W. & Frydl, K. (eds.). Committee on Law and Justice, Division of Behavioral and Social Sciences and Education. Washington, DC, National Academies Press.

Pierce, G., Spaar, S., & Briggs, L. R. (1986). *The character of police work: Strategic and tactical implications*, Boston, MA, Center for Applied Social Research, Northeastern University.

Reppetto, T. (1976). "Crime prevention and the displacement phenomenon," *Crime & Delinquency*, 22, 166 – 177.

Roncek, D. W. (2000). Schools and crime. In Goldsmith, V. Mcguire, P. G., Mollenkopf, J. H., & Ross, T. A. (eds.), *Analyzing crime patterns: Frontiers of practice*, Thousand Oaks, CA, Sage Publications, 153 – 165.

Sampson, R. J., Raudenbush, S. W., & Earls, F. (1997). "Neighborhoods and violent crime: A multilevel study of collective efficacy," *Science*, 277, 918 – 924.

Scherdin, M. J. (1992). "The halo effect: Psychological deterrence of electronic security systems," In Clarke, R. V. (ed.), *Situational crime prevention: Successful case studies*. Albany, NY, Harrow and Heston.

Shaw, C. R., & Mckay, H. D. (1942 [1969]). *Juvenile delinquency and urban areas. A study of rates of delinquency in relation to differential characteristics of local communities in American cities*, Chicago, University of Chicago Press (Revised ed.).

Sherman, L. W. (1990). "Police crackdowns: Initial and residual deterrence," In Tonry, M. & Morris, N. (eds.), *Crime and Justice: A Review of Research*, vol. 12, Chicago, University of Chicago Press, 1 – 42.

Sherman, L. W. (1995). "Hot spots of crime and criminal careers of places," In Eck, J. E. & Weisburd, D. (eds.), *Crime and place, Crime Prevention Studies*, vol. 4, Monsey, NY, Criminal Justice Press, 35 – 52.

Sherman, L. W., And Rogan, D. P. (1995). "Effects of gun seizures on gun violence: 'Hot spots' patrol in Kansas City," *Justice Quarterly*, 12, 673 – 694.

Sherman, L. W., & Weisburd, D. (1995). "General deterrent effects of police patrol in crime hot spots: A randomized controlled trial," *Justice Quarterly*, 12, 625 – 648.

Sherman, L. W., Gartin, P. R., & Buerger, M. E. (1989). "Hot spots of predatory crime: Routine activities and the criminology of place," *Criminology*, 27, 27 – 56.

Skogan, W. G. (1976). "Efficiency and effectiveness in big-city police departments,"

Public Administration Review, 36, 278 – 286.

Smith, W. R. , Frazee, S. G. , & Davison, E. L. (2000). "Furthering the integration of routine activity and social disorganization theories: Small units of analysis and the study of street robbery as a diffusion process,"*Criminology*, 38, 489 – 523.

Spelman, W. (1995). "Criminal careers of public places," In Eck, J. E. & Weisburd,D. (eds.),*Crime and place*, *Crime Prevention Studies*, vol. 4. Monsey, NY, Willow Tree Press.

Taniguchi, T. A. , Rengert, G. F. , & Mccord E. S. (2009). "Where size matters: Agglomeration economies of illegal drug markets inPhiladelphia," *Justice Quarterly*, 26, 670 – 694.

Taylor, R. B. (1997). "Social order and disorder of street blocks and neighborhoods: Ecology, microecology, and the systemic model of social disorganization,"*Journal of Research in Crime and Delinquency*, 34, 113 – 155.

Taylor, R. B. (1998). "Crime and small-scale places: What we know, what we can prevent, and what else we need to know," In Taylor, R. B. , Bazemore, G. , Boland, B. , Clear, T. R. , Corbett, R. P. J. , Feinblatt, J. , Berman, G. , Sviridoff, M. & Stone, C. (eds.), *Crime and place: Plenary papers of the 1997 Conference on Criminal Justice Research and Evaluation*, Washington, DC: National Institute of Justice, 1 – 22.

Taylor, R. B. (1999). *Crime, grime, fear, and decline: A longitudinal look*. Research in Brief. Washington, DC, National Institute of Justice, U. S. Department of Justice.

Taylor, R. B. (2001). *Breaking away from broken windows: Baltimore neighborhoods and the nationwide fight against crime, grime, fear, and decline*. Boulder, CO, Westview Press.

Taylor, R. B. , Gottfredson, S. D. , & Brower, S. (1984). "Block crime and fear: Defensible space, local social ties, and territorial functioning,"*Journal of Research in Crime and Delinquency*, 21, 303 – 331.

Teichman, D. (2005). "The market for criminal justice: Federalism, crime control, and jurisdictional competition,"*Michigan Law Review*, 103, 1831 – 1876.

Tracy, P. E. , & Kempf-Leonard, K. (1996). *Continuity and discontinuity in criminal careers*. New York, Plenum Press.

U. S. Census Bureau. (2010). 2009 Current Population Survey, Annual Social and

Economic Supplement, Washington, DC, Author.

Weisburd, D. (2008). "Place-based policing," *Ideas in American Policing*. Washington, DC, Police Foundation.

Weisburd, D., & Green, L. (1994). "Defining the street level drug market," In D. Mackenzie, D. & Uchida, C. (eds.), *Drugs and crime: Evaluating public policy initiatives*, Thousand Oaks, CA: Sage Publications, 61 – 76.

Weisburd, D., & Green, L. (1995). "Policing drug hot spots: The Jersey City Drug Market Analysis Experiment," *Justice Quarterly*, 12, 711 – 736.

Weisburd, D., & Mazerolle, L. G. (2000). "Crime and disorder in drug hot spots: Implications for theory and practice in policing," *Police Quarterly*, 3, 331 – 349.

Weisburd, D., & Eck, J. E. (2004). "What can the police do to reduce crime, disorder, and fear?", *The Annals of the American Academy of Political and Social Science*, 593, 42 – 65.

Weisburd, D., & Braga, A. A. (2006). "Hot spots policing as a model for police innovation," In Weisburd, D. & Braga, A. A. (eds.), *Police Innovation: Contrasting perspectives*, New York, Cambridge University Press, 225 – 244.

Weisburd, D., Maher, L., & Sherman, L. (1992). "Contrasting crime general and crime specific theory: The case of hot spots of crime," In Adler, F. & Laufer, W. (eds.), *New Directions in criminological theory*, *Advances in Criminological Theory*, vol. 4. New Brunswick, NJ: Transaction Press, 45 – 69.

Weisburd, D., Morris, N. A., & Groff, E. R. (2009). "Hot spots of juvenile crime: A longitudinal study of arrest incidents at street segments in Seattle, Washington," *Journal of Quantitative Criminology*, 25, 443 – 467.

Weisburd, D., Groff, E. R., & Yang, S.-M. (Forthcoming). *Understanding developmental crime trajectories at place: Social disorganization and opportunity perspectives at micro units of geography*. Washington, DC, National Institute of Justice, U. S. Department of Justice.

Weisburd, D., Bushway, S., Lum, C., & Yang, S-M. (2004). "Trajectories of crime at places: A longitudinal study of street segments in the city of Seattle," *Criminology*, 42, 283 – 321.

Weisburd, D., Wyckoff, L. A., Ready, J., Eck, J. E., Hinkle, J. C., & Gajewski, F. (2006). "Does crime just move around the corner? A controlled study of spatial displacementand diffusion of crime control benefits," *Criminology*, 44, 549 – 592.

Wolfgang, M. E. , Figlio, R. , & Sellin, T. (1972) , *Delinquency in a birth cohort.* Chicago, University of Chicago Press.

Wolfgang, M. , Thornberry, T. P. , & Figlio, R. M. (1987). *From boy to man, from delinquency to crime*, Chicago, University of Chicago Press.

基于地点的警务

大卫·威斯勃德（David Weisburd）

希伯来大学

警务实践通常将视点集中在人身上，而且往往从报警人来电之后开始。它关注甄别谁是犯罪嫌疑犯，并终止对嫌疑犯的逮捕以及这个过程所需要经历的整个刑事司法程序。有时警察的注意力还得放在更广泛的社区问题和"社区照顾"上（Kahan and Meares，1998，Mastrofski，1999），期待警察既能确保社区安全又要处理好如近年来的国土安全威胁问题（Waddington and Neyroud，2007）。但是，尽管警察的任务更为广泛，警务实践的核心在于人，无论是被害者还是罪犯，他们都是警务工作的关键。

警方专业人士可能会反对警务实践的上述描述。他们认为，近几年来警方已经开始探索的不仅仅是罪犯和受害者，还有包括与犯罪背景有关的情境和地点。为了支持这论点，他们可能会注意到，全国各地警察机构已经开始把注意力集中在犯罪热点上，犯罪地图已经成为最前沿的执法的核心特征（Weisburd and Lum，2005）。此外，他们可能认为，犯罪地点是最近许多警务创新的重要组成部分，例如计算机统计（Silverman，1999）、犯罪热点警务（Sherman and Weisburd，1995；Weisburd and Braga，2006）、问题导向警务（Eck，2003）。从这个意义上讲，许多具有前瞻性的警察机构已开始认识到如果警察期望对犯罪采取些措施或其他相关问题，那么地点和人的因素一样需要得到充分的关注。

然而，事实还是事实，例如，当诸如问题导向的警务创新在实践的时候，如何抓获罪犯和通过刑事司法系统处置他们仍然是警察的主要犯罪预防战略（Weisburd and

Braga，2006）。此外，尽管对犯罪地图非常感兴趣，但是信息系统的重心依旧是集中在受害者和罪犯身上。

尽管警察已经开始关注类似犯罪热点的问题，美国的警察数据库告诉我们很少犯罪的情境。相应地，尽管诸如计算机统计等重要的警务战略创新需要警察关注问题地点，当前的警务活动继续是在按地理来组织维持社会治安的单位，如警察辖区或责任区，但是，它们事实上和最近研究所发现的作为真正犯罪意义上的犯罪地点几乎毫无关系。

在这篇文章中，我想说，警方应该把地点，而不是人作为警务实践的中心。我的观点不仅是简单地在警务实践中考虑地点因素，而是要使地点成为警察实用数据库、警务活动的地理组织、打击犯罪和治安混乱警务战略等等方面重要的组成部分，还要对以城市为背景的警察角色进行定义。就本文来说，比起基于人的警务，基于地点的警务作为警察行动的焦点会更有效，因为对于警察行动来说它提供一个更加稳定的目标，更强有力的证据基础，碰到更少的道德及法律问题。这些优势表明警方把重点从参与犯罪的人转移到犯罪行为的情境中。这绝不再是那些已经促进和发展关注犯罪背景的警务变革的警察领导层们的一个激进想法（Bratton，1998；Bueermann，1999；Maple and Mitchell，1999）。另外，警察学方面的学者们提出地点在推断犯罪起因和犯罪预防等方面的重要性也已经有将近三十年了（Eck and Weisburd，1995；Sherman，Gartin and Buerger，1989；Sherman and Weisburd，1995；Spelman and Eck，1989a，1989b；Weisburd，2004；Weisburd，Bushway，Lum，and Yang，2004）。基于地点的警务代表着新的一轮警务变革，尽管它需要重新思考警务实践关键的组织单位。

再次声明，简单的支持基于地点的警务是不够的，我将会提出实际上警察应该如何有效地实施与此相关的做法。当然，在推出新的方法之前，警察会遇到新的问题和机会来采取和更新警务措施。我在这方面的建议应该是被认为完善政策以推进警务事业。警方已经在过去的二十年里表现出了他们对于推进警务革命和创新的浓厚兴趣（Skogan and Frydl，2004；Weisburd and Braga，2006b）。基于地点的警务是发展过程中的一个自然进程。

一、什么是地点？

在我们展开讨论基于地点警务的优点前，来定义我所说的地点是很重要的。基于地点警务不是简单地将警务战略在地理单元上开展实施。传统警务由于警察需要按规定在较大区域内划分操作区块,比如警察部门的辖区和责任区,在这个意义上传统警务可以被认为是基于地点的警务。事实上,在基于地点警务中,地点指的是地理聚集的不同水平,而不是传统有警察局执行官和规划者的区域。地点在此是指微观上很小的分析单位,如建筑物或地址、街区、街道或路段(Eck and Weisburd,1995)。当犯罪集中在这些地方时,它们通常就会被叫做热点。

犯罪地点有两种非常有价值的阐述,它们在解释"地点"对于理解犯罪和警察干预方面的重要作用上有不同指向。在明尼阿波利斯的热点试验(1995)中,劳伦斯·谢尔曼(Lawrence Sherman)和我划定了增加巡逻的街区或路段(见图1)。

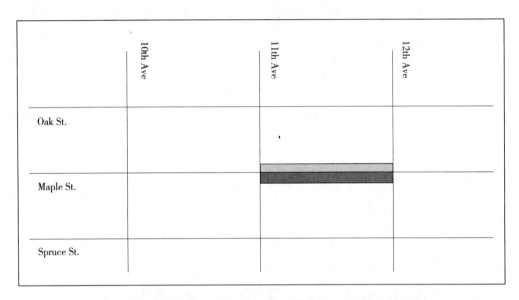

图1　明尼阿波利斯市热点区域巡逻试验中的一个试验点的样本

我们使用街区,一部分原因是它们代表了一个容易被警察识别的分析单元,为警察干预提供自然的环境。但是,我们与其他学者们一样也承认,下列因素使得街区或路段成为地点警务中的一种特别有用的分析单位:街区居民的视觉亲近,相互关联的角色义务,共同准则和行为的接受度,周期性的活动规律,街道的物理界限划定,以及街区的历史演变(Hunter and Baumer,1982;Taylor, Gottfredson and Brower,1984)。

在泽西市的位移和扩散项目(Weisburd, Wyckoff, Ready, Eck, Hinkle and Gajewski,2004;Weisburd, Wyckoff, Ready and Eck, Hinkle and Gajewski,2006)中,我和我的同事尝试鉴别出警方注意中离散的地点。但在这项研究中我们试图审查具体类型的犯罪市场。这种市场往往遍布在犯罪的大面积路段。图2是泽西市卖淫市场划定的犯罪干预界限。

这个案例中包括的是一组城市街区,但重要的是,它比以往作为犯罪干预和犯罪

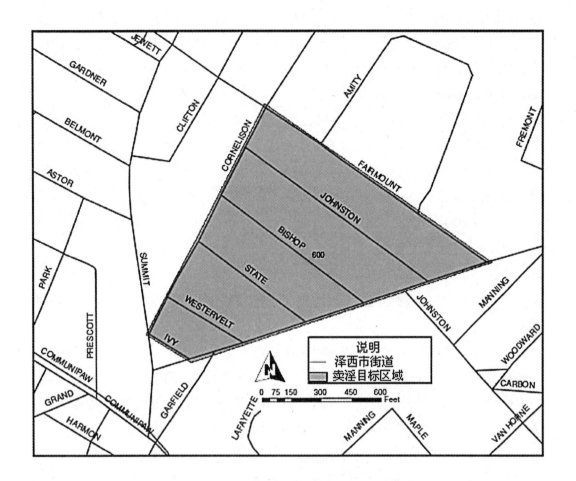

图2 泽西市犯罪位移和效益扩散项目的地点

科学研究的重点社区或者警察辖区要小得多。移动项目和明尼阿波利斯试验说明因警察利益和犯罪基本结构的不同,分析的地点单元也会发生变化。如果警察大范围地采取这种方法,那么定义基于地点警务的分析单元会需要更多的投入和研究(Weisburd,Bruinsma,and Bernasco,即将出版)。

二、什么是基于地点警务?

当我要解释为什么地点警务模式应该成为现代警务的焦点时,我认为有必要先定义什么是基于地点警务。其核心是关注犯罪聚集的地方以及与导致该地犯罪发生的相关因素。从这个意义上来讲,基于地点警务理论上是建立在"日常行为理论"(Cohen and Felson,1979;Felson,1994)基础上的。这个理论主张犯罪就是合适的目标(如受害者)，缺乏"有能力的监护人"(如警察)，以及有动机的、潜在的违法人出现这三方面共同作用而导致的。当然，这一切都必须发生在一定的地点和情境背景中，并据此基于地点警务认为上述因素会在某些特殊地点上有机结合(Brantingham and Brantingham，1981，1984)。

基于地点警务模式的策略可以如热点巡逻一样简单，就如同明尼阿波利斯(Minneapolis)热点试验，警察采取的干预措施就是分派更多的巡逻力量在犯罪聚集的地方(犯罪热点)。基于地点警务也会采用复杂的方法来改善有些地方的犯罪问题。例如，泽西城毒品市场分析项目(Jersey City Drug Market Analysis Project)(Weisburd and Green，1995)，一个三步骤项目(包括识别和分析问题，作出应对反应，和维护犯罪控制效果)就用来缓解毒品热点的问题。在泽西城问题导向警务项目(Jersey City Problem-Oriented Policing Project)(Braga，Weisburd，Waring，Mazerolle，Spelman and Gajewski，1999)中，问题导向警务理念被用来针对暴力犯罪热点小区域制定特殊的策略。

基于地点警务中的"地点管理者"往往是要改善犯罪和犯罪相关问题的中心人物(Eck，1994；Eck and Weisburd，1995)。例如，发现了酒吧间招待和保镖规范行为的方式与饮酒中的暴力形成有很大的关系(Homel and Clark，1995)。像业主、管理员、酒吧间招待、门卫，甚至生活或居住在该地的人都可以成为地点警务模式中的重要资源(Scott，2005)。一种基于地点警务的方法就是用民事补救措施来"说服或强迫非违约方的第三者承担行为的责任以防止或结束犯罪或滋扰行为的发生"(Mazerolle and Roehl 1998：1)。在这种情况下，警察可以使用滋扰和撤销诉讼法规促使房东和业主来帮助警察控制犯罪。

三、地点警务的优点

在给出了我认为的"地点"的定义，例举了基于地点警务策略的例子后，接下来我想谈谈为什么基于地点警务会成为警务中的一个中心战略和实践方法。基础和应用研究证据有力地支持了对地点的更深入重视。正如我下面要详细描述的，就警力资源分配来讲，基于地点警务相比以人为主的警务模式可能更有效。对警方的犯罪干预来说，它比基于违法者的犯罪干预，更具有时间稳定性，也有针对性。也许更为重要的是，正如我下面提到，基于地点警务的有效性有令人信服的实验证据支持。

四、基于地点警务的效益

由于人们总是期望最大限度地描述警务的特征,因此,对警察战略的效益评估也有很多不同方法。我认为从警务效益这个定义开始是合理的,警务效益是指策略更有效,并达到能用较少目标实现同样犯罪预防的实效。这样的定义表明更有效的策略同样是更有实际价值的。当然,不论确定的目标怎么样,用相似的策略才能得出这样的结论。效益在警务活动中是很重要的,因为警力资源是有限的。

在某种程度上,犯罪集中小部分潜在目标上,警务效益就可以最大化。就地点而言,基础研究指出犯罪高密度地集中在某些地点上。第一个展开这方面研究论证的是劳伦斯·谢尔曼在20世纪80年代后期做的研究。谢尔曼审查了明尼阿波利斯的报警地址,发现一年内该市50%的犯罪报警电话集中在约3.5%的地址上(Sherman,Gartin, and Buerger,1989)。最近,我与同事(Weisburd, Bushway, Lum, and Yang,2004)得出类似水平的犯罪不仅集中在西雅图的街区,而且一些特定的地点报告的犯罪案件集中度,在过去长达14年,保持相当的稳定。(见图3)

相应的,还有一系列的研究表明,忽略对特定分析单位的定义,犯罪的集中在地理微观层面是显著存在的(Brantingham and Brantingham,1999;Crow and Bull,1975;Pierce, Spaar and Briggs,1988;Roncek,2000;Sherman *et al.*,1989;Weisburd and Green,1994;Weisburd, Maher and Sherman,1992)。对于特定种类的犯罪类型来说,这种集中程度更大。比如,我和我的同事发现西雅图市的29,849的街区中有86个街区发生了该市青少年犯罪的三分之一(Weisburd, Morris 和 Groff)。

值得注意的是,在这些小地理单元的犯罪聚集群不能够简单掩盖那些发生在较大地理范围内的犯罪趋势,比如社区。例如,研究表明,那些被认为是小镇中治安良好的区域,但往往其中的某些街区却具有高犯罪率,而那些被认为是治安堪忧的区域,却也有着相对犯罪率极低的地段(Weisburd and Green,1994)。在最近的一个青少年犯罪热点的研究中表明,微观地点单位的犯罪随着不同的街道而有所差异(Groff, Weisburd,and Morris,即将出版)。实用地理统计数据能确定空间独立性,格勒夫等人表明相邻街区随着时间的推移呈现不同层次和类型的犯罪。

正如已经指出的,犯罪是集中在某个地点,值得注意的是犯罪同时又会在罪犯中聚集,这是30多年前沃尔夫冈(Wolfgang)、菲戈里欧(Figlio)和塞琳(Sellin)(1972)在研究中提出的。犯罪是更集中在地点上还是更集中在罪犯上呢? 我们尝试着拿

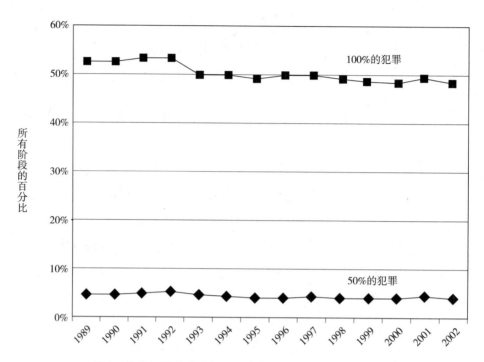

图3　华盛顿州西雅图市 3000 个街段上犯罪案件的集中度

资料来源:威斯勃德等(*Weisburd et al.*),(2004)。

1989 年到 2002 年间西雅图的犯罪案件作比较。我们的结果表明,当用目标作为标准时,的确更有效地集中在地点上。用这种方法我们发现了研究期间平均约 1500 个路段占了每年 50% 的犯罪量。在同一时期,6108 个罪犯实施了每年 50% 的犯罪。简单地说,当警方的注意在人上而不是地点上时,他们需要瞄准之前目标量的 4 倍才能够发现同样程度的犯罪。

五、基于地点目标的稳定性

到目前为止的讨论,整体评估警方战略有效性时忽略了一个主要问题。警务目标的稳定性是加强警务实践的一个重要考虑因素。如果一个分析单元犯罪率存在着很高的不稳定性,那么警方策略的有效性就降低了。例如,犯罪分子在不同时间内实施违法行为波动很大,在某一时期达到高峰,接着又十分低调。对这些罪犯实施监禁所投入的资源就可能没有什么真正的预防犯罪的效益,尽管说它有利于惩治犯罪。相同地,如果用于制定预防犯罪的新方案,而识别和追踪的目标很困难,那么策略的有效性将会受到质疑。

或许除了犯罪生涯中的可变性和不稳定性,在犯罪学中就没有其他的事实成立。差异性中一个首要因素就是大部分罪犯都属早龄犯罪,相对来说犯罪比较早(Blumstein, Cohen, Roth and Visher, 1986;Wolfgang *et al.*, 1987;Gottfredson and Hirschi,1990;Tracy and Kempf-Leonard,1996;Laub and Sampson,2003)。但是也存在着证据证明,大部分罪犯的犯罪行为存在着高不稳定性,尽管是从短期阶段来看。这可能和基于地点的犯罪发展模式形成鲜明对比,后者相对呈现时间稳定性。在我们的西雅图基于地点的犯罪趋势研究中(Weisburd *et al.*, 2004),我们发现不仅仅是大约相同数量的路段占据了每年50%的犯罪量,而且1989年非常高和非常低犯罪率的路段到2002年也大致处在相似的位置上。这在图4中表明,用纳金和其同事研发的分组轨迹分析方法将犯罪轨迹中的路段标出来(Nagin, 1999;Nagin and Tremblay, 2001)。然而尽管数据轨迹都有发展趋势,但是,令人震惊的是地点随着时间的推移呈现相对稳定的犯罪发展动态。

这种稳定性进而说明基于地点警务不仅是针对目标数量有效,而且是在警务战略应用在特殊目标上也是更高效的。地点,简单地说,就是不动目标。将警务战略用在一个高案发率的犯罪热点,并不是说来年该区域的案发率就会明显下降。犯罪地点的时间稳定性使得犯罪地点成为警力资源重点投入的对象。

地点是不变的对象,从另一种意义上说,不同于罪犯,它始终在一个地方。美国的国家统计局关于美国住房调查显示,美国人每7年搬一次家(美国住房调查科,2005年)。有理由假设罪犯迁移比这个更频繁。研究往往表明,追踪犯罪进行调查研究的难度很大(Wolfgang *et al.*, 1987;Laub and Sampson,2003),根据以往的经验,警方用最新所知的地址寻找罪犯,但是,罪犯往往已不住那儿了。基于地点的警务模式提供的目标始终是在同一个地方。对投入在犯罪预防上的警察资源来说,这并非微不足道。

六、基于地点警务的有效性

虽然传统和经验为刑事司法从业者提供了指导,但是学者、从业者和决策者越来越达成一种共识,认为犯罪行为的控制应该建立在科学证据的基础上,也就是"什么是有效"的证据(Cullen and Gendreau, 2000;MacKenzie, 2000;Sherman, 1998;Sherman, Farrington, Welsh and MacKenzie,2002)。尽管基于证据的范式在其他领域也在发展,包括犯罪和司法领域(Farrington and Weisburd, 2007;Nutley and Davies,

1999；Davies，Nutley and Smith，2000），但这种趋势也许是卫生专业领域最为突出，"循证医学"的理念获得了政府部门和专业人士的支持（Millenson，1997；Zuger，1997）。以证据为准则，基于地点警务获得了大力支持。事实上，国家研究理事会在仔细审查警务实践和警务时，得出结论："关于犯罪热点而开展的警力资源研究现在提供有力证据证明了其有效性"（Skogan and Frydl，2004：250）。

国家研究理事会的结论是对过去十年中九个一系列关于基于地点警务的研究中得出的（Braga，2001）。其中，五项随机试验的研究被认为是该项目有成效的最可靠证明（Campbell and Boruch，1975；Shadish，Cook and Campbell，2002；Weisburd，2003；Wilkinson，1999）。这五项也关注了犯罪位移的问题，认为犯罪位移是警方对某一特殊地点进行犯罪预防的结果。一直以来反对犯罪地理预防的原因也是它仅仅是空间上打击犯罪，而犯罪是会转移到其他没有受相同打击力度的地方去（Reppetto，1976）。这种空间位移论对基于地点干预的整个犯罪预防价值是一种威胁，因为如果犯罪只会简单地转移到另一个街角，那么，很小范围内的犯罪预防其价值是相当有限的。

重要的是，布拉干和美国国家研究委员会审查的9个研究中有8个（所有的研究都采用实验方法）数据表明，基于地点警务方法有利于犯罪预防，并且有统计的显著性。没有一个探讨空间位移的研究发现明显的犯罪从一个地方转移到其他地方的证据。事实上，五分之四的实验研究存在着"犯罪控制利益扩散"的现象（Clarke and Weisburd，1994），也就是说临近这些地点周围地带也获得了犯罪预防的效果，尽管他们不是警方战略的重点。

鉴于空间转移的常用假设，值得一提的是最近《警察基础》中一项研究，其重点就是专门关于这个问题的，参考了我以前提到的关于"地点"的定义（Weisburd *et al.*，2004；Weisburd *et al.*，2006）。不同于先前的研究，泽西城位移和扩散项目目的不在于评估特定的警察干预的影响力。相反，它的重点在于探索因热点警务战略而引起的犯罪空间位移，在时间上的快速转移程度。本研究的结果与以往的研究相一致，是在对目标地区测试该方案结果的过程中形成的（如上所述）。不存在着立即空间转移的情况。但是存在有利证据证明犯罪控制利益的空间扩散现象。

这项研究为我们提供了定性数据在收集和理解方面的明显优势，使得我们了解到基于地点警务为什么会有目标影响而无空间位移影响的结果。违法者并没有知觉所有的地方都拥有同样的作案机会。举个例子，容易接触客户是贩毒分子的一个关键标准，同样的，较少居民的居住就减少有关卖淫活动向警方报警的事件。实施犯罪活动的地点特殊性需求，也决定犯罪不可能在一个城市内轻易地转移。事实上，证明这种特点

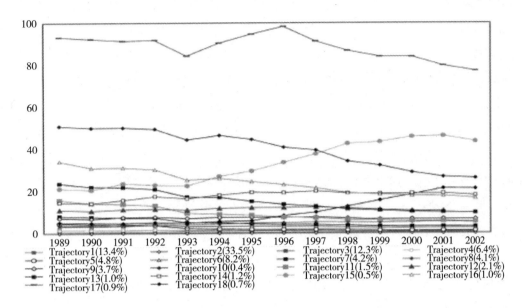

图 4　西雅图市 18 个犯罪事件轨迹（1989—2002 年）

备注：圆括号里面的百分比代表每个轨迹涉及的街段所占西雅图市街段的比例。

资料来源：Weisburd *et al.*，（2004）。

的地点相对来说比较少。反过来，罪犯分子从犯罪地点转移需要十分的努力并且承担着风险。正如一位贩毒者告诉我们："你很难在一个不是你居住的地方做生意，因为那不是你的地盘。这就是人们如何自取灭亡（Weisburd *et al.*，2006：578）。"此外，罪犯相对地对自己的家和地盘感到舒适些，也比较偏好于和周围的人交流。就像一个妓女解释说的，"在我自己的地方，我知道这里的人。在'山上'，我根本不知道镇的那一头人的情况"（Weisburd *et al.*，2006：579）。

不管是什么导致空间位移现象的缺失，但是这些研究结果都加强基于地点警务工作的证据基础。如国家研究会报道，警务学者已经开发了相应的犯罪预防方法，说明基于地点警务得到大力支持。

七、法律和道德的关注

警察常常抱怨他们对犯罪束手束脚。虽然说警务工作受法律约束的程度一直是争议产生的源泉（Bittner，1967；Ohlin and Remington，1993；Skogan and Frydl，2004；Vollmer，1933；Wickersham Commission，1931；Wilson，1950），显而易见的，基于地点警务所提供的警务干预目标是较少受到传统法律监督保障的。习惯法和我们传统法律对地方的考虑会比对人的考虑要少。但不是说警察在地方上想做什么就能做什么的。然而，宪法和程序法对于目标地点有时候还是比较宽松的。

当一个地方成为犯罪目标或值得特殊需要保护时，对于个体违法者就容易达到执法合法化。例如，卡汗（Dan Kahan）和梅尔斯（Tracey Meares）注意到，执法人员"不必取得授权，甚至不需要有可疑原因就能够在检查站让驾驶人员停下，对进入机场或政府楼的所有人员进行检查。"这也就意味着在特定地点，当公共安全放在中心考虑时，在其他地方违反个人权利的警务活动在这些地方就容易被接受。犯罪集中的地方通常是符合这个原则，而事实上，在许多城市里毒品市场就会受到特别的关注。另一个例子就是安全学校地带，因为学校存在易受伤害的潜在的受害者，所以特殊的警务活动就比较容易展开。宪法问题就显得很复杂，因为它并不能在每个情况下都将入侵合法化。然而，政治家、法官、普通市民事实上都有种直觉，认为警察应当允许在某些有特殊问题的地方使用自由裁量权来开展警务实践，如在获得居民的支持，且犯罪聚集的地方。

因此，基于地点的警务在制定犯罪预防战略而确定目标时，就避开了许多限制。但重要的是，基于地点的警务又是一种更少胁迫的警务方法，从长远来看，使犯罪预防策略更加人性化。要使基于地点警务成功，警察有必要扩大他们的工具箱，充分考虑到他们的目标对象是地点而不是人①。相对执法来讲，民法对中止基于地点的犯罪更为有效（Mazerolle and Roehl，1998），正如切赫（Cheh）（1991：1329）发现的，"警察和检察官都接受民事策略，不仅仅是因为他们动用武器可能会导致反社会行为，还因为民事补救可以提供快速的解决方法，又符合刑事审判中严谨的宪法保护。"不论出于何种原因，犯罪预防的战略从刑法考虑转移到从民法或行政法考虑，其结果就是犯罪预防措施更少地建立在逮捕和监禁犯人为目的的传统执法理念上。

八、提高预防，降低监禁

在过去的二十年里，美国的监禁率越来越高。在监狱上的开支已经远远超出教育和医疗保障支出的两倍（Hughes，2006）。道德上的代价是230万的美国人待在监狱里（Sabol，Couture，and Harrison，2007），受到了不人道的对待和人格上的侮辱。基于地点警务旨在减少地区内犯罪机会，而不是等待着犯罪的发生然后逮捕犯罪嫌疑人。成功

---

① 我非常感激特雷西·米尔斯对这些问题的洞察和领悟。

的犯罪预防项目不需要很高的逮捕率,特别是采用对违法者开展劝阻、引导方式时,比如通过"第三方警务"的方式(Mazerolle and Ransley,2005)。从这个意义上来讲,基于地点警务的预防犯罪方法能够提升公共安全度,同时又减少了监禁带来的人力和财政上的损失。如果基于地点警务能够成为警务活动的重心,而不是逮捕罪犯,那么我们很可能会看到在相同时期内监狱里人口的下降,而且犯罪预防措施效率会大大提升。

九、必须做什么?

目前为止,我得出了,基于地点警务提高了警务实践的效益和将警力资源分配到具有犯罪状况相对稳定的目标;其有效性获得了令人信服的证据支持,并且它能够减少警务实践中的法律障碍和长期的基于人的警务模式带来的社会和道德的代价。但正如我所说的,很多警察会说,警务活动已经开始以地点为主。我们该如何完善基于地点警务的大项目呢?

首先重要的是要认识到地点事实上始终都是警察关注的焦点。正如 Carolyn Block(1988)在讨论警察对犯罪地图的兴趣中指出的,"犯罪地图并没有什么新奇之处。当标针问世时,标针地图就已经出现在警察局长的办公桌后面的墙上。"此外,过去十年里,犯罪热点已经成为美国警务工作中共有的主题。在最近的一项研究中,我和拉姆(Cynthia Lum)(2005)发现拥有 100 名以上宣誓警察的 125 个样本警察局中 62% 声称已经采用了计算机犯罪地图。其中,80% 做了关于犯罪热点的分析,并有三分之二将犯罪热点用在巡逻工作上。这十年来,计算机统计已经在更多的美国警察局广泛应用(Weisburd, Mastrofski, McNally and Greenspan, 2001;Weisburd, Mastrofski, McNally, Greenspan, and Willis,2003)。尽管 Compstat 这项创新目的在于将警方倾尽全力到特定的目标,增加组织的控制和承担责任,但是它也提倡犯罪地理分析的创新。

我的立场比较理性,而不仅是简单的倡导警方将新的策略放入到警察干预的篮子里。要使基于地点的警务模式取得成功,警察必须要在理解和处理犯罪方面改变他们的分析单位。劳伦斯·谢尔曼曾嘲讽说,"为什么我不多想想'在什么地方做的'而不是'谁做的'?"(Sherman,1995:37)。直到现在,警务仍然将人作为警务实践的中心。这在数据收集和警察组织结构中可以体现出来。基于地点警务需要警察结构上有根本的改变以便应对犯罪和解决其他社区问题。

比如,警察收集的数据需要建立别于历来以罪犯及其特征为中心的数据系统。

事实上,新增的基于地理的标识并不是最初的案件、逮捕、报警等数据。在 20 世纪 80 年代末,研究人员试图从警方采集的数据中分析犯罪地点,但案发地点却十分模糊,因此,以失败告终。经常会出现同一个地址上有多个名称,也有些是真实的地址,有些只是商店或机构的名称。这些地址名称标识包括可能的排列方式计分,而且基于这样的设计,地址标识符往往不能够说明这些地址在城市的东南西北方向。在过去的十年里,警察对案发地点的识别已有很大进步,部分原因是记录管理系统的显著改进,也有部分原因是地理信息系统的引进。但令人吃惊的是,大多数地方的警察都不能够在他们的数据系统中简单地识别出一个地址。

在逮捕人员数据库里,通常都是记录罪犯的年龄、性别、文化程度和人口统计学数据。但很少有数据告诉我们这些地方的特征和警察执法活动的环境。一个成功的基于地点警务项目是需要警察实时搜集大量的关于这些地方的信息。我们必须要像了解犯罪嫌疑人一样了解这些犯罪高发的地方。在对特定地点进行警务干预时就需要用到这些数据。由于无法经常性地收集信息或很难从其他警署获取信息,就会限制基于地点警务战略的展开。布洛克(Carolyn Block)和格林(Lynn Green)(1994)在他们称之为 GeoArchive(地理档案库)里就已经明确这类数据库的重要性。

相对于基于地点警务而言,传统以人为中心警务在发展数据资源上的失败在于警察中领导者对警察所处的位置不感兴趣。对警察定位追踪的技术往往称为自动车辆定位器技术。在过去的几十年里,国内不只一个警察机构用这种技术来进一步了解警察日常巡逻与犯罪之间的关系。我们需要知道的不仅仅是犯罪发生的地点,而且还要知道警察所处的位置。这些信息帮助我们验证见警率如何影响一个地方的犯罪,以便我们设计出更好的巡逻策略。出于这样的理念,我和警察基金会,伊丽莎白(Elizabeth)、格洛夫(Groff)、琼斯(Greg Jones)已经同达拉斯警察局开始共同进行一项革新项目。但在某种意义上讲,警察运用基于地点警务的方法会失败仅仅因为它才刚开始运用在犯罪预防的实践中。

当今警务地理组织也没能认识到地点在发展警务战略中的重要性。调动安排大辖区内的警察是出于犯罪都是在大地理水平活动的假设。然而,警察管辖区或责任区很少能拟合像社区之类更大的地理单位,从而不太适合基于地点警务模式。或许,警察应该考虑将巡逻力量按照相似犯罪程度或趋势来分配到微观的地方。这种围绕地点警察组织重构,就能够集中策略思想和资源来解决共同的问题。基于地点警务下的警察组织重构可能还有其他形式,但是显然现在的辖区或责任区并没有真正考虑到犯罪的地理分布和其在小范围内的聚集情况。

管理地方治安必定有一个从以抓获和起诉犯罪嫌疑人为目的转移到降低区域内

犯罪可能性为目的的过程。侧重于执法的警务并不是新的说法,事实上它是格尔斯坦(Herman Goldstein)早在1979年提出的问题导向警务模式的中心理念。他与其他学者已经投入了将近30年,尝试让警察将重心从逮捕和起诉犯罪嫌疑人转到更多关注解决犯罪问题上。但这些呼吁最多只是引起警方的注意,并没有过多地听从,而逮捕犯罪嫌疑人仍然是执法的主要任务,即便在警务变革过程中也是如此(Braga and Weisburd,2006)。但这又有什么好奇怪的呢?在警察文化中,一个基于人的警务已经成主导,自然而然地警察就会继续集中对付犯罪嫌疑人和逮捕他们。

基于地点警务使重心转移成为可能,因为它将犯罪地点定为犯罪预防的中心,而不再是犯罪嫌疑人。警察的工作重心就会从仅仅查处犯罪嫌疑人转移到改善地方环境。衡量这种方式的成功与否不在于警察逮捕了多少犯罪嫌疑人,而在于作为人们居住、旅游、工作的地方是不是更加安全和谐。如先前提出的,地点警务模式比起传统执法模式需要警察做更多的工作。

在这样基于地点警务的模式下,警察需要关心的不仅仅是地方,犯罪嫌疑人,受害人,还要考虑潜在的"非警察监护者"。如果要提高一个地方的安全度,那么自然要考虑到如Eck等人提到的"地方管理人"(Eck,1994;Eck and Wartell,1996)。"第三方警务"(Mazerolle and Ransley,2005)也就成为了基于地点警务工作的一部分。但更广泛地讲,警察的工作范围也就拓宽到所有人,因为他们也都是犯罪问题存在的因素之一。

在提倡开展基于地点警务的同时,值得一提的是警察也不能放弃对涉及犯罪的人的重视。事实上,我并不是说要忽视人,而是说要在犯罪发生的背景下去看待人。说人不应该成为警务活动的中心并不是否定他们是组成犯罪的构成要件之一。区别在于警察如何恰到好处地协调信息和犯罪预防之间的关系。另外,可能还是有些犯罪更适合从人这方面来入手,这也应该是理解基于地点警务的核心内容。虽然没有确凿的科学证据证明累犯预防项目或者受害者犯罪预防项目有效,但高危犯罪人群和受害人明显是要引起警方的特别关注。

十、结束语

本文主要讨论了基于地点警务的优点。如我所述的,基础调查表明犯罪行为都是在小的地理范围内进行,如路段或者是小的街区群落。这些地方就可以成为警察干预的稳定的目标,而不像犯罪分子是移动的目标。评估研究提供了有力的实验证据证明基于地点警务模式的有效性,驳斥了实施干预措施后犯罪只不过在小范围内转移的假设。事实上,证据表明这种预防方式更可能给周围地区带来犯罪控制扩散性效益。

相关研究表明警方以人为主的警务模式转移到为以地为主的警务模式,只是时间问题。在过去几十年里,这种转变已经是警务改革的主流趋势,它将需要我们在警务数据采集、警务活动组织等方面要有根本的改变,特别是对警察观念的变化。到现在为止警察还是认为警察工作是要抓获犯罪行为人。现在是时候该改变警察的观点,需要警察能深刻认识到犯罪预防的关键在于改善犯罪滋生的环境。

[参考文献见英文原作]

(金 诚 沈如意 译)

Place-Based Policing

David Weisburd

Hebrew University

Police practices are focused primarily on people and often begin when people call the police. They are focused on identifying offenders who commit crimes, and end with the arrests of those offenders and their processing through the criminal justice system. Police attention is also directed at times to broader community problems and " community caretaking" (Kahan and Meares, 1998; Mastrofski, 1999), and the police are expected to play a role in securing communities in emergencies and more recently in response to homeland security threats (Waddington and Neyroud, 2007). But despite the broader mandate of the police, the core practices of policing assume that people, whether victims or offenders, are the key units of police work.

Police professionals might take exception to this portrait of policing. They will argue that police in recent years have begun to think not only about offenders and victims but also about the situations and places that are the context of crime. To bolster this argument, they might note that police agencies throughout the country have begun to focus in on crime hot spots and that crime mapping has become a central feature of cutting-edge law enforcement (Weisburd and Lum, 2005). Moreover, they could argue that the location of crime is a key component of many recent police innovations, such as Compstat (Silverman, 1999), hot spots policing (Sherman and Weisburd, 1995; Weisburd and Braga, 2006a), and problem-oriented policing (Eck, 2003). In this sense, many forward-looking police agencies have begun to recognize that places as well as people need to be considered if police are to do something about crime and other related problems.

It is still the case, however, that catching criminals and processing them through the criminal justice system remains the predominant police crime prevention strategy, and this is true even, for example, when innovative approaches such as problem-oriented policing are employed (Braga and Weisburd, 2006). Moreover, despite interest in crime mapping, information systems in policing continue to be centered on victims and offenders. Databases in American policing tell us little about the context of crime, despite the fact that police have begun to focus on such contexts as hot spots of crime. In turn, despite important strategic innovations in policing, like Compstat that demand that the police attend to problem places, policing today continues to be geographically organized into units such as police precincts or beats that have little to do with the crime places that recent research has identified as central to understanding crime.

In this essay, I am going to argue that police should put places rather than people at the center of police practices. My point is not simply that places should be considered in policing but that they should become a key component of the databases that police use; of the geographic organization of police activities; of the strategic approaches that police employ to combat crime and disorder; and in the definitions of the role of the police in urban settings. My essay will show that place-based policing, as opposed to person-based policing, is more efficient as a focus of police actions; provides a more stable target for police activities; has a stronger evidence base; and raises fewer ethical and legal problems. These benefits of place-based policing suggest that the police should shift their primary focus from the people involved in crimes to the contexts of criminal behavior. This is no longer a radical idea for police administrators who have fostered and developed innovations that are concerned with the context of crime (Bratton, 1998; Bueermann, 1999; Maple and Mitchell, 1999). Police scholars in turn have pointed to the importance of places in crime causation and crime prevention for almost three decades (Eck and Weisburd, 1995; Sherman, Gartin, and Buerger, 1989; Sherman and Weisburd, 1995; Spelman and Eck, 1989a, 1989b; Weisburd, 2004; Weisburd, Bushway, Lum, and Yang, 2004). Place-based policing in this context represents an evolution in policing even if it demands a reconsideration of the key organizing units of police practice.

Recognizing that it is not enough to simply argue in favor of place-based policing, I will conclude by suggesting practical ways in which the police must change to effectively implement these practices. Of course, in advancing new approaches, the police in the field will adopt and innovate as they identify new problems and opportunities. My suggestions in this regard should be seen as ideas for implementing policies that can advance the policing industry. Police over the last two decades have shown a remarkable degree of interest in innovation to advance police practices (Skogan and Frydl, 2004; Weisburd and Braga, 2006b). Place-based policing represents a natural progression in this process.

WHAT IS A PLACE?

Before we turn to the benefits of place-based policing, it is important to begin by defining what I mean by place. Place-based policing is not simply the application of police strategies to units of geography. Traditional policing in this sense can be seen as place-based, since police have routinely defined their units of operation in terms of large areas, such as police precincts and beats. In place-based policing, place refers to a very different level of geographic aggregation than has traditionally interested police executives and planners. Places in this context are very small micro units of analysis, such as buildings or addresses; block faces, or street segments; or clusters of addresses, block faces, or street segments (Eck and Weisburd, 1995). When crime is concentrated at such places, they are commonly called hot spots.

Two illustrations of crime places are useful since they point to the different ways that place may be important in understanding crime and in police interventions. In the Minneapolis Hot Spots Experiment (1995), Lawrence Sherman and I identified street segments or street blocks for increased patrol presence (see Figure 1).

We used street blocks in part because they represented a unit of analysis that was easily identified by police and could provide a natural setting for police interventions. But we also recogniged, as have other scholars, that such factors as the visual closeness of residents of a block; interrelated role obligations; acceptance of certain common norms and behavior; common, regularly recurring rhythms of activity; the physical boundaries of the street; and the historical evolution of the street segment make the street block a particularly useful unit for analysis for policing places (Hunter and Baumer, 1982; Taylor, Gottfredson, and Brower, 1984).

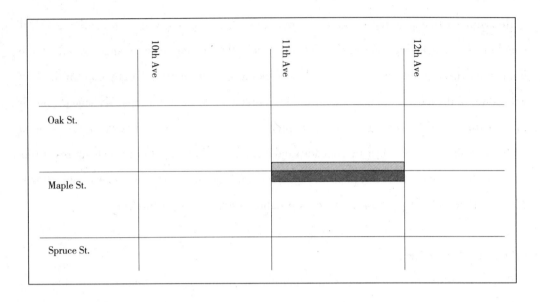

Figure 1   Place in the Minneapolis Hot spots Experiment

In the Jersey City Displacement and Diffusion Project (Weisburd, Wyckoff, Ready, Eck, Hinkle, and Gajewski, 2004; Weisburd, Wyckoff, Ready, Eck, Hinkle, and Gajewski, 2006), my colleagues and I also sought to identify a discrete place for police attention. But in this study we sought to examine specific types of criminal markets. Such markets often spread across street segments in a larger area of Criminal activity. Figure 2 illustrates the boundaries of a prostitution market identified for inter vention in Jersey City.

Included in this case is a group of city blocks but, importantly, this is still much smaller than the neighborhoods or police precincts that have often been the focus of police interventions and scientific study of crime. The displacement project and the Minneapolis experiment illustrate more generally the ways in which unites of place might differ depending on the interests of the police and the underlying structure of crime problems. This issue of defining units of analysis for place-based policing is one that certainly will demand more attention if police adopt this approach on a large scale (see also Weisburd, Bruinsma, and Bernasco, forthcoming).

WHAT IS PLACE-BASED POLICING?

While my intention is to explain why policing places should become a central focus of modern policing, it is useful to define initially what is meant by place-based policing. At its core is a concern with focusing in on places where crimes are concentrated and it begins

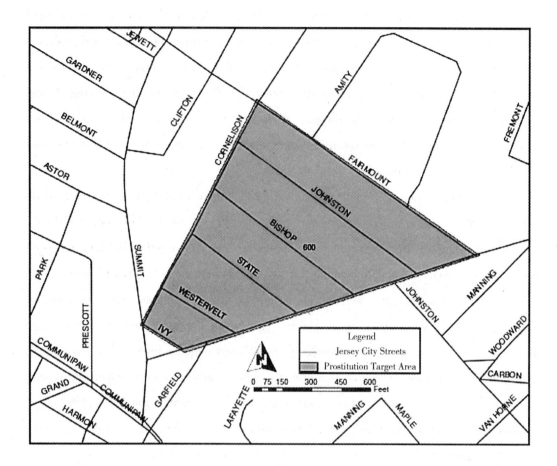

Figure 2　Place in the Jersey City Displacement and Diffusion Project

with an assumption that there is something about a place that leads to crimes occurring there. In this sense, place-based policing is theoretically based on "routine activities theory" (Cohen and Felson, 1979; Felson, 1994), which identifies crime as a matter of the convergence of suitable targets (e. g. , victims), an absence of "capable guardians" (e. g. , police), and the presence of motivated or potential offenders. Of course, this all must occur in the context of a place or situation, and accordingly place-based policing recognizes that there is something about specific places that leads to the convergence of these elements (Brantingham and Brantingham, 1981, 1984).

The strategies of place-based policing can be as simple as hot spots patrol, as was the case in the Minneapolis Hot Spots Policing Experiment, where the police intervention involved placing more patrol resources at places where crime is concentrated (hot spots). But place-based policing can also take a much more complex approach to the amelioration of crime problems at places. In the Jersey City Drug Market Analysis Project (Weisburd and Green, 1995), for example, a three-step program (including identifying and analyzing problems, developing tailored responses, and maintaining crime control gains) was used to reduce problems at drug hot spots. In the Jersey City Problem-Oriented Policing Project (Braga, Weisburd, Waring, Mazerolle, Spelman, and Gajewski, 1999), a problem-oriented policing approach was taken in developing a specific strategy for each of the small areas defined as violent crime hot spots.

In place-based policing, "place managers" are often central figures in trying to do something about crime and crime-related problems (Eck, 1994; Eck and Weisburd, 1995). For example, the way in which bartenders and bouncers regulate behavior has been found to be strongly related to violence in drinking establishments (Homel and Clark, 1995). Place managers, such as business owners or managers, bartenders, doormen, or simply people who live and work at places, can be an important resource for policing places (Scott, 2005). A related approach to place-based policing involves the use of civil remedies to "persuade or coerce non-offending third parties to take responsibility and action to prevent or end criminal or nuisance behavior" (Mazerolle and Roehl, 1998: 1). In such cases, the police might use nuisance and abatement statutes to induce landlords and property owners to aid the police in controlling crime at places.

THE ADVANTAGES OF POLICING PLACES

Having defined what I mean by places and provided some initial examples of place-based policing strategies, I want to turn to why place-based policing makes sense as a central strategic and practical approach to policing. The basic and applied research evidence strongly supports a greater focus on places. As I detail below, place-based policing provides an approach that is likely to be more efficient than person-based policing in terms of the allocation of police resources. It also provides a focus for police interventions that is relatively stable across time and more easily targeted than offender-based crime prevention. Perhaps most importantly, as I will show, there is convincing experimental evidence for the effectiveness of place-based policing.

THE EFFICIENCY OF PLACE-BASED POLICING

The efficiency of police strategies can be defined in a number of different ways, depending on the features of policing that one might want to maximize. I think it is reasonable to begin with a definition of police efficiency that suggests that strategies are more efficient to the extent that they offer police the same crime prevention value with a smaller number of targets. Such a definition implies that more efficient tactics are also more cost effective. Of course, this would be the case only if the strategies used are similar, irrespective of the targets identified, a point I will return to later. Efficiency is important in policing because police resources are limited.

To the extent that crime is concentrated among a small number of potential targets, the efficiency of policing can be maximized. In the case of places, basic research has pointed to a tremendous concentration of crime at place. The first major study to point this out was conducted by Lawrence Sherman in the late 1980s. Sherman examined crime calls to the police at addresses in Minneapolis and found that about 3.5 percent of the addresses in Minneapolis in one year produced about 50 percent of the crime calls (Sherman, Gartin, and Buerger, 1989). More recently, my colleagues and I (Weisburd, Bushway, Lum, and Yang, 2004) have shown not only that a similar level of crime concentration exists at street segments in Seattle, but also that the concentration of reported crime incidents at micro places is stable over a fourteen-year period (see Figure 3).

There are, in turn, a series of studies that suggest that significant concentration of crime at micro levels of geography exists, regardless of the specific unit of analysis defined (Brantingham and Brantingham, 1999; Crow and Bull, 1975; Pierce, Spaar, and Briggs, 1988; Roncek, 2000; Sherman et al., 1989; Weisburd and Green, 1994; Weisburd, Maher, and Sherman, 1992). This concentration seems to be even greater for specific types of crime. For example, my colleagues and I found that 86 street segments out of 29,849 account for one third of the total number of juvenile crime incidents in Seattle (Weisburd, Morris, and Groff, in progress).

It is important to note that such clustering of crime at small units of geography does not simply mask trends that are occurring at a larger geographic level, such as communities. Research has shown, for example, that in what are generally seen as good parts of town there are often streets with strong crime concentrations, and in what are often defined as bad neighborhoods, many places are relatively free of crime (Weisburd and Green, 1994). The extent to which crime at micro units of place varies from street to street is illustrated in a recent study of hot spots of juvenile crime (Groff, Weisburd, and Morris, forthcoming).

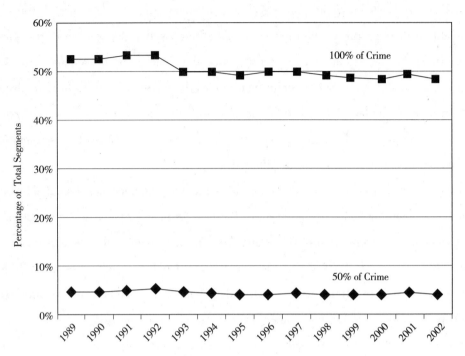

Figure 3   Concentration of Crime Incidents Across 30,000

Street Segments in Seattle, Washington

Source: Weisburd, Bushway, Lum, and Yang 2004.

Using geographic statistics that identify spatial independence, Groff *et al.* , show that street segments right next to each other tend to have very different levels and patterns of crime over time.

Having said that crime is concentrated at place, it is important to note that crime is also concentrated among offenders, a fact pointed out in research by Wolfgang, Figlio, and Sellin (1972) more than thirty years ago. Is crime more concentrated at places than among offenders? We tried to make this comparison using crime incidents from Seattle over the 1989 to 2002 time period. Our results suggest that when using targets as a criterion, places are indeed a more efficient focus than offenders. Using this approach, we found that on average about 1,500 street segments accounted for 50 percent of the crime each year during this period. During the same period, 6,108 offenders were responsible for 50 percent of the crime each year. Simply stated, the police have to approach four times as many targets to identify the same level of overall crime when they focus on people as opposed to places.

THE STABILITY OF PLACE-BASED TARGETS

The discussion so far ignores a major issue in assessing the overall efficiency of police strategies. Stability of police targets is an important consideration in developing police practices. If there is high instability of crime across time at a unit of analysis, then police strategies will be less efficient. For example, let us say that criminals vary in offending greatly over time with a very high peak in one time period and very low activity in subsequent periods. Investment of resources in incarceration of such offenders may have little real crime prevention benefit, though of course it may satisfy important considerations of just punishments for criminals. Similarly, if it is very hard to identify and track targets for crime prevention initiatives, the efficiency of strategies will also be challenged.

There is perhaps no more established fact in criminology than the variability and instability of offending across the life course. A primary factor in this variability is the fact that most offenders age out of crime, often at a relatively young age (Blumstein, Cohen, Roth, and Visher, 1986; Wolfgang *et al.* , 1987; Gottfredson and Hirschi, 1990; Tracy and Kempf-Leonard, 1996; Laub and Sampson, 2003). But there is also evidence of strong instability in criminal behavior for most offenders even when short time periods are observed. This may be contrasted with developmental patterns of crime at place, which suggest much stability in crime incidents over time. In our Seattle study of crime trends at places (Weisburd *et al.* , 2004), we found not only that about the same number of street segments were responsible for 50 percent of the crime each year, but also that the street segments that tended to evidence very low or very high activity at the beginning of the period of study in 1989 were similarly ranked at the end of the period in 2002. This is illustrated in Figure 4, where street segments are placed in crime trajectories using group-based trajectory analyses developed by Nagin and colleagues (Nagin, 1999; Nagin and Tremblay, 2001). While there are developmental trends in the data, what is most striking is the relative stability of crime at place over time.

This stability in turn suggests that place-based policing will not only be more efficient in terms of the number of targets but also in the application of police strategies to specific targets. Places, simply put, are not moving targets. A police strategy that is focused on very high crime rate hot spots is not likely to be focusing on places that will naturally become cool a year later. The stability of crime at place across time makes crime places a particularly salient focus for investment of police resources.

Places are not moving targets in another important sense in that, unlike offenders, they stay in one place. The American Housing Survey from the United States Census Bureau shows that Americans move once every seven years (American Housing Survey Branch, 2005). It is reasonable to assume that offenders move even more often than this. Studies have often noted the difficulty of tracking offenders for survey research (Wolfgang *et al.*, 1987; Laub and Sampson, 2003), and it is a common experience of the police to look for an offender and find that he or she no longer lives at the last known address. Place-based policing provides a target that stays in the same place. This is not an insignificant issue when considering the investment of police resources in crime prevention.

THE EFFECTIVENESS OF PLACE-BASED POLICING

Although tradition and experience often provide the only guidance for criminal justice practitioners, there is a growing consensus among scholars, practitioners, and policy makers that crime control practices and policies should be rooted as much as possible in scientific evidence about "what works" (Cullen and Gendreau, 2000; MacKenzie, 2000; Sherman, 1998; Sherman, Farrington, Welsh, and MacKenzie, 2002). This trend is perhaps most prominent in the health professions where the idea of "evidence-based medicine" has gained strong government and professional support (Millenson, 1997; Zuger, 1997), though the evidence–based paradigm is also developing in other fields, including crime and justice (see Farrington and Weisburd, 2007; Nutley and Daviesm, 1999; Davies, Nutley, and Smith, 2000). Using evidence as a criterion, there is substantial support for place-based policing. Indeed, the National Research Council, in its careful review of police practices and polices, concluded that "... [S]tudies that focused police resources on crime hot spots provide the strongest collective evidence of police effectiveness that is now available" (Skogan and Frydl, 2004: 250).

The National Research Council conclusions are based on a series of nine studies examining place-based policing over the previous decade (Braga, 2001). Of these, five studies were randomized experiments, which are generally seen as representing the most reliable evidence of program effectiveness (Campbell and Boruch, 1975; Shadish, Cook, and Campbell, 2002; Weisburd, 2003; Wilkinson and Task Force on Statistical Inference, 1999). Five studies also looked at the problem of displacement of crime as a result of crime prevention efforts at specific places. One long-standing objection to focusing crime prevention geographically is that it will simply shift or displace crime to other places not receiving the same level of police attention (Reppetto, 1976). Such spatial displacement represents a threat to the overall crime prevention value of place-based interventions, since there is little value in crime prevention at very small units of geography if crime will simply move around the corner.

Importantly, eight of the nine studies (and all of the studies using experimental methods) reviewed by Braga (2001) and the National Research Council panel showed statistically significant crime prevention benefits for the place-based policing approach. None of the studies examining spatial displacement found evidence of significant displacement to other places. Indeed, four of five studies examining this problem found evidence of a "diffusion of crime control benefits" (Clarke and Weisburd, 1994), meaning that areas close by the sites receiving the intervention actually showed crime prevention gains despite the fact that they were not the focus of police strategies.

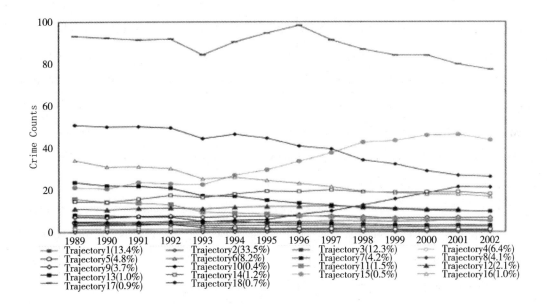

Figure 4   Trajectories of Crime for Street Segments in Seattle(1989 - 2002)

Source: Weisburd, Bushway, Lum, and Yang 2004.

Given the common assumption of spatial displacement, it is worthwhile to note a recent Police Foundation study that focused specifically on this question and that was referred to earlier when I discussed the definition of places (Weisburd *et al.* , 2004; Weisburd *et al.* , 2006). Unlike earlier studies, the Jersey City Displacement and Diffusion Project was not designed to assess the impacts of particular police interventions. Rather, it was singularly focused on examining to what extent there was immediate spatial displacement as a result of hot spots policing strategies. The findings in this study follow earlier results that were developed in the context of tests of program outcomes at targeted areas (described above). There was no evidence of immediate spatial displacement. There was, however, strong evidence of spatial diffusion of crime control benefits.

That study provided us with the advantage of qualitative data collection to understand why place-based policing has target impacts without the type of spatial displacement outcomes that are commonly assumed. We found that offenders did not perceive all places as having the same opportunities for crime. For example, easy access for clients was a critical criterion for drug dealers, as was the presence of relatively few residents who might call the police about prostitutes. The need for special characteristics of places to carry out criminal activity meant that crime could not simply displace to every place in a city. Indeed, the number of places evidencing such characteristics might be relatively small. In turn, spatial movement of offenders from crime sites often involved substantial effort and risk by offenders. As one drug dealer told us, "... [Y]ou really can't deal in areas you aren't living in, it ain't your turf. That's how people get themselves killed" (Weisburd *et al.*, 2006: 578). Moreover, offenders, like non-offenders, come to feel comfortable with their home turf and the people that they encounter. As a prostitute explained, "In my area, I know the people. Up on 'the hill', I don't really know the people at that end of town" (Weisburd *et al.*, 2006: 579).

Whatever the explanation for the lack of spatial displacement outcomes, these research results reinforce the evidence base for place-based policing. As reported by the National Research Council, place-based policing is supported by the strongest evidence that policing scholars have yet to develop for a crime prevention approach.

LEGAL AND ETHICAL CONCERNS

Police often complain that their hands are tied in doing something about criminals. While the extent of legal constraints on policing are the source of much debate (Bittner, 1967; Ohlin and Remington, 1993; Skogan and Frydl, 2004; Vollmer, 1933; Wickersham Commission, 1931; Wilson, 1950), it is clear that place-based policing offers a target for police interventions that is less protected by traditional legal guarantees. The common law and our legal traditions have placed less concern over the rights of places than the rights of individuals. It is not that police can do what they like at places. Rather, the extent of constitutional and procedural guarantees has at times been relaxed where places are targeted.

When it is established that places are crime targets or deserve special protection, it becomes easier to legally justify enforcement in regard to individual offenders. For example, Dan Kahan and Tracey Meares (1998: 1172) note that law enforcement officials "needn't obtain a warrant or even have probable cause ... to stop motorists at sobriety checkpoints or to search all individuals entering airports or government buildings." This means that at certain places, where issues of public safety are a central concern, it is possible to justify policing activities that would be unacceptable if carried out against individuals in other places. Places where crime is concentrated are often seen to meet this criterion, as is the case in many cities that have designated drug market areas for special attention. Safe school zones are another example of the identification of places that allow special activities by the police, in this case because of the vulnerability of potential victims. The constitutional issues here are complex and do not simply justify intrusion in every case. Nonetheless, politicians, judges, and, indeed, ordinary citizens have an intuition that police should be allowed appropriate discretion to police certain places that exhibit specific problems, such as concentrated crime, when there is the support of residents. [1]

Place-based policing, accordingly, provides a target for police that may lead to fewer constraints in terms of the development of crime prevention strategies. But, importantly, it also suggests an approach to policing that may lead to less coercive and, in the long term, more humane crime prevention practices. To be successful in place-based policing, it is often necessary for police to expand their toolbox to take into account the fact that their targets are places and not people. The civil law rather than law enforcement is often the most successful method for interrupting crime at place (Mazerolle and Roehl, 1998). As Cheh has observed (1991: 1329), "Police and prosecutors have embraced civil strategies not only because they expand the arsenal of weapons available to reach anti-social behavior, but also because officials believe that civil remedies offer speedy solutions that are unencumbered by the rigorous constitutional protections associated with criminal

---

[1] I am indebted to Tracey Meares for her insights on these issues.

trials. " Whatever the reason for the shift in tactics from ones that rely on the criminal law to ones that rely on civil or administrative law, the end result is crime prevention strategies that are less reliant on traditional law enforcement practices that often lead to the arrest and imprisonment of offenders.

INCREASING PREVENTION WHILE DECREASING INCARCERATION

Over the last two decades, we have begun to imprison Americans at higher and higher rates. Spending on prisons has increased at more than double the rate of spending on education and health care (Hughes, 2006). The moral cost is that fully 2. 3 million Americans everyday are in prisons or jails (Sabol, Couture, and Harrison, 2007), institutions that are often dehumanizing and degrading. Policing places puts emphasis on reducing opportunities for crime at places, not on waiting for crimes to occur and then arresting offenders. Successful crime prevention programs at places need not lead to high numbers of arrests, especially if methods are developed that discourage offenders, for example through "third party policing" (Mazerolle and Ransley, 2005). In this sense, place-based policing offers an approach to crime prevention that can increase public safety while decreasing the human and financial costs of imprisonment for Americans. If place-based policing was to become the central focus of police, rather than the arrest and apprehension of offenders, we would likely see at the same time a reduction of prison populations and an increase in the crime prevention effectiveness of the police.

WHAT MUST BE DONE?

In my comments so far, I have tried to establish that place-based policing increases the efficiency of policing and focuses police resources on more stable targets; has a convincing evidence base regarding its effectiveness; and provides a focus for policing that can reduce legal barriers to police strategies and lessens the long-term social and moral consequences of person-based policing. But as I noted at the outset, many police practitioners would argue that policing already is concerned with places. What must change to implement a broad program of place-based policing?

It is important to start out by recognizing that places have indeed always been a concern for the police. As Carolyn Block (1998) has noted in discussing interest in crime mapping among police, "Crime maps are nothing new. Pin maps have graced walls behind police chiefs' desks since pins were invented." Moreover, over the last decade, hot spots policing approaches have become a common staple of American policing. In a recent study, Cynthia Lum and I (2005) found that 62 percent of a sample of 125 departments with 100 or more sworn officers claimed to have adopted computerized crime mapping. Of these, 80 percent claimed to conduct hot spots analysis and two-thirds use hot spots policing as a patrol strategy. Compstat has also been adopted widely by larger American police agencies over the last decade (Weisburd, Mastrofski, McNally, and Greenspan, 2001; Weisburd, Mastrofski, McNally, Greenspan, and Willis, 2003). And though Compstat is an innovation that seeks to concentrate police efforts on specific goals and increase organizational control and accountability, it has encouraged geographic analysis of crime as one of its innovations.

But my position is more radical than simply advocating that police add a new strategy to the basket of police interventions. For place-based policing to succeed, police must change their unit of analysis for understanding and doing something about crime. As Lawrence Sherman has quipped, "Why aren't we thinking more about 'wheredunit' rather than 'whodunit'?" (Sherman, 1995: 37). Policing today continues to place people at the center of police practices. This is reflected in how data are collected, as well as how the police are organized. Place-based policing demands a fundamental change in the structure of police efforts to do something about crime and other community problems.

For example, police data has developed historically out of a system that was focused on offenders and their characteristics. Indeed, the addition of a place-based identifier was not initially a source of much concern in incident, arrest, or police call databases. In the late 1980s, researchers who tried to analyze the locations of crime using police databases were often frustrated by an inability to identify where a crime occurred. There were often multiple names given to similar addresses, some based on the actual address and some on the names given to stores or other institutions at that address. Such name identifiers often included scores of possible permutations, and address identifiers often failed to identify whether the address was in the south, north, east, or west of cities with such designations. Over the last decade, police have become much better at identifying where the crime is located, in part because of significant advances in records management systems and in part because of advances in geographic information systems. But it is striking how police in most jurisdictions have failed to go very much beyond the simple identification of an address in their data systems.

In the case of arrest databases, it is common to collect data on age, gender, and often education and other demographic characteristics of offenders. But it is rare for such databases to tell us much about the nature of the places that are the context of police activities. A successful program of place-based policing would require that the police routinely capture rich data about places. We should know as much about the places that are hot spots of crime as we do about offenders who commit crimes. Such data should be regularly available to police when they decide to focus interventions on specific places. The failure to collect such data routinely, or to gain such data from other agencies, limits the ability of police to develop effective place-based policing strategies. Carolyn Block and Lynn Green (1994) have already suggested the importance of such databases in what they have called a GeoArchive.

The failures of traditional person-centered policing to develop data sources relevant for place-based policing is also evidenced in the lack of interest of police executives in knowing where the police are. While technologies for tracking the whereabouts of police, often termed automated vehicle locator technologies, have been available for decades, not a single police agency in the country has used these technologies to try to understand the routine relationships between police patrol and crime. We need to know not only where crime is but also where the police are. This information would allow us to identify how police presence affects crime at place and to design more effective patrol strategies. The Police Foundation, with Elizabeth Groff, Greg Jones, and I, has just begun an innovative program in collaboration with the Dallas Police Department with this aim in mind. But it is in some sense indicative of the failure of police to take a place-based approach that this technology has only now begun to be applied to practical crime prevention.

The geographic organization of policing today also fails to recognize the importance of places in developing police strategies. By arranging police in large precincts and beats, the police have assumed that the common denominator of crime is found at large geographic levels. While it might be argued that precincts and beats are seldom fit for even larger geographic units such as communities, they are particularly ill fit for place-based policing. Perhaps police should consider dividing patrol according to micro places that have similar crime levels and developmental trends over time. Such a reorganization of police around places would focus strategic thinking and resources on solving common problems. The reorganization of police for place-based policing might also take other forms, but it is clear that today's precincts or beats do not take into account what we know today about the geographic distribution of crime and its concentration at relatively small crime places.

In policing places, there must also be a shift from arresting and prosecuting offenders to reducing the opportunities for crime at place. The idea that police were too focused on law enforcement is not a new one, and indeed was a central concern of Herman Goldstein when he introduced the idea of problem-oriented policing in 1979. Goldstein and others have for almost three decades tried to influence the police to be less focused on arrest and prosecution of individual offenders and more focused on solving crime problems. But these calls have at best been only partially heeded by the police, and there is much evidence that law enforcement and arrest of offenders remains the primary tool of policing even in innovative programs (Braga and Weisburd, 2006). But why should we be surprised? In a police culture in which person-based policing is predominant, it is natural for police officers to continue to focus on offenders and their arrest.

Place-based policing provides an opportunity to finally shift this emphasis, because it places the crime place rather than the offender at the center of the crime prevention equation. It changes the central concern of police to improving places rather than simply processing offenders. Success in this context must be measured not in terms of how many arrests the police make but in terms of whether places become safer for the people who live, visit, or work in such places. As noted earlier, policing places requires the expansion of the toolbox of policing far beyond traditional law enforcement.

In this context, place-based policing requires that police be concerned not only about places, offenders, and victims but also about potential non-police guardians. If the goal of the police is to improve safety at places, then it is natural in policing places to be concerned with what Eck and others have termed "place managers" (Eck, 1994; Eck and Wartell, 1996). "Third party policing" (Mazerolle and Ransley, 2005) is also a natural part of place-based policing. But, more generally, place-based policing brings the attention of the police to the full range of people and contexts that are part of the crime problem.

In advocating place-based policing, it is important to note that police should not abandon concern with people involved in crimes. Indeed, I am not suggesting that people should be ignored, but rather that they should be seen in the context of where crime occurs. Saying that people should not be at the center of the crime equation does not mean that they are not an integral part of that equation. The difference is in good part how the police should organize information and crime prevention efforts. Moreover, there may be some crimes that are better understood by focusing on people rather than places, and this should also be a central component of our understanding of place-based policing. Though there is as yet little solid scientific evidence that repeat offender or victim crime prevention programs are effective (Weisburd and Eck, 2004), it is clear that very high-rate criminals or victims should be the subjects of special police attention.

CONCLUSION

My discussion has centered on the benefits of place-based policing. As I have illustrated, basic research suggests that the action of crime is at very small geographic units of analysis, such as street segments or small groups of street blocks. Such places also offer a stable target for police interventions, as contrasted with the constantly moving targets of criminal offenders. Evaluation research provides solid experimental evidence for the effectiveness of place-based policing and contradicts the assumption that such interventions will just move crime around the corner. Indeed, the evidence available suggests that such interventions are much more likely to lead to a diffusion of crime control benefits to areas nearby.

Research accordingly suggests that it is time for police to shift from person-based policing to place-based policing. While such a shift is largely an evolution in trends that have begun over the last few decades, it will nonetheless demand radical changes in data collection in policing, in the organization of police activities, and particularly in the overall world view of the police. It remains true today that police officers see the key work of policing as catching criminals. It is time to change that world view so that police understand that the key to crime prevention is in ameliorating crime at place.

References

American Housing Survey Branch. 2005. *American Housing Survey for the United States: 2005.* Washington, DC: Housing and Household Economic Statistics Division, U. S. Census Bureau.

Bittner, Egon. 1967. The police on skid-row: A study of peacekeeping. *American Sociological Review* 32: 699 – 715.

Block, Carolyn R. 1998. The GeoArchive: An information foundation for community policing. In *Crime Mapping & Crime Prevention*, *Crime Prevention Studies*, *vol. 8*, eds. David Weisburd and Tom McEwen, 27 – 81. Monsey, NY: Criminal Justice Press.

Block, Carolyn R. and Lynn A. Green. 1994. *The GeoArchive Handbook: A Guide for Developing a Geographic Database as an Information Foundation for Community Policing.* Chicago: Illinois Criminal Justice Information Authority.

Blumstein, Alfred, Jacqueline Cohen, Jeffrey Roth, and Christy Visher (eds). 1986. *Criminal Careers and "Career Criminals."* Washington, DC: National Academies Press.

Braga, Anthony A. 2001. The effects of hot spots policing on crime. *Annals of the American Academy* 578: 104 – 125.

Braga, Anthony A., David Weisburd, Elin J. Waring, Lorraine Green-Mazerolle, William Spelman, and Francis Gajewski. 1999. Problem-oriented policing in violent crime places: A randomized controlled experiment. *Criminology* 37: 541 – 580.

Braga, Anthony A. and David Weisburd. 2006. Problem-oriented policing: The disconnect between principles and practice. In *Police Innovation: Contrasting Perspectives*, eds. David Weisburd and Anthony A. Braga, 133 – 154. Cambridge, UK: Cambridge University Press.

Brantingham, Paul J. and Patricia L. Brantingham. 1981. *Environmental Criminology.* Beverly Hills, CA: Sage.

Brantingham, Paul J. and Patricia L. Brantingham. 1984. *Patterns in Crime.* New York: Macmillan.

Brantingham, Patricia L. and Paul J. Brantingham. 1999. A theoretical model of crime hot spot generation. *Studies on Crime and Crime Prevention* 8: 7 – 26.

Bratton, William (with Peter Knobler). 1998. *Turnaround: How America's Top Cop Reversed the Crime Epidemic.* New York: Random House.

Bueermann, James. 1999. *Transforming Community Policing for the 21st Century: Risk-focused Policing.* Redlands, CA, Police Department. Unpublished paper.

Campbell, Donald T. and Robert F. Boruch. 1975. Making the case for randomized assignment to treatments by considering the alternatives: Six ways in which quasi-experimental evaluations in compensatory education tend to underestimate effects. In *Evaluation and Experiment*: *Some Critical Issues in Assessing Social Programs*, eds. Carl Bennett and Arthur Lumsdaine. New York: Academic Press.

Cheh, Mary M. 1991. Constitutional limits on using civil remedies to achieve criminal law objectives: Understanding and transcending the criminal-civil law distinction. *Hastings Law Journal* 42: 1325 – 1413.

Clarke, Ronald V. and David Weisburd. 1994. Diffusion of crime control benefits: Observations on the reverse of displacement. In *Crime Prevention Studies*, *vol. 2*, ed. Ronald V. Clarke, 165 – 183. Monsey, NY: Criminal Justice Press.

Cohen, Lawrence E. and Marcus Felson. 1979. Social change and crime rate trends: A routine activity approach. *American Sociological Review* 44: 588 – 608.

Crow, Wayman and James Bull. 1975. *Robbery Deterrence*: *An Applied Behavioral Science Demonstration*, *Final Report*. La Jolla, CA: Western Behavioral Science Institute.

Cullen, Francis T. and Paul Gendreau. 2000. Assessing correctional rehabilitation: Policy, practices, and prospects. In *Policies*, *Processes*, *and Decisions of the Criminal Justice System*, *Vol. 3*, ed. Julie Horney, 109 – 175. Washington, DC: National Institute of Justice, U. S. Department of Justice.

Davies, Huw T. O. , Sandra Nutley and Peter C. Smith. 2000. *What Works*: *Evidence-Based Policy and Practice in Public Services*. London: Policy Press.

Eck, John. E. 1994. Drug markets and drug places: A case-control study of the spatial structure of illicit drug dealing. PhD Dissertation. College Park: University of Maryland.

Eck, John E. 2003. Police problems: The complexity of problem theory, research and evaluation. In *Problem-Oriented Policing*: *From Innovation to Mainstream*, *Crime Prevention Studies*, *vol. 15*, ed. Johannes Knutsson. Monsey, NY: Criminal Justice Press.

Eck, John E. and David Weisburd. 1995. Crime places in crime theory. In *Crime and Place*, eds. John E. Eck and David Weisburd. Monsey, NY: Criminal Justice Press.

Eck, John E. and Julie Wartell. 1996. *Reducing Crime and Drug Dealing by Improving Place Management*: *A Randomized Experiment*. Washington, DC: National Institute of Justice.

Farrington, David and David Weisburd. 2007. The Campbell Collaboration Crime and

Justice Group. The Criminologist, January/February.

Felson, Marcus. 1994. *Crime and Everyday Life: Implications and Insights for Society.* Thousand Oaks, CA: Pine Forge Press.

Goldstein, Herman. 1979. Improving policing: A problem-oriented approach. *Crime & Delinquency* 25: 236 – 258.

Gottfredson, Michael and Travis Hirschi. 1990. *A General Theory of Crime.* Stanford, CA: Stanford University Press.

Groff, Elizabeth, David Weisburd, and Nancy Morris. Forthcoming. Where the action is at places: examining spatio-temporal patterns of juvenile crime at places using trajectory analysis and GIS. In *Putting Crime in Its Place: Units of Analysis in Spatial Crime Research*, eds. David Weisburd, Gerben Bruinsma, and Wim Bernasco. New York: Springer Verlaag.

Homel, Ross and Jeff Clark. 1995. The prediction and prevention of violence in pubs and clubs. In *Crime Prevention Studies Vol. 3*, ed. Jeff Clark. Monsey, NY: Criminal Justice Press.

Hughes, Kristen A. 2006. *Justice Expenditure and Employment in the United States*, 2003. Washington, DC: Bureau of Justice Statistics, U.S. Department of Justice.

Hunter, Albert J. and Terry L. Baumer. 1982. Street traffic, social integration, and fear of crime. *Sociological Inquiry* 52: 122 – 131.

Kahan, Dan M. and Tracey L. Meares. 1998. The coming crisis of criminal procedure. *Georgetown Law Journal* 86; 1153 – 1184.

Laub, John H. and Robert J. Sampson. 2003. *Shared Beginnings, Divergent Lives: Delinquent Boys to Age 70.* Cambridge, MA: Harvard University Press.

MacKenzie, Doris L. 2000. Evidence-based corrections: Identifying what works. *Crime & Delinquency* 46: 457 – 471.

Maple, Jack and Chris Mitchell. 1999. *The Crime Fighter: Putting the Bad Guys Out of Business.* New York: Doubleday.

Mastrofski, Stephen. 1999. *Policing for People. Ideas in American Policing* series. Washington DC: Police Foundation.

Mazerolle, Loraine and Jan Roehl. 1998. Civil remedies and crime prevention. In *Crime Prevention Studies*, *Vol. 9*, eds. Loraine Mazerolle and Jan Roehl. Monsey, NY: Criminal Justice Press.

Mazerolle, Lorraine and Janet Ransley. 2005. *Third Party Policing*. Cambridge, UK: Cambridge University Press.

Millenson, Michael L. 1997. *Demanding Medical Excellence: Doctors and Accountability in the Information Age*. Chicago: University of Chicago Press.

Nagin, Daniel S. 1999. Analyzing developmental trajectories: A semiparametric, group-based approach. *Psychological Methods 4*: 139 – 157.

Nagin, Daniel S. and Richard E. Tremblay. 2001. Analyzing developmental trajectories of distinct but related behaviors: A group-based method. *Psychological Methods* 6: 18 – 34.

Nutley, Sandra, and Huw T. O. Davies. 1999. The fall and rise of evidence in criminal justice. *Public Money & Management* 19: 47 – 54.

Ohlin, Lloyd and Frank Remington (eds.). 1993. *Discretion in Criminal Justice: The Tension Between Individualization and Uniformity*. Albany: State University of New York Press.

Pierce, Glenn L., Susan Spaar, and LeBaron R. Briggs. 1988. *The Character of Police Work: Strategic and Tactical Implications*. Boston: Center for Applied Social Research, Northeastern University.

Reppetto, Thomas A. 1976. Crime prevention and the displacement phenomenon. *Crime & Delinquency* 22: 166 – 177.

Roncek, Dennis W. 2000. Schools and crime. In *Analyzing Crime Patterns: Frontiers of Practice*, eds. Victor Goldsmith, Philip McGuire, John H. Mollenkopf, and Timothy A. Ross, 153 – 165. Thousand Oaks, CA: Sage.

Sabol, William J., Heather Couture, and Paige M. Harrison. 2007. *Prisoners in 2006*. Washington, DC: Bureau of Justice Statistics, U. S. Department of Justice.

Scott, Michael. 2005. Shifting and sharing police responsibility to address public safety problems. In *Handbook of Crime Prevention and Community Safety*, ed. Nick Tilley. Cullompton, Devon: Willan Publishing.

Shadish, William R., Thomas D. Cook, and Donald T. Campbell. 2002. *Experimental and Quasi-Experimental Designs for Generalized Causal Inference*. Boston: Houghton Mifflin.

Sherman, Lawrence W. 1995. Hot spots of crime and criminal careers of place. In *Crime and Place, Crime Prevention Studies*, *vol.* 4, eds. David Weisburd and John E. Eck, 35 – 52. Monsey, NY: Criminal Justice Press.

Sherman, Lawrence W. 1998. *Evidence-Based Policing. Ideas in American Policing* series. Washington, DC: Police Foundation.

Sherman, Lawrence W., Patrick R. Gartin, and Michael E. Buerger. 1989. Hot spots of predatory crime: Routine activities and the criminology of place. *Criminology* 27: 27 – 55.

Sherman, Lawrence W. and David Weisburd. 1995. General deterrent effects of police patrol in crime 'hot spots': A randomized, controlled trial. *Justice Quarterly* 12: 625 – 648.

Sherman, Lawrence W., David P. Farrington, Brandon C. Welsh, and Doris L. MacKenzie (eds.). 2002. *Evidence-Based Crime Prevention.* New York: Routledge.

Silverman, Eli B. 1999. *NYPD Battles Crime: Innovative Strategies in Policing.* Boston, MA: Northeastern University Press.

Skogan, Wesley and Kathleen Frydl. (eds). 2004. *Fairness and Effectiveness in Policing: The Evidence.* Washington, DC: National Academies Press.

Spelman, William and John E. Eck. 1989a. The police and the delivery of local government services: A problem-oriented approach. In *Police Practice in the '90s: Key Management Issues*, ed. James Fyfe. Washington, DC: International City Management Association.

Spelman, William and John E. Eck. 1989b. Sitting ducks, ravenous wolves, and helping hands: New approaches to urban policing. *Public Affairs Comment* 35: 1 – 9.

Taylor, Ralph B., Stephen D. Gottfredson, and Sidney Brower. 1984. Block crime and fear: Defensible space, local social ties and territorial functioning. *Journal of Research in Crime and Delinquency* 21: 303 – 331.

Tracy, Paul E. and Kimberly Kempf-Leonard. 1996. *Continuity and Discontinuity in Criminal Careers.* New York: Plenum Press.

Vollmer, August. 1933. Police progress in the past twenty-five years. *Journal of Criminal Law and Criminology* 24: 161 – 175.

Waddington, P. J. and Peter Neyroud (eds.). 2007. Policing terrorism. *Policing: A Journal of Policy and Practice* 1 (1).

Weisburd, David. 2004. The emergence of crime places in crime prevention. In *Developments in Criminological and Criminal Justice Research*, eds. Gerben E. B. Bruinsma, Henk Elffers, and Jan de Keijser. Cullompton, Devon: Willan Publishing.

Weisburd, David. 2003. Hot spot policing experiments and criminal justice research: Lessons from the field. *Annals of the American Academy of Political and Social Science* 559: 220 – 245.

Weisburd, David, Lisa Maher, and Lawrence Sherman. 1992. Contrasting crime general and crime specific theory: The case of hot spots of crime. *Advances in Criminological Theory* 4: 45 – 69.

Weisburd, David and Lorraine Green. 1994. Defining the drug market: The case of the Jersey City DMA System. In *Drugs and Crime: Evaluating Public Policy Initiatives*, eds. Doris L. MacKenzie and Craig D. Uchida, 61 – 76. Newbury Park, CA: Sage.

Weisburd, David and Lorraine Green. 1995. Policing drug hot spots: The Jersey City Drug Market Analysis experiment. *Justice Quarterly* 12: 711 – 735.

Weisburd, David, Stephen Mastrofski, Ann Marie McNally, and Rosann Greenspan. 2001. Compstat and Organizational Change: Findings from a National Survey. Report submitted to the National Institute of Justice by the Police Foundation under award number 98-IJ-CX-007.

Weisburd, David, Stephen D. Mastrofski, Ann Marie McNally, Rosann Greenspan, and James Willis. 2003. Reforming to preserve: Compsat and strategic problem solving in American policing. *Criminology and Public Policy* 2 (3): 421 – 455.

Weisburd, David, Shawn Bushway, Cynthia Lum, and Sue-Ming Yang. 2004. Trajectories of crime at places: A longitudinal study of street segments in the city of Seattle. *Criminology* 42: 283 – 322.

Weisburd, David and John Eck. 2004. What can police do to reduce crime, disorder and fear? *Annals of the American Academy of Political and Social Science.* 593: 42 – 65.

Weisburd, David and Cynthia Lum. 2005. The diffusion of computerized crime mapping in policing: Linking research and practice. *Police Practice and Research* 6: 419 – 434.

Weisburd, David and Anthony A. Braga. 2006a. Hot spots policing as a model for police innovation. In *Police Innovation: Contrasting Perspectives*, eds. David Weisburd and Anthony A. Braga, 225 – 244. Cambridge, UK: Cambridge University Press.

Weisburd, David andBraga, Anthony A. 2006b. Introduction: Understanding police innovation. In *Police Innovation: Contrasting Perspectives*, eds. David Weisburd and Anthony A. Braga, 1 – 23. Cambridge, UK: Cambridge University Press.

Weisburd, David, Laura A. Wyckoff, Justin Ready, John E. Eck, Joshua C. Hinkle, and

Frank Gajewski. 2004. Does crime just move around the corner? A study of displacement and diffusion in Jersey City, NJ, Executive Summary. Final report to the National Institute of Justice by the Police Foundation under award number 97-IJ-CX0055. http://www.ncjrs.gov/pdffiles1/nij/grants/211679.pdf

Weisburd, David, Laura A. Wyckoff, Justin Ready, John E. Eck, Joshua C. Hinkle, and Frank Gajewski. 2006. Does crime just move around the corner? A controlled study of spatial displacement and diffusion of crime control benefits. *Criminology* 44: 549 – 592.

Weisburd, David, Nancy Morris, and Elizabeth Groff. In progress. Hot spots of juvenile crime: A longitudinal study of street segments in Seattle, Washington.

Weisburd, David, Gerben Bruinsma, and Wim Bernasco (eds.). Forthcoming. *Putting Crime in Its Place: Units of Analysis in Spatial Crime Research.* New York: Springer Verlaag.

Wickersham Commission. 1931. Wickersham report on police. *The American Journal of Police Science* 2: 337 – 348.

Wilkinson, Leland and Task Force on Statistical Inference. 1999. Statistical methods in psychology journals: Guidelines and explanations. *American Psychologist* 54: 594 – 604.

Wilson, Orlando W. 1950. *Police Administration.* New York: McGraw-Hill.

Wolfgang, Marvin, Robert M. Figlio, and Thorsten Sellin. 1972. *Delinquency in a Birth Cohort.* Chicago: University of Chicago Press.

Wolfgang, Marvin, Terence P. Thornberry, and Robert M. Figlio. 1987. *From Boy to Man, From Delinquency to Crime.* Chicago: University of Chicago Press.

Zuger, Abigail. 1997. New way of doctoring: by the books. *New York Times*, 16 Dec.

警务、毒品与20世纪90年代纽约市凶杀案的下降

史蒂文·F.梅斯纳(STEVEN F. MESSNER)

纽约州立大学奥尔巴尼分校

桑德罗·加力(SANDRO GALEA)

密西根大学

肯尼思·J.塔迪福(KENNETH J. TARDIFF)

康乃尔大学

梅利莎·特蕾西(MELISSA TRACY)

密西根大学

安杰拉·不恰雷利(Angela Bucciarelli)
京卡·马卡姆·派珀(Tinka Markham Piper)
维多利亚·弗赖伊(Victoria Frye)
大卫·弗拉霍夫(David Vlahov)

纽约医药研究院城市流行病学研究中心

20世纪90年代,纽约市凶杀案下降的水平一直是大众媒体密切关注的目标,也是学术研究的焦点。基本事实已经为人熟知。凶杀案在短时间内突然间急剧下降。在1990年,有记录的凶杀案有2245起,到了1998年却降到了633起,下降了72%(Karmen,2000:24)。尽管其他大城市在20世纪90年代的凶杀案也有下降的趋势,

焦点还是对准了纽约,只因其在美国众多城市中具有"美国媒体首都"的不同寻常地位(Fagan,Zimring,and Kim,1998:1227)。就像卡门(Karmen,2000:29)说的,"关于新兴的趋势和最前沿的发展的消息在主流媒体销售点的后院传播极为迅速"。

尽管大众对20世纪90年代纽约市凶杀案骤减印象深刻,对此现象的成因却成为时下讨论的一个主要话题。主流媒体和政府官员将此成效均归功于威廉姆布莱登担任纽约市警察局局长的时候实行的警务策略(Bratton,1998;Conklin,2003;Kelling and Bratton,1998)。布莱登(Bratton)的警务改革可以归纳为"零容忍警务"、"生活质量警务"、"破窗警务"以及"秩序维护警务"(Eck and Maguire,2000;Kelling and Coles,1996)。从一个"业内人士"的角度来看这些警务活动对纽约市凶杀案的贡献,柯林和布莱登(Kelling and Bratton,1998,1227)说"没有另外有价值的其他理论……被提出来反驳我们的信仰,那就是警方行动起到了关键的作用"。

然而,在犯罪学领域,专家对警务策略在凶杀案下降中所起的杰出作用,特别是在全国范围内,提出了质疑。批评者告诫说,尽管警务策略可能对凶杀案的下降起到了一定的作用,但是其他的原因也可能起到了相同甚至更重要的作用(Bowling,1999;Eck and Maguire,2000;Joanes,2000;Levitt,2004;National Research Council,2004)。其中最多提及的解释是凶杀案的下降与高纯度可卡因市场的变化有关(Blumstein and Rosenfeld,1998;Blumstein,Rivara and Rosenfeld,2000;Rosenfeld,2002)。支持者提出,高纯度可卡因的传播与凶杀案的趋势在时间上呈重合现象。当高纯度可卡因市场开始出现的时候,凶杀案开始上升,而当市场开始萎缩的时候,凶杀案也开始下降。

这两个解释显然不是相互排斥的。警务策略和与毒品相关的活动变化都可能导致纽约市凶杀案的下降。尽管经过缜密的推测,但是事实上,几乎没有直接的证据可以说明警务策略和毒品对凶杀案有怎样的影响。到目前为止,两个最具严谨的研究是柯林(Kelling)、苏泽(Sousa)(2001)和哈考特(Harcourt)、路德维格(Ludwig)(2006)①。基于合并的、横向的时间序列设计,将警察服务区作为分析单元,柯林(Kelling)和苏泽(Sousa)发现轻罪的逮捕与暴力犯罪(谋杀,强奸,抢劫以及严重伤害)的综合测量显著相关,这与"破窗警务"的理念是一致的。他们没有发现因可卡

---

① 罗森菲尔德(Rosenfeld)、菲尔嫩戈(Fernango)以及鲍默(Baumer)(2005)做的一个严密的关于警察勤务对凶杀案发案下降作用的分析,在3个城市进行:波士顿,纽约,弗吉尼亚的里士满。他们运用曲线增长分析模式得出20世纪90年代纽约市凶杀案发案率的趋势与其他大城市并无异常,这使得我们对布莱登警务政策的作用产生了极大的怀疑。作者承认他们的数据不允许对三个干预变量本身进行评估(2005:422)。他们对自己的研究的评价是对当时正在进行的地方执法工作对犯罪率干预的评估的一种新的尝试(2005:440)。

因的使用量的减少而导致凶杀案减少的证据。相反的,在对这些数据的重新分析之后,哈考特(Harcourt)、路德维格(Ludwig)提出,当回归模型拓展到包括更多复杂的控制因素后,轻罪的逮捕对暴力犯罪的下降低于统计显著性。在哈考特(Harcourt)、路德维格(Ludwig)的模型中,可卡因使用的测量仍然不显著,这和之前的结果相一致。

本篇论文建立在柯林(Kelling)、苏泽(Sousa)和哈考特(Harcourt)、路德维格(Ludwig)先前的工作基础之上,并在若干方面进行了扩展。首先,除了检验警务策略和可卡因对凶杀案的影响外,我们将凶杀案分为涉枪案件与非涉枪案件。在先前的研究中,这两类案件在纽约市的凶杀案中呈现不同的趋势,因此区别对待是十分必要的(Fagan, Zimring, and Kim, 1998:1319-20;Karmen,2000:117)。其次,在柯林(Kelling)和苏泽(Sousa)的研究中,毒品活动的指标来源于纽约市整个区域内医院出院数据,因此,指标过于粗糙,是个替代性的数据;我们运用更加精确的指标,数据来源可以精确到了各个警察服务区。第三,我们把重罪逮捕的测量引入到了我们的分析中。这个措施可以使我们去检验,特别是在一些轻罪行为中,如果掺杂较多的警务执法是否会有同比的明显作用。我们的分析因此比先前"纽约市谋杀谜"中对两个嫌疑人中的角色分析更加完善(Karmen,2000)。

一、研究背景

柯林(Kelling)和苏泽(Sousa)(2001:1-3)的研究是在警察勤务与犯罪预防相关性争论非常盛行的背景下开展的。他们引用了长期以来的主流思想,由英国伦敦市政警察局创始人罗伯特·比尔(Robert Peel)提出的,即警察的根本任务是预防犯罪和维护秩序。柯林(Kelling)和苏泽(Sousa)认为这个观点在20世纪50年代以前一直得到广泛认同。在这个时期,围绕着"警察真正做什么"这个问题展开,而研究结果也对传统思维上的警务对犯罪的作用提出了挑战。这些研究发现了一些关于犯罪的普遍认识倾向,强调社会不公平、种族歧视、贫困等因素是"犯罪的根源"。这类犯罪根源论对警务在犯罪预防中的作用持怀疑甚至是否定的态度,也就是说,他们认为警察在犯罪预防中根本没有起一点作用。

尽管在20世纪70年代至80年代,对警察的怀疑论成为了学术界的主流思想,柯林(Kelling)和苏泽(Sousa)还是提出了不同的意见。包括戈尔茨坦(Goldstein)(1979)关于"问题导向警务"的理念。根据这个理论,进入警察注意视线的事件正是需要解决的问题,警察的工作就是去解决这些问题。第二个理念,就是引起了广泛影响的"破窗警务",通过威尔逊(Wilson)和柯林(Kelling)(1982)发表在亚特兰大月刊上的文章而逐渐为大家所熟知。这个理念的根本前提是认为无序和不文明行为加剧了居民的恐惧,导致他们陆续搬离所住地方,因此减弱了非正式的社会控制,也"鼓励"了那些侵犯者。① 基于此,警察可以通过对一些轻微违法行为的处理,比如无序行为,卖淫嫖娼(修理破窗)来减少严重犯罪的发生,维护秩序。

纽约市的警察官员开始一项周密的计划,准备将"破窗"警务推行到实践中去(Kelling and Bratton,1998)。柯林(Kelling)起先是与纽约交通当局合作在地铁警局推广主动警务,后来当布莱登(Bratton)当选纽约市警察局局长之后,将主动警务延伸到纽约警察局的其他部门(Kelling and Sousa,2001:2)。在布莱登(Bratton)的领导下,警务改革涵盖了一系列特殊的策略(Conklin,2003:31-5;Karmen,2000:83-140)。布莱登(Bratton)倡导精确而及时的统计数据为决策提供信息。他还提倡数据计算机化,热点地图绘制,这种策略被广泛称之为 COMPSTAT(比较统计数据)。他还在警察局引入了企业管理的方法,在给予地区警察局指挥官更多权力的同时,也要求他们对自己的工作绩效负责。纽约市警察局的警务改革是多方面的,据布莱登(Bratton)说,"关键策略"是对影响生活质量违法行为的严格执法。比如地铁中的逃票行为,挑衅型乞讨,公共场合饮酒及酗酒行为,以及妓女拉客行为(Conklin,2003:37)。地区警察局指挥官遵从了布莱登(Bratton)的指挥,1998 年的非重罪类违法行为拘捕率是 1989 年的 2 倍,与此期间重罪的拘捕数却减少了(Solomon,2003)。

20 世纪 90 年代纽约市凶杀案急剧下降与警务策略干预在时间和空间上相符合。但是,犯罪学家们质疑了警务策略对纽约市的凶杀案下降起到主要作用这一观点,他们列举了一些其他的解释。其中一个被广泛关注的是毒品市场,特别是可卡因市场,它在许多大城市已成为致命暴力死亡的主要原因。

毒品论最早是由布卢姆斯坦(Blumstein)(1995)提出来解释 20 世纪 80 年代到 90 年代初美国大城市里所谓的"凶杀潮"的。根据布卢姆斯坦(Blumstein)(1995)所说,到了 20 世纪 80 年代中期,许多大城市对可卡因需求开始迅猛增长,并迅速在全国传播开来。在全国各个地方,对毒品日益增长的需求使得他们需要招收一批未成年男青年来做毒品交易工作。毒品市场通常伴随着暴力(Goldstein,1985),因此,这些新进的雇员就需要购置枪支求得自保。随着携带枪支从事毒品交易的人越来

---

① 威尔逊(Wilson)和柯林(Kelling)的破窗理论可以看做是强调维护秩序重要性的通用警务的一种发展。泰勒(Taylor)(2001:ch.3)开展了关于警务的"粗暴理论"不同发展的讨论,参见斯科根(Skogan, 1990)。

多,那些没有参加毒品交易的人,尤其是在青少年,也开始携带枪支以求自我防卫。随着枪支在人群中逐渐普及化,人际间的冲突变得越来越血腥,也导致了更高的凶杀率。后来,大约在20世纪90年代初,吸食毒品的人数下降了(Golub and Johnson)。毒品需求量的下降,减少了招收更多毒品交易者的需求,也使毒品市场趋于稳定,随着"毒品潮"的退去,凶杀率开始下降。

在过去的几十年间,许多证据支持了毒品市场/武器竞赛与凶杀案的发展趋势相关联。这个论断与文件记录的杀人案人口统计学数据相符合(Blumstein and Rosenfeld,1998;Cook and Laub,2002;Rosenfeld,2002)。在快速的下降以及反弹后,像瘟疫般迅速增长的凶杀案,往往与年轻的非洲裔美国籍男青年有关,这部分人正是假设中因毒品市场的扩张而招收,后来因市场萎缩而退出的从事毒品交易的人群。除此之外,在20世纪80年代末期,在青年中凶杀案的增长很大程度上取决于涉枪凶杀案的增长。[1] 这个结果与我们所获知的那些新雇的贩毒者之间开展的购枪等武器竞争也是一致的。此外,有证据显示凶杀案比率的上升和下降的时间段与毒品市场的扩张与萎缩也一致。往往是城市越大,人口密度越大的沿海城市(毒品更可能传播)更容易成为"凶杀潮"的先驱之地(Messner et al.,2005)。研究还提出,通过对非法涉毒活动的评估可以解释美国大城市中凶杀率的变化(Ousey and Lee,2002)。最后,毒品市场竞争/武器竞赛改变凶杀案发案率理论的最吸引人的特征是质量对称。它从理论上说明凶杀案的升降趋势在逻辑上与流行相一致(Blumstein and Rosenfeld,1998:1209)[2]。

总之,基于破窗理论的警务,纽约市凶杀案发生了令人瞩目的下降率,这把警务策略对犯罪预防是否有作用这一基本问题推到了犯罪学研究的最前线。结果是富有争议的,甚至是针锋相对的(Eck and Maguire,2000:225)。此外,正如埃克(Eck)、麦圭尔(Maguire)所发现的,纽约市试验是非常重要的,因为布莱登的特殊策略已经成为可以在任何地方施行的,用来预防犯罪的"蓝本",而实际上,全世界的警察部门也都在纽约市试验的基础上开展了类似的警务(2000:228)。因此,相较于其他可能因素,尤其是毒品因素,评估破窗警务对纽约市凶杀案下降的真实影响和实际效果,至今仍是犯罪学优先探讨的主题。

---

① 温特穆特(Wintemute,2000:53)认为最近的凶杀案趋势(不仅仅是青少年凶杀案)都是由涉枪凶杀案件的趋势主导的。

② 库克(Cook)和劳布(Laub)(2002:145)质疑,凶杀潮的下降趋势实际上只不过是上升趋势的一个镜像而已,特别是当我们把侵犯者的性别、民族等以及是否使用武器考虑进去之后。

二、先前的评估

在柯林(Kelling)和苏泽(Sousa)(2001:3)看来,他们面临一个挑战,即引入一个研究设计,用来切实评估是否警务策略,尤其是"破窗"警务能有效解释最近纽约市犯罪趋势。柯林和苏泽(Kelling and Sousa)的研究设计的一个主要的特征是综合纽约警察局各个管辖区域横向和纵向的数据。实质上,他们不是把纽约市当作一个单一的城市,而是将其视为与警察管辖区域一致的 75 个不同的城市(2001:4)。每个区域都有其特有的警务活动,毒品市场以及社会结构的特征。调查中发现,在1989—1998 年期间,它们的暴力犯罪呈现出了不同的趋势。基于纽约市综合的横向和时间序列数据,当影响整个城市的因素得到有效控制时,不同变量之间的联系则可以得到测量和检验。

在柯林(Kelling)和苏泽(Sousa)的多元分析中,因变量是在区域级层次上对 4 种暴力侵害类案件的综合评估,分别是谋杀、强奸、抢劫以及严重伤害案件。最主要的自变量是以警察服务区一级的轻罪拘捕,它是用来衡量破窗警务的指标。① 另外三个变量被用来衡量可能导致暴力犯罪下降的其他原因。为掌握人口统计学数据,评估中的指标还包括了"男性青年"(每个区域就读公立学校男性人数),还有两个用来衡量经济状况的数据(失业人数)及滥用毒品类型(涉毒出院登记)。鉴于数据的来源限制,涉毒出院登记的数据根据行政区划分的数据,而不是警察局管辖区的数据。涉毒出院登记数据包括了整个调查时间段,对男性青年和失业的数据来源于 1990 年的统计数字。

柯林(Kelling)和苏泽(Sousa)用分层线性模型来评估破窗警务对纽约市凶杀案的影响的假设。他们把时间作为第一层变量,把其他自变量作为第二层变量。结果显示暴力犯罪时间趋势存在区域显著差异。此外,他们在时间断面上检验第二层变量的效应时,发现轻罪逮捕得出了预期的负效应:即轻罪逮捕平均数高的区域,暴力犯罪下降更多。男性青年和行政区域内贩毒没有获得统计上的显著性,而是行政区域内的失业与犯罪有出乎意料的反向结果(高失业率,高犯罪下降率)。总之,柯林(Kelling)和苏泽(Sousa)得出的结果支持了他们的主要假设:"破窗警务与区域内的

---

① 在 20 世纪 80 年代早期基于数据的研究中,桑普森(Sampon)和科恩(Cohen)(1988)引进了一种创造性的测量方法,"攻击型警务"——对在每个警察影响下的无序行为以及驾驶的拘捕(DUI)。他们报告在一个大城市中这个评估的结果与抢劫案的发生率呈负相关,这与震慑犯罪论的观点一致。最近的研究中,麦克唐娜(Macdonald)(2002)使用了比较研究法,再次验证桑普森和科恩早前的发现。

暴力犯罪联系密切,而其他观点则没有体现出来。"

哈考特(Harcourt)、路德维格(Ludwig)最近对这个结论提出了挑战,他们指出了柯林(Kelling)和苏泽(Sousa)的两级分层增长模型的一个重要的错误,这个模型着重研究了暴力犯罪的变化(每个区域内在1989—1998年之间的暴力犯罪的线性趋势)及其对应的轻罪拘捕的等级(1989—1998的平均拘捕数)。在这种情况下,分析实际上忽视了1989—1998年间不同区域内所有轻罪拘捕随时间变化的特征(Harcourt and Ludwig,2006:293)。这个方法不仅遗漏了这一点重要的信息,也容易得出关于警务活动与暴力犯罪之间错误的结论。因为,轻罪逮捕率的平均水平与暴力犯罪的初始水平是高度相关的。因此,我们有理由推断,从20世纪80年代"凶杀潮"期间经历了不同寻常的高犯罪率的区域,在20世纪90年代会有一个犯罪率大幅度下降期,这只是一个简单的回归平均数问题。

哈考特(Harcourt)、路德维格(Ludwig)用几个经验性的阐述对柯林(Kelling)和苏泽(Sousa)的结论提出质疑。哈考特(Harcourt)、路德维格(Ludwig)在测量暴力犯罪,轻罪逮捕率及控制变量时用了与柯林(Kelling)和苏泽(Sousa)同样的数据。除此之外,哈考特(Harcourt)、路德维格(Ludwig)还在研究中引入了大量基于普查路段水平的社会人口统计学特征指标。同时,研究还包括调查期间每个区域增加配备的警力,调查早期暴力犯罪的状况,以及调查先期(1984—1989)暴力犯罪的变化。

哈考特(Harcourt)、路德维格(Ludwig)重复了柯林(Kelling)和苏泽(Sousa)运用HLM分层线性模型统计框架下,获得的关键系数,然后他们遵循与柯林和苏泽"相同的直觉"研究方法,估计了一系列的模型(Harcourt and Ludwig,2006:294)。然而,他们用了更常见的实践,应变量用每个区域在1989—1998年期间暴力犯罪实际的变化代替了以前的时间线性趋势。[①] 他们发现,轻罪逮捕的平均数值与暴力犯罪成负相关,这与柯林和苏泽(Kelling and Sousa)的结论是一致的。尽管,警务变量仍然保持统计上显著的反向,但是无论测量研究初期暴力犯罪的情况,还是研究的过程中暴力犯罪的变化趋势,警务变量的重要性都在减少。然而,当所有的控制变量都被加入进行评估的时候,轻罪拘捕的效应低于统计显著性。哈考特(Harcourt)、路德维格(Ludwig)还估计了区别模型,在一定的控制条件下,暴力犯罪的变化是如何随着轻罪逮捕的变化而变化的。对暴力犯罪的变化与轻罪拘捕的变化在控制变量下进行了单线差别模式的评估,这些分析的结果没能支持破窗理论。哈考特(Harcourt)、路德

――――――――――――

① 哈考特(Harcourt)与路德维格(Ludwig)假定暴力犯罪在时间序列上不存在线形,对暴力犯罪的线性时间趋势模型提出质疑。

维格(Ludwig)得出结论,认为他们对纽约市的数据的再分析使得他们得出苏格兰裁定:"无法证明"(2006:276)①。

三、我们的研究

我们采用先前对纽约市的警务变化影响评估基本相同的研究设计,这是一个综合的横向的时间序列设计,但是在许多方面对原来的设计重新定位与扩展。我们将主要的注意力放在凶杀案中上。犯罪学家普遍认为官方的凶杀案数据比其他侵害类案件都更加可靠,因为凶杀案是最可能会被上报并记录在案的。举例来说,奥布赖恩(O'brien)(1996)介绍说,在1973—1992年间,"犯罪统一报告"中所记录的一些非致命暴力犯罪(强奸、抢劫以及重伤侵害类案件)在全国的上升是由于警察勤务的大量投入而获得的产出,并非暴力事件的上升。这种测量误差对任何评价"破窗"警务作用都有重要的影响。因为非致命暴力多的原因似乎与强调警察对犯罪案件进行记录有关,对致力于切实减少犯罪的努力背道而驰。

另外,我们将凶杀案归分为涉枪侵害案件与非涉枪案件。费根(Fagan)、齐姆林(Zimring)、金(Kim)(1998:1319)通过对20世纪80年代中期到90年代纽约市凶杀案的研究,区分出两种在时间趋势上不相关联的凶杀案:涉枪凶杀案和非涉枪凶杀案。非涉枪案件在警务改革之前就已经出现了下降的趋势且平稳下降。这个趋势并不能说明布莱登(Bratton)推行的警务改革对凶杀案有实质性的影响。相反,涉枪案件的下降与警务改革在时间上却是有很好的吻合(Fagan, Zimring, and Kim, 1998:1319)②。此外,据费根(Fagan)、齐姆林(Zimring)、金(Kim)(1998:1322)所提及的,诸如纽约市推行的维护治安技术,"如果警察运用到执勤中,增加对枪支的搜查,那么对涉枪案件会有特殊的效果"。通过加大轻微违法行为的查处,威慑枪支的携带

---

① 哈考特(Harcourt)与路德维格(Ludwig)对纽约市管辖区水平的数据的再次分析后,他们对科马克(Corman)和莫坎(Mocan)的研究进行了严格的评估(2002)。科马克(Corman)和莫坎(Mocan)详尽地分析了纽约市每月的时间序列数据,发现他们破窗警务对抢劫和飞车抢劫(而不是谋杀)有抑制作用。哈考特(Harcourt)与路德维格(Ludwig)认为研究设计中还存在不足,即研究设计仅仅依靠管辖区域一个变量进行的研究,而且纽约市的数据可以用其他的观点来解释。哈考特(Harcourt)与路德维格(Ludwig)还运用运动—机会(MTO)实验来进行评估,迁移到一个不利因素少、环境无序少的邻里社区是否会减少犯罪行为。但是他们最终发现这并没有减少侵害类犯罪的数量,他们认为这是对破窗警务理念的强有力的反驳。

② 费根(Fagan)、齐姆林(Zimring)和金(Kim)(1998:1320)提醒,对警务和其他因素来说,分析因果责任是非常困难的。他们推测,作为一个发案率下降的原因,纽约市的警务模式与枪支导向警务一致,而不是与不加区分的生活质量干预警务相一致(Fagan, Davis, 2003)。

可能会导致凶杀案的下降。但是,这种效应可能只针对涉枪案件而不是非涉枪案件(Karmen,2000:117)。因此,无论在经验还是理论的角度,比起非涉枪凶杀案,破窗警务更能够解释涉枪凶杀案的变化。

我们修改了一个以前的研究中重要的变量:毒品使用的类型,特别是可卡因。先前对纽约市破窗警务的评估使用了市级医院所提供的出院人员登记记录,而暴力犯罪数据则来自于更低一层的区级。就像哈考特(Harcourt)、路德维格(Ludwig)(2006:317)所发现的,这样的测量误差很有可能减弱他们之间的关系,使相关系数趋向于零(无联系)。因此我们有理由推测,滥用毒品的重要性在先前的研究中被低估了。我们使用不同的数据资源:它来源于医药工作者对事故死亡者的毒品含量的信息登记记录。这个数据有两个令人欢喜的特征,通过地理定位我们可以了解其所住的具体地址,以及对所在区域(而不是市级大区域)的毒品使用情况有个初步的评估。此外,有些事故伤者表现假装和其他正常人没有什么不一样,使得出院登记信息很有可能不足以完全代表公众中的毒品使用者数量的巨大(Galea *et al.*,2003)。

我们还把另外一个警务指标引入到我们的分析中来:重罪拘捕率。那些剧增的轻罪拘捕区域同时也被视作是警察勤务活动频繁的区域,任何有关破窗警务的明显作用都未能真正体现出来。凶杀案的下降最多的区域可能就是警务活动全面加强的地方。这个结果更符合一般震慑犯罪的解释而不是对违反生活质量行为的大面积镇压和整顿。

最后,我们还对另外一个暴力侵害行为进行了模型估计,即抢劫罪的发案率,用来佐证我们分析结果的有效性。我们基于以往的研究,建立更为细致的多变量模型,考虑了凶杀案研究文献中曾提及的潜在的社会人口统计学相关变量,同时,将研究期间警力的变化作为一个指标进行评估。

四、数据和方法

这个研究的数据主要来源于三个方面:纽约市首席医学检验办公室,纽约市警察局,以及美国统计局。纽约市首席医学检验办公室对纽约市 1990—1999 年期间所有发生的凶杀、自杀以及事故死亡案件,通过标准化的人工复核并建立了医学文件加以鉴定。纽约市首席医学检验办公室对所有的非自然死亡人员负有调查的义务。因此,纽约市所有的凶杀、自杀、事故死亡事件都是由纽约市首席医学检验办公室复核,并进行规定绘制图表以便数据的提取。此外,纽约市首席医学检验官从 1990 年到现在都是同一个人,所以,纽约市首席医学检验办公室对案件的形式、分类、毒理学的概念,政策以及其他方面在调查研究期间保持一致。

关于死亡的原因、死亡的周边环境(是否使用枪支)以及毒理学等信息都是由训练有素的摘录员按照规范的流程和数据形式,从纽约市首席医学检验办公室文件中收集的。纽约市首席医学检验办公室的调查员们通过对死者的用药历史,社会环境以及死亡的环境、尸检报告、实验数据对每个案件的死因进行复核。在1990—1999年期间,任何由纽约市首席医学检验办公室经手的案子都被精确定位到每个警察管辖区域,这里他们使用了一种叫ArcGIS 9.0软件来确定受伤的位置(ESRI,Redlands,CA,美国环境系统研究所公司,雷德兰兹,加利福尼亚)。只有准确的受伤现场的案子才被包括在我们的分析中。

研究单元是纽约市警察管辖区域。警察管辖区域是区域水平上的单位,对于评估破窗理论是很有帮助的。因为警察执法就是以每个管辖区为单位开展的(Fagan,West and Holland,2003:1566)。第34号区和第35号区(分别是华盛顿高地与因伍德)被看作是一个区,因为他们在1994年才分开。中央公园(22区),因为没有一个人在此处居住,所以没有包括在内。因此,在计算比率时,没有人口分母值。

(一)因变量

我们的因变量包括总凶杀案发案率、涉枪案件以及非涉枪案件的发案率、抢劫案件发案率。凶杀案的数据来源于纽约市首席医学检验办公室,抢劫的数据则来源于纽约市警察局,比率是按照每100000人来计算的,人口基数按照1990年统计的人口总数。

(二)自变量

两个最主要的自变量(轻罪拘捕数与毒品使用)都是时变的变量。纽约市警察局按照常规收集了每个辖区内不同原因的逮捕数据。从纽约警察局收集了1990年到1999年间所有轻罪逮捕的数据,借此来表征破窗导向警务,这和以往的研究一致。(Corman and Mocan ,2006;Harcourt and Ludwig,2006;Kelling and Sousa,2001)轻罪拘捕率也是以每十万人口来计算的,运用1990年人口数作为分母。另外一个主要的自变量是毒品的使用程度,用从纽约首席医学检验办公室获得的每个区域内事故死亡者的比率来表示,这些死者的毒理学结果是对可卡因呈阳性。[①]

---

① 我们对毒品的评估首先假设在每个区域之间的事故死亡的风险是不变的。为了评估风险的差异可能对结果导致的影响程度,我们在凶杀案回归模型中加入了总事故死亡率(作为变化值)。把这个加入进来使得对其他几个协变量的参数估计影响最小。事故死亡率与凶杀案总数、涉枪凶杀案、非涉枪凶杀案案件有显著相关:当事故死亡率上升时,凶杀案呈上升趋势。

(三)控制变量

我们引入了过于宏观研究中与凶杀案有关的大量的社会人口统计学特征作为控制变量(Land McCall and Cohen,1990)。这些变量是以十年为统计周期的,因此,我们将这些变量视为不变的固定变量,并都采用1990年的统计数据。具体的变量包括:

男性比例:调查区域中男性的比例

年龄小于35岁的比例:调查区域内年龄在35周岁以下的人口比例

黑人比例:调查区域内黑人的比例

女性当家的比例:调查区域内女性掌管家庭主要事务的家庭比例

社会救济人口比例:调查区域内接受社会救济的人口比例

低于贫困指标2倍人口比例:调查区域内收入低于贫困指标2倍的人口比例

高中以下学历人口比例:调查区域内25周岁以上的教育程度低于高中的人口比例

失业比例:调查区域内15周岁以上未就业的人口比例

这些社会人口统计控制变量的来源是美国统计总结文件3号(SF3)。网络信息共享平台(Infoshare Online,2007)收集的是普查区间水平的统计数据,这些数据需要整合成警察局管辖区域水平的数据。

因为有些社会经济变量(高中以下学历的人口比例,低于贫困指标2倍的人口比例,女性当家的人口比例,社会救济人口比例)具有高度的内部相关性,我们用主成分分析法,每个区域建构一个整合的社会经济状况值,这和以往对凶杀案的宏观研究方法是一致的(Land McCall and Cohen,1990)。综合分值是通过对4个项目的分数累积相加获得,每个项目的权重是由它们的因素负荷来确定的。这个综合指标与分数呈反向的关系,即分数越高,社会经济地位越低(Range,23.4 – 189.0)。

除了管辖区的社会人口统计学指标之外,我们还加进了另外两个控制变量:武器可得性与警力。武器研究者通常认为,在缺少精确的官方数据或者具有代表性的调查数据的情况下,最可靠的武器可得性数据是用枪自杀的案件比例(Azreal, Cook and Miller,2004;Cook and Ludwig,2006; Kleck,2004)[1]。我们测量武器可得性是用每年每个区域内使用枪支自杀的比例来表示。警力指标就是每年由纽约市警察局分派到每个区级警察局的人数[2]。上述两个变量的数据都是一年一变的,因此,这些变

---

[1] 克莱克(Kleck, 2004)认为自杀的间接测量适用于横向研究,建议纵向研究中不能使用任何标准化的间接数据。相反,沃金、库克、米勒、路德维格(Azreal, Cook, and Miller,2004;Cook, and Ludwig,2006)认为涉枪自杀的比例在两种研究中都是一个重要的间接测定指标。

[2] 我们非常感谢在与伯纳德·哈考特(Bernard Harcourt)和延斯·路德维格(Jens Ludwig)的私人谈话中提供的关于警力的数据。

量都以年变化来表示。

最后,我们对重罪也进行了策略,数据由纽约市警察局从1990—1999年间按辖区进行收集。重罪的拘捕率也是以每十万人口来表示,用1990年人口统计数值为基数得来的,此数值以年变变量加入到了回归模型中。我们加入这个变量来评估警务活动是否得到全方位的提升,或者破窗警务只是对凶杀案的下降有着特别的贡献。

纽约市1990年到1999年间一共14151起凶杀案,我们能够成功地定位于警察管辖区水平的有12971起案件(占原始数据的91.7%)。被选入凶杀案件和其他被剔除的案件并没有明显系统性差别。变量的一元统计分析见附表A。

(四)分析框架

所有的分析都以变化着的混合模型为基础,我们通过将t+1年与t年相对应的值做差而得出相邻年度之间变化的量作为自变量与因变量。因此,所有的模型多遵守以下等式:

$$\triangle Yij = ai + \beta\triangle Xij + \gamma X'i + eij + r \times eij - 1$$

$\triangle Yij$代表因变量在时间t到t+1时间段内,在第i个管辖区,第j个时间间隔内的变化。$\triangle Xij$代表第i个管辖区在第j时间段的自变量的变化的矢量。$X'i$是1990年统计的不随时间变化的人口统计学特征矢量。r是自相关系数。我们使用了随机截距模型来说明自变量与应变量之间的在基础关系上的潜在差异,以及用自回归相关性结构来说明区域内相关性。

我们首先对所有的凶杀案进行了分析,我们研究了轻罪拘捕率单变量的变化对凶杀案案件的影响。接着我们使用了与柯林(Kelling)和苏泽(Sousa)相类似的预测变量来评估这个模型。这个模型的指标包括了毒品使用,以及年龄、性别和失业率等控制变量。然后我们增加其他的控制变量到这个模型中。在增加的分析中,我们将凶杀案分成涉枪与非涉枪案件,我们对于分类模型来讲,只进行整个模型的评估。最后,我们扩展了模型,将重罪的拘捕变量也加入进去,我们就全部预测变量,对所有的凶杀案、分类的凶杀案案件以及抢劫案件发案率的影响进行了评估。

五、研究结论

所有的凶杀案发案率的最初结果见表1。模型1表明轻罪拘捕率对凶杀案发案率的变化呈现出了双变量效应。与柯林(Kelling)和苏泽(Sousa)以及破窗警务的理念一致,统计所得的系数呈负值,并且呈统计显著性(β=-.0013,p<.001)。随着一个地区的轻罪逮捕率上升,谋杀率就下降。

在模型2里,我们也引进了在柯林(Kelling)和苏泽(Sousa)研究中出现过的相似的控制变量,轻罪拘捕率的变化对其影响仍然没有变化,而且保持了明显的负值。对年龄、性别并未达到统计显著水平,而失业率的系数却是显著的,并获得了意料之外的反向关系。这些结果与柯林(Kelling)和苏泽(Sousa)的研究发现类似。但是,与之前的结果不同的是,我们毒品使用这个指标的来源于辖区一级而非市一级的数据是正向的,并且呈统计显著:随着事故死亡者毒品检验呈阳性的比例减少,凶杀案也呈减少的趋势。

表1　预测1990—1999[a]年纽约市警察局辖区凶杀案变化的随机效果模型

	模型1	模型2	模型3
轻罪逮捕率的变化	-.0013 ***	-.0013 ***	-.0012 **
吸食可卡因的变化[b]		.0761 *	.0760 *
男性比例		-.0148	-.0268
35岁以下人口比例		-.1046	-.0448
失业比例		-1.1755 *	-.8458
武器可得性的变化[c]			-.0047
黑人比例			.0052
社会经济状况综合指数[d]			-.0233
警力的变化[e]			.0030

＊p<.05;＊＊p<.01;＊＊＊p<.001. N=666 辖区—时间。

a 1990 年美国统计局所公布的各区域的人口数用于计算比率。

b 事故死亡毒品检测呈阳性比例的年度变化。

c 自杀事件中,使用枪支比例的年度变化。

d 社会经济状况综合指标在警察局管辖区水平的社会经济变量包括:高中以下学历的比例,低于贫困线2倍的人口比例,女性当家的家庭比例,接受社会救济的家庭比例。

e 警察局管辖区水平的警察人数年度变化。

模型3引入了其他控制变量,轻罪拘捕率的变化对凶杀案的效应并没有受到影响。回归参数显示一个辖区内每十万人口增加833个轻罪拘捕数则对应减少区域内的1个凶杀案。为了更进一步解释轻罪这个变量的作用,我们将其他协变量保持平均值,预测凶杀案发生率随着轻罪逮捕率的变化情况。结果如图1所示。轻罪逮捕率变化为25%时,凶杀案发案减少了2.51。而轻罪逮捕变化达到75%时,凶杀案的下降率又增加了1%(-3.47),这个差别是极其明显的。当轻罪逮捕率变化为10%时,凶杀案的发案率每十万人口减少1.7起,当轻罪逮捕率变化达到90%时,凶杀案发案率每十万人口减少4.3起。也就是说,我们的统计模型表明,轻罪逮捕率变化达到90%的时候,凶杀案的发案率变化是轻罪逮捕率变化为10%的时候的2.5倍。

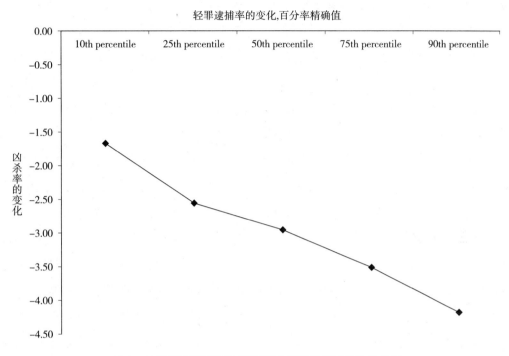

图1　凶杀案变化率与地区轻罪逮捕变化率百分比的关系

从模型3里,也发现吸食毒品对凶杀案仍然有正向的显著作用。[①] 回归参数显示吸食毒品增加13%,每个区域凶杀案会增加1起。相反,其他预测变量的系数都没有出现显著效应。社会人口统计学特征变量没有出现显著效应,是意料之外的,但是,研究采用混合统计模型用来预测凶杀案的年变化,使用了轻罪逮捕率、可卡因逮捕、武器的可得性、警力等时变指标,而社会人口统计学特征值则是不随时间变化的固定值。因此,社会人口统计学指标只能解释横向变量,不能反映辖区内随着时间变化的特征。在用平均值代替时变测量的横向研究中,期望的社会经济特征变量对凶杀案的影响是可以观察的。不利的社会经济状况对预测凶杀案的发生率有很强的、显著的作用:社会经济水平越是恶劣地区,凶杀案的发案率越高。

---

① 考虑均值回归的可能性,我们在凶杀案模型中加入了两个指标,这两个指标描述了研究时间段之前年份凶杀案增长情况:1989年和1984年,凶杀案数量的简单差值;以1984年的数据为基准,这个差值的百分比。轻罪逮捕率变化和吸食毒品的变化没有受到新增变量的影响。伯纳德·哈考特(Bernard Harcourt)和延斯·路德维格(Jens Ludwig)提供了20世纪90年代以前的有关凶杀案的数据。

表 2 是对表 1 中的模型进一步深化研究,分别预测涉枪凶杀案与非涉枪凶杀案的发案率。结果对轻罪逮捕率的变化和吸食毒品的变化带来的凶杀案发案率的变化给出了重要的解释。两种测量都得出对涉枪凶杀案有显著效应,而非涉枪凶杀案则没有。轻罪逮捕率的结果与费根(Fagan)、齐姆林(Zimring)、金(Kim)(1998:1319)同纽约市警务理念的变化与涉枪凶杀案下降的趋势相"吻合",而与非涉枪凶杀案趋势不符合的结论相似。同样的,吸食毒品也对涉枪凶杀案呈现一定影响,与布卢姆斯坦(Blumstein)的高纯度可卡因论有着一致的理念。毒品市场的萎缩和扩张通过市场供货主体间武器装备竞争影响凶杀案的发案率,同时也暗示毒品吸食的类型的变化影响着涉枪凶杀案件,而不是非涉枪凶杀案件的发生。

如果说枪支在纽约市凶杀案发案率中起着突出的作用,为什么在我们的模型中,对枪支可得性指标却没有呈现显著效应? 一个可能性是因为指标是无效的,但是在先前研究中已对这种测量提供了较高有效性的证明(Azreal,Cook,and Miller,2004;Cook and Ludwig,2006;Kleck,2004)。或者说,枪支可得性与凶杀案之间的因果关系不是直接的,其替代值和凶杀案之间的关系不能很好地反映出来。例如,库克(Cook)、路德维格(Ludwig)(2006:386)说,枪支普及导致高凶杀案发案率的根本机制是"枪支从合法的所有人转移到了非法的所有人中,而不是合法所有者的措施使用的增加"。因此,通常把是否持有枪支的测量当作一个研究武器与凶杀案关系的途径是个错误的思路。

在表 3 中,我们考虑了轻罪逮捕率的明显效应事实上是不存在可能性的,因为一般来讲,这段时间内由于加大了对一些轻微违法行为的打击,同样,也促进了对严重违法犯罪行为的查处力度(比如重罪的逮捕)。事实上,轻罪逮捕率的变化与重罪逮捕率的变化有着正向、显著相关($r=.305$),如果在回归模型中用重罪逮捕率的变化代替轻罪逮捕率的变化,其研究结果会是高度相似的(虽无直接结果,但是可以得出)。然而,当重罪与轻罪逮捕率变化同时都被考虑进凶杀案发案率模型中时,只有轻罪逮捕率显示出了预料中的负向的统计显著性,不仅是在总的模型中显著,在涉枪凶杀案中也显著,但不包括对非涉枪凶杀案。

表 2　预测 1990—1999[a] 年纽约市警察管辖区涉枪与非涉枪凶杀案发案率变化的随机效应模型

	凶杀案类型	
	涉枪	非涉枪
轻罪逮捕率的变化	- .0010 ***	- .0002
吸食可卡因的变化[b]	.0749 **	.0012

	凶杀案类型	
	涉枪	非涉枪
男性比例	-.1226	.0958
35 周岁以下人口比例	-.0225	-.0223
失业人口比例	-.2709	-.5749
枪支持有的变化[c]	.0137	-.0184
黑人比例	-.0154	.0206
社会经济状态[d]	-.0185	-.0049
警力的变化[e]	.0055	-.0026

* $p<.05$；** $p<.01$ ***；$p<.001$. $N=666$ 区域一年份。

a 1990 年美国统计局所公布的各区域的人口数用于计算比率。

b 事故死亡毒品检测呈阳性比例的年度变化。

c 自杀事件中,使用枪支比例的年度变化。

d 社会经济状况综合指标在警察局管辖区水平的社会经济变量包括:高中以下学历的比例,低于贫困线 2 倍的人口比例,女性当家的家庭比例,接受社会救济的家庭比例。

e 警察局管辖区水平的警察人数年度变化。

表 3 的最后一列用来评估轻罪逮捕率与除凶杀案以外的其他暴力违法行为之间的关系:如抢劫。与凶杀案的结果类似,轻罪逮捕率的增长与抢劫发案率的下降有显著的联系。有意思的是,吸食毒品却与抢劫没有显著效应。[①]

表 3　预测 1990—1999[a] 年纽约市警察局辖区随着重罪逮捕率的变化,凶杀案总数、涉枪凶杀案、非涉枪凶杀案和抢劫案件变化的随机效应模型

	违法类型			
	凶杀案总数	涉枪凶杀案	非涉枪凶杀案	抢劫
轻罪逮捕率变化	-.0011 **	-.0009 **	-.0003	-.0375 ***
重罪逮捕率变化	-.0010	-.0012	.0002	.0221
吸食可卡因的变化[b]	.0747 *	.0733 **	.0014	.9924
男性比例	-.0379	-.1354	.0976	-19.5133 **
35 周岁以下的人口比例	-.0296	-.0050	-.0247	6.0517 *
失业人口比例	-.9600	-.4031	-.5569	-121.3400 ***
武器持有变化比例[c]	-.0045	.0139	-.0185	.2001

---

① 为了证实这个研究的稳定性,我们把监禁情况的变化作为一个新的指标。测量涉及辖区内每十万人逮捕入狱的人数,这个指标与轻罪逮捕率的变化值相似。监禁的变化在任何模型中对犯罪率没有任何影响,而对监禁率变化加以控制后,对参数估计影响达到最小,并没有改变统计显著性。监禁数据来源于纽约市刑事司法服务部门,由理查德·罗森菲尔德(Richard Rosenfeld)友情提供。

	违法类型			
	凶杀案总数	涉枪凶杀案	非涉枪凶杀案	抢劫
黑人比例	.0063	.0142	.0204	.6100
社会经济状况综合指标[d]	−.0242	−.0194	−.0047	1.1976
警力变化[e]	.0053	.0082	−.0029	−.0285

＊p<.05；＊＊p<.01 ＊＊＊；p<.001. N=666 区域—年份。

a 1990 年美国统计局所公布的各区域的人口数用于计算比率。

b 事故死亡毒品检测呈阳性比例的年度变化。

c 自杀事件中,使用枪支比例的年度变化。

d 社会经济状况综合指标在警察局管辖区水平的社会经济变量包括:高中以下学历的比例,低于贫困线 2 倍的人口比例,女性当家的家庭比例,接受社会救济的家庭比例。

e 警察局管辖区水平的警察人数年度变化。

六、总结与概述

本研究对两个用来解释 20 世纪 90 年代纽约市凶杀案急剧下降成因的理论进行再次评估,即:破窗警务理论与可卡因/毒品活动理论。本研究的创新点有:(1)对涉枪与非涉枪凶杀案进行了单独分析。(2)对毒品检测使用了更优的数据,选用了事故死亡者的可卡因毒理学检验。(3)引入重罪逮捕率这个变量,用来从全面加强警务活动中,区分出生活质量违法事件警务活动对凶杀案的效应。本研究是基于 1990—1999 年间纽约市 74 个区综合的、横向的、时间序数据开展研究的,所有变量的测量都是在适合区一级的水平上进行的。混合回归模型的结果都非常支持对纽约市凶杀案的两种分析,但同时也得出了一些新结果。

我们发现轻罪逮捕率的变化与凶杀案发案率的变化呈反向关系。这个结果具有统计显著性。这在开始阶段对社会人口统计学变量、改变警力水平、重罪逮捕率的变化等变量进行控制的模型中也出现同样的结果,这些发现支持了柯林(Kelling)和苏泽(Sousa)的结论:新型的警务政策在纽约市凶杀案下降中起到了非凡的作用。

当我们按是否使用武器对凶杀案进行分类分析时,发现警务对涉枪凶杀案,而不是非涉枪凶杀案有显著效应。这个发现反映了环境影响了枪支使用模式。就全国而言,调查期间,比对其他如因争论而导致的谋杀案件来说,枪支的使用在重罪和有组织犯罪中更加常见(司法统计局,2006)。看起来警务政策在重罪有关的凶杀事件或者同伙活动中有更重要的影响,而对于因争吵而导致凶杀的事件则作用不大。我们研究表明轻罪逮捕率对涉枪凶杀案而不是非涉枪凶杀案的重要影响与费根、齐姆林、金（Fagan, Zimring, and Kim, 1998:1322）所得出的关于破窗警务实践的观点在一定程度上是符合的。费根（Fagan）、齐姆林（Zimring）、金（Kim）（1998:1322）认为破窗警务的一个目标是"让枪支从大街上消失"。执法策略让警察和民众有更多时间的接触，也帮助警察掌握更多线索，更有希望找到并抓获一些可能导致涉枪凶杀案的非法枪支。

研究中发现吸食毒品（可卡因）的变化对凶杀案的发案率变化有显著效应。从事故死亡者的毒理分析得出，如果毒品使用人数下降，凶杀案也趋于下降。与轻罪逮捕率的结果一样，吸食毒品效应也可以用是否使用武器来区分，吸食毒品对涉枪凶杀案而不是对非涉枪凶杀案起作用。这个结果与理论上关于切断毒品市场与非法枪支使用之间联系的观点一致。

但本研究还存在一些局限性。我们对毒品活动指标没有区分高纯度可卡因和其他形式的可卡因，只能反映吸食毒品的程度而不能反映毒品市场运作的特征。例如，吸食可卡因与可卡因的买卖在地理上并不一定相吻合，因此，可以认为可卡因致死或受伤的地方可能不足以反映该地方毒品交易频繁性水平。这个研究的结果只能间接解释凶杀案下降的"高纯度可卡因市场"论断。

一般来说，合理推测在非实验性设计中是不可靠的，而且在研究中对一些变量的忽视也是不可避免的。当前值得关注的是许多无法测量的警务特征与轻罪逮捕率相关。虽然把警力水平和重罪逮捕率作为控制变量进行考虑，但是纽约市加强维护治安，减少扰乱秩序行为的警务实践是警察局进行组织变革和任务重组的组成部分（全国研究会议，2004:230）。因此，轻罪逮捕率系数很有可能包含着警务变革的其他方面因素，这些警务活动伴随着维护秩序警务被有选择地吸收到各个管辖区。对不同警务模型的绩效研究可以得出最成功的警务改革是各种警务活动有机组合的"一揽子警务模式"，而不是简单的执法活动（Weisburd and Eck, 2004:42）。因此可以推断，维护治安的警务活动与其他被正式在更大范围内有效的其他警务实践一起对纽约市凶杀案的发案率的减少起到了积极的作用。分析轻罪逮捕率与凶杀案发案率之间成反比的精确机制，为今后进一步研究提出了新的挑战。

此外，数据的可得性限制了相对于社会人口统计学变量的改善，警务变化和毒品活动对凶杀案下降的重要影响评估。这些人口统计学变量在一些宏观的研究中被认为与暴力犯罪有关。本研究的模型包括了一系列的社会人口统计学变量，但是这些都是来源于统计数据而且都是随时间的变化保持不变的。因此，我们可以关注到在十年之前,各辖区之间人口统计学水平上的可预测差异,但是在理论上不能将社会条件的变化与凶杀案相联系。① 尽管我们只能推测,警务策略与社会趋势都导致了纽约市涉枪凶杀案的下降(Fagan, Zimring, and Kim, 1998:1320)。

另外一个值得引起我们注意的问题是本研究的结论和先前哈考特(Harcourt)、路德维格(Ludwig)(2006)的观点存在差异。我们选用了类似的模型,将犯罪变化向逮捕率变化进行回归,但是得到了不同的结论。其中一个很明显的差异是因变量,本研究中凶杀案与抢劫都作为因变量,而在之前哈考特(Harcourt)、路德维格(Ludwig)的模型是一个综合模型,对刑事凶杀案、强奸、重罪侵害类案件以及抢劫做了综合的评估。然而,当我们在回归模型中用综合暴力犯罪来替代时,轻罪逮捕率与吸食毒品仍然重复着凶杀案和抢劫案相类似的结果。对毒品使用的结果不同不足为奇;因为我们的研究是在区一级数据而不是市一级数据的基础之上,但是轻罪拘捕率的不同结果是令人疑惑的。我们包括了一些和哈考特(Harcourt)、路德维格(Ludwig)类似的控制变量,但是还是存在着一些结论的差别。以后研究的重要方向是在相应的研究中将变量分开来进行评估,可以得出不同的结论。

最后,针对轻罪逮捕率与凶杀案的发案率之间成反比的结论,对警务政策的执行提几点建议。地方政府部门在有限的资源分配中面临不同的选择,对警务变革的投资应该以改善城市生活质量为目标对各种策略进行必要的权衡。另外,维护治安秩序的警务活动存在一定的风险,已经早已被意识到。这些政策给了警察相当的支配权,在某些情况下,可能导致其过度使用暴力、酷刑以及偏见的执法(Skogan, 1990:164; Greene, 1999)。事实上,有批评者提出纽约市破窗警务所需要的社会支出远远大于表面上所获得的利益(Karmen, 2000:120)。因此,尽管本研究得出警务改革有助于减少犯罪,但还要提出与以往研究相同的观点,即要对警务变革的支出与收益进行仔细的计算,以及在实施主动警务的过程中使社会正义与犯罪控制能达到明智的权衡(Sampson and Cohen, 1988:186)。

[参考文献和附件见英文原作]

(丁靖艳　袁立华　译)

---

① 要注意的是,我们的研究仅仅是在短期内对警察勤务的作用进行评估。费根(Fagan)、外斯特(West)以及霍兰(Holland)(2003)认为监禁对邻里的生态社会有不利的影响,从长远来看,可能会导致犯罪行为的发生。在附注13 里,同时期的监禁的变化在我们的模型中评估得出对凶杀案的变化没有影响,但是某种程度上,主动警务导致了更多的监禁,监禁折射了社会以及心理上的邻里生活的结构。费根(Fagan)、外斯特(West)和霍兰(Holland)(2003:1589)猜测,长期的警察勤务可能与短期的评估结果恰恰相反。

Policing, Drugs, and the Homicide Decline in New York City in the 1990s

Steven F. Messner

University at Albany, University of New York

Sandro Galea

University of Michigan

Kenneth J. Tardiff

Cornell University

Melissa Tracy

University of Michigan

Angela Bucciarelli
Tinka Markham Piper
Victoria Frye
David Vlahov

Center for Urban Epidemiologic Studies New York Academy of Medicine

The decline in homicide levels in New York City over the course of the 1990s has been the source of intense scrutiny in the popular press and in the scholarly literature. The basic facts are well known. Levels of homicide fell abruptly and precipitously over a relatively short period of time. In 1990, 2,245 criminal homicides were recorded. This figure dropped to 633 in 1998, which is a decrease of 72 percent (Karmen, 2000: 24). Although other major cities also exhibited falling homicide rates during the 1990s, special attention has been directed toward the New York City experience, caused in part by the city's preeminent status as the "media capital of the United States" (Fagan, Zimring, and Kim, 1998: 1277). As Karmen (2000: 29) observes, "word travels fast about cutting-edge developments and emerging trends in the 'backyard' of major media outlets."

Although little disagreement exists about the impressive scope of the homicide decline in New York City during the 1990s, the reasons for this phenomenon are the subject of vigorous debate. The popular media and public officials have assigned much credit to policing strategies implemented by William Bratton while serving as the head of the New York Police Department (Bratton, 1998; Conklin, 2003; Kelling and Bratton, 1998). Bratton's innovations encompassed a range of policies that have been loosely characterized under rubrics such as "zero tolerance policing," "quality-of-life policing," "broken windows policing," and "order maintenance policing" (Eck and Maguire, 2000; Kelling and Coles, 1996). In an "insider's" assessment of the contribution of this kind of policing to the homicide decline in New York City, Kelling and Bratton (1998: 1227) observe that "no credible alternatives ... have been put forth to contradict our belief that police action played a pivotal role."

The criminological community, however, has generally responded to such claims about the prominent role of policing as an explanation for the declining homicide levels in New York City, in particular, and in the nation, in general, with a good deal of skepticism. Critics have cautioned that, although policing might have played some role in the homicide drop, other factors are likely to be as important or more important (Bowling, 1999; Eck and Maguire, 2000; Joanes, 2000; Levitt, 2004; National Research Council, 2004). One of the most highly touted alternatives to the policing explanation involves changes in crack cocaine markets (Blumstein and Rosenfeld, 1998; Blumstein, Rivara, and Rosenfeld, 2000; Rosenfeld, 2002). Proponents of this position point to a temporal overlap between homicide trends and the spread of crack cocaine. Homicides began to increase around the time that crack-cocaine markets emerged and started to decline when crack markets began to shrink.

These two explanations are not, of course, mutually exclusive. Both policing and changes in drug-related activities may have contributed to the drop in homicides in New York City. Yet despite extensive speculation, actually very little direct evidence exists on the relative impact of policing and drugs. Two of the most rigorous studies to date are those of Kelling and Sousa (2001) and Harcourt and Ludwig (2006). [1] On the basis of a pooled, cross-sectional time-series design with police precincts serving as units of analysis, Kelling and Sousa find that the number of misdemeanor arrests is significantly related to a composite measure of violent crime (murder, rape, robbery, and felonious assault), which is consistent with the thesis of "broken windows" policing. They detect no evidence for a role of decreasing use of cocaine. In contrast, in a reanalysis of these data, Harcourt and Ludwig report that the effect of misdemeanor arrests on violent crime falls below statistical significance when the regression model is expanded to include a more comprehensive array of controls. The measure of cocaine use is not significant in the Harcourt and Ludwig models, which is similar to the earlier findings.

In this article, we build on and extend the prior work by Kelling and Sousa and Harcourt and Ludwig in several respects. First, in addition to examining the impact of policing and cocaine on total levels of homicide, we disaggregate homicides into categories of gun-related and non-gun-related. This procedure is very useful because past research has demonstrated that these two forms of homicide exhibit distinct trends in New York City over the period under examination (Fagan, Zimring, and Kim, 1998). Moreover, theoretical reasons exist to expect that the effects of both policing and drug markets are likely to have been particularly pronounced for gun homicides (Fagan, Zimring, and Kim, 1998: 1319 – 20; Karmen, 2000: 117). Second, whereas the indicator of drug activity in the Kelling and Sousa research is a rough proxy measure based on hospital discharge data for the boroughs in New York City, we employ a more refined indicator, measured at the appropriate precinct level. Third, we introduce into the analyses a measure of felony arrests. This measure enables us to examine the extent to which any apparent effect of more vigorous enforcement of relatively minor crimes in particular is confounded with more vigorous policing in general. Our analyses thus provide a more thorough assessment than previously conducted of the role of the two major suspects in the "New York Murder Mystery" (Karmen, 2000).

---

[1] Rosenfeld, Fernango, and Baumer (2005) have conducted a highly sophisticated analysis of the impact of policing on the homicide decline in three cities: Boston, New York, and Richmond, VA. They apply growth curve analysis and report that the New York City homicide trend did not deviate significantly from other large cities in the 1990s, which raises questions about the role of the Bratton policing strategies. The authors acknowledge that their data do not allow for an evaluation of the "three interventions *per se*" (2005: 422), and they characterize their work as "a point of departure for ongoing evaluation of the impact of local law enforcement interventions on crime rates" (2005: 440).

THE RESEARCH CONTEXT

Kelling and Sousa (2001: 1 - 3) locate their study within the context of a more general debate about the relevance of policing for crime prevention. They call attention to the "long-prevailing" view enunciated by Sir Robert Peel, founder of London's Metropolitan Police, that the primary mission of the police is to prevent crime and disorder. This view, Kelling and Sousa maintain, was widely accepted until the 1950s. Around this time, basic questions were raised about what the police actually do, and the resulting research challenged the conventional wisdom about the impact of the police on crime. These findings fostered a general orientation toward crime that emphasizes "collective 'root causes' like social injustice, racism, and poverty" (2001: 3). The "root causes" orientation toward crime causation, in turn, is conducive to a highly skeptical stance about policing, i.e., the view that the police really do not matter when it comes to preventing crime.

Although the skeptical appraisal of the role of the police tended to dominate discourse during the 1970s and 1980s, Kelling and Sousa identify dissenting voices. These voices include the Goldstein (1979) arguments about "problem-oriented policing." According to this perspective, incidents coming to the attention of the police are best regarded as manifestations of underlying problems, and the proper role of the police is to address these problems. A second idea that has become particularly influential is that of "broken windows" policing, which was originally popularized through the *Atlantic Monthly* article by Wilson and Kelling (1982). The underlying premise of this approach is that disorder and incivility frighten residents and lead them to withdraw, thereby weakening informal social control and emboldening offenders. [1] The police can, accordingly, reduce levels of serious crimes by enforcing minor violations, such as disorderly conduct and prostitution (fixing broken windows), and maintaining order.

Police officials in New York City embarked on a deliberate effort to put "broken windows" theory into practice (Kelling and Bratton, 1998). Kelling initially worked with New York City transportation authorities to develop proactive policing in the subways and then with Bratton to implement such policies more generally in the city after Bratton became the head of the New York City Police Department (NYPD) (Kelling and Sousa, 2001: 2). The

---

[1] The Wilson and Kelling arguments about "broken windows" can be viewed as a variant of a more general approach to policing that emphasizes the importance of maintaining order. Taylor (2001: ch. 3) provides an extended discussion of different variants of the "incivilities thesis" of policing. See also Skogan (1990).

policing reforms under Bratton's leadership encompassed an array of specific tactics (Conklin, 2003: 31 - 5; Karmen, 2000: 83 - 140). Bratton emphasized the importance of accurate and current statistics to inform decision making, and he promoted the use of computerized data and maps of "hot spots," which is a method often referred to as "Compstat." He also introduced corporate-style management techniques, which gave precinct commanders more authority but also held them accountable for improvements (or the lack thereof) in their precincts (Conklin, 2003: 39). The policing reforms in New York City were thus multifaceted, but the "lynchpin strategy," according to Bratton himself, was the "strict enforcement of laws against quality-of-life offenses such as subway turnstile jumping, aggressive panhandling, drinking and being drunk in public, and soliciting prostitutes" (Conklin, 2003: 37). Precinct commanders evidently heeded the Bratton directives; more than twice as many non-felony arrests were made in 1998 as in 1989, whereas the number of felony arrests actually decreased over this period (Solomon, 2003).

The dramatic decline in homicide in New York City during the 1990s thus coincided with a deliberate policy intervention. However, criminologists have called for caution in attributing the homicide drop in New York City primarily to innovations in policing, citing various alternative interpretations. One of the more highly regarded alternatives emphasizes the critical role of drug markets, in particular crack-cocaine markets, as a major source of lethal violence in large cities (Bowling, 1999).

The "crack-cocaine" thesis was originally introduced by Blumstein (1995) to account for the so-called homicide epidemic in urban America during the 1980s and early 1990s. According to Blumstein (1995), the demand for crack cocaine emerged in select cities in the mid-1980s and spread thereafter to other parts of the nation. Within any given locale, the increased demand for crack led to the recruitment of young minority males to serve as drug dealers. Violence typically surrounds drug markets (Goldstein, 1985), and thus, these new recruits acquired firearms for protection. The increased gun toting of those involved in crack-cocaine trafficking then diffused throughout the community at large, especially to other youths, as those not involved in the drug trade took up arms for self-defense. As guns spread through the general population, interpersonal disputes became more lethal, which resulted in a rising homicide rate. Subsequently, the number of crack users dropped off, beginning in some cities in the early 1990s (Golub and Johnson, 1997). This decrease in the demand for crack alleviated the pressures for the recruitment of more drug dealers and brought some stability to drug markets. As the crack epidemic began to subside, homicide rates started to fall.

Several types of evidence lend credibility to the drug market/arms race explanation for homicide trends over recent decades. The argument is consistent with the documented demographics of homicide (Blumstein and Rosenfeld, 1998; Cook and Laub, 2002; Rosenfeld, 2002). The epidemic-like pattern of rapid increase followed by sharp reversal and decline was most pronounced among young African-American males, which is precisely the population that is hypothesized to have been recruited into, and subsequently out of, crack-cocaine markets. In addition, the growth in homicides among young people during the late 1980s was driven largely by the increase in homicides committed with handguns. [1] This finding is consistent with the claims about the accelerating arms race spawned by the acquisition of guns by newly recruited drug dealers. Furthermore, the evidence indicates that the "timing" of the increases and declines in homicide across cities is consistent with the drug-market thesis. The larger, denser cities along the coasts—those most susceptible to the spread of cocaine— tended to be in the "vanguard" in the homicide epidemic (Messner et al., 2005). Research also suggests that measures of illegal drug activity can explain changes in homicide rates across metropolitan areas in the United States (Ousey and Lee, 2002). Finally, an attractive feature of the drug market/arms race thesis of changing homicide levels is its symmetrical quality. It accounts for both the rise and the fall of homicide levels in a logically consistent fashion (Blumstein and Rosenfeld, 1998: 1209). [2]

In sum, the impressive decline in homicides in New York City that coincided with concerted efforts to implement "broken windows" theory has positioned the general question of the impact of policing on crime prevention at the forefront of criminological discourse. The resulting debates have been vigorous, even "rancorous" (Eck and Maguire, 2000: 225). Moreover, as Eck and Maguire observe, the New York City experience is particularly important because the specific strategies of Bratton have been offered as a "blueprint" for reducing crime that should be applicable anywhere, and because police

---

[1] Wintemute (2000: 53) observes that recent trends in overall homicides (not merely youth homicides) "were driven almost entirely by trends in handgun homicide."

[2] Focusing specifically on youth violence, Cook and Laub (2002: 145) question whether the "downside" of the homicide epidemic is, in fact, a mirror image of the "upside," specifically with respect to the sex, race, and ethnicity of offenders and to weapon use.

agencies throughout the world have, in fact, implemented similar strategies based on the New York City experience (2000: 228). Assessing the actual impact of "broken windows" policing on the homicide decline in New York City, in comparison with the effects of credible alternative factors, in particular with drugs, is thus a topic of high priority for criminological inquiry.

PRIOR ASSESSMENTS

Kelling and Sousa (2001: 3) confront this challenge by introducing a design that, in their view, allows for the "most definitive assessment of whether police tactics—particularly 'broken-windows' policing—explain recent crime trends in New York City." The key feature of the Kelling and Sousa research design is the pooling of cross-sectional and longitudinal data for New York City police precincts. In essence, rather than treating New York City as a single city, they view it as 75 different cities corresponding to the respective police precincts (2001: 4). The precincts vary with respect to police activity, drug markets, and social structural characteristics, and they exhibit differing trends in violent crime over the period under investigation: 1989 – 1998. With the pooled, cross-sectional, time-series data, the relationships among the variables of interest within New York City can be examined while effectively controlling for factors that affected the city at large.

The dependent variable in the Kelling and Sousa multivariate analysis is a composite measure of complaints at the precinct level for four violent offenses: murder, rape, robbery, and felonious assault. The key independent variable is precinct-level arrests for misdemeanors, which serves as the indicator of "broken windows" policing. [1] Three additional measures are included to represent variables that have been offered as possible alternatives to the policing explanation for the violent crime decline. To capture demographics, they include an indicator of "young males" (the number of males enrolled in public schools in each precinct). The two other measures reflect economic conditions (number of unemployed persons) and patterns of drug use (hospital discharges for

---

[1] In a study based on data for the early 1980s, Sampson and Cohen (1988) introduce a creative measure of "aggressive policing"—arrests for disorderly conduct and driving under the influence (DUI) per police officer. They report that this measure is negatively related to robbery rates for a sample of large cities, which is consistent with the deterrence perspective. A more recent study by MacDonald (2002) using a comparable measure reaffirms the earlier findings of Sampson and Cohen.

cocaine-related incidents). Because of data limitations, unemployment and hospital discharges are measured at the borough rather than at the precinct level. The data on hospital discharges are available over time, whereas the measures of young males and unemployment are based on 1990 census data.

Kelling and Sousa use hierarchical linear modeling (HLM) to assess their hypothesis about the effects of "broken windows" policing. They treat time as a level 1 variable, and the independent variables as level 2 variables. Their results indicate that the time trends in violent crime complaints vary significantly across precincts. Moreover, when they examine the effects of the level 2 variables on the time slopes, they find that the measure of misdemeanor arrests yields the expected negative effect: Precincts with a high average number of misdemeanor arrests experienced a greater decline in violent crime. The coefficients for the measures of young males and borough cocaine fail to attain statistical significance, whereas the coefficient for borough unemployment is significant in the counterintuitive negative direction (higher unemployment, greater crime decline). Overall, Kelling and Sousa conclude that the results support their main hypotheses: " ' [B] roken windows' policing is strongly associated with the decline in violent crime in precincts, while major competing explanations are not" (2001 : 10).

Harcourt and Ludwig (2006) have recently challenged this conclusion. They identify a problematic feature of the Kelling and Sousa two-level, hierarchical growth model. This model "basically relates *changes* in violent crimes (each precinct's linear trend in violent crime over the 1989 – 98 period) against the *levels* of misdemeanor arrests (average arrests from 1989 to 1998). " In so doing, the analysis effectively "throws away all of the over-time variation in misdemeanor arrests across precincts from 1989 to 1998" (Harcourt and Ludwig, 2006 : 293). This approach not only sacrifices useful information, but it also makes the analysis susceptible to a spurious relationship between policing and violent crime because the average level of misdemeanor arrests is strongly correlated with initial levels of violent crime. It is thus plausible to speculate that precincts that experienced an unusually high increase in violent crime during the "epidemic" period of the 1980s would yield the greatest decrease in the 1990s as a result of a simple reversion to the mean.

Harcourt and Ludwig challenge the Kelling and Sousa conclusions with several empirical illustrations. Harcourt and Ludwig use similar data to that used by Kelling and Sousa to measure violent crime, misdemeanor arrests, and the control variables. In addition,

Harcourt and Ludwig incorporate measures for a wide range of sociodemographic characteristics recorded at the census tract level, which are then aggregated to the precinct level. They also include a measure of the number of police officers assigned to each precinct to account for increases in manpower during the period, a measure of the level of violent crime at the beginning of the period, and a measure of change in violent crime for earlier years (1984 – 1989).

Harcourt and Ludwig first replicate the key coefficients reported by Kelling and Sousa using the HLM statistical framework. They then estimate a series of models that follows "the same intuition" of the Kelling and Sousa approach (Harcourt and Ludwig, 2006: 294). However, instead of modeling the linear time trend in violent crimes, they follow more conventional practices and model their dependent variable as the actual change in violent crime over the 1989 – 1998 period for each precinct. [1]They find that the average number of misdemeanor arrests exhibits a significant negative relationship with changes in violent crime, which is consistent with Kelling and Sousa. The introduction of the measure of violent crime at the beginning of the period, as well as the measure of changes in violent crime in the years preceding the period, reduces the magnitude of the policing variable, although it remains statistically significant in a negative direction. However, after the full complement of control variables is entered, the effect of misdemeanor arrests falls below statistical significance. Harcourt and Ludwig also estimate a first-difference model wherein changes in violent crime are related to changes in misdemeanor arrests, along with controls. The results of these analyses offer no support for the broken windows thesis. Overall, Harcourt and Ludwig conclude that their reanalysis of the New York City data leads them to a Scotch verdict: "not proven" (2006: 276). [2]

---

[1]　Harcourt and Ludwig (2006: 294) question the modeling of the linear time trend, given the nonlinearity in the time series for violent crime.

[2]　After their reanalysis of the New York City precinct-level data, Harcourt and Ludwig critically evaluate research by Corman and Mocan (2002). Corman and Mocan analyze monthly, time-series data for New York City at large and find support for the broken windows thesis for robbery and motor vehicle theft (but not for murder). Harcourt and Ludwig illustrate the limitations of research designs that rely on a single jurisdiction and show how the New York City data are consistent with alternative interpretations. Harcourt and Ludwig also report evidence from the Moving to Opportunity (MTO) experiment to assess whether movement to less-disadvantaged, less-disorderly neighborhoods is associated with reduced criminal behavior. They find that, in general, relocation to less disorderly communities does not reduce offending, which they regard as strong evidence contrary to the "broken windows" thesis.

THE CURRENT STUDY

We adopt the same basic research design of these previous assessments of the impact of changes in policing in New York City—a pooled, cross-sectional, time-series design—but reorient and extend the analysis in several ways. We focus primary attention on the offense of homicide. Criminologists generally agree that the official data on homicide are superior to those for other offenses because homicides are likely to be reported and recorded. O'Brien (1996) demonstrates, for example, that the apparent increase in national rates of nonlethal violent crimes (rape, robbery, and aggravated assault) in the *Uniform Crime Reports* over the 1973—1992 period can be plausibly attributed to increases in police productivity rather than to increases in violent incidents. This type of measurement error is particularly consequential in any effort to assess the impact of "broken windows" policing. Such policing is likely to be associated with increased pressures for recording, which would operate in the opposite direction of any genuine crime-reducing effect.

In addition, our homicide data allow us to distinguish between gun-related and non-gun-related offenses. Fagan, Zimring, and Kim (1998: 1319) have examined homicide trends in New York City from the mid-1980s through the 1990s and have concluded that "two separate types of homicides with two discrete time trends" exist: gun and non-gun homicides. Non-gun homicides begin their decline before the widely publicized policing changes and exhibit a fairly steady decline. Such a trend does not suggest that innovations during the Bratton regime had substantial impact. In contrast, "the temporal fit between policing changes and gun homicide declines is a good one" (Fagan, Zimring, and Kim, 1998: 1319). [1]Moreover, as Fagan, Zimring, and Kim note (1998: 1322), the order maintenance techniques implemented in NYC ". . . can have gun-specific results if police use them to produce gun search opportunities." The more vigorous enforcement of minor infractions might accordingly contribute to a decline in homicides by deterring casual gun toting, which is an effect that would be expected for gun-related, but not necessarily non-gun-related, incidents (Karmen, 2000: 117). Broken windows policing would thus seem to be a more plausible candidate for the explanation of gun-related than non-gun-related

---

[1] Fagan, Zimring, and Kim (1998: 1320) caution that it is extremely difficult to "parse causal responsibility" for policing and other factors. They speculate that "the pattern of policing in New York City is more consistent with gun-oriented policing than with indiscriminate quality-of-life interventions as a cause of decline" (1998: 1322; see also Fagan and Davies, 2003).

homicides on both empirical and theoretical grounds.

We also improve on the measurement of a key variable considered in previous research: drug use patterns, in particular, cocaine use. The prior assessments of broken windows policing in New York City have used hospital discharge data, which are available at the borough level, whereas violent crime has been measured at the lower, precinct level of aggregation. As Harcourt and Ludwig (2006: 317) observe, the resulting measurement error is likely to attenuate the relationship and bias the coefficient toward zero. It is thus plausible to speculate that the importance of cocaine use has been underestimated in prior analyses based on drug data for New York City boroughs. We rely on a different data source: medical examiner records of cocaine levels among persons who were accident decedents. This data source has two highly desirable features. Through geocoding, addresses can be determined and a measure of drug use can be constructed that refers to the appropriate precinct (rather than borough) level. In addition, accident victims are likely to mimic persons in the general population, whereas hospital discharge data might under-represent cocaine use among the public at large (see Galea *et al.*, 2003).

Our analysis also extends prior work by introducing an alternative indicator of policing: felony arrest rates. Precincts with increasing misdemeanor arrests might be characterized by more intensive enforcement activity of the police in general, and any apparent effect of "broken windows" policing might actually be spurious. Homicide declines might be most prominent in those precincts where police activity of all kinds intensified. This result would be more consistent with a general deterrence interpretation than an interpretation that credits crackdowns on quality-of-life offenses.

Finally, we estimate models for another violent offense, robbery rates, to determine the robustness of the results, and we build on the earlier work by explicitly considering multivariate models that take into account potentially confounding sociodemographic covariates that are well established in the homicide literature (Land, McCall, and Cohen, 1990) as well as an indicator of police manpower changes that occurred during the period under investigation.

DATA AND METHODS

Data for this study were collected from three principal sources: the Office of the Chief

Medical Examiner (OCME) of New York City, the NYPD, and the U.S. Census Bureau. All cases of homicides, suicide, and accident deaths in New York City from 1990 to 1999 were identified through standardized manual review and abstraction of medical files in the OCME of New York City. The OCME is responsible for investigating all deaths of people believed to have died from unnatural causes. Thus, all homicide, suicide, and accident deaths in New York City are reviewed by the OCME and would have been included in the charts used for data extraction. In addition, the Chief Medical Examiner has been the same person from 1990 to the current time in New York City, so the forms, classification of cases, toxicology, policies, and other aspects of the OCME have remained the same over the time period covered in this study.

Data regarding cause of death, circumstances of death (including use of a gun), and toxicology were collected from the OCME files by trained abstractors using a standardized protocol and data collection forms. The OCME investigators used the medical history of the decedent, the circumstances and environment of the death, autopsy findings, and laboratory data, to attribute the cause of death to each case reviewed. All OCME cases from 1990 to 1999 were then geocoded to the police precinct level by address of injury using ArcGIS software, version 9.0 (ESRI, Redlands, CA). Only cases with a valid address of injury were included in the analysis.

The units of analysis for the research are New York City police precincts. Police precincts are useful area-level units for the assessment of the broken windows thesis because law enforcement is organized at the precinct level (Fagan, West, and Holland, 2003: 1566). Precincts 33 and 34, covering the Washington Heights and Inwood areas, were treated as one precinct because they were split only in 1994. The Central Park precinct (Precinct 22) was excluded a priori because no one resides in this precinct, and thus, no population denominator is available for rate estimation.

Dependent Variables

Our dependent variables are total homicide rates, gun-related and non-gun-related homicide rates, and robbery rates. Homicide deaths were collected from the OCME and robberies from the NYPD; rates were calculated per 100000 population using data from the 1990 census as the relevant denominator.

Independent Variables

The two key independent variables (misdemeanor arrests and cocaine use) are both time-varying variables. The NYPD routinely collects data on all police arrests for various causes by precinct. Data were collected from the NYPD on all misdemeanor arrests by precinct from 1990 to 1999 to represent "broken windows"-oriented policing, which is consistent with prior research (Corman and Mocan, 2002; Harcourt and Ludwig, 2006; Kelling and Sousa, 2001). Misdemeanor arrest rates were also expressed as rates per 100000 population using 1990 census population counts as the relevant denominator. The other key independent variable is level of cocaine use, measured as the proportion of accident decedents whose toxicology results were positive for cocaine in each precinct and recorded from OCME data. [1]

Control Variables

We introduce controls for a wide range of sociodemographic characteristics of precincts that have been linked with homicide rates in past macrolevel research (Land, McCall, and Cohen, 1990). Data for these variables are available only for decennial years, and thus, they are measured as time invariant fixed at the 1990 census year. The specific measures are as follows:

Percent male. Percent persons in a given precinct who were male.

Percent under age 35. Percent persons in a given precinct under age 35 years.

Percent black. Percent persons in a given precinct who were black.

Percent female-headed households. Percent households in a given precinct with a self-reported female head of household.

Percent of population on public assistance. Percent persons in a given precinct receiving pubic assistance.

Percent under 200 *percent poverty.* Percent persons in a given precinct earning less money annually than the 200 percent poverty margin.

---

[1] Our measure of cocaine use implicitly assumes that the risk of accidental death does not vary systematically across precincts. To assess the extent to which the results might be sensitive to differentials in this risk, we included a measure of the overall accidental death rate (as a change score) in our regression models for homicide. The inclusion of this measure has minimal impact on the parameter estimates for other covariates. The accidental death rate is significantly related to total, gun-related, and non-gun-related homicides: Increases in accidental deaths are associated with increases in homicides.

Percent persons with less than high-school education: Percent persons in a given precinct over the age of 25 years with less than a high-school education.

Percent unemployed: Percent persons in a given precinct over the age of 15 years who were unemployed.

The data source for these sociodemographic control variables is the U. S. Census Summary File 3 (SF3). Infoshare Online (2007) was used to provide census data at the tract level, which were aggregated to the police precinct level.

Because some socioeconomic variables (percent of persons with less than high-school education, percent of persons under 200 percent poverty, percent of female-headed households, and percent of persons on public assistance) are highly intercorrelated, we conducted principal component analysis to construct an aggregate socioeconomic status score for each precinct, which is consistent with conventional practices in macrolevel homicide research (Land, McCall, and Cohen, 1990). The composite score was created by summing the four items, each weighted by its factor loading in the analysis. The composite index is scored in the direction of disadvantage: the greater the score, the poorer the socioeconomic status (range, 23.4 – 189.0).

In addition to the indicators of sociodemographic characteristics of precincts, we include controls for two other variables: a proxy for firearm availability and a measure of manpower levels. Researchers on firearms generally agree that, in the absence of accurate administrative data or representative survey data, the most reliable proxy measure for firearm availability is the percentage of suicides committed with a gun (Azrael, Cook, and Miller, 2004; Cook and Ludwig, 2006; Kleck, 2004). [1]Our measure of firearm availability is the proportion of suicide deaths where guns were used per precinct per year. The indicator of manpower is the number of police officers assigned to each precinct in each year by the NYPD. [2]Data on the firearm proxy and police manpower are available on an annual basis, and thus, these variables are expressed as annual change scores.

---

[1]　Kleck (2004) reports that the suicide proxy measure is valid for cross-sectional research but advises against using any standard proxies for longitudinal analyses. In contrast, Azrael, Cook, and Miller (2004) and Cook and Ludwig (2006) conclude that the percentage of suicides involving guns is a useful proxy for both kinds of analyses.

[2]　We are grateful to Bernard Harcourt and Jens Ludwig for providing the data on police manpower in a personal communication.

Finally, we also include a measure of felony arrests, collected from the NYPD by precinct from 1990 to 1999. Felony arrest rates are computed as rates per 100,000 population using 1990 census population counts as the relevant denominator and are entered into regression models as annual change scores. We include this variable to assess whether increased police activity at all levels or broken windows policing specifically contributed to the decline in homicides.

Of the 14,151 homicides that occurred in New York City from 1990 to 1999, we were able to successfully geocode 12,971 cases to the police precinct level (91.7 percent of original sample). No systematic differences were found between homicide cases included in the analysis and cases excluded from the analysis. Univariate statistics for the variables in the analysis are reported in appendix A.

Analytic Framework

All analyses are based on "change" mixed models where we calculated year-to-year change for the key dependent and independent variables by subtracting the relevant value at year t from the value for the subsequent year $t + 1$. Therefore, all models are of the following form:

$$\Delta Y_{ij} = \alpha_i + \beta \Delta X_{ij} + \gamma X'_i + e_{ij} + r \times e_{ij-1}$$

where ΔY_{ij} is the change in the dependent variable between times t and $t + 1$ for the ith precinct in the jth time interval, ΔY_{ij} is a vector of the change in the independent variables of interest for the ith precinct in the jth time interval, X'_i is the vector of time invariant baseline demographic characteristics measured in 1990, and r is the autocorrelation coefficient. We use random intercept models to account for potential differences in baseline relations between key independent and dependent variables and account for intra-precinct correlation using an autoregressive correlation structure.

Our first set of analyses examines total homicides. We begin with an examination of the effect of changes in the misdemeanor arrest rate alone on changes in total homicide rates. Next, we estimate a model with predictor variables analogous to that examined by Kelling and Sousa. This model includes the indicator of cocaine use and the controls for age/sex structure and unemployment. We then introduce the additional control variables into the models. In additional analyses, we disaggregate homicides into gun-related and non-gun-related categories. We only report estimates for the full model for the disaggregated analyses. Finally, we expand the model to include the measure of felony arrests, and we estimate the effects of the full complement of predictor variables on total and disaggregated homicides and on robbery rates.

RESULTS

Initial results for total homicide rates are given in table 1. Model 1 shows the bivariate effect of changes in the misdemeanor arrest rate on changes in the homicide rate. Consistent with the Kelling and Sousa findings and the thesis of broken windows policing, the coefficient is negative and statistically significant ($\beta = -.0013$, $p < .001$). As the misdemeanor arrest rate in a precinct increases, the homicide rate decreases.

In model 2, control variables similar to those considered by Kelling and Sousa are introduced. The effect for the measure of changes in the misdemeanor arrest rate is unchanged within rounding, and it remains significantly negative. The measures of age/sex structure fail to attain a level of statistical significance, whereas the coefficient for unemployment is significant but in the unexpected negative direction. These findings are all similar to those reported by Kelling and Sousa. However, in contrast with this earlier research, our indicator of cocaine use, measured at the appropriate precinct level rather than at the borough level, is positive and statistically significant: As the proportion of accident victims with positive cocaine toxicology decreases, the homicide rate declines as well.

Table 1   Random Effects Models Predicting Change in Homicide Rates for NYC Police Precincts, 1990—1999[a]

	Model 1	**Model** 2	**Model** 3
Change in misdemeanor arrest rate	−.0013 ***	−.0013 ***	−.0012 **
Change in cocaine use[b]		.0761 *	.0760 *
Percent male		−.0148	−.0268
Percent under age 35 years		−.1046	−.0448
Percent unemployed		−1.1755 *	−.8458
Change in firearm availability[c]			−.0047
Percent black			.0052
SES composite[d]			−.0233

	Model 1	**Model** 2	**Model** 3
Change in manpower[e]			.0030

ABBREVIATION: SES = socioeconomic status.

* $p < .05$; ** $p < .01$; *** $p < .001$. $N = 666$ precinct-years.

[a] 1990 U. S. Census precinct population used to calculate rates.

[b] Annual change in proportion of accident decedents with positive cocaine toxicology.

[c] Annual change in proportion of suicides where guns were used.

[d] SES composite index includes the following socioeconomic variables aggregated to the police precinct level: percent less than high-school education, percent less than 200 percent poverty, percent female-headed households, and percent receiving public assistance.

[e] Annual change in size of police force in precinct.

The additional control variables are entered in model 3. The effect for changes in misdemeanor arrests withstands these additional controls. The regression parameter suggests that an increase of 833 misdemeanor arrests for a police precinct of 100,000 population would be associated with about one less homicide in that precinct. To further illustrate the magnitude of the effect of the misdemeanor arrest variable, we estimated predicted values for the change in homicide rates at varying percentiles of changes in misdemeanor arrests with the other covariates fixed at their mean values. The results are displayed in figure 1. For precincts in the 25th percentile of change in misdemeanor arrests, the predicted change in homicide rates is a drop of 2.51. The predicted fall in the homicide rate increases by about 1 for precincts in the 75th percentile (-3.47). The contrasts are striking at the extremes. For precincts in the 10th percentile of change in misdemeanor arrest rates, the predicted change in homicide rates is a decrease of 1.7 per 100,000. For precincts in the 90th percentile of change in misdemeanor arrest rates, the predicted decrease in homicide rate is 4.2 per 100,000. In other words, our statistical model suggests that the decrease in homicide was 2.5 times greater for precincts in the 90th percentile compared with those in the 10th percentile of change in misdemeanor arrest rate. The findings in model 3 also reveal that the measure of cocaine use retains its significant, positive effect. [1] The regression parameters suggest that a 13 percent increase in cocaine

---

[1]   To consider the possibility of mean reversion, we also estimated models that include two indicators of the growth in homicide in the years immediately preceding the time period under investigation: the simple difference in the homicide count between 1989 and 1984 and this difference as a proportion of the 1984 value. The effects of changes in misdemeanor arrests and cocaine use are unaffected by these additional controls. Bernard Harcourt and Jens Ludwig generously supplied the data for the measures of homicide before the 1990s.

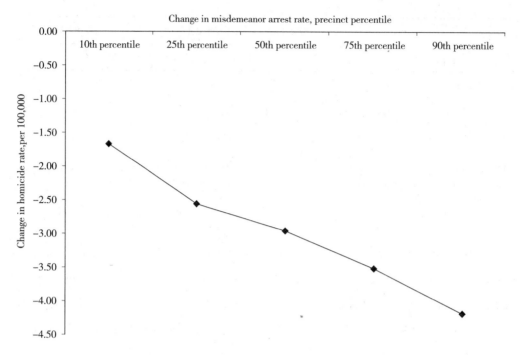

Figure 1   Change in Homicide Rates Associated with Different Changes in Misdemeanor Arrest Rates by Precinct Percentile of Change in Misdemeanor Arrest Rates

use, as reflected by the proxy measure, would be associated with about one more homicide per precinct. The coefficients for the remaining predictor variables, in contrast, are not significant. The null effects for the sociodemographic characteristics might seem to be surprising, but recall that our "mixed" statistical models predict annual changes in homicide rates using time-varying indictors of misdemeanor arrests and cocaine arrests (as well as the firearm proxy and manpower measure), along with the time-invariant measures of sociodemographic characteristics. The sociodemographic characteristics, thus, can only explain cross-sectional variation and not variation over time within precincts. In a cross-sectional analysis with average values used in place of the time-varying measures (not shown but available on request), the expected impact of socioeconomic conditions on levels of homicide is observed. The indicator of socioeconomic disadvantage emerges as a strong and significant predictor of homicide rates: The more disadvantaged precincts exhibit significantly higher average levels of homicide.

Table 2 presents the fully specified model from table 1, which now predicts gun-related and non-gun-related homicides separately. The results reveal an important specification of the impact of changes in misdemeanor arrests and changes in drug use. Both measures exert significant effects on gun-related homicides but not on non-gun-related homicides. The pattern for misdemeanor arrests is consistent with the Fagan, Zimring, and Kim (1998: 1319) observation that the timing of policing changes in New York City "fits" gun homicide declines but not trends in non-gun-related homicides. Similarly, the restricted impact of cocaine use on gun-related homicide is consistent with key elements of the Blumstein crack-cocaine thesis. The expansion and contraction of crack markets allegedly affected homicide rates through an associated arms race, which implies that changing patterns of drug use should affect gun-related homicides but not necessarily non-gun-related homicides.

If guns played a prominent role in changes in homicide rates in New York City, why is the coefficient for the gun availability proxy nonsignificant in our models? One possibility is that the proxy is invalid, but previous research has provided reasonably strong validation of this measure (Azrael, Cook, and Miller, 2004; Cook and Ludwig, 2006; Kleck, 2004). Alternatively, the causal linkage between general gun availability and homicides may be indirect and not well reflected in the relationship between the proxy and changes in homicides. Cook and Ludwig (2006: 386) argue, for example, that the primary mechanism by which gun prevalence produces high homicide rates is "through the transfer of guns from 'legal' to 'illegal' owners, rather than through increased gun misuse by otherwise legal owners." Accordingly, the general measure of gun availability may be too blunt an instrument to capture the kind of access to firearms that is likely to be related to homicides.

In table 3, we consider the possibility that the apparent effect of misdemeanor arrests is actually spurious because of more intensive policing in general, as reflected in more vigorous enforcement of serious law infractions (i. e., felony arrests). Changes in misdemeanor arrests are, in fact, positively and significantly correlated with changes in felony arrests ($r = .305$), and if the measure of changes in felony arrests is substituted for the measure of changes in misdemeanor arrests in the regression models, the pattern of results is highly similar for the two policing measures (results not shown but available on request). However, when both policing measures are included in the same equation predicting homicides in the models in table 3, only the misdemeanor arrest measure is statistically significant in the expected negative direction for total and gun-related homicide but not for non-gun-related homicide.

Table 2 Random Effects Models Predicting Change in Gun-Related and Non-Gun-Related Homicide Rates for New York City Police Precincts, 1990—1999[a]

	Type of Homicide	
	Gun-Related	Non-Gun-Related
Change in misdemeanor arrest rate	−. 0010 ***	−. 0002
Change in cocaine use[b]	. 0749 **	. 0012
Percent male	−. 1226	. 0958
Percent under age 35 years	−. 0225	−. 0223
Percent unemployed	−. 2709	−. 5749
Change in firearm availability[c]	. 0137	−. 0184
Percent black	−. 0154	. 0206
SES composite[d]	−. 0185	−. 0049
Change in manpower[e]	. 0055	−. 0026

ABBREVIATION: SES = socioeconomic status.

$*p < .05$; $** p < .01$; $*** p < .001$. $N = 666$ precinct-years.

[a] 1990 U. S. Census precinct population used to calculate rates.

[b] Annual change in proportion of accident decedents with positive cocaine toxicology.

[c] Annual change in proportion of suicides where guns were used.

[d] SES composite index includes the following socioeconomic variables aggregated to the police precinct level: percent less than high-school education, percent less than 200 percent poverty, percent female-headed households, and percent receiving public assistance.

[e] Annual change in size of police force in precinct.

The results in the final column of table 3 also allow us to conduct an assessment of the robustness of the results for homicide across another violent offense: robbery. Similar to the results for homicide, increases in misdemeanor arrests are significantly associated with decreases in robbery rates. Interestingly, the effect of changes in cocaine use is not significant for robbery. [1]

---

[1] As an additional assessment of the robustness of the findings, we have introduced an indicator of change in levels of incarceration to the models. The measure refers to the number of prison admissions by precinct of arrest per 100,000 population, which is expressed as a change score analogous to the measure of change in misdemeanor arrests. The measure of change in incarceration has no effect on crime rates in any models, and controlling for change in incarceration rates has minimal impact on the parameter estimates and doos not ofter statistical significance. The in carceration data are from the New York State Division of Criminal Justice Service and Were Kindly provided by Richard Rosenfeld.

Table 3 Random Effects Models Predicting Changes in Total, Gun-Related, and Non-Gun-Related Homicide Rates and Robbery Rates for New York City Police Precincts, 1990—1999,[a] With Change in Felony Arrests

	Type of Offense			
	Total Homicides	Gun-Related Homicides	Non-Gun-Related Homicides	Robberies
Change in misdemeanor arrest rate	−.0011 **	−.0009 **	−.0003	−.0375 ***
Change in felony arrest rate	−.0010	−.0012	.0002	.0221
Change in cocaine use[b]	.0747 *	.0733 **	.0014	.9924
Percent male	−.0379	−.1354	.0976	−19.5133 **
Percent under age 35 years	−.0296	−.0050	−.0247	6.0517 *
Percent unemployed	−.9600	−.4031	−.5569	−121.3400 ***
Change in firearm availability[c]	−.0045	.0139	−.0185	.2001
Percent black	.0063	.0142	.0204	.6100
SES composite[d]	−.0242	−.0194	−.0047	1.1976
Change in manpower[e]	.0053	.0082	−.0029	−.0285

ABBREVIATION: SES = socioeconomic status.

$* p < .05$; $** p < .01$; $*** p < .001$. $N = 666$ precinct-years.

[a] 1990 U.S. Census precinct population used to calculate rates.

[b] Annual change in proportion of accident decedents with positive cocaine toxicology.

[c] Annual change in proportion of suicides where guns were used.

[d] SES composite index includes the following socioeconomic variables aggregated to the police precinct level: percent less than high-school education, percent less than 200 percent poverty, percent female-headed households, and percent receiving public assistance.

[e] Annual change in size of police force in precinct.

SUMMARY AND CONCLUSIONS

This research has reexamined the two leading interpretations for the dramatic decline in homicide rates in New York City in the 1990s: the "broken windows policing" thesis and the "crack-cocaine/drug activity" thesis. We have gone beyond prior work by 1) examining gun-related and non-gun-related homicides separately, 2) using a superior measure of drug activity based on cocaine toxicology of accident decedents, and 3) including a measure of felony arrests to help distinguish the effects of increased policing of "quality-of-life" offenses from intensified policing more generally. Our analyses have been based on pooled, cross-sectional, time-series data for 74 New York City precincts over the 1990—1999 period, with all variables measured at the appropriate precinct level. The results of our mixed-regression models offer qualified support for each of the two leading explanations of the homicide decline in New York City, but they also raise some important questions.

We find that changes in misdemeanor arrest rates are negatively related to changes in total homicide rates. This effect is statistically significant, and it persists in the models controlling for sociodemographic characteristics at the beginning of the time period, changing levels of police manpower, and for changes in felony arrests. These findings support the Kelling and Sousa general claim that the implementation of new policing policies played a nontrivial role in the homicide decline in New York City.

We also observe that, when homicides are disaggregated by weapon use, the effect of changes in policing is significant for gun-related, but not for non-gun-related, homicide. This observation may reflect patterns of gun use by circumstances. For the nation at large, during the time period under investigation, guns were more likely to be used in felony and gang-related incidents than in other kinds of homicides, such as homicides evolving out of arguments (Bureau of Justice Statistics, 2006). It seems likely that policing policies will have more of an impact on homicides associated with felonies and gang activities than on argument-related homicides. The observation of an effect of misdemeanor arrests on gun-related homicides, but not on non-gun-related homicides, is also consistent with arguments advanced by Fagan, Zimring, and Kim (1998: 1322) that the kinds of changes in policing associated with broken windows theory might be effective, at least in part, by "taking guns off the street." Enforcement tactics resulting in greater police/citizen contacts presumably increase opportunities to search for, and apprehend, illegal guns that might otherwise be used in gun-related homicides.

We also find a significant effect of changes in cocaine use on changes in homicide rates. Declining cocaine use, as indicated by the toxicology of accident victims, is associated with decreasing homicide levels. Similar to the results for misdemeanor arrests, the effect of the cocaine measure is specified by weapon use; it emerges for gun-related homicides but not for non-gun-related homicides. These results are in accord with theoretical arguments about the close connection between crack-cocaine markets and the illegal use of guns.

We recognize that some limitations are associated with our analysis. The indicator of drug activity does not discriminate between crack cocaine and other forms of cocaine, and it reflects the levels of use rather than the features of the drug market operations. It is possible, for example, that patterns of cocaine use do not "map" closely with patterns of drug buying and selling, which implies that cocaine deaths by place of injury might not reflect the level of drug market activity. The findings for this measure thus bear indirectly on some specific claims of the "crack-cocaine market" thesis of the homicide decline.

More generally, causal inference is inherently precarious in nonexperimental designs, and the possibility of omitted variables bias cannot be dismissed. One particularly important concern for current purposes is that some unmeasured features of policing are correlated with misdemeanor arrests. We have included controls for levels of police manpower and felony arrests, but the practice of intensive policing of disorderly behavior in New York City was implemented as part of a larger constellation of organizational change and a reorientation of the mission of the NYPD (National Research Council, 2004: 230). Accordingly, the coefficient for misdemeanor arrests might be capturing other aspects of policing that were selectively adopted across precincts along with the intensive policing of disorder. Research on the effectiveness of various forms of policing has revealed that the most successful innovations have been those that combine highly focused police efforts with "an expansion of the tool box of policing beyond simple law enforcement" (Weisburd and Eck, 2004: 42). It is thus plausible to speculate that the policing of disorder operated in concert with other police practices that have been shown to be effective in a wide range of contexts to reduce levels of homicide in New York City. Clarifying the precise mechanisms underlying the finding of a negative effect of misdemeanor arrests on homicides is an important challenge for future research.

In addition, data availability inhibits the assessment of the importance of changes in policing or drug activity on the homicide decline relative to improvements in the kinds of social conditions that have been linked with violent crime in the macro-criminological literature. Our models include a wide range of measures of sociodemographic characteristics as controls, but these measures are based on census data and are time invariant. We thus can take into account appreciable differences in the levels of sociodemographic characteristics across precincts at the beginning of the decade, but we cannot estimate the relationships between changes in theoretically relevant social conditions and changes in homicide. [1]Although we can only speculate, it seems likely that both law enforcement and social trends are likely to have contributed to declining gun homicide in New York City (see Fagan, Zimring, and Kim, 1998: 1320).

Another issue that requires more consideration is the reason for the discrepancies between our findings and the previous results of Harcourt and Ludwig (2006). We employ a similar modeling strategy, regressing crime changes on arrest changes, yet arrive at divergent conclusions. One obvious difference between the two studies is the dependent variable. Homicide and robbery serve as the dependent variables in the analyses reported above, whereas Harcourt and Ludwig model a composite measure of violent crime based on the sum of criminal homicides, rapes, felonious assaults, and robberies. However, when we substitute a composite violent crime measure in our regression models, the results for misdemeanor arrests and the cocaine measure replicate those for homicide and robbery. The differences across studies for the cocaine measure are perhaps not surprising, given that our proxy is measured at the precinct rather than at the borough level, but the varying results for misdemeanor arrests are perplexing. We have included a range of control variables similar to those of Harcourt and Ludwig, but some differences in model specification exist. An important task for future research is to isolate those design features of the respective studies that can account for the divergent findings.

We close with a caution about the policy implications of our findings of significant negative effects of changes in misdemeanor arrests on changes in homicide rates. Local governmental officials confront difficult choices in the allocation of scarce resources, and thus, investments in policing policies must be weighed against alternative strategies for improving the quality of life in the city. Moreover, the potential dangers associated with policing disorder have long been recognized. These strategies grant the police considerable discretion, which under certain circumstances may be conducive to the excessive use of force, brutality, and prejudicial enforcement (Skogan, 1990: 164; see also Greene,

---

[1] Note also that our analyses are confined to relatively short-term effects of policing. Research by Fagan, West, and Holland (2003) suggests that incarceration has adverse consequences for the social ecology of neighborhoods that increase the likelihood of crime in the long run. As reported in footnote 13, an indicator of contemporaneous change in incarceration rates has no effect on change in homicide rates in our sample, but to the extent that proactive policing leads to increased incarceration, and incarceration stains "the social and psychological fabric of neighborhood life," as suggested by Fagan, West, and Holland (2003: 1589), the long-term effect of policing might be contrary to its short-term effect.

1999). Indeed, critics have suggested that the social costs associated with broken windows policing in New York City have exceeded any ostensible benefits (Karmen, 2000: 120). Thus, although our analyses suggest that innovations in policing hold promise for crime reduction, we echo earlier calls for careful cost/benefit calculations and a judicious balancing of the goals of crime control and social justice in deliberations about the implementation of forms of proactive policing (Sampson and Cohen, 1988: 186).

References

ArcGIS, version 9. 0. 2004. ESRI, Redlands, CA.

Azrael, Deborah, Philip J. Cook, and Matthew Miller. 2004. State and local prevalence of firearms ownership: Measurement, structure, and trends. *Journal of Quantitative Criminology* 20:43 – 62.

Blumstein, Alfred. 1995. Youth violence, guns, and the illicit-drug industry. *Journal of Criminal Law and Criminology* 86:10 – 36.

Blumstein, Alfred, and Richard Rosenfeld. 1998. Explaining recent trends in U. S. homicide rates. *Journal of Criminal Law and Criminology* 88:1175 – 216.

Blumstein, Alfred, Frederick P. Rivara, and Richard Rosenfeld. 2000. The rise and decline of homicide. *Annual Review of Public Health* 21:505 – 41.

Bowling, Benjamin. 1999. The rise and fall of New York murder. *British Journal of Criminology* 39:531 – 54.

Bratton, William J. , with Peter Knobler. 1998. *Turnaround: How America's Top Cop Reversed the Crime Epidemic.* New York: Random House.

Bureau of Justice Statistics. 2006. Homicide Trends in the U. S. : Homicide Circumstances. U. S. Department of Justice. http://www. ojp. usdoj. bjs/ homicide/ circumst. htm.

Conklin, John E. 2003. *Why Crime Rates Fell.* Boston, MA: Allyn and Bacon.

Cook, Philip J. , and John H. Laub. 2002. After the epidemic: Recent trends in youth violence in the United States. In *Crime and Justice: A Review of Research*, Vol. 29, ed. Michael Tonry. Chicago, IL: University of Chicago Press.

Cook, Philip J. , and Jens Ludwig. 2006. The social costs of gun ownership. *Journal of*

Public Economics 90:379 – 91.

Corman, Hope, and Naci Mocan. 2002. *Carrots, Sticks and Broken Windows.* NBER Working Paper 9061. http://www. nber. org/papers/w9061.

Eck, John E., and Edward R. Maguire. 2000. Have changes in policing reduced violent crime? An assessment of the evidence. In *The Crime Drop in America*, eds. Alfred Blumstein and Joel Wallman. Cambridge, UK: Cambridge University Press.

Fagan, Jeffrey, and Garth Davies. 2003. Policing guns: Order maintenance and crime control in New York. In *Guns, Crime, and Punishment in America*, ed. Bernard E. Harcourt. New York: New York University Press.

Fagan, Jeffrey, Valerie West, and Jan Holland. 2003. Reciprocal effects of crime and incarceration in New York City neighborhoods. *Fordham Urban Law Journal* 30: 155 1 – 602.

Fagan, Jeffrey, Franklin E. Zimring, and June Kim. 1998. Declining homicide in New York City: A tale of two trends. *Journal of Criminal Law and Criminology* 88:1277 – 323.

Galea, Sandro, Jennifer Ahern, David Vlahov, Phillip O. Coffin, Crystal Fuller, Andrew C. Leon, and Kenneth J. Tardiff. 2003. Income distribution and risk of fatal drug overdose in New York City neighborhoods. *Drug and Alcohol Dependence* 70:139 – 48.

Goldstein, Herman. 1979. Improving policing: A problem-oriented approach. *Journal of Crime and Delinquency* 25:236 – 58.

Goldstein, Paul J. 1985. The drugs/violence nexus: A tripartite conceptual framework. *Journal of Drug Issues* 14:493 – 506.

Golub, Andrew Lang, and Bruce D. Johnson. 1997. *Crack's Decline: Some Surprises Across U. S. Cities.* National Institute of Justice Research Brief. Washington, DC: U. S. Department of Justice.

Greene, Judith A. 1999. Zero tolerance: A case study of police policies and practices in New York City. *Crime & Delinquency* 45:171 – 87.

Harcourt, Bernard E., and Jens Ludwig. 2006. Broken windows: New evidence from New York City and a five-city social experiment. *University of Chicago Law Review* 73: 27 1 – 320.

Infoshare Online. 2007. www. infoshare. org.

Joanes, Ana. 2000. Does the New York City Police Department deserve credit for the decline in New York City's homicide rates? A cross-city comparison of policing strategies and homicide rates. *Columbia Journal of Law and Social Problems* 33:265 – 311.

Karmen, Andrew. 2000. *New York Murder Mystery: The True Story Behind the Crime Crash of the* 1990s. New York: New York University Press.

Kelling, George L., and William J. Bratton. 1998. Declining crime rates: Insiders' views of the New York City story. *Journal of Criminal Law and Criminology* 88:1217 – 231.

Kelling, George L., and Catherine M. Coles. 1996. *Fixing Broken Windows: Restoring Order and Reducing Crime in Our Communities*. New York: Simon and Schuster.

Kelling, George L., and William H. Sousa, Jr. 2001. *Do Police Matter? An Analysis of the Impact of New York City's Police Reforms*. New York: Center for Civic Innovation at the Manhattan Institute.

Kleck, Gary. 2004. Measures of gun ownership levels for macro-level crime and violence research. *Journal of Research in Crime and Delinquency* 41:3 – 36.

Land, Kenneth C., Patricia L. McCall, and Lawrence E. Cohen. 1990. Structural covariates of homicide rates: Are there any invariances across time and social space? *American Journal of Sociology* 95:922 – 63.

Levitt, Steven D. 2004. Understanding why crime fell in the 1990s: Four factors that explain the decline and six that do not. *Journal of Economic Perspectives* 18:163 – 90.

MacDonald, John M. 2002. The effectiveness of community policing in reducing urban violence. *Crime and Delinquency* 48:592 – 618.

Messner, Steven F., Glenn D. Deane, Luc Anselin, and Benjamin Pearson-Nelson. 2005. Locating the vanguard in rising and falling homicide rates across U. S. cities. *Criminology* 43:661 – 96.

National Research Council. 2004. *Fairness and Effectiveness in Policing: The Evidence. Committee to Review Research on Police Policy and Practices*, eds. Wesley Skogan and Kathleen Frydel. Committee on Law and Justice, Division of Behavioral and Social Sciences and Education. Washington, DC: The National Academies Press.

O'Brien, Robert M. 1996. Police productivity and crime rates: 1973—1992. *Criminology* 34:183 – 207.

Ousey, Graham, and Matthew R. Lee. 2002. Examining the conditional nature of the illicit drug market-homicide relationship: A partial test of the theory of contingent causation. *Criminology* 40:73 – 102.

Rosenfeld, Richard. 2002. Crime decline in context. *Contexts: Understanding People in Their Social Worlds* 1:25 – 34.

Rosenfeld, Richard, Robert Fernango, and Eric Baumer. 2005. Did *Ceasefire*, *Compstat*, and *Exile* reduce homicide? *Criminology & Public Policy* 4:419 – 50.

Sampson, Robert J., and Jacqueline Cohen. 1988. Deterrent effects of the police on crime: A replication and theoretical extension. *Law & Society Review* 22:163 – 89.

Skogan, Wesley. 1990. *Disorder and Decline: Crime and the Spiral of Decay in American Neighborhoods*. Berkeley, CA: University of California Press.

Solomon, Freda F. 2003. *The Impact of Quality-Of-Life Policing*. New York City Criminal Justice Agency Research Brief, No. 3.

Taylor, Ralph B. 2001. *Breaking Away from Broken Windows: Baltimore Neighborhoods and the Nationwide Fight Against Crime, Grime, Fear, and Decline*. Boulder, CO: Westview.

Weisburd, David, and John E. Eck. 2004. What can police do to reduce crime, disorder, and fear? *Annals of the American Academy of Political and Social Science* 593:42 – 5.

Wilson, James Q., and George L. Kelling. 1982. Broken windows: The police and neighborhood safety. *Atlantic Monthly* 249:29 – 38.

Wintemute, Garen. 2000. Guns and gun violence. In *The Crime Drop in America*, eds. Alfred Blumstein and Joel Wallman. Cambridge, UK: Cambridge University Press.

Steven F. Messner is the Distinguished Teaching Professor of Sociology at the University at Albany, State University of New York. His research focuses on social organization and crime, the spatial patterning of crime, and crime in China.

Sandro Galea is an associate professor in the Department of Epidemiology at the University of Michigan School of Public Health. His research interests include the role of social and economic factors in shaping population health.

Kenneth J. Tardiff is a professor of psychiatry and public health in the Department of Psychiatry at the Weill School of Medicine, Cornell University. His research interests include homicide and other violence, suicide, and accidental drug overdoses.

Melissa Tracy is a research analyst in the Department of Epidemiology at the University of Michigan School of Public Health. Her research interests include determinants of mortality and morbidity in urban areas.

Angela Bucciarelli is a research analyst with the Center for Urban Epidemiologic Studies at the New York Academy of Medicine. Areas of particular interest are spatial analytic methods and geographic information systems (GIS) technology applied to public health research.

Tinka Markham Piper is a senior project director with the Center for Urban Epidemiologic Studies at the New York Academy of Medicine. Her research interests include changing trends in fatal injury (homicide, suicide, and drug overdose) in urban areas.

Victoria Frye is a research investigator at the Center for Urban Epidemiologic Studies at The New York Academy of Medicine and an adjunct assistant professor at New York University. Dr. Frye studies the distribution and determinants of intimate partner violence against women and the roles of sociostructural and socially interactive factors in maintaining intimate partner violence at the neighborhood level.

David Vlahov is the director of the Center for Urban Epidemiologic Studies at the New York Academy of Medicine. His research interests include the epidemiology of behavior and of infectious disease transmission in urban areas.

Appendix A. Univariate Statistics for New York City Police Precincts, 1990—1999 ($N = 74$)[a]

	Mean	SD
Homicides per 100,000[b]	20.7	22.2
Gun-related homicides per 100,000[b]	14.8	16.9
Non-gun-related homicides per 100,000[b]	5.9	7.5
Robberies per 100,000[b]	1126.0	977.7
Misdemeanor arrests per 100,000[b]	4769.1	4981.9
Felony arrests per 100,000[b]	2403.9	2120.7
Cocaine use[b,c]	8.0	10.6
Percent male	47.0	2.3
Percent under age 35 years	52.1	7.5
Percent unemployed	4.5	1.2
Firearm availability[b,d]	18.8	20.6
Percent black	27.5	27.2
Percent with less than high-school education	32.8	13.7
Percent under 200% poverty	37.0	16.8
Percent female-headed households	20.1	11.7

continued

	Mean	SD
Percent receiving public assistance	5. 6	3. 7
SES composite score[e]	91. 1	41. 8
Police force in precinct[b]	220. 5	60. 4

ABBREVIATIONS: SD = standard deviation, SES = socioeconomic status.

[a] Demographic characteristics based on 1990 U. S. Census.

[b] Data available for each year 1990—1999.

[c] Proportion of accident decedents with positive cocaine toxicology.

[d] Proportion of suicides where guns were used.

[e] SES composite index includes the following socioeconomic variables aggregated to the police precinct level: percent less than high-school education, percent less than 200 percent poverty, percent female-headed households, and percent receiving public assistance.

解读失业、凶杀与福利国家的联系

理查德·罗森菲尔德(Richard Rosenfeld)

密苏里圣路易斯大学

史蒂文·F. 梅斯纳(Steven F. Messner)

纽约州立大学奥尔巴尼分校

经济因素对犯罪率的影响是定量科学研究犯罪学的一个重要方向和议题。很多卓越的理论成果都诠释了恶化的经济状况,尤其是失业率的增加,会对犯罪率产生正面或者负面的影响(Cantor and Land, 1985)。但是这些研究成果所得出的经济因素及其所诱发犯罪的关联性却是模棱两可的(Chiricos, 1987;Cook and Zarkin, 1985;Greenberg, 2001)。半个世纪前,一位极有影响力的犯罪学家从当时的研究成果中总结出了这样的推断:"显而易见,经济因素与犯罪的关联性是极不确定的,因此无法得出清晰和明确的结论"(Vold,1958:181)。虽然后继的研究者开始逐步得出一些规律性的结论,比如犯罪主要集中发生在贫困地区(Pratt and Cullen, 2005;Sampson, Morenoff, and Gannon-Rowley 2002),但是经济运行和犯罪之间的天然联系仍旧是一个不解之谜。

一个虽然不起眼却始终坚持的关于福利国家与国家凶杀率之间关联性的研究部分是:慷慨的福利保障政策和低凶杀率是一对孪生兄弟(Fiala and LaFree,1988;Gartner,1990;Messner and Rosenfeld, 1997)。另外,先前的研究也发现福利国家制约着人口老龄化(Pampel and Gartner, 1995)、收入不均衡(Savolainen, 2000)、家庭不和谐(Gartner, 1991)等因素对凶杀率的影响:慷慨的福利保障能够有效削弱这些因素对凶杀率的影响。

　　我们依然采用分两步走的研究惯例。前一步调查研究经济状况对犯罪率的影响,后一步再添加福利国家这一变量,从而在此次调查研究中系统地阐述我们的假设。我们假设与失业率相挂钩且受社会经济状况制约的福利国家状况与整个国家的凶杀率之间存在一定的关联。在那些有着慷慨福利保障政策的国家,失业率对凶杀率的影响较弱;反之,则要强。我们对 13 个工业发达国家在 1971 年至 2001 年期间进行了追踪调查。我们的研究分析主要基于制度性社会失范论(Messner and Rosenfeld, 2007;Rosenfeld and Messner, 2006)。

一、研究背景

　　从经济学与社会学的角度,大量丰富的犯罪学理论成果早已阐释了犯罪率是伴随着经济状况的发展变化而不断变化的。经济学理论揭示了个人如果粗略地估算了相对利益、合法或者不合法行为所要付出的代价,就会在当不遵守规则时的纯收益(收益减去花费)超出了遵守规则时的纯收益的情况下,选择违反规则(Becker, 1968;Pyle, 2000)。失业率的增加与收入的减少降低了遵守规则带来的利益,却使犯罪成为更具诱惑力的行为选择方式!

　　社会学理论也同样假定在行为获得的利益和必须付出的代价面前能够做出理性的选择,但社会学家通常比经济学家更专注于探究这些理性选择是如何在社会文化环境中产生的。在默顿的经典著作《社会结构与异化》(1938)中,他指出:这个社会过度强调人应该在财富上获得成功才有价值,相对而言,却并不那么强调获取这些成功的途径的合法性,从而将会导致产生更多的"颠覆性"手段,比如通过犯罪手段,尤其是那些通过正当合法途径只能获取微乎其微的利益的人。也就是说,随着失业率的增加和个人收入的减少,这些采用颠覆性手段的人群数量就会不断增加。另外,我们从经典的社会控制论中也能得到同样的揭示:不断恶化的经济状况将会使人们逐步失去对固有传统秩序的依赖和联系,因此抑制犯罪的枷锁和纽带也将会被不断削弱和打破(Hirschi, 1969)。

　　从之前经济学和社会学的角度来看,研究者主要侧重于研究犯罪者的犯罪动机以及如何抑制这些动机的产生。相较之下,如果我们从犯罪机会的角度入手,则将目光直接投向了受害群体的特点和类型,并能预见到不断恶化的经济状况与犯罪率是呈负相关联系的。日常活动犯罪理论家认为经济状况的衰退,会伴随着有吸引力的作案目标的减少和监视守卫力量的增强,能够减少犯罪的机会(Cohen and Felson,1979;Cohen, Felson and Land, 1980)。举例来说,由于失业率的增加,会有更多人待在家里,从而会减少入室盗窃的现象;并且人们在外出的时候也不会带上太多有价值的东西,也能间接减少抢劫案件的发生。

当然这些假设的犯罪动机和犯罪机会的过程并不是互相排斥的。在犯罪动机和犯罪机会的共同作用下,整个犯案的程度会不断变化,并且随着时间段的不同而呈现出不同的特点。事实上,很多研究者都认为,因经济因素产生的对被害人的犯罪机会的影响往往是在短时间内突发的,但是对犯罪动机的影响却很有可能是长久酝酿的(Cantor and Land, 1985)。这其中确切的本质联系目前仍没有得到充分的科学阐释,最有效的方法是通过统计建模来处理和分析,但这仍旧是理论上的论述(Greenberg,2001;Cantor and Land, 2001)。

(一)福利国家和犯罪率

我们从经济学和社会学这两个角度,综合考虑福利国家对经济因素与犯罪率两者关系的影响。虽然它们有着不同的历史根源,现代福利国家旨在缓和市场经济给个体和家庭带来的不利影响(Esping-Andersen, 1990)。通过失业保险、医疗保险、养老金、子女津贴、儿童保健津贴、育婴假和收入补贴等法定授权形式使得那些因持续的高失业率或者经济萧条不能维持生计的人能够更好地渡过难关。在经济学原理中,福利国家在经济衰退的时候,能增加人们遵纪守法带来的纯收益而减少犯罪带来的纯收益。在默顿(Merton)(1938)看来,福利国家能够减少那些为了实现社会文化价值目标而采用非法手段的可能性。从社会控制论的角度来看,福利国家的保护性在于能使人们即使在失业的时候,也能继续维持与社会的联系,遵守社会的秩序。所有的阐释都印证了一个命题:强大的福利国家能够削弱由经济下滑所带来的犯罪率的增加。

在社会经济状况衰退时期,预期的国家福利对犯罪目标和守卫监视力量的影响并不是那么清晰。福利保障的收入价值重估会减少市价跌落给犯罪目标造成的价值影响。与此同时,不断上升的失业率会增加犯罪目标的监守力量,因为即使有着优厚的福利保障所带来的价值,失业的人也一定会比有工作的人有更多的时间待在家里。因此福利国家对犯罪机会的影响比对犯罪动机的影响更为适度。

先前的研究成果已经表明,在那些有着慷慨福利的时期,国家的凶杀率水平低(Fiala and LaFree, 1988;Gantner, 1990;Messner and Rosenfeld, 1997)。最近一份以100个国家为样本的关于凶杀率调查报告(Antonaccio and Tittle, 2007)将记录的福利待遇和资本财富分配的均衡性和密度的数据相结合制成了索引量表。他们发现一个与其他研究一致的结论,这些指数的高低与犯罪率有着很大的关联。社会资本财富集中度数值高且福利分配均衡度数值低的国家,除去一些控制变量,就会呈现出较高的凶杀率。

另外,一些研究也显示在强大的福利国家的背景下,通过一定的福利国家条件,可以有效遏制凶杀产生的犯罪倾向因素。萨沃莱宁(Savolainen)(2000)通过分析两份有重叠但仍有所不同的跨国性研究样本资料,指出收入不均对凶杀率的影响在那些福利保障较薄弱的国家要更大。加特纳(Gartner)(1991)则用相似的研究手段致力于家庭压力带来的影响。通过一份1965年到1980年期间对17个发达国家进行的追踪调查,她发现由于未成年少女怀孕、未婚生子和离婚等家庭因素而引发的婴幼儿和青少年被杀害的比例在那些福利保障相对较差的国家和时期内要高。潘佩尔(Pampel)和加特纳(Gartner)(1995)也在一份针对发达国家的追踪研究报告中发现涉及不同年龄结构的凶杀率构成与上述研究呈现同样的结果。大量生活在"集体主义"这个指标较低国家的青少年和年轻人,其产生凶杀倾向的可能性大(这个指标包括了福利的慷慨度、集体协商、民主制度对比多数民主、左倾政党统治以及非暴力的政治冲突)。

所有这些研究成果都阐释了就制度框架而言,健全的福利国家(或者其他集体主义政治协商)能够减弱市场经济给个人、家庭和各年龄段成员带来的诱发犯罪的倾向。比如潘佩尔(Pampel)和加特纳(Gartner)(1995:245)主张:社会体系促进了集体对于提高生活水平和对于保护社会团结政策的责任,可以缓解人群间相互造成的不利影响。这些制度框架都反映和保护了社会远离市场兴衰带来的冲击(247)。类似的逻辑方法也被应用于研究制度框架对高生育率、少女怀孕、单身妈妈、家庭不健全等影响和结果的塑造。经济压力、社会孤立以及社会关心支持的缺乏在无法避免的时候,年轻的单身母亲可以通过社会政策措施的调控来推进社会对于福利的集体责任,从而减少对孩子造成的虐待与杀害。

通过福利国家,政府能够充分保护市场给个人和家庭带来的冲击,更进一步讲,可以有效缓和经济危机和促进社会团结。但研究者也推测,福利国家对凶杀率的调节作用也反映了一种文化价值取向,即避免人与人之间的暴力冲突(Gartner,1991:238)。福利国家反映和强化了对于个人福利集体责任的伦理,提升了情境或者干预了有潜在暴力倾向的人。从另一个角度说,集体主义价值取向能让人们在追求个人利益的时候换位思考,考虑到他人的权益,而不是一味地通过暴力手段追逐个人利益和解决与他人的矛盾。

（二）制度性社会失范论

犯罪学中的制度性社会失范论是作为过往研究中用于解释现代福利国家的保护性和降低暴力作用的一个恰当有用的框架（Savolainen，2000）。这个理论扩展了默顿（Merton）在1938年提出的关于高犯罪率与社会失范之间，以及超出分层体系的社会不平等与社会制度的复杂构成和现代社会之间全方位的联系。这样的社会体系必须平衡有时会产生的竞争，也要平衡经济、家庭、政治和教育等制度的需要。由此在各个社会制度间产生的彼此联系则被称作社会公共制度均势。在有些社会中，比如美国，自由市场经济主导着社会公共制度均势的平衡。其他制度的功能和目标不断的削弱，当出现制度冲突的时候，非经济制度能不断地适应市场需求。另外，道德规范行为模式、语言、市场逻辑规律在非经济领域的社会生活中发挥了重要的作用。（Messner and Rosenfeld，2007:74-84）这种制度模式不仅反映了同时也催化了社会文化思潮，正如默顿（Merton）（1938）所言，这种社会文化思潮颂扬经济上取得的成功，且不再强调通过合理途径获取成功。市场对于制度结构的支配以及不择手段的文化价值取向轮流地破坏社会的控制，支持着非经济制度功能，刺激犯罪率的攀升。

在绝大多数发达社会中，政策在调节市场经济和促成福利保障的过程中都起到了重要的作用。国家关于失业保险、医疗保险、社会保险、儿童津贴以及其他法律措施的政策能够保护公民远离因市场经济衰退而受到的影响。通过促进消费，国家也能加快经济的复苏。但是这些政策的调整作用和福利保障作用会削弱市场经济对制度结构的主宰。先前对福利国家和凶杀率的研究表明发达社会中通过制度结构的调整来抑制暴力犯罪还是最主要的途径。

二、当前的研究成果

关于福利国家对收入不均衡、家庭压力、劳动力过剩的缓和作用，涉及市场运行的压力和市场的兴衰的研究文献都是属于间接研究。而关于经济状况与犯罪的研究文献都是采用对市场波动尤其是失业率的直接测量，而不是考虑失业率或者其他市场经济因素对犯罪的影响是如何作为福利国家条件的。结合分析福利国家是如何缓解市场经济对犯罪率的影响，我们能从每一个研究领域中获得启示。当前研究中我们将失业率作为衡量市场行为结果的指标，要是我们把目光集中到先前的研究成果，也会发现他们也将失业率作为经济繁荣与否的显著指标。基于同样的理由，我们在前人研究的基础上，着力解释凶杀这种最严厉犯罪的变量来研究失业率对全国凶杀率的影响。另外,凶杀这种类型的犯罪研究在很长一个阶段都可以使用到最为可信的跨国的数据。

三、数据和研究方法

本次研究中我们使用的凶杀率测量数据来自于世界卫生组织。这些数据是基于对死亡原因的探究,被权威医疗部门认证,并排除了有自杀企图的情况,而且这些数据在国际范围内通常有其他方式可以用来替代记录。依照惯例,我们计算凶杀率是以 10 万人为基准的。失业率源自于国际货币基金组织(http://www. imf. org/external/data. htm)和世界经济合作发展组织(http://www. oecd. org/)。我们的福利国家测量数据源自于《各国社会福利保障权威比较》(Scruggs, 2004)。我们使用变量"总体福利慷慨度"来表明各个国家的失业救济金、医疗保险金和退休金的普遍性和延伸性。这三种救济金的种类为收入重置价值制定了标准(救济金的多少与生产工人的平均工资的比值),包括资格条件,受益期限和劳动力百分比。这些通过三类救济金测算的最后得分加在一起的总得分就形成了总体上的福利慷慨度数值(Scruggs, 2004)。

我们的模型也包含了人口规模的大小和 15 岁至 24 岁的人群的百分比。这些数据都来自于 1970 年至 2004 年全美人口数量统计年鉴。另外,我们也引进了虚拟变量来固定不同国家和不同年份的影响,以线性趋势来表现凶杀率和国家特有的凶杀案件的变化趋势。国家通过国家间不可测的不变时的多样性资源达到控制,年份通过模拟估算国家间变异来源的时间变化来达到条件,共同的和特有的国家确定趋势在国家之间随着时间的推移控制着额外变量。实际的变量(凶杀率、失业率、社会福利慷慨程度、人口规模以及年龄结构)随着自然对数的分解而变化,产生的系数是可信且有弹性的(预测的结果将有 1% 上下的浮动)。这些原始变量的具体统计和描述都反映在表 1 中。

表 1　相关系数与描述性统计(样本数为 403)[a]

	(1)凶杀	(2)失业	(3)慷慨程度	(4)人口规模	(5)年龄结构
(1)	—				
(2)	.103	—			
(3)	-.350	-.084	—		

	(1)凶杀	(2)失业	(3)慷慨程度	(4)人口规模	(5)年龄结构
(4)	.873	.185	-.408	—	
(5)	.281	.088	-.280	.103	—
平均值	1.84	5.79	27.24	4.49E+07	15.06
标准差	2.11	3.05	8.22	6.21E+07	1.83
最小值	.53	.70	11.00	3.91E+06	11.00
最大值	10.55	12.00	45.40	2.85E+08	19.74

a 变量单位为原米。

反观各个国家的一系列凶杀率在一定程度上并不是一成不变的。在经过首要系列变动之后,才能逐步呈现出趋于稳定的状态。因此我们选取了一系列有首要差别的凶杀率样本,以及其他回归分析中的有效变量,并选取一个特例。我们研究的兴趣点在市场波动是如何影响凶杀率的变化的,首要差异性也与以上的研究方法一致。这个特例就是福利的慷慨程度。跟以往的研究一样,我们着眼于福利保障的不同程度是如何影响凶杀率与市场经济环境两者之间的关系。因此,在我们的研究分析中,福利慷慨的指标按不同程度被区分。

最初的检验同样表明异方差误差项在模型间回归,而相关误差在模型间和模型内回归。因此我们采用切实可行且普遍适用的最小平方估计量(FGLS)来估算我们的模型,从而在异方差性,相关模型间误差和模型内连续相关性面前得出一致的系数。

我们的模型是以 13 个工业发达国家在 1971 年到 2001 年期间的数据为样本进行估算的。将这些国家在这期间的所有数据加以运用组合,制成 403 个有差异性的样本。在测量中,我们尽量让样本中缺失的数据降低到最低,因此我们的样本比起先前那些用于研究凶杀率与福利国家关系的样本要小一些。虽然如此,基于我们的研究有大量的变量存在,并以覆盖更多的福利国家为目的,我们的研究对象从那些有优厚的福利保障制度的国家,例如瑞典、挪威和丹麦到福利保障制度政策相对较差的美国、英国和日本。我们的研究分析报告覆盖了 31 年期间能运用到的福利国家慷慨度的数据(Scruggs,2004)。因为美国的凶杀率是非常高的,我们从中分析得出的多重研究结果,既有包含美国的,也有不包含美国的。

四、结 论

在表 1 中,展示了从 1971 年到 2001 年期间调查的 13 个发达国家的平均凶杀率程度,从中我们发现,在图中显示的美国的凶杀率要比别的国家高。美国的凶杀率是接下来几个高凶杀率国家(加拿大、澳大利亚、意大利)的凶杀率的四倍多,是那些排在列表末端的几个国家(英国、挪威、荷兰和日本)凶杀率的八倍多。虽然在测量凶杀时对数和差分的运算会减少这个差距,但这仍无法改变美国与其他国家相比在凶杀率上的巨大差距。

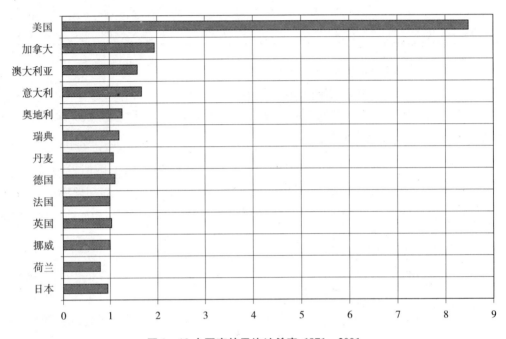

图1　13个国家的平均凶杀率,1971—2001

　　美国在衡量福利保障慷慨度的样本列表中接近底部,只比日本高一点,在英国和澳大利亚的下面。正如注释中所说,北欧国家有着最高的福利保障慷慨度得分(见图表二)。美国较高的凶杀率和较低水平的福利保障慷慨程度则会反映出"美国例外论"的可能性,这是一种失业率对凶杀率的显著影响,这种影响超出了其他发达国家等福利国家对凶杀率与市场行为间联系的影响。通过多种样本比较的结果,包含美国或是不包含美国的,我们证实了这种可能性,这在先前的研究中是没有的(Gartner, 1990,1991;Pampel and Gartner,1995)。

　　表1依据分析得出的真实数据(在原稿中)展示了双变量间的联系。这与先前的研究一致(Savolainen, 2000;Messner and Rosenfeld, 1997),国家的凶杀率和福利慷慨度得分之间存在一定的负相关(r=-.350, p <.01)。有着更慷慨福利保障的国家更倾向于有着较低的凶杀率。我们发现在人口规模和凶杀率之间有着很强的正相关(r =.873, p <.01),一定程度上反映了美国高凶杀率与大规模人口之间的联系。失

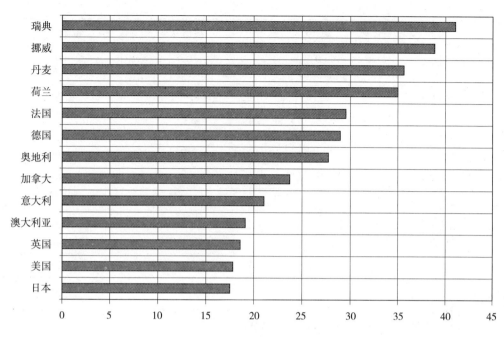

图2   13个国家的平均社会福利慷慨度，1971—2001

业率与凶杀率的联系在统计上的显示是有显著关联的，但是影响并不是很大（r = .103，p<.05）。最后，我们在我们的样本中发现了失业率与福利慷慨度之间虽然有联系，但是并不显著（r = -.084）。在调查研究的过程中，样本中一些有着优秀慷慨福利的国家正在经受着高增长的失业率。举例来说，法国的失业率20世纪后20年始终徘徊在10%左右。然而在新的世纪，强大的福利国家并不意味着就能完全保证就业了。福利国家是否能缓和失业率对凶杀率的影响才是我们此次多元变量研究的中心。

表2中展示了我们模型回归分析的结果。研究结果并不是用普通的线性趋势来指示，特定的全国性的趋势以及虚变数来描绘出不同国家不同年份间的固定影响。列表的第一列展现了在每年失业率、人口规模大小、年龄构成和福利慷慨度的变化对凶杀率的变化影响的回归值。没有一样对凶杀率有着显著的影响。这也就说明了某些国家对失业率的控制和对福利保障的高层次发展并没有促使其国内的凶杀率与别国相比有更大的差异。

表2   关于失业、慷慨程度指标、年龄结构和人口规模[a]的国家凶杀率的 FGLS 衰退

	模型 1	模型 2[b]	模型 3[b,c]
失业	-.044 (.029)	-.008 (.032)	-.027 (.036)

	模型 1	模型 2[b]	模型 3[b,c]
慷慨程度	.039 (.068)	.055 (.067)	.091 (.070)
人口规模	-.793 (.621)	-.990 (.636)	-.700 (.711)
年龄结构	-.138 (.168)	-.186 (.169)	-.379 * (.188)
Unem x Gen	— (—)	-.213 * (.086)	-.214 * (.098)
LL	399.13	401.34	361.73
Wald Chi[2]	1013.66 **	1070.19 **	1081.48 **
N	390	390	360

** $p < .01$ * $p < .05$（双层）。

[a] 组内或组间异方差于义最小平方模型相关误差。模型包括普通线性趋势、国家间趋势、国家和年份的固定影响（结果抑制）。所有变量滞后（以 e 为基础），并且除了慷慨程度，第一差分。

[b] 失业和慷慨程度均值中心。

[c] 美国省略了。

　　这个微不足道的失业率的影响与先前研究得出的失业率对凶杀率的影响是一致的（Pyle, 2000）。相比先前代表性的研究,福利慷慨度对凶杀率缺乏有效影响,除去其他因素,从中我们发现有较低的凶杀率的国家有着较强大的福利国家（Fiala and LaFree, 1988;Messner and Rosenfeld, 1997;Savolainen, 2000）。结论的不同可归因于研究规格的不同,尤其是当前的凶杀率的研究中包含了的某些不可测量的异质源。

　　第二列显示了与第一列中相同测量的系数,并且显示了失业率与福利慷慨度之间相互作用的因素。这两个测量是这个模型的中心平均值。交叉项代表了在一定的福利慷慨度的条件下,失业率变化对凶杀率变化的影响。如果我们的假设是正确的话,该测量系数应该是负的,表示在低福利慷慨度下失业率对凶杀率强烈的影响。这就是我们所发现的（ b = -.213 , p < .05 ）。我们也发现在这个方程式里,失业率变化对凶杀率的影响是微乎其微的。通过集中预测,这是在平均水平的福利慷慨度上预测失业率对凶杀率的效果（Aiken and West, 1991;36—40,Jaccard and Turrisi, 2003;23—26）。

　　正如表 2 中第三列所表明的那样,当把美国拿出我们的分析研究时,这些结果一点都没有改变。结果显示,一般在高度发达国家,福利国家是以失业率对凶杀率的影响为条件的。我们的研究结果不仅仅只是简单地将美国的高凶杀率和低福利保障人为地放在一起进行比较。

虽然我们发现了失业率对凶杀率存在有条件的有效的影响,且这个影响量是适度的。图3反映了在平均福利慷慨度下,失业率的变化对凶杀率的变化的影响量的评估,存在一标准值的偏差以及存在最大值和最小值。图3表明了评估的要点是通过表2的模型二中的系数进行计算(Aiken and West,1991:9—14)。我们在样本中根据各国福利慷慨度的均值不同,用不同斜率的斜线来展示随着福利慷慨度不同,失业率与凶杀率之间的联系。正如期望的一样,关于失业率对凶杀率影响强度的评估,可以通过降低福利慷慨度,在福利慷慨度达到最大限度(b = .171),来加强失业率对凶杀率的影响;反之通过提升福利慷慨度,来削弱其对凶杀率的影响。另外,我们发现在有着北欧国家特点的福利慷慨度下,失业率对凶杀率有着较小的、负面的影响。

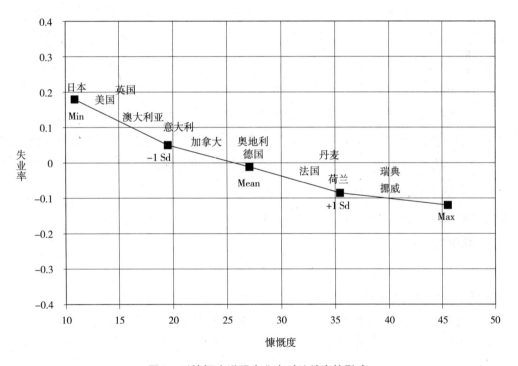

图3 以慷慨度说明失业率对凶杀率的影响

因为我们选取的样本始终围绕着最高福利国家和最低福利国家的巨大差异,(见图2),那些适度的失业率的影响并不能归因于福利慷慨度测量限制的变化。从这些福利国家的情况我们总结得出自20世纪70年代开始,失业率的变化会导致凶杀率较小但却是可见的影响。

五、总　结

当前研究融合了宏观犯罪学研究的两个重要部分:一是关于失业率和犯罪联系的传统研究,另一个是最近更多的关于福利国家对凶杀率影响的研究。根据工业发达国家福利条件的不断改善,我们假设失业率对凶杀率的影响是变化的。通过保护个人来抵抗市场力量的冲击,我们推断具有普遍性和慷慨性的福利保障政策应该可以削弱失业率对凶杀率的影响。这个假设与先前的研究相一致,在优质福利的国家,福利国家可以减弱劳动力过剩,收入不均人群,家庭破裂对凶杀率的影响(Gartner,1990,1991;Pampel and Gartner, 1995;Savolainen, 2000)。制度性社会失范论把这些理论成果以及最新的研究统称为如何在社会制度体系下有效地平衡市场经济的竞争以及其他制度是如何促进社会文化和社会经济状况来降低严重犯罪的犯罪率的(Messner and Rosenfeld, 2007;Rosenfeld and Messner, 2006)。

我们的理论假设被一份涉及13个工业发达国家并历时30年的关于凶杀率、失业率和福利保障政策的追踪调查所证实。失业率变化对全国凶杀率变化的影响,在那些福利慷慨程度低的国家则要强。甚至在那些福利慷慨程度低的国家,失业率对于凶杀率的影响也是适度存在的,但也是有意义的。即使在我们的样本中,那些福利慷慨度最低的,失业率加倍(比如:增加100%)所带来的对凶杀率影响的增加比例也不超过20%。

或许我们已经发现失业率对犯罪率的影响比对凶杀率的影响要强,尤其是那些有着明显侵财性动机的犯罪。另外,失业率并不是唯一的或许也不是最好的用于衡量经济因素对犯罪影响的指标 。近期对美国以及对一些区域的研究成果也表明市场行为的结果和对经济状况的集体认知作为更宽泛的指标所具有的影响要更强(Arvanites and Defina, 2006;Rosenfeld and Fornango, 2007)。在我们的研究分析报告中,我们已经使用了失业率和凶杀率,这是基于数据的实用性以及为了与之前的研究保持一致性。将来的研究应该扩展研究的范围,包含其他的经济的和犯罪的指标,或许可以使用更小的国家样本,从而可以得到必要的时间序列。

也有可能我们的研究结果混淆了在工业发达国家所谓的在失业率影响下的犯罪机会和犯罪动机对凶杀率的影响。留给将来研究的一个重要问题就是有着优质福利的国家在经济萎缩时期,犯罪机会是如何产生影响的。通过改变犯罪者犯罪动机的强度或者限制这些动机,我们假定慷慨的福利保障政策会削弱失业率对凶杀率的影响。但是如果福利国家的强度同样缓解了失业率和犯罪受害机会的关系,在此条件下广义的福利国家范围内,失业对犯罪的影响或许会被颠倒。我们发现在数据中,那些有着高度福利慷慨度的国家对此影响的显示是微弱的(见图3)。抽离犯罪动机和犯罪机会这两个因素,考虑失业率对于犯罪的影响,会在观念认识和方法上面临挑战(Paternoster and Bushway, 2001)。将来的研究应该针对这点来获得对福利国家是如何以失业率和其他市场结果对犯罪率的影响为条件的全面了解。

但是也许现有研究中对我们影响最为深远的来自于我们的主要结论。当我们将先前的研究与之相结合,并且在今后的调查研究中进行重演,我们的研究发现将会对美国现有的新自由主义的政策规定产生疑问而且会在其他地方鼓励削减社会福利,而将这些福利投入到刺激经济增长当中去。首先,此类措施建议必须证明这样的社会投入不会减缓而是刺激经济增长(Lindert, 2004)。再次,这些建议需要淡化或者可以不顾市场力量的破坏性后果,波拉尼(Polanyi)(2001【1944】)称之为自我约束性市场。福利国家要成为一种必要的并能与现代市场经济相抗衡的力量,而且越来越多的证据证明那种会极大削弱福利国家并且为了支持经济发展而进行制度偏袒的国家政策,可能会威胁到,使之暴露在无约束的市场力量面前,而这个保护机制恰恰是在一个发达资本主义民主国家维护社会和谐稳定的保证力量。

注 释

1. 现有的理论陈述(Messner and Rosenfeld, 2007; Rosenfeld and Messner, 2006)主要着眼于经济状况、家庭因素、政策和教育等,但是现代社会制度的完整结构应该也包括相应的宗教思想和大众传媒。

2. 德汉姆(Durkheim)(1958)提出了国家作为先进社会"失范"经济的调节者这一关键角色的经典论断。德汉姆(Durkheim)对国家所释放的能力的认识,或许过于乐观(Varga,2006)。

3. 马里兰大学的加里·拉弗雷(Gany LaFree)教授收集了这些凶杀数据,并为本次研究提供了相关的凶杀数据资料。

4. http://unstats. un. org/unsd/demographic/products/dyb/dyb2. htm.

5. 不管怎么样,慷慨度的衡量展示了相较之下的年龄不同所带来的差别。

6. 对固定样本数据采用普遍的最小平方的估算。所有的模型回归在 Stata9.2 软件中采用模型数据广义最小二乘法的命令。我们对每个模型采取分开的 AR(1) 过程。

7. 在某些研究数据中,并没有失业率与社会福利慷慨度。通过插入相近的可替代数据,我们弥补了这些空缺的数据。这些样本包括澳大利亚、奥地利、加拿大、丹麦、法国、德国、意大利、日本、荷兰、挪威、瑞典、英国和美国。其中在 1989 年之前,德国的数据主要取自于西德。

8.我们也针对福利慷慨度对凶杀率的影响尝试了非线性研究。虽然我们也在非线性的研究中发现了福利慷慨度的影响,并对此进行了二次说明,但通过使用 BIC 数据分析,显示非线性研究并没有比线性研究有更多影响,结果暗示非常高程度的社会福利慷慨度对凶杀率的影响却是十分小的。因此,当前的研究分析主要致力于福利保障慷慨度对凶杀率的线性影响。

[参考文献见英文原作]

(展万程　翁一帆 译)

Unemployment, Homicide,
and the Welfare State

Richard Rosenfeld

University of Missouri-St. Louis

Steven F. Messner

University at Albany, State University of New York

The impact of economic conditions on crime rates has been a major source of inspiration and controversy in quantitative investigations of crime. There are good theoretical reasons to expect that deteriorating economic conditions, especially increasing unemployment, should influence crime rates, either positively or negatively (Cantor and Land, 1985). But the research literature linking crime to economic conditions has been at best ambiguous (Chiricos, 1987; Cook and Zarkin, 1985; Greenberg, 2001). A half century ago an influential criminological theorist drew the following conclusion from the existing research: "The obvious inference is that the general relations of economic conditions and criminality are so indefinite that no clear or definite conclusion can be drawn" (Vold, 1958:181). Although subsequent research has established some regularities, such as a concentration of crime in disadvantaged places (Pratt and Cullen, 2005; Sampson, Morenoff, and Gannon-Rowley, 2002) the nature of the relationships between the functioning of the economy and criminal offending remains something of a mystery.

A considerably smaller but more consistent body of research links the welfare state to national homicide rates: more generous social welfare policies are associated with lower homicide rates (Fiala and LaFree, 1988; Gartner, 1990; Messner and Rosenfeld, 1997). In addition, prior research has found that the welfare state conditions the effect of large age cohorts (Pampel and Gartner, 1995), income inequality (Savolainen, 2000), and family stressors (Gartner, 1991) on homicide rates: generous welfare policies weaken the effect of these conditions on homicide.

We draw on these two research traditions-the former investigating the effect on crime rates of economic conditions and the latter the additive and conditioning effects of the welfare state-in formulating the hypothesis under investigation in the current study. We hypothesize that the welfare state conditions the effect of economic conditions, indexed by the unemployment rate, on national homicide rates. In nations with more generous welfare policies the effect of unemployment on homicide should be weaker than in those with less generous welfare policies. We test this hypothesis with panel data on 13 advanced industrial nations over the period 1971 to 2001. Our analysis is guided by the institutional-anomie theory of crime (Messner and Rosenfeld, 2007; Rosenfeld and Messner, 2006).

BACKGROUND

Economic and sociological theories of crime offer ample justification for expecting that crime rates should vary with changing economic conditions. Economic theories predict that persons calculate, if crudely, the comparative benefits and costs of legal and illegal behavior and will break the law when the net benefits (benefits minus costs) of doing so exceed the net benefits of conformity (Becker, 1968; Pyle, 2000). Rising unemployment rates and falling incomes reduce the benefits of conformity and make crime an increasingly attractive behavioral choice.

Sociological theories also posit that persons choose rationally between the benefits and costs of alternative lines of action, but sociologists generally devote more attention than do economists to the social and cultural contexts in which rational choices are made. In his classic essay on "social structure and anomie," Merton (1938) proposes that societies that place a strong emphasis on the value of economic success and correspondingly less emphasis on the legitimate means of attaining success will have high rates of "innovative" behavior, including crime, especially among persons for whom the benefits of pursuing legitimate means of success are minimal. By implication, the population of innovators will grow with rising unemployment or falling incomes. The same prediction follows from classical social control theory. A deteriorating economy implies that people have less of a "stake in conformity," and thus the bonds that might restrain the impulses to commit crimes are weakened (Hirschi, 1969).

The preceding economic and sociological perspectives focus on the offender's motivation to commit crime and the restraints on such motivation. By contrast, so-called opportunity perspectives direct attention to the characteristics and activity patterns of crime victims and predict the opposite relationship between deteriorating economic conditions and crime. Routine activity theorists argue that economic decline should reduce criminal opportunities by reducing target attractiveness and increasing guardianship (Cohen and Felson, 1979; Cohen, Felson, and Land, 1980). As unemployment rates increase, for example, more people stay at home, reducing burglary, and carry less of value with them when they are away from home, reducing robbery.

These hypothesized motivational and opportunity processes are not, of course, mutually exclusive. Both might operate to varying degrees and on different time scales. Indeed, researchers have proposed that the effect of economic conditions on opportunities for victimization is virtually instantaneous, whereas the impact on motivations is likely to be lagged (Cantor and Land, 1985). The exact nature of these processes has yet to be explicated fully, and the most effective ways to "decouple" them in statistical modeling remains a matter of controversy in the literature (Greenberg, 2001; Cantor and Land, 2001).

The Welfare State and Crime

Consider now the impact of the welfare state on the relationship between economic conditions and crime rates, from both economic and sociological perspectives. Although they have disparate historical origins, modern welfare states are intended to cushion the harmful effects of market economies on individuals and families (Esping-Andersen, 1990). Entitlements in the form of unemployment insurance, health insurance, old-age pensions, child allowances, subsidized child care, parental leave, and income supplements enable persons to better withstand periods of protracted unemployment or depressed market incomes. In economic terms, the welfare state increases the net benefits of continued conformity during economic downturns and reduces the net benefits of crime.

From Merton's (1938) perspective, the welfare state should lessen the likelihood persons will turn to illegitimate means to pursue culturally valued goals. From a social control perspective, the protections of the welfare state should help sustain bonds to the conventional order despite periods of unemployment. In all of these cases, a strong welfare state should weaken the impact of economic downturns on crime rates.

The expected effect of the welfare state on target attractiveness and guardianship during periods of economic decline is less clear. The income replacement value of welfare benefits should lessen the effect of falling market incomes on the value of crime targets. But rising unemployment should increase target guardianship regardless of welfare generosity because, even with generous unemployment benefits, unemployed workers are bound to spend more time at home than employed workers. The impact of the welfare state on criminal opportunities, therefore, is probably more modest than its effect on criminal motivation.

Prior research has shown lower levels of homicide in nations and during periods of high welfare generosity (Fiala and LaFree, 1988; Gartner, 1990; Messner and Rosenfeld, 1997). In a recent study of homicide rates for a sample of 100 nations, Antonaccio and Tittle (2007) combine indicators of welfare policies with measures of union density and inequality to create "capitalism" index. They observe a significant positive effect of this index on homicide rates, which is consistent with other research on the welfare state. Nations with higher scores on the capitalism measure, and thus lower scores on the measures of the generosity of welfare policies, exhibit higher homicide rates, net of a range of control variables.

In addition, several studies have revealed a conditioning or contextual influence of the welfare state such that the effect of criminogenic conditions on homicide rates is reduced in the context of a strong welfare state. Savolainen (2000) reports that the impact of income inequality on homicide rates is stronger in nations with comparatively weak and restrictive welfare policies in cross-sectional analyses of two datasets with overlapping but slightly different samples. Gartner (1991) pursues a similar line of inquiry focusing on indicators of family stress. In a panel study of 17 developed nations over the period 1965—1980, she finds that the effects on infant and child homicide rates of family stress factors such as teen births, non-marital births, and divorce are stronger in nations and periods with low levels of state spending on social welfare programs. Pampel and Gartner (1995) discover the same pattern of results in a panel study of developed nations for the effect of population age structure on homicide rates: Large cohorts of adolescents and young adults have a stronger effect on homicide rates in nations with low scores on a "collectivism" scale (an index combining welfare generosity, corporatist bargaining arrangements, parliamentary vs. majoritarian democracy, leftist party rule, and nonviolent political conflict).

Each of these studies interprets the conditioning effect of strong welfare states (or other "collectivist" political arrangements) in terms of the *institutional context* developed to mitigate the criminogenic effects of market economies on individuals, families, or age cohorts. Pampel and Gartner (1995:245) argue, for example, that "societal institutions promoting collective responsibility for living standards and solidaristic policies of social protection can cushion the harmful impact of membership in large cohorts." Such an institutional context "both reflects and promotes goals of social protection from market vicissitudes" (247). The same logic applies to how the institutional context shapes the experience and consequences of high fertility, adolescent pregnancy, single motherhood, and family disruption. The economic stress, social isolation, and lack of social support experienced by young, single mothers are mitigated, if not eliminated, by social policies and practices that promote collective responsibility for social welfare, resulting in less child abuse and homicide (Gartner, 1991:232).

The welfare state, then, protects individuals and families from the full brunt of market forces, most directly, by alleviating economic hardship and also by promoting social solidarity. But researchers speculate that its conditioning effects on homicide may also reflect a *cultural* orientation that inhibits interpersonal violence (Gartner, 1991:238). An ethic of collective responsibility for individual welfare, reflected and reinforced by the welfare state, may promote interventions in situations or with persons with a high potential for violence. More generally, a communal orientation that encourages people to consider the interests of others when pursuing personal goals is incompatible with the use of violence to advance self-interest or solve interpersonal disputes.

Institutional-Anomie Theory

The institutional-anomie theory of crime is an appropriate and useful framework for explaining the protective and violence-reducing effects of the modern welfare state revealed in past research (Savolainen, 2000). The theory extends Merton's (1938) foundational arguments linking high crime rates to anomie and social inequality beyond the stratification system to the full range of social institutions constituting complex, modern societies. Such societies must balance the sometimes competing requisites and claims of economic, familial, political, and educational institutions. [1] The resulting interrelationship among institutions has been termed the *institutional balance of power*. In some societies-the United States is the paradigmatic case-the free-market economy dominates the institutional balance of power. The functions and goals of other institutions are devalued, and non-economic roles tend to be accommodated to market requirements when role-conflicts emerge. In addition, the norms, language, and logic of the marketplace penetrate into non-economic spheres of social life (Messner and Rosenfeld, 2007:74 - 84). This institutional pattern both reflects and promotes an anomic cultural ethos that, following Merton (1938), extols the virtues of economic success and de-emphasizes the legitimate means for pursuing success. Market dominance of the institutional structure and a "by any means necessary" cultural orientation, in turn, undermine the social control and support functions of non-economic institutions and stimulate high rates of crime.

In most developed societies, the polity plays an important role in regulating the market economy and promoting social welfare. [2] State policies on unemployment insurance, health insurance, social security, child allowances, and other entitlements protect persons from the full impact of market downturns. By bolstering consumer spending, they may also speed economic recovery. But the regulatory and welfare functions of the polity are weakened to the extent that the market economy dominates the institutional structure. Prior research on the welfare state and homicide suggests that this is a primary path by which the institutional structures of developed societies are implicated in criminal violence.

THE CURRENT STUDY

The research literature on the moderating influence of the welfare state on income inequality, family stressors, and large youth cohorts makes reference to market forces and "vicissitudes" but does not measure them directly. At the same time, the literature on economic conditions and crime employs direct measures of market oscillations, typically the unemployment rate, but does not consider how unemployment or other market effects on crime may be conditioned by the welfare state. Each research area could benefit from their combination in analyses of how market effects on crime rates are moderated by the welfare state. Given the attention devoted to it in prior research and its salience as a measure of e-conomic wellbeing, we use the unemployment rate as our measure of market outcomes in the current study. For the same reasons-to build on prior research and to explain variation in the most serious of criminal offenses-we examine the effect of unemployment on national homicide rates. In addition, homicide is the offense type for which the most reliable cross-national data are available over an extended time period.

DATA AND METHODS

The homicide measure used in this study is from the World Health Organization. These data are based on "cause of death" reports from medical authorities and thus exclude attempted homicides, which are not always recorded in a comparable manner across nations. Following conventional procedures, we use the homicide rate per 100, 000 population (*homicide*).[3] The unemployment rates (*unemploy*) are from the International Monetary Fund (http://www. imf. org/external/data. htm) and Organization for Economic Cooperation and Development (http://www. oecd. org/). Our measure of the welfare state is from the Comparative Welfare Entitlements Dataset (Scruggs, 2004). We use the variable "Overall Generosity Score" to indicate the universality and extensiveness of each nation's unemployment, sickness, and pension benefits (*generosity*). The three benefit types were coded for their income replacement value (ratio of the benefit value to the average wage for production workers), qualifying conditions, benefit duration, and percentage of the labor force covered. Aggregate scores for these dimensions were then summed across the three benefit types to form the Overall Generosity Score (Scruggs, 2004).

Our models also contain controls for population size (*population*) and percentage of the population ages 15 – 24 (*age comp*). Both indicators are from the United Nations Demographic Yearbooks for 1970 to 2004.[4] In addition, we introduce fixed effects in the form of dummy variables for nation and year, a common linear trend for the homicide rate, and nation-specific homicide trends. The nation effects control for unmeasured time-invariant sources of heterogeneity across nations, the year effects condition the model estimates on time varying sources of variation within nations, and the common and country-specific deterministic trends control for additional heterogeneity within nations over time. The substantive variables (homicide, unemployment, welfare generosity, population size, and age composition) are transformed to their natural logs for analysis, which yields coefficients interpretable as elasticities (the percentage change in the outcome given a 1% change in the predictor). Descriptive statistics for these variables in original metric are presented in Table 1.

Table 1   Correlation Matrix and Descriptive Statistics(N=403)[a]

	(1) Homicide	(2) Unemploy	(3) Generosity	(4) Population	(5) Age Comp
(1)	—				
(2)	.103	—			
(3)	−.350	−.084	—		
(4)	.873	.185	−.408	—	
(5)	.281	.088	−.280	.103	—
Mean	1.84	5.79	27.24	4.49E+07	15.06
StD	2.11	3.05	8.22	6.21E+07	1.83
Min	.53	.70	11.00	3.91E+06	11.00
Max	10.55	12.00	45.40	2.85E+08	19.74

[a] Variables in orignal metric

Inspection of the logged homicide series for each nation indicated that the series are nonstationary in levels. Stationarity was induced after taking the first difference of the series.. We therefore employ the first-differenced series for homicide and the other substantive variables in our regression analyses, with one exception. Given our interest in how market *volatility* influences change in homicide rates, first differencing is appropriate on substantive grounds as well. The exception is welfare generosity. As in prior research, we are interested in how differences in the *level* of welfare generosity affect the relationship between changing market conditions and homicide. [5] Therefore, the *generosity* indicator is entered in (logged) levels in our analyses.

Preliminary inspection also indicated heteroskedastic error terms in the between-panel regressions and correlated errors in both the between- and within-panel regressions. We therefore use a feasible generalized least squares estimator (FGLS) to estimate our models, which yields unbiased and consistent coefficients in the presence of heteroskedasticity, correlation of the between-panel errors, and serial correlation of the within-panel errors. [6]

Our models are estimated for a sample of 13 advanced industrial nations over the period

1971—2001. Data are available for all of these nations throughout the period, yielding a balanced panel design with 403 observations (13 ∗ 31) before differencing. We constructed the sample to minimize missing data on our main measures, resulting in a sample somewhat smaller than those used in prior research on the welfare state and homicide.[7] Nonetheless, for the purposes of our analysis ample variation exists across nations in welfare generosity, ranging from the expansive welfare regimes of Sweden, Norway, and Denmark to the more restrictive policies of the United States, Britain, Australia, and Japan. The 31-year period covered by the analysis was determined by the a-vailability of the welfare generosity data (Scruggs, 2004). Because the United States is an extreme outlier in homicide rates, we present results from the multivariate analysis for samples including and excluding the U. S.

RESULTS

The degree to which the homicide rate in the United States surpasses the rates of other advanced nations is illustrated in Figure 1, which presents the average homicide rates between 1971 and 2001 for the 13 nations under investigation. The U. S. homicide rate is over four times the rates of the next highest nations (Canada, Australia, and Italy) and more than eight times those of the nations at the bottom of the list (the United Kingdom, Norway, the Netherlands, and Japan). Logging and differencing the homicide measure reduces but does not eliminate the sizable homicide gap between the United States and the other nations.

The United States falls close to the bottom of the sample on the summary measure of welfare generosity, just below the United Kingdom and Australia and above Japan. As noted, the Scandinavian nations have the highest welfare generosity scores (see Figure 2). The United States' very high homicide rate and low level of welfare generosity raises the possibility that an observed effect of unemployment on homicide by welfare generosity may reflect "American exceptionalism" rather than the general impact of the welfare state on the relationship between homicide and market outcomes among developed nations. We address this possibility by comparing our multivariate results for samples with and without the United States, which has not been done in prior research (Gartner, 1990, 1991; Pampel and Gartner, 1995).

Table 1 presents bivariate correlations based on the pooled data for the substantive

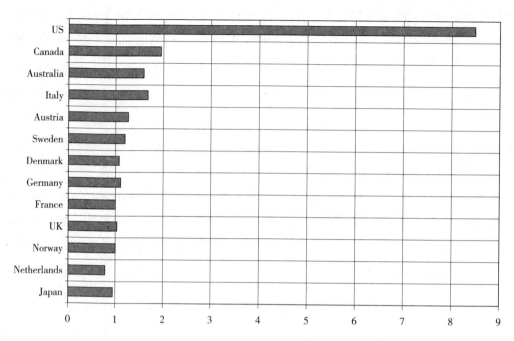

Figure 1 Average Homicide Rates in 13 Nations, 1971—2001

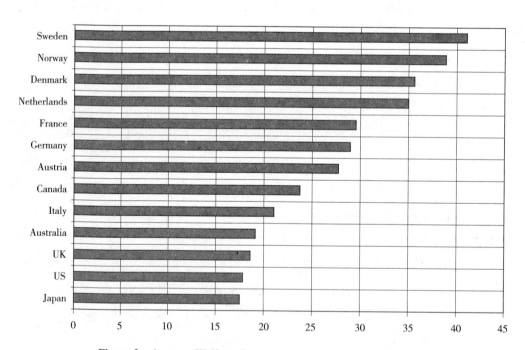

Figure 2 Average Welfare Generosity in 13 Nations, 1971—2001

variables in the analysis (in original metric). Consistent with prior research (Savolainen, 2000; Messner and Rosenfeld, 1997), a moderate, negative correlation exists between the national homicide rate and welfare generosity score ($r = -.350$, $p < .01$). Nations with more generous welfare states tend to have lower homicide rates. We observe a very strong, positive correlation between population size and homicide ($r = .873$, $p < .01$), in part reflecting the comparatively high homicide rate and large population of the United States. The correlation between the unemployment rate and homicide rate is statistically significant but small ($r = .103$, $p < .05$). Finally, a small and non-significant association exists between unemployment and welfare generosity in our sample ($r = -.084$). During the period under investigation, several of the nations with the most generous welfare states in the sample experienced large increases in unemployment rates. For example, France's unemployment rate hovered around 10% during the last decades of the 20th century. In the contemporary era, a strong welfare state is no guarantee of full employment. Whether the welfare state moderates the effect of unemployment on homicide is the focus of our multivariate analysis.

The results of our panel regressions are presented in Table 2. Results are not shown for the common linear trend indicator, country-specific trends, and dummy variables representing fixed effects for each nation and year. The first column of the table presents the results from a regression of year-over-year change in homicide on year-over-year change in unemployment, population size, and age composition, and the level of welfare generosity. None of the predictors has a significant effect on homicide. In this specification, nations displaying greater change in unemployment or higher levels of welfare generosity do not exhibit larger changes in homicide rates than other nations.

Table 2   FGLS Regression of National Homicide Rates on Unemployment , Generosity Index , Age Composition , and Population Size[a]

	Model 1	Model 2[b]	Model 3[b,c]
Unemploy	-.044 (.029)	-.008 (.032)	-.027 (.036)
Generosity	.039 (.068)	.055 (.067)	.091 (.070)
Population	-.793 (.621)	-.990 (.636)	-.700 (.711)
Age Comp	-.138 (.168)	-.186 (.169)	-.379 * (.188)
Unem x Gen	— (—)	-.213 * (.086)	-.214 * (.098)
LL	399.13	401.34	361.73

	Model 1	Model 2[b]	Model 3[b,c]
Wald Chi[2]	1013. 66 **	1070. 19 **	1081. 48 **
N	390	390	360

** p<. 01 * p<. 05 (two-tailed).

[a] Heteroskedastic feasible generalized least squares models with within-and between-panel correlated errors. Models contain common linear trend, within-country trends, county and year fixed effects (results suppressed). All variables logged (base e) and , except Generosity , first differenced.

[b] Unemploy and Generosity mean-centered.

[c] U S omitted.

The negligible unemployment effect is consistent with prior studies of unemployment effects on homicide rates (Pyle, 2000). The absence of a significant effect of welfare generosity on homicide contrasts with prior cross-sectional studies, which have found lower homicide rates in nations with stronger welfare states, net of other determinants (Fiala and LaFree, 1988; Messner and Rosenfeld, 1997; Savolainen, 2000). The difference in results probably is attributable to specification differences, especially the inclusion in the current study of controls for unmeasured sources of heterogeneity in homicide rates.[8]

Column two displays the coefficients for the same measures shown in column one and also the coefficient for the interaction of *unemploy* and *generosity*. The two measures have been mean-centered in this model. The product term represents the effect of change in unemployment on change in homicide conditioned on the level of welfare generosity. If our hypothesis is correct, the coefficient on this measure should be negative, representing a stronger effect of unemployment on homicide at lower levels of generosity. That is what we find ($b=-.213$, $p<.05$). We also find a negligible effect of the change in unemployment on the change in homicide in this equation. With centered predictors, this is the predicted effect of unemployment on homicide at the mean level of welfare generosity (see Aiken and West, 1991:36－40; Jaccard and Turrisi, 2003:23－26).

These results do not change appreciably when the United States is removed from the analysis, as shown in the third column Table 2. It appears that the welfare state conditions the impact of unemployment on homicide across highly developed nations generally. Our results are not simply an artifact of the comparatively high homicide rates and low welfare generosity in the United States.

Although we find a significant conditional effect of unemployment on homicide, its magnitude is modest. Figure 3 displays the estimated magnitude of the effect of the change in unemployment on the change in homicide at the mean level of welfare generosity, one standard deviation below and above the mean, and the minimum and maximum values. The point estimates shown in Figure 3 were calculated using the coefficients from Model 2 of Table 2 (see Aiken and West, 1991:9 - 14). We have also arrayed the nations in our sample according to their mean generosity score along the line representing the "simple slope" of the unemployment-homicide relationship by levels of welfare generosity. As expected, the estimated effect of unemployment on homicide strengthens with falling levels of welfare generosity, reaching a maximum value (b = . 171) at the observed minimum generosity score, and weakens with rising levels of generosity. In addition, we observe small, negative unemployment effects at the high levels of welfare generosity characteristic of the Nordic countries.

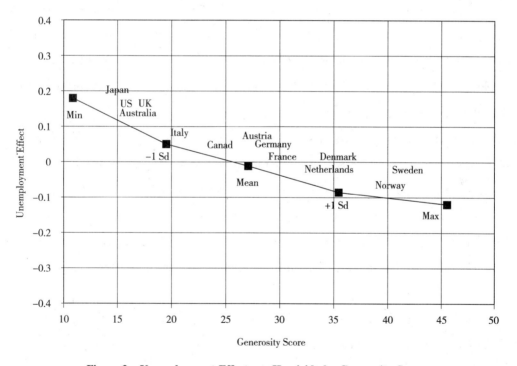

Figure 3   Unemployment Effects on Homicide by Generosity Score

Because our sample encompasses large differences between the most and least generous welfare states (see Figure 2) , the modest unemployment effects are not due to constricted variation on the generosity measure. We conclude that changes unemployment rates have resulted in discernible but small changes in the homicide rates across the observed range of welfare states since the 1970s.

CONCLUSIONS

The current study integrates two important bodies of macro-criminological research: a long tradition of research on unemployment and crime and more recent studies of the influence of the welfare state on homicide. We hypothesized that the effect of unemployment on homicide should vary according to the extensiveness of social welfare provisions in advanced industrial societies. By protecting persons against the full brunt of market forces, we reasoned that universalistic and generous social welfare policies should dilute the impact of unemployment on homicide. This hypothesis is consistent with prior research showing weaker effects of large youth cohorts, income inequality, and family disruption on homicide rates in stronger welfare states (Gartner, 1990, 1991; Pampel and Gartner, 1995; Savolainen, 2000). The institutional-anomie theory of crime situates these studies and the current one in a general account of how social systems that effectively balance the competing claims of a market economy and other institutions foster cultural and social conditions conducive to low rates of serious crime (Messner and Rosenfeld, 2007; Rosenfeld and Messner, 2006).

We find support for our hypothesis in a panel study of homicide, unemployment, and social welfare policies over a 30-year period in 13 advanced industrial nations. The effect of changes in the unemployment rate on changes in national homicide rates is stronger at lower levels of welfare generosity. Even at low levels of welfare generosity the impact of unemployment on homicide is modest, but it is not trivial. A doubling of the unemployment rate (i. e., a 100% increase) yields just under a 20% increase in homicide at the lowest generosity levels in our sample.

We might have found stronger unemployment effects for offenses other than homicide, especially those with an overt economic motivation. In addition, the unemployment rate is not the only and perhaps not the best measure of economic conditions with an impact on crime. Recent research on U. S. states and regions has shown stronger effects on crime rates of broader indicators of market outcomes and collective perceptions of economic conditions (Arvanites and Defina, 2006; Rosenfeld and Fornango, 2007). We have used the unemployment and homicide rate in our analysis for reasons of data availability and to remain consistent with prior research. Future research should expand this investigation to incorporate other economic and crime indicators, perhaps with smaller samples of nations for which the requisite time series are available.

It also is possible that our results confound so-called opportunity and motivation effects of unemployment on homicide in the advanced industrial nations (Cantor and Land, 1985). A key question for future research is how criminal opportunities are affected during economic contractions in nations with strong welfare states. We have assumed that generous social welfare policies weaken the positive effect of unemployment on homicide by altering the strength of offenders' motivations to commit crime or the restraints on these motivations. But if the strength of the welfare state also moderates the relationship between unemployment and the opportunities for victimization, the "net" impact of unemployment on crime could be reversed under conditions of an expansive welfare state. We find faint indications of such an effect at high levels of welfare generosity in our data (see Figure 3). Unpacking the motivation and opportunity effects of unemployment on crime poses difficult conceptual and methodological challenges (Paternoster and Bushway, 2001). Future research will have to address this issue to gain a comprehensive understanding of how the welfare state conditions the impact of unemployment and other market outcomes on crime.

But perhaps the most important implications of the current study derive from our main result. When combined with those of prior studies and if replicated in future research our findings raise questions about current neoliberal policy prescriptions in the United States and elsewhere that encourage cutbacks in social welfare spending to stimulate economic growth. First, such proposals must contend with evidence that social spending does not retard and may stimulate growth (Lindert, 2004). Second, they downplay or ignore the socially disruptive consequences of unbridled market forces, what Polanyi (2001 [1944]) referred to as the "self-regulating market." The welfare state emerged as a necessary institutional counterweight to the modern market economy. The accumulating evidence suggests that policies that would substantially weaken the welfare state and tilt the institutional balance of power in favor of the economy might threaten to undo the social protections from uncontrolled market forces that have guaranteed a modicum of social peace in the advanced capitalist democracies.

Notes

1. Existing statements of the theory (Messner and Rosenfeld, 2007; Rosenfeld and

Messner, 2006) focus on the economy, family, polity, and education but a full treatment of the institutional structure of modern societies would also incorporate religious institutions and the mass media (see Messner and Rosenfeld, 2006).

2. Durkheim (1958) provides a classic statement on the critical role of the state as a regulator of the intrinsically "anomic" economies of the advanced societies. For a critique of Durkheim's rather optimistic view of the "liberating" capacities of the state, see Varga (2006).

3. Professor Gary LaFree of the University of Maryland compiled the homicide data and kindly provided the homicide series for the current study.

4. http://unstats. un. org/unsd/demographic/products/dyb/dyb2. htm.

5. In any case, the *generosity* indicator exhibits comparatively little year-to-year change.

6. See Greene, 2003, on the use of generalized least squares estimators with panel data. All regressions are performed using the xtgls option in Stata 9. 2. We specify separate AR (1) processes within each panel.

7. In a few instances data for unemployment and welfare generosity were missing. We imputed the missing data by interpolating from adjacent values. The sample of nations consists of Australia, Austria, Canada, Denmark, France, Germany, Italy, Japan, Netherlands, Norway, Sweden, United Kingdom, and the United States. Prior to 1989 data for Germany are for West Germany.

8. We also tested for a nonlinear effect of welfare generosity on homicide. Although we found evidence of nonlinearity in a quadratic specification of the welfare generosity effect, implying smaller effects on homicide at very high levels of welfare generosity, model comparisons using BIC statistics revealed no improvement in fit of the nonlinear over the linear model. The current analysis, therefore, focuses on the linear effect of welfare generosity on homicide.

References

Aiken, Leona S. and Stephen G. West. 1991. *Multiple Regression: Testing and Interpreting Interactions*. Thousand Oaks, CA: Sage.

Antonaccio, Olena and Charles R. Tittle. 2007. "A Cross-National Test of Bonger's Theory of Criminality and Economic Conditions. "*Criminology* 45:925 − 958.

Arvanites, Thomas M. and Robert H. Defina. 2006. "Business Cycles and Street Crime. " *Criminology* 44:139 − 164.

Becker, Gary. 1968. " Crime and Punishment: An Economic Approach. " *Journal of Political Economy* 73:169 − 217.

Cantor, David, and Kenneth C. Land. 1985. "Unemployment and Crime rates in the Post-World War II United States: A Theoretical and Empirical Analysis. " *American Sociological Review* 50: 317 − 332.

____. 2001. "Unemployment and Crime Fluctuations: A Comment on Greenberg. " *Journal of Quantitative Criminology* 17:329 − 342.

Chiricos, Theodore. 1987. "Rates of Crime and Unemployment: An Analysis of Aggregate Research Evidence. " *Social Problems* 34:187 − 212.

Cohen, Lawrence E. , and Marcus Felson. 1979. "Social Change and Crime Rate Trends: A Routine Activities Approach. " *American Sociological Review* 44: 588 − 608.

Cohen, Lawrence E. , Marcus Felson, and Kenneth C. Land. 1980. "Property Crime Rates in the United States: A Macrodynamic Analysis, 1947 − 1977; with Ex Ante Forecasts for the Mid-1980s. " *American Journal of Sociology* 86: 90 − 118.

Durkheim, Emile. 1958. *Professional Ethics and Civic Morals*. Translated by Cornelia Brookfiled. Glencoe, IL: Free Press.

Esping-Andersen, Gosta. 1990. *The Three Worlds of Welfare Capitalism*. Princeton, NJ: Princeton University Press.

Fiala, Robert and Gary LaFree. 1988. "Cross-National Determinants of Child Homicide. " *American Sociological Review* 53:432 − 445.

Gartner, Rosemary. 1990. "The Victims of Homicide: A Temporal and Cross-National Comparison. " *American Sociological Review* 54:92 − 106.

____. 1991. "Family Structure, Welfare Spending, and Child Homicide in Developed Democracies. " *Journal of Marriage and the Family* 53:231 − 240.

Greenberg, David F. 2001. "Time Series Analysis of Crime Rates. " *Journal of Quantitative Criminology* 17:291 − 327.

Greene, William H. 2003. *Econometric Analysis*. Fifth edition. Upper Saddle River, NJ: Prentice-Hall.

Hirschi, Travis. 1969. *Causes of Delinquency*. Berkeley, CA: University of California

Press.

Jaccard, James and Robert Turrisi. 2003. *Interaction Effects in Multiple Regression*. Second edition. Thousand Oaks, CA: Sage.

Lindert, Peter H. 2004. *Growing Public: Social Spending and Economic Growth Since the Eighteenth Century*. New York: Cambridge University Press.

Merton, Robert K. 1938. "Social Structure and Anomie." *American Sociological Review* 3: 672 – 682.

Messner, Steven F. and Richard Rosenfeld. 1997. "Political Restraint of the Market and Levels of Criminal Homicide: A Cross-National Application of Institutional-Anomie Theory." *Social Forces* 75: 1393 – 1416.

____. 2006. "The Present and Future of Institutional-Anomie Theory." *Advances in Criminological Theory* 15: 127 – 148.

____. 2007. *Crime and the American Dream*. Fourth Edition. Belmont, CA: Wadsworth.

Pampel, Fred C. and Rosemary Gartner. 1995. " Age Structure, Socio-Political Institutions, and National Homicide Rates." *European Sociological Review* 11: 243 – 260.

Paternoster, Raymond, and Shawn Bushway. 2001. "Theoretical and Empirical Work on the Relationship Between Unemployment and Crime." *Journal of Quantitative Criminology* 17: 391 – 407.

Polanyi, Karl. 2001 [1944]. *The Great Transformation*. Boston: Beacon.

Pratt, Travis C., and Francis T. Cullen. 2005. " Assessing Macro-level Predictors and Theories of Crime: A Meta-analysis." In Michael Tonry, ed., *Crime and Justice: A Review of Research*. Volume 32. Chicago: University of Chicago Press.

Pyle, David. 2000. "Economists, Crime, and Punishment." In *The Economic Dimensions of Crime*, eds. Nigel G. Fielding, Alan Clarke, and Robert Witt. New York: St. Martin's.

Rosenfeld, Richard and Robert Fornango. 2007. "The Impact of Economic Conditions on Robbery and Property Crime: The Role of Consumer Sentiment." *Criminology* 45: 735 – 769.

Rosenfeld, Richard and Steven F. Messner. 2006. "The Origins, Nature, and Prospects of Institutional-Anomie Theory." In Stuart Henry and Mark Lanier, eds. *The Essential Criminology Reader*. Boulder, CO: Westview.

Sampson, Robert J. , Jeffrey D. Morenoff, and T. Gannon-Rowley. 2002. " Assessing ' Neighborhood Effects': Social Processes and New Directions in Research. " *Annual Review of Sociology* 28: 443 – 78.

Savolainen, Jukka. 2000. "Inequality, Welfare State, and Homicide: Further Support for the Institutional Anomie Theory. " *Criminology* 38:1021 – 1042.

Lyle Scruggs (2004) *Welfare State Entitlements Data Set: A Comparative Institutional Analysis of Eighteen Welfare States*, Version 1. 1 (http://sp. uconn. edu/ ~ scruggs/wp. htm).

Varga, Ivan. 2006. " Social Morals, the Sacred and State Regulation in Durkheim's Sociology. " *Social Compass* 54 (4) :457 – 466.

Vold, George B. 1958. *Theoretical Criminology*. New York: Oxford University Press.

责任编辑:张　立
装帧设计:周涛勇
责任校对:周　昕

图书在版编目(CIP)数据

国际犯罪学大师论犯罪控制科学/刘建宏 主编. -北京:人民出版社,2012.7
ISBN 978－7－01－010963－3

Ⅰ. ①国… 　Ⅱ. ①刘… 　Ⅲ. ①犯罪控制-文集 　Ⅳ. ①D917.6-53

中国版本图书馆 CIP 数据核字(2012)第 127244 号

国际犯罪学大师论犯罪控制科学
GUOJI FANZUIXUE DASHI LUN FANZUI KONGZHI KEXUE

主编 刘建宏　副主编 金　诚

人民出版社 出版发行
(100706　北京朝阳门内大街 166 号)

北京中科印刷有限公司印刷　新华书店经销

2012 年 7 月第 1 版　2012 年 7 月北京第 1 次印刷
开本:787 毫米×1092 毫米 1/16　印张:36.25
字数:650 千字　插页:8　印数:0,001-3,000 册

ISBN 978－7－01－010963－3　定价:98.00 元(共二册)

邮购地址 100706　北京朝阳门内大街 166 号
人民东方图书销售中心　电话 (010)65250042　65289539